Lee and Gaensslen's

ADVANCES IN FINGERPRINT TECHNOLOGY

THIRD EDITION

Lee and Gaensslen's
ADVANCES IN FINGERPRINT TECHNOLOGY

THIRD EDITION

EDITED BY ROBERT S. RAMOTOWSKI

CRC Press
Taylor & Francis Group
Boca Raton London New York

CRC Press is an imprint of the
Taylor & Francis Group, an **informa** business

CRC Press
Taylor & Francis Group
6000 Broken Sound Parkway NW, Suite 300
Boca Raton, FL 33487-2742

Printed and bound in India by Replika Press Pvt. Ltd.
Version Date: 20120727

International Standard Book Number: 978-1-4200-8834-2 (Hardback)

Library of Congress Cataloging-in-Publication Data

Ramotowski, Robert.
Lee and Gaensslen's advances in fingerprint technology / Robert Ramotowski. -- 3rd ed.
p. cm.
Rev. ed. of: Advances in fingerprint technology / edited by Henry C. Lee, R.E. Gaensslen. 2nd ed.
Includes bibliographical references and index.
ISBN 978-1-4200-8834-2 (alk. paper) -- ISBN 978-1-4200-8837-3 (alk. paper)
1. Fingerprints. 2. Fingerprints--Data processing. I. Advances in fingerprint technology. II. Title. III. Title: Advances in fingerprint technology.

HV6074.A43 2013
363.25'8--dc23 2012028772

Visit the Taylor & Francis Web site at
http://www.taylorandfrancis.com

and the CRC Press Web site at
http://www.crcpress.com

Contents

Preface

The first and second editions of *Advances in Fingerprint Technology* were published first by Elsevier and then later by CRC Press, LLC (now the Taylor & Francis Group). Drs. Henry C. Lee and Robert E. Gaensslen served as the editors of these two editions. Having both retired since the publication of the second edition, the Taylor & Francis Group offered me the opportunity to prepare the updated third edition of the book. I enthusiastically accepted their gracious offer and decided to modify the title of this edition of the book to reflect the important contributions that the two original editors made to this series. I would like to thank the Taylor & Francis Group for providing me the opportunity to revise and update, *Lee and Gaensslen's Advances in Fingerprint Technology, third edition.*

When the second edition of this book was published back in 2001, the primary concern of the fingerprint field was the ramifications that stemmed from several Daubert hearings, which challenged the admissibility of fingerprint evidence. Now in 2012, the major concern centers on the implications of the recommendations outlined in the 2009 report by the National Research Council (NRC) of the National Academies, *Strengthening Forensic Science in the United States—A Path Forward.* This report highlighted perceived deficiencies throughout the various forensic sciences. In particular, Chapter 5 addressed specific concerns associated with friction ridge analysis. A broad recommendation of the NRC report was that there was a strong need for additional research in many areas of the forensic sciences, including pattern recognition disciplines like friction ridge analysis.

There have been a considerable number of advances in the area of fingerprint detection, imaging, and interpretation in the last 11 years since the second edition was published. This third edition has been completely updated with new material, covering nearly 500 pages and with more than 1500 references (nearly double the amount contained in the previous edition). I also decided to eliminate the chapters on the history of fingerprinting and identification of latent prints, as these subjects have been more than adequately covered in the previous two editions. These topics no longer represent "advances" in fingerprint technology.

The book has been restructured into two parts. Part I consists of Chapters 1 through 7, which provide a detailed review of current, widely used development techniques (as well as some older, historical methods). These chapters will cover powder methods, amino acid reagents, metal deposition methods, lipid reagents, vapor/fuming methods, blood reagents, and miscellaneous methods for challenging surfaces. Part II consists of Chapters 8 through 16, which describe more recent advances as well as novel, emerging technologies that have just begun to reach maturity. Chapter 8 provides comprehensive details about work performed by the UK Home Office regarding the use of powders and brushes. While a relatively old and simple technique, the method receives a new and fresh perspective in this chapter. Chapter 9 takes an old and new look at advances with blood reagents. The chapter highlights the transition from previously carcinogenic peroxidase reagents to new and safer protein staining methods. Chapter 10 provides a comprehensive overview of the vacuum metal deposition technique. The authors describe the new research that has been done to enlighten the reader about the mechanism of this complex process. Chapter 11 looks at the cyanoacrylate fuming process. There have been numerous studies published over the past decade that have provided new perspectives on both activation and polymerization mechanisms. Chapter 12 provides an update on ninhydrin analogs. Recent developments with

1,2-indanedione/zinc as well as natural products like genipin and lawsone are described. Chapter 13 covers the emerging trends in print development using nanotechnology. A comprehensive review of novel methods involving metal-based nanoparticles, quantum dots, and other kinds of nanoparticles is provided. Chapter 14 covers the important topic of how to handle latent print recovery and decontamination at scenes contaminated with chemical, biological, radiological, nuclear, and explosive materials. These types of crime scenes are likely to become more common as instability throughout the world continues to increase. Chapter 15 describes a model for quantitatively interpreting and assessing minutiae in a print. Such research will address some of the concerns outlined in the NRC report by providing quantitative support to previously held qualitative opinions. Chapter 16 covers methods for digital and chemical imaging of latent prints and describes the recent developments over the past ten years that have greatly expanded the options for examiners to nondestructively capture latent prints *in situ*. The content of all of these chapters has not been covered in such detail anywhere else in the literature.

One minor issue that needs to be addressed at this point concerns terminology. As will be evident after reading the various chapters contained in this book, the authors are from many different parts of the world. As such, the terms "fingerprint" and "fingermark" will be used throughout the book. There can be confusion over the usage of these terms, since they are not necessarily interchangeable. Of particular concern has been the lack of internal consistency with this terminology within some recent articles and publications.

The term "fingermark" has been defined by Champod et al.* as

> ...traces left (unknowingly) by a person on an object (sometimes referred to as the "unknown," "latent," or "questioned" mark). Almost by definition, the mark implies a lesser quality impression that includes latent, partial, distorted, reversed (tonally or laterally), or superimposed impressions.

The definition for "fingerprint" was then described as "...a record or comparison print taken for identification, exclusion, or database purposes (sometimes referred to as a "known" print)." Thus, the term "fingermark" would be synonymous with "latent print" or "latent fingerprint," while the term "fingerprint," as defined by Champod et al., would be consistent with the traditional usage of "fingerprint" or "inked fingerprint" as it is commonly used in the United States.

In conclusion, it should be noted that the views expressed by the authors in these chapters do not necessarily reflect the official position of their employers or the editor. In addition, vendor and product names are provided for illustrative purposes only, and their inclusion does not imply endorsement by either the editor, authors, or their employers.

* Champod C, Lennard C, Margot P, Stoilovic M. (2004) *Fingerprints and Other Ridge Skin Impressions*. CRC Press, Boca Raton, FL p. 183.

Acknowledgments

I would like to thank all of the contributors to this revised third edition for their tireless efforts and cooperation to complete this effort. I would also like to thank the staff at Taylor & Francis Group, with special appreciation to Becky Masterman, Kathryn Younce, Jennifer Stair, and Moureharry Saranyaa for patiently explaining the editorial process to a novice like myself and making the whole effort comparatively painless. I would like to acknowledge Brendan Westphal, visual information specialist, United States Secret Service, for his input for the final cover art design. I would also like to recognize Dr. Andy Becue, from the University of Lausanne, for taking considerable time out of his busy schedule to comprehensively review Chapters 1 through 7. I am grateful for his detailed comments and corrections. Special thanks are in order for the encouragement offered by the members of the Washington, DC, chapter of the League of Extraordinary Gentlemen. Finally, I would also like to acknowledge Dr. Antonio Cantu for also providing comments on Chapters 1 through 7. It is to him, my mentor, colleague, and friend, that I would like to dedicate this third edition of *Lee and Gaensslen's Advances in Fingerprint Technology*. Thank you for inspiring me to pursue research in the area of latent print detection.

Editors

Robert S. Ramotowski is currently employed as the chief research scientist within the Forensic Services Division of the United States Secret Service, where he has worked as a research scientist for more than 18 years. His job duties include the coordination of forensic research activities within the laboratory (as well as between other entities, including academia, industry, and other domestic and international law enforcement laboratories), particularly in the areas of latent print visualization, questioned document analysis, instrumental analysis, and ink and paper chemistry. He has published more than two dozen articles on latent print and document chemistry and given or conducted more than 50 lectures and workshops in more than a dozen countries. He was awarded distinguished membership status in the International Association for Identification in 2008.

Dr. Henry C. Lee is one of the world's foremost forensic scientists. His work has made him a landmark in modern-day forensic sciences. He has been a prominent player in many of the most challenging cases of the last 50 years. Dr. Lee has worked with many law enforcement agencies from 46 countries and helped solve more than 8000 cases. In recent years, his travels have taken him to England, Bosnia, China, Germany, Singapore, Croatia, Brunei, Thailand, the Middle East, and other countries around the world. Dr. Lee currently serves at the University of New Haven (UNH) as distinguished chair professor. He is also the founder of the Henry C. Lee Institute of Forensic Science and serves as director of the Forensic Research & Training Center and as director of UNH National Cold Case Center.

Dr. Lee's testimony figured prominently in the O. J. Simpson, Jason Williams, Peterson, and Kennedy Smith trials and in convictions of the "Wood chipper" murderer as well as thousands of other murder cases. He has assisted local and state police in their investigations of other famous crimes, such as the murder of Jon Benet Ramsey in Boulder, Colorado; the 1993 suicide of White House Counsel, Vincent Foster; the kidnapping of Elizabeth Smart; the death of Chemdra Levy; the reinvestigation of the Kennedy assassination; and the Casey Anthony case.

Dr. Lee is currently the director of Forensic Research and Training Center and distinguished chair professor in Forensic Science of University of New Haven. He was the chief emeritus for Connecticut State Police from 2000 to 2010 and was the commissioner of public safety for the State of Connecticut from 1998 to 2000. He has also served as Connecticut's chief criminalist and director of State Police Forensic laboratory from 1978 to 2000. Dr. Lee was the driving force in establishing a modern state police communication system, community-based police services sex offender and DNA databank, major crime investigation concepts, and advanced forensic science services in Connecticut.

In 1975, Dr. Lee joined the University of New Haven, where he created the school's Forensic Sciences program. He has also taught as a professor at more than a dozen universities, law schools, and medical schools. Though challenged with the demands on his time, Dr. Lee still lectures throughout the country and world to police, universities, and civic organizations. He has authored hundreds of articles in professional journals and has authored and coauthored more than 40 books, covering areas such as DNA, fingerprints, trace evidence, crime scene investigation, and crime scene reconstruction.

He is the author for some best sellers, such as *Famous Crime Revisited; Cracking Cases: The Science of Solving Crimes; Blood Evidence*; and *Creaking More Cases*. In addition, his textbooks such as *Forensic Science, Physical Evidence*, and *Henry Lee's Crime Scene Handbook* have been widely adopted in medical legal and forensic professions. He has appeared in many TV shows and movies. His television serial *Trace Evidence—Dr. Henry Lee File* has received high rating and has been showing around the world.

Dr. Lee has been the recipient of numerous medals and awards, including the 1996 Medal of Justice from the Justice Foundation and the 1998 Lifetime Achievement Award from the Science and Engineer Association. He has also been the recipient of the Distinguished Criminalist Award from the American Academy of Forensic Sciences; the J. Donero Award from the International Association of Identification; the ACFE Lifetime Achievement Award from the American College of Forensic Examiner in 2000; the Medal of Honor from Ellis Island Foundation in 2004; Congressional Recognition for Outstanding Services from the U.S. Congress in 2004; the Presidential Medal of Honor from the Croatian president in 2005; the Medal of Service from the Ministry of Interior, Taiwan, Republic of China, 2006; the Friendship Award from the People's Republic of China; and the Gusi Peace Award from the Philippines in 2008. He was elected a distinguished fellow of the American Academy of Forensic Science (AAFS) in 1992. He was invited as one of the overseas Chinese delegates to attend the 2011 People's Congress in China.

Dr. Lee was born in China and brought up in Taiwan. He first worked for the Taipei Police Department, attaining the rank of captain. He came to the United States with his wife, Margaret, in 1965. He received his BS in forensic science from John Jay College in 1972. Dr. Lee continued his studies in biochemistry at NYU, where he received his master's degree in 1974 and his PhD in 1975. He has also received special training from the FBI Academy, ATF, RCMP, and other organizations. He is a recipient of 20 honorary degrees: doctorate degrees of science from the University of New Haven, University of Connecticut; honorary doctorate of law from Roger Williams Law School, Michell College, American International University and Taiwan Scientific Technology University; honorary doctorate degree in Humem Letters from the University of Bridgeport, St. Joseph College, Armstrong University, in recognition of his contributions to law and science, etc.

R.E. Gaensslen received his BS in biology from the University of Notre Dame in 1965 and his PhD in biochemistry from Cornell University, Ithaca, New York, in 1971. He is a professor emeritus in the Department of Forensic Science at the University of Illinois at Chicago.

Prof. Gaensslen was formerly professor and director of graduate studies, forensic science, University of Illinois at Chicago; professor and director of forensic science at the University of New Haven; visiting fellow at the National Institute of Law Enforcement and Criminal Justice; and associate professor at the John Jay College of Criminal Justice, City University of New York.

Prof. Gaensslen has authored or coauthored several books and chapters in edited volumes and has edited or coedited four books. He has also published over 60 papers in the refereed scientific literature. He has given over 130 presentations at scientific meetings and to general audiences. He has also organized, coordinated, and participated in dozens of workshops and training courses for forensic science laboratory as well as law enforcement personnel.

Prof. Gaensslen is a fellow of the Criminalistics Section, American Academy of Forensic Sciences. He has received the Paul L. Kirk Distinguished Criminalist Award from the Criminalistics Section, and was made a distinguished fellow by the academy in 2000. He is a life member of the Northeastern Association of Forensic Scientists. He was editor of the Journal of Forensic Sciences from 1992 to 2000 and has been an associate editor from 2000 to the present. He was also professor emeritus in the Forensic Science Group, Department of Biopharmaceutical Sciences, University of Illinois at Chicago.

Prof. Gaensslen has been project director/principal investigator on numerous grants and contracts for training and research. Some of his most recent projects include serving as co-principal investigator on an NIJ-funded grant to estimate the prevalence of drug-facilitated sexual assault and on two studies funded by the Midwest Forensic Resources Center at Ames Lab, Ames, Iowa.

Contributors

Joseph Almog
Casali Institute of Applied Chemistry
The Hebrew University of Jerusalem
Jerusalem, Israel

Helen L. Bandey
Centre for Applied Science and Technology
Home Office
Hertfordshire, United Kingdom

Andy Bécue
Institute of Police Science
School of Criminal Sciences
University of Lausanne
Lausanne, Switzerland

Stephen M. Bleay
Centre for Applied Science and Technology
Home Office
Hertfordshire, United Kingdom

Antonio A. Cantú
Forensic Services Division
United States Secret Service
Falls Church, Virginia

Bruce Comber
Forensic and Data Centres
Australian Federal Police
Canberra, Australia

Andrew P. Gibson
Centre for Applied Science and Technology
Home Office
Hertfordshire, United Kingdom

Chris Lennard
Faculty of Applied Science
National Centre for Forensic Studies
University of Canberra
Canberra, Australia

Linda A. Lewis
Chemical Sciences Division
Oak Ridge National Laboratory
Oak Ridge, Tennessee

Cedric Neumann
Eberly College of Science
The Pennsylvania State University
University Park, Pennsylvania

Gemma Payne
Forensic and Data Centres
Australian Federal Police
Canberra, Australia

Robert S. Ramotowski
Forensic Services Division
Department of Homeland Security
United States Secret Service
Washington, District of Columbia

Vaughn G. Sears
Centre for Applied Science and Technology
Home Office
Hertfordshire, United Kingdom

Naomi Speers
Forensic and Data Centres
Australian Federal Police
Canberra, Australia

Milutin Stoilovic
Australian Federal Police
Monash, Australia

Della Wilkinson
Forensic Science and Identification Services
Royal Canadian Mounted Police
Ottawa, Canada

1

Powder Methods

Robert S. Ramotowski

CONTENTS

1.1 Fingerprint Powders

Powders are perhaps the oldest means for visualizing prints and have been in use since the late nineteenth century [1]. Over the years, a considerable number of organic and inorganic materials have been used to make powders. Several references provide a detailed description of the early development and chemistry of powder formulations [1–3]. However, most of this information is of historical interest, since powders are now largely purchased from commercial sources.

The powder development process is essentially a mechanical or physical phenomenon. Powders adhere to moist and tacky latent print residue; however, this attraction decreases over time as the residue begins to dry out. Thomas studied the underlying physics of this adhesion process [4]. An electrostatic potential was applied to a powder-coated aluminum surface in an effort to detach the powder particles. The stress required to remove particles from ridge deposits was calculated to be $2.2 \times 10^6 N/m^2$, while only $\sim 10^3 N/m^2$ was required to remove particles from the furrows. Frictional charging (caused by contact of the brush fibers with the print residue) was found to play only a very minor role in the powder adhesion process.

There are a number of categories of powder types (e.g., traditional, magnetic, luminescent, thermoplastic, and nanoparticles), each of which will be briefly discussed in this chapter. However, a review of more recent advances in conventional and nanoparticle powders will be covered in subsequent chapters.

1.1.1 Traditional Powders

Historically, fingerprint powders were often made using toxic substances, which contained inorganic heavy metals (e.g., lead, mercury) and aromatic organic compounds (e.g., soot/lampblack, aniline dyes). One particularly toxic early method involved dusting lead acetate or carbonate onto paper and then fuming the substrate with hydrogen sulfide to produce brown-colored ridge detail [2]. Traditional powders consisted of resinous polymeric material for adhesion and a colorant for developing contrast [5]. Common adhesive materials were starch, kaolin, rosin, and silica gel. The majority of early recipes for powders used inorganic salts for colorants; however, the trend has now shifted more to organic colorant compounds.

Dyes have been suggested for use as powders since the early twentieth century. In 1906, Stockis suggested the use of a mixture of lycopodium powder and the azo dye, Sudan black III [2]. In 1920, Mitchell mentioned the use of methylene blue to detect prints on paper [6]. Most of these dyes fell out of use when more efficient chemical methods were introduced. However, xanthene dyes mixed with inexpensive insoluble salts have recently been recommended by Sodhi and Kaur [5]. Other dye powders with luminescent characteristics have once again found use after the introduction of laser and alternate light source.

Nonmagnetic, metallic powders were introduced to reduce moisture absorption (common with powders based on chalk or talc) and to improve durability and the photographic recording contrast of developed prints [7]. Examples of these powders included bronze, gold, or aluminum metal flakes. These fine-lining metal flakes were typically used as pigments in metallic paints. Ultimately, the aluminum metal flake powder found the most widespread use and became the standard powder recommended by the U.K. Home Office [8].

1.1.2 Magnetic Powders

The first reported use of a magnetic applicator and powder was by MacDonell in 1961 [9]. The invention of the Magna brush allowed for surfaces to be processed without streaking caused by the interaction of conventional brush fibers with the latent print residue. Excess powder could be removed from the substrate by cleaning the powder from the Magna brush and then passing it over the print. Powder that had not adhered to the print would be attracted to the magnet on the brush. Modifications to the original Magna brush design were reported by Ball [10]. He also reported on the construction of a large-scale magnetic applicator to aid in the processing of larger surface areas [11]. Eight quarter-inch diameter magnetic rods were placed in between wooden dowels in order to construct a continuous brush head of powder.

Commercial magnetic powders were initially composed of a two-component system—a nearly spherical, magnetic iron carrier (~50 μm in diameter) and a copper or aluminum nonmagnetic flake developer (~10–20 μm in diameter) [12]. It was thought that a one-component, purely magnetic flake powder could perform the dual functions of carrier and developer more efficiently. Attempts to improve magnetic powders were undertaken in the late 1980s [13]. Initial studies focused on optimizing the particle size and stearic acid levels. Stearic acid is usually added during the milling process to promote the production of smooth, reflective surfaces. It also improves adhesion of such powders to latent print residue. In fact, Goode and Morris reported that when stearic acid was removed from the production process, the effectiveness of the flake powders produced diminished significantly [14]. Optimum development was achieved when the particle size was 10–25 μm in diameter and had a stearic acid content of 3–5 wt.% [12].

An effort to investigate the effect of particle morphology on the effectiveness of magnetic powders was reported by James et al. [15]. Irregularly shaped powders with rough surfaces and jagged edges were found to produce darker print development while spherical powders with smooth, rounded surfaces produced lighter print development. In comparison to nonmagnetic aluminum flake powder, the new magnetic powders reportedly performed better on rougher surfaces, while the flake powder did slightly better on smooth surfaces. Additional work was done to improve the magnetic wand applicator using rare earth magnets. Applicators of different sizes, including one that could hold up to 200 g of powder (compared to the ~2 g of powder that commercial wands could hold), were developed and tested.

During field trials, the new magnetic flake powders, marketed in the United Kingdom as Magneta Flake by K9 Scenes of Crime Products Ltd. performed well on a variety of substrates. Milne reported on identifiable prints developed in a series of different crime scenes in east London after aluminum powder failed to produce sufficient detail [16]. Bailey reported that magnetic powder was superior to non-magnetic powder on a series of ceramic cups [17].

1.1.3 Luminescent Powders

Fluorescent powders were introduced in the late 1970s after the laser began to be used for visualizing latent prints. Dalrymple et al. first reported the use of coumarin-6 as a fluorescent powder in conjunction with an argon ion laser in 1977 [18]. Thornton described a modified coumarin-6 powder in which the dye was mixed with conventional black powder in a ratio of 1:100 and dissolved in ethanol [19]. After the solvent evaporated, the powder was dusted onto different surfaces. The black powder appeared to act as a carrier for the fluorescent coumarin-6 dye. Prints not apparent in the visible mode could subsequently be imaged in the fluorescent mode using a laser.

Menzel and Duff expanded the list of fluorescent dye powders to include Mars red, several lake pigments (produced by precipitating a dye with a metallic salt), and several metal-free pigments [20]. Ultimately, the lake pigments and Mars red were deemed too toxic for general use. Naphthol red B, a metal-free pigment, was found to be comparable to Mars red in intensity and performance. Rhodamine dyes (6G and B), acridine yellow, Nile blue perchlorate, oxazine 1 perchlorate, 3,3′-diethyloxadicarbocyanine iodide, and 3,3′-diethylthiatricarbocyanine iodide were also suggested as candidates for fluorescent dye powders [21].

Menzel also suggested the use of phosphorescent powders [22]. Emission lifetimes for fluorescent materials are on the order of nano- to microseconds (i.e., 1×10^{-9}–1×10^{-6} s), while for phosphorescent materials the timeframe is measured in milliseconds (i.e., 1×10^{-3} s). These powders could help limit background fluorescence from the substrate by taking advantage of these differences in luminescence lifetimes. For example, once an excitation source was cut off from a sample, the background fluorescence lifetime would quickly decay; however, a phosphor-developed print would continue to luminesce for a significantly longer period of time. This time difference, although very small, allowed the background interference to be nearly completely eliminated.

A rare earth–doped phosphor (strontium aluminate) powder was used in experiments using a similar approach, which is referred to as time-resolved imaging [23]. After illumination with long-wave UV radiation for 2 min, the luminescence from the phosphor-dusted print was separated from the background fluorescence. Fluorescence lifetime imaging has also been used successfully to visualize fluorescent powder-dusted prints [24]. Nanosecond-scale, time-resolved imaging was described by Seah et al. [25]. Because of this high resolution, even fluorescence (not phosphorescence) from magnetic powders could be resolved and eliminated from the background substrate fluorescence.

1.1.4 Thermoplastic Powders

In 1967, Jones recommended the use of photocopy toners to visualize latent prints as well as using heat to fix them to the substrate [26]. Good results were obtained even on a paper towel. Micik recommended a similar process but used dry ink instead of toner to initially visualize the print [27]. Ball described the use of a modified mixture of iron-based magnetic photocopy toner to develop latent prints using a magnetic brush [28]. A toner-based technique was also developed by Gert de Waal of the South African Criminal Bureau and reported by Putter [29]. After heating the sample to darken and fuse the toner, good results were obtained on items like foil wrappers from cigarette packs. Singla and Jasuja reported a modified toner method that did not require application of heat to fuse the toner [30]. Dry photostat toners were dusted onto the surface and then fixed by carefully spraying ethyl ether from a distance of about 10 cm. Different colored toners could be used for different colored surfaces.

1.1.5 Nanotechnology Powders

In the past decade, there has been considerable interest in using nano-sized particles (between 1×10^{-9}–1×10^{-6} m in diameter) as powders for latent print development. One such technology involved the use of quantum dots, which are semiconductor nanocrystals exhibiting special optical properties that are dependent upon their size [31]. As a result, the emission wavelength characteristics can be tuned to a desired wavelength by modifying their particle size. Quantum dots have been reported to fluoresce up to 20 times brighter than conventional dyes [32]. However, there are serious health and safety concerns about dusting with such nanoparticle powders, especially those that contain cadmium (this will be covered in more detail in a subsequent chapter).

Menzel reported on the use of cadmium sulfide nanocrystals capped with dioctyl sulfosuccinate [33]. Although applied as a post-cyanoacrylate dye stain, the technique showed the promise of enhancing latent prints. Combining these quantum dots with functionalized dendrimers (roughly spherical polymers that have extensive, highly functionalized branched chains) added the possibility of chemical, rather than physical, interactions between latent print residue and quantum dot powders. Initially, the generation 4 Starburst® (PAMAM) dendrimer was used because it could bond chemically (via amide linkages) to the carboxylic acid or ester groups present in latent print residue [34]. A complete overview of nanoparticle technology for latent print development will be provided in a subsequent chapter.

1.1.6 Anti-Stokes Powders

These powders are comprised of specialized materials that exhibit upconversion or anti-Stokes emissions. In the conventional fluorescence emission process, lower wavelength (higher energy) radiation is used to convert a material to its excited state. The material returns to its ground state by emitting a photon at a longer wavelength (lower energy). The difference in excitation and emission wavelengths is referred to as the Stokes shift. An example would be using the 514.5 nm line of an argon ion laser to excite rhodamine 6G dye, which would emit at a maximum wavelength of approximately 555 nm.

When upconversion materials are excited with longer wavelength (lower energy) radiation sources like high-powered, near-infrared lasers, multiple photons can be absorbed. The emission of a single photon occurs at a shorter wavelength (higher energy). The difference in wavelengths is referred to as the anti-Stokes shift. An example of this was reported by Ma et al. who excited $NaYF_4$ doped with erbium and ytterbium at 980 nm and observed an emission in the green portion of the spectrum (495–570 nm) [35]. The material produced good results on some difficult surfaces, including Australian polymer banknotes.

Overall, the primary advantage of using near-infrared excitation sources is that very few substrates absorb in that region of the spectrum. Thus, the excited substrates do not emit visible fluorescence that could compete with that emanating from the anti-Stokes-powdered print. For example, when a Coca Cola can is illuminated with green light, the red-colored background luminesces strongly. When illuminated at 980 nm, the same background emits little or no background fluorescence. Although still a very recent development in latent print visualization field, these upconversion materials were studied extensively by Elicia Bullock, a student at the University of Technology, Sydney, Australia [36].

Reagent application

Care must be exercised when using conventional fingerprint brushes. Latent prints can be very fragile and easily damaged or destroyed by the lack of proper technique. James et al. studied the various factors that could lead to print damage, including a variety of powder and brush types [37]. Magnetic applicators were found to produce less damage than standard zephyr or squirrel hair brushes. They also noted that sebaceous-rich prints are more prone to smearing, although this tends to decrease as the print ages. Temperature and humidity conditions were also found to be a factor. In an effort to produce a brush-less application method for powders, an aerosol spray method was introduced by Bonura in 1960 [38]. However, a review of the new technique by the Subcommittee on Fingerprints of the Science and Practice Committee of the International Association for Identification (IAI) found that its performance was less effective than conventional black powder [39].

In some cases, prints have been reportedly revived by "huffing" or breathing warm moisture onto the print prior to powdering [40]. It is thought that as a print dries out, salts and minerals are still left behind. These chemicals would then absorb water from warm, moist breath and rehydrate the print, making it more amenable to powdering. Delano recommended the use of a commercial vaporizer instead of huffing in order to prevent an examiner from inhaling the powder [41]. Importantly, this method would significantly reduce DNA contamination of the print and surface by an examiner using the huffing method. Fortunato and Walton reported the use of this technique to improve recovery of prints from skin [42]. In some cases, application of warm moisture from breath has been done after the print has been powdered, but just prior to lifting the impression [43].

1.2 Powder Suspension Techniques

Powder suspensions are typically a mixture of water, powder, and surfactant. While the specific choice of these ingredients can have a significant impact on the reagent's performance, the technique has gained widespread acceptance as a robust technique that can be used on a wide variety of surface types.

1.2.1 Small Particle Reagent

Small particle reagent (SPR) as a method for visualizing latent prints dates back to the mid-1970s, when Morris and Wells (working for the Atomic Weapons Research Establishment, Aldermaston, United Kingdom) patented it in 1977 [14]. These initial reagents consisted of an insoluble powder mixed with a dilute surfactant solution (similar to today's powder suspension methods). The powders used in this reagent needed to have particle sizes that ranged between 1 and 10 μm (although very small-sized particles performed poorly) and included molybdenum disulfide, graphite, cobalt oxide, lead oxide, photocopier toner, and Monastral blue dye. Molybdenum disulfide was found to produce the best and most consistent results. It was also inexpensive and did not suffer from batch-to-batch variations, like other materials evaluated.

The development of SPR grew out of a need to develop prints on nonporous items that had been wetted or subjected to long immersion times in water. In fact, some tests have shown that items submerged in water for more than 30 days can still yield prints when SPR is used [44]. Many diverse types of surfaces are amenable to SPR processing, including exotic items such as raw ivory [45].

It was assumed that since SPR developed prints on wetted surfaces, it must be interacting with the lipid fraction of the latent print (although apparently not the same material as physical developer). The use of spot tests indicated that SPR interacted with compounds like oleic and linoleic acids, glycerol esters, cholesterol, and squalene. Interestingly, Goode and Morris reported that SPR could be used on wetted paper, including surface-coated and waxy papers (e.g., packaging used for commercial explosives). Reynoldson and Reed conducted an operational trial that compared SPR and VMD [46]. They found that VMD produced nearly twice as many prints as SPR on polyethylene bags. In 23% of the cases, VMD produced prints while this occurred in only 5% of the cases with SPR.

The presence of a surfactant was found to be critical to the success of SPR. Although the type of surfactant was not found to be important (i.e., nonionic, cationic, etc.), the chemical's "tail" had to contain at least eight carbon atoms. Recommendations for a specific surfactant concentration were also found to be unnecessary. However, too low of a concentration caused random deposition and too high of a concentration resulted in little or no deposition of powder. Goode and Morris recommended a mixture of Tergitol 7 and choline chloride. Their original recommended formula involved creating a surfactant stock solution (8 mL Tergitol 7, 4 g choline chloride, and 500 mL distilled water), which would then be used to create a working solution (10 g of molybdenum disulfide, 50 mL surfactant stock solution, and 900 mL distilled water). The addition of choline chloride was later found to be unnecessary [46]. Haque et al. agreed, noting that good results could be obtained with their iron oxide suspension without the choline chloride [47]. The authors speculated that the function of this additive might have been to render the sebaceous materials in the latent print more hydrophilic. Pounds et al. also found that the presence of choline chloride was not necessary and also recommended the use of molybdenum disulfide dispersed in Manoxol OT [48].

Jasuja et al. reported on the use of a nonsynthetic-based detergent derived from the dried fruit of the *Sapindus mukorossi* plant [49]. The fruit contained saponin, a natural and biodegradable substitute for synthetic detergents. The authors prepared several SPRs by combining powders (e.g., black charcoal) with the detergent solution. The detergent solution was prepared by adding 15 g of powder with 100 mL of the detergent solution (1 mL of saponin in 125 mL of distilled water). One dried fruit could produce up to 5 mL of saponin, which could then produce 600 mL of the SPR reagent. The naturally derived detergent SPRs performed as well as ones containing synthetic detergents; however, they provided the additional advantage of a significant cost savings.

When preparing the reagent, molybdenum disulfide should be added in small amounts while constantly stirring the mixture. When finished, the mixture should be vigorously shaken and also just prior to use. The material can be applied by spraying, by dipping, or in the form of an aerosol foam. If the dipping method is used, the articles need to be placed face down into the SPR solution for approximately 30–60 s. The article is then transferred to a water bath and is gently agitated to remove excess reagent. The article should then be allowed to dry completely.

An interesting additional processing step was recently described by Cohen et al. [50]. The authors had noted that after processing a taxi involved in a carjacking with molybdenum-disulfide-based SPR, additional print detail could be obtained by wiping the dry residual SPR with paper towels. It also appeared that the stronger the wiping action, the better the prints. After the wiping process, the background turned yellowish-brown and a sulfurous odor was detected (presumed to be hydrogen sulfide gas released by a catalytic oxidation–reduction chemical reaction [51]). The prints could not be lifted from the surface with a tape but could be removed with water and a damp cloth.

1.2.2 Black Powder Suspensions

The first black powder suspension method appeared to have been developed in Japan in the early 1990s. This method was reported by Burns after a trip to Matsuyama City in Japan in 1992 [52]. This simple mixture of water, detergent, and powder would eventually be marketed as Sticky-side Powder™ by the Lightning Powder Company. Numerous other commercially available products have been marketed since the 1990s. The reagent was initially applied to the adhesive side of tape either by immersion or painting. However, black powder suspensions have been used successfully on a variety of nonporous surfaces, including Tyvek shipping envelopes [53].

Given the simple and relatively inexpensive components used to make black powder suspensions, there have been a number of efforts conducted to make customized versions of these commercially available reagents. Kimble experimented with several different powders, including Lightning black powder, Lightning REDWOP powder, Delta dual fingerprint powder, Sirchie silver metallic powder, and Sirchie galvanic powder [54]. A diluted Kodak Photo-Flo 200 solution was used as the surfactant. Results comparable to Sticky-side Powder were achieved for several of the powder suspensions. Another black powder suspension reagent, composed of Lightning black powder and the concentrated liquid detergent Liqui-Nox™, has been described as Alternate Black Powder [55].

The U.K. Home Office performed numerous studies on black powder suspensions beginning in 1999 [8]. Two different reagents were ultimately recommended, one carbon based (CBPS) and another one based on iron oxide (FeBPS). The CBPS reagent was found to work better on adhesive surfaces, while the FeBPS reagent was reported to work better on nonporous surfaces [56]. On tapes with rubber-based adhesives, the Home Office recommended that cyanoacrylate fuming be done prior the use of CBPS. For acrylic-based adhesive tapes, CBPS was recommended without prior cyanoacrylate fuming.

1.2.3 White Powder Suspensions

An attempt to formulate a powder suspension technique that worked on dark-colored surfaces was reported by Frank et al. in 1993 [57]. A number of different white powders were tried, including barium sulfate, talc, titanium dioxide, zinc oxide, zinc carbonate, and basic zinc carbonate. The best results were achieved with a mixture consisting of 0.66 g of zinc carbonate, 20 mL of water, 0.06 g of Tergitol-7, and 55 g of diethyl ether as a propellant. As with the molybdenum disulfide optimization trials, the authors noted that smaller zinc carbonate particles (~2 μm) performed better than larger ones (~6 μm).

A titanium dioxide version of white powder suspension was reported by Wade in 2002 [58]. The author used SPR-W (Sirchie), which is a mixture of titanium dioxide, Tergitol 7, and water. Improvement in development was observed when Kodak Photo-Flo was added (a ratio of two parts SPR-W to one part Photo-Flo was used). Print detail was developed on both sides of a black electrical tape. A paste version was attempted using Kerr-McGee's CR-880 (a paint grade TiO_2 that has an average particle size of 0.22 μm) and equal parts of water and Photo-Flo. Different samples of the rutile and anatase forms of titanium dioxide were tested and the rutile form (specifically, Kemira 820) was found to perform best. The use of distilled water was recommended to reduce background interference. Development on light-colored tapes could be achieved using an alternate light source with the excitation wavelength set in the 300–400 nm range and an orange cutoff filter. Williams et al. also reported excellent results with titanium dioxide [59]. The authors noted successful development by mixing SPR-W with Photo-Flo (2:1 ratio) and immersing the item in the reagent. They recommended a rinse that consisted of a 1:1 mixture of tap water and Photo-Flo to improve contrast on duct and electrical tapes.

Three types of white powder suspension reagents were recently compared [60]. The three types (Wetwop™, Wet Powder, and an HOSDB white powder suspension) were all titanium oxide based. Latent prints were aged for 24 h prior to immersion in tap water for 6 h. The prints were then dried and aged up to 8 days. Results indicated that no appreciable differences were observed for recovery rates of prints during the aging study. Overall, Wetwop was found to be the best white powder suspension reagent evaluated. A follow-up study compared the white Wetwop to vacuum metal deposition (VMD) [61]. Latent prints were aged for 24 h prior to immersion in tap water for 6 h. The prints were dried and aged up to 28 days. Results indicate that the two methods performed comparably on the various wetted nonporous surfaces. The authors recommend that if VMD fails to produce ridge detail, then a powder suspension technique should be attempted.

White powder suspensions were also investigated for use in the enhancement of bloody fingerprints [62]. The authors compared Wetwop and an HOSDB white powder suspension (WPS) formulation. The reagents were applied to the prints using a camel hair brush. Results indicated that WPS used on dark backgrounds produced better results than using either acid violet 17 or acid black 1. The best overall processing sequence was found to involve processing with the acid dyes followed by WPS.

1.2.4 Fluorescent Powder Suspensions

The development of a fluorescent powder suspension technique was considered ideal, as it could work on dark, light, or multicolored surfaces. Springer et al. reported such a technique in 1995 [63]. Rhodamine 6G and Basic Yellow 40 were used to prepare "powder" suspensions. The BY-40 SPR was found to work best and was prepared by mixing 100 mL of a 0.1% BY 40 solution (in ethanol) with 100 mL of the Home Office MoS_2 SPR stock solution [8]. Another fluorescent SPR, Liqui-Drox, was reported by Hollars et al. in 2000 [64]. The reagent was a mixture of 20% Ardrox P-133D, 40% Liqui-Nox (an industrial detergent), and 40% distilled water. The adhesive surface was painted with this material and then rinsed with distilled water after 10 s. After the item was dry, a long-wave ultraviolet source was used to excite any fluorescent ridge detail. Any developed prints should be photographed immediately, as fading can occur significantly within 12 h. This technique was reported not to visualize any latent prints on the nonadhesive side of tapes.

Jasuja et al. used zinc carbonate as a "carrier" for a series of fluorescent powders, including rhodamine B, rhodamine 6G, acridine orange, anthracene, cyano blue, and Basic Yellow 40 [65]. Latent prints used in the study were either fresh or submerged in water for up to 96 h. The best results were obtained with cyano blue. The reagent was created by preparing two solutions: a dye solution (0.01 g of cyano blue dissolved in 10 mL of distilled water) and a zinc carbonate solution (7.5 g dissolved in a mixture of 1 mL of the detergent Labolene and 125 mL of distilled water). This solution was reported to remain stable for up to 12 days. A short-wave ultraviolet source was required to excite fluorescence (the optimal excitation wavelength for cyano blue is <280 nm).

Sodhi et al. reported on a similar fluorescent SPR using eosin Y [66]. The reagent was prepared by mixing 5.0 g of zinc carbonate in 75 mL of distilled water and then adding 0.01 g of eosin Y and 0.3 mL of the commercial detergent GenteelIR. Latent prints immersed in water for up to 36 h produced clear and sharp print detail. Developed prints were viewed using 505–550 nm excitation and a red filter. This eosin Y SPR was also reported to produce good development on compact discs without harming the data stored on the medium [67]. An additional washing step involving the use of a 1:1 mixture of ethanol–water and wiping with cotton was required to clear the developed prints.

1.2.5 Operational Usage and Sequencing

There have been some comments regarding the proper role for powder suspensions in the overall processing sequence. A number of papers have noted that prefuming items like tapes or nonporous items can cause the performance of powder suspensions to decrease dramatically. Scott reported that for latex and nitrile gloves as well as various tapes, cyanoacrylate fuming of these items prior to the use of powder suspensions failed to produce any additional ridge detail [68]. In contrast, prints of excellent quality were developed on these surfaces when fuming was not performed. Another study examined the best way to process balled-up tape. The authors concluded that if the tape samples had been processed first with cyanoacrylate fuming, the use of alternate powder suspensions would produce poor results [69].

Onstwedder et al. report on the effect of SPR processing on subsequent firearms analysis [70]. Because molybdenum disulfide can be used as a lubricant, there was concern that the reagent could have an impact on the internal workings of a firearm. The firearms were immersed in water for up to 35 days, refrigerated in water overnight, and then processed with the original Morris SPR reagent. Each side of the firearm was immersed into the SPR solution three times for 45–60 s. This method was compared with allowing the submerged firearms to dry, and then subjecting them to cyanoacrylate fuming and black powder. The SPR reagent was found to produce more suitable prints than the CA fuming/black powder sequence. The latter processing sequence was found to have a more significant impact on the subsequent firearms analysis.

Powder suspensions have been successfully used on a variety of different surfaces. The traditional molybdenum-based SPR was reported to work well on glass bottles soaked with arson accelerants [71]. Accelerants tested included gasoline, kerosene, diesel oil, a 1:1 mixture of gasoline and diesel oil, mineral oil, turpentine, paint thinner (Nitro 21), and toluene. With SPR, prints could still be recovered with 50%–60% success rates 13 days after treatment with the accelerant. A follow-up study evaluated several SPR reagents for processing these items [72]. The best SPR reagent contained 8–12 mL of detergent (Tergitol 7) per liter of water and 200 g per liter of molybdenum disulfide powder. SPRs were also found to be successful at recovering latent prints from a variety of objects exposed to temperatures of 200°C from arson scenes [73]. Objects exposed to firefighting media (e.g., water, foam) could also be recovered. An added benefit of this process was that upon application, the detergent in the SPR reagent effectively removed soot.

The Israel National Police were the first to report the use of both black and white SPR as an aerosol spray in 1992. With these products, dimethyl ether was used as a propellant.

Similar products were reported by Ishizawa et al. in 1999 [74]. Because the authors were applying for a patent on these sprays, the exact nature of all of the constituents was not provided in their publication. However, the product was found to contain a mixture of 3–7 g of powder (mixtures of agalmatolite (80%), lithopene (10%), and zinc oxide (10%) for white SPR and carbon black (45%) and carbon graphite (55%) for black SPR) per 100 mL of fixer (which contained denatured amino silicone, dimethyl silicone, isopropyl alcohol, water, and other proprietary chemicals).

The adhesive type used on tapes was found to significantly influence the performance of SPRs [73]. Two adhesive types, rubber (styrene and butadiene) and acrylic (ethyl, butyl, and ethyl-hexyl acrylates), were investigated. The iron-based HOSDB powder suspension was found to work well on rubber-based adhesives, but poorly on acrylic-based ones. A similar result was observed with the HOSDB titanium-oxide-based powder suspension. Overall, acrylic tapes processed with powder suspensions resulted in significant background development. The study also revealed that carbon black (powdered graphite) outperformed iron-oxide-based powder suspensions on adhesive tapes. The iron-oxide-based formulation recommended by HOSDB involved mixing 20 mL of detergent solution (25 mL of Triton X detergent with 35 mL of ethylene glycol and 40 mL of distilled water) with 20 g of iron oxide powder [75]. Overall for nonwetted surfaces, regular powders were found to be the most effective process on smooth nonporous surfaces and superglue fuming/dye stain was found to be the most effective for rough, nonporous surfaces.

Reagent preparation

SPR/black powder suspension

For light surfaces there are two options, the traditional molybdenum-disulfide-based reagent or the iron oxide one.

Israel National Police SPR [51]

Detergent solution	
Dioctylsulfosuccinate, sodium salt (98%)	10 mg
Water (tap)	90 mL
Stock solution	
Molybdenum disulfide	100 mg
Detergent solution	15 mL
Water (tap)	1000 mL
Working solution	
Stock solution	100 mL
Water (tap)	1000 mL

1. Carefully mix the reagents in the order they are listed to create the detergent and stock solutions.
2. To prepare the working solution, add 100 mL of the stock solution and dilute it up to 1 L with tap water.
3. Working solutions are typically prepared as needed and disposed of after processing has been completed.
4. For stock or detergent solutions, the appropriate information (e.g., chemical contents, preparer's initials, date, reliability test result) should be recorded on the container's label.

HOSDB iron oxide powder suspension [75]:

Detergent solution	
Triton X detergent	25 mL
Ethylene glycol	35 mL
Distilled water	40 mL
Working solution	
Detergent solution	100 mL
Water (tap)	1000 mL

1. Carefully mix the reagents in the order they are listed to create the detergent solution.
2. To prepare the working solution, combine 20 mL of the detergent solution with 20 g of iron oxide powder (obtained from Fisher Scientific, product number I/1100/53).
3. Stir the mixture until an even consistency has been achieved.
4. Working solutions are typically prepared as needed and disposed of after processing has been completed.
5. For the detergent solutions, the appropriate information (e.g., chemical contents, preparer's initials, date, reliability test result) should be recorded on the container's label.

   Note that commercially available powder suspensions like Wetwop, Sticky-side Powder, and Wet Print can also be used. The HOSDB iron oxide powder suspension is typically used on nonadhesive surfaces.

White powder suspension
For dark surfaces, the use of white particle suspensions is recommended.

Sirchie SPR-W (immersion) [59]

SPR-W*	2 parts
Kodak Photo-Flo 200	1 part

1. Carefully mix the reagents in a pan large and deep enough to accommodate the evidence.
2. Stir the mixture until an even consistency has been achieved.
3. Working solutions are typically prepared as needed and disposed of after processing has been completed.

Williams and Elliot (dipping) [59]

Titanium dioxide (Kemira 820 rutile)	1 g
Kodak Photo-Flo 200	10 mL
Water (tap)	10 mL

1. Carefully add titanium dioxide, Photo-Flo, and water and mix thoroughly.
2. Working solutions are typically prepared as needed and disposed of after processing has been completed.

---

* As of December 2010, the Sirchie website now describes SPR-W as SPR200 (white).

Fluorescent powder suspension
For multicolored surfaces, there are a number of different fluorescent SPR formulations available, but the two commonly encountered examples are provided in the following.

Israel National Police Fluorescent SPR [63]

Basic yellow stock solution	
Basic Yellow 40	1 g
Ethanol	1 L
SPR stock solution [8]	
Water (tap)	500 mL
Tergitol 7	4 mL
Molybdenum disulfide (ROCOL AS Powder)	50 g
Working solution	
Basic Yellow 40 stock solution	100 mL
SPR stock solution	100 mL

1. Carefully mix the reagents in the order they are listed to create the BY40 and SPR stock solutions.
2. To prepare the working solution, combine 100 mL of the BY40 stock solution with 100 mL of the SPR stock solution.
3. Stir the mixture until an even consistency has been achieved.
4. Working solutions are typically prepared as needed and disposed of after processing has been completed.
5. For the stock solutions, the appropriate information (e.g., chemical contents, preparer's initials, date, reliability test result) should be recorded on the container's label.

Excitation of developed prints is achieved by setting the alternate light source (ALS) wavelength to 450 nm and viewing the emission with a 549 nm cutoff filter.

Liqui-Drox [64]

Working solution	
Ardrox P-133D	200 mL
Liqui-Nox detergent	400 mL
Distilled water	400 mL

1. The solution should be mixed thoroughly until it has a thick consistency and milky-yellow color.
2. The solution should be constantly agitated to maintain the suspension.
3. Working solutions are typically prepared as needed and disposed of after processing has been completed.

Excitation of developed prints is achieved using long-wave ultraviolet light and viewed with either yellow or orange goggles.

Reagent application

There are several different application methods that can be used to treat items of different sizes and surface characteristics [59]. Most commercial products can be used as purchased via the spraying or aerosol methods. Other application methods may require slight modifications to the formulas listed earlier. All appropriate personal protective equipment should be used when preparing and using this reagent. Run the appropriate positive and negative controls to ensure that the reagent solution is working properly. When processing has been completed, all chemicals should be disposed of properly according to the appropriate federal, state, and local environmental laws.

Spraying method
In this form of application, either commercially prepared products or custom systems [57] can be used. Processing involves spraying the surface with the reagent and then rinsing with water. A recent article by Cohen et al. [50] recommended wiping the surface with a paper towel to enhance the development on smooth surfaces. This should only be done after any visible print detail has been imaged.

Immersion method
The powder suspension mixture should be prepared by combining two parts of powder suspension with one part of Kodak Photo-Flo 200. Sufficient reagent should be prepared to completely submerge the item. Place the item into the solution for at least 1 min and agitate the solution carefully to avoid having the item impact the sides of the tray. Agitation is required to keep the particles in suspension. The item should then be placed into a tap water rinse bath until the desired contrast has been achieved. Spraying the rinse solution or placing it under a stream of water should be avoided since ridge detail could be lost on some surfaces. The item should then be allowed to air dry.

Dipping method
Sufficient reagent should be prepared to completely submerge the item. The item should be carefully dipped into the reagent several times over a period of 2–3 min. The solution should be agitated to prevent fallout of the suspended particles. The item should be slowly removed from the solution and then rinsed in a tap water bath. If hazing of the background occurs, rinsing the item in a bath of equal parts tap water and Kodak Photo-Flo 200 may improve contrast.

Pasting method
A mixture of equal parts of powder suspension and Kodak Photo-Flo 200 should be used. Several ounces of this mixture should be placed in a beaker and allowed to stand for at least 20 min to allow the mixture to separate. The excess liquid the top should be carefully decanted until only the paste at the bottom remains. Using a fine hair brush saturated with paste, apply it to the item's surface using very light pressure. The entire surface should be coated and then immediately rinsed off with running tap water or by submerging the item in a rinse bath of equal parts tap water and Kodak Photo-Flo 200. Exposure of the item to the powder suspension paste should be for no more than a few seconds (especially when processing tapes).

References

1. Lee HC, Gaensslen RE. (2001) Methods of latent fingerprint development. In: Lee HC, Gaensslen RE, Eds., *Advances in Fingerprint Technology*, 2nd edn. CRC Press, Boca Raton, FL.
2. Olsen RD. (1978) *Scott's Fingerprint Mechanics*. Charles C. Thomas, Springfield, IL.

3. Moenssens AA. (1971) *Fingerprint Techniques*. Chilton Book Company, Radnor, PA.
4. Thomas GL. (1978) The physics of fingerprints and their detection. *J Phys E Sci Instrum* 11:722–731.
5. Sodhi GS, Kaur J. (2001) Powder method for detecting latent fingerprints: a review. *Forensic Sci Int* 120:172–176.
6. Mitchell CA. (1920) The detection of finger-prints on documents. *Analyst* 45:122–129.
7. Chapel CE. (1941) *Finger Printing: A Manual of Identification*. Coward McCann, Inc., New York.
8. Bowman V, ed. (2004) *Manual of Fingerprint Development Techniques*, 2nd edn. (2nd revision). Home Office: Police Scientific Development Branch, Sandridge, U.K.
9. MacDonell HL. (1961) Bristless brush development of latent fingerprints. *Ident News* 11(3):7–9, 15.
10. Ball RD. (1983) D.I.Y. magnetic powder applicator. *Fingerprint Whorld* 8(31):74.
11. Ball RD. (1983) Blanket coverage. *Fingerprint Whorld* 9(33):14–16.
12. James JD, Pounds CA, Wilshire B. (1991) Magnetic flake fingerprint technology. *J Forensic Ident* 41(4):237–247.
13. James JD, Pounds CA, Wilshire B. (1991) Flake metal powders for revealing latent fingerprints. *J Forensic Sci* 36(5):1368–1375.
14. Goode GC, Morris JR. (1983) Latent fingerprints: a review of their origin, composition and methods for detection. AWRE Report No. 002/83.
15. James JD, Pounds CA, Wilshire B. (1992) New magnetic applicators and magnetic flake powders for revealing latent fingerprints. *J Forensic Ident* 42(6):531–542.
16. Milne R. (1996) Magnetic fingerprint powder. A field trial of K9 magneta flake powder. *Fingerprint Whorld* 22(85):113–116.
17. Bailey JA. (2003) An evaluation of magnetic and nonmagnetic fingerprint powders on ceramic materials. *J Forensic Ident* 53(2):162–168.
18. Dalrymple BE, Duff JM, Menzel ER. (1977) Inherent fingerprint luminescence—detection by laser. *J Forensic Sci* 22(1):106–115.
19. Thornton JI. (1978) Modification of fingerprint powder with coumarin-6 laser dye. *J Forensic Sci* 23(3):536–538.
20. Menzel ER, Duff JM. (1979) Laser detection of latent fingerprints—treatment with fluorescers. *J Forensic Sci* 24(1):96–100.
21. Menzel ER, Fox KE. (1980) Laser detection of latent fingerprints: preparation of fluorescent dusting powders and the feasibility of a portable system. *J Forensic Sci* 25(1):150–153.
22. Menzel ER. (1979) Laser detection of latent fingerprints—treatment with phosphorescers. *J Forensic Sci* 24(3):582–585.
23. Liu L, Zhang Z, Zhang L, Zhai Y. (2009) The effectiveness of strong afterglow phosphor powder in the detection of fingermarks. *Forensic Sci Int* 183:45–49.
24. Seah LK, Wang P, Murukeshan VM, Chao ZX. (2006) Application of fluorescence lifetime imaging (FLIM) in latent finger mark detection. *Forensic Sci Int* 160:109–114.
25. Seah LK, Dinish US, Phang WF, Chao ZX, Murukeshan VM. (2005) Fluorescence optimization and lifetime studies of fingerprints treated with magnetic powders. *Forensic Sci Int* 152:249–257.
26. Jones RG. (1967) Fused finger prints. *Fingerprint Ident Mag* 48:11–14.
27. Micik W. (1974) Dry ink works better than toner. *Fingerprint Ident Mag* 55:11–15.
28. Ball R. (1982) Copy-book technique. *Fingerprint Whorld* 7(28):82–83.
29. Putter PJ. (1984) Toner technique. *Fingerprint Whorld* 10(37):23.
30. Singla AK, Jasuja OP. (1992) Developing and fixing latent fingerprints: a simple method. *Can Soc Forensic Sci J* 25(2):119–121.
31. Dilag J, Kobus H, Ellis AV. (2009) Cadmium sulfide quantum dot/chitosan nanocomposites for latent fingermark detection. *Forensic Sci Int* 187:97–102.
32. Jamieson J, Bakhshi R, Petrova D, Pocock R, Imani M, Seifalian AM. (2007) Biological applications of quantum dots. *Biomaterials* 28:4717–4732.
33. Menzel ER, Savoy SM, Ulvick SJ, Cheng KH, Murdock RH, Sudduth MR. (2000) Photoluminescent semiconductor nanocrystals for fingerprint detection. *J Forensic Sci* 45(3):545–551.

34. Bouldin KK, Menzel ER, Takatsu M, Murdock RH. (2000) Diimide-enhanced fingerprint detection with photoluminescent CdS/dendrimer nanocomposites. *J Forensic Sci* 45(6):1239–1242.
35. Ma R, Bullock E, Maynard P, Reedy B, Shimmon R, Lennard C, Roux C, McDonagh A. (2011) Fingermark detection on non-porous and semi-porous surfaces using $NaYF_4$:Er,YB up-converter particles. *Forensic Sci Int* 207:145–149.
36. Bullock E. (2006) Anti-stokes up-converters for use in latent fingermark detection. Honors thesis, University of Technology Sydney, Sydney, New South Wales, Australia.
37. James JD, Pounds CA, Wilshire B. (1991) Obliteration of latent fingerprints. *J Forensic Sci* 36(5):1376–1386.
38. Bonura MJ. (1960) The Bonura method of spraying fingerprint powders. *Ident News* 10(5):4–6.
39. Anon. (1960) Pressurized spray fingerprint powders. *Ident News* 10(2):5.
40. Wilson JC. (1974) Developing latent prints on plastic bags. *Ident News* 24(9):13–14.
41. Delano RA. (1978) The use of a vaporizer in the recovery of latent prints on plastic bags. *Ident News* 28(10):6–7.
42. Fortunato SL, Walton G. (1998) Development of latent fingerprints from skin. *J Forensic Ident* 48(6):704–717.
43. Phillips J. (1980) Breath of life (1). *Fingerprint Whorld* 6(22):36.
44. Polimeni G, Foti BF, Saravo L, De Fulvio G. (2004) A novel approach to identify the presence of fingerprints on wet surfaces. *Forensic Sci Int* 146S:S45–S46.
45. Azoury M, Clark B, Geller B, Levin-Elad M, Rozen E. (2001) Latent print detection on raw ivory of african elephants. *J Forensic Ident* 51(5):496–503.
46. Reynoldson TE, Reed FA. (1984) Operational trial comparing metal deposition with small particle reagent for the development of latent fingerprints on polythene. Scientific Research and Development Branch (SRDB) Publication 12/84.
47. Haque F, Westland AD, Milligan J, Kerr MF. (1989) A small particle (iron oxide) suspension for detection of latent fingerprints on smooth surfaces. *Forensic Sci Int* 41:73–82.
48. Pounds CA, Jones RJ. (1981) The use of powder suspensions for developing latent fingerprints. part 1. Formulation development. Home Office Central Research Establishment (HOCRE) Report No. 4.
49. Jasuja OP, Singh GD, Sodhi GS. (2007) Small particle reagent: a saponin-based modification. *J Forensic Ident* 57(2):244–251.
50. Cohen D, Cohen EH. (2010) A significant improvement to the SPR process: more latent prints were revealed after thorough wiping of small particle reagent-treated surfaces. *J Forensic Ident* 60(2):152–162.
51. Levin Elad M. (2009) Modified SPR and fluorescent cyanoacylates: new directions in the fingerprint lab. Presented at the International Fingerprint Research Group Meeting, Lausanne, Switzerland.
52. Burns DS. (1994) Sticky-side powder: the Japanese solution. *J Forensic Ident* 44(2):133–138.
53. Personal communication with John Morgan, May 25, 2011.
54. Kimble GW. (1996) Powder suspension processing. *J Forensic Ident* 46(3):273–280.
55. Trozzi TA, Schwartz RL, Hollars ML. (2001) *Processing Guide for Developing Latent Prints*. U.S. Department of Justice, Federal Bureau of Investigation, Washington, DC.
56. Anon. (2007) *Fingerprint and Footwear Forensics Newsletter*. HOSDB Publication No. 59/07.
57. Frank A, Almog J. (1993) Modified SPR for latent fingerprint development on wet, dark objects. *J Forensic Ident* 43(3):240–244.
58. Wade DC. (2002) Development of latent prints with titanium dioxide (TiO_2). *J Forensic Ident* 52(5):551–559.
59. Williams NH, Elliott KT. (2005) Development of latent prints using titanium dioxide (TiO_2) in small particle reagent, white (SPR-W) on adhesives. *J Forensic Ident* 55(3):292–305.
60. Nic Daéid N, Carter S, Laing K. (2008) Comparison of three types of white powder suspensions for the recovery of fingerprints on wetted nonporous surfaces. *J Forensic Ident* 58(5):590–599.

61. Nic Daéid N, Carter S, Laing K. (2008) Comparison of vacuum metal deposition and powder suspension for the recovery of fingerprints on wetted nonporous surfaces. *J Forensic Ident* 58(5):600–613.
62. Au C, Jackson-Smith H, Quinones I, Jones BJ, Daniel B. (2011) Wet powder suspensions as an additional technique for the enhancement of bloodied marks. *Forensic Sci Int* 204:13–18.
63. Springer E, Bergman P. (1995) A fluorescent small particle reagent (SPR). *J Forensic Ident* 45(2):164–168.
64. Hollars ML, Trozzi TA, Barron BL. (2000) Development of latent fingerprints on dark colored sticky surfaces using liqui-drox. *J Forensic Ident* 50(4):357–362.
65. Jasuja OP, Singh GD, Sodhi GS. (2008) Small particle reagents: development of fluorescent variants. *Sci Justice* 48:141–145.
66. Sodhi GS, Kaur J. (2010) Fluorescent small particle reagent. part I: a novel composition for detecting latent fingerprints on wet non-porous items. *Fingerprint Whorld* 36(141):150–153.
67. Sodhi GS, Nigam D, Kaur M, Kaur R, Kaur S. (2010) Fluorescent small particle reagent. part II: detection of latent fingerprints on compact disks. *Fingerprint Whorld* 36(141):154–158.
68. Scott M. (2009) Does CA fuming interfere with powder suspension processing? *J Forensic Ident* 59(2):144–151.
69. Wilson HD. (2010) RAY dye stain versus gentian violet and alternate powder for development of latent prints on the adhesive side of tape. *J Forensic Ident* 60(5):510–523.
70. Onstwedder J, Gamboe TE. (1989) Small particle reagent: developing latent prints on water-soaked firearms and effect on firearms analysis. *J Forensic Sci* 34(2):321–327.
71. Shelef R, Levy A, Rhima I, Tsaroom S, Elkayam R. (1996) Development of latent fingerprints from incendiary bottles. I. Development of latent fingerprints from unignited incendiary bottles. *J Forensic Ident* 46(5):556–560.
72. Elkayam R, Rhima I, Shelef R. (1996) Development of latent fingerprints from incendiary bottles. II. Optimization of small particle reagent for the development of latent fingerprints from glass surfaces washed with accelerant fluids. *J Forensic Ident* 46(5):561–564.
73. Bleay S, Sears V. (2007) Powder suspensions. Magnificent or myth? Presented at the International Fingerprint Research Group Meeting, Canberra, Australia.
74. Ishizawa F, Takamura Y, Fukuchi T, Shimizu M, Ito M, Kanzaki M, Hasegawa T, Miyagi A. (1999) New sprays for the development of latent fingerprints. *J Forensic Ident* 49(5):499–504.
75. Sears V, Downham R, MacPhee D, Jones B, Reynolds A. (2009) Powder suspensions part II. Presented at the International Fingerprint Research Group Meeting, Lausanne, Switzerland.

2

Amino Acid Reagents

Robert S. Ramotowski

CONTENTS

2.1 Ninhydrin

The synthesis of ninhydrin (originally described as 1,2,3-triketohydrindene, but also referred to as 1,2,3-indanetrione) was first reported by Professor Siegfried Ruhemann, of the University Chemical Laboratories at Cambridge University, England, in 1910 [1]. He had attempted to synthesize 1,2-indanedione by reacting 1-indanone with *p*-nitrosodimethylaniline (and then hydrolyzing the subsequently formed imine to the desired product), but instead formed the now famous triketone [2]. Of particular interest to forensic scientists was Ruhemann's choice to react this new compound with ammonia.

He noted that if "the aqueous solution of the mixture of both substances is kept for a short time, it turns a deep reddish-violet, and no longer reduces silver nitrate" [1].

Ruhemann also observed that an aqueous solution of the triketohydrindene colored the skin purple upon contact. He also observed an intense blue coloration when it was reacted with α-amino acids, including glycine, alanine, and valine [3]. He later reported that triketohydrindene could also visualize proteins and their hydrolytic products [4]. The compound hydrindantin was also isolated and found to react in a similar fashion as triketohydrindene with α-amino acids. It was later determined that hydrindantin is an intermediate in the overall ninhydrin reaction. In 1911, Ruhemann reported the corrected structure for the reaction product between triketohydrindene and ammonia, which he called diketohydrindylidene-diketohydrindamine [5]. This product eventually became known as Ruhemann's purple in his honor.

In 1913, Abderhalden and Schmidt also noted the incredible sensitivity of the reaction between this new reagent and sweat [6]. Even with very dilute solutions of triketohydrindene (>1:10,000) a colored reaction still could be observed with amino acids [7]. They cautioned that if sweat from fingers came in contact with glassware used to make the solution, the contamination would produce the colored reaction regardless of whether or not the original sample contained such material. They were also the first to use the term ninhydrin to refer to the triketohydrindene molecule.

2.1.1 Chemistry and Reaction Mechanism

When ninhydrin reacted with an α-amino acid, ammonia and carbon dioxide evolved, along with an aldehyde with one less carbon than the parent amino acid. Certain amino acids did not evolve ammonia or form Ruhemann's purple. Examples of these compounds include proline, hydroxyproline, and tryptophan. Sunlight and the presence of oxidizing agents have been reported to decrease the yield and stability of Ruhemann's purple. Although Ruhemann had essentially established the structure of the product of ninhydrin and compounds containing amine functionalities, it is now represented either as a completely delocalized system or as a zwitterion with a positive charge on the nitrogen.

In general, the formation of Ruhemann's purple involves three steps [2]. The final product of this reaction requires two molecules of ninhydrin for each molecule of amino acid. The reaction involves the initial attack of the amine function on ninhydrin, followed by the oxidation and reduction steps that lead to intermediates, and then finally the formation of Ruhemann's purple from these compounds. The rate determining step appeared to involve a nucleophilic displacement of an OH group from the ninhydrin hydrate by a nonprotonated amino group [8,9]. A more recent study using ab initio quantum calculations further refined previously proposed ninhydrin mechanisms [10]. Removal of the Ruhemann's purple complex can be achieved by using dilute (1%–3%) ammonia [11].

The interaction of ninhydrin and amines has been proven to be a second-order reaction. The rate of reaction between ninhydrin and an amino acid has been established as a function of the ionization constant of the amino group on the amino acid anion [12]. The rate of reaction of some amines can be significantly slower than others [8]. Thus, a low color yield for a particular compound may only indicate an incomplete reaction. Certain amino acids form little or no Ruhemann's purple. Imino acids (e.g., proline), aromatic amines (e.g., aniline), nucleic acids (e.g., guanine), multifunctional amino acids (e.g., asparagine, tryptophan), and nonamino acids (e.g., fructose) react with ninhydrin to produce products other than Ruhemann's purple. Amino acids such as lysine and cysteine produce low color yields because their reaction with ninhydrin yields mostly side products.

Other explanations include hydrolytic, oxidative, and photolytic instability as well as side reactions forming interfering colored compounds. Steric factors may also play a role in the slower reaction rates [12].

The reaction is also influenced by the pH of the solvent system used [13]. Although the presence of organic solvents makes the accurate measurement of pH impossible, it is possible to estimate this value based on the fact that the rate of reaction between ninhydrin and an amino acid is a function of the ionization constant of the amino group on the amino acid anion. Since most amino acids have their optimum reactivity at a pH around 5, this value was recommended. Goode and Morris recommended an optimum pH of approximately 4 [13]. They speculated that the acid is required to neutralize the variable amounts of alkali present in different papers (since maximum color development was found to occur under acidic conditions). There are a number of different ninhydrin formulations that contain varying amounts of acid, typically glacial acetic acid.

The amount of color formed during the reaction of ninhydrin and amino acids does not always correspond to theoretical predictions [14]. Several processes could be responsible for the diminished amount of color formation, including the slow reaction of ninhydrin with some amines, an unfavorable reaction equilibrium that could favor the formation of other products, competition due to side reactions, and compounds that form interfering colored products with ninhydrin (including non-nitrogenous compounds like hydroxyl- and keto-aldehydes and acids). Ramminger et al. noted that the ninhydrin reaction on paper surfaces had several disadvantages [15]. The primary issue was that when the solvent had evaporated, the resulting dry environment essentially stopped the reaction from occurring. It was also noted that if insufficient ninhydrin was available, a 1:1 reaction between the amino acid and ninhydrin molecules took place and Ruhemann's purple was not formed. They recommend treating a sample several times, alternating between the developing reagent and a blank solvent wash.

Ninhydrin is known to react with more than just primary amino acids. Proteins and peptides can react with ninhydrin, but usually they do not produce the theoretical yield of Ruhemann's purple. Some have suggested the use of proteolytic enzymes to help digest proteins into amino acids that would theoretically increase the color yield. The use of trypsin to enhance ninhydrin development was first reported in 1961 [16]. Menzel et al. evaluated trypsin and pronase as possible candidates for sequential treatment of prints both before and after ninhydrin [17]. The technique worked for relatively fresh prints, but not for one that was 2 weeks old. During the development process, overheating the sample could lead to smudged ridge detail and significant background development, as trypsin itself can react with ninhydrin. This may be due to the fact that the enzyme cannot sufficiently penetrate the dried-out print residue, which has not migrated into the paper fibers, to produce any appreciable color yield improvement. A subsequent study found particle size to be a significant factor [18]. Finely powdered, lyophylized Sigma Type III trypsin gave the most enhancement with virtually no background interference. Pounds et al. reported on the use of antibodies and lectins to improve ninhydrin development [19]. Monoclonal anti-H (blood antigen) produced the most consistently effective results. Results on nonporous surfaces were found to be significantly better than on porous ones.

There are differences in the reactivity of ninhydrin for different people [20]. In some cases, donors who had moist palms failed to produce strong ninhydrin development. Conversely, a donor deemed excellent actually had a very low moisture level measured on his hands. The critical factor appears to be the amino acid concentration present in the sweat rather than the subject's diet. Godsell reported that approximately 15% of test subjects were found to produce very faint or no reaction to ninhydrin [21]. Similar results were reported by Edwards et al. [22]. They found a correlation between donor age and intensity of the ninhydrin reaction. While 15% of test subjects older that 25 were found to be negative to the reaction, only 5% of those younger than 25 were found not to produce a reaction.

2.1.2 Forensic Applications

After Ruhemann's discovery, the use of ninhydrin to visualize amino acids separated by paper chromatography increased dramatically. However, a curious phenomenon began to be observed. When handling paper chromatogram with bare hands, a person was likely to leave behind fingerprints that would be visualized along with the amino acids. In fact, one publication recommended handling paper chromatograms with forceps to avoid leaving prints behind [23]. It was not until 1954 that a procedure was published for deliberately targeting latent prints on paper with ninhydrin [24]. Odén and von Hofsten used a 0.2% w/v solution of ninhydrin in acetone and acetic acid (0.4%) to spray paper surfaces. After drying, the items were then heated at 80°C for a few minutes. Maximum development of ridge detail was observed over a period of 24–48 h after application of the spray.

If the item to be processed with ninhydrin has been stored in ideal conditions (dark, low oxygen, and relatively steady temperatures), then it is possible to develop some relatively old prints. Oden and von Hofsten reported that 12 year old prints from a grammar book were able to be visualized using this method [24]. In 1978, a 6 year old print was reported to have been developed on a murder confession letter in Rhodesia (now Zimbabwe) [25]. In one particular case, a box full of 40 year old student notebooks was processed with ninhydrin, which yielded fingerprints that could be identified to at least one of the students who had made entries in that particular book (the adult prints were used for comparison) [26]. Foster noted that 30 year old prints had been developed and in one case an 11 year old print was developed and identified to a suspect [27]. When stored properly, ninhydrin developed prints can resist fading for a substantial period of time. Burns reported that a ninhydrin developed palm print was still present on a menu card 27 years after processing [28]. Interestingly, the application of metal salts (e.g., copper) was reported to stabilize the Ruhemann's purple complex and prevent color fading almost indefinitely (see Section 2.2) [29].

In 1969, Crown reported a nonpolar, petroleum ether–based formulation for ninhydrin that did not affect inks [30]. Ninhydrin was first dissolved in methanol (40 mL) and then mixed with petroleum ether F (boiling point range 30°C–60°C) to make a 0.75% w/v working solution. The mixture had to be shaken in a separatory funnel to produce two distinct layers. The pale yellow fraction was removed and used to process documents. This solution was reported to be unstable (<24 h) and needed to be made just prior to processing. It was later determined that addition of 1% v/v acetic acid into the Crown formulation improved sensitivity by a factor of 5 and color intensity by a factor of 4 [13]. Mooney reported a ninhydrin formula that involved mixing ninhydrin directly into ethyl ether [31]. Constant agitation from the use of a magnetic stirrer completely dissolved the ninhydrin and the working solution did not run inks or dyes. It also was reported to work well on genuine U.S. currency.

In 1974, Morris and Goode introduced a nonflammable, nonpolar ninhydrin formulation based on 1,1,2-trichloro-1,2,2-trifluoroethane (Fluorisol or CFC-113) [32]. This reagent was a much safer alternative to the petroleum ether solution recommended by Crown. Ninhydrin was first dissolved in acetic acid and absolute ethanol. A portion of this stock solution was then mixed with Fluorosil to make the concentration of the overall working solution 0.5% w/v. Samples were heated for 20 min at 60°C or 2 min at 120°C. This formulation was also noted to dissolve typewriter correction fluid on documents [33]. In 1975,

Linde recommended a 1.0% w/v solution of ninhydrin in acetone and water (3% v/v). This solution was sprayed onto documents, which were then processed in an oven set between 100°C and 120°C for 5–30 min. Tighe introduced "Freon Plus Two" in 1984 [34]. This reagent involved dissolving ninhydrin in methanol and ethyl acetate and then creating the working solution with Freon. The methanol often needed to be heated to fully dissolve the ninhydrin crystals.

In 1987, the Vienna Convention for the Protection of the Ozone Layer drafted the Montreal Protocol on Substances That Deplete the Ozone Layer, which would eventually phase out solvents like Freon by the mid-1990s. Nonessential use was banned in the United States in 1995. A number of research efforts were launched to find a suitable replacement that was nonflammable, nontoxic, volatile, and nonpolar (to minimize damage to inks).

Watling et al. introduced a heptane-based alternative reagent [35]. Ninhydrin was first dissolved in absolute ethanol and then diluted with heptane. The authors noted that HPLC-grade heptane must be used; otherwise, the ninhydrin may precipitate out of the solution. Jungbluth reported on the success of using a mixture of hydrochlorofluorocarbons (HCFCs) [36]. Genesolv 2010 (a mixture of HCFC-123* (10%) and HCFC-141b†), Genesolv 2020 (a mixture of HCFC-123 (20%) and HCFC-141b), and Genesolv 2000 (1,1-dichloro-1-fluoroethane or HCFC-141b) were compared to see if they would be suitable replacements for CFC-113. A water-based formula was reported during the 2007 IAI Conference in San Diego, California.‡ Good results were reported for copy, notebook, and newspaper [37].

The U.K. Home Office began an extensive search for a suitable replacement for CFC-113 in the early 1990s [38–40]. Initial studies focused on HCFC-141b, HCFC-225ca/cb, and flammable solvents such as cyclohexane and heptane. Of all of the reagents tested, only the acidified heptane formula§ was comparable to CFC-113 performance. This reagent was not investigated further due to its flammability. The use of supercritical carbon dioxide as a solvent was reported to produce good result, but small chamber size limited broader application of the method [41]. A subsequent study investigated the use of 1,1,1,2,3,4,4,5,5,5-decafluoropentane (HFC4310mee, also known as Vertrel XF) and 1-methoxynonafluorobutane (HFE 7100). Interestingly, if an alcohol (e.g., ethyl) and acid (e.g., acetic) were present in solution, this could lead to the formation of ethyl acetate and water (which can blur ridge detail). The addition of ethyl acetate to this solution shifted the equilibrium toward the starting materials (ethanol and acetic acid) and prevents water formation. In the U.K. Home Office laboratory and pseudooperational trials, HFE 7100 performed the best with virtually no running of inks [42]. Similar results were reported by Petruncio [43].

Solvent-free applications of ninhydrin have been proposed. Ludas introduced the dry ninhydrin technique in 1992 [44]. This technique involved placing documents between pieces of filter paper that had been soaked in a ninhydrin solution (35 g of ninhydrin in 500 mL of ethanol or methanol). The item and filter paper were then placed in a towel and ironed with steam for several minutes. Schwarz et al. reported on the sublimation of ninhydrin under vacuum [45]. Optimum conditions for the sublimation reaction involved the use of a vacuum chamber set to a pressure of 2–5 mbar, addition of 50 mg of ninhydrin, and a heating source set to 150°C for 30 min.

* HCFC-123 is also known by its chemical name, 2,2-dichloro-1,1,1-trichloroethane.

† HCFC-141b is also known by its chemical name, 1,1-dichloro-1-fluoroethane.

‡ To prepare this reagent, 5 g of ninhydrin were dissolved into a liter of water and then placed into a steam iron.

§ This reagent was prepared by mixing 5 g ninhydrin, 75 mL ethanol, 25 mL ethyl acetate, 3 mL acetic acid, and 1 L heptane.

The use of lasers to enhance visible ninhydrin development has been proposed. German reported that the use of an argon ion laser enhanced the ridge detail on porous surfaces, especially brown paper bags [46]. Herod et al. used a 4.5 W argon ion laser to pump a dye laser tuned to 580 nm (producing approximately 1 W of power at this wavelength) to enhance weakly developed ninhydrin prints [47]. Using an Oriel G 772-6300 emission filter, they reported observing additional ridge detail fluorescing in the red to near infrared portion of the spectrum.

The use of highly concentrated, oversaturated ninhydrin solutions has been noted to cause paper fibers to swell, which can obscure indented writing and striations [48]. Moore reported on the effect of the electronic detection apparatus (ESDA) process on the subsequent development of latent prints [49]. Less than 2% of prints developed in this experiment were found to undergo significant enough deterioration to the point of causing an acceptable print to become unidentifiable. These cases occurred when documents were humidified for more than 30 min. Azoury et al. found that subjecting documents to high humidity environments for only a few minutes could have a negative effect on ninhydrin development [50].

Quality control standards for evaluating the reliability of a given ninhydrin solution have been proposed [51]. Nielson advocated the use of a serial dilution of a mixture of amino acids (based on the summary published by Knowles [52]) for testing ninhydrin working solutions [53]. Schwarz dispensed a solution of a mixture of amino acids onto test sheets using a bubble jet printer [54].

Premixed sprays are commercially available from several forensic vendors. Their formulations are proprietary and can vary considerably. Depending on the amount of polar solvents used, ink running could be a potential problem. Some of the earlier commercial products (e.g., Chem Print™, Criminalistics, Inc., Miami, FL) contained methanol and xylene, in addition to petroleum ether.

Propellants, atomizers, or compressors can be used to prepare in-house sprays. Spraying tends to be less efficient that dipping since variable amounts of the ninhydrin reagent are exposed to the item's surface. Caution must also be taken to avoid inhaling the aerosol particles. The use of such sprays in a fume hood is self-evident; however, it should be noted that fume hoods are not optimized for removal of aerosol particles. Additional personal protective equipment (e.g., respirators) may be required.

Reagent preparation*

Working solution (petroleum ether)

Ninhydrin	6 g
Ethanol	50 mL
Petroleum ether	950 mL

1. Add the ninhydrin to the ethanol and mix thoroughly until it has completely dissolved.
2. The solution should be slowly diluted with the petroleum ether.
3. The appropriate information (e.g., chemical contents, preparer's initials, date, reliability test result) should be recorded on the container's label.
4. The final working solution is stable for 3–6 months.

* This formulation is currently used by the U.S. Secret Service. There are literally dozens of different published and unpublished formulations for ninhydrin. The ones provided here provide a range of different options. The HFE 7100 reagent is nonflammable and the heptane reagent was found by the U.K. Home Office to perform as well as the original nonflammable CFC-113-based version. Readers are encouraged to make their own choices based on factors such as safety, cost, and performance.

Working solution (heptane) [7]

Ninhydrin	5 g
Ethanol	75 mL
Ethyl acetate	25 mL
Acetic acid	3 mL
Heptane	1 L

1. This is a modification of the heptane formulation first proposed by Watling and Smith [35]. The ninhydrin should be dissolved first into the ethanol, ethyl acetate, and acetic acid.
2. Once completely dissolved, the mixture should be diluted slowly with heptane.
3. The appropriate information (e.g., chemical contents, preparer's initials, date, reliability test result) should be recorded on the container's label.
4. The solution is stable for months when stored at ambient conditions.

Working solution (HFE 7100) [41]

Ninhydrin	5 g
Ethanol	45 mL
Ethyl acetate	2 mL
Acetic acid	5 mL
HFE 7100	1 L

1. The ninhydrin should be dissolved first into the ethanol, ethyl acetate, and acetic acid.
2. Once completely dissolved, the mixture should be diluted slowly with HFE 7100.
3. The appropriate information (e.g., chemical contents, preparer's initials, date, reliability test result) should be recorded on the container's label.
4. The solution is stable for months when stored at ambient conditions. This reagent is nonflammable.

Reagent application

1. All appropriate personal protective equipment should be used when preparing and using this reagent.
2. Run the appropriate positive and negative controls to ensure that the reagent solution is working properly.
3. Items should be immersed in the working solution for a few seconds. This allows the entire paper surface to be exposed to the full concentration of ninhydrin.* Spraying tends to be less efficient that dipping since variable amounts of the ninhydrin reagent is exposed to the item's surface.
4. The item should be allowed to air dry and then should be placed in a humidity-controlled oven set at 65% RH and 80°C [38]. Depending on the paper type and thickness, most items require development under these conditions for only

* The pretreatment of paper with cyanoacrylate ester fumes was not found to inhibit subsequent treatment with ninhydrin or zinc chloride [69].

5–10 min. Large environmental chambers may require additional time to return to the temperature and humidity set points. If longer exposure times are used, the color of the Ruhemann's purple product changes from a dark purple to a lighter magenta color. Background development also increases as development time increases.

5. The purple-colored product should be viewed under white light (with a green filter) or under green light as well.* Although it does not fluoresce at room temperature, immersion in liquid nitrogen could produce weak fluorescence.
6. The purple-colored product was reported to be stable almost indefinitely if stored in the dark.
7. When processing has been completed, all chemicals should be disposed of properly according to the appropriate federal, state, and local environmental laws.

2.2 Metal Salt Enhancement

The use of group 12 (or IIb) metal salts to stabilize the color of Ruhemann's purple (RP) has been known since the early 1950s [55]. Kawerau et al. recommended a 0.8% w/v solution of copper nitrate in acidified (nitric acid) ethanol. However, this solution was used only to stabilize the visible-colored product. Morris et al. explored the use of metal salts in the early 1970s [56]. By the end of that decade, lasers were in use for detecting inherent fluorescence in latent print deposits [57]. RP by itself is not fluorescent when excited by long-wave ultraviolet radiation. Herod and Menzel used an argon ion laser to pump a dye laser (power output of 1 W at ~580 nm) to view ninhydrin fluorescence in the red to near-infrared portion of the spectrum [47]. This was especially true for weakly developed ninhydrin prints. A subsequent study was the first to report the efficacy of a zinc chloride solution to significantly enhance ninhydrin fluorescence [58]. This fluorescence was much stronger than that observed by Herod and Menzel [47]. An acidified, Freon TF® and ethanol-based zinc chloride solution was recommended. Improved contrast with existing prints was reported to occur on porous and nonporous surfaces.

Kobus et al. reported on the use of a xenon arc lamp to excite ninhydrin-developed prints posttreated with zinc chloride [59]. To achieve optimal fluorescence, items had to be immersed in liquid nitrogen, at −196°C or 77 K. This lower temperature results in a higher quantum yield for the zinc–RP complex and can increase the fluorescence intensity significantly. In most instances, treatment of the purple-colored RP molecule with zinc chloride results in the formation of an orange-colored metal complex that has enhanced fluorescence even at room temperature. In cases where the intensity of the RP complex is strong, treatment with zinc chloride resulted in a red rather than the expected orange-colored metal complex. Stoilovic et al. noted that treatment of the RP molecule with zinc salts produced an orange-colored complex [60]. Treatment with cadmium, mercury, nickel, cobalt, calcium, iron, copper, and silver yielded a red complex, while magnesium produced

* According the RGB color model, green and magenta form a primary/secondary color pair. When a green filter is used to view the magenta-colored ninhydrin development, the print appears to darken (which could improve contrast).

a blue one. Only complexes with group IIb metals were found to produce measurable fluorescence at liquid nitrogen temperatures. A recent study reported the use of indium chloride in combination with an LED array for excitation, to produce orange-colored fluorescent complexes [61].

A number of studies have been conducted to investigate the structure of the product formed between Ruhemann's purple and metal salt. Based on unpublished observations, Wieland reported a Ruhemann's purple-to-metal ratio of 2:1. Others subsequently confirmed this ratio, but others found a 1:1 ratio as well. Lennard et al. used x-ray diffraction studies to determine that the complex formed had a 1:1 ratio of metal-to-chelating agent for zinc, cadmium, and mercury [62]. However, they noted that additional complexes with different ratios could form under different experimental conditions. These metals formed six-coordinate complexes with the metal occupying one site, Ruhemann's purple three, and water molecules in the remaining two sites. The latter observation was offered as an explanation for the need for moisture in the fingerprint enhancement process.

Davies et al. reported that different complexes could be formed, based on the relative humidity level and the concentration of Ruhemann's purple [63]. Strongly colored, ninhydrin-treated prints tended to form red complexes with a 2:1 ratio. These complexes were found to fluoresce at room temperature. Interestingly, different 2:1 complexes were found to form when a pure amino acid was used instead of natural sweat. Weakly developed ninhydrin treated prints tended to produce the orange complex with a 1:1 ratio. On paper, the concentration of RP was found to be the dominant factor, with lower concentrations favoring the orange-colored 1:1 complex.

Liberti et al. reported that exposure to natural or artificial light and excess moisture had a detrimental effect on the luminescence of Zn–RP complexes [64]. Light exposure produced significant fading, depending on the intensity of the source and exposure time. The presence of excess water was found to lead to the formation of a red, nonfluorescent complex. An increase in the moisture content of the paper could be the result of the presence of certain paper additives, the solvents used, and the hygroscopic nature of zinc chloride.

Menzel et al. reported that the fluorescence of the cadmium–RP complex was significantly less than the zinc–RP complex [65]. A total of 21 different metal salts were evaluated in that study, including rare earth compounds. No significant effects related to the associated anion species (e.g., chloride, nitrate, perchlorate) or hydration were found. They noted that the higher the degree of planarity of the final metal–RP complex, the stronger the fluorescence. Although initial results with rare earth–RP complexes were disappointing, a subsequent study found that europium and terbium complexes did exhibit luminescence [66]. This luminescence occurred via intramolecular energy transfer from the RP ligand (good absorber) to the rare earth ions (good emitters) [67]. The peak emission for the europium complex was observed at 615 nm (using a dye laser tuned at 579 nm for excitation). With luminescence lifetimes on the order of milliseconds (~0.4 ms for europium and 1.3 ms for terbium), these rare earth complexes were reported to be good candidates for time-resolved imaging (to remove highly fluorescent background interferences) [68]. Terbium complexes were also found to exhibit good luminescence when excited in the short-wave ultraviolet region [67]. Maximum emission occurred in the green portion of the spectrum, centered at 545 nm.

The ninhydrin–zinc chloride process has also been used to stain both untreated and cyanoacrylate-fumed prints on nonporous surfaces [69]. Menzel et al. reported some success with using the ninhydrin/zinc chloride sequence for smooth surfaces (with no pretreatment), as long as it was applied using a light, fine mist. For prefumed prints, the development times for the ninhydrin/zinc chloride process were found to be longer than for untreated ones, most likely due to the need for the reagent to penetrate the cyanoacrylate polymer. Although side-by-side comparisons were not made in this study, Menzel et al. noted that prior fuming of prints on paper was generally not found to inhibit the subsequent reaction with ninhydrin and zinc chloride.

Reagent preparation*

Stock solution

Zinc chloride	3.7 g
Methanol	10.0 mL

1. Stir the zinc chloride until it is completely dissolved in methanol.
2. This solution should be stored in a glass bottle and should remain stable indefinitely.
3. The appropriate information (e.g., chemical contents, preparer's initials, date, reliability test result) should be recorded on the container's label.

Working solution

Zinc chloride Stock Solution	1 part
Petroleum ether	5 parts

1. Slowly add the petroleum ether to the zinc chloride solution and thoroughly mix the solutions.
2. Store the working solution in a glass bottle.
3. Some separation may occur between the petroleum ether and methanol over time. The working solution should be used for only a short period of time.
4. The appropriate information (e.g., chemical contents, preparer's initials, date, reliability test result) should be recorded on the container's label.

Reagent application

1. All appropriate personal protective equipment should be used when preparing and using this reagent.
2. Run the appropriate positive and negative controls to ensure that the reagent solution is working properly.
3. The ninhydrin-treated item should be completely dry prior to application of zinc chloride.
4. The zinc chloride reagent can be applied either by immersing the item into the solution or by spraying it as a fine mist.
5. The treated item should be briefly developed in a similar fashion as ninhydrin (80°C and 65% RH), especially in dry environments. Heat and humidity can be supplied using a conventional steam iron; however, caution should be exercised since scorching and excess background development can result from the uneven application of this method.

* The use of zinc salts, like zinc chloride or zinc nitrate, after ninhydrin has essentially been replaced by the use of more sensitive, highly fluorescent compounds (e.g., DFO, 1,2-indanedione) prior to ninhydrin application.

6. The magenta-colored RP complex should turn orange after application of zinc chloride (it should turn red after the application of cadmium or mercury salts).
7. Optimal illumination conditions for the RP–zinc complex involve excitation at 490 nm with an emission peak at 550 nm.
8. The fluorescence can be enhanced by immersing the item in a liquid nitrogen bath. Caution must be exercised when using liquid nitrogen as it can cause severe frostbite or burns upon contact with skin.
9. When processing has been completed, all chemicals should be disposed of properly according to the appropriate federal, state, and local environmental laws.

2.3 Ninhydrin Analogs

An analog is a chemical compound that has a similar structure and similar chemical properties to those of another compound, but differs from it by a single element or a group. The first to prepare a ninhydrin analog was probably Ruhemann in 1912, when he synthesized triketomethylenedioxyhydrindene. At that time, these compounds were not considered for their potential to develop latent prints. It was not until the early 1980s that research groups began to look at synthesizing modified ninhydrin compounds. The dual goals of producing such an analog are to produce a compound that has intense, visible colored development (as good as or superior to ninhydrin) as well as a superior room temperature fluorescence. Over the course of the next few decades, several groups worked toward this goal, including the Israel National Police, the U.S. Secret Service, and the Australian Federal Police. During that time, nearly 100 new analogs were synthesized and evaluated for their potential to develop visible and fluorescent prints [70].

2.3.1 First Analogs

Almog et al. were the first to synthesize and evaluate an analog of ninhydrin specifically for development of latent prints [71]. The first three analogs were benzo[e]ninhydrin, benzo[f]ninhydrin, and 5-chloro-5-methoxyninhydrin. The benzo[f] analog, first synthesized in 1957 by Meier and Lotter [72], was found to produce dark green (nearly black) colored prints, whose intensity was comparable to that produced by ninhydrin itself. Menzel et al. reported that the new compound had an absorption maximum in solution at 530 nm (540 nm with reactions on paper with latent prints) and produced intense fluorescence when excited with a 532 nm Nd:YAG laser [73]. The use of zinc chloride as a posttreatment for the benzo[f]ninhydrin reaction with latent prints produced an orange-colored fluorescence, whose intensity was significantly stronger than that from ninhydrin–$ZnCl_2$. Safaryn reported that benzo[f]ninhydrin-$ZnCl_2$ fluorescence represented a 10-fold increase over that from ninhydrin–$ZnCl_2$ [74]. The emission maximum appeared to center around 550 nm, depending on the excitation wavelength.

As promising as benzo[f]ninhydrin appeared to be, there were some significant limitations. The most problematic was its cost. Initially, it was very cost prohibitive to synthesize because of expensive starting materials and low yields. Further research produced cheaper and more efficient ways to synthesize the analog [75]. However, even when first commercially available by Aldrich, the cost was a staggering $514.50 per gram in 1999 [76]. This would compare unfavorably to a price of less than $1.00 per gram for ninhydrin, even at 2012 prices. Other potential drawbacks included variable colored prints (depending on the substrate and the development conditions), decreased solubility in polar solvents, and inferior development (both in contrast and quantity of prints) on certain substrates versus ninhydrin [77]. The novel synthesis and evaluation of a related compound, naphtha[f]ninhydrin, was reported by Hallman et al. [78]. This compound did not appear to have been evaluated as a fingerprint reagent, but it would most likely suffer from some of the similar drawbacks noted for benzo[f]ninhydrin.

Several bisninhydrin analogs have also been reported [79]. In principle, these compounds could react to form polymeric RP species. 4,4′-bisninhydrin and 5,5′-bisninhydrin were synthesized, but were found to have low solubility in typical solvents and no enhanced chromogenic or fluorogenic properties. Kobus et al. reported on analogs containing oxygen, sulfur, and selenium [80]. Promising candidates for visual color development included the 5-methylselenium-, 5-nitrophenyl-, benzo[f]furo-, and 5-thiophenylninhydrin analogs. The benzo[f]furoninhydrin analog appeared to exhibit a fluorescence intensity that was superior to DFO.

2.3.2 Aryl, Alkyl, and Alkoxy Analogs

The next major milestone in the search for promising new ninhydrin analogs occurred in 1986 [81]. A series of analogs were synthesized in this preliminary study, including 4-nitroninhydrin, 5-nitroninhydrin, tetrachloroninhydrin, and tetrabromoninhydrin (which contain electron withdrawing groups) as well as 4-methoxyninhydrin, 5-methoxyninhydrin, and 5,6-dimethoxyninhydrin (which contained electron-donating groups). The subsequent follow-up study determined that 5-methoxyninhydrin was the most promising candidate [82]. In general, Lennard et al. noted that the presence of an electron-donating group (e.g., methoxy) was found to enhance fluorescence, while the presence of an electron-withdrawing group (e.g., chlorine) was found to reduce fluorescence intensity. Substitution at the 5-position on the ninhydrin molecule was found to be a key factor in producing a good fluorescent compound (significantly more so than substitution at the 4-position).

However, 5,6-dimethoxyninhydrin (with two electron-donating groups) was found to exhibit no room temperature fluorescence. The presence of these two groups was thought to lead to steric hindrance in the final coordination complex, thus forcing it to lose planarity. With regard to the molecules containing single atom electron-withdrawing groups, as the mass of the atom increased (e.g., from chlorine to iodine), the fluorescence decreased (this is known as the "heavy atom" effect). The presence of acetic acid in the reagent was also found to be necessary, as reagent solutions prepared without it took more than three times as long to develop. The only major drawback with 5-methoxyninhydrin was its cost of production (comparable to benzo[f]ninhydrin).

Additional synthetic studies were conducted on different classes of ninhydrin analogs. One focused on the evaluation of vicinal triketones for their ability to develop prints [83]. Compounds such as dihydrophenalene and alloxan were found to produce colored prints on paper. A number of aminoninhydrins were also explored as potential candidates for fingerprint development [84]. The dimethylamino and amino groups contained unshared pairs of electron and thus were some of the strongest electron-donating groups known. Electron-donating groups have typically produced good fluorescent analogs. Two of the compounds synthesized, 5-dimethylaminoninhydrin and 5-aminoninhydrin, showed some promising fluorescence characteristics. The initial color of the reaction product of the analog and L-alanine varied from yellow to blue/purple.

An attempt to increase the solubility of alkoxy-ninhydrin analogs lead to the synthesis of four chain-elongated compounds based on 5-methoxyninhydrin [85]. The ethoxy, *n*-propoxy, isobutoxy, and isoamyloxy analogs were prepared and tested for fluorescence and solubility in nonpolar solvents. While solubility in hexane increased as the chain length increased, the fluorescence intensity decreased significantly. Two proposed hypotheses for this behavior included a decrease in extended conjugation between the alkoxy group and aromatic ring and a decrease in coplanarity of the RP complex due to the steric hindrance of the hydrocarbon side chains.

Almog et al. reported on the enhanced sensitivity of "dual fingerprint reagents" [86]. These reagents would be one-step processes that combined strong initial color development with strong luminescence qualities. This could be achieved either by a single compound (for which no ideal candidate has yet been discovered) or by mixing an analog with a zinc salt in a combined reagent. The latter method was attempted by creating reagents with 5-methoxy and 5-methylthioninhydrin (5-MTN) that had an overall zinc (or cadmium) concentration of 0.2%. The best results were obtained with the 5-MTN/zinc chloride mixture, which developed fluorescent prints with an intensity comparable to DFO (an additional advantage was that the initial pink color of the 5-MTN mixture was observed to be considerably stronger than the color developed by DFO).

2.3.3 Sulfur Analogs

One of the most successful classes of ninhydrin analogs was the one that incorporated sulfur. Among some of the first compounds to be synthesized were thieno[f]ninhydrin and 5-methylthioninhydrin (5-MTN) [87,88]. Interestingly, the thieno[e]ninhydrin analog did not exhibit good fluorogenic properties [79]. However, Cantu et al. found thieno[f]ninhydrin to be the most fluorescent analog synthesized up to that time (including being superior to 5-MTN) [89]. A subsequent study found that a series of different 5-thioninhydrins showed considerable promise [90]. A comprehensive evaluation of 5-MTN was reported by Wallace-Kunkel et al. [91]. Although results indicated that 5-MTN was superior to ninhydrin (and could be used in place of it in laboratories that did not use other fluorescent reagents), its fluorescence intensity was found to be significantly less than that produced by 1,2-indanedione. These new analogs reacted with amino acids to produce purple-colored reaction products like ninhydrin; however, reaction with zinc chloride changed the color to pink and yielded strong fluorescence. One possible explanation for the apparent success of 5-methylthioninhydrin and thieno[f]ninhydrin would be that these compounds had resonance structures that exhibited an extended *p*-quinoid structure, due to the release of electron density from sulfur into the aromatic system [79]. Both benzo[e]ninhydrin and thieno[e]ninhydrin adopted an *o*-quinoid structure, which was not favorable.

Two additional analogs, 5-(2-thienyl)ninhydrin (2-THIN) and 5-(3-thienyl)ninhydrin, were also reported to exhibit strong fluorescence upon secondary treatment with zinc chloride [92,93]. 2-THIN was found to be superior to DFO in the absorption mode (i.e., stronger initial color) as well as the fluorescence mode after zinc nitrate treatment [94]. However, high production costs associated with the synthesis of these two thienyl compounds made their operational usage unlikely.

One exception to the rule of enhanced fluorescence noted with sulfur analogs was thianinhydrin [95]. Only weak fluorescence was detected at the concentration and excitation power used. Two additional sulfur analogs were reported and these were modeled using HyperChem and AM1 Hamiltonian [96]. Both 3-thiononinhydrin and 1,3-dithiononinhydrin were computationally determined to have good potential as fluorogenic fingerprint reagents. However, the authors were not able to confirm this operationally since they were unable to synthesize either compound.

More recently, ninhydrin thiohemiketals have been suggested as a new visualization method that would incorporate nanotechnology [97]. The idea behind this method was to enhance the ability of gold nanoparticles to covalently bind to thiol compounds in the latent print residue. This process could be further enhanced by first reacting a thiol-modified ninhydrin with the amino acids in the print. In general, the gold nanoparticles could subsequently bind to the thiol portion of the modified ninhydrin and then be further amplified with a silver physical developer solution. The sensitivity of such a reagent was likely to be much greater than current processes because it works via a nonlinear mechanism (a potential for exponential amplification of the gold labeled residues) rather than the traditionally linear approach (i.e., one molecule of amino acid reacting with two ninhydrin molecules to form RP).

Interestingly, 5-methylthioninhydrin is currently the only commercially available ninhydrin analog (Sigma-Aldrich once sold benzo[f]ninhydrin and 5-methoxyninhydrin, but both are no longer in stock). BVDA currently markets 5-methylthioninhydrin and also provides a recommended reagent formulation in their product brochure [98]. The cost of the reagent is comparable to 1,2-indanedione. They recommended using the hemiketal form of the analog since it would react with moisture in the paper to form the more familiar hydrate (the common form of ninhydrin).

Reagent preparation [98]

Working solution (5-MTN Hemiketal)

5-MTN hemiketal	3.4 g
Glacial acetic acid	10 mL
Isopropanol	25 mL
Ethyl acetate	145 mL
Methyl *t*-butyl ether	100 mL
Petroleum ether	720 mL

1. The reagent should be prepared first by combining the 5-MTN hemiketal with the acetic acid, isopropanol, and ethyl acetate and stirring for 10–15 min.
2. When the 5-MTN hemiketal has fully dissolved, the methyl *t*-butyl ether and petroleum ether can then be slowly added.
3. The appropriate information (e.g., chemical contents, preparer's initials, date, reliability test result) should be recorded on the container's label.
4. The working solution is stable for extended periods of time at room temperature. Some precipitation of 5-MTN may occur if the reagent is stored at reduced temperatures.

Working solution (zinc chloride)

Zinc chloride	30 g
Methyl t-butyl ether	500 mL
Ethanol (anhydrous)	20 mL
Glacial acetic acid	20 mL
Hydrocarbon solvent	500 mL

1. The zinc chloride should be dissolved first in a mixture of the methyl *t*-butyl ether and ethanol. This can take at least 30–60 min with constant stirring.
2. After the zinc chloride has fully dissolved, add the acetic acid and then dilute this solution with the hydrocarbon solvent (e.g., petroleum ether, pentane, heptane).
3. The appropriate information (e.g., chemical contents, preparer's initials, date, reliability test result) should be recorded on the container's label.
4. The zinc chloride working solution is reported to be stable indefinitely.

Reagent application

1. All appropriate personal protective equipment should be used when preparing and using this reagent.
2. Run the appropriate positive and negative controls to ensure that the reagent solution is working properly.
3. Items should be immersed in the working solution for a few seconds and then allowed to thoroughly air dry in a fume hood.
4. The recommended development conditions involve storage in the dark at room temperature for at least 2 days at 80% RH.
5. Due to the high concentration of zinc chloride in the reagent, it is recommended that posttreatment of items be done with an aerosol sprayer.
6. The treated item should be viewed under white light and also in the fluorescence mode. Optimal conditions involve illumination at 525 nm and viewing/imaging using a Schott OG550 or other similar filter.
7. When processing has been completed, all chemicals should be disposed of properly according to the appropriate federal, state, and local environmental laws.

2.4 1,8-Diazafluoren-9-One

The synthesis of 1,8-diazafluoren-9-one (DFO) was first reported by Druey and Schmidt in 1950. There was no indication that either chemist noted the potential reaction of this compound with amino acids to produce a fluorescent product. In the late 1980s, a collaboration between the U.K. Home Office Central Research and Support Establishment and The Queen's University (Belfast, Northern Ireland) began to revisit this compound and evaluate its potential for fingerprint visualization [99,100]. This discovery was first reported at the International Association for Identification Educational Conference in Pensacola, Florida, in July 1989. They reported a strongly fluorescent product with amino acids and latent prints that had an excitation maximum at 470 nm and an emission maximum at 570 nm.

The synthesis of DFO analogs was reported by Frank et al. in 1993 [101]. This was done in an attempt to increase the fluorescence intensity of the product between these new analogs and amino acids. The first analog prepared was 1-monoazafluoren-9-one, but it did not produce any fluorescence after reaction with amino acids. Although the intended compound, dibenzo-1,8-diazafluorenone, was not able to be synthesized, two promising candidates (dipyridyl ketone and pyrimidine ketone) were found to produce intensely fluorescent products with amino acids. When excited at 365 nm, these compounds were reported to be superior to DFO. However, the cost of the new analogs made their commercialization impractical.

2.4.1 Chemistry and Reaction Mechanism

A study of the reaction mechanism of DFO and L-alanine was reported by Wilkinson [102]. This study confirmed that the reaction product between DFO and amino acids was analogous to the complex formed between ninhydrin and amino acids. The structure of the complex consists of two DFO molecules connected by a central nitrogen atom via the 9-position on each ring. The structure had extensive electron delocalization and was in very close agreement with the structure proposed by Grigg [99]. Wilkinson provided further information on the reaction mechanism as well. It appeared that DFO first reacted with the solvent to form a hemiketal, which facilitated an attack from the nitrogen (from the amino acid) at the electron-deficient carbonyl group on the DFO molecule. Following decarboxylation, hydrolysis occurred at the nitrogen–carbon double bond to form an aromatic amine. This compound further reacted with another DFO molecule to create the final complex.

Most current sequencing recommendations use DFO prior to ninhydrin. Application of ninhydrin has a quenching effect on the fluorescence of DFO-treated prints. However, Corson et al. recommended that DFO could also be used in a nonfluorescent application to enhance the contrast of ninhydrin-developed prints [103]. The authors reported that on numerous occasions, the use of DFO on post-ninhydrin-treated prints yielded additional, undetected ridge detail. The effect of treating prints processed with DFO with metal salt solutions was explored by Conn et al. in 2001 [104]. Conformational analysis of the reaction product between DFO and amino acids determined that only a relatively small out-of-plane angle occurred in the reaction product between DFO and amino acids. This would suggest that there was little improvement in π-orbital overlap to be gained by complexing with metal salts such as zinc nitrate.

There has been a debate over whether or not an item should be prehumidified prior to processing with DFO. Preliminary data in favor of prehumidification was presented by Brennan et al. in 2003 [105]. The best results were obtained by double-dipping items into a freshly prepared DFO solution and using development conditions of 30°C and 60% RH. Brennan detailed the construction of a special glove box for humidifying samples and reported improved results for 1,2-indanedione and DFO [106]. The Home Office reported that they had evaluated different relative humidity levels (18%, 45.5%, and 73%) and had observed no differences in the visible or fluorescence intensities of developed prints [107]. Sears noted that although some water is required for the DFO reaction (the use of molecular sieves to dry the solvents renders DFO ineffective), the prehumidification of paper did not improve latent print development [108].

2.4.2 Forensic Applications

An evaluation of DFO and 5-methoxyninhydrin was reported by Lennard et al. in 1990 [109]. In contrast to Grigg et al., the authors found that the maximum absorption for DFO was between 520 and 560nm. Champod et al. characterized the broad excitation spectrum of DFO to be from 430 to 580nm, with maxima at 460, 530, and 560nm [110]. The detection limits for 5-methoxyninhydrin and DFO were reported to be (under white light) 50 and 100ng of amino acid, respectively, and (in fluorescence mode) 3ng for both compounds [109]. DFO was found to produce a lower background fluorescence than 5-methoxyninhydrin, although DFO often left a yellowish stain on processed items. A subsequent evaluation by Stoilovic described a modified DFO formula that increased its long-term stability [111]. The previously reported formula was observed to destabilize after only a few days. The modification involved adding chloroform to the stock solution.* The use of a heating press (set at 180°C for 10 s) was found to produce equal development compared to the traditional oven heating method.

Initial formulations for DFO relied on the use of banned chlorofluorocarbons as carrier solvents [112]. There have been a number of attempts to find suitable replacement solvents for the Freon 113† that was used in the original formulation. Jungbluth recommended replacing Freon with 2,2-dichloro-1,1,1-trifluoroethane, also known as HCFC-123 or Genesolv 2020‡ [36]. Masters et al. described an evaluation of a xylene- and petroleum ether-based formula§ [113]. Didierjean et al. proposed a formulation whose concentration remained at 0.025% w/v, but included twice the amount of methanol¶ [114]. This reagent was found to produce very strong, fluorescent prints on a variety of substrates, except plastic fiber mailing envelopes and genuine U.S. currency. The U.K. Home Office recommended two replacement solvents for DFO, HFE 7100** and HFC 4310mee†† [115]. The HFE 7100 formulation was found to be slightly superior to both the CFC and HFC formulations. Alternatively, hydrocarbon solvent-based formulations have also been used operationally.

The use of DFO to develop prints on thermal papers often led to the darkening of the paper and a loss of contrast between any developed prints and the background. Several attempts were made to address this problem. The first involved a solventless contact process [116]. The technique involved application of the reagent via presoaked and dried filter papers. The item would be placed between two DFO-soaked sheets and then wrapped with a paper towel. The development step involved placing a steam iron filled with a 5% acetic acid solution on top of the paper towel for 1 min and then transferring the item to a mounting press set at 100°C for 10 min. The method resulted in developed prints without any background interference or damage to writing inks.

The U.K. Home Office reported several modifications to their recommended DFO processing method for thermal papers. Initially, the Home Office recommended doubling the amount of methanol in the reagent to help clear the black coloration [117]. Treated items required an additional 15–30 s of soaking time in the modified solution to completely remove the background coloration. A more recent recommendation involved the use of an ethanol prewash for 5–10 s prior to using the standard DFO formulation [118]. Schwarz et al. described a modified DFO method for obtaining prints on thermal papers [119]. The authors recommended the use of a two-stage process involving a petroleum ether–based DFO reagent, followed by a clearing solution (the authors referred to this as a "whitening" solution) called G3. The G3 solution was composed of an equimolar (12.5 mmol) mixture of 4-pyrrolidino-pyridine, oenantholactam, 1-octyl-2-pyrrolidone, and 1-cyclohexyl-pyrrolidone in ethanol and petroleum ether. Interestingly, upon processing ninhydrin-treated prints on thermal paper with the G3 solution, the developed prints turned blue and there was no damage to any ballpoint inks present on the item.

---

* The stock solution consisted of 2.4 g DFO in 150 mL chloroform, 300 mL methanol, and 30 mL glacial acetic acid. The working solution was prepared by combining 80 mL of the stock solution with 1000 mL of 1,1,2-trichlorotrifluoroethane (Arklone P).

† The chemical name for Freon 113 is 1,1,2-trichloro-1,2,2-trifluoroethane (CAS No. 76-13-1)

‡ The formulation involved mixing 0.05 g DFO, 4 mL methanol, 2 mL acetic acid, and 94 mL Genesolv 2020.

§ The stock solution contained 1 g of DFO dissolved in 180 mL of methanol and 20 mL of acetic acid. The working solution was prepared by mixing 60 mL of the stock solution with 50 mL acetone, 10 mL isopropanol, 50 mL xylene, and 830 mL of petroleum ether.

¶ The formula contained 0.25 g DFO mixed with 40 mL methanol, 20 mL acetic acid and 940 mL HFE 7100.

** HFE 7100 is a mixture of two inseparable isomers, 2-(difluoromethoxymethyl)-1,1,1,2,3,3,3-heptafluoropropane (CAS No. 163702-08-7) and 1,1,1,2,2,3,3,4,4-nonafluoro-4-methoxy-butane (CAS No. 163702-07-6).

†† The chemical name for HFC 4310mee is 1,1,1,2,2,3,4,5,5,5-decafluoropentane (CAS No. 138495-42-8).

2.4.3 Impact on DNA

The effect of DFO treatment on subsequent DNA recovery and analysis was reported by Zamir et al. [120]. In two threat cases, neither the envelopes nor the letters yielded any prints after treatment with DFO. However, after phenol/chloroform extraction, six STR loci were obtained from the items in both cases. DNA recovery from DFO-treated bloodstains was also reported to be successful, with little impact observed from the chemical processing [121]. A subsequent study by Raymond et al. showed that DFO treatment appeared to have the least effect on DNA recovery compared to the rest of the common porous-item processing techniques [122].

Reagent formulation

Nonflammable formulation [123]

DFO	250 mg
Methanol	30 mL
Acetic acid	20 mL
HFE71DE*	275 mL
HFE 7100	725 mL

Hydrocarbon formulation [124]

DFO	500 mg
Methanol	100 mL
Ethyl acetate	100 mL
Acetic acid	20 mL
Petroleum ether	780 mL

1. For both reagent formulations, the DFO should be dissolved first in a mixture of the methanol/acetic acid (nonflammable formulation) and methanol/acetic acid/ethyl acetate (hydrocarbon formulation). This mixture should be stirred continuously until the DFO completely dissolves.
2. Once the DFO has dissolved completely, the carrier solvent should then be added slowly to the DFO solution, while constantly stirring. The solution should be stirred for a few minutes after the carrier has been added.
3. The reagent solution should be stored in a glass bottle, in the dark, and at a relatively constant temperature. Temperature extremes should be avoided (especially cold) as this could destabilize the reagent and lead to precipitation of DFO from the solution.
4. The appropriate information (e.g., chemical contents, preparer's initials, date, reliability test result) should be recorded on the container's label.

Reagent application

1. All appropriate personal protective equipment should be used when preparing and using this reagent.
2. Run the appropriate positive and negative controls to ensure that the reagent solution is working properly.

* HFE71DE is a 1:1 mixture (by weight) of HFE 7100 (which itself is a mixture of two isomers) with *trans*-1,2-dichloroethylene.

3. The reagent can be applied to a porous surface either by dipping, spraying, or painting. The dipping method is the most efficient.
4. Once the item has been allowed to air dry in a fume hood, the items should be placed in an oven set at 100°C for 20 min. The items should be heated at ambient humidity—no additional moisture should be added to the oven chamber. Although not ideal, an iron (no steam setting) can be used to provide heat. Caution must be exercised since scorching and background overdevelopment can occur.
5. The items can then be viewed under white light to observe any visible color development.
6. For fluorescence examination, a light source (e.g., laser, ALS) with suitable wavelength characteristics should be used. DFO has excitation maxima at approximately 530 and 560 nm (with the strongest emission occurring at 576 nm). A suitably filtered alternate light source can be used for excitation of the DFO-treated prints. A red filter (e.g., Schott OG 590) should be used for viewing the fluorescence emission.
7. When processing has been completed, all chemicals should be disposed of properly according to the appropriate federal, state, and local environmental laws.

2.5 1,2-Indanedione

Although mentioned in the literature as far back as 1912, the compound 1,2-indanedione (1,2-diketohydrindene) was first synthesized and reported by Cava et al. in 1958 [125]. Dr. Joullié's research group at the University of Pennsylvania was the first to investigate its potential use as a fingerprint reagent in the mid-1990s. 5-Methylthio-1,2-indanedione was the first analog to be synthesized in 1996. The parent compound was evaluated in 1996 and found to show considerable promise as a fluorescent fingerprint visualization reagent. A total of eight 1,2-indanedione analogs were synthesized and tested [126]. The study determined that a strong link between the heat and humidity conditions and the fluorescence intensity. Results also indicated that both the presence of an acid (in this case acetic acid) and zinc nitrate posttreatment significantly enhanced the color and fluorescence of the reaction product. A subsequent paper described the possibility of mixing the 1,2-indanedione and zinc nitrate into a single reagent [127].

2.5.1 Chemistry and Reaction Mechanism

The reaction of 1,2-indanedione and its analogs with amino acids has been described by Petrovskaia et al. [128]. The first step in the reaction is the formation of an imine followed by decarboxylation to form a 1,3-dipolar species (with variable geometries). The next step involves the formation of 2-amino-1-indanone. The final reaction complex was formed upon reaction with another 1,2-indanedione molecule. The result was a Ruhemann's purple-like structure, which has been named Joullié's pink (JP)* [97]. Alaoui et al. described two fluorescent products, 1,2-di(carboxymethylimino)indane and 2-carboxymethyliminoindanone,

* Professor Madeleine Joullié and her research group at the University of Pennsylvania were the first to synthesize numerous 1,2-indanediones and evaluate them for their abilities to develop latent prints.

obtained from the reaction of 1,2-indanedione and glycine [129]. Lennard et al. reported that the reaction of different amino acids with 1,2-indanedione yielded products with different colors and fluorescence intensities [130].

While the formation of hemiketals appears to be essential for the reaction of DFO with amino acids, the opposite was found to be true with 1,2-indanedione [131]. In the presence of alcohols, 1,2-indanedione forms a very stable hemiketal. This stable hemiketal appears to have a significantly reduced reactivity toward amino acids. Wiesner et al. recommended using ethyl acetate instead of alcohols in 1,2-indanedione formulations [132]. The reaction rate of 1,2-indanedione was also described. 1,2-Indanedione was found to react at a rate similar to that of ninhydrin, but at a faster rate than DFO. This study also found that acetic acid did not affect the fluorescence intensity of the reaction product. However, it was reported to have a detrimental effect on the clarity of the developed prints. This trend was also observed by Kasper et al. [133].

Recent reaction mechanism studies have further elucidated the role of water and zinc in the formation of the JP reaction product [134]. Both appear to have a positive influence on the reaction's outcome. Performing the reaction at ambient humidity appeared to quench undesirable side reaction that would decrease the yield of JP (and thus reduce fluorescence). The zinc ions have been found to interact with one of the critical reaction intermediates to stabilize it and thus increase the yield of JP. This would also increase the eventual fluorescence of the reaction (as well as latent prints treated with 1,2-indanedione/zinc). Finally, the presence of zinc chloride also slowed the rate of degradation of the JP product in high humidity environments.

2.5.2 Forensic Applications

Numerous other laboratories have conducted evaluations of these compounds. Interestingly, these investigations have produced conflicting results. Almog et al. found that zinc chloride posttreatment of the prints did not enhance fluorescence [135]. Overall, the authors found that 1,2-indanedione was at least as good as DFO in visualizing latent prints. Roux et al. evaluated both 1,2-indanedione and the dimethoxy analog [136]. These compounds were found to be at least as sensitive as DFO in detecting amino acids. The detection limits were determined to be 2.4×10^{-3} mg/mL for DFO and 7.6×10^{-5} mg/mL for the two 1,2-indanediones. The authors recommended the use of a heat press (set at 120°C for 15 s), which they found to be superior to conventional oven heating. They also found that the carrier solvent had an impact of fluorescence intensity. HFE 7100 was found to be the best carrier solvent.

The Home Office performed several evaluations of 1,2-indanedione. Merrick et al. described an optimized formula for the new reagent* [115]. When compared to three different DFO formulations (each in either Freon 113, HFC 4310mee, or HFE 7100), the indanedione reagent produced the weakest results. Gardner et al. reported on an equimolar evaluation of DFO and 1,2-indanedione [137]. Besides the advantage in improved solubility of the compound in nonpolar solvents, little practical difference in performance was observed between the two reagents when treating pseudooperational materials (e.g., envelopes, newspapers, train tickets). Sears et al. compared DFO with a 1,2-indanedione/zinc solution [138]. The optimized IND-Zn solution† was found to produce superior results only on brown paper, newsprint, and magazine paper.

---

* The formula involved mixing 2510 mg of 1,2-indanedione with 90 mL of ethyl acetate and 10 mL of acetic acid. The final reagent volume was achieved by the addition of 1000 mL of HFE 7100.

† The HOSDB optimized IND–Zn formulation was prepared by mixing 0.125 g of 1,2-indanedione, 45 mL ethyl acetate, 5 mL acetic acid, 0.25 mL zinc chloride stock solution, and 500 mL of HFE 7100. The zinc chloride stock solution was prepared by mixing 0.2 g zinc chloride with 5 mL of absolute ethanol.

Wallace-Kunkel reported on the relative effectiveness of six different indanedione formulations [139]. Although a formulation recommended by BVDA produced the best results, the solution was reported as unstable. The authors modified the BVDA formulation by substituting HFE 7100 for petroleum ether.* Development of samples was done using a heat press set at 165°C for 10s. Successful fingerprint development (excitation at 532nm with OG590 long pass filter) was reported on wallpaper, untreated wood, thermal paper, and green and yellow fluorescent paper. Overall, the optimized formulation was found to be more sensitive than either DFO or ninhydrin. In a direct comparison with DFO, 1,2-indanedione was found to develop 50% more fingerprints than DFO and 46% more than when using DFO-ninhydrin sequential processing.

Although mixing 1,2-indanedione and zinc salts into a combined reagent had been reported back in the mid-1990s [127], the first to create a successful fingerprint reagent was Stoilovic et al. [140]. This work was first presented in 2006 [141]. One important observation reported in this study was that in drier climates, humidity was required to develop optimum fluorescence. They reported that combining the zinc chloride into the 1,2-indnaedione reagent made it less susceptible to environmental conditions.† The excitation and emission maxima were found to nearly overlap (λ_{ex} was reported to be 550nm and λ_{em} was 559nm). Overall, the 1,2-indanedione/zinc reagent was found to significantly outperform DFO. Russell et al. also published a modified IND–Zn reagent [142]. The optimized reagent formulation‡ was reported to produce results that were superior to the Australian Federal Police formulation.

Bicknell et al. observed a similar trend in performance [143]. The optimized reagent solution used petroleum ether as the carrier solvent, since no advantage was found using HFE 7100.§ Moisture (either from the ambient relative humidity of the room or from the paper) was reported to play a critical role in maximizing fluorescence intensity. It appeared that if the ambient relative humidity was below 70%, ninhydrin development conditions (80°C, 65% RH) were required, whereas if the value was above 70% DFO development conditions were required (i.e., 20min at 100°C). When 58 naturally handled envelopes were processed with DFO followed by 1,2-indanedione/zinc, 116 prints were developed with 1,2-indanedione/zinc (84 of which were not detected first by DFO). DFO failed to develop any prints beyond those developed by the 1,2-indanedione/zinc reagent.

1,2-Indanedione has also been recommended for developing prints on thermal papers. However, the presence of acetic acid and the use of heat lead to a blackening of the printed side of the thermal receipt. Stimac recommended an optimized formulation¶ based on

* The optimized formula recommended mixing 1g of 1,2-indanedione with 10mL of acetic acid, 90mL of ethyl acetate, and 900mL of HFE 7100.

† The optimized formulation involved mixing 1g of 1,2-indanedione, 30mL dichloromethane, 60mL ethyl acetate, 10mL acetic acid, and 900mL HFE 7100. The zinc chloride stock solution was prepared by mixing 0.4g of zinc chloride with 10mL absolute ethanol, 1mL ethyl acetate, and 190mL of HFE 7100. The final reagent was prepared by mixing 2mL of the zinc chloride stock solution per 100mL of 1,2-indanedione reagent solution.

‡ This reagent was prepared by mixing 5g of 1,2-indanedione, 150mL dichloromethane, 300mL ethyl acetate, 50mL acetic acid, 0.5mL, and 450mL HFE 7100 to create a stock solution. The zinc chloride stock solution is prepared by mixing 8g of zinc chloride in 200mL absolute ethanol. The final reagent is prepared by mixing 3mL of the zinc chloride stock solution with 500mL of the 1,2-indanedione stock solution. Then, 50mL of this solution was diluted with 450mL of HFE 7100.

§ The optimized formulation involved mixing 1g of 1,2-indanedione, 30mL dichloromethane, 60mL ethyl acetate, 10mL acetic acid, and 900mL HFE 7100. The zinc chloride stock solution was prepared by mixing 0.4g of zinc chloride with 10mL absolute ethanol, 1mL ethyl acetate, and 190mL of HFE 7100. The final reagent was prepared by mixing 8mL of the zinc chloride stock solution per 100mL of 1,2-indanedione reagent solution.

¶ The optimized formulation involved mixing 2g of 1,2-indanedione with 70mL ethyl acetate and 930mL of HFE 7100.

the work by Wiesner [144]. Samples treated with this reagent were allowed to develop at room temperature over a period of 24h. This reagent was able to develop ridge detail on 47% of randomly acquired thermal receipt samples (overall 18% were suitable for identification purposes). Patton et al. reported on the use of a dry contact method for developing prints with 1,2-indanedione/zinc [145]. An acid-free HFE 7100-based reagent was found to work best when prints were allowed to develop at ambient temperature for 48h. Although the developed prints were not as intense as ones developed with the Australian Federal Police's special thermal paper 1,2-indanedione/zinc formulation [146],* the dry contact method could be used in cases where documents are fragile or international travel is required. Schwarz et al. describe the use of an 1,2-indanedione/zinc solution and heat followed by a special clearing solution to visualize prints on thermal papers [147]. The clearing solution G3 decolorizes the thermal papers within seconds, leaving clear prints with good contrast.

Wallace-Kunkel surveyed dozens of laboratories around the world in 2004 to gauge the familiarity with 1,2-indanedione and its use in casework [148]. 1,2-Indanedione was found to routinely be used in casework in 14% of laboratories (compared to 11% using DFO routinely). Of those who used 1,2-indanedione routinely, 60% reported that it worked better than DFO (only 10% rated DFO as the superior reagent).

2.5.3 Impact on DNA

The effect of 1,2-indanedione treatment of items on subsequent recovery of DNA has been investigated [149]. Although all nine loci were identified after processing, there was less success as the time gap between processing and DNA analysis increased (this is especially common in laboratories with large case backlogs). Significant degradation was reported to occur in as little as 6 days. At least partial DNA profiles were obtained post-1,2-indanedione using Profiler plus and both Chelex and Qiamp extraction methods on thermal and carbonless papers [150]. Partial profiles were obtained even with time gaps of 21 days between processing and DNA analysis. It should be noted that this study was done using 1,2-indanedione and not the currently recommended 1,2-indanedione/zinc.

Reagent preparation

Working solution (U.S. Secret Service)

1,2-Indanedione	0.8 g
Ethyl acetate	90 mL
Glacial acetic acid	10 mL
Zinc chloride stock solution	80 mL
Petroleum ether	820 mL

Zinc chloride stock solution

Zinc chloride	0.4 g
Absolute ethanol	10 mL
Ethyl acetate	1 mL
Petroleum ether	190 mL

* This reagent was prepared by mixing 0.75g of 1,2-indanedione, 15mL dichloromethane, 35mL ethyl acetate, 0.5mL zinc chloride stock solution, and 450mL HFE 7100. The zinc chloride stock solution is prepared by mixing 8g of zinc chloride in 200mL absolute ethanol.

Working solution (Australian Federal Police) [140]

1,2-Indanedione	1 g
Dichloromethane	30 mL
Ethyl acetate	60 mL
Glacial acetic acid	10 mL
Zinc chloride stock solution	20 mL
HFE 7100	900 mL

Zinc chloride stock solution

Zinc chloride	0.4 g
Absolute ethanol	10 mL
Ethyl acetate	1 mL
HFE 7100	190 mL

1. 1,2-Indanedione should be completely dissolved in the ethyl acetate and glacial acetic acid.
2. The zinc chloride stock solution should be added, followed by the slow addition of petroleum ether. If flammability is a concern, HFE 7100 can be substituted for the petroleum ether.
3. The solution should be mixed thoroughly. The solution can sometimes have a cloudy appearance. This will typically go away and become clear in about 24 h.
4. Store this solution in a dark glass or plastic bottle.
5. The appropriate information (e.g., chemical contents, preparer's initials, date, reliability test result) should be recorded on the container's label.
6. The shelf life of this solution is at least one month if stored in the dark at room temperature.

Reagent application

1. All appropriate personal protective equipment should be used when preparing and using this reagent.
2. Run the appropriate positive and negative controls to ensure that the reagent solution is working properly.
3. Items should be immersed in the working solution for a few seconds.
4. Development of the items is dependant upon the ambient humidity of the laboratory. If the relative humidity is above 70% then the items should be developed in an oven set at 100°C for 20 min. When the humidity level drops below 70%, an environmental chamber set at 80°C and 65% RH should be used for 20 min.
5. If a steam press is to be used for development, treated items should be processed at 165°C for 10 s.
6. The pink-colored product should be viewed under white light and also in the fluorescence mode. Optimal conditions involve illumination at 525 nm and viewing/imaging using a Schott OG550 or other similar filter.
7. When processing has been completed, all chemicals should be disposed of properly according to the appropriate federal, state, and local environmental laws.

2.6 Miscellaneous Amino Acid Reagents

2.6.1 *p*-Dimethylaminocinnamaldehyde

The compound *p*-dimethylaminocinnamaldehyde (pDMAC) was first used for fingerprint visualization in the mid-1970s [151]. While it was initially introduced to the fingerprint community for producing visible prints [151], the first indications of its luminescence potential was reported in 1977 [152] and subsequently in 1979 [153]. Aldehydes and ketones react with primary amines to form imines (N-substituted imines also known as Schiff bases) and secondary amines to form enamines [154]. Through a condensation reaction, pDMAC is known to form colored compounds of these types [155]. The color of the reaction products can be made more intense by the addition of dilute acids. A recent article confirmed that pDMAC appeared to preferentially react with amino acids rather than urea or sodium chloride [156].

At first, this compound was thought to react with urea specifically, rather than amino acids. This was encouraging since more of the total nitrogen in sweat was contained in urea than in amino acids [152]. It was selected as a viable candidate to replace ninhydrin because it reacted at room temperature in approximately 2 min and produced an intense magenta-colored product. The color was found to be pH-dependent and the addition of more dilute acid kept the reaction product magenta-colored. If the pH increased above neutral, the reaction product would be bright yellow in color. One drawback noted was that the prints must be imaged within about a 4 h time span, since the background continued to develop, thus reducing contrast. However, it was noted that even if the background obscured the print, it still could be visualized in the fluorescence mode using an argon ion laser. The magenta-colored development could be completely removed from the substrate by immersion in a 3.0% nitric acid solution. However, operationally, the results were found to be less impressive, as the reagent produced diffused ridge detail with prints more than 5–10 days old [13]. Another study found the operational usefulness of pDMAC to be less than 72 h [157]. It also stated that the best acid for the reagent overall was 5-sulfosalicylic acid.

In the mid-1990s, the use of pDMAC was revived. Two independent research groups had examined the potential use of the compound for its fluorescent properties rather than its visible colored ones. Although both techniques involved vapor phase reactions, they employed significantly different approaches. The first method involved the direct heating of the pDMAC compound in a fume hood [158]. Items were passed through the vapor stream to produce fluorescent prints, which were viewed by using both 350 and 530 nm (550 nm emission filter) excitation and the appropriate blocking filters for viewing. Brennan used this process to develop prints on thermal papers that were heat-sensitive. An alternative approach was also contemporaneously developed [159]. This method involved the use of "dry" pDMAC to produce prints by a vapor transfer mechanism. The item to be processed was placed between two sheets of photocopy paper that had been soaked in pDMAC and allowed to dry. The item typically remained in contact with these sheets overnight to allow for development. Often, there were no visible signs of a reaction, but when illuminated with an argon ion laser, fluorescent prints could be observed.

Subsequent attempts have been made to produce analogs of pDMAC, to see if improvements could be made [160]. None of these compounds were found to be superior to pDMAC.

Reagent preparation [159]

pDMAC stock solution

pDMAC	0.25 g
Ethanol	50 mL

Acid stock solution

5-Sulfosalicylic acid	1 g
Ethanol	50 mL

1. pDMAC and 5-sulfosalicylic acid are readily soluble in ethanol. Ensure that both compounds have completely dissolved before preparing the working solution.
2. The working solution is prepared by mixing equal amounts of the two stock solutions together.
3. Filtering may be required after mixing the two solutions together.
4. The appropriate information (e.g., chemical contents, preparer's initials, date, reliability test result) should be recorded on the container's label.
5. The shelf life of this solution was reported to be at least 1 month if stored in the dark at room temperature.

Reagent application

1. All appropriate personal protective equipment should be used when preparing and using this reagent.
2. Run the appropriate positive and negative controls to ensure that the reagent solution is working properly.
3. Blotter papers should be immersed in the working solution until they have been entirely soaked (they should turn yellow if they are alkaline).
4. The papers should be allowed to air dry.
5. The item to be processed should be placed in between two dried blotter papers (containing the pDMAC). This "sandwich" should then be placed in a sealable plastic bag.
6. The development typically takes between 12 and 24 h. The item may not appear to have any visible color change (or it may have a slight yellow tint).
7. Fluorescent prints can be viewed by using blue-green excitation and an orange filter to view the emission.
8. When processing has been completed, all chemicals should be disposed of properly according to the appropriate federal, state, and local environmental laws.

2.6.2 NBD Chloride

The use of the fluorogenic reagent NBD chloride (also known as 4-chloro-7-nitrobenzo-2-oxa-1,3-diazole or 4-chloro-7-nitrobenzofurazan) to react with amino acids was first reported in 1968 [161]. It was first evaluated for use as a fingerprint visualization reagent by Salares et al. in 1979 [162]. The authors found that the excitation maximum for this compound was 465 nm.

Subsequently, the compound was evaluated for routine use and compared to ninhydrin [163,164]. The reagent was prepared by dissolving 0.1 g of NBD chloride into 10 mL of acetonitrile and then diluting the solution to a final volume of 100 mL with 1,1,1-trichloro-2,2,2-trifluoroethane. Prints were developed by dipping the items into the solution, followed by heating in an oven set at 110°C for 10 min. The excitation and emission maxima were determined to be 480 and 544 nm, respectively. The authors reported a lack of selectivity with the NBD chloride reagent. It reacted with certain additives in paper (optical brighteners) as well as with water. Predrying of papers helped to reduce this background development. A comparison of NBD chloride with the nonflammable ninhydrin formulation reported by Morris and Goode [32] found that both reagents produced similar results with older prints; however, NBD chloride had a slight advantage with more recent prints (3–9 months old). A subsequent study recommended that the reagent be used as a post-ninhydrin treatment [164].

Five ether derivatives of NBD chloride (containing either alkoxy or aryl-oxy substituents at the 4-position) were synthesized and evaluated by Almog et al. [165]. The compounds were tested by dipping and in the vapor phase. Solutions were prepared by using the formulation reported by Warrener et al. [163], except that the ratio of acetonitrile to Freon used was 1:99 (instead of 1:9). All of the NBD ethers were found to work better than NBD chloride, with less background fluorescence and discoloration. NBD chloride has significant health and safety issues, including being classified as a potent mutagen [166].

2.6.3 Dansyl Chloride

The compound dansyl chloride (also known as 1-dimethylaminonaphthalene-5-sulfonyl chloride) has been used to label both amino acids and proteins [167–169]. Sanger was the first to observe that free, unprotonated α-amino acid groups of peptides reacted with 2,4-dinitrofluorobenzene to form dinitrophenyl derivatives. Subsequent hydrolysis with hydrochloric acid cleaved all of the peptide bonds except for the derivatized N-terminal amino acid, which could then be isolated and analyzed. Updated versions of this procedure employed even more sensitive derivatizing agents, like dansyl chloride. This reagent formed a highly fluorescent derivative with amino acids and proteins and was reported to be 100 times more sensitive than Sanger's original method.

Dansyl chloride was evaluated as a fingerprint reagent by Lee et al. in 1979 [170]. A subsequent evaluation by Clark et al. [171] found that the dansyl chloride reagent produced highly fluorescent fingerprints. The reagent was prepared by mixing 10 mg of dansyl chloride into 20 mL of acetone. The solution was sprayed onto the paper surfaces and then heated in an oven set at 50°C for 1 min. The excitation and emission maxima for this compound were reported as 337 and 492 nm, respectively. Kinoshita et al. reported that the addition of cycloheptaamylose could enhance the fluorescence of the reaction product with dansyl chloride [167].

2.6.4 *o*-Phthalaldehyde

o-Phthalaldehyde (OPA) has been used as an antimicrobial pesticide and as a disinfectant for sterilizing medical and dental equipment [172]. Shore et al. appeared to be the first to report the reaction between OPA and amines, which formed intensely fluorescent products [173]. Cohn et al. used a 0.1% w/v methanolic solution of OPA as a fluorometric assay for glutathione [174]. Fluorophore formation was found to be pH dependent, decreasing rapidly below a pH of 8. Roth reported the use of OPA to form highly fluorescent products with most amino acids [175]. However, the amino acid cysteine and imino acids proline and hydroxyproline failed to produce a fluorescent product. A reagent solution containing OPA, 2-mercaptoethanol (a reducing agent), and a borate buffer (pH 9.5) was found to have a sensitivity as low as 1 nanomole of alanine. The reaction proceeded over the course of 2–5 min at room temperature. The reaction products, 1-alkyl-2-alkylthio-substituted isoindoles, had excitation and emission maxima at 330 and 465 nm, respectively [176]. Benson et al. reported that the addition of Brij detergent and a 10-fold increase in the 2-mercaptoethanol concentration increased the detection limit to the picomole range (1×10^{-12} mole) [177]. The OPA reagent was reported to be 5–10 times more sensitive than fluorescamine (see Section 2.6.5).

The first application of this compound to visualize latent prints was reported by Mayer et al. in 1977 [178,179]. The reagent was prepared by first dissolving 2.5 g of boric acid into 95 mL of distilled water. The pH of this solution was adjusted to 10.4 using 6 M potassium hydroxide. Next, 0.3 mL of 30% Brij 35 detergent solution and 0.2 mL of 2-mercaptoethanol were added. To this solution, a mixture of 0.24 g of *o*-phthalaldehyde dissolved in 2 mL of methanol was added to make the final reagent. The reagent was applied to surfaces as a fine spray (Babington nebulizer). The reaction proceeded rapidly at room temperature. Long-wave ultraviolet radiation was used to excite the developed prints.

Fischer described an OPA formulation that did not include 2-mercaptoethanol [180]. Both acetone- and Freon-based solutions* were prepared and compared to ninhydrin. Prints were processed with OPA by dipping the papers into the reagent for approximately 15 s and then allowing them to air dry. A steam iron was used to expedite development along with a 1% nitric acid/acetone solution. Overall the reaction of OPA with latent prints produced fluorescence detail as good as ninhydrin–zinc chloride and it did not appear to be influenced by humidity conditions.

2.6.5 Fluorescamine

The compound fluorescamine (also known as 4-phenylspiro[furan-2(3H),1′-phthalan]-3–3′-dione) has been used to label amino acids for analysis by a wide variety of instrumental techniques [181]. It has also been used in the toxicological analysis of amphetamine and its differentiation from methamphetamine [182]. Weigele et al. appear to be the first to report the use of this compound to detect primary amino acids [183]. It was first introduced as a potentially sensitive latent print reagent by Lee in 1978 [184] and reported later in 1979 [185]. Menzel reported on the use of an argon ion laser with UV option (10 mW) to excite fluorescamine-treated prints in the 333.6–363.8 nm range [153]. The values for the excitation and emission maxima have been reported to be 390 and 465/475 nm, respectively [186].

The fluorescamine reaction begins with nucleophilic addition of the amine nitrogen to the compound's double bond [181]. This results in the breaking of a C–O bond and the loss of the compound's chiral center. A second nucleophilic attack by the amino acid nitrogen on the (former) chiral carbon closes the five-membered ring and forms a fluorescent product with two chiral centers. The reaction ultimately produces four fluorescent stereoisomers. The compound is known to hydrolyze rapidly in water to produce nonfluorescent products [187]. Suitable solvents for this compound include acetone, dioxane, dimethylsulfoxide, tetrahydrofuran, and acetonitrile.

* The acetone solution was prepared by dissolving 0.25 g OPA in 100 mL of acetone and the Freon solution was prepared by dissolving 0.25 g OPA in 5 mL denatured ethanol and then diluting the solution up to 100 mL. A 1% nitric acid solution was prepared by carefully adding 1 mL of concentrated nitric acid into 99 mL of acetone. This reagent was sprayed onto the paper surface after application of OPA.

2.6.6 Genipin

Gardenia jasminoides is a fragrant, flowing evergreen tropical plant, most commonly found in Vietnam, southern China, Taiwan, Japan, and India. The compound genipin was first described as an amino acid reagent in the 1960s [188,189]. It was prepared by β-glucosidase hydrolysis of geniposide (extracted from the fruit of the *Gardenia jasminoides* plant). Upon reaction with amino acids, the initially colorless genipin formed a blue product. Unlike ninhydrin, genipin produced a slightly different product for each amino acid. The molar absorptivity of this blue pigment was found to be at least twice the value of the corresponding ninhydrin reaction product [190]. The reaction product of genipin and the amino acids glutamic acid and asparagine was reported to be 11 times more intense.

The blue-colored product of the dual reagent was determined to be fluorescent, with a maximum excitation wavelength of 540 nm and a maximum emission at 610 nm. This red-shift in fluorescence provided an advantage on brown wrapping paper and documents written with fluorescent inks [191]. The optimal working solution concentration was found to be 0.17% w/v. Increasing the concentration beyond this amount did not improve the intensity of fluorescence. The working solution has a pH of 6.8. Deviations from this relatively neutral pH caused a decrease in sensitivity. In a comparison between genipin, ninhydrin, and DFO, ninhydrin and genipin produced equivalent visible-colored print development, while DFO exhibited a significantly higher fluorescence intensity.

Reagent preparation [191]

Working solution

Genipin	1.71 g
Ethanol	57 mL
Ethyl acetate	86 mL
HFE 7100	857 mL

1. Genipin should be completely dissolved in the ethanol and ethyl acetate before diluting the mixture to 1 L with HFE 7100. If flammability is not a major concern, petroleum ether can be substituted for the HFE 7100.
2. Store this solution in a dark glass or plastic bottle.
3. The appropriate information (e.g., chemical contents, preparer's initials, date, reliability test result) should be recorded on the container's label.
4. The shelf life of this solution is reported to be at least 1 month if stored in the dark at room temperature.

Reagent application

1. All appropriate personal protective equipment should be used when preparing and using this reagent.
2. Run the appropriate positive and negative controls to ensure that the reagent solution is working properly.
3. Items should be immersed in the working solution for a few seconds.
4. The item should be allowed to air dry and then should be placed in a humidity-controlled oven set at 80% RH and 75°C–85°C for approximately 15 min.
5. The blue-colored product should be viewed under white light and also in the fluorescence mode. Optimal conditions involve illumination at 590 nm and viewing/imaging through a 620 nm cut-off filter (Kodak gelatin red filter No. 92).

6. The colored and fluorescent products were reported to be stable for at least 6 months.
7. When processing has been completed, all chemicals should be disposed of properly according to the appropriate federal, state, and local environmental laws.

2.6.7 Lawsone

Lawsone (2-hydroxy-1,4-naphthoquinone) reacts with amino acids to form a purple-brown colored product [192]. Lawsone is a naphthoquinone, a group of compounds known to react and form colored products with amino acids. It is also assumed to be the compound responsible for the staining properties of henna, a natural product obtained from the leaves of *Lawsonia inermis*. Henna has been a traditional hair and skin dye for millennia. The optimum working solution concentration was reported to be 0.1% w/v (or 1 mg/mL) in a 1:4 mixture of ethyl acetate and HFE 7100. A petroleum ether–based solution was found to perform equally well if a substitute solvent was desired. Processing latent prints treated with lawsone in a heat press set at 150°C for 0.5–1 h produced purple-brown-colored prints [193]. However, more uniform development was observed after heating samples in an oven set between 140°C and 170°C for 1 h. The maximum excitation wavelength was determined to be 590 nm and emission could be viewed through a Wratten NA29 filter.

Reagent preparation [192]

Working solution

Lawsone	50 mg
Ethyl acetate	10 mL
HFE 7100	40 mL

1. Lawsone should be completely dissolved in the ethyl acetate before diluting the mixture with HFE 7100. If flammability is not a major concern, petroleum ether can be substituted for the HFE 7100.
2. Store this solution in a dark glass or plastic bottle.
3. The appropriate information (e.g., chemical contents, preparer's initials, date, reliability test result) should be recorded on the container's label.
4. The shelf life of this solution has not been determined.

Reagent application

1. All appropriate personal protective equipment should be used when preparing and using this reagent.
2. Run the appropriate positive and negative controls to ensure that the reagent solution is working properly.
3. Items should be immersed in the working solution for a few seconds.
4. The item should be allowed to air dry and then should be placed in an oven set between 140°C and –170°C for approximately 1 h. The oven produced more consistent development than the use of a shirt press.
5. The purple-brown-colored product should be viewed under white light and also in the fluorescence mode. Optimal conditions involve illumination at 590 nm and viewing/imaging through a 640 nm cut-off filter (Wratten NA29).
6. When processing has been completed, all chemicals should be disposed of properly according to the appropriate federal, state, and local environmental laws.

References

1. Ruhemann S. (1910) Cyclic di- and tri-ketones. *Trans Chem Soc* 97:1438–1449.
2. Joullié MM, Thompson TR, Nemeroff NH. (1991) Ninhydrin and ninhydrin analogs. Synthesis and applications. *Tetrahedron* 47(42):8791–8830.
3. Ruhemann S. (1910) Triketohydrindene hydrate. *Trans Chem Soc* 98:2025–2031.
4. Ruhemann S. (1911) Triketohydrindene hydrate part III. Its relation to alloxan. *Trans Chem Soc* 99:792–800.
5. Ruhemann S. (1911) Triketohydrindene hydrate part V. *Trans Chem Soc* 99:1486–1492.
6. Abderhalden E, Schmidt H. (1913) Some observations and tests on triketohydrindene hydrate. *Z Physiol Chem* 85:143 (translated from German).
7. Abderhalden E, Schmidt H. (1911) On the use of triketohydrindene hydrate for tracing proteins and their stages of decomposition. *Z Physiol Chem* 72:37 (translated from German).
8. Friedman M. (2004) Applications of the ninhydrin reaction for analysis of amino acids, peptides, and proteins to agricultural and biomedical sciences. *J Agric Food Chem* 52(3):385–406.
9. Lamothe PJ, McCormick PG. (1972) Influence of acidity on the reaction of ninhydrin with amino acids. *Anal Chem* 44(4):821–825.
10. Petraco ND, Proni G, Jackiw JJ, Sapse A-M. (2006) Amino acid alanine reactivity with the fingerprint reagent ninhydrin. A detailed ab initio computational study. *J Forensic Sci* 51(6):1267–1275.
11. Shulenberger WA. (1963) Questioned document news and views. *Ident News* 13(3):9–10,14.
12. Friedman M, Sigel CW. (1966) A kinetic study of the ninhydrin reaction. *Biochemistry* 5:478–485.
13. Goode GC, Morris JR. (1983) Latent fingerprints: a review of their origin, composition and methods for detection. AWRE Report No. 022/83.
14. Friedman M, Williams LD. (1974) Stoichiometry of formation of Ruhemann's purple in the ninhydrin reaction. *Bioorg Chem* 3:267–280.
15. Ramminger U, Nickel U, Geide B. (2001) Enhancement of an insufficient dye-formation in the ninhydrin reaction by a suitable post treatment process. *J Forensic Sci* 46(2):288–293.
16. McLaughlin AR. (1961) Developing latent prints on absorbent surfaces. *Fingerprint Ident Mag* 42(8):3–16.
17. Menzel ER, Everse J, Everse KE, Sinor TW, Burt JA. (1984) Room light and laser development of latent fingerprints with enzymes. *J Forensic Sci* 29(1):99–109.
18. Everse K, Menzel ER. (1986) Sensitivity enhancement of ninhydrin-treated latent fingerprints by enzymes and metal salts. *J Forensic Sci* 31(2):446–454.
19. Pounds CA, Hussain JI. (1987) Biological and chemical aspects of latent fingerprint detection. In: *Proceedings of the International Forensic Symposium on Latent Prints*, Laboratory & Identification Divisions, Federal Bureau of Investigation, FSRTC FBI Academy, Quantico, VA, U.S. Government Printing Office, Washington, DC, pp. 9–13.
20. Almog J, Sheratzki H, Elad-Levin M, Sagiv AE, Singh GD, Jasuja OP. (2011) Moistened hands do not necessarily allude to high quality fingerprints: the relationship between palmar moisture and fingerprint donorship. *J Forensic Sci* 56(S1):S162–S165.
21. Godsell J. (1963) Fingerprint techniques. *J Forensic Sci Soc* 3(2):79–87.
22. Edwards CJ, Hockey JA, Hudson FL. (1966) Some observations on the detection of fingerprints using ninhydrin. *J Forensic Sci Soc* 6:183–184.
23. Levy AL, Chung D. (1953) Two-dimensional chromatography of amino acids on buffered papers. *Anal Chem* 25(3):396–399.
24. Odén S, von Hofsten B. (1954) Detection of fingerprints by the ninhydrin reaction. *Nature* 173(4401):449–450.
25. Papenfus R. (1982) Age and ninhydrin. *Fingerprint Whorld* 8(30):39.
26. Lambourne G. (1982) Ninhydrin record? *Fingerprint Whorld* 8(30):18.
27. Foster HH. (1976) Ninhydrin development of latent impressions. *Fingerprint Ident Mag* 57(6):3–5.

28. Burns G. (1982) Ninhydrin longevity. *Fingerprint Whorld* 7(28):98–99.
29. Odén S. (1957) Process of developing fingerprints. *Ident News* 7(1):1–2.
30. Crown DA. (1969) The development of latent fingerprints with ninhydrin. *J Crim Law Criminol Pol Sci* 60(2):258–264.
31. Mooney DG. (1973) Additional notes on the use of ninhydrin. *Ident News* 23(10):9–11.
32. Morris JR, Goode GC. (1974) NFN—an improved ninhydrin reagent for the detection of latent prints. *Pol Res Bull* 24:45–53.
33. Leadbetter MJ. (1982) Fluorisol ninhydrin and typewriter correcting fluid. *Fingerprint Whorld* 7(28):92.
34. Tighe DJ. (1984) Freon—plus two. Presented at the U.S. Postal Inspection Service Crime Laboratories, Washington, DC, March 13, 1984.
35. Watling WJ, Smith KO. (1993) Heptane: an alternative to the Freon/ninhydirn mixture. *J Forensic Ident* 43(2):131–134.
36. Jungbluth WO. (1993) Replacement for Freon 113. *J Forensic Ident* 43(3):226–233.
37. Black J. (2008) Ninhydrin formulation introduced by Koreans. SWGFAST Members Forum, posted July 16, 2008.
38. Hewlett DF, Sears VG. (1997) Replacements for CFC113 in the ninhydrin process: part 1. *J Forensic Ident* 47(3):287–299.
39. Hewlett DF, Sears VG, Suzuki S. (1997) Replacements for CFC113 in the ninhydrin process: part 2. *J Forensic Ident* 47(3):300–306.
40. Hewlett DF, Sears VG. (1996) Formulation of amino acid reagents—search for a safe effective replacement for CFCs. In: Almog J, Springer E, Eds., *Proceedings of the International Symposium on Fingerprint Detection and Identification*. Hemed Press, Jerusalem, Israel, pp. 99–108.
41. Hewlett DF, Winfield PGR, Clifford AA. (1996) The ninhydrin process in supercritical carbon dioxide. *J Forensic Sci* 41(3):487–489.
42. Hewlett DF, Sears VG. (1999) An operational trial of two non-ozone depleting ninhydrin formulations for latent fingerprint detection. *J Forensic Ident* 49(4):388–396.
43. Petruncio AV. (2000) A comparative study for the evaluation of two solvents for use in ninhydrin processing of latent print evidence. *J Forensic Ident* 50(5):462–468.
44. Ludas M, Nin Dry. (1992) A non-destructive ninhydrin application for bank robbery demand notes and check forgery cases. Presented at the 77th Annual International Association for Identification Educational Conference, Atlantic City, NJ.
45. Schwarz L, Frerichs I. (2002) Advanced solvent-free application of ninhydrin for detection of latent fingerprints on thermal paper and other surfaces. *J Forensic Sci* 47(6):1274–1277.
46. German ER. (1981) You are missing ninhydrin developed prints. *Fingerprint Whorld* 7(26):40–42.
47. Herod DW, Menzel ER. (1982) Laser detection of latent fingerprints: ninhydrin. *J Forensic Sci* 27(1):200–204.
48. Moenssens AA. (1968) Ninhydrin development of latent finger prints: a careful reappraisal. *Fingerprint Ident Mag* 49(3):11–14,23.
49. Moore DS. (1988) The electrostatic detection apparatus (ESDA) and its effects on latent prints on paper. *J Forensic Sci* 33(2):357–377.
50. Azoury M, Gabbay R, Cohen D, Almog J. (2003) ESDA processing and latent fingerprint development: the humidity effect. *J Forensic Sci* 48(3):564–570.
51. Mooney DG. (1966) Development of latent fingerprints and palmprints by ninhydrin. *Ident News* 16(8/9):4–6.
52. Knowles AM. (1978) Aspects of physiochemical methods for the detection of latent fingerprints. *J Phys E Sci Instrum* 11:713–721.
53. Nielson JP. (1987) Quality control for amino acid visualization reagents. *J Forensic Sci* 32(2):370–376.
54. Schwarz L. (2009) An amino acid model for latent fingerprints on porous surfaces. *J Forensic Sci* 54(6):1323–1326.
55. Kawerau E, Wieland T. (1951) Conservation of amino acid chromatograms. *Nature* 168(4263):77–78.

56. Morris JR, Goode GC, Godsell JW. (1973) Some new developments in the chemical detection of latent fingerprints. *Pol Res Bull* 21:31–36.
57. Dalrymple BE, Duff JM, Menzel ER. (1977) Inherent fingerprint luminescence—detection by laser. *J Forensic Sci* 22(1):106–115.
58. Herod DW, Menzel ER. (1982) Laser detection of latent fingerprints: ninhydrin followed by zinc chloride. *J Forensic Sci* 27(3):513–518.
59. Kobus HJ, Stoilovic M, Warrener RN. (1983) A simple luminescent post-ninhydrin treatment for the improved visualization of fingerprints on documents in cases where ninhydrin alone gives poor results. *Forensic Sci Int* 22:161–170.
60. Stoilovic M, Kobus HJ, Margot PAJ, Warrener RN. (1986) Improved enhancement of ninhydrin developed fingerprints by cadmium complexation using low temperature photoluminescence techniques. *J Forensic Sci* 31(2):432–445.
61. Takatsu M, Shimoda O, Onishi K, Onishi A, Oguri N. (2008) Detection of pretreated fingerprint fluorescence using an LED-based excitation system. *J Forensic Sci* 53(4):823–827.
62. Lennard CJ, Margot PA, Sterns M, Warrener RN. (1987) Photoluminescent enhancement of ninhydrin developed fingerprints by metal complexation: structural studies of complexes formed between Ruhemann's purple and group IIb metal salts. *J Forensic Sci* 32(3):597–605.
63. Davies PJ, Kobus HJ, Taylor MR, Wainwright KP. (1995) Synthesis and structure of the zinc(II) and cadmium(II) complexes produced in the photoluminescent enhancement of ninhydrin developed fingerprints using group 12 metal salts. *J Forensic Sci* 40(4):565–569.
64. Liberti A, Calabrò G, Chiarotti M. (1995) Storage effects on ninhydrin-developed fingerprints enhanced by zinc complexation. *Forensic Sci Int* 72(3):161–169.
65. Menzel ER, Bartsch RA, Hallman JL. (1990) Fluorescent metal–Ruhemann's purple coordination compounds: applications to latent fingerprint detection. *J Forensic Sci* 35(1):25–34.
66. Menzel ER, Mitchell KE. (1990) Intramolecular energy transfer in the europium–Ruhemann's purple complex: application to latent fingerprint detection. *J Forensic Sci* 35(1):35–45.
67. Alaoui IM, Menzel ER. (1994) Emission enhancement in terbium–Ruhemann's purple complexes. *Forensic Sci Int* 66(3):203–211.
68. Mekkaoui AI, Menzel ER. (1993) Spectroscopy of rare earth–Ruhemann's purple complexes. *J Forensic Sci* 38(3):506–520.
69. Menzel ER, Burt JA, Sinor TW, Tabuch-Ley WB, Jordan KJ. (1983) Laser detection of latent fingerprints: treatment with glue containing cyanoacrylate ester. *J Forensic Sci* 28(2):307–317.
70. Hansen DB, Joullie MM. (2005) The development of novel ninhydrin analogs. *Chem Soc Rev* 34:408–417.
71. Almog J, Hirshfeld A, Klug JT. (1982) Reagents for the chemical development of latent fingerprints: synthesis and properties of some ninhydrin analogs. *J Forensic Sci* 27(4):912–917.
72. Meier R, Lotter HG. (1957) Uber benz- und naphthoindantrione. *Chem Berichte* 90:222–228.
73. Menzel ER, Almog J. (1985) Latent fingerprint development by frequency doubled neodymium: yttrium aluminum garnet (Nd:YAG) laser: benzo[f]ninhydrin. *J Forensic Sci* 30(2):371–382.
74. Safaryn JE, Joullié MM. (1985) Quarterly research report to the U.S. Secret Service, August 1985.
75. Heffner R, Safaryn JE, Joullié MM. (1987) A new synthesis of benzo[f]ninhydrin. *Tetrahedron Lett* 52:6539–6543.
76. Aldrich Catalog, 1998–1999, cat No. 31078-6.
77. Almog J, Sears VG, Springer E, Hewlett DF, Walker S, Wiesner S, Lidor R, Bahar E. (2000) Reagents for the chemical development of latent fingerprints: scope and limitations of benzo[f] ninhydrin in comparison to ninhydrin. *J Forensic Sci* 45(3):538–544.
78. Hallman JL, Bartsch RA. (1991) Synthesis of naphtho[f]ninhydrin. *J Org Chem* 56(21):6243–6245.
79. Hark RR, Hauze DB, Petrovskaia O, Joullié MM. (2001) Synthetic studies of novel ninhydrin analogs. *Can J Chem* 79:1632–1654.
80. Kobus HJ, Pigou PE, Jahangiri S, Taylor B. (2002) Evaluation of some oxygen, sulfur, and selenium substituted ninhydrin analogues, nitrophenylninhydrin and benzo[f]furoninhydrin. *J Forensic Sci* 47(2):254–259.

81. Lennard CJ, Margot PA, Stoilovic M, Warrener RN. (1986) Synthesis of ninhydrin analogues and their application to fingerprint development: preliminary results. *J Forensic Sci Soc* 26:323–328.
82. Lennard CJ, Margot PA, Stoilovic M, Warrener RN. (1988) Synthesis and evaluation of ninhydrin analogues as reagents for the development of latent fingerprints on paper surfaces. *J Forensic Sci Soc* 28(1):3–23.
83. Almog J. (1987) Reagents for chemical development of latent fingerprints: vicinal triketones—their reaction with amino acids and with latent fingerprints on paper. *J Forensic Sci* 32(6):1565–1573.
84. Almog J, Hirshfeld A, Frank A, Sterling J, Leonov D. (1991) Aminoninhydrins: fingerprint reagents with direct fluorogenic activity—preliminary studies. *J Forensic Sci* 36(1):104–110.
85. Ohta H, Ogasawara K, Suzuki Y, Sugita R, Suzuki S. (2001) Examination of 5-alkoxyninhydrins as latent fingerprint visualization reagents. *Can Soc Forensic Sci J* 34(2):73–79.
86. Almog J, Klein A, Davidi I, Cohen Y, Azoury M, Levin-Elad M. (2008) Dual fingerprint reagents with enhanced sensitivity: 5-methoxy- and 5-methylthioninhydrin. *J Forensic Sci* 53(2):364–368.
87. Heffner RJ, Joullié MM. (1991) A synthesis of two novel benzo[f]ninhydrin analogs: 6-methoxybenzo[f]ninhydrin and thieno[f]ninhydrin. *Synth Commun* 21(8,9):1055–1069.
88. Heffner RJ, Joullié MM. (1991) Synthetic routes to ninhydrins. Preparation of ninhydrin, 5-methoxyninhydrin, and 5-methylthioninhydrin. *Synth Commun* 21(21):2231–2256.
89. Cantu AA, Leben DA, Joullié MM, Heffner RJ, Hark RR. (1993) A comparative examination of several amino acid reagents for visualizing amino acid (glycine) on paper. *J Forensic Ident* 43(1):44–67.
90. Almog J, Hirshfeld A, Frank A, Grant H, Harel Z, Ittah Y. (1992) 5-Methylthio ninhydrin and related compounds: a novel class of fluorogenic fingerprint reagents. *J Forensic Sci* 37(3):688–694.
91. Wallace-Kunkel C, Lennard C, Stoilovic M, Roux C. (2006) Evaluation of 5-methylthioninhydrin for the detection of fingermarks on porous surfaces and comparison. *Ident Can* 29(1):4–13.
92. Hauze DB, Petrovskaia O, Joullié MM. (1996) New reagents for the development of fingerprints. In: Almog J, Springer E, Eds., *Proceedings of the International Symposium on Fingerprint Detection and Identification*. Hemed Press, Jerusalem, Israel, pp. 119–123.
93. Hark RR. (1996) Chemical detection of fingerprints—synthesis of arylated ninhydrin analogs. In: Almog J, Springer E, Eds., *Proceedings of the International Symposium on Fingerprint Detection and Identification*. Hemed Press, Jerusalem, Israel, pp. 127–135.
94. Lennard C. (1994) Evaluation of 5-(2-thienyl)ninhydrin: preliminary results. Unpublished data, February.
95. Hauze DB, Joullié MM. (1997) Novel synthesis of thianinhydrin. *Tetrahedron* 53(12):4239–4246.
96. Elber R, Frank A, Almog J. (2000) Chemical development of latent fingerprints: computational design of ninhydrin analogues. *J Forensic Sci* 45(4):757–760.
97. Almog J, Glasner H. (2010) Ninhydrin thiohemiketals: basic research towards improved fingermark detection techniques employing nano-technology. *J Forensic Sci* 55(1):215–220.
98. http://usa.bvda.com/productinfo.php?file=methylthioninhydrin (accessed on February 19, 2011).
99. Grigg R, Mongkolaussavaratana T, Pounds CA, Sivagnanam S. (1990) 1,8-Diazafluorenone and related compounds. A new reagent for the detection of α-amino acids and latent fingerprints. *Tetrahedron Lett* 31(49):7215–7218.
100. Pounds CA, Grigg R, Mongkolaussavaratana T. (1990) The use of 1,8-diazafluoren-9-one (DFO) for the fluorescent detection of latent fingerprints on paper. A preliminary evaluation. *J Forensic Sci* 35(1):169–175.
101. Frank FJ, Handlin N. (1993) Development of a latent fingerprint detection chemical: dibenzo-1,8-diazafluorenone. *MAFS Newsletter* July, pp. 22–31.
102. Wilkinson D. (2000) Study of the reaction mechanism of 1,8-diazafluoren-9-one with the amino acid, L-alanine. *Forensic Sci Int* 109:87–103.
103. Corson WB, Lawson JE, Kuhn KE. (1991) Alternate applications of DFO for non-fluorescent visualization. *J Forensic Ident* 41(6):437–445.

104. Conn C, Ramsay G, Roux C, Lennard C. (2001) The effect of metal salt treatment on the photoluminescence of DFO-treated fingerprints. *Forensic Sci Int* 116:117–123.
105. Brennan J, Archer N. (2003) Prehumidification: its effect on amino acid reagents. Preliminary observations. Presented at the International Fingerprint Research Group Meeting, St. Albans, Hertfordshire, U.K., May 2003.
106. Brennan J. (2005) Effect of humidity on DFO development. Presented at the International Fingerprint Research Group Meeting, The Hague, the Netherlands, April 2005.
107. Anon. (2004) DFO: effects of pre-humidification. Fingerprint Development and Imaging Update. PSDB Publication. April, p. 6.
108. Sears V. (2003) DFO development. Presented at the International Fingerprint Research Group Meeting, St. Albans, Hertfordshire, U.K., May 2003.
109. Lennard CJ, Massonnet G, Margot P. (1990) A comparison between DFO (1,8-diaza-9-fluorenone) and 5-methoxyninhydrin for the development of latent fingerprints on paper surfaces. Presented at the 12th Meeting of the International Association of Forensic Sciences, Adelaide, South Australia, Australia.
110. Champod C, Lennard C, Margot P, Stoilovic M. (2004) *Fingerprints and Other Ridge Skin Impressions*. Boca Raton, FL: CRC Press, LLC, pp. 128–131.
111. Stoilovic M. (1993) Improved method for DFO development of latent fingerprints. *Forensic Sci Int* 60:141–153.
112. Hardwick S, Kent T, Sears V, Winfield P. (1993) Improvements to the formulation of DFO and the effects of heat on the reaction with latent fingerprints. *Fingerprint Whorld* 19(73):65–69.
113. Masters N, Morgan R, Shipp E. (1991) DFO, its usage and results. *J Forensic Ident* 41(1):3–10.
114. Didierjean C, Debart M-H, Crispino F. (1998) New formulation of DFO in HFE7100. *Fingerprint Whorld* 24(94):163–167.
115. Merrick S, Gardner SJ, Sears VG, Hewlett DF. (2002) An operational trial of ozone-friendly DFO and 1,2-indanedione formulations for latent fingerprint detection. *J Forensic Ident* 52(5):595–606.
116. Bratton RM, Juhala JA. (1995) DFO—dry. *J Forensic Ident* 45(2):169–172.
117. Anon. (2005) Thermal papers—no more problems! Fingerprint Development and Imaging Update. HOSDB Publication No. 6/2003, April, p. 5.
118. Anon. (2006) Use of DMAC on thermal papers. *Fingerprint and Footwear Forensics Newsletter*. HOSDB Publication No. 58/06, October, p. 3.
119. Schwarz L, Klenke I. (2007) Enhancement of ninhydrin- or DFO-treated latent fingerprints on thermal paper. *J Forensic Sci* 52(3):649–655.
120. Zamir A, Oz C, Geller B. (2000) Threat mail and forensic science: DNA profiling from items of evidence after treatment with DFO. *J Forensic Sci* 45(2):445–446.
121. Roux C, Gill K, Sutton J, Lennard C. (1999) A further study to investigate the effect of fingerprint enhancement techniques on the DNA analysis of bloodstains. *J Forensic Ident* 49(4):357–376.
122. Raymond JJ, Roux C, du Pasquier E, Sutton J, Lennard C. (2004) The effect of common fingerprint detection techniques on the DNA typing of fingerprints deposited on different surfaces. *J Forensic Ident* 54(1):22–44.
123. Bowman V, ed. (2004) *Manual of Fingerprint Development Techniques*, 2nd edn. (2nd revision). Police Scientific Development Branch, Home Office, Sandridge, U.K.
124. Trozzi TA, Schwartz RL, Hollars ML. (2001) *Processing Guide for Developing Latent Prints*. U.S. Department of Justice, Federal Bureau of Investigation, Washington, DC.
125. Cava MP, Little RL, Napier DR. (1958) Condensed cyclobutane aromatic systems. V. the synthesis of some α-diazoindanones: ring contraction in the indane series. *J Am Chem Soc* 80:2257–2263.
126. Ramotowski R, Cantu AA, Joullié MM, Petrovskaia O. (1997) 1,2-Indanediones: a preliminary evaluation of a new class of amino acid visualizing compounds. *Fingerprint Whorld* 23(90):131–140.
127. Hauze DB, Pterovskaia O, Taylor B, Joullié MM, Ramotowski R, Cantu AA. (1998) 1,2-Indanediones: new reagents for visualizing the amino acid components of latent prints. *J Forensic Sci* 43(4):744–747.

128. Petrovskaia O, Taylor BM, Hauze DB, Carroll PJ, Joullié MM. (2001) Investigations of the reaction mechanisms of 1,2-indanediones with amino acids. *J Org Chem* 66:7666–7675.
129. Alaoui IM, Menzel ER, Farag M, Cheng KH, Murdock RH. (2005) Mass spectra and time-resolved fluorescence spectroscopy of the reaction product of glycine with 1,2-indanedione in methanol. *Forensic Sci Int* 152:215–219.
130. Lennard A, Stoilovic M, Lennard C. (2006) Reaction between amino acids and ninhydrin, DFO, and 1,2-indanedione. Presented at the 17th Symposium of the Australian-New Zealand Forensic Science Society, Perth, Western Australia, Australia, April.
131. Wilkinson D. (2001) Spectroscopic study of 1,2-indanedione. *Forensic Sci Int* 114:123–132.
132. Wiesner S, Springer E, Sasson Y, Almog J. (2001) Chemical development of latent fingerprints: 1,2-indanedione has come of age. *J Forensic Sci* 46(5):1082–1084.
133. Kasper SP, Minnillo DJ, Rockhold AM. (2002) Validating IND (1,2-indanedione). *Forensic Sci Commun*;4(4):http://www2.fbi.gov/hq/lab/fsc/backissu/oct2002/kasper.htm (accessed on February 25, 2011).
134. Spindler X, Shimmon R, Roux C, Lennard C. (2011) The effect of zinc chloride, humidity and the substrate on the reaction of 1,2-indanedione-zinc with amino acids in latent fingermark secretions. *Forensic Sci Int* 212:150–157.
135. Almog J, Springer E, Wiesner S, Frank A, Khodzhaev O, Lidor R, Bahar E, Varkony H, Dayan S, Rozen S. (1999) Latent fingerprint visualization by 1,2-indanedione and related compounds: preliminary results. *J Forensic Sci* 44(1):114–118.
136. Roux C, Jones N, Lennard C, Stoilovic M. (2000) Evaluation of 1,2-indanedione and 5,6-dimethoxy-1,2-indanedione for the detection of latent fingerprints on porous surfaces. *J Forensic Sci* 45(4):761–769.
137. Gardner SJ, Hewlett DF. (2003) Optimization and initial evaluation of 1,2-indanedione as a reagent for fingerprint detection. *J Forensic Sci* 48(6):1288–1292.
138. Sears V, Batham R, Bleay S. (2009) The effectiveness of 1,2-indanedione-zinc formulations and comparison with HFE-based 1,8-diazafluoren-9-one for fingerprint development. *J Forensic Ident* 59(6):654–678.
139. Wallace-Kunkel C, Lennard C, Stoilovic M, Roux C. (2007) Optimization and evaluation of 1,2-indanedione for use as a fingermark reagent and its application to real samples. *Forensic Sci Int* 168:14–26.
140. Stoilovic M, Lennard C, Wallace-Kunkel C, Roux C. (2007) Evaluation of a 1,2-indanedione formulation containing zinc chloride for improved fingermark detection on paper. *J Forensic Ident* 57(1):4–18.
141. Wallace-Kunkel C, Stoilovic M, Lennard C, Roux C. (2006) 1,2-Indanedione—Where are we now? Presented at the 17th Symposium of the Australian-New Zealand Forensic Science Society, Perth, Western Australia, Australia, April.
142. Russell SE, John GL, Naccarato SL. (2008) Modifications to the 1,2-indanedione/zinc chloride formula for latent print development. *J Forensic Ident* 58(2):182–192.
143. Bicknell DE, Ramotowski RS. (2008) Use of an optimized 1,2-indanedione process for the development of latent prints. *J Forensic Sci* 53(5):1108–1116.
144. Stimac JT. (2003) Thermal paper: latent friction ridge development via 1,2-indanedione. *J Forensic Ident* 53(3):265–271.
145. Patton ELT, Brown DH, Lewis SW. (2010) Detection of latent fingermarks on thermal printer paper by dry contact with 1,2-indanedione. *Anal Methods* 2:631–637.
146. Stoilovic M, Lennard C. (2006) *Fingerprint Detection and Enhancement*, 3rd edn. Australian Federal Police, Canberra, Australian Capital Territory, Australia, pp. 90, 122, 124.
147. Schwarz L, Hermanowski M-L. (2011) Using indanedione-zinc, heat, and G3 solution sequentially to detect latent fingerprints on thermal paper. *J Forensic Ident* 61(1):30–37.
148. Wallace-Kunkel C, Roux C, Lennard C, Stoilovic M. (2004) The detection and enhancement of latent fingermarks on porous surfaces—a survey. *J Forensic Ident* 54(6):687–705.
149. Azoury M, Zamir A, Oz C, Wiesner S. (2002) The effect of 1,2-indanedione a latent fingerprint reagent, on subsequent DNA profiling. *J Forensic Sci* 47(3):586–588.

150. Yu P-H, Wallace MM. (2007) Effect of 1,2-indanedione on PCR-STR typing of fingerprints deposited on thermal and carbonless paper. *Forensic Sci Int* 168:112–118.
151. Morris JR. (1976) British patent 1423025.
152. Melton CW, Myers WC. (1977) Development of improved and new methods for the detection and recovery of latent fingerprints. Battelle Columbus Laboratories.
153. Menzel ER, Duff JM. (1979) Laser detection of latent fingerprints—treatment with fluorescers. *J Forensic Sci* 24(1):96–100.
154. Solomons TWG. (1988) *Organic Chemistry*, 4th edn. John Wiley & Sons, New York, p. 757.
155. Feigl F. (1939) *Qualitative Analysis by Spot Tests: Inorganic and Organic Applications*. Nordemann Publishing Company Inc., New York.
156. Lee JL, Bleay SM, Sears VG, Mehmet S, Croxton R. (2009) Evaluation of the dimethylamino-cinnemaldehyde contact transfer process and its application to fingerprint development on thermal papers. *J Forensic Ident* 59(5):545–568.
157. Sasson Y, Almog J. (1978) Chemical reagents for the development of latent fingerprints. I: scope and limitations of the reagent 4-dimethylamino-cinnamaldehyde. *J Forensic Sci* 23(4):852–855.
158. Brennan J, Bramble S, Crabtree S, Wright G. (1995) Fuming of latent fingerprints using dimethylaminocinnamaldehyde. *J Forensic Ident* 45(4):373–380.
159. Ramotowski R. (1996) Fluorescence visualization of latent fingerprints on paper using p-dimethylaminocinnamaldehyde (PDMAC). In: Almog J, Springer E, Eds., *Proceedings of the International Symposium on Fingerprint Detection and Identification*. Hemed Press, Jerusalem, Israel, pp. 91–94.
160. Personal communication from Dr. Madeleine Joullié to Dr. Tony Cantu (March 22).
161. Ghosh P, Whitehouse M. (1968) 7-Chloro-4-nitrobenzofurazan: a new fluorogenic reagent for amino acids and other amines. *Biochem J* 108:155–156.
162. Salares VR, Eves CR, Carey PR. (1979) On the detection of fingerprints by laser excited luminescence. *Forensic Sci Int* 14:229–237.
163. Warrener RN, Kobus HJ, Stoilovic M. (1983) An evaluation of the reagent NBD chloride for the production of luminescent fingerprints on paper: I. Support for a xenon arc lamp being a cheaper and valuable alternative to an argon ion laser as an excitation source. *Forensic Sci Int* 23:179–188.
164. Stoilovic M, Warrener RN, Kobus HJ. (1984) An evaluation of the reagent NBD chloride for the production of luminescent fingerprints on paper: II. A comparison with ninhydrin. *Forensic Sci Int* 24:279–284.
165. Almog J, Zeichner A, Shifrina S, Scharf G. (1987) Nitro-benzofurazanyl ethers—a new series of fluorogenic fingerprint reagents. *J Forensic Sci* 32(3):585–596.
166. Nelson JO, Warren PF. (1981) NBD-chloride is a potent mutagen in the salmonella mutagenicity assay. *Mutat Res* 88:351–354.
167. Kinoshita T, Iinuma F, Tsuji A. (1974) Microanalysis of proteins and peptides. I. Enhancement of the fluorescence intensity of dansyl amino acids and dansyl proteins in aqueous media and its application to assay of amino acids and proteins. *Chem Pharm Bull* 22(10):2413–2420.
168. Walker JM. (1994) The dansyl-edman method for peptide sequencing. *Methods Mol Biol* 32: 329–334.
169. Walker JM. (1994) The dansyl method for identifying n-terminal amino acids. *Methods Mol Biol* 32:321–328.
170. Lee HC, Attard AE. (1979) The use of dansyl chloride in latent print detection (abstract). In: *Proceedings of American Forensic Science Annual Meeting*, Atlanta, GA.
171. Clark S, Quigley MN, Tezak J. (1993) Chemical detection of latent fingerprints. *J Chem Educ* 70(7):593–595.
172. Anon. (2007) Chemical information profile for *o*-phthalaldehyde. Supporting Nomination for Toxicological Evaluation by the National Toxicology Program. Integrated Laboratory Systems, Inc., Research Triangle Park, NC, April.
173. Shore PA, Burkhalter A, Cohn VH. (1959) A method for the fluorometric assay of histamine in tissues. *J Pharmacol Exp Ther* 127:182–186.

174. Cohn VH, Lyle J. (1966) A fluorometric assay for glutathione. *Anal Biochem* 14:434–440.
175. Roth M. (1971) Fluorescence reaction for amino acids. *Anal Chem* 43(7):880–882.
176. Anon. (2003) *o*-Phthalaldehdye reagent. Pickering Laboratories Reagent Bulletin for Post-Column Liquid Chromatography.
177. Benson JR, Hare PE. (1975) *o*-Phthalaldehyde: fluorogenic detection of primary amines in the picomole range. Comparison with fluorescamine and ninhydrin. *Proc Natl Acad Sci* 72(2):619–622.
178. Mayer SW, Meilleur CP, Jones PF. (1977) The use of ortho-phthalaldehyde for superior visualization of latent fingerprints. *Ident News* 27(9):13–14.
179. Haylock SE. (1978) Ortho-phthalaldehyde. *Fingerprint Whorld* 4(14):52–53.
180. Fischer JF. (1990) A modified *o*-phthalaldehyde technique using blue-green light excitation for developing luminescent latent prints. *J Forensic Ident* 40(6):327.
181. Skelley AM, Mathies RA. (2003) Chiral separation of fluorescamine-labeled amino acids using microfabricated capillary electrophoresis devices for extraterrestrial exploration. *J Chrom A* 1021:191–199.
182. Nowicki HG. (1976) Studies on fluorescamine: part I—applications of fluorescamine in forensic toxicological analysis. *J Forensic Sci* 21(1):154–162.
183. Weigele M, DeBernardo SL, Tengi JP, Leimgruber W. (1972) Novel reagent for the fluorometric assay of primary amines. *J Am Chem Soc* 94(16):5927–5928.
184. Lee HC. (1978) Advantages and disadvantages of fluorescamine and *o*-phthalaldehyde for the detection of latent prints. Presented at the International Association of Identification Conference, Austin, TX, 27 August.
185. Lee HC, Attard AE. (1979) Comparison of fluorescamine, *o*-phthalaldehyde, and ninhydrin for the detection and visualization of fingerprints. *J Pol Sci Admin* 7(3):333–335.
186. Anon. (2005) Fluorescamine. Sigma Product Information. Product Number F 9015. January 2005.
187. De Bernardo S, Weigele M, Toome V, Manhart K, Leimgruber W, Böhlen P, Stein S, Udenfriend S. (1974) Studies of the reaction of fluorescamine with primary amines. *Arch Biochem* 163:390–399.
188. Djerassi C, Gray JD, Kincl FA. (1960) Naturally occurring oxygen heterocyclics. IX. Isolation and characterization of genipin. *J Org Chem* 25:2174–2177.
189. Djerassi C, Nakano T, James AN, Zalkow LH, Eisenbraun EJ, Shoorlery JN. (1961) Terpenoids. XLVII. The structure of genipin. *J Org Chem* 26:1192–1206.
190. Almog J, Cohen Y, Azoury M, Hahn T-R. (2004) Genipin—a novel fingerprint reagent with colorimetric and fluorogenic activity. *J Forensic Sci* 49(2):255–257.
191. Levinton-Shamuilov G, Cohen Y, Azoury M, Chaikovsky A, Almog J. (2005) Genipin, a novel fingerprint reagent with colorimetric and fluorogenic activity, part II: Optimization, scope and limitations. *J Forensic Sci* 50(6):1367–1371.
192. Jelly R, Lewis SW, Lennard C, Lim KF, Almog J. (2008) Lawsone: a novel reagent for the detection of latent fingermarks on paper surfaces. *Chem Commun* 3513–3515.
193. Jelly R, Lewis SW, Lennard C, Lim KF, Almog J. (2009) Naphthoquinones as novel reagents for the detection of latent fingermarks on paper surfaces. Presented at the International Fingerprint Research Group Meeting, Lausanne, Switzerland, June.

3

Metal Deposition Methods

Robert S. Ramotowski

CONTENTS

3.1 Silver Nitrate

The Italian scientist Camillo Golgi was the first to use a mixture of potassium dichromate and silver nitrate to stain tissue samples in 1873. Pierre Aubert was allegedly the first to use silver nitrate to detect latent prints as far back as 1877 [1]. With regard to processing porous items, the silver nitrate technique was used almost exclusively in the early twentieth century until being supplemented by ninhydrin in 1954. Silver nitrate solutions typically varied between 3% and 10% w/v, although Cuthbertson reported that 1% w/v was the optimum concentration [2]. Although aqueous silver nitrate solutions were commonly used, an alcohol-based formulation had the advantage of drying faster. Olsen reported that a special silver nitrate formulation, developed by Nicoletti at the Denver Police Department Crime Laboratory, worked well on dynamite wrappers [3].*

The mechanism of the reaction is relatively simple. Silver nitrate reacts with the chlorides present in the latent print to form silver chloride via a double replacement reaction (i.e., if the chloride was present in the latent print residue as sodium chloride then the reaction products would be silver chloride and sodium nitrate). Since the silver chloride bond is weak, exposure of the treated surface with short-wave ultraviolet radiation would convert silver chloride to metallic silver. The print would appear to be brown to grayish-black in color. Historically, silver nitrate has been used sequentially after iodine and ninhydrin. One report indicated that silver nitrate produced an additional 10% of identifiable latent prints in this sequence [4]. Goode and Morris hypothesize that the additional prints were a by-product of the formation of a silver–ninhydrin complex, which could produce better color contrast (similar to the use of zinc chloride after ninhydrin) [5].

There are two main drawbacks to using silver nitrate. The first is the strong background coloration that occurs due to silver interacting with the background substrate and the second involves the difficulty in controlling the speed of the photochemical reaction (with the short-wave ultraviolet [UV] lamp) [5]. The presence of a complexing agent, disodium ethylenediamine tetracetic acid (Na_2EDTA), and a reducing agent (thiourea), has been reported to significantly reduced background interferences. Excess silver present in the substrate background can be removed via complexation with Na_2EDTA. The presence of thiourea, which chemically reduces silver chloride to silver metal, eliminates the need for reduction by short-wave UV radiation. The reagent required the use of three separate solutions to produce optimum development.

Olsen noted that there is a difference in background development between aqueous and alcohol-based silver nitrate reagents [3]. To illustrate this point, a latent palm print was cut in half and each half was treated with either the aqueous or alcohol-based silver nitrate reagent. After 3 years, the half treated with the aqueous reagent was completely blackened while the half treated with the alcohol-based reagent was still clearly visible.

Clearing solutions have been used to remove the silver from both the developed print and background. This prevents the inevitable darkening of the background, which reduces the contrast of the print (as well as any printing or writing on the document). Typically, a 2% w/v solution of mercuric nitrate in distilled water (in some cases nitric acid was also added on a 2% v/v basis) was used to remove silver stains [3]. These solutions are no longer recommended as they are extremely toxic and are very expensive to dispose of properly. Other less toxic chemicals used as clearing solutions included Chlorox® and hyposodium sulfite.

Humidity plays a large role in limiting the effectiveness of the silver nitrate development process. The diffusion of chloride ions under humid conditions effectively limits the technique to prints less than a few weeks old [2]. The rate of chloride ion diffusion was once suggested as a possible method for determining the age of a deposited print [6], but there

* The reagent is prepared by making three stock solutions. Each stock solution was prepared by mixing 6g of silver nitrate in 10mL of distilled water followed by the addition of 100mL of alcohol. The alcohols were methanol, ethanol, and isopropanol, respectively. The ethanol solution must be added to one of the other solutions first to ensure that the final reagent was stable.

is no record of any further work being performed on this effort. Significant deterioration (with respect to silver nitrate development) was observed in prints maintained at 60% RH for 15 days [2]. At 80% and 100% RH conditions, significant deterioration occurred in as little as 2 days and 1 day, respectively. At relative humidity values ranging between 0% and 40%, no deterioration was observed up to 22 days. Latent prints exposed to water are rarely developed with silver nitrate. However, under more optimal conditions, it is possible to develop up to 8 month old prints [7].

Although used primarily for paper and cardboard, silver nitrate can also be an effective reagent for untreated wood [8]. The reagent has also been used to develop latent prints in more unusual circumstances. A partial palm impression was developed using a 6% w/v silver nitrate solution in methanol on a cow horn [9]. Loveridge reported that shoeprints had been recovered from paper and cloth using silver nitrate [10]. A dilute solution of physical developer (PD) has been used to enhance weakly developed silver nitrate prints [11]. An unusual alternative was proposed for uneven silver nitrate development within a single print [12]. A 200 kV Van de Graaf generator was successfully used to darken an underdeveloped portion of the print without overdeveloping the rest of the print or background. It appears that the electron bombardment was sufficient to finish breaking the silver chloride bonds.

Other silver salts have been suggested as alternatives to silver nitrate [13]. The perchlorate and chromate salts were evaluated by the Royal Canadian Mounted Police (RCMP) and University of Ottawa. These compounds were dissolved in a suitable organic solvent (e.g., toluene, xylene) and could be applied using an aerosol spray. Another process investigated involved the use of silver perchlorate and camphor on nonporous items like polyethylene. First, a thin coating of camphor (6%–8% in *n*-hexane) was either sprayed onto the surface of the item or heated as a vapor. After waiting 3 min, the silver perchlorate (3% in acetone) was applied. After an additional 15 min, the sample was placed in a photographic developer for 5 min and then immersed in a PD until optimum contrast was achieved.

Reagent preparation (water based)

Staining solution [14]

Silver nitrate	30 g
Distilled/RO–DI wate	1000 mL

1. Silver nitrate dissolves quickly in water. A clear solution should be formed. If a cloudy solution forms, the water quality is insufficient and the reagent will need to be made again.
2. This solution should be stored in a dark-colored glass bottle and should be stored in the dark.
3. The appropriate information (e.g., chemical contents, preparer's initials, date, reliability test result) should be recorded on the container's label.

Reagent preparation (alcohol based)

Staining solution [14]

Silver nitrate	30 g
Distilled/RO–DI water	100 mL
Ethanol	1000 mL

1. Silver nitrate should be mixed with the distilled/reverse osmosis–deionization (RO–DI) water first and then the ethanol should be added.
2. Stir this solution until it has formed a homogeneous solution.
3. This solution should be stored in a dark-colored glass bottle and stored in the dark.
4. The appropriate information (e.g., chemical contents, preparer's initials, date, reliability test result) should be recorded on the container's label.

Reagent application

1. All appropriate personal protective equipment should be used when preparing and using this reagent.
2. Run the appropriate positive and negative controls to ensure that the reagent solution is working properly.
3. This reagent can be applied by dipping, spraying, and brushing. For smaller items, dipping is the more effective method. For larger items, spraying or brushing is the most practical method.
4. When dipping items, the article needs to remain in the reagent long enough only to become saturated (a few seconds).
5. Treatment with silver nitrate and posttreatments should be done in a low-light environment (no direct sunlight) to minimize background development.
6. For larger objects, cotton balls or a paint brush may be used to apply the reagent.
7. Excess reagent solution needs to be removed by using absorbent blotter material and then allowed to dry (a hair dryer can be used to accelerate the drying process).
8. The treated item should then be exposed to short-wave UV radiation long enough to develop ridge detail but not to overdevelop the background.
9. Record the image as soon as possible since the contrast between the print and background will continue to deteriorate over time.
10. When processing has been completed, all chemicals should be disposed of properly according to the appropriate federal, state, and local environmental laws.

3.2 Physical Developer

PD has been a successful and reliable process for detecting latent prints not only on water-soaked porous items, but nonsoaked evidence as well. The mechanism of the process is quite complex and is covered comprehensively elsewhere [15]. Overall, the process involves an oxidation–reduction reaction, which uses an iron-based developer to reduce silver nitrate to a grayish-colored silver metal on the latent print residue. Although PD appears to react with the water-insoluble fraction of the latent print residue, it likely reacts with a wide variety of compounds rather than one specific class of chemicals. Morris found that triglycerides, wax esters, and hydrocarbons were potential triggering compounds for PD [16]. PD has also been noted to react with EDTA [16] and monounsaturated lipids. Colloidal silver has also been used as a stain for proteins [17]. Whatever PD reacts with, it must be relatively stable with respect to time. A recent publication reported that 55 year old prints on electricity bills were developed by PD [18]. On those same items, sequential treatment with 1,8-diazafluoren-9-one (DFO) failed to produce any reaction and ninhydrin produced only faint, spotty ridge detail. Subsequent processing with PD visualized a total of seven identifiable prints. Other sources report that PD was able to visualize a 30 year old print [19] on test material and an approximately 8 year old print as well [20].

PD had been in use for a considerable period of time prior to its introduction as a latent print visualization reagent in the early 1970s. These developers had been used to process images from photographic plates for decades. As with the anecdotal reports of scientists observing fingerprints developing on their paper chromatograms containing amino acids after spraying them with ninhydrin solutions, similar observations were noted with prints developing on the edges of handled photographic plates [5]. In 1972, Collins and Thomas, from the Atomic Weapons Research Establishment (AWRE), used these relatively unstable developers to enhance metalized prints (which had been previously processed with metal vapor deposition) [20]. When these solutions were used in an attempt to develop prints on items like paper and fabric, the results were disappointing because the solutions remained stable for only a few minutes after preparation (the silver would eventually precipitate out of solution).

3.2.1 Chemistry and Mechanism

The first use of stabilized PDs for latent print visualization was at the AWRE by Morris, who was under contract from the U.K. Home Office [16]. His work was based on research that had been conducted by Dippel, Jonker, and van Beek at the Philips Research Laboratories in Eindhoven, the Netherlands in the 1960s [21,22]. These reagents consisted of silver nitrate, Fe^{2+}/Fe^{3+} redox couple, citric acid, and (eventually) surfactants. Philips had been working on creating stabilized PDs that did not suffer from spontaneous nucleation (caused by the presence of both the reducing agent, ferric nitrate, and the metal ion Ag^{+} in the developer), which caused the rapid precipitation of metal from the developer. Using microelectrophoresis, Jonker and Molenaar observed that the metal nuclei spontaneously formed in the solution had a negative charge. In order to protect these negatively charged colloids from the other positively charged metal ions, they advocated the use of positively charged surface-active molecules (i.e., surfactants or detergents). The use of cationic (i.e., positively charged) surfactants (e.g., *n*-dodecylamine acetate) caused the developing silver colloid to change from a negative to a positive charge. This prevented aggregation with other positively charged silver ions in the developer. This slowed the unwanted consumption of silver ions, thus making more of them available to visualize prints.

The nonionic (i.e., no charge) surfactant present in today's PD (either Synperonic N or Tween 20) was once thought only to assist in keeping the cationic surfactant soluble. Indeed, Jonker noted that the addition of *n*-dodecylamine acetate to the PD resulted in the near immediate precipitation of the surfactant [22]. The addition of a nonionic surfactant was thought to be necessary to stabilize the developer. However, recent work has indicated that the nonionic surfactant acts as a protecting group that can further stabilize the developing colloidal particle [23]. Particles deposited by the PD process appear to be well-formed spheres approximately 5–10 μm in diameter when fully grown. However, upon closer inspection, the spherical particles are composed of silver "plates," which cause the particle to have an irregular shape. The particles appear dark because the irregular surface traps incident light in the open spaces between plates.

Workers at the AWRE and Police Scientific Development Branch (PSDB) worked throughout the 1970s to optimize the Philips' stabilized PD [24–26]. This work culminated in the writing of the first operational user's guide for the process in 1981 [27]. In this guide, the author mentioned for the first time the need to use an acid prewash prior to the immersion of evidence in PD. Thick stock or heavily coated papers can require substantially more soaking time to fully neutralize. The overall purpose of the prewash is to neutralize as much calcium carbonate in the paper as possible. Most papers today have a slightly basic pH due to the presence of calcium carbonate, which is used as an inexpensive filler. The presence of calcium carbonate in the paper can act as nucleation sites that can spontaneously draw the silver out of the developer and cause the entire paper surface to turn black [28].

According to Hardwick, the choice of maleic acid was made because it was compatible with all but one of the papers included in experimental trials. As it turns out, the only criteria for selecting an acid for the prewash appears to be that it must be chlorine free. Chlorinated acids (e.g., hydrochloric acid) could leave behind chlorine residues in the paper, which could lead to the formation of silver chloride. Exposure of the silver chloride to light would cause it to turn dark and decrease the background contrast. Other acids have been used successfully for the prewash step, including acetic [29], nitric [30], and malic [31] acids. A recent study that compared nitric and malic acid prewashes for the PD process found that a 2.5% w/v malic acid solution provided the best fingerprint development, although a 0.24% v/v nitric acid prewash produced less background interference with about half of the papers tested [31]. They noted that more concentrated malic acid solutions led to higher background interference.

The quality of the water used in the PD process is very important. Morris was one of the first to specify that purified water be used [16]. He noted that the water had to have a specific resistance of higher than 2 MΩ/cm and that it also had to be filtered before use. This value would be similar to high-grade distilled water (resistivity values greater than 0.1 MΩ/cm), which is produced by heating water in a closed chamber and condensing the steam. Ultrapure water can have resistivity values greater than 18 MΩ/cm. This water is obtained from RO–DI treatment systems. Reverse osmosis involves removing large ions and molecules from water by passing it through selective membranes at high pressures. Deionization involves passing the water through various ion exchange resins to remove unwanted constituents. A simple test was described by Hardwick to determine whether or not a particular batch of water was suitable for use with the PD process [27]. The test involved placing a few crystals of silver nitrate into a beaker containing the water sample. If any cloudiness developed, then the water was unsuitable. If the water remained clear, it was suitable for use with PD.

With working solutions prepared using the nonionic surfactant Synperonic N, the shelf life was about 7–14 days. Interestingly, when Tween 20 was used to replace Synperonic N, the shelf life of the working solution increased up to 2 months [31]. Barford et al. report that their PD working solutions, if allowed to "rest" for 2–3 weeks prior to use, worked better than freshly prepared PD solutions. Freshly prepared solutions worked but resulted in more substantial background development. Of considerable interest was their observation that their working PD solutions could last up to 3 months without reduction in development efficiency. They speculated that a yellow-colored batch of *n*-dodecylamine acetate (compare to the mostly white-colored version purchased today), provided by the PSDB, may have contained contaminates that could have stabilized the working solution. Morris speculated that the stability of working PD solutions could potentially be extended beyond even 3 months [15].

Commercial PD kits are available from several forensic product vendors. A review of several of these commercial kits found that the majority work reasonably well [27]. However, there were some issues regarding the accuracy of the instructions provided in the technical notes provided with these kits. Also, it is difficult to know the age of the solutions that are provided with each kit. While the shelf life of silver nitrate is essentially indefinite (if kept in the dark), the shelf life of the combined redox/detergent solution is not well known. Another study comparing commercial PD kits with those prepared from component chemicals, found overall that their performances were similar [32].

3.2.2 Sequencing

PD can be used successfully after reagents like 1,2-indanedione/zinc, DFO, ninhydrin, secondary metal salt treatments (e.g., zinc chloride), Oil Red O, and iodine, but not after silver nitrate. Processing silver nitrate–treated articles with PD will result in a complete blackening of the item. Other impression evidence, like shoeprints, may also develop with PD [33]. Silver has also been known to nucleate in paper folds and creases. Tongs with grip marks should be avoided as these patterns may be transferred to the paper and developed with PD. It is also very important not to overload the processing tray with exhibits. Enough reagent solution should be placed into the tray to ensure that each paper item flows freely without getting stuck to each other. Agitation is critical. An inexpensive mechanical shaker can be constructed to perform this task [34]. If two paper items become stuck together during the acid prewash, then the overlapping areas will not be exposed to the acid and the calcium carbonate will not be neutralized. Gray- to black-colored blotches will result in those areas.

3.2.3 Reagent Reliability Testing

Reliability testing of the working PD solution is strongly recommended. This should be done not only after the working solution has been prepared (to see if it was prepared correctly), but also as the working solution ages. At the U.S. Secret Service, the author worked on creating a fast, qualitative spot test that could be used to gauge the health of the working PD solution [36]. The test involved spotting a dilute mixture of gold chloride onto Whatman filter paper and allowing it to dry. The spot test could then be placed directly into the PD working solution. The acid prewash step was not required because the paper did not contain calcium carbonate or other fillers. If the solution had been made properly, the gold chloride spot would darken within 3–5 s. If the spot did not turn a dark gray-black color or took substantially longer than 5 s to react, then a second test would be run. If that test showed similar results, then the solution would be discarded. This process is similar to a spot test described by Feigl, in which silver detection limits as low as 0.005 μg have been reported [37]. Recent research has revealed that the gold chloride spot tests do not remain sufficiently stable over time [36]. The results of these studies have led to a recommendation that tetrasodium EDTA be used in place of the gold chloride (both for stability and economic reasons). Other laboratories have used ascorbic acid or oleic acid [38].

The current formulation used in the U.S. Secret Service's laboratory consists of five different solutions. It should be noted that distilled water can be used in place of the RO–DI water described in this formula (see the following footnotes).

Reagent preparation

Redox solution

Ferric nitrate nonahydrate	30 g
Ferrous ammonium sulfate hexahydrate*	80 g
Citric acid monohydrate	20 g
RO–DI water	900 mL

1. The chemicals should be mixed sequentially in the order listed earlier.
2. Each chemical should be allowed to completely dissolve prior to adding the next chemical.
3. Store the solution in a glass or plastic container.
4. The appropriate information (e.g., chemical contents, preparer's initials, date, reliability test result) should be recorded on the container's label.
5. The shelf life of this solution is approximately 6 months.

Detergent solution

n-Dodecylamine acetate	3 g
Tween 20†	3 mL
RO–DI water	1000 mL

1. The two detergents listed must be added in the order in which they appear in the list given earlier. In particular, the *n*-dodecylamine acetate is not very soluble in water and takes a considerable amount of time to fully dissolve (which can take up to 30–45 min).
2. After the addition of the Tween 20 the solution may have a slightly cloudy appearance.‡
3. Store the solution in a glass bottle.
4. The appropriate information (e.g., chemical contents, preparer's initials, date, reliability test result) should be recorded on the container's label.
5. The shelf life of this solution is ~6–12 months.

Silver nitrate solution

Silver nitrate	10 g
RO–DI water	50 mL

* Care must be exercised when adding the ferrous ammonium sulfate to the solution [31]. Barford et al. report that adding this chemical to the redox solution can cause a drop of 2°C–3°C (4°F–6°F), which can cause the citric acid to not dissolve properly. Any undissolved particles can act as spontaneous nucleation sites when the silver nitrate solution is added, resulting in uncontrolled precipitation. The authors recommended that the temperature range of the redox solution should remain between 17°C–23°C (63°F–73°F) at all times during the mixing process. If the temperature falls below 17°C (63°F), some of the chemicals may precipitate out of the solution.

† Synperonic N has traditionally been used as the nonionic surfactant in the PD formulation. It can be substituted on a 1:1 basis for Tween 20 in the detergent solution given. However, if distilled water is used in place of the RO–DI water, the relative amounts of the two detergents will have to be adjusted. Because there are more ions present in distilled water compared to RO–DI water, more detergent is required to achieve a suitable balance for the overall physical development process. For distilled water, the amounts of *n*-dodecylamine acetate and Tween 20 (or Synperonic N) would be 4 g and 4 mL, respectively [40]. The FBI recommended 3 g and 4 mL, respectively [14].

‡ After a period of several days, it is possible that excess surfactant may precipitate out of the working solution as a white-colored sediment [28,31]. This may affect the efficiency of the working solution.

1. Add the silver nitrate into the water and mix thoroughly.
2. Since silver nitrate is quite soluble in water, the process should not take more than a few minutes and the resulting solution should be colorless and clear.
3. Store the solution in a dark glass bottle.
4. The appropriate information (e.g., chemical contents, preparer's initials, date, reliability test result) should be recorded on the container's label.
5. The shelf life of this solution is indefinite if kept sealed and in the dark.

Acid prewash solution

Malic acid	25 g
RO–DI water	1000 mL

1. Add the malic acid into the water and stir until it is completely dissolved. In this step, maleic acid can be substituted on a 1:1 basis for malic acid.
2. Store the solution in a glass bottle.
3. The appropriate information (e.g., chemical contents, preparer's initials, date, reliability test result) should be recorded on the container's label.
4. The shelf life of this solution is indefinite.

PD working solution

Redox solution	900 mL
Detergent solution	40 mL
Silver nitrate solution	50 mL

1. Slowly add the detergent solution to the 900 mL of Redox Solution. Allow this solution to stir for at least 5–10 min to ensure that the detergents are fully incorporated into the solution.
2. Next, slowly add the silver nitrate solution to the mixture and allow it to stir for at least 5 min.
3. When the mixing is complete, the working PD solution should be transferred to a dark, amber-colored bottle.
4. The appropriate information (e.g., chemical contents, preparer's initials, date, reliability test result) should be recorded on the container's label.
5. The shelf life of the Tween 20–based PD working solution has been reported to be up to 2 months.

Reagent application

Prior to immersing any paper items into the final working PD solution, all extraneous metallic items (e.g., staples, paper clips) should be removed as these items can act as nucleation sites for PD. In fact, sufficient metal can be transferred to the paper from these items such that their latent images can be developed even if they are removed. Tongs with smooth grips should be used for handling the items in solution (to avoid developing grip marks on the item).

1. All appropriate personal protective equipment should be used when preparing and using this reagent.
2. Run the appropriate positive and negative controls to ensure that the reagent solution is working properly.

3. Place the porous items in a distilled or RO–DI water bath for about 5–10 min.*
4. Carefully drain off the water and then add the acid to the same tray.
5. The items should remain in the malic acid for at least 10–15 min, although thicker coated papers may require significantly more time.†
6. After a sufficient period of time, carefully drain off the malic acid solution and then add the PD working solution into the same tray. A water rinse between steps is not required.
7. The items should remain in the working PD solution until sufficient gray-black ridge development has occurred.‡
8. Once sufficient development has occurred, carefully drain off the working PD solution into a receptacle for proper disposal.
9. The items can now be rinsed in tap water§ (check your local regulations about whether or not the water rinses need to be collected for disposal) at least three to four times or until the rinse water appears completely clear (no traces of yellow, cloudy material).
10. The final assessments should only be done after the items have been rinsed and completely dried.
11. When processing has been completed, all chemicals should be disposed of properly according to the appropriate federal, state, and local environmental laws.

3.2.4 Bleach Toning

One of the more common post-PD processing techniques involves the use of dilute bleach. First reported by Phillips et al. [19], bleach improves the contrast of PD development in two ways, by lightening the background (by decolorizing residual stains) and by darkening the gray-colored print detail. The latter effect is caused by the formation of black-colored silver oxide, which results from the interaction of the silver with hypochlorite (household bleach is a ~5% solution of sodium hypochlorite). It should be noted that bleach does not remove silver stains. On the contrary, the bleach will darken the color of any silver, whether it is present in the print or the background. It has been reported that the use of the bleach intensifier can lead to a 10% increase in identifiable prints [19].

* The purpose of this initial rinse is to remove Ruhemann's purple stains from the document as well as any other water-soluble contaminants. It can also soften wrinkles and creases in the paper and thus prevent silver deposition in those areas. Multiple washes may be required to remove more substantial contamination. Care must be exercised with fragile papers.

† It is important to note that leaving a paper item in this solution longer than 10–15 min is generally safe; however, leaving it in for too short a period of time can lead to complete blackening of the item. As the calcium carbonate is being neutralized, carbon dioxide is given off in the form of small bubbles (resembling effervescence). Some use the disappearance of these bubbles as a sign that the paper is fully neutralized, but these bubbles can be difficult to observe.

‡ A compromise often has to be reached at this stage as some prints on the item may develop at faster rates than others. Also, the background will appear to be darker than it actually is when immersed in the PD working solution. When the item is fully dried, the background tends to lighten significantly.

§ If reprocessing the item with physical developer is anticipated, then distilled or RO–DI water must be used at this stage. As mentioned before, traces of chlorine from the tap water can be left behind in the paper fibers and can lead to the formation of silver chloride. This can cause the paper background to turn completely dark when exposed to the physical developer and light.

Reagent preparation

Bleach intensifier [19]

Household bleach (5% sodium hypochlorite)	1 part
Tap water	1 part

1. The water and bleach should be mixed just prior to use.
2. If stored in a glass bottle, the shelf life of this solution is indefinite.

Reagent application

1. All appropriate personal protective equipment should be used when preparing and using this reagent.
2. Run the appropriate positive and negative controls to ensure that the reagent solution is working properly.
3. The PD-processed item should have been thoroughly rinsed with water before this step. Traces of even small amounts of redox solution left on the item can react with the bleach to produce highly toxic gases.
4. The item should be immersed in the intensifier solution for about 2–3 min.
5. After that time, the item should be thoroughly rinsed with tap water to remove all traces of the bleach.
6. The item should be completely dried prior to evaluating the ridge detail.
7. When processing has been completed, all chemicals should be disposed of properly according to the appropriate federal, state, and local environmental laws.

3.2.5 Potassium Iodide Toning

In 1998, Dr. George Saunders proposed the use of potassium iodide as a means of improving the contrast of PD prints developed on dark or heavily patterned surfaces. The toning solution is composed of the standard redox solution (from PD) and a 20% w/v aqueous solution of potassium iodide. The mixture of these two solutions generates iodine (I_2), which combines with iodide ions (I^-) to form triodide ions (I_3^-) [39]. Papers that contain starch will then react with the triodide ions to form a blue-black-colored starch–iodine complex. The silver in the print is converted to a white-yellow-colored compound, silver iodide, and the background (if it contains starch) turns a dark blue-black color. This process does not develop any additional detail. It can only improve the contrast for ridge detail visualized by the PD process. Most inexpensive papers contain sufficient starch and thus work well with this toning solution.

Reagent preparation

Potassium iodide (KI) toning solution [15]

20% w/v potassium iodide solution (in RO–DI water)	1 part
Redox solution	19 parts

1. Add 20 g of potassium iodide into 100 mL of RO–DI water and mix thoroughly.
2. Prepare the redox solution in the same way as for the PD reagent.
3. Mix the redox and potassium iodide solutions just prior to use.

Reagent application

1. All appropriate personal protective equipment should be used when preparing and using this reagent.
2. Run the appropriate positive and negative controls to ensure that the reagent solution is working properly.
3. The silver PD print is first treated with the bleach intensifier solution as described in the previous section.
4. Place the item into the redox/KI solution. The reaction occurs relatively rapidly, converting the print to a white-yellow color and the background to a dark blue-black color.
5. When sufficient contrast is achieved between the print and the background, the print will need to be photographed in the solution. If removed from the solution, the contrast almost immediately begins to decrease and the print detail may be lost.
6. When processing has been completed, all chemicals should be disposed of properly according to the appropriate federal, state, and local environmental laws.

3.2.6 Miscellaneous Toning Processes

There are several other possible post-PD treatment options. In the 1970s, the U.K. Home Office developed a radioactive toning process for PD prints on dark or highly patterned surfaces [25,26]. The process involved processing the PD print with a solution containing a radioactive isotope of sulfur (^{35}S). Solutions containing radioactive sodium sulfide or thiourea were used to convert the silver PD to silver sulfide. This radioactive product could then be imaged using radiographic film (i.e., autoradiography). The inherent health and safety risks associated with this process make it impractical, although good results were achieved on certain patterned surfaces. A process for converting the silver PD print to a fluorescent product was developed and reported by Kyle [40]. This reagent was based on a dye-toning solution first reported by Crabtree and Ives [41] and involved the use of rhodamine 610 and potassium ferrocyanide [15]. This solution renders the silver PD prints luminescent (using 514.5 nm excitation and a Schott KV 550 long pass filter) in less than 10 min.

3.3 Multimetal Deposition

3.3.1 Multimetal Deposition (MMD I)

Colloidal gold has been reported to bind with proteins since at least 1939 [42]. Its application for visualizing latent prints was first suggested by Saunders as a process known as multimetal deposition (MMD, or referred to now as MMD I) [43]. Saunders employed a modified procedure first reported by Frens [44] to produce the colloidal gold particles. This method produces gold colloid particle sizes with an average diameter of 30 nm. He also took advantage of the use of a modified PD to enhance the gold deposited on the friction ridge detail. This two-step process was based on a method developed by Holgate et al. [45]. They proposed a new and very sensitive immunogold-silver staining method that was the first to suggest the use of a secondary silver colloid enhancement step for improved labeling of proteins. Using this work as a guide, Saunders developed a universal latent print developer, one that would develop prints on porous and nonporous surfaces [46]. In 1990, the U.S. Secret Service and the Los Alamos National Laboratory (George Saunders) shared an R&D 100 award for this achievement.

The method suffered from some significant drawbacks. First, the method was very complicated and required a considerable amount of time and finesse to prepare all of the necessary solutions. The cost of the overall reagent was also a factor as the process involved colloidal gold and silver solutions. In addition, the process required dedicated and scrupulously clean glassware for preparing and using the reagent. Saunders reported good results on nonporous surfaces, including adhesive/nonadhesive sides of tapes (e.g., plastic, bandage, masking, strapping, cellophane), credit cards, computer disks, Styrofoam, bags, coins, foil, Mylar, and glass. However, MMD did not appear to work on cartridge casings [47] and its use was reported to have a potentially negative impact on subsequent ballistic analyses [48].

Operationally, the process did not turn out to work well routinely on porous surfaces. Too much of the colloidal gold remained behind in the paper fibers (even after multiple water rinses) and caused high background levels when the modified PD step was used. Nevertheless, Saunders reported good results with MMD on variety of porous substrates, including bank checks, government checks, counterfeit currency, envelopes, yellow tablet paper, photographic paper, and newsprint. Because of the nonspecific binding of colloidal gold (caused by the presence of proteins on the surface of the substrate), genuine U.S. currency, leather, clothing, and skin were not recommended for processing with MMD. Saunders noted that for porous surfaces, MMD could be used after ninhydrin or superglue, but not after zinc chloride treatment. It appeared that divalent ions (zinc from the zinc chloride) interfered with gold colloid formation and stability.

Reagent preparation

This version of the multimetal deposition reagent was introduced by Saunders in 1989. The method was a modification of the technique used by Frens to produce 30 nm sized colloidal gold particles.

Solution A (tetrachloroauric acid trihydrate)		
	Etrachloroauric acid trihydrate	1 g
	RO–DI water	10 mL
Solution B (sodium citrate)		
	Sodium citrate tribasic dehydrate	1 g
	RO–DI water	100 mL
Solution C (0.1 M citric acid)		
	Citric acid monohydrate	4.8 g
	RO–DI water	50 mL
Solution D (polyethylene glycol)		
	Polyethylene glycol	1 mL
	RO–DI water	100 mL
Solution E (colloidal gold)		
	Solution A (tetrachloroauric acid trihydrate)	1 mL
	Solution B (sodium citrate)	15 mL
	Tween 20	5 mL
	Solution C (citric acid)	>1 mL
	Solution D (polyethylene glycol)	10 mL
	RO–DI water	1000 mL

1. Mix the RO–DI water and 1 mL of the tetrachloroauric acid trihydrate solution (Solution A) thoroughly.
2. Heat the solution until it reaches a gentle boil.
3. Add 15 mL of sodium citrate (Solution B) and continue to boil the solution until it turns a port-wine color.
4. Turn off the heat and, while still hot, add 5 mL of Tween 20 surfactant and mix thoroughly.
5. When sufficiently cool, add 10 mL of polyethylene glycol (Solution D) and mix thoroughly.
6. Adjust the pH of the solution to 2.7 by adding aliquots of citric acid (Solution C).
7. If necessary, restore the solution volume to 1 L with RO–DI water.
8. Store the colloidal gold solution in a scrupulously clean glass bottle and refrigerate.
9. The appropriate information (e.g., chemical contents, preparer's initials, date, reliability test result) should be recorded on the container's label.
10. The solution will remain stable for approximately 3 months.

Solution F (silver nitrate)

Silver nitrate	20 g
RO–DI water	100 mL

Solution G (modified redox)

Ferric nitrate nonahydrate	16 g
Ferrous ammonium sulfate hexahydrate	44 g
Citric acid monohydrate	11 g
Tween 20	0.25 mL
RO–DI water	1000 mL

1. The chemicals listed should be mixed in the order given.
2. The modified redox (Solution G) will appear yellow in color and may be slightly cloudy.
3. Store the solution in a glass or plastic container.
4. The appropriate information (e.g., chemical contents, preparer's initials, date, reliability test result) should be recorded on the container's label.
5. The solution has a 3–6 month shelf life.

Solution H (modified PD)

Solution G (modified PD redox)	990 mL
Solution F (silver nitrate)	10 mL

1. Add the two solutions together and mix thoroughly.
2. The working modified PD solution is very unstable and must be used immediately after mixing. This solution will last no more than 15–20 min before the silver begins to precipitate out.

Reagent application

1. All appropriate personal protective equipment should be used when preparing and using this reagent.
2. Run the appropriate positive and negative controls to ensure that the reagent solution is working properly.
3. Using a clean glass tray, cover the items with RO–DI water and agitate for approximately 10 min.*
4. Place the items in a new, clean glass tray and add the colloidal gold solution.
5. Allow the items to agitate in the colloidal gold solution for at least 30–45 min. Do not allow the items to overdevelop in this solution.
6. Rinse the items in several RO–DI water baths to remove as much of the colloidal gold from the background as possible (this is especially important for paper items and less so for nonporous substrates).
7. Examine the item for signs of visible prints (when wet the prints will appear purple and when dry will have a metallic, gold-colored appearance).
8. Place the item into a freshly prepared modified PD solution and agitate for approximately 5–15 min or until optimal development has been achieved.† Monitor the development progress carefully as development can occur rapidly.
9. Rinse the items with tap or RO–DI water to remove all traces of the modified PD solution. Rinsing should continue until the water no longer shows any sign of cloudy yellow material (for tap water).
10. Allow the item to dry completely prior to making any visual assessments.
11. When processing has been completed, all chemicals should be disposed of properly according to the appropriate federal, state, and local environmental laws.

3.3.2 Multimetal Deposition II

In an effort to improve the operational performance of MMD I, Schnetz and Margot proposed a modification known as MMD II [49]. They used a modification of the method originally reported by Slot and Geuze [50]. This method produced more homogeneity in the colloidal gold solution, producing 14 nm sized particles. The smaller particles appeared to give superior development compared to the 30 nm particles recommended by Saunders. This new method produced finer ridge detail structure, including pores and ridge edges. However, the overall color intensity of the developed print was often weaker than that observed with MMD I. This difference was attributed to the modified PD used. A second treatment with a fresh batch of the modified PD typically produced darker prints more consistent with the MMD I process.

Schnetz and Margot significantly modified the PD used to amplify the colloidal gold particles. After testing several different reducing agents and sources of silver ions they ultimately settled on hydroquinone and silver acetate [51]. This new developer tended to

* Do not use an acid prewash (e.g., maleic or malic acids). Saunders noted that exposing the item to an acid wash could cause interference with the gold deposition process.

† As much as is practicable, avoid exposing the modified PD solution to light. It is very unstable and the silver colloids will precipitate out of solutions faster if the solution is exposed to room light.

work more slowly than the iron(II)/iron(III)/silver nitrate system and produced lighter gray-colored images of the latent prints. The background interference with the new developer was reported to be significantly less than with the original modified PD reagent.

They also measured the effect of reagent pH, Tween 20 concentration, reagent temperature, and cleanliness of the glassware. Reagent pH was found to be absolutely critical for successful latent print development. If the pH was allowed to rise above 3.1, the positively charged materials in the fingerprint residue would begin to lose their affinity for the colloidal gold particles [52]. The pH of the reagent needed to be maintained at a range of 2.5–2.8. Constant monitoring of pH during the processing of porous items was required, as the presence of alkaline materials like calcium carbonate could cause the pH of the reagent to increase above 3. The Tween 20 concentration in the original MMD formulation (0.5% w/v) was found to be too high. A 0.1% w/v solution was recommended. Lower concentrations of Tween 20 lead to higher background interferences while higher concentrations can lead to a washout effect. Temperature had no measurable effect on the MMD II process; thus, the normal range of ambient laboratory temperatures was found to be acceptable. Glassware cleanliness was also found to be a critical factor in the success of this reagent. Schnetz and Margot strongly recommend the use of siliconized glassware and high-quality water for all solutions. Coating the interior surface of the glassware with silane compounds prevented scratches and contaminants on the glassware from prematurely nucleating the gold from the colloidal solution.

Overall, MMD II was found to perform significantly better than the original MMD I [50,51]. Regarding the overall processing sequence, cyanoacrylate fuming was found to inhibit MMD. However, if there is little or no cyanoacrylate development on the nonporous item, MMD II can be used successfully in some cases. Application of a dye stain (e.g., rhodamine 6G or basic yellow 40) did improve subsequent MMD development on nonporous items. Both dye stain molecules contain nitrogen sites that could be protonated at low pH values and thus act as nucleation sites for the colloidal gold. For most nonporous surfaces, vacuum metal deposition was found to develop superior ridge detail compared to MMD II. An attempt was made to amplify MMD deposited colloidal gold with zinc deposited under vacuum in a VMD chamber. Although a small amount of zinc deposited on the surfaces of the ridges producing some weak development, this processing sequence did not prove to be successful. With semiporous items (e.g., latex/nitrile gloves, polystyrene, waxed paper), MMD II produced superior results to VMD on all surfaces except for Australian polymer banknotes. With porous substrates, conventional PD was found to be superior to MMD II and more reliable and reproducible. Apparently the binding of gold to the paper fibers was stronger than the binding of gold to the latent print residue.

Reagent preparation

This version of the multimetal deposition reagent was introduced by Schnetz and Margot in 2001.* The method is a modification of the technique used by Slot and Geuze to produce 14 nm sized colloidal gold particles.

Glassware deactivation (siliconization)

1. Soak glassware overnight in a bath of 10% Extran (sodium 2-ethylhexyl sulfate).
2. Rinse the glassware in hot water followed by a cold water rinse.
3. Heat all items in an oven (set at 100°C) until completely dry.

* The modified MMD process was first discussed at the International Symposium on Fingerprint Detection and Identification, held at Ne'urim, Israel, in 1995. No abstract or paper referring to this presentation was included in the conference proceedings.

4. Cool items to room temperature.
5. Soak items for ~5 s in the treatment solution (4 mL 3-aminopropyltriethoxysilane in 200 mL acetone).
6. Rinse the items twice in acetone.
7. Rinse the items twice in distilled water.
8. Dry in an oven (set at 42°C) for 24 h.

Solution A (tetrachloroauric acid trihydrate)	
Tetrachloroauric acid trihydrate	1 g
RO–DI water	10 mL
Solution B (sodium citrate)	
Sodium citrate tribasic dehydrate	1 g
RO–DI water	100 mL
Solution C (citric acid)	
Citric acid monohydrate	1.05 g
RO–DI water	50 mL
Solution D (tannic acid)	
Tannic acid	0.1 g
RO–DI water	10 mL
Solution E (colloidal gold)	
Solution A (tetrachloroauric acid trihydrate)	0.5 mL
Solution B (sodium citrate)	20 mL
Tween 20	0.5 mL
Solution C (citric acid)	>1 mL
Solution D (polyethylene glycol)	0.1 mL
RO–DI water	475 mL

1. Add 0.5 mL of tetrachloroauric acid trihydrate to 400 mL of RO–DI water and mix thoroughly.
2. In a separate container, mix 75 mL of RO–DI water, 20 mL of sodium citrate, and 0.1 mL of tannic acid.
3. Heat the two solutions separately to 60°C.
4. When the temperatures have reached 60°C, quickly add the sodium citrate/tannic acid solution to the gold chloride solution and mix thoroughly.
5. Bring the mixture to the boiling point (at which point the solution will turn a ruby red color).
6. Allow the solution to cool to room temperature.
7. Store this solution in a polyethylene bottle in a refrigerator at 4°C.
8. The appropriate information (e.g., chemical contents, preparer's initials, date, reliability test result) should be recorded on the container's label.
9. Immediately before use, restore the solution to room temperature and then add 0.5 mL of Tween 20 and mix thoroughly.
10. Adjust the pH of the solution to a range of 2.5–2.8 with the citric acid solution.

Solution F (silver acetate)

Silver acetate*	0.2 g
RO–DI water	100 mL

Solution G (buffer solution)†

Citric acid	128 g
Sodium citrate	118 g
RO–DI water	500 mL

Solution H (hydroquinone solution)

Solution G	200 mL
Hydroquinone	1 g

1. The chemicals listed should be mixed in the order given.
2. The modified PD redox solution will appear colorless.
3. The reagent should be used as soon as it is prepared.

Reagent application

1. All appropriate personal protective equipment should be used when preparing and using this reagent.
2. Run the appropriate positive and negative controls to ensure that the reagent solution is working properly.
3. For nonporous items, a quick rinse in RO–DI water is recommended. For porous items, a 2 min soak in RO–DI water is recommended.‡
4. Process the item in the MMD II colloidal gold solution (Solution E) for ~20 min. Gentle agitation is recommended.
5. Rinse the item thoroughly (especially porous substrates) with RO–DI water.
6. Add 100 mL of RO–DI water to 100 mL of the hydroquinone/buffer solution to create a working solution. Soak the item in this solution for 2–5 min.
7. Transfer the item to a glass tray containing a freshly prepared modified PD solution, comprised of 100 mL silver acetate solution (Solution F) and 100 mL of the hydroquinone/buffer solution (Solution H).§
8. Allow the items to soak in the reagent for approximately 20 min. Very gentle agitation is advised.
9. Rinse the item thoroughly with RO–DI water.
10. Rinse the item thoroughly with tap water.
11. Allow the item to dry completely prior to making any visual assessments.
12. When processing has been completed, all chemicals should be disposed of properly according to the appropriate federal, state, and local environmental laws.

* Silver acetate dissolves in water very slowly. It can take more than 30 min to completely dissolve.
† The three components of this solution are added together in an approximate ratio of 24:22:50.
‡ As with the Saunders' MMD method, MMD II does not require any acid prewash solution for the porous substrates.
§ This solution should be prepared just prior to use. After 10–20 min, this solution may turn dark gray but it will not affect the results.

3.3.3 Multimetal Deposition III/IV

Jones et al. described additional modifications to the MMD process [53]. They described a modification of the MMD II method by Brennan at the Forensic Science Service (London, United Kingdom) as MMD III. This hybrid method used the 30nm sized particles from the Saunders' process and the hydroquinone/silver acetate developer recommended by Schnetz. Jones et al. mention a fourth possible combination of the reagents, which had never been previously evaluated. This reagent, known as MMD IV, used the 14nm sized particles from the Schnetz method and the conventional iron (II)/iron (III)/silver nitrate developer used in the conventional PD process. Reagents with the 14nm colloidal gold particles gave greater detail and stronger development than the 30nm sized particle reagents. The reagents using the hydroquinone/silver acetate developer produced superior ridge detail, but the iron (II)/iron (III)/silver nitrate developer gave darker development. As with the MMD II reagent, a second treatment of the item in a fresh hydroquinone/silver acetate developer solution could significantly improve the results.

3.3.4 Fluorescent MMD

An effort to develop a fluorescent version of the MMD reagent was reported by Becue et al. [55]. The process involved the use of a colloidal gold solution followed by the *in situ* generation of zinc oxide (ZnO) particles, which selectively deposited on gold nanoparticles. The ZnO particles were generated by combining zinc nitrate and dimethylamine-borane (DMAB). When exposed to long-wave ultraviolet radiation, the ZnO-labeled ridge detail would fluoresce around 580nm. The process involved five basic steps: the initial 2–3min rinse in RO–DI water; a 5–15min soak in a pH 2.65 colloidal gold solution; another 2–3min rinse in RO–DI water; a 30min soak in the zinc nitrate/DMAB solution; and a final 2–3min rinse in RO–DI water. Good results were obtained on transparent polypropylene, black polyethylene bags, black polystyrene, and aluminum foil. On the latter substrate, the developed image was reversed (i.e., ridge detail was dark and the background was fluorescent). This indicated that either the gold or ZnO nanoparticles had a greater affinity for the aluminum rather than the latent print residue. A comparison of this new fluorescent method to the MMD II process showed both to be comparable in the visible mode, but the new MMD showed enhanced contrast in the fluorescence mode. However, due to the limitation of this method to nonporous surfaces, its use as an alternative to MMD II is currently not recommended.

3.3.5 Single Metal Deposition

Single metal deposition (SMD) was initially proposed by Stauffer et al. as a simpler and cheaper alternative to MMD [56]. The authors sought to correct for two disadvantages inherent in the MMD process, the labor-intensive nature of the reagent's preparation (specifically the added silver processing step) and its production of dull gray ridge detail. The authors note that SMD can achieve similar results to MMD II with one less step, one less reagent, and at a lower cost. SMD used the same colloidal gold solution as MMD II, but used a gold-based developer instead of the more traditional silver-based ones. The hydroquinone prebath and the hydroquinone/silver acetate steps were replaced with a single hydroxylamine/gold chloride step. The surface of the print ridges where gold is deposited from the colloidal gold step acts as a nucleation site for the reduced gold from the gold chloride developer. This resulted in a significant increase in the size of the deposited gold rather than creation of new gold particles.

The authors [56] noted that SMD can achieve similar results to MMD II with one less step, lower cost, and almost no risk of over development.

The developer was prepared by mixing two different stock solutions. The first involved the use of a 10% w/v tetrachloroauric acid solution (this is the same one used in the preparation of the colloidal gold solution in MMD and is referred to as Solution I). Approximately 695 mg of hydroxylamine hydrochloride was then dissolved in 100 mL of RO–DI water (Solution II). Both of these solutions could be stored for months before use if Solution I is kept refrigerated at 4°C. The developer was created just prior to use by mixing 200 mL of Solution I with 1 mL of Solution II. This developer could last up to 30 min.

The optimized immersion time in the gold developer was reported to be 20 min [57]. Shorter soaking times lead to inhomogeneous ridge development. The ideal stirring speed was determined to be 70 rpm. Increased speeds lead to more background development and slower speeds lead to inhomogeneous development (observed as irregular densities throughout the ridge pattern). The optimal ratio of gold to hydroxylamine was found to be 1:1, which was consistent with the stoichiometry of the reaction. The optimal concentration used for these two components was reported to be 3×10^{-4} M.

Of the seven different surfaces tested with SMD, only the nonadhesive side of masking tape developed inferior ridge detail when compared to MMD. The other surfaces evaluated showed very similar development. Overall, because both SMD and MMD rely on the deposition of gold from the colloidal gold step, they were found to be similar in both sensitivity and reactivity (and also have the same associated advantages and disadvantages). The primary advantages are reduced cost and time/complexity in preparation of the reagent.

3.4 Vacuum Metal Deposition

3.4.1 Background

The deposition of thin metal films under vacuum on nonporous surfaces for the detection of latent fingerprints was first suggested to the U.K. Home Office by Professor S. Tolansky in 1963 [58]. This suggestion was based on previous work from the 1930s that described the coating of condenser paper with a two-step process of gold and zinc [59]. Other observations indicated that zinc typically would not condense on grease films even if the surface had previously been coated with a thin layer of gold [60]. Theys et al. described a metal deposition process for visualizing latent prints on various kinds of paper in 1968 [61]. The process involved the vaporization of a mixture of metal powders (73% zinc, 21.5% antimony, 5.5% copper) at temperatures up to 1540°C and pressures of 10^{-4} or 10^{-5} torr. Good development was observed with prints up to 2 years old on uncoated and typing papers. However, subsequent analysis of the deposited metal film from this process indicated that it was pure zinc (no copper or antimony was found) [62]. In the early 1970s, the U.K. Police Scientific Development Branch sponsored work on metal deposition at the Royal Holloway College with the goal of making this process an operational technique. This work focused on developing prints on paper and cloth/fabric substrates using gold followed by cadmium. In conventional VMD processing, cadmium was soon replaced by zinc for health and safety reasons. It took nearly two decades for the vacuum metal deposition (VMD) technique to reach North America. The first reported use of VMD to identify a suspect in casework there was described by Murphy in 1991 [63]. Three identifiable prints were developed on a milk carton left behind by the suspect at the scene of a robbery.

3.4.2 Reaction Mechanism

For the VMD process to work effectively, a reduced pressure environment is required. At standard room temperature, air molecules (as well as others) move rapidly and experience frequent collisions [64]. Mean free path is a term that describes the average distance that a large number of molecules travel between collisions. At standard atmospheric pressure (760 torr), the mean free path would be approximately 6.6×10^{-6} cm. At the standard pressures used during the VMD process (10^{-4}–10^{-5} torr), the mean free path would range between 50 and 500 cm. Thus, at reduced pressures, molecules can travel much longer distances without colliding with other molecules. This allows evaporated gold or zinc to travel relatively unimpeded in a vacuum chamber from the filament source to the substrate surface.

Although the chemistry and physics of vacuum vapor deposition is quite complex, a number of studies have been conducted to determine how and why the process works. Jones examined the VMD process in detail [65]. The deposition of the gold layer on a substrate was found to be independent of the presence of latent print residue. The gold density was determined to be the same for the latent print as it was for the background. The thickness of a discontinuous gold film deposited can be as low as one Angstrom (i.e., 1×10^{-10} m). However, the overall structure of the film is dependent upon the bonds formed between the gold atoms and the substrate. Since adhesion forces between the gold atoms are greater than the forces between the atoms and the surface, ellipsoid-shaped clusters are formed. Due to differences in molecular structure, cluster density and size can vary on different substrates. Because of these differences, the subsequent deposition of zinc can be either positive (zinc deposits on ridges only) or negative (zinc deposits on the background only).

Grant et al. investigated the inhibition of VMD coating as a function of the type of polyethylene surface [66]. On matte-textured substrates, the background surface was coated with zinc while the latent print ridges were not. The reverse was found to be true for glossy surfaces. Glossy surfaces were also found to require significantly more time during the zinc coating stage. The presence of a slip agent (e.g., Erucamide, oleamide) resulted in development similar to that of glossy surfaces (i.e., only the fingerprint ridges were coated with zinc) while its absence resulted in development similar to matte surfaces. The type of polyethylene was also determined to be a factor. All of the glossy bags were made from low-density polyethylene (LDPE) and the matte bags were high-density polyethylene (HDPE).

Jones et al. also investigated this phenomena of positive or negative development for commonly encountered plastics like LDPE (group I) and HDPE (group II) [67]. The authors determined that the differences in surface structure of these plastics produced different gold film structures. The morphology of these clusters was determined to have a significant influence on the subsequent deposition of zinc. For group I plastics, low amounts of gold produce negative-type development. As the amount of gold deposited increases, positive-type (or "reverse") development occurred. When the amount of gold deposited was relatively low, negative-type development occurred on group II plastics. However, as the amount of gold deposited increased, overdevelopment could occur. When an excess amount of gold was deposited, no development occurred on group I plastics while normal, but poor quality, negative-type development occurred on group II plastics.

A subsequent study with polypropylene (PP), polyvinyl chloride (PVC), and polyethylene terephthalate (PET) also noted the influence of polymer type on VMD development [68]. The ability to recover poorly developed zinc prints after initially exposing them to an excess amount of gold was also investigated [67]. Exposure of the sample to air resulted in the formation of a coating of zinc oxide, which effectively deactivated nearly the entire surface coating. A subsequent application of 1.5 times the recommended amount of gold would allow normal development with zinc to occur (the excess is required because some gold may be absorbed into the existing clusters on the surface).

3.4.3 Alternatives to the Conventional Gold–Zinc Process

Initially, the recommended sequence for VMD was gold followed by cadmium [58]. However, cadmium was replaced by zinc for health and safety reasons. Current protocols now recommend the evaporation of gold followed by zinc at approximately 1.5×10^{-4} torr (2×10^{-4} mbar). At this pressure, gold will evaporate at a temperature of 1132°C and zinc at 235°C. The use of metals other than gold, cadmium, and zinc has been reported. Kent et al. initially investigated a wide variety of metals and metal combinations [58]. Silver, copper, aluminum, bismuth, chromium, magnesium, platinum, lead, antimony, and tin were evaluated individually and in combination with either cadmium or zinc. Gossage reported on the efficacy of sequences involving silver, tin, zinc, chromium-zinc, gold-zinc, copper-zinc, aluminum-copper, aluminum-copper-zinc, and chromium-aluminum-copper [69]. Silver, tin, chromium-zinc, and chromium-aluminum-copper performed the best on substrates that produced poor results with the gold-zinc sequence.

Silver, as a single metal deposition technique, had been used initially to reduce background printing interference on counterfeit credit cards, making tool marks from embossing machines easier to visualize [70]. Philipson and Bleay reported on the use of an optimized silver single metal deposition technique for surfaces that were not amenable to the conventional gold/zinc sequence [71]. The authors recommended the sequential treatment of items with the conventional gold/zinc process and then with silver if the previous technique failed to develop latent prints. Although they noted that the amount of silver required was dependent on substrate type, multiple applications of the silver technique could be used to achieve sufficient intensity and contrast. The same authors had also reported that the use of silver as a single metal treatment after the gold/zinc process produced additional prints in 10% of cases [72]. This modified VMD technique produced good results on glossy-printed card stock, the lubricated inside of a condom wrapper, plastic drinking bottles, and thick plastic carrier bags. The use of an aluminum single metal VMD was initially developed by BOC Edwards and was evaluated by Gunaratne et al. [73]. The results for prints on Mylar® that had been aged up to 48 h indicated that the aluminum VMD method significantly outperformed the conventional gold/zinc process. However, for prints aged up to 90 days on Mylar, both methods tended to lose their sensitivity and were equally effective.

3.4.4 Sequencing

The effect of fuming an item with cyanoacrylate prior to VMD processing was examined by Jones et al. [68]. Prior cyanoacrylate fuming of polymer substrates made of PET or PVC resulted in better quality prints being developed with subsequent VMD processing. With PP substrates, there was no improvement in print quality noted. However, there continues to be debate as to where VMD should be placed in the overall nonporous processing sequence. The current Home Office recommendations suggest that VMD be used first before other techniques such as powders and cyanoacrylate fuming [74]. Others recommend that cyanoacrylate fuming be done prior to VMD [11]. Margot and Lennard note that significant improvement in ridge detail was achieved when this sequence was followed, but not when the processes were reversed in order.

3.4.5 Operational Usage

VMD has been used to successfully develop prints in cases where previous treatments had failed. In one particular case, several fingerprints and a palm print were developed on a heavily contaminated black trash bag recovered from a 4 year old homicide investigation [75]. Prior processing of the bag with cyanoacrylate fumes did not reveal any ridge detail. The RCMP described a series of cases in which VMD produced important fingerprint evidence [76]. Case successes described included: 6 year old prints developed on two large plastic garbage bags; a single latent print developed on a plastic bag that had been in a river for 18h; several prints obtained from baby bottle liners contaminated with cocaine residue; a single print developed on a plastic garbage bag exposed to the outdoor environment for 5 days; and finger-, palm-, and shoeprint impressions developed on plastic. VMD was reported to be the best method for developing latent prints more than 6 months old on polymer banknotes [77]. For especially problematic surfaces, pretreatment of the item with ion bombardment from a glow discharge was reported to improve latent print recovery (especially on cloth and polyethylene) [78].

Success rates for polyethylene samples stored indoors for up to 1 month ranged from 50% to 75% [58]. Similar results were obtained for samples stored outside for up to 2 weeks. In a field trial, 622 polyethylene exhibits from 61 cases were treated with VMD. Identifiable prints were developed in 30 of those cases. It was noted that the VMD technique had little success on heavily plasticized polyvinyl chloride substrates. However, good results were obtained with test prints on cotton poplins, cotton, and nylon using gold followed by either zinc or cadmium [79]. Abe reported on the successful development of a print on a synthetic fabric using a combination of gold and cadmium [80]. Misner reported that the VMD process detected more latent prints than cyanoacrylate fuming followed by dye staining [81]. Older prints were more likely to be developed using VMD than cyanoacrylate fuming and dye staining. In another study, VMD was found to be superior to cyanoacrylate fuming on prints older than 24 months (84.2% recovery rate versus 59.6%) [82]. The effect of contamination of polyethylene drug bags on the VMD process was investigated by Ziv and Springer [83]. The presence of drug residues typically prevented the condensation of gold and zinc onto these surfaces. In an effort to remove these residues without harming latent prints that may be present, several different solvent washes were evaluated. Best results were achieved with either distilled water or a 5% ethanol/distilled water treatment.

References

1. Moenssen AA. (1971) *Fingerprint Techniques*. Radnor: Chilton Book Company, p. 120.
2. Cuthbertson F. (1969) Chemistry of Fingerprints. AWRE Report 013/69.
3. Olsen RD. (1978) *Scott's Fingerprint Mechanics*. Springfield, IL: Charles C. Thomas, p. 295.

4. Caton HE. (1974) Physical and chemical aspects of latent print development. In *Proceedings of the Conference on the Science of Fingerprints*. London, England: Home Office Police Scientific Development Branch, pp. 177–183.
5. Goode GC, Morris JR. (1983) Latent fingerprints: a review of their origin, composition and methods for detection. AWRE Report No. 022/83.
6. Angst E. (1962) Procédés pour la détermination de l'âge d'empreintes dactyloscopiques sur le papier. *Rev Int Criminol Pol Tech Sci* 16:134–146.
7. Chapel CE. (1941) *Fingerprinting. A Manual of Identification*. New York: Coward McCann.
8. Bowman V. (ed.) (1998) *Manual of Fingerprint Development Techniques*. St. Albans: Home Office, Police Scientific Development Branch.
9. Watling WJ. (1974) Process for developing latent fingerprints on cow horns. *J Forensic Ident* 24(6):3–4.
10. Loveridge FH. (1984) Shoe print development by silver nitrate. *Fingerprint Whorld* 10(38):58.
11. Margot P, Lennard C. (1994) *Fingerprint Detection Techniques*. Lausanne, Switzerland: Institut de Police Scientifique et de Criminologie.
12. Belcher GL. (1983) Generating silver nitrate latents. *Fingerprint Whorld* 9(34):58.
13. Kerr FM, Westland AD, Haque F. (1981) Observations on the use of silver compounds for fingerprint visualization. *Forensic Sci Int* 18:209–214.
14. Trozzi TA, Schwartz RL, Hollars ML. (2001) *Processing Guide for Developing Latent Prints*. Washington, DC: U.S. Department of Justice, Federal Bureau of Investigation.
15. Cantu AA. (2001) Silver physical developers for the visualization of latent prints on paper. *Forensic Sci Rev* 13:29–64.
16. Morris JR. (1975) The detection of latent fingerprints on wet paper samples. SSCD Memo No. 367.
17. Berson G. (1983) Silver staining of proteins in polyacrylamide gels: increased sensitivity by a blue toning solution. *Anal Biochem* 134:230–234.
18. Anon. (2003) What is the oldest fingerprint that you have developed? Fingerprint Development and Imaging Update Publication No. 26/2003, Home Office Police Scientific Development Branch.
19. Phillips CE, Cole DO, Jones GW. (1990) Physical developer: a practical and productive latent print developer. *J Forensic Ident* 40(3):135–147.
20. Rimmer B, Tuthill H. (1985) Physical developer—an evaluation and some modifications. *Ident Canada* 8(4):3–7.
21. van Beek LKH. (1973) The PD photographic process. *Philips Tech Rev* 33(1):1–13.
22. Jonker H, Molenaar A, Dippel CS. (1969) Physical development recording systems: III. Physical development. *Photograph Sci Eng* 13(2):38–43.
23. Aslan K, Pérez-Luna VH. (2002) Surface modification of colloidal gold by chemisorption of alkanethiols in the presence of a nonionic surfactant. *Langmuir* 18:6059–6065.
24. Fuller AA, Thomas GM. (1974) The physical development of fingerprint images. Technical Memorandum 26/74.
25. Knowles AM, Lee D, Wilson D. (1977) Development of latent fingerprints on patterned papers and papers subjected to wetting. Technical Memorandum 12/77.
26. Knowles AM, Lee D, Wilson D. (1978) Development of latent fingerprints on patterned papers and papers subjected to wetting. Technical Memorandum 5/78.
27. Hardwick SA. (1981) User guide to physical developer—a reagent for detecting latent fingerprints. User Guide No. 14/81, Home Office Police Scientific Development Branch.
28. Ramotowski R. (1996) Importance of an acid prewash prior to the use of physical developer. *J Forensic Ident* 46(6):673–677.
29. Ramotowski R. (2000) A comparison of different physical developer systems and acid pretreatments and their effects on developing latent prints. *J Forensic Ident* 50(4):363–384.
30. Barford AD, Brennan JS, Hooker RH, Price CJ. (1991) Operational experiences in the use of physical developer for detecting latent marks. Unpublished manuscript.

31. Wilson JD, Cantu AA, Antonopoulos G, Surrency MJ. (2007) Examination of the steps leading up to the physical developer process for developing fingerprints. *J Forensic Sci* 52(2):320–329.
32. Houlgrave SM, Ramotowski R. (2011) Comparison of different physical developer working solutions. Part. I. Longevity studies. *J Forensic Ident* 61(6):575–593.
33. Swofford HJ. (2010) The efficacy of commercial vs. noncommercial physical developer solutions and sequential enhancement of friction ridge impressions using potassium iodide. *J Forensic Ident* 60(1):19–33.
34. Morton S. (1983) Shoe print development by PD treatment. *Fingerprint Whorld* 9(34):61–62.
35. Emmons BW. (1993) Physical developer rocker. *J Forensic Ident* 43(5):457–460.
36. Houlgrave SM, Ramotowski R. (2011) Comparison of different physical developer working solutions. Part. II. Reliability studies. *J Forensic Ident* 61(6):594–605.
37. Feigl F. (1972) *Spot Tests, Inorganic Applications.* Amsterdam, the Netherlands: Elsevier Publishing Co.
38. Personal communication with Dr. Lothar Schwarz, January 25, 2010.
39. Bowman V, ed. (2004) Manual of fingerprint development techniques 2nd edition (2nd revision). Home Office: Police Scientific Development Branch, Sandridge, UK.
40. Cantu AA, Leben D, Wilson K. (2003) Some advances in the silver physical development of latent prints on paper. Proceedings of the Society of Photographic Instrumentation Engineers, Sensors, and Command, Control, Communications, and Intelligence Technologies for Homeland Defense and Law Enforcement II 5071:164–167.
41. Kyle KR. (2003) Latent Fingerprint Detection. Summary Report for Project STP-018-99. Special Technologies Laboratory, unpublished report.
42. Crabtree JI, Ives CI. (1928) Dye toning with single solutions. *Soc Mot Pict Eng* 12(36):967–974.
43. Kausche GA, Rusha H. (1939) Die siehtbarmachung tier adsorption von metallkolloiden an ewißkörper. I. Die reaktion kolloides gold—tabakmosaikvirus. *Kolloid Z* 89:21–26.
44. Saunders GC. (1989) Multimetal deposition technique for latent fingerprint visualization. Final Progress Report to the U.S. Secret Service, Washington, DC, unpublished report.
45. Frens G. (1973) Controlled nucleation for the regulation of the particle size in monodisperse gold solutions. *Nat Phys Sci* 241:20–22.
46. Holgate CS, Jackson P, Cowen PN, Bird CC. (1983) Immunogold-silver staining: new method of immunostaining with enhanced sensitivity. *J Histochem Cytochem* 31(7):938–944.
47. Saunders G. (1989) Multimetal deposition technique for latent fingerprint development. Presented at the International Association for Identification, 74th Annual Education Conference, Pensacola, FL.
48. Saunders GC, Cantu AA. (1996) Evaluation of several techniques for developing latent fingerprints on unfired and fired cartridge cases. In: Almog J, Springer E (eds.) *Proceedings of the International Symposium on Fingerprint Detection and Identification.* Jerusalem, Israel: Hemed Press, pp. 155–160.
49. Donche A. (1994) Development of latent fingerprints on cartridge casings. *Fingerprint Whorld* 20(75):13–19.
50. Schetz B, Margot P. (2001) Technical note: latent fingermarks, colloidal gold and multimetal deposition (MMD). Optimisation of the method. *Forensic Sci Int* 118:21–28.
51. Slot JW, Geuze HJ. (1985) A new method of preparing gold probes for multiple-labelling cytochemistry. *Eur J Cell Biol* 38:87–93.
52. Skutelsky E, Goyal V, Alroy J. (1987) The use of avidin-gold complex for light microscopic localization of lectin receptors. *Histochemistry* 86:291–295.
53. Becue A, Cantu AA. (2012) Fingermark detection using nanoparticles. In: Ramotowski RS (ed.) *Lee and Gaensslen's Advances in Fingerprint Technology*, 3rd edn. Boca Raton, FL: CRC Press.
54. Jones N, Lennard C, Stoilovic M, Roux C. (2003) An evaluation of multimetal deposition II. *J Forensic Ident* 53(4):444–488.

55. Jones N. (2002) Metal deposition techniques for the detection and enhancement of latent fingerprints on semi-porous surfaces. PhD dissertation. University of Technology Sydney, Sydney, New South Wales, Australia.
56. Becue A, Scoundrianos A, Champod C, Margot P. (2008) Fingermark detection based on the in situ growth of luminescent nanoparticles—towards a new generation of multimetal deposition. *Forensic Sci Int* 179:39–43.
57. Stauffer E, Becue A, Singh KV, Thampi KR, Champod C, Margot P. (2007) Single metal deposition (SMD) as a latent fingermark enhancement technique: an alternative to multimetal deposition (MMD). *Forensic Sci Int* 2007:168:e5–e9.
58. Durussel P, Stauffer E, Becue A, Champod C, Margot P. (2009) Single-metal deposition: optimization of this fingermark enhancement technique. *J Forensic Ident* 59(1):80–96.
59. Kent T, Thomas GL, Reynoldson TE, East HW. (1976) A vacuum coating technique for the development of latent fingerprints on polythene. *J Forensic Sci Soc* 16:93–101.
60. Bosch R. (August 1937) British Patent 510642.
61. Pollak JE. (March 1936) British Patent 492681.
62. Theys P, Turgis Y, Lepareux A, Chevet G, Ceccaldi PF. (1968) New technique for bringing out latent fingerprints on paper: vacuum metallization. *Int Crim Pol Rev* 217:106–108.
63. Hambley DS. (1972) The physics of vacuum evaporation development of latent fingerprints. PhD dissertation, University of London, Royal Holloway College, London, U.K.
64. Murphy MP. (1991) A vacuum metal identification. *J Forensic Ident* 41(5):318–320.
65. Hill RJ. (1986) *Physical Vapor Deposition*. Berkeley, CA: The BOC Group, Inc.
66. Jones N, Stoilovic M, Lennard C, Roux C. (2001) Vacuum metal deposition: factors affecting normal and reverse development of latent fingerprints on polyethylene substrates. *Forensic Sci Int* 115:73–88.
67. Grant H, Springer E, Ziv Z. (1996) Vacuum metal deposition inhibition on polythene bags. In: Almog J, Springer E, Eds., *Proceedings of the International Symposium on Fingerprint Detection and Identification*. Jerusalem, Israel: Hemed Press, pp. 203–214.
68. Jones N, Stoilovic M, Lennard C, Roux C. (2001) Vacuum metal deposition: developing latent fingerprints on polyethylene substrates after the deposition of excess gold. *Forensic Sci Int* 123:5–12.
69. Jones N, Mansour D, Stoilovic M, Lennard C, Roux C. (2001) Influence of polymer type, print donor and age on the quality of fingerprints developed on plastic substrates using vacuum metal deposition. *Forensic Sci Int* 124:167–177.
70. Gossage GD. (2004) The effectiveness of selected metals in the vacuum metal deposition process for developing latent fingerprints. Masters thesis, California State University, Los Angeles, CA.
71. Morris RN, Gilmour CL, Laturnus PL, Yamashita AB. (1997) Vacuum metal deposition of silver as an aid in credit card examinations. *J Forensic Ident* 47(1):57–63.
72. Philipson D, Bleay S. (2007) Alternative metal processes for vacuum metal deposition. *J Forensic Ident* 57(2):252–273.
73. Bleay S, Philipson D. (2005) Alternative metal processes for VMD. Presented at the International Fingerprint Research Group Meeting, The Hague, the Netherlands.
74. Gunaratne A, Knaggs C, Stansbury D. (2007) Vacuum metal deposition: comparing conventional gold/zinc VMD to aluminum VMD. *Ident Canada* 30(2):40–62.
75. Anon. (1996) Vacuum metal deposition puts pressure on unsolved homicide cases. *The Print* 12(6):15.
76. Batey GW, Copeland J, Donnelly DL, Hill CL, Laturnus PL, McDiarmid CH, Miller KJ, Misner AH, Tario A, Yamashita AB. (1998) Metal deposition for latent print development. *J Forensic Ident* 48(2):165–175.
77. Flynn J, Stoilovic M, Lennard C. (1999) Detection and enhancement of latent fingerprints on polymer banknotes: a preliminary study. *J Forensic Ident* 49(6):594–612.

78. Thomas GL, Kent T. (1975) On the use of a glow discharge to remove contamination prior to fingerprint development by metal deposition. Home Office Police Scientific Development Branch Research Note 25/75.
79. Godsell JW. (1972) Fingerprints—use of radio-active gas and vacuum metal deposition for the development of latent fingerprints on paper and fabrics. *Pol Res Bull* 19:16–21.
80. Abe S. (1983) Development of latent fingerprints by vacuum deposition technique. *Rep Natl Res Inst Pol Sci* 31(4):377–379.
81. Misner AH. (1992) Latent fingerprint detection on low density polyethylene comparing vacuum metal deposition to cyanoacrylate fuming and fluorescence. *J Forensic Ident* 42(1):26–33.
82. Masters NE, DeHaan JD. (1996) Vacuum metal deposition (VMD) and cyanoacrylate detection of older latent prints. In: Almog J, Springer E, Eds., *Proceedings of the International Symposium on Fingerprint Detection and Identification*. Jerusalem, Israel: Hemed Press, pp. 197–202.
83. Ziv Z, Springer E. (1996) Additional methods for pre-treatment of drug contaminated polythene bags prior to vacuum metal deposition of latent fingerprints. In: Almog J, Springer E, Eds., *Proceedings of the International Symposium on Fingerprint Detection and Identification*. Jerusalem, Israel: Hemed Press, pp. 179–196.

4

Lipid Reagents

Robert S. Ramotowski

CONTENTS

4.1 Sudan Black

Sudan Black B (also known as solvent black 3) is a fat-soluble diazo dye that was initially used for staining tissue sections. The dye was first prepared in Germany in the early 1930s and was proposed as a myelin stain in 1935 by Lison and Dagnelie [1]. Around the same time in England, it was proposed as a stain for fats. Its use as a dye stain for visualizing latent prints was first reported by Mitsui et al. in 1980 [2]. This formulation contained the dye along with ethylene glycol, ethanol or methanol, and water. This reagent successfully recovered latent prints on paper submerged in water for up to 10 days [3]. The reagent has also been recommended for rough, nonporous surfaces that have been wetted or have been contaminated with greasy or sticky substances [4].

Prior to the introduction of Sudan black, water-soaked papers were often dried and processed with black Magna powder. A comparison of the two techniques on water-soaked porous items found that Magna powder–developed latent prints were of a higher quality than Sudan black–developed prints [5]. When Magna powder was used after application of Sudan black, improved latent print detail was observed in 57% of cases (in the remaining 43% there was no change in quality). When Sudan black was used after application of Magna powder, no improvement in quality was observed. The age of the latent prior to immersion in water did not appear to affect the quality of the developed latent prints; however, the immersion time was found to have a significant effect. Only 25% of the samples were recovered after immersion in water for 1 week.

Sudan black was used in combination with cyanoacrylate fuming in a homicide investigation to recover latent fingerprint evidence on a concrete abutment from a parking lot [6]. The abutment was made of Portland cement and was coated with an unknown mold release agent, which left the top and sides with a matte surface. A number of techniques were tested on a similar matrix and produced ridge detail. However, due to latent print quality, strong contrast, and print longevity, the method chosen was cyanoacrylate fuming followed by Sudan black staining. When this procedure was used on the actual crime scene evidence, only smudges were developed. In another homicide investigation, successful recovery of a print was achieved on a clear, plastic bag used to cover the victim [7]. The bag was processed twice with cyanoacrylate fumes and followed by application of the dye stain Ardrox. No identifiable prints were found. Several applications of Sudan black followed by rinsing produced a print that was later identified to the suspect in the case.

Sudan black has also been used to visualize prints on glass jar contaminated with petroleum jelly [8]. Sudan black did not actually stain the petroleum jelly–stained print; however, it did create contrast by staining the underlying jar label. The print was then photographed using oblique lighting and then lifted with Mokrosil™. The U.K. Home Office recommended an alternate Sudan black formulation for use at crime scenes in 2005 [9]. This reagent required the use of the solvents 1-methoxy-2-propanol and water to prepare the working solution.* Its use is recommended on nonporous surfaces that are too sticky for processing with powders and where cyanoacrylate fuming would not be an effective alternative. They also note that since 1-methoxy-2-propanol has a flash point above 48°C, it is much safer to use at scenes than the more flammable ethanol-based reagents. The University of Lausanne also experimented with alternate Sudan black formulations.† An acetone–water-based reagent was created and tested against the Home Office formulation. The results (not published) indicated that it produced better results than the 1-methoxy-2-propanol-based reagent.

Reagent preparation [10]

Working solution

Sudan black	15 g
Ethanol	1000 mL
Distilled/RO-DI water	500 mL

1. Sudan black should be dissolved first in the ethanol. Water is then added and the solution mixed thoroughly.
2. Some of the Sudan black dye may not completely dissolve and will remain in suspension in the working solution.
3. This solution should be stored in a glass bottle and is stable indefinitely.
4. The appropriate information (e.g., chemical contents, preparer's initials, date, reliability test result) should be recorded on the container's label.

Reagent application

1. All appropriate personal protective equipment should be used when preparing and using this reagent.
2. Run the appropriate positive and negative controls to ensure that the reagent solution is working properly.

* The working solution was prepared by dissolving 10 g of Sudan black into 500 mL of 1-methoxy-2-propanol. This solution needs to be stirred vigorously for at least 1 h prior to adding 500 mL of purified water. This working solution should be stirred for at least 1 h before being used. The shelf life of the working solution has been reported to be approximately 1 month.

† The working solution was prepared by dissolving 2.1 g of Sudan black into 500 mL of acetone and stirring vigorously. After stirring, 500 mL of water was added. This solution was then vigorously stirred prior to use.

3. This reagent is typically applied by immersing items into a glass tray containing the working solution for approximately 2 min.
4. The item should then be removed and rinsed thoroughly with tap water and then allowed to dry.
5. When processing has been completed, all chemicals should be disposed of properly according to the appropriate federal, state, and local environmental laws.

4.2 Oil Red O

4.2.1 Chemistry and Mechanism

Oil red O (ORO) is a lipophilic dye from the diazo family (similar to the fingerprint stain Sudan Black B). ORO (also known as Solvent Red 27) was recommended by French in 1926 as a substitute for Sudan III because it exhibited a much greater depth of color upon staining [11]. Some studies have indicated that the commercially available samples of ORO are actually composed of at least four different colored constituents [12,13]. Rather than a specific chemical reaction, it is an increase in entropy (i.e., the measure of disorder or randomness in a closed system) caused when the dye partitions into the lipid fraction of a latent print that drives the reaction mechanism [14]. Interestingly, Salama et al. found that for a supposedly lipid-only stain, ORO was able to interact with a considerable number of chemicals (51 out of 66 substances evaluated as compared to 20 positive results for PD).

In discussing with which components of latent print residue ORO reacts, an interesting theory was proposed by Cantu et al. [15]. Although latent print residue has traditionally been divided into water-soluble (e.g., amino acids, salts) and water-insoluble (e.g., lipids, large proteins) categories, the latter can actually be subdivided even further. The water-insoluble category could be characterized by a robust fraction (which appears to interact with physical developer) and a labile fraction (which appears to interact with lysochromes like ORO).

The labile fraction (i.e., the components likely to undergo changes in the short term) would be composed of more traditional lipids like saturated/unsaturated fatty acids and triglycerides. These materials oxidize rather quickly when exposed to air (but not upon exposure to water). This portion of the residue can be washed away by solvents having low dielectric constant values (e.g., petroleum ether) but not by solvents having high dielectric constants (e.g., water, methanol). A solvent's dielectric constant can be loosely compared to its dipole moment (defined as a measure of the equality of sharing bonding electrons between atoms). As such, a molecule like hexane shares its bonding electrons nearly equally amongst its constituent atoms and would be expected to have a low dipole moment (~0 C-m)* as well as a low dielectric constant (2.02). This theoretical interpretation was confirmed by Salama et al., who observed that hydrocarbon solvents (which have low dielectric constant values) had a detrimental effect on ORO print development, but solvents like HFE 7100 and HFC-4310mee (which have higher dielectric constant values) did not [14]. Dielectric constant values for commonly encountered solvents can be found in Table 4.1 [16].

* The SI unit of measure for dipole moments is the Coulomb-meter (abbreviated as C-m). The more traditional CGS unit of measure for dipole moments is called the Debye (abbreviated as D).

TABLE 4.1
Values for the Dielectric Constant and Dipole Moment for Selected Solvents

	Boiling Point (°C)	Dielectric Constant	Dipole Moment (Debye)
Acetone	56.3	20.7	2.88
Acetonitrile	81.6	37.5	3.92
1-Butanol	117.7	17.8	1.66
Chloroform	61.2	4.80	1.01
Cyclohexane	80.7	2.02	0
Ethyl acetate	77.1	6.02	1.78
Ethyl alcohol	78.0	24.3	1.69
Ethyl ether	34.6	4.34	1.15
Heptane	98.4	1.92	0
Hexane	68.7	1.90	0
Methanol	64.7	32.6	1.70
Methylene chloride	39.8	9.08	1.60
Methylethyl ketone	79.6	18.5	2.78
Pentane	36.1	1.84	0
Petroleum ether	30–60	1.87	0
1-Propanol	97.2	20.1	1.68
2-Propanol	82.3	18.3	1.66
Toluene	110.6	2.40	0.36
Water	100	78.5	1.85
o-Xylene	144.4	2.57	0.62
p-Xylene	138.5	2.27	0

Source: The values in this table were obtained primarily from Lide, D.R., *CRC Handbook of Chemistry and Physics*, 71st edn., CRC Press, Boca Raton, FL, 1990, pp. 8–44.

The robust fraction would be composed of large, water-insoluble proteins (and similar materials like lipoproteins), which can bind strongly to the cellulose in paper via hydrogen bonding. This bonding allows these residues to remain on paper for fairly long periods of time. Neither a solvent with high nor low dielectric constant values would be expected to have a significant influence on the robust fraction. This hypothesis was also confirmed by Salama et al. [14]. Indeed, the U.K. Home Office reported that 55-year-old prints on an electricity bill had been recovered with PD [17].

4.2.2 Operational Usage

The first reported forensic application of ORO was for the visualization of lip prints in 2002 [18]. ORO, Sudan III, and Sudan Black B were evaluated both in powder and solution form. It was noted that these lysochromes do not work as well on aged samples (up to 20 days). Sudan Black B was found to work the best, followed by ORO and Sudan III. This work was subsequently expanded to visualizing latent lip prints on human skin in 2006 [19]. In this work, ORO was applied in powder form with a brush (as with conventional fingerprint powders) and rinsed with distilled water.

Beaudoin introduced ORO as a staining solution for latent prints on porous substrates in 2004 [20]. The goal of this work was to determine if this new reagent could develop latent prints on wetted papers as effectively as physical developer (although at this stage no direct comparison was attempted). Latent prints were placed on a variety of different porous substrates, aged for a few days, and then soaked briefly in water. Good results were obtained for all paper types, including brown Kraft paper bags and brown corrugated cardboard. Prints developed by ORO appear as red-colored ridge detail on a pink-stained background. Although there can be significant background staining with some papers, the contrast is still sufficient to observe ridge detail. Attempts to replicate these results on glass and other nonporous surfaces were unsuccessful.

A subsequent study involved directly comparing the new ORO reagent with physical developer [21]. A number of different papers were evaluated, including seven different thermal papers. For the thermal papers, prints were deposited, soaked for 2 h in tap water, and then aged up to 30 days prior to processing. For the white photocopier and brown Kraft papers, prints were deposited, soaked in tap water for up to 24 h, and then aged up to 30 days prior to processing. Overall, ORO was reported to outperform PD on all of the thermal paper types investigated. One drawback noted was that the use of ORO caused any writing or printed material present on the paper to be lost; however, this did result in the developed prints having better contrast against the background. Although ORO outperformed PD on standard photocopier paper, the reverse was observed with brown Kraft paper.*

Salama et al. also did a comprehensive evaluation of ORO and compared its effectiveness to PD [14]. The authors looked at modifications to the Beaudoin ORO formulation to see if improvements could be made, especially by removing the filtration step. *Conn's Biological Stains* noted that the presence or absence of impurities can have a significant effect on the relative success or failure of a stain [1]. Also, the addition of certain materials (e.g., dextrins) to hydro-alcoholic solutions of ORO enhanced the staining of fats and decreased the amount of dye precipitating from the solution. Salama et al. found that removing the sodium hydroxide from the reagent formulation resulted in no latent prints being visualized [14]. The authors surmised that sodium hydroxide ionized the ORO by removing a proton from the hydroxide group (this causes a shift to the ketone resonance form). Overall, despite many different alterations, the original formulation of Beaudoin was ultimately found to work the best.

Salama et al. evaluated more than a dozen different porous substrates, along with adhesive tapes, glass slides, and plastic vial caps. Latent prints were aged up to 8 weeks under ambient conditions and some were subjected to various water treatments (including immersion in tap water for up to 24 h). ORO produced good quality development on the majority of porous substrates tested as well as wet and dry plastic and glass substrates up to 4 weeks old. Because of strong red background staining, ORO was not successful on either the nonadhesive or the adhesive side of tapes tested. ORO performed

* This observation may be explained by a better understanding of the nature of Kraft papers (the word Kraft means "strong" in German). These papers are produced by the alkaline sulfate process (also known as the "Kraft process" because the resulting paper is stronger than what is produced with the acidic sulfite process). These types of paper products are required when heavier than normal stress demands are expected (e.g., grocery bags, mailing envelopes). These papers often appear gold to brown in color because the lignin content is not completely removed. Lignin is a poly-aromatic compound that has a tar-like brown-black-colored appearance. It tends to be highly lipophilic (i.e., it can dissolve lipids). Although the lipid fraction of latent print residue would initially be attracted to lignin, over time that residue may be drawn into the paper matrix and begin to diffuse. It would be expected that as a latent print ages on such a surface, the ability of a reagent like ORO to visualize it would decrease because of that phenomenon. Another issue involves the oxidation of lipids contained in latent print residue [22]. As latent print residue ages, the lipids oxidize and the print matrix itself hardens, rendering the ability of ORO to partition into it less likely. Because PD is thought to react with the robust faction (which is more polar and would not be drawn into the nonpolar lignin matrix), it would not react in a similar fashion to ORO.

particularly well on Kraft envelopes (in contrast to Rawji and Beaudoin [21]), the shiny side of brown paper, and white photocopy paper.

Wood and James reported that ORO produced at least as good fingerprint development compared to physical developer on four paper types [23]. With intentionally charged (i.e., sebaceous loaded) prints, ORO appeared to outperform PD. Prints were also soaked in three types of water (tap, rain, and river) as well as petrol for 1 h. Neither technique was able to develop any prints on the petrol-soaked papers. Wood and James extended their study by looking at latent print persistence after immersion in water and unleaded petrol [24,25]. Prints on paper and unplasticized PVC were immersed for up to 1 week prior to processing. For the prints soaked in water up to 1 week, ORO was found to be the best technique (outperforming PD at each time interval). Ninhydrin was found to be the best reagent for the petrol-soaked papers, but only up to a 24 h soak.

Regarding ORO's placement in the overall processing sequence for porous substrates, Salama et al. found that ORO could still develop prints after all routine amino acid treatments had been used (including those using HFE 7100 and HFC 4310mee) [14]. The worst performance was observed when 1,8-diazafluoren-9-one (DFO) was followed by ninhydrin, zinc chloride, and then finally ORO. Although sequencing ORO after PD appeared to produce the best results, the authors ultimately recommended using ORO prior to PD (because of the destructive nature of PD).

As the latent prints began to age, the overall performance of ORO decreased as the performance of physical developer increased. While ORO performed significantly better on fresh prints, this result gradually declined up to the fourth week. At this point, PD produced more prints with better contrast than ORO. The authors recommended that if the print age was known to exceed 4 weeks, then PD should be used. However, a recent case has been reported in which a 21-year-old print was visualized with ORO [25]. The case involved a murder and a subsequent attempt to set the victim's car on fire to cover the crime. When the car did not catch fire, the paper material (used to start the fire) was recovered but not processed at the time. Subsequent processing with DFO more than two decades after the incident did not produce positive results; however, treating the items with ORO revealed two prints.

4.2.3 Reagent Sequencing Considerations

If ORO is to be used in a processing sequence for porous items, it should be used prior to physical developer [26,27]. It has also been noted that latent prints less than 1 month old gave better results than older ones (for which PD is known to produce superior results). Also, if amino acid reagents like DFO, 1,2-indanedione-zinc, or ninhydrin are to be used prior to ORO in the sequence (i.e., for documents that have not been wetted or soaked in water), then solvents with higher dielectric constants should be used (e.g., acetone, ethanol, methanol) as the dominant carrier. However, it should be noted that solvents with higher dielectric constants are also more polar and will tend to remove inks.

Reagent preparation [25]

Staining solution

Oil red O	1.54 g
Methanol	770 mL
Sodium hydroxide	9.2 g
Deionized water	230 mL

1. The ORO should first be dissolved into the methanol and mixed thoroughly.
2. The sodium hydroxide should then be dissolved into the water and mixed thoroughly.
3. Mix the two solutions together thoroughly. Filtering is required to remove undissolved solids.
4. Store the staining solution in a brown bottle and away from light.
5. The appropriate information (e.g., chemical contents, preparer's initials, date, reliability test result) should be recorded on the container's label.
6. The solution has been reported to remain stable for up to 8 months.

Buffer solution

Sodium phosphate monobasic monohydrate	101.5 g
Sodium phosphate dibasic heptahydrate	339 g
Distilled water	4 L

1. Mix the sodium phosphate monobasic monohydrate into 1 L of distilled water and mix thoroughly.
2. Mix the sodium phosphate dibasic heptahydrate into 1 L of distilled water and mix thoroughly.
3. Combine the two solutions and mix thoroughly.
4. Add sufficient distilled water to achieve a final volume of 4 L.
5. The appropriate information (e.g., chemical contents, preparer's initials, date, reliability test result) should be recorded on the container's label.

Reagent application

1. All appropriate personal protective equipment should be used when preparing and using this reagent.
2. Run the appropriate positive and negative controls to ensure that the reagent solution is working properly.
3. Immerse the item in the staining solution and agitate for 60–90 min.*
4. Cover the processing tray (plastic wrap or parafilm will suffice) to prevent the evaporation of methanol from the staining solution.
5. Remove the item from the solution and allow excess reagent to be drained off and then place it into the buffer solution (to adjust the pH of the paper back to ~7, which makes it more stable). This should take only a couple of minutes to complete.
6. Allow the item to air dry before evaluating the development.
7. When processing has been completed, all chemicals should be disposed of properly according to the appropriate federal, state, and local environmental laws.

* It has been observed that processing times tend to increase as the age of the print increases.

4.3 Nile Red

Möhlau and Uhlmann were the first to report the synthesis of Nile red (9-diethylamino-5H-benzo[α]phenoxazine-5-one) and other phenoxazine dyes in 1896. It is an intensely fluorescent lipid dye that was first inadvertently discovered as a contaminant of Nile blue by Smith in 1907 [28]. It was later determined that Nile red was responsible for the fluorescence observed upon reaction with the hydrophobic lipid portions of cellular material. The dye is poorly soluble in water but does dissolve in a variety of organic solvents. In predominantly aqueous solutions, the dye will preferentially partition from this environment into certain hydrophobic lipid materials. Nile red was reported to interact and fluoresce in the presence of compounds like cholesterol, oleic acid [29], phospholipids, cholesteryl esters, and triglycerides [28]. Greenspan noted that Nile red was able to stain a wider variety of lipid compounds that were not detected using ORO [30]. It was first investigated for use in visualizing latent prints in the early 1990s by Saunders [31]. Saunders initially determined that the dye worked well but only on relatively fresh prints (less than 2 days old). He recommended a stock solution using either dimethylsulfoxide or acetone and then a dilute aqueous working solution.

Subsequent work investigated Nile red's ability to enhance cyanoacrylate fumed prints. Day et al. compared the dye's effectiveness to rhodamine 6G [32]. They used solutions prepared in acetone (10 μg/mL) and ethanol (10 μg/mL). Excitation was achieved using a wavelength range between 457 and 514 nm. Although the study was somewhat limited in scope, Nile red produced a stronger fluorescent signal than rhodamine 6G and good results were obtained on plastic bags and handgun surfaces.

A more detailed investigation of the dye was recently conducted by Deppe in 2010 [33]. The compound was first evaluated as a lipid dye for latent prints that had been soaked in water. On porous substrates, the reagent was compared to ninhydrin, 1,2-indanedione/zinc, ORO, and PD. Prints were placed on the substrates, soaked in water for 1 h, dried, and then aged up to 6 weeks. As expected, the amino acid reagents (which react with water-soluble components) did not produce any prints. Nile red developed slightly more intense and clearer prints than ORO on nonrecycled papers, although the performance of both reagents diminished slightly as the content of recycled material increased (up to 80%–100%). In contrast to previous observations, Nile red was able to develop prints up to 15 weeks old as well as ones that had been submerged in water for up to 4 weeks. In comparison to PD, Nile red performed more consistently and had significantly less background staining. When comparing ORO and PD to Nile red overall, Deppe noted the relatively shorter preparation and processing times (as well as increased contrast from the fluorescence) as major advantages for the latter technique. However, it should be noted that only PD has been reported to reliably develop very old latent prints [17].

On nonporous surfaces, cyanoacrylate fuming was performed prior to staining with either Nile red or rhodamine 6G. Treatment of the nonporous substrates did not involve soaking in water prior to processing. Of the two nonporous surfaces tested, rhodamine 6G appeared to work better on glass while Nile red developed more ridge detail on aluminum foil.

Sequential treatments were also investigated. When Nile red was used after ninhydrin or 1,2-indanedione/zinc, the development was ill-defined. A possible explanation for this phenomenon could be that the solvents used in these two reagents are typically more nonpolar (e.g., petroleum ether or in this case HFE 7100), which can potentially dissolve lipids. These solvents are capable of dissolving lipids contained in the latent print (the material with which Nile red reacts). Deppe speculated that residual amino acids might be interfering with the Nile red reaction and recommended a maleic acid prewash (pH ~4). However, this did not completely solve the problem and further work on refining sequences involving Nile red on porous substrates is still needed.

Reagent preparation [33]

Stock solution

Nile red	1 mg
acetone	1 mL

Working solution

Stock solution	100 μL
Deionized water	99.9 mL

1. When preparing the stock solution, it should be stirred until the Nile red has completely dissolved in the acetone.
2. When preparing the working solution, the deionized water should be added to the stock solution and mixed thoroughly.
3. The appropriate information (e.g., chemical contents, preparer's initials, date, reliability test result) should be recorded on the container's label.
4. As prepared, the working solution has a light violet color. This solution is not very stable and loses effectiveness with 30–60 min after preparation.

Reagent application [33]

There are two different procedures for using Nile red, as a lipid dye and as a post-cyanoacrylate stain. As a lipid stain on porous items, significant diffusion (smudging) of developed ridge detail has been observed with papers containing a high content of recycled fibers.

Single stain

1. All appropriate personal protective equipment should be used when preparing and using this reagent.
2. Run the appropriate positive and negative controls to ensure that the reagent solution is working properly.
3. The items to be processed a placed in a glass tray containing the working solution for 10–20 s. Older prints may require longer soaking times in the reagent.
4. Processed items are then placed into a deionized water bath for 5 min while agitating gently. The items should be allowed to air dry.
5. To view the fluorescence, an excitation wavelength of 490 nm should be used in conjunction with a 555 nm viewing filter.
6. When processing has been completed, all chemicals should be disposed of properly according to the appropriate federal, state, and local environmental laws.

Post-cyanoacrylate stain

1. All appropriate personal protective equipment should be used when preparing and using this reagent.
2. Run the appropriate positive and negative controls to ensure that the reagent solution is working properly.

3. The items should be placed in the working solution for up to 1 h while gently agitating the solution.
4. A deionized water rinse solution should then be used for approximately 5 min before allowing the items to air dry.
5. To view the fluorescence, an excitation wavelength of 490 nm should be used in conjunction with a 555 nm viewing filter.
6. When processing has been completed, all chemicals should be disposed of properly according to the appropriate federal, state, and local environmental laws.

4.4 Europium Chelates

Europium is a part of the lanthanide element series within the periodic table. The lanthanide element series range from lanthanum (atomic number 57) through lutetium (atomic number 71), and includes europium, gadolinium, and terbium. Although lanthanides emit radiation at high quantum efficiencies, they absorb excitation radiation rather poorly [34]. However, when chelated to suitable organic ligands that can absorb the excitation radiation and intramolecularly transfer that energy back to the lanthanide metal ion (e.g., europium), strong fluorescence can result. Chelation is the formation of a bond (or bonds) between a ligand and a metal ion. A ligand is a neutral molecule or ion that possesses a lone electron pair that can be used to form a bond to a metal ion [35].

These bonds are typically referred to as coordinate covalent bonds. A ligand that can form one bond with the metal ion is referred to as a monodentate ligand. Ligands that form two bonds with the metal ion are called bidentate ligands (when three bonds are formed, the term tridentate ligand is used). The intramolecular transfer of energy between ligands and rare-earth compounds was first reported in 1942 [36]. Europium compounds were preferentially chosen because of the element's high luminescence efficiency, large Stokes shifts (i.e., the difference between the excitation and emission wavelengths), and long luminescence lifetimes (on the order of milliseconds for phosphorescence) [37]. This latter property made them attractive compounds for time-resolved imaging techniques that could significantly diminish interference caused by substrate background fluorescence [38].

A number of organic lipids have been proposed for interaction with lanthanides including theonyltrifluoroacetone, 1,10-phenanthroline [37,39,40], trioctylphosphine oxide (TOPO), tributylphoshine oxide, 2-phenanthroline [41], and tris(6,6,7,7,8,8,8-heptafluoro-2,2-dimethyl-3,5-octanedionato) [42] (abbreviated as [Eu(fod)$_3$]). Allred et al. [37,40] characterized the interaction of such rare-earth metal complexes with latent print residue as a multistep chemical reaction. They propose that the europium first reacted with a conjugating ligand (e.g., ethylenediamminetetraacetic acid [EDTA] via transesterification or acid anhydride formation) to form a nonluminescent complex. This complex then reacted with the fingerprint residue. This was followed by reaction with the sensitizing ligands (e.g., 1,10-phenanthroline and theonyltrifluoroacetone) to form a luminescent complex. Allred et al. noted that this three-step process was able to render lipid materials (like margarine) highly fluorescent. In addition, even fresh prints soaked in water were also observed to fluoresce strongly after treatment with this reagent. However, prints aged more than a few days showed a significant decrease in fluorescence intensity and developed prints faded dramatically within 24h.

Menzel reported another simplified version of a europium chelate reagent [43]. This one-step method involved only the use of one bidentate ligand, 1,10-phenanthroline. This reagent was reported to work well on brown Kraft paper and nylon cloth. In contrast to the complex explanation described previously for the mixed ligand reagent, a much simpler reaction mechanism was proposed for this process [44]. Europium is capable of forming 9-coordinate complexes (i.e., nine single or mixed bonds between ligands and the central metal atom can be formed). 1,10-Phenanthroline forms three bidentate coordinate bonds to the europium (for a total of six coordination bonds). The remaining three open sites are occupied by water. Since water is known to quench fluorescence, the resulting complex is not fluorescent.

A possible mechanism for the reaction of this europium complex with latent print residue has been proposed [44]. When this reagent comes in contact with the hydrophobic (i.e., water-fearing) portion of the latent print residue, the water molecules are stripped off as the complex partitions into the print. The now empty ligand bonding sites become occupied by lipid molecules and the resulting complex is highly fluorescent. Interestingly, if the europium complex is dissolved in pure methanol, rather than water, the complex itself is fluorescent and will stain the background heavily as well as the print. This mechanism helps to explain why it is not successful in developing older prints. As latent print residue ages, water quickly evaporates, removing in excess of 99% of the original weight of the residue [45]. As this occurs, the print becomes dried out and hardens. Now exposed to air, lipids begin to oxidize and break down. The ability of a large complex to partition into this unfavorable environment decreases significantly over a relatively short period of time.

Reagent preparation [39]

Solution I

Methanol	80 mL
Acetone	20 mL
Europium chloride hexahydrate	75 mg
EDTA excess	

Solution II

1,10-Phenanthroline	75 mg
Methanol	40 mL
Acetone	10 mL

Solution III

Thenoyltrifluoroacetone	45 mg
Methanol	40 mL
Acetone	10 mL

1. Each solution is prepared by mixing the chemicals in the order in which they are listed.
2. Each solution should be mixed until the contents have thoroughly dissolved.
3. The appropriate information (e.g., chemical contents, preparer's initials, date, reliability test result) should be recorded on each container's label.
4. Each solution can be stored in a glass bottle and is stable for at least 6 months.

Modified reagent preparation [43]

Working solution

Europium chloride hexahydrate	0.366 g
1,10-Phenanthroline	0.541 g
acacia*	0.1 g
Methanol	50 mL
Water	950 mL

1. The reagent is prepared by completely dissolving the first three chemicals in the methanol.
2. The water is then slowly added to this mixture until a final volume of 1 L is achieved.
3. The appropriate information (e.g., chemical contents, preparer's initials, date, reliability test result) should be recorded on the container's label.
4. This solution can be stored in a glass bottle and is stable for at least 6 months.

Reagent application

1. All appropriate personal protective equipment should be used when preparing and using this reagent.
2. Run the appropriate positive and negative controls to ensure that the reagent solution is working properly.
3. Each solution is sequentially sprayed onto the item. The time interval between the application of each solution is no more than a few minutes. Because acetone and methanol are relatively volatile, they tend to evaporate before damage to the latent print residue can occur.
4. The complete reaction occurs within a few minutes after the application of the third solution.
5. To view the fluorescence, a long-wave ultraviolet excitation source is needed. The emission can be viewed by the naked eye in the orange-red portion of the visible spectrum (no filter is required).
6. When processing has been completed, all chemicals should be disposed of properly according to the appropriate federal, state, and local environmental laws.

Good results on relatively fresh prints were observed with surfaces like brown Kraft paper, white notepad paper [39], and U.S. currency [40]. With the $Eu(fod)_3$ complex, dipping times in excess of 20 s resulted in decreased print development [42]. For items processed with $Eu(TTA)_3 \cdot 2TOPO$ [41], an immersion time of 5 s was reported along with a 5 s water wash.

Modified reagent application

1. All appropriate personal protective equipment should be used when preparing and using this reagent.
2. Run the appropriate positive and negative controls to ensure that the reagent solution is working properly.
3. The item is immersed into the solution for a few seconds, removed, and then allowed to air dry.

* Acacia, also known as gum Arabic, is a gum or sap derived from certain species of acacia plants. It is used here in a powdered form.

4. To view the fluorescence, a short-wave ultraviolet excitation source is needed. The emission can be viewed by the naked eye in the orange-red portion of the visible spectrum (no filter is required).
5. When processing has been completed, all chemicals should be disposed of properly according to the appropriate federal, state, and local environmental laws.

Little to no background fluorescence is observed with most porous substrates. However, the process is limited to relatively fresh prints (less than a few days old).

References

1. Lille RD, Stotz EH, Emmel VM. (1977) *H.J. Conn's Biological Stains*. St. Louis, MO: Sigma Chemical Company.
2. Mitsui T, Katho H, Shimada K, Wakasugi Y. (1980) Development of latent prints using a Sudan black B solution. *J Forensic Ident* 30(8):9–10.
3. Mitsui T, Katho H, Shimada K. (1981) Development of latent prints using a Sudan black B solution. *Fingerprint Whorld* 6(24):84–85.
4. Anon. (1995) Sudan black. *Minutiae*:3.
5. Stone RS, Metzger RA. (1981) Comparison of development techniques Sudan black B/black magna powder for water-soaked porous items. *J Forensic Ident* 31(1):13–14.
6. Munroe RGR. (1994) Latent fingerprint development on a cement matrix. *Can Soc Forensic Sci J* 27(1):1–4.
7. Monday TD. (2004) Progressive processing: a matter of persistence. *J Forensic Ident* 54(4):438–441.
8. Snyder C. (2009) Methods for developing and preserving prints in petroleum jelly. *J Forensic Ident* 59(2):153–171.
9. Anon. (2005) Solvent black 3 for scenes of crime. *Fingerprint Development and Imaging Newsletter*, HOSDB Publication No. 20/05.
10. Trozzi TA, Schwartz RL, Hollars ML. (2001) *Processing Guide for Developing Latent Prints*. U.S. Department of Justice, Federal Bureau of Investigation, Washington, DC.
11. Anon. (1977) *H.J. Conn's Biological Stains*, 9th edn. Ed. Lillie RD. Williams & Wilkins Company, Baltimore, MD.
12. Jencks WP, Durrum EL, Jetton MR. (1955) Paper electrophoresis as a quantitative method: the staining of serum lipoproteins. *J Clin Invest* 34(9):1437–1448.
13. Kutt H, Tsaltas TT. (1959) Staining properties of Oil Red O and a method of the partial purification of the commercial product. *Clin Chem* 5(2):149–160.
14. Salama J, Aumeer-Donovan S, Lennard C, Roux C. (2008) Evaluation of the fingermark reagent Oil Red O as a possible replacement for physical developer. *J Forensic Ident* 58(2):203–237.
15. Cantu A, Burow D, Wilson J. (2007) On some properties of the Oil Red O fingerprint visualization reagent. Presented at the International Fingerprint Research Group Meeting, Canberra, Australian Capital Territory, Australia, 2007.
16. Lide DR. (1990) *CRC Handbook of Chemistry and Physics*, 71st edn. CRC Press, Boca Raton, FL, pp. 8–44.
17. Anon. (2003) What is the oldest fingerprint that you have developed? Fingerprint Development and Imaging Update Publication No. 26/2003, Home Office Police Scientific Development Branch, November.
18. Castelló A, Alvarez M, Miquel M, Verdu F. (2002) Long-lasting lipsticks and latent prints. *Forensic Sci Commun* 4(2).

19. Navarro E, Castelló A, López JL, Verdú F. (2006) Crinimalystic sic.: effectiveness of lysochromes on the developing of invisible lipstick-contaminated lipmarks on human skin. A preliminary study. *Forensic Sci Int* 158:9–13.
20. Beaudoin A. (2004) New technique for revealing latent fingerprints on wet, porous surfaces: Oil Red O. *J Forensic Ident* 54(4):413–421.
21. Rawji A, Beaudoin A. (2006) Oil Red O versus physical developer on wet papers: a comparative study. *J Forensic Ident* 56(1):33–54.
22. Mong GM, Petersen CE, Claus TRW. (1999) Advanced fingerprint analysis project: fingerprint constituents. Pacific Northwest National Laboratory (PNNL) Report 13019, 1999.
23. Wood MA, James T. (2009) ORO. The physical developer replacement. *Sci Justice* 49:272–276.
24. Wood MA, James IT. (2009) Latent fingerprint persistence and development techniques on wet surfaces. *Fingerprint Whorld* 35(135):90–100.
25. Beaudoin A. (2011) Oil Red O: fingerprint development on a 21-year-old cold case. *J Forensic Ident* 61(1):50–59.
26. Rawji A, Beaudoin A. (2007) Oil Red O versus physical developer for wet substrates: a comparative study. *Ident Canada* 30(1):4–18.
27. Guigui K, Beaudoin A. (2007) The use of Oil Red O in sequence with other methods of fingerprint development. *J Forensic Ident* 57(4):550–581.
28. Greenspan P, Mayer EP, Fowler SD. (1985) Nile red: a selective fluorescent stain for intracellular lipid droplets. *J Cell Biol* 100:965–973.
29. Fowler SD, Greenspan P. (1985) Application of Nile red, a fluorescent hydrophobic probe, for the detection of neutral lipid deposits in tissue sections. Comparison with Oil Red O. *J Histochem Cytochem* 33(8):833–836.
30. Greenspan P, Fowler SD. (1985) Spectrofluorometric studies of the lipid probe, Nile red. *J Lipid Res* 26:781–789.
31. Saunders G. (1993) Nile red. Presented at the International Fingerprint Research Group Meeting, Washington, DC, May.
32. Day KJ, Bowker W. (1996) Enhancement of cyanoacrylate developed latent prints using Nile red. *J Forensic Ident* 46(2):183–187.
33. Deppe J. (2010) Methods/reagents to reveal fingerprints that have been in wet or very humid condition (on porous surfaces). Thesis (for International Internship for Diploma Studies in Germany), University of Technology Sydney, Sydney, New South Wales, Australia.
34. Menzel ER. (1997) Lanthanide-based fingerprint detection. *Fingerprint Whorld* 23(88):45–51.
35. Zumdahl SS. (1989) *Chemistry*, 2nd edn. D.C. Heath and Company, Lexington, KT, p. 908.
36. Weissman SI. (1942) Intramolecular energy transfer, the fluorescence of complexes of europium. *J Chem Phys* 10:214–217.
37. Allred CE, Murdock RH, Menzel ER. (1997) New lipid-specific, rare earth-based chemical fingerprint detection method. *J Forensic Ident* 47(5):542–556.
38. Murdock RH, Menzel ER. (1993) A computer interfaced time-resolved imaging system. *J Forensic Sci* 38(3):521–529.
39. Allred CE, Menzel ER. (1997) A novel europium-biconjugate method for latent fingerprint detection. *Forensic Sci Int* 85:83–94.
40. Allred CE, Lin T, Menzel ER. (1997) Lipid-specific latent fingerprint detection: fingerprints on currency. *J Forensic Sci* 42(6):997–1003.
41. Wilkinson D. (1999) A one-step fluorescent detection method for lipid fingerprints; $Eu(TTA)_3{\cdot}2TOPO$. *Forensic Sci Int* 99:5–23.
42. Caldwell JP, Henderson W, Kim ND. (2001) Luminescent visualization of latent fingerprints by direct reaction with a lanthanide shift reagent. *J Forensic Sci* 46(6):1332–1341.
43. Menzel ER. (1999) *Fingerprint Detection with Lasers*, 2nd edn. New York: Marcel Dekker.
44. Personal communication between Dr. Tony Cantu and Dr. Malka Linder, May 4, 1999.
45. Ramotowski RS. (2001) Composition of latent print residue. In: Lee HC, Gaensslen RE, Eds. *Advances in Fingerprint Technology*, 2nd edn. CRC Press, Boca Raton, FL, pp. 63–104.

5

Vapor/Fuming Methods

Robert S. Ramotowski

CONTENTS

5.1 Cyanoacrylate Fuming

Dr. Harry Coover first worked with cyanoacrylate monomers in 1942 while searching for a material to make clear plastic gun sights. He rejected the material as being too sticky. Cyanoacrylates were also synthesized by Ardis in 1949. The first accidental discovery of the powerful adhesive properties inherent in ethyl cyanoacrylate occurred in 1951 [1]. While attempting to measure the refractive index of freshly synthesized ethyl cyanoacrylate monomer, Joyner and Shearer (working for Coover at Eastman) found that the glass prism faces of the refractometer became firmly bonded together. Ultimately the methyl-based adhesive, Eastman 910, would be marketed as Super Glue® in 1958.

Coover saw the potential of this new product as a tissue adhesive. During the Vietnam War, cyanoacrylates were used by mobile army surgical hospitals to stabilize uncontrolled bleeding. A thin film of adhesive sprayed onto a wound resulted in almost immediate cessation of the bleeding. An attempt to introduce this procedure back in the United States failed due to reports of carcinogenicity in some animal testing and the process failed to obtain Food and Drug Administration (FDA) approval. Studies had indicated that higher esters of cyanoacrylate (e.g., octyl) were significantly less toxic than the methyl and ethyl esters. Cyanoacrylates are currently used in some surgical procedures [2].

Cyanoacrylate fuming is one of the most common techniques used to visualize latent prints on nonporous surfaces. Developed prints appear white in color, after the cyanoacrylate monomer has polymerized on the latent print residue. The discovery of the cyanoacrylate fuming process for latent print development can be traced back to 1977 [3]. In May of that year, Fuseo Matsumura, a trace evidence examiner at the Saga Prefectural Crime Laboratory of the National Police Agency of Japan, observed that his fingerprint ridges were visible on microscope slides while mounting forensic samples from a murder case. His colleague, latent print examiner Masato Soba, performed some preliminary research and noted that cyanoacrylates had potential for detecting latent prints on several surfaces, including the adhesive surface of tape. In September 1979, the technique was demonstrated to U.S. Army Crime Laboratory Latent Print Examiners, who eventually transferred the technology to their laboratory in Georgia.

In May of 1979, L.W. Wood, from the Police Headquarters in Northampton, United Kingdom, noticed that his fingerprints developed on a film tank that he had repaired with cyanoacrylate. In 1980, the information was relayed to the Home Office Central Research Establishment, whose personnel concluded that the process was promising. In mid-1980, Louis Bourdon, from Ontario, Canada, applied for patents in both Canada and the United States for using cyanoacrylates to develop latent prints. The U.S. patent was issued on October 27, 1981 [4]. A patent infringement claim was made by attorneys representing Bourdon to police agencies working with the cyanoacrylate fuming technique. They were temporarily forced to halt work with the new technique until a successful rebuttal to the infringement claims was made by the U.S. Army judge advocate general.

It is interesting to note that during the first few years of processing evidence with cyanoacrylate fumes no acceleration methods were used. The amount of time required for development to occur varied from hours to days [5]. Items were initially fumed in thin layer chromatography tanks, fish tanks, and Petri dishes [6]. Several different chemical acceleration methods were attempted. Early attempts involved the use of chemicals like triethyldiamine dipropylene ester, *N,N,N′,N′*-tetramethylethylenediamine, various triol polyesters, and other amines, esters, and ethers [7]. Ultimately, the use of absorbent cotton soaked in a 0.5 N solution of sodium hydroxide (and dried) was found to produce good results when mixed with cyanoacrylate. Polymerization could also be initiated by the presence of the cellulose fibers in the cotton. White fumes were observed approximately 15–20 s after combining the glue and sodium hydroxide-soaked cotton and lasted for about 1–2 min. Sodium carbonate was also suggested as a catalyst [8]. A mixture of baking soda and sawdust has also been recommended as an accelerant [9].

The application of heat to accelerate the fuming process was proposed in 1983 [10]. One method involved heating a metal block to 100°C and then placing an aluminum foil pan containing the glue on top. Prints generally developed within 5–10 min, but 30 min was recommended. The methyl-cyanoacrylate monomer was preferred because of its higher volatility. A light bulb was also suggested as a heat source to accelerate fuming [11]. The glue was placed on a watch glass that was suspended above the light bulb. Fuming commenced 3–5 min after the bulb was switched on and optimum development was obtained in 7–12 min.

Cyanoacrylate in gel form, known commercially as "Hard Evidence," was also reported and determined to be superior to the sodium hydroxide/cotton and heat acceleration method [12]. After peeling apart a resealable pouch, the cyanoacrylate gel was exposed and began polymerizing. The addition of water vapor to facilitate this reaction was found to be critical. One method for generating water vapor for the fuming process involved freezing the item for 10–20 min [13]. The item was then be placed into a chamber and fumed as it thawed. Another similar effort involved the mixing of cyanoacrylate with petroleum jelly (1 cc of Vaseline to four drops of cyanoacrylate) spread between acetate sheets [14].

There have also been several attempts to create a one-step colored cyanoacrylate fuming process. One early effort involved the use of iodine crystals in conjunction with a cotton pad soaked with sodium hydroxide [15]. Prints were successfully developed on lined notebook paper and a wax-coated plastic cup. The solid, dried-out polymeric form of the cyanoacrylate has been reported to develop ridge detail as well as the liquid form [16]. The liquid monomer can be derived *in situ* as a vapor from the heated solid polymer.

5.1.1 Chemistry and Mechanism

The mechanism of cyanoacrylate polymerization has been studied extensively. Generally, basic compounds are reported to initiate or act as catalysts for the reaction [17]. Because of the enhanced stabilization that occurs with the propagating anion of cyanoacrylates (due to the presence of two electron withdrawing groups, nitrile and ester), even weakly basic compounds like water, polar solvents, and halide ions can act as initiators. These electron-rich compounds are known as nucleophiles. Nucleophiles are electron pair donors (i.e., Lewis bases) and generally seek a positively charged (i.e., electron deficient) center to neutralize their electric charges [18]. Hetero-carbon multiple bonds like the double bond in carbonyls (C=O) or the triple bond in a nitrile group (C≡N) have large differences in electric charge between molecules (in each case the carbon would have a partially positive charge and the oxygen or nitrogen would have a partially negative charge).

Nucleophilic attack on the cyanoacrylate monomers occurs at these partially positive sites via either simple or conjugate addition. After the first successful attack, a relatively stable intermediate compound is formed that has both a positive and negative charge (known as a zwitterion, from the German word for "hybrid"). Reaction of this species with additional monomer units extends the growth of the nascent polymer. Propagation of the polymer continues until either the supply of nucleophile or monomer runs out or a chain termination agent is introduced [17]. Chain termination occurs when the reaction intermediate is deactivated (e.g., the addition of water) and is no longer capable of reacting with nucleophiles.

The reaction of cyanoacrylate monomers with latent print residue is far more complex and less well understood. The mechanism described earlier occurs under clean laboratory conditions and with pure compounds. These conditions are rarely, if ever, achieved at crime scenes or in forensic laboratories. Substrates are often contaminated and exposed to harsh environmental conditions. However, several recent efforts have attempted to study this interaction and make hypotheses as to what components of latent print residue initiate the polymerization and what chemicals may aid in rejuvenating older prints. Given the complexity of the composition of latent print residue [19], it is not surprising that there are still many questions yet to be answered.

One of the first attempts to describe the cyanoacrylate reaction mechanism was by Lee and Gaensslen in 1984 [20]. The authors asserted that microscopic amounts of water and other bases initiated the polymerization and that cyanoacrylate vapors reacted with lipids, fatty acids, amino acids, and proteins in latent print residue. An attempt to use basic substances to enhance the sensitivity of cyanoacrylate fumes to latent print residues was first reported in the late 1990s [21]. Polymer density was quantitatively measured via carbonyl bond absorbance (which follows the Beer-Lambert law) as recorded by Fourier transform infrared spectroscopy. The authors found that prefuming with ammonia led to a significant increase in methyl-2-cyanoacrylate polymer formation on latent print ridges.

Czekanski et al. proposed a rather unique explanation for the reaction mechanism [22]. In addition to reporting that nonpolar hydrocarbons (e.g., undecane, dodecane, and hexadecane) could initiate polymerization, the authors reported that film thickness and viscosity did have an impact on the initiation reaction but not molecular weight or density. Film thickness was also found to influence reaction time. The authors proposed a possible reaction mechanism model that suggested that cyanoacrylate monomers either diffused into a latent print residue to a saturation point or were desorbed. A similar reaction occurred on the background substrate, but neither water nor monomer would accumulate. This model involved gas-phase partitioning into a thin film—analogous to what occurs in a gas chromatographic column (although the model suggested a static rather than a dynamic exchange/flow of chemical species). The authors concluded that a variety of compounds could possibly serve as the "stationary phase" that traps monomers in the print residue.

The effect of water exposure on the successful development of cyanoacrylate-fumed prints was investigated by Moores and Bandey [23]. Prints of varying ages (1 h, 1 day, and 5 days) were immersed in either fresh or salt water (34 g/L) for 1 h. Overall, water-soaking significantly reduces the chances of developing prints with cyanoacrylate, although results for salt water–immersed samples were better than those for fresh water–soaked ones. Development of good print detail varied inversely to the age of the latent prior to immersion.

5.1.2 Cyanoacrylate Pretreatments

Lewis et al. reported that the initiators for ethyl-2-cyanoacylate appeared to be water-soluble components and that humidity did not appear to have a significant impact on the polymerization process [24]. The authors also noted that acetic acid vapors could effectively "rejuvenate" aged prints, apparently by dissolving the dried out initiator material in the latent print. Aged oily prints were easier to develop than aged clean ones, possibly due to lipid materials forming emulsions in the residue, thus retaining moisture. Wargacki et al. subsequently reported that the carboxylate group is the primary initiation site for polymerization and performed significantly better than a primary amine [25]. They also noted that polymer formation was directly linked to the presence of hydrogen ions, which act as termination agents. Thus, a higher concentration of hydrogen ions (i.e., a lower pH or acidic environment) led to lower accumulations of cyanoacrylate polymer. Wargacki et al. also noted that, although exposing prints to both ammonia and acetic acid vapors prior to fuming increased polymer formations, acetic acid appeared to outperform ammonia by at least a factor of two [26].

A validation study of different pretreatments was recently reported by Pinto and Stevenson [27]. The authors evaluated a number of prefuming treatments on six substrates including acetic acid, ammonia, acetic acid followed by ammonia, and ammonia followed by acetic acid. Split depletion print series were used to directly compare each pretreatment with a control sample (which received no pretreatment). The authors reported that a significant increase in the ridge thickness of the fumed prints occurred if an acetic acid pretreatment was used (0.12–0.31 mm for regular fuming versus 0.21–0.53 mm for enhanced fuming). The use of both acetic acid and ammonia led to a decrease in developed print quality.

McLaren et al. investigated the use of a 10% w/v aqueous methylamine as a pretreatment for "rejuvenating" older prints on polyethylene prior to cyanoacrylate fuming [28]. Methylamine is an effective Lewis base and its increased absorbance of water promotes chain propagation and polymerization. However, in contrast to Wargacki et al. [26], the authors found that ammonia pretreatments produced significantly more consistent results than either heated water vapor or acetic acid.

The effect of hydrogen chloride (HCl) or chlorine exposure on latent prints was reported by McDonald et al. [29]. Under normal conditions, amines present in a latent print can be N-chlorinated and make them less reactive toward reagents like ninhydrin; however, low-humidity conditions can inhibit this reaction. In addition, the hydrolysis reaction that occurs when chlorine dissolves in water produces hypochlorous and hydrochloric acids, which can inhibit reactions with amino acids. In addition, the formation of additional hydrogen ions can also inhibit the subsequent cyanoacrylate fuming process (this can occur if the hydrogen chloride concentration exceeds $20\,mg/m^3$, while values below $5\,mg/m^3$ had no adverse effect). However, pretreatment of such HCl-exposed prints with triethylamine and ethanolamine significantly improved the quality of the cyanoacrylate-fumed prints.

5.1.3 Atmospheric CA Fuming

Operationally, there is a distinct contrast between fuming objects in a controlled environment (e.g., a specifically designed fuming cabinet in a laboratory) and an uncontrolled one (e.g., a crime scene). One of the first to build a controlled, dedicated cyanoacrylate fuming cabinet (known as the "Sandridge" superglue cabinet) was the U.K. Home Office Police Scientific Development Branch in 1985 [30]. The PSDB group subsequently published environmental recommendations of 80% ± 2% relative humidity (RH) and a heating temperature of 140°C [31]. To fume items in this chamber, 3 g of cyanoacrylate, placed into an aluminum dish, was required. However, after processing was completed, this cabinet required mechanical extraction of excess cyanoacrylate fumes before the items could be removed. A detailed validation study was performed by the Home Office to see if the original recommendations were accurate and reproducible [32]. Paine et al. reported that the results indicated that the original recommendation for approximately 80% RH produced the best quality and contrast of developed prints, which was consistent with the Home Office recommendations from the 1980s. They also found that sebaceous-loaded prints were less susceptible to changes in RH than eccrine-loaded ones.

Another purposely built cabinet was reported by Barclay in 1986 [33]. The large cabinet had the advantage of a water filtration system to remove the toxic cyanoacrylate fumes. In 1995, Stokes and Brennan described a custom-built, self-scrubbing fuming chamber [34]. The importance of keeping chambers clean and free of cyanoacrylate polymer buildup was reported by Weaver and Clary [35]. They used a dilute sulfuric acid solution (1:12) to coat the chamber walls (to inhibit polymer growth) and thus theoretically made more cyanoacrylate monomers available to react with the latent print residue.

At the crime scene, many different methods have been used to fume objects *in situ* because it is not practical to remove oversized or irregularly shaped items. The use of a cyanoacrylate fuming wand was first proposed by Weaver [36]. A review of this technology was reported by Froude [37]. The wand was essentially a butane-heated torch in which solid cyanoacrylate polymer was vaporized at high temperatures. This results in a rapid, short-lived burst of fumes that could be applied to a localized area. Froude noted several disadvantages associated with the fuming wand. Additional disadvantages included the following: the very high temperatures generated by the wand could melt or damage fragile items, extensive and cumbersome personal protective equipment would be required to use the wand outside of a fume hood, the cartridges were found to last only 60 s, and the high temperatures generated by the wand could produce dangerous decomposition products like acrylonitrile and hydrogen cyanide. Overall, the conventional fuming process was found to produce better print development.

A method for processing cars using a custom-built system for pumping heated cyanoacrylate fumes into the vehicle was reported by Tissier et al. [38]. The temperature was not controlled within the vehicle and humidity levels could only be increased by placing a cup of hot water into the car. A similar methodology was reported by Karlinszky and Harkai [39]. Large-scale fuming of crime scenes has also been reported [40]. Heavy plastic tent-type enclosures were used in residential interiors. The size of the spaces fumed ranged from 8,000 to 12,000 ft^3 (226–340 m^3). For such a scene, 100 mL of cyanoacrylate monomer was split between several hot plates, which were heated to 66°C (150°F). The fuming was allowed to continue overnight.

A commercial product for processing large scenes was reported by Bandey and Kent in 2003. The use of the SUPERfume process, manufactured by Foster and Freeman, Ltd., was compared against laboratory fuming cabinet development and aluminum flake powdering [30]. Basic Yellow 40 in water was used for subsequent staining of cyanoacrylate development. Six donors supplied a series of nine depletion prints on 19 different surfaces (done in triplicate). Within each triplicate, one panel was aged for 1 day, another for 1 week, and the other for 1 month. The results obtained from the laboratory fuming cabinet were superior to fuming at the scene, mostly due to the greater control of temperature and humidity. The report noted that a change in temperature of 1°C resulted in a change of 5% relative humidity. Small localized variations in temperature could lead to drastic changes in humidity conditions and lead to a decrease in cyanoacrylate polymer formation. Since different surfaces develop print detail at different rates, it is easier to observe and stop the fuming process when it is conducted in a chamber than when it is conducted in a sealed room.

One of the most common issues with atmospheric fuming of items was the potential for overdevelopment of the print. Heat sources, like hot plate or heat blower, were used to see if excess polymer could be removed [41]. At temperatures between 70°C and 80°C, the polymer began to volatilize rapidly. This can clear up overdeveloped portions of the print and increase contrast dramatically. However, inattention can lead to loss of all detail, which apparently cannot be redeveloped by refuming with cyanoacrylate.

5.1.4 Vacuum Cyanoacrylate Fuming

The use of reduced pressures for processing items with cyanoacrylate fumes originated in Canada in 1987 [42]. The prototype chamber first built by Watkins was delivered to the Royal Canadian Mounted Police (RCMP) Forensic Identification Support Section in Ottawa in 1989 [43]. This system operated at a reduced pressure of approximately 300 mtorr (equivalent to 0.4 mbar)* and required 20 min to develop suitable impressions. A simpler and cheaper version, using a bench top desiccator, was introduced in 1994 [44]. An early validation experiment found that prints developed in the new vacuum chamber were superior in contrast to those developed by the traditional atmospheric method. A subsequent evaluation found distinct differences in the physical appearance of the cyanoacrylate polymer formed by both methods [45]. Using scanning electron microscopy, prints developed under reduced pressure appeared as a layer of solid polymer while those developed at atmospheric pressure appeared as a tangled network of fibers. In the reduced pressure process, no humidity was present. As the pressure was reduced, all traces of water vapor were removed. The results of this study also indicated that a majority of samples processed via the reduced pressure process were equal or superior to those visualized at atmospheric pressure with heat and humidity. These results were also corroborated by the Institut de Recherche Criminelle de la Gendarmerie Nationale (France) [42].

In another validation study, distinctly different results were obtained by the U.K. Home Office [46]. The authors noted that although both techniques were capable of developing high-quality prints in certain situations, overall, the atmospheric heat and humidity process was the superior visualization technique. This was particularly true as the age of the latent print increased. The use of the methyl or ethyl monomer of cyanoacrylate was found to make no difference for either development method. Interestingly, the authors observed that the reduced pressure technique produced higher background reactions than for prints visualized at atmospheric conditions. They speculate that the tangled fiber structure of the polymers grown at atmospheric conditions provided greater surface area for dye stains to attach than the more solid and smooth structures produced at reduced pressure. One purported advantage of the reduced pressure process is that the inside of plastic bags is also treated during the process. Kent and Winfield asserted that this was of little operational value as these items would eventually be sliced open to apply dye stains. Similar conclusions were reached by Chan and Kinsella [47].

Mixed results were observed with firearms processed by the two methods [47]. Some prints developed with the reduced pressure method were subsequently enhanced when reprocessed with the atmospheric heat/humidity method. Certain metallic surfaces responded better to one technique than the other. Reduced pressure fuming was the superior method for blue-steel firearms, while atmospheric fuming was better with weapons with light-colored or polished surfaces like chrome. Mixed results were also obtained by Bessman et al. [48]. The reduced pressure method produced better results on substrates like glass, plastic page protectors, and Styrofoam whereas the atmospheric heat/humidity method visualized prints better on plastic substrates in general (e.g., Glad sandwich bags, black plastic bags). Both methods produced similar results with clear plastic bags, sandwich bags, and clear plastic cups. Neither method produced satisfactory development on duct tape or aluminum foil.

* Vacuum chambers from different manufacturers can report pressure values in different units. The pressure value cited in reference [43] is in millitorr units. The SI unit for pressure is the pascal (Pa), which is equal to one newton per square meter (N/m^2 or kg/ms^2). The value of 300 mtorr would be equivalent to 40.0 Pa.

5.1.5 Sequencing

Enhancement of cyanoacrylate-fumed ridge detail typically involves the subsequent use of powders and chemical dye stains. In some instances, the use of powders after cyanoacrylate ester fuming could lead to spotty ridge detail [49]. The fuming process was observed to dry out residues on the surface of certain types of evidence, leading to poor or no ridge detail development. In contrast, magnetic powders were reported to be very effective on glue-treated items [10]. Menzel first reported the use of a methanolic solution rhodamine 6G as a post-cyanoacrylate dye stain [50]. Although not as effective as other reagents, ninhydrin-zinc chloride was also explored as a post-glue treatment for a print on aluminum foil. The reagent did react with the glue polymer, but longer reaction times were required. Stoilovic et al. recommended the use of Coumarin 540, a dye that can be excited by the use of a filtered xenon arc lamp (430–470 nm) or the 488 nm line of an argon ion laser [51]. The use of a water-tracing dye (possibly Ardrox, but not specifically identified in the article), which fluoresced yellow-green under short-wave ultraviolet, as a stain for cyanoacrylate was also reported [52]. Since then, many new dyes and dye combinations have been described for use after cyanoacrylate fuming [53].

Vacuum metal deposition (VMD) has been compared to cyanoacrylate fuming. One comparison found that VMD was slightly superior to cyanoacrylate fuming/dye stain, especially for aged prints [54]. Another comparison on glass slides also found differences between the two techniques based on the age of the latent print [55]. For prints less than 2 months old, both methods produced similar results. However, on older prints (24 months), VMD performed significantly better than cyanoacrylate fuming. The authors recommended sequencing cyanoacrylate fuming followed by VMD to obtain the best results.

Thiburce et al. reported on the optimization of the cyanoacrylate fuming—Bluestar sequence for detecting blood prints at a crime scene [56]. A control slide bearing spots of sodium hydroxide (a known cyanoacrylate catalyst) was developed to ensure than the polymerization level was optimal. The authors noted that from casework experience, cyanoacrylate fuming of washed blood could inhibit subsequent application of Bluestar. In addition, high levels of cyanoacrylate polymer on the print were also found to inhibit the Bluestar reaction. However, using the control slide with sodium hydroxide control spots, the level of polymerization could be controlled to prevent overdevelopment.

Operationally, cyanoacrylate fuming can interfere with a number of other forensic examinations. Fuming has been reported to interfere with attempts to recover digital data from compact discs [57]. Templin and Nielson concluded that cyanoacrylate fuming did not affect trigger pull measurements for pistols and revolvers, although they did not evaluate the impact of dye stains or organic solvents [58]. Early methods for analyzing blood and biological fluids were often adversely impacted by prior fuming with cyanoacrylate [20]. However, modern advances in the extraction and analysis of DNA from forensic samples have largely eliminated these concerns. Shipp et al. reported that a restriction fragment length polymorphism (RFLP) profile could be obtained from cyanoacrylate-fumed bloodstains [59]. Zamir et al. were able to successfully recover at least five short tandem repeats (STR) markers from fumed prints on adhesive tapes [60]. Stein et al. [61] and von Wurmb et al. [62] also reported successful recovery and analysis of DNA from cyanoacrylate-fumed samples.

In an effort to preserve fragile latent prints from the domestic and international shipping process, the U.S. Army Criminal Investigation Laboratory instituted a policy requiring that all nonporous evidence be treated with cyanoacrylate fuming prior to submission [63]. This would include fuming in the field prior to removal of items from the crime scene. During a period of 9 months (June 1988 through February 1989), 60% of cases were fumed in the field. For those items fumed in the field, an average of 3.29 latent prints were developed per case (0.21 identifications per case) compared to 1.06 per case (0.04 identifications per case) in the laboratory. This data tended to support the claim that a significant amount of latent prints were being wiped off or damaged during handling, packaging, and shipping.

5.1.6 Cyanoacrylate Dye Stains

In general, the choice of dye stain (or dye stain combination) should be made in conjunction with an examination of the nature of the item. The background's ability to fluoresce under certain wavelengths or the propensity of a particular dye stain to adhere strongly to certain surfaces should be taken into consideration. It is important to choose a dye stain with an appropriate Stokes shift for the surface being examined. In order to optimally view the fluorescent prints, the choice of the proper emission filter is also critical.

5.1.6.1 Ardrox

In 1987, Vachon and Sorel introduced the use of Ardrox 970-P-10 (marketed in the United States as Ardrox P133D) as a long-wave ultraviolet excited dye stain for cyanoacrylate prints [64]. Ardrox was initially applied by soaking the item in an undiluted solution for 10 min (followed by rinsing); however, reduced processing times could be achieved by using a 2% solution in methanol and Freon [65] or 1% in isopropanol and acetonitrile [66]. A more recent formula for Ardrox has been reported (see the following).

Reagent preparation [67]

Working solution

Ardrox P133D	2 mL
Acetone	10 mL
Methanol	25 mL
Isopropanol	10 mL
Acetonitrile	8 mL
Petroleum ether	945 mL

1. The various chemicals and solvents should be mixed thoroughly in the order listed.
2. The final addition of petroleum ether should be done slowly to ensure that separation into different layers does not occur.
3. The appropriate information (e.g., chemical contents, preparer's initials, date, reliability test result) should be recorded on the container's label.
4. The working solution has a shelf life of approximately 6 months and should be stored in a glass bottle until ready for use.

Reagent application

1. All appropriate personal protective equipment should be used when preparing and using this reagent.
2. Run the appropriate positive and negative controls to ensure that the reagent solution is working properly.

3. The dye can be applied either by spraying, dipping, or by squirting from a wash bottle.
4. Cold water can be used to rinse away heavy background staining.
5. The absorption maximum for Ardrox is reported to be 380 nm, with an emission maximum of 500 nm [53]. A long-wave UV source or filtered alternate light source (ALS) can be used.
6. Treated prints should be viewed with a yellow or orange filter.
7. When processing has been completed, all chemicals should be disposed of properly according to the appropriate federal, state, and local environmental laws.

5.1.6.2 Basic Yellow 40

This dye is also known as BY40, C.I. Basic Yellow, and Maxilon Brilliant Flavine 10GFF.

Reagent preparation [68]

Alcohol-based working solution

Basic Yellow 40	2 g
Ethanol	1000 mL

1. The BY40 and ethanol should be mixed thoroughly.
2. The appropriate information (e.g., chemical contents, preparer's initials, date, reliability test result) should be recorded on the container's label.
3. The working solution should be stored in a glass bottle until ready for use.

Water-based working solution*

Basic Yellow 40	1 g
Photo-Flo	2 mL
Water	1000 mL

1. The BY40 should be combined with the water and Photo-Flo and mixed thoroughly.
2. The appropriate information (e.g., chemical contents, preparer's initials, date, reliability test result) should be recorded on the container's label.
3. The working solution should be stored in a glass bottle until ready for use.

Reagent application

1. All appropriate personal protective equipment should be used when preparing and using this reagent.
2. Run the appropriate positive and negative controls to ensure that the reagent solution is working properly.
3. The dye can be applied either by spraying, dipping, or by squirting from a wash bottle.
4. Cold water can be used to rinse away heavy background staining.
5. The excitation wavelength for this reagent is centered around 460 nm (blue).

* The Home Office Police Scientific Development Branch developed a water-based formulation for Basic Yellow 40 for crime scene use. Although the aqueous BY40 has health and safety advantages, it may not work as well as the ethanol-based formulation on some surfaces.

6. The emission maximum is centered around 490 nm and treated prints should be viewed with an orange filter.
7. When processing has been completed, all chemicals should be disposed of properly according to the appropriate federal, state, and local environmental laws.

5.1.6.3 MBD

MBD is the abbreviation for 7-(*p*-methoxybenzylamino)-4-nitrobenze-2-oxa-1,3-diazole.

Reagent preparation [67]

MBD stock solution

MBD	1 g
Acetone	1000 mL

1. The MBD and acetone should be mixed thoroughly.
2. The appropriate information (e.g., chemical contents, preparer's initials, date, reliability test result) should be recorded on the container's label.
3. The working solution should be stored in a glass bottle until ready for use.

MBD working solution

MBD stock solution	10 mL
Methanol	30 mL
Isopropanol	10 mL
Petroleum ether	950 mL

1. The MBD stock solution and solvents should be mixed thoroughly in the order listed.
2. The final addition of petroleum ether should be done slowly to ensure that separation into different layers does not occur.
3. The appropriate information (e.g., chemical contents, preparer's initials, date, reliability test result) should be recorded on the container's label.
4. The working solution has a shelf life of approximately 6 months and should be stored in a glass bottle until ready for use.

Reagent application

1. All appropriate personal protective equipment should be used when preparing and using this reagent.
2. Run the appropriate positive and negative controls to ensure that the reagent solution is working properly.
3. The dye can be applied either by spraying, dipping, or by squirting from a wash bottle.
4. Cold water can be used to rinse away heavy background staining.
5. The maximum excitation wavelength for this reagent is centered at 465 nm.
6. The emission maximum for this dye is centered at 515 nm and treated prints should be viewed with an orange filter.
7. When processing has been completed, all chemicals should be disposed of properly according to the appropriate federal, state, and local environmental laws.

5.1.6.4 Rhodamine 6G

Rhodamine 6G is a basic xanthene analog dye. The first mention of the use of rhodamine dyes for latent print detection was by Menzel and Duff in 1979 [69].

Reagent preparation [67]

Stock solution

Rhodamine 6G	1 g
Methanol	1000 mL

1. The rhodamine and methanol should be mixed thoroughly.
2. The appropriate information (e.g., chemical contents, preparer's initials, date, reliability test result) should be recorded on the container's label.
3. The working solution should be stored in a glass bottle until ready for use.

Working solution

R6G stock solution	3 mL
Acetone	15 mL
Acetonitrile	10 mL
Methanol	15 mL
Isopropanol	32 mL
Petroleum ether	925 mL

1. Rhodamine 6G stock solution and solvents should be mixed thoroughly in the order listed.
2. The final addition of petroleum ether should be done slowly to ensure that separation into different layers does not occur.
3. The appropriate information (e.g., chemical contents, preparer's initials, date, reliability test result) should be recorded on the container's label.
4. The working solution has a shelf life of approximately 6 months and should be stored in a glass bottle until ready for use.

Reagent application

1. All appropriate personal protective equipment should be used when preparing and using this reagent.
2. Run the appropriate positive and negative controls to ensure that the reagent solution is working properly.
3. The dye can be applied either by spraying, dipping, or by squirting from a wash bottle.
4. Cold water can be used to rinse away heavy background staining.
5. The excitation wavelength for this reagent is approximately 525 nm.
6. The emission maximum for rhodamine 6G is approximately 555 nm and treated prints should be viewed with orange goggles.
7. When processing has been completed, all chemicals should be disposed of properly according to the appropriate federal, state, and local environmental laws.

5.1.6.5 MRM 10

MRM 10 is a combination of three different dye stain stock solutions, MBD, rhodamine 6G, and Basic Yellow 40 (Maxilon Brilliant Flavine 10 GFF).

Reagent preparation [67]

Stock solution A

Rhodamine 6G	1 g
Methanol	1000 mL

1. The rhodamine and methanol should be mixed thoroughly.
2. The appropriate information (e.g., chemical contents, preparer's initials, date, reliability test result) should be recorded on the container's label.
3. The working solution should be stored in a glass bottle until ready for use.

Stock solution B

Basic Yellow 40	2 g
Methanol	1000 mL

1. The BY 40 and methanol should be mixed thoroughly.
2. The appropriate information (e.g., chemical contents, preparer's initials, date, reliability test result) should be recorded on the container's label.
3. The working solution should be stored in a glass bottle until ready for use.

Stock solution C

MBD	1 g
Acetone	1000 mL

1. The MBD and acetone should be mixed thoroughly.
2. The appropriate information (e.g., chemical contents, preparer's initials, date, reliability test result) should be recorded on the container's label.
3. The working solution should be stored in a glass bottle until ready for use.

Working solution

Stock solution A	3 mL
Stock solution B	3 mL
Stock solution C	7 mL
Methanol	20 mL
Isopropanol	10 mL
Acetonitrile	8 mL
Petroleum ether	950 mL

1. The stock solutions and solvents should be mixed thoroughly in the order listed.
2. The final addition of petroleum ether should be done slowly to ensure that separation into different layers does not occur.
3. The appropriate information (e.g., chemical contents, preparer's initials, date, reliability test result) should be recorded on the container's label.
4. The working solution has a shelf life of approximately 6 months and should be stored in a glass bottle until ready for use.

Reagent application

1. All appropriate personal protective equipment should be used when preparing and using this reagent.
2. Run the appropriate positive and negative controls to ensure that the reagent solution is working properly.
3. The dye can be applied either by spraying, dipping, or by squirting from a wash bottle.
4. Cold water can be used to rinse away heavy background staining.
5. The excitation wavelength range for this reagent is broad, between 365 and 530 nm.
6. Treated prints should be viewed with an orange filter.
7. When processing has been completed, all chemicals should be disposed of properly according to the appropriate federal, state, and local environmental laws.

5.1.6.6 RAM

RAM is a combination of three different dye stain solutions, rhodamine 6G, Ardrox, and MBD.

Reagent preparation [67]

Stock solution A

Rhodamine 6G	1 g
Methanol	1000 mL

1. The rhodamine and methanol should be mixed thoroughly.
2. The appropriate information (e.g., chemical contents, preparer's initials, date, reliability test result) should be recorded on the container's label.
3. The working solution should be stored in a glass bottle until ready for use.

Stock solution B

MBD	1 g
Acetone	1000 mL

1. The MBD and acetone should be mixed thoroughly.
2. The appropriate information (e.g., chemical contents, preparer's initials, date, reliability test result) should be recorded on the container's label.
3. The working solution should be stored in a glass bottle until ready for use.

Working solution

Stock solution A	3 mL
Ardrox P133D	2 mL
Stock solution B	7 mL
Methanol	20 mL
Isopropanol	10 mL
Acetonitrile	8 mL
Petroleum ether	950 mL

1. The stock solutions and solvents should be mixed thoroughly in the order listed.
2. The final addition of petroleum ether should be done slowly to ensure that separation into different layers does not occur.
3. The appropriate information (e.g., chemical contents, preparer's initials, date, reliability test result) should be recorded on the container's label.
4. The working solution has a shelf life of approximately 30 days and should be stored in a glass bottle until ready for use.

Reagent application

1. All appropriate personal protective equipment should be used when preparing and using this reagent.
2. Run the appropriate positive and negative controls to ensure that the reagent solution is working properly.
3. The dye can be applied either by spraying, dipping, or by squirting from a wash bottle.
4. Cold water can be used to rinse away heavy background staining.
5. The excitation wavelength range for this reagent is broad, between 365 and 530 nm.
6. Treated prints should be viewed with an orange filter.
7. When processing has been completed, all chemicals should be disposed of properly according to the appropriate federal, state, and local environmental laws.

5.1.6.7 RAY

RAY is a dye stain that incorporates rhodamine 6G, Ardrox, and Basic Yellow 40 and was first reported by Olenik in 1994 [70]. The dye stain was recently compared to Gentian violet and alternate black powder for its ability to develop prints on the adhesive side of tapes [71].

Reagent preparation [71]

Working solution

Basic Yellow 40	0.5 g
Glacial acetic acid	10 mL
Rhodamine 6G	0.05 g
Ardrox	4 mL
Isopropanol	450 mL
Acetonitrile	40 mL

1. The dyes and solvents should be mixed thoroughly in the order listed.
2. The appropriate information (e.g., chemical contents, preparer's initials, date, reliability test result) should be recorded on the container's label.
3. The working solution should be stored in a glass bottle until ready for use.

Reagent application

1. All appropriate personal protective equipment should be used when preparing and using this reagent.
2. Run the appropriate positive and negative controls to ensure that the reagent solution is working properly.

3. The dye can be applied either by spraying, dipping, or by squirting from a wash bottle.
4. Cold water can be used to rinse away heavy background staining.
5. The excitation wavelength range for this reagent is broad, between 450 and 550 nm.
6. Treated prints should be viewed with either an orange or red filter.
7. When processing has been completed, all chemicals should be disposed of properly according to the appropriate federal, state, and local environmental laws.

5.1.6.8 Thenoyl Europium Chelate

Thenoyl europium chelate (TEC) was first introduced in 1993 by Misner et al. [72]. It was described as an alternative to other dye stains, like Ardrox and rhodamine 6G, which have broad emission in areas that overlap commonly encountered substrates. In addition, TEC dye was reported to actually penetrate into the cyanoacrylate polymer, thus concentrating more dye and creating significantly stronger fluorescence. Other cyanoacrylate dye stains were found to react primarily at the surface of the cyanoacrylate [73]. TEC was reported to have a broad excitation centered at 350 nm (long-wave ultraviolet), but a very sharp emission at 614 nm.

The use of methyl ethyl ketone (MEK) in the dye formulation was found to be critical [74]. In optimum quantities, MEK allowed the TEC dye to penetrate into the cyanoacrylate polymer. The maximum volume percent of MEK was found to be 22% (with the remainder being water). The pH of the reagent was also found to be critical, with the optimum range between 7 and 8. Fluorescence intensities dropped off dramatically outside this narrow pH range. At low pH values, the hydrogen ion could compete with the metal ion to chelate to the enolate ion, while at high pH values the metal ion would form hydrated hydroxides rather than chelate complexes. The fluorescence could also be negatively impacted by the presence of buffers, such as citrate. The authors speculate that the carbonyl groups on the citrate ion extracted the europium metal ion and disrupted the formation of the thenoyl chelate.

A variation of this reagent was suggested by Lock et al. [75]. The stock solution was prepared by mixing 0.5 g EuTTAPhen in 60 mL of *n*-propanol and 40 mL of acetonitrile. The working solution was prepared by mixing 5 mL of the stock solution into 95 mL of petroleum ether. The excitation maximum for the chelate was determined to be centered around 350 nm with a narrow band (20 nm) emission centered around 612 nm. This reagent was also mixed with Basic Yellow 40 to create a new stain that had more excitation and emission wavelength ranges available to view print fluorescence.

Reagent preparation [74]

Stock solution

Europium trichloride hexahydrate	0.5 g
Distilled water	800 mL
Thenoyltrifluoroacetone	1.0 g
Methyl ethyl ketone	200 mL

1. Combine the europium trichloride and water together and stir until completely dissolved.
2. Combine the thenoyltrifluoroacetone and MEK together and stir until completely dissolved.

3. The aqueous solution is slowly poured into the MEK solution and then stirred vigorously for 5 min.
4. Because the chelate is not entirely soluble in the MEK/water mixture, it may have a faint milky appearance. Sonication for approximately 5 min can be helpful.
5. The appropriate information (e.g., chemical contents, preparer's initials, date, reliability test result) should be recorded on the container's label.

Working solution

Stock solution	100 mL
Methyl ethyl ketone	180 mL
Distilled water	720 mL

1. Combine the stock solution with 180 mL of methyl ethyl ketone.
2. Dilute the resulting solution with water and stir until a homogenous solution is obtained.
3. The appropriate information (e.g., chemical contents, preparer's initials, date, reliability test result) should be recorded on the container's label.

Reagent application

1. All appropriate personal protective equipment should be used when preparing and using this reagent.
2. Run the appropriate positive and negative controls to ensure that the reagent solution is working properly.
3. The TEC reagent is typically applied by the use of a wash bottle.
4. Once the MEK has evaporated the area of interest can be washed with a rinse (containing 80% methanol, 15% water, and 5% Tergitol 7).
5. For larger items, a 10-fold dilution of the reagent described earlier will be required to minimize background development.
6. Items can be immersed into this solution but should be checked for development at regular time intervals.
7. The methanol-based rinse solution can also be used for these items as well.
8. When processing has been completed, all chemicals should be disposed of properly according to the appropriate federal, state, and local environmental laws.

5.1.6.9 Gentian Violet

Gentian violet (also known as methyl violet 10B or C.I. basic violet 3) is part of a broader class of dyes called triarylmethines (these dyes have traditionally been referred to as "triarylmethanes", but this nomenclature is incorrect since the central carbon is actually sp^2 hybridized. These were some of the first synthetic dyes produced during the latter half of the nineteenth century. They are commonly used in ballpoint ink formulations. The use of gentian violet as a post-cyanoacrylate dye stain was reported by Kobus et al. in 1983 [76]. The authors noted that samples fumed with cyanoacrylate needed an additional 2 h of exposure to the atmosphere to complete the polymerization process. Freshly fumed prints were found not to adequately absorb the dye stain. Gentian violet was found to produce good results on polyethylene, but not on metallic surfaces like aluminum. The ability of a variety of biological stains and commercial fabric dyes to stain cyanoacrylate-fumed prints was reported by Kempton et al. [77]. Most of the biological stains tested (with the exception of gentian violet) failed to adequately stain cyanoacrylate-fumed prints as efficiently as hot solutions of the commercial fabric dyes. Gentian violet was also used to develop a print on a cyanoacrylate-fumed surface (a closed-circuit camera system) when conventional powders and fluorescent dye stains (due to strong background fluorescence from the substrate) were ineffective [78].

Reagent preparation

Staining solution

Gentian violet	1 g
Distilled/RO-DI water	1000 mL

1. Gentian violet should be mixed with the water and stirred until it has completely dissolved.
2. The appropriate information (e.g., chemical contents, preparer's initials, date, reliability test result) should be recorded on the container's label.
3. This solution should be stored in a glass bottle and is stable indefinitely.

Reagent application

1. All appropriate personal protective equipment should be used when preparing and using this reagent.
2. Run the appropriate positive and negative controls to ensure that the reagent solution is working properly.
3. Items to be processed should be placed into a tray containing the staining solution. The solution should be continually agitated during the entire development time.
4. For larger objects, spraying or painting may be used to apply the reagent.
5. Distilled or RO-DI water can be used to rinse excess reagent from the substrate surface.
6. When processing has been completed, all chemicals should be disposed of properly according to the appropriate federal, state, and local environmental laws.

5.1.6.10 Sudan Black

In a manner similar to Gentian violet, Sudan black (Solvent Black 3) can also be used as a post cyanoacrylate fuming dye. Its dark black color can create good contrast on lighter-colored surfaces. There are several examples in the literature of the use of Sudan black in this fashion. Munroe reported on the use of Sudan black in conjunction with cyanoacrylate fuming to recover latent fingerprint evidence on a concrete abutment from a parking lot [79]. A series of laboratory tests were conducted on concrete to validate the sequence. However, when this procedure was used on the actual crime scene evidence, only smudges were developed. Monday reported the successful recovery of a print on a clear, plastic bag used to cover a homicide victim [80]. The bag was processed twice with cyanoacrylate fumes and followed by application of the dye stain Ardrox; however, no identifiable prints were found. After several applications of Sudan black and rinsing yielded an identifiable print. A recommended formula for Sudan black was provided in the chapter on lipid reagents.

5.1.7 One-Step Fluorescent Cyanoacrylate Fuming

The idea of using a dye that can copolymerize with methyl cyanoacrylate fumes began back in the late 1980s. With funding from the National Institutes of Justice, the Alaska Department of Public Safety Laboratory, in coordination with Minnesota Mining and Manufacturing (3M), developed a fuming wand with a special cartridge that contained a magenta-colored dye from the styryl family [81]. When the cartridge was heated, the dye would copolymerize with the methyl cyanoacrylate to produce pink-colored, fluorescent prints in one step. An argon ion laser was used to excite the developed prints and a red-orange filter (approximately 600 nm) was used to view the fluorescence. Recently, a new product (CN Yellow) was introduced [82]. After testing more than 800 potential dyes, a dye was selected with an excitation range between 415 and 470 nm and emission between 450 and 650 nm. A future product with an excitation range of 505–540 nm was to be developed. Another new product, PolyCyano UV,* has also shown some promise for developing fluorescent cyanoacrylate prints in one step [83].

Other attempts have been made to chemically alter the structure of the cyanoacrylate to incorporate functional groups that would promote the formation of a fluorescent polymer on latent print residue. The Bundeskriminalamt (Wiesbaden, Germany) and Fresenius Technical University collaborated on such an effort between 1991 and 1994 [84]. To date, none of these efforts has proven to be successful. Recent efforts have once again focused on creating new cyanoacrylate monomers that contain either colored or fluorescent functional groups [85]. Various compounds were trialed, including adducts of cyanoacrylic acid-anthracene, esters of cyanoacrylic acid-anthracene, and ethyl cyanoacrylate-anthracene. Unfortunately, the compounds evaluated decomposed before becoming volatile and thus failed to form colored or fluorescent prints.

5.1.8 Health and Safety

There are a number of health and safety issues associated with cyanoacrylate ester fuming. Several sources have discussed the dangers involved with inhalation of the cyanoacrylate vapors [86]. Another serious complication caused by heating cyanoacrylate monomers or polymers is the formation of hydrogen cyanide gas. One source lists the critical temperature point at 205°C (400°F) [87]. Another source reports that heating to temperatures as low as 120°C (250°F) can increase toxicity, and temperatures as high as 205°C (400°F) can generate hydrogen cyanide [88]. At 222°C (431°F) 6.2 μg of hydrogen cyanide was detected while at 274°C (525°F) 108 μg were measured. The optimum temperature range for heating cyanoacrylates was found to be between 88°C and 99°C (190°F –210°F). There is also a danger caused by the compound's relatively low flash-point of 83°C (181°F) [89].

Recently, Fung et al. made quantitative measurements of the amount of hydrogen cyanide (HCN) generated from heating ethyl cyanoacrylate at different temperatures [90]. The amount of cyanide anion (CN^-) was then measured using either the sodium picrate or picrate-resorcinol methods. When the ethyl cyanoacrylate was heated to 180°C, no HCN was detected. However, beginning at temperatures as low as 200°C, a 1 g sample of Loctite Hard Evidence heated for 30 min generated 10 μg of HCN. A significant increase in HCN was detected at temperatures above 260°C. At 280°C, the same material generated 100 μg

* This product was originally developed in Japan and marketed by Lukia Co., Ltd. For additional information, see: http://www.fosterfreeman.com/index.php?option=com_content&view=article&id=273 (accessed November 10, 2011).

of HCN. Heating the polymeric form of cyanoacrylate typically generated more HCN than the corresponding amount of the liquid monomer.

The authors noted that in Australia, the time-weighted average concentration limit for workplace exposure to hydrogen cyanide is 11 mg/m^3. HCN is considered lethal at concentrations from 100 mg/m^3. These levels would not be reached using conventional procedures where heating temperatures are limited to approximately 120°C. However, exposure levels could become more significant when improvised delivery systems are used (e.g., at crime scenes). Fung et al. measured the temperatures generated by a commercially available fuming wand [91]. This device was found to produce a temperature of about 290°C at the tip and 350°C at the center of the cyanoacrylate cartridge. Caution should be taken with these types of devices as significant amounts of HCN could be generated at these elevated temperatures.

5.2 Iodine

The year 1876 is often cited throughout the literature as the first reported use of iodine vapors by Aubert to visualize latent prints [92]. However, a recent discovery by Quinche and Margot traced the advent of iodine fuming back to 1863 [93]. Paul Jean Coulier had used iodine vapors to detect document alterations, but inadvertently observed that latent print impressions could also be detected by this technique. His observation was very similar to that of scientists in the early twentieth century, who noted that their prints developed on paper chromatograms when sprayed with ninhydrin. Coulier's method involved the use of a mixture of iodine and fine sand (4:100). The paper was placed over the mixture and was allowed to develop for 15–60 min. Of additional interest was Coulier's observation that these developed prints could be used to identify the person who originally touched the paper. This would make Coulier among the first to suggest the use of fingerprints for identification purposes.

Mitchell noted that iodine was one of the most sensitive latent print detection reagents available in the 1920s [94]. In his article, he reported that Coulier (as well as Aubert) had suggested the technique many years before. Mitchell also mentions the use of osmium and ruthenium tetroxide as potential fuming agents (these will be discussed later). The method was a mainstay in most fingerprint development texts up until the late 1980s [92,95–97]. Iodine fuming was recommended in the first edition of the Home Office Manual in 1986, but was eliminated in subsequent revisions. As more sensitive visualization techniques were developed, iodine gradually began to be phased out of most laboratories by the late twentieth century.

5.2.1 Chemistry and Mechanism

Iodine is part of the group 17 ("nonmetal elements") of the periodic table, which are better known as the halogens. It was discovered in 1811 by Bernard Courtois, who was attempting to find a new source of saltpeter (potassium nitrate) to make gunpowder during the Napoleonic Wars. It is the first element in the series to exist in a solid form (bromine is a liquid and chlorine and fluorine are gases). The only other solid halogen is astatine, which is incredibly rare (only a millionth of a gram has ever been produced) and intensely radioactive. Iodine was best known for its antiseptic qualities (these were alcohol-based solutions that were also known as "tincture of iodine") and its use in the form of potassium iodide tablets to prevent absorption of radioactive iodine by saturating the thyroid gland.

Halogens are very capable of selectively adding across carbon–carbon double bonds (*trans* addition) of unsaturated hydrocarbons (e.g., oleic acid) [98]. Iodine can do this at room temperature without a catalyst. In fact, it is used to quantitatively determine the number of double bonds in unsaturated compounds (a process known as determining the iodine number). This was once considered a mechanism for the iodine reaction with latent print residue. Although unsaturated compounds can be found in these deposits, their chemical reaction with iodine leads to the formation of colorless products.

The mechanism is more likely due to physical absorption rather than a chemical addition reaction. This would also tend to explain the fugitive nature of the developed print (i.e., the reaction process is reversible). Almog et al. noted several observations that supported that conclusion [99]. First, they observed that the rate of reaction for the addition of iodine across a carbon–carbon double bond was very slow. This would be in contrast to the nearly instantaneous coloration observed when iodine fumes come in contact with latent prints. Secondly, the successful fixation of iodine-developed prints requires the presence of free iodine (not bound by a carbon–iodine bond). Finally, the use of test prints prepared using solutions free of fatty materials (i.e., free of compounds with carbon–carbon double bonds) still produced colored impressions upon exposure to iodine fumes.

Almog et al. believed that water appeared to be a key factor in the iodine reaction [99]. For relatively fresh prints, there was an attractive force generated by the constant dipole of water and the induced dipole of iodine. This process was thought to be enhanced by the presence of inorganic salts in the latent print deposit. By developing an apparatus that simultaneously generated steam and iodine fumes, the authors were able to develop dark purple prints that were up to 110 days old. This was thought to be due to adsorbed iodine reacting with starch in the paper in the presence of excess water.

5.2.2 Iodine Fixation

One of the main drawbacks of the iodine fuming process is the lack of permanence of the developed prints. Generally, prints will fade within a number of days. One of the first fixatives was mentioned by Coulier in 1863 and involved the use of silver acetonitrate and gallic acid [93]. Mitchell noted that the use of silver salts followed by thiosulfate could achieve similar results [94]. Bridges mentioned that the use of an aqueous calcium chloride and potassium bromide solution was found to produce superior results, compared to a 10% tannic acid solution (applied by brush) [95]. Two different solutions (one containing gum Arabic, alum, and formaldehyde and the other acetone, gun cotton, absolute ethanol, and ether) were also recommended and applied as a spray. Palladium chloride, which turns iodine prints dark brown, was also recommended [96]. Starch solutions have been used to fix iodine prints since the 1930s (initially reported in Europe) [92]. These starch solutions were typically sprayed onto a surface using an atomizer or similar device. Tap water will also temporarily stabilize the print and cause it to turn a dark blue color [100]. It can be applied by soaking a piece of cotton, the use of an atomizer, or by steam from an iron.

Transferring of the iodine-developed prints onto a silver plate has been used since it was publicized by McMorris during the mid-1930s [101]. Either a thoroughly cleaned tin or silver plate was pressed against a processed surface for about 5 s. The plate was then exposed to a light source (for at least 30 s), after which the image would gradually become visible. Silver was found to be more effective than tin. A silver-plated copper Daguerreotype plate was found to be a more economic alternative, without compromising development quality [102].

One of the more significant advances in rendering iodine prints more permanent was reported by Trowell in 1975 [103]. The author noted that iodine reacted with a number of different compounds to produce colored products. Tetrabase (*p,p′*-tetramethyldiaminodiphenylmethane), in the presence of an oxidizing agent like iodine, was found to undergo a redox reaction that resulted in a blue-green-colored product. A 0.2% w/v solution was typically prepared in Freon 113 (1,1,2-trichlorotrifluoroethane) and applied by dipping the material into the solution or by placing the iodine print on a pad consisting of tetrabase powder dispersed in a silicone rubber putty (0.2 g per 10 g of uncured silicone rubber).

None of these fixatives is practical for routine operational use (particularly from a health and safety standpoint). A significant breakthrough was reported by Mashiko and Hizaki in 1977 [104]. The compound 7,8-benzoflavone was found to stabilize the fading of iodine developed prints (via inclusion upon drying), producing a dark purple-colored product. The reagent was prepared by first dissolving 0.3 g of 7,8-benzoflavone in 10 mL of chloroform and then adding 90 mL of cyclohexane. The authors reported successful development on a document containing a latent print that was soaked in water for 1 h. The print was split and one-half processed with ninhydrin and the other iodine-benzoflavone. Good detail was developed on the iodine-benzoflavone side while the ninhydrin side produced only a smudge. The benzoflavone method does not produce a permanently colored print. Ozone (present in air) begins to break down the complex in less than 1 week. To remove the color, a solution of acetone and hydrogen peroxide (an aggressive oxidizing agent) could be used.

Haque et al. reported that a combination of iodine and benzoflavone in one solution enhanced the reaction [105]. The reagent was typically applied to a surface using an aerosol sprayer. Prints up to several weeks old were successfully developed using this reagent on surfaces such as bond papers, newsprint, checks, Kraft paper, cardboard, paper towels, and painted items. In the event that decolorization was required, ammonia vapor, ammonium hydroxide, or dilute sodium or potassium hydroxide solutions could be used.

5.2.3 Operational Usage

Over the years, there have been many methods reported for the application of iodine to porous and nonporous surfaces.

5.2.3.1 Vapor Method

The use of iodine vapors was first reported by Coulier in 1863 [93]. Prints were developed at room temperature without any other catalyst. The vapor method was in use at the Federal Bureau of Investigation's Technical Laboratory as early as the mid-1930s [106]. The fuming method was typically conducted at room temperature in a fuming box with a clear glass front for observation. A small amount of iodine crystals (~1.0 g) was placed into an evaporating dish and placed in the bottom center of the cabinet. Items to be processed were suspended above the evaporating dish. Heat (~50°C) could be applied to speed up the process. In 1948, examiners with the San Diego Police Laboratory introduced modifications to the technique, including the "iodine vaporizer" and the "vapor frame" [107].

The most well-known portable vapor method for iodine involves the use of a fuming "gun." Such devices have been reported as far back as the 1930s [106]. The basic construction of such a device involved the packing of a glass tube with iodine (~0.5 g) and calcium chloride crystals separated by glass wool [95]. Devices with two separate glass chambers have also been reported [100]. A device with separate tubes for each component can also be used. A rubber tube was used to supply warm breath, which was first dried by the calcium chloride and then passed through the glass wool to the iodine crystals. The temperature of the air is sufficient to sublimate the iodine crystals and produce violet fumes, which were then expelled from the device. Interestingly, the use of such a device to fume physical developer prints appeared to enhance their contrast [108]. In some cases, new ridge detail not visualized by physical developer was observed.

These devices are no longer recommended because of the danger of inhaling toxic iodine fumes. In fact, the corrosive nature of iodine vapors could degrade any rubber components of a fuming gun, which could lead to leaks. A variation of the traditional fuming gun that eliminated the need for human breath to sublime the iodine was introduced by Ross in 1956 [92]. This device used an electric lamp to heat the iodine crystals and pressurized, heated air (generated from squeezing a rubber bulb) to expel the vapors. A power source was required for the lamp. This innovative device still did not eliminate the hazards associated with inhaling the expelled fumes.

Another interesting variation of this fuming method was introduced by MacDonell and was called the porous glass iodine fuming technique [109]. Dry iodine powder (called Driodine) was mixed with porous glass (96% silica, 4 nm pore diameter). As this mixture is spread over a surface, the impregnated iodine in the porous glass was released as a vapor at a controlled rate. A variation of this involved impregnating an absorbent material (e.g., paper towel) with iodine and sandwiching it between two glass plates [97].

5.2.3.2 Dusting Method

Iodine crystals can be ground into a fine dust and used in a similar fashion to other conventional powders [96]. Care must be exercised to avoid leaving the iodine powder in contact too long with the paper surface, since background discoloration could occur. A variation of this technique involved placing the iodine powder directly onto the surface. The substrate is then agitated back and forth until development was observed. Overdevelopment of the print detail and background were noted as possible disadvantages of this technique. A modification of this technique involved mixing iodine powder with finely ground chalk (1:2 ratio) to produce better development and contrast [110].

5.2.3.3 Solution Method

Several different reagent solutions have been reported. Haque et al. proposed a more modern version that involved mixing the iodine and 7,8-benzoflavone together into one working solution. This solution was found to be unstable and must be used within 1 h [105]. Pounds and Hussain reported that a reagent, prepared by combining 2 mL of a 10% w/v 7,8-benzoflavone solution with 100 mL of a 0.1% w/v iodine solution (in cyclohexane), could be painted onto large surfaces at crime scenes [111].

Reagent preparation [105]

Stock solution

7,8-Benzoflavone	1.0 g
Methylene chloride	33 mL
Cyclohexane	300 mL

1. 7,8-Benzoflavone should be mixed with the methylene chloride until it is completely dissolved.
2. The cyclohexane should be carefully added and stirred to create a homogeneous mixture.
3. This solution should be stored in a glass or plastic bottle.
4. The appropriate information (e.g., chemical contents, preparer's initials, date, reliability test result) should be recorded on the container's label.

Working solution

Iodine crystals	0.3 g
Stock solution	150 mL

1. The iodine crystals should be added to the stock solution and mixed thoroughly.
2. The working solution should be prepared only when needed. Once mixed, the solution must be used within 1 h.

Reagent application

1. All appropriate personal protective equipment should be used when preparing and using this reagent.
2. Run the appropriate positive and negative controls to ensure that the reagent solution is working properly.
3. The working solution should be transferred to a spraying device (e.g., spray bottle, atomizer).
4. The item should be lightly sprayed multiple times to develop optimum contrast. Heavier spraying can lead to blurring.
5. The dark blue-colored product will last only 2–7 days. Images of developed print detail should be taken as soon as possible.
6. When processing has been completed, all chemicals should be disposed of properly according to the appropriate federal, state, and local environmental laws.

5.3 Miscellaneous Fuming Techniques

Historically, many chemicals have been used in vapor form to visualize latent prints on a variety of different substrates. Most of these historical methods have been abandoned due to their acute toxicities. Some of these materials include hydrogen fluoride, hydrochloric acid, hydrobromic acid, mercuric iodine, hydrogen sulfide, and nitric acid [96]. More recently, a series of fluorogenic reagents was evaluated in the vapor phase [112]. The reagents evaluated (excited using ultraviolet radiation) included anthracene, anthranilic acid, perylene, rhodamine B, rhodamine 6G, 7-diethylamino-4-methylcoumarin, triphenylcarbinol, and antimony trichloride. Anthranilic acid produced the best results on fresh prints while anthracene performed best on prints a few days old. Neither compound worked well when used as a powder to dust surfaces. There are some additional historical and some novel fuming methods described in the following sections.

5.3.1 Osmium/Ruthenium Tetroxide

Osmium (atomic number 76) and ruthenium (atomic number 44) are part of the group 8 elements of the periodic table and are also part of the platinum group metals. These two compounds are typically separated from each other in their tetroxide forms. The use of these compound for the visualization of latent prints dates back at least to 1920 [94]. Mitchell noted that the use of osmium tetroxide in the vapor form would be expected to be more sensitive than osmic acid, but not as sensitive as iodine vapor. He also speculated that ruthenium tetroxide or other volatile ruthenium salts would also be effective latent print reagents. These compounds are well known in organic chemistry as strong oxidizing compounds. They will oxidize most hydrocarbons to a cyclic ester and then form a vicinal diol via hydrolysis [113]. However, these compounds are not likely to be colored. They can directly stain lipids in their vapor form and have been used for improving contrast in transmission and scanning electron microscopy specimens.

Although classic fingerprint texts continued to mention the use of these two compounds well into the 1970s [96], their use was limited by cost, toxicity, and their tendency to explode violently when heated [114]. However, a new method was reported that eliminated the need for heating and generated the compounds via a chemical reaction [115]. Ruthenium tetroxide (RTX) vapor was produced by mixing a 0.1% w/v aqueous solution of ruthenium chloride with an 11.3% w/v aqueous solution of ammonium cerium nitrate in equal volumes (in a closed chamber). Upon reaction with sebaceous material in the latent print residue, a black-colored product, ruthenium dioxide, was reported to form. The authors also reported that dark surfaces could be processed with this method and then lifted onto white lifting media to create contrast. Results were reported to be significantly better with sebaceous material than with eccrine residues. RTX fuming was also reported to not inhibit development if used prior to 1,8-diazafluoren-9-one (DFO) (fluorescence) or ninhydrin treatments; however, the use of RTX fuming after these techniques was found to be detrimental.

Dipping items into the aforementioned solution was reported to produce better results than the vapor fuming process [113]. However, interest in the fuming method was renewed upon the publication of a significant refinement of the original method [116]. In the new method, ruthenium tetroxide was dissolved in a saturated halogenide (e.g., tetradecafluorohexane). This produced a yellow, nonflammable reagent that could be applied to surfaces via a simple spraying device. Brownish-black prints could be developed on a variety of surfaces, including regular and thermal paper, leather, vinyl, wood, and human skin. In the latter case, RTX was found to work better on dead bodies than with live skin samples [117]. Items could be dipped directly into the reagent solution as well. The developed prints can also be lifted from dark surfaces to improve contrast. When using the reagent in a nonlaboratory setting, extreme care must be taken to avoid skin contact with or inhalation of the vapors.

A comprehensive evaluation of this new RTX method was conducted by Flynn et al. [118]. The authors formulated a cheaper alternative to the commercially available RTX solution using HFE 7100. Although this alternative was found to produce less background staining, the reagent solution was less stable and began to breakdown after 24 h. Increasing the concentration of ceric ammonium nitrate from 0.5% w/v to 5% w/v increased the stability up to 2 months. When compared to iodine-benzoflavone, RTX produced good results only on relatively fresh prints (generally less than 3 days old). Iodine-benzoflavone was able to develop ridge detail up to 5 days old on surfaces like brick and raw wood. RTX was also determined to significantly impact sequential processing.

It had a detrimental effect when used prior to powdering and cyanoacrylate fuming with rhodamine 6G staining. Ultimately, the authors concluded that safety risks associated with the RTX reagent would limit its usage at crime scenes.

5.3.2 Flame/Soot Method

The flame process was first used on an experimental basis in 1904 and was reported to work well on older prints that did not respond well to traditional powdering methods [96]. Research was conducted during the 1950s by examiners at the U.S. Army Criminal Investigation Laboratory. The best materials for creating the dark-colored soot were found to be soft resinous pine, camphor, pine tar, and nitrocellulose plastics. Medlin preferred the soft resinous pine wood [119]. For creating light-colored "soot" particles, magnesium and titanium tetrachloride [120] were recommended. When organic materials like camphor are burned, a yellow diffusion flame is produced (similar to a candle). The flame itself is composed of incandescent carbon/soot particles. Soot is formed when there is an excess amount of fuel (e.g., camphor) and limited source of oxidant (i.e., oxygen).

The flame process was traditionally used after powdering methods failed to produce any ridge detail. The item was typically passed over the top of the flame until sufficient soot was deposited on the substrate. Excess soot could be removed with a feather or fiberglass brush. The technique could be used on a variety of surfaces, including unpainted tin and the rough surface of a padlock [121], handguns, cartridge casings [122], and stained glass [123]. In fact, prints may be naturally developed by soot at arson scenes, where items may be protected from intense heat or water damage. One study noted that prints could be recovered in such situations (using a cold water rinse to remove excess soot), even on a light fixture that was directly above the point of origin of the fire [124]. Successful recovery of prints in rooms adjacent to the point of origin was also noted.

5.3.3 Disulfur Dinitride

Recently, the use of disulfur dinitride under reduced pressure to visualize latent prints has been reported [125,126]. Preliminary results indicated that prints could be developed on a variety of substrates, including aluminum foil, paper, cotton, plastics, adhesive tapes, and pottery. Disulfur dinitride (S_2N_2) can be generated by the thermal cracking of S_4N_4 in the presence of silver wool. The resulting S_2N_2 was found to interact with as yet unknown constituents of latent prints to form the dark blue/black $(SN)_x$ polymer. The amount of time required to fully visualize a latent print can vary from 10 to 60 min. Recently, Bleay et al. observed that on metallic surfaces, the technique could visualize prints after they had been removed [127]. A minimum deposition time of 30 min was required before removal. Once the print was removed, it appeared that the S_2N_2 polymerized preferentially on the oxide-free surface of the metal. It should be noted that in their pure forms, S_2N_2 and S_4N_4 are friction-sensitive and could decompose explosively above 30°C.

References

1. O'Connor JT. (1994) Sticking with winners. *Chem Tech*:51–57.
2. Bot GM, Bot KG, Ogunranti JO, Onah JA, Sule AZ, Hassan I, Dung ED. (2010) The use of cyanoacrylate in surgical anastomosis: an alternative to microsurgery. *J Surg Tech Case Rep* 2:44–48.

3. German E. http://onin.com/fp/cyanoho.html (accessed 9/7/10).
4. Bourdon LP. (1981) U.S. Patent 4,297,383.
5. Kendall FG. (1982) Super glue® fuming for the development of latent fingerprints. *Ident News* 32(2):3–5.
6. Norkus PM. (1982) Glue it. *Ident News* 32(2):6.
7. Kendall FG, Rehn BW. (1982) Rapid method of super glue fuming for the development of latent fingerprints. *Ident News* 32(6):3–4.
8. Martingale WE. (1983) Cyanoacrylate fuming as a method for rapid development of latent fingerprints utilizing anhydrous sodium carbonate as a dry catalyst. *Ident News* 33(11):13.
9. Sampson WC. (1994) Effective and cost efficient catalyst (sawdust). *J Forensic Ident* 44(2):191–192.
10. Olenik JH. (1983) Super glue—a modified method. *Ident News* 33(1):9–10.
11. Besonen JA. (1983) Heat acceleration of the super glue fuming method for development of latent fingerprints. *Ident News* 33(2):3–4.
12. Mock JP. (1984) Super glue fuming techniques—a comparison between methods of acceleration. *Ident News* 34(11):7, 10.
13. Sahs PT, Wojcik RJ. (1984) Moisture catalyst for cyanoacrylate fuming. *Ident News* 34(9):9–10.
14. Gilman PL, Sahs PT, Gorajczyk JS. (1985) Stabilized cyanoacrylate. *Ident News* 35(3):7.
15. Grimm MR, Taylor RA. (1984) Super glue sticks it to the bad guys! *Ident News* 34(3):7, 11.
16. Almog J, Gabay A. (1986) A modified super glue® technique—the use of polycyanoacrylate for fingerprint development. *J Forensic Sci* 31(1):250–253.
17. Woods J, Guthrie J, Rooney J, Kelly L, Doyle A, Noonan E. (1989) Vapour deposition of poly(alkyl-2-cyanoacrylate) resist coatings: a new electron-beam/deep-ultra-violet photoresist technology. *Polymer* 30:1091–1098.
18. Solomons TWG. (1988) *Organic Chemistry*, 4th edn. John Wiley & Sons, New York.
19. Ramotowski RS. (2001) Composition of latent print residue. In: Lee HC, Gaensslen RE. (Eds.) *Advances in Fingerprint Technology*, 2nd edn. CRC Press, Boca Raton, FL.
20. Lee HC, Gaensslen RE. (1984) Cyanoacrylate fuming. *Ident News* 34(6):8–14.
21. Burns DT, Brown JK, Dinsmore A, Harvey KK. (1998) Base-activated latent fingerprints fumed with a cyanoacyrlate monomer. a quantitative study using Fourier-transform infra-red spectroscopy. *Anal Chim Acta* 362:171–176.
22. Czekanski P, Fasola M, Allison J. (2006) A mechanistic model for the superglue fuming of latent prints. *J Forensic Sci* 51(6):1323–1328.
23. Moores E, Bandey H. (2003) Effectiveness of superglue on articles that have been wetted. Presented at the International Fingerprint Research Group Meeting, St. Albans, Hertfordshire, U.K., May.
24. Lewis LA, Smithwick RW, Devault GL, Bolinger B, Lewis SA. (2001) Processes involved in the development of latent fingerprints using the cyanoacrylate fuming method. *J Forensic Sci* 46(2):241–246.
25. Wargacki SP, Lewis LA, Dadmun MD. (2007) Understanding the chemistry of the development of latent fingerprints by superglue fuming. *J Forensic Sci* 52(5):1057–1062.
26. Wargacki SP, Lewis LA, Dadmun MD. (2008) Enhancing the quality of aged latent fingerprints developed by superglue fuming: loss and replenishment of initiator. *J Forensic Sci* 53(5):1138–1144.
27. Pinto VJ, Stevenson SH. (2010) Analysis of aged fingerprints and enhancement of the cyanoacrylate fuming method. *Ident Canada* 33(2):44–65.
28. McLaren C, Lennard C, Stoilovic M. (2010) Methylamine pretreatment of dry latent fingermarks on polyethylene for enhanced detection by cyanoacrylate fuming. *J Forensic Ident* 60(2):199–222.
29. McDonald D, Pope H, Miskelly GM. (2008) The effect of chlorine and hydrogen chloride on latent fingermark evidence. *Forensic Sci Int* 179:70–77.
30. Bandey H, Kent T. (2003) Superglue treatment of crime scenes: a trial of the effectiveness of the Mason Vactron SUPERfume process. Home Office Police Scientific Development Branch Publication No. 30/03.
31. Kent T, ed. (1986) *Manual of Fingerprint Development Techniques*, 1st edn. U.K. Home Office, Police Scientific Development Branch, Sandridge, U.K.

32. Paine M, Bandey HL, Bleay SM, Wilson H. (2011) The effect of relative humidity on the effectiveness of the cyanoacrylate fuming process for fingermark development and on the microstructure of the developed marks. *Forensic Sci Int* 212:130–142.
33. Barclay F. (1986) Cyanoacrylates—filtration, recovery, and re-use. *Fingerprint Whorld* 12(46):37–38.
34. Stokes M, Brennan J. (1995) A free standing cabinet for cyanoacrylate fuming. *Forensic Sci Int* 71(3):181–190.
35. Weaver DE, Clary EJ. (1989) Cyanoacrylate inhibitor. *J Forensic Ident* 39(3):175–176.
36. Weaver DE, Clary EJ. (1993) A one-step fluorescent cyanoacrylate fingerprint development technology. *J Forensic Ident* 43(5):481–492.
37. Froude JH. (1996) The super glue fuming wand: a preliminary evaluation. *J Forensic Ident* 46(1):19–31.
38. Tissier P, Didierjean J-C, Prud'homme C, Pichard J, Crispino F. (1999) A "cyanoacrylate case" to develop fingerprints in cars. *Sci Justice* 39(3):163–166.
39. Karlinszky L, Harkai G. (1990) Detection of latent fingerprints: application of cyanoacrylate for the inside of cars. *Forensic Sci Int* 46:29–30.
40. Weaver DE. (1993) Large scale cyanoacrylate fuming. *J Forensic Ident* 43(2):135–137.
41. Springer E. (1996) Two techniques for improving fingerprint yield. In: Almog J, Springer E, Eds. In: *Proceedings of the International Symposium on Fingerprint Detection and Identification*. Hemed Press, Jerusalem, Israel, pp. 109–113.
42. Hebrand J, Donche A, Jaret Y, Loyan S. (1996) Revelation of fingerprints with cyanoacrylate vapours traditional treatment/vacuum treatment. In: Almog J, Springer E, Eds., *Proceedings of the International Symposium on Fingerprint Detection and Identification*. Hemed Press, Jerusalem, Israel, pp. 67–78.
43. Campbell BM. (1991) Vacuum chamber cyanoacrylate technique evolution. *RCMP Gazette* 53(12):12–16.
44. Yamashita AB. (1994) Use of a benchtop desiccator for vacuum cyanoacrylate treatment of latent prints. *J Forensic Ident* 44(2):149–158.
45. Watkin JE, Wilkinson DE, Misner AH, Yamashita AB. (1994) Cyanoacrylate fuming of latent prints: vacuum versus heat/humidity. *J Forensic Ident* 44(5):545–556.
46. Kent T, Winfield P. (1996) Superglue fingerprint development—atmospheric pressure and high humidity, or vacuum evaporation? In: Almog J, Springer E, Eds., *Proceedings of the International Symposium on Fingerprint Detection and Identification*. Hemed Press, Jerusalem, Israel, pp. 59–66.
47. Chan A, Kinsella H. (2002) Cyanoacrylate fuming: latent fingerprint development under atmospheric and vacuum conditions. *Ident Canada* 25(3):9–12.
48. Bessman CW, Nelson E, Lipert RJ, Coldiron S, Herrman TR. (2005) A comparison of cyanoacrylate fuming in a vacuum cabinet to a humidity fuming chamber. *J Forensic Ident* 55(1):10–27.
49. Hamm ED. (1984) Cyanoacrylate, maybe! *Ident News* 34(5):5,13–14.
50. Menzel ER, Burt JA, Sinor TW, Tubach-Ley WB, Jordan KJ. (1983) Laser detection of latent fingerprints: treatment with glue containing cyanoacrylate ester. *J Forensic Sci* 28(2):307–317.
51. Stoilovic M, Kobus HJ, Warrener RN. (1983) Luminescent enhancement of fingerprints developed with super glue: a case example. *Fingerprint Whorld* 9(33):17–18.
52. Olsen RD. (1984) A practical fluorescent dye staining technique for cyanoacrylate-developed latent prints. *Ident News* 34(4):5,11–12.
53. Mazzella WD, Lennard CJ. (1995) An additional study of cyanoacrylate stains. *J Forensic Ident* 45(1):5–18.
54. Misner AH. (1992) Latent fingerprint detection on low density polyethylene comparing vacuum metal deposition to cyanoacrylate fuming and fluorescence. *J Forensic Ident* 42(1):26–33.
55. Masters NE, DeHaan JD. (1996) Vacuum metal deposition and cyanoacrylate detection of older latent prints. *J Forensic Ident* 46(1):32–45.
56. Thiburce N, Becue A, Champod C, Crispino F. (2011) Design of a control slide for cyanoacrylate polymerization: application to the CA-Bluestar sequence. *J Forensic Ident* 61(3):232–249.

57. Jasuja OP, Singh GD, Sodhi GS. (2007) Development of latent fingerprints on compact discs and its effects on subsequent data recovery. *Forensic Sci Int* 156(2–3):237–241.
58. Templin RH, Nielson JP. (1988) Evaluation of the effects of cyanoacrylate processing on pistol and revolver trigger pull. *J Forensic Ident* 38(4):161–164.
59. Shipp E, Roelofs R, Togneri E, Wright R, Atkinson D, Henry B. (1993) Effects of argon laser light, alternate source light, and cyanoacrylate fuming on DNA typing of human bloodstains. *J Forensic Sci* 38(1):184–191.
60. Zamir A, Springer E, Glattstein B. (2000) Fingerprints and DNA: STR typing of DNA extracted from adhesive tape after processing for fingerprints. *J Forensic Sci* 45(3):687–688.
61. Stein C, Kyeck SH, Henssge C. (1996) DNA typing of fingerprint reagent treated biological stains. *J Forensic Sci* 41(6):1012–1017.
62. von Wurmb N, Meissner D, Wegener R. (2001) Influence of cyanoacrylate on the efficiency of forensic PCRs. *Forensic Sci Int* 124:11–16.
63. Perkins DG, Thomas WM. (1991) Cyanoacrylate fuming prior to submission of evidence to the laboratory (editorial). *J Forensic Ident* 41(3):157–162.
64. Vachon G, Sorel J. (1987) New fingerprint development process. In: *Proceedings of the International Forensic Symposium on Latent Prints.* Laboratory & Identification Divisions, Federal Bureau of Investigation, FSRTC, FBI Academy, Quantico, VA. U.S. Government Printing Office, Washington, DC.
65. McCarthy MM. (1990) Evaluation of ardrox as a luminescent stain for cyanoacrylate processed latent impressions. *J Forensic Ident* 40(2):75–80.
66. Olenik J. (1992) Ardrox: an alternate solvent system. *J Forensic Ident* 42(6):513–516.
67. Trozzi TA, Schwartz RL, Hollars ML. (2001) *Processing Guide for Developing Latent Prints.* U.S. Department of Justice, Federal Bureau of Investigation, Washington, DC.
68. Bowman V, Ed. (2009) *Manual of Fingerprint Development Techniques*, 2nd edn. Home Office Police Scientific Development Branch, Sandridge, U.K.
69. Menzel ER, Duff JM. (1979) Laser detection of latent fingerprints—treatment with fluorescers. *J Forensic Sci* 24(1):96–100.
70. Olenik JH. (1994) Cyanoacrylate Fluorescent Enhancement. *Minutiae* 24:5.
71. Wilson HD. (2010) RAY dye stain versus gentian violet and alternate powder for the development of latent prints on the adhesive side of tape. *J Forensic Ident* 60(5):510–523.
72. Misner A, Wilkinson D, Watkin J. (1993) Thenoyl europium chelate: a new fluorescent dye with a narrow emission band to detect cyanoacrylate developed fingerprints on non-porous substrates and cadavers. *J Forensic Ident* 43(2):154–165.
73. Wilkinson DA, Misner AH. (1994) A comparison of thenoyl europium chelate with ardrox and rhodamine 6G for the fluorescent detection of cyanoacrylate prints. *J Forensic Ident* 44(4):387–406.
74. Wilkinson DA, Watkin J. (1993) Europium aryl-β-diketone complexes as fluorescent dyes for the detection of cyanoacrylate developed fingerprints on human skin. *Forensic Sci Int* 60:67–79.
75. Lock ERA, Mazzella WD, Margot P. (1995) A new chelate as a fluorescent dye for cyanoacrylate pretreated fingerprints—EuTTAPhen: europium thenoylTrifluoroacetone ortho-phenanthroline. *J Forensic Sci* 40(4):654–658.
76. Kobus HJ, Warrener RN, Stoilovic M. (1983) Two simple staining procedures which improve the contrast and ridge detail of fingerprints developed with "super glue" (cyanoacrylate ester). *Forensic Sci Int* 23:233–240.
77. Kempton JB, Rowe WF. (1992) Contrast enhancement of cyanoacrylate-developed latent fingerprints using biological stains and commercial fabric dyes. *J Forensic Sci* 37(1):99–105.
78. Stitt W. (1997) New use for gentian violet. *J Forensic Ident* 47(3):274–275.
79. Munroe RGR. (1994) Latent fingerprint development on a cement matrix. *Can Soc Forensic Sci J* 27(1):1–4.
80. Monday TD. (2004) Progressive processing: a matter of persistence. *J Forensic Ident* 54(4):438–441.
81. Weaver DE, Clary EJ, Rao SP. A one step fluorescent cyanoacrylate fingerprint development technology (undated report).

82. Weaver DE. (2008) One step fluorescent cyanoacrylate co-polymerization success. Presented at the International Association for Identification, 93rd Annual Education Conference, Louisville, KY.
83. Hahn W, Ramotowski R. (2012) Evaluation of a novel one-step fluorescent cyanoacrylate fuming process for latent print visualization. *J Forensic Ident*, 62(3):277–296.
84. Spring M, Gros L, Deinet W. (1995) Visualisation of latent fingerprints with cyanoacrylates. Project Report Summary (December).
85. Springer E. (2011) Fluorescent cyanoacrylate. Technical Support Working Group T-3036 Final Report.
86. Anon. (1984) Toxicity Investigations (editorial). *Fingerprint Whorld* 9(35):i.
87. Masters NE. (1995) *Safety for the Forensic Identification Specialist*. Lightning Powder Company, Inc., Salem, OR, pp. 146–147.
88. Mock JP. (1985) Cyanoacrylates and heat—a word of caution. *Fingerprint Whorld* 11(41):16–17.
89. http://msds.chem.ox.ac.uk/ET/ethyl_cyanoacrylate.html (accessed on 9/12/10).
90. Fung TC, Grimwood K, Shimmon R, Spindler X, Maynard P, Lennard C, Roux C. (2011) Investigation of hydrogen cyanide generation from the cyanoacrylate fuming process used for latent fingermark detection. *Forensic Sci Int* 212:143–149.
91. Fung TC, Grimwood K, Shimmon R, Spindler X, Maynard P, Lennard C, Roux C. (2011) Investigation of hydrogen cyanide generation from the cyanoacrylate fuming process used for latent fingermark detection. Presented at the International Fingerprint Research Group Meeting, Linköping, Sweden, June.
92. Moenssens AA. (1971) *Fingerprint Techniques*. Chilton Book Company, Radnor, PA.
93. Quinche N, Margot P. (2010) Coulier, Jean-Paul (1824–1890): a precursor in the history of fingermark detection and their potential use for identifying their source (1863). *J Forensic Ident* 60(2):129–134.
94. Mitchell CA. (1920) Detection of finger-prints on documents. *Analyst* 45:122–129.
95. Bridges BC. (1942) *Practical Fingerprinting*. Funk & Wagnalls, New York.
96. Olsen R.D. (1978) *Scott's Fingerprint Mechanics*. Charles C. Thomas, Springfiled, IL.
97. Goode GC, Morris JR. (1983) Latent fingerprints: a review of their origin, composition and methods for detection. AWRE Report No. 002/83.
98. Neal AL. (1971) *Chemistry and Biochemistry: A Comprehensive Introduction*. McGraw-Hill, New York.
99. Almog J, Sasson Y, Anati A. (1979) Chemical reagents for the development of latent fingerprints. II: controlled addition of water vapor to iodine fumes—a solution to the aging problem. *J Forensic Sci* 24(2):431–436.
100. Fogleman EL. (1980) Iodine development. *Ident News* 30(7):11–14.
101. Foley JF. (1972) Development of latent fingerprints—iodine silver transfer method. *Ident News* 22(3):14.
102. Hinds JF. (1977) The iodine-silver plate transfer method of obtaining fingerprints from difficult surfaces. *Can Soc Forensic Sci J* 10(1):27–30.
103. Trowell F. (1975) A method for fixing latent fingerprints developed with iodine. *J Forensic Sci Soc* 15:189–195.
104. Mashiko K, Hizaki MI. (1977) Latent fingerprint processing iodine 7,8-benzoflavone method. *Ident News* 27(11):3–5.
105. Haque F, Westland A, Kerr FM. (1983) An improved non-destructive method for detection of latent fingerprints on documents with iodine-7,8-benzoflavone. *Forensic Sci Int* 21(1):79–83.
106. Anon. (1937) The chemical development of latent fingerprints on paper. *Sparks Anvil* 5(7):3–4.
107. Scott WR. (1954) Miscellaneous materials subcommittee report. *Ident News* 4(3):3,7.
108. Beecroft W. (1989) Enhancement of physical developer prints. *RCMP Gazette* 51(2):17.
109. MacDonell HL. (1961) Recent developments in the processing of latent fingerprints. *Ident News* 11(9):6–7.
110. Grodsky M. (1957) Variations in latent print techniques. *Fingerprint Ident Mag* 39(6):16–19.

111. Pounds CA, Hussain JI. (1987) Biologic and chemical aspects of latent fingerprint detection. In: Proceedings of the International Forensic Symposium on Latent Prints. Laboratory & Identification Divisions, Federal Bureau of Investigation, FSRTC, FBI Academy, Quantico, VA. U.S. Government Printing Office, Washington, DC, pp. 9–13.
112. Almog J, Gabay A. (1980) Chemical reagents for the development of latent fingerprints. III: visualization of latent fingerprints by fluorescent reagents in the vapor phase. *J Forensic Sci* 25(2):408–410.
113. Margot P, Lennard C. (1994) *Fingerprint Detection Techniques*, 6th ed. University of Lausanne, Lausanne, Switzerland.
114. Blackledge RD. (1998) Re: Latent fingerprint processing by the ruthenium tetroxide method [letter to the editor]. *J Forensic Ident* 48(5):557–559.
115. Mashiko K, German ER, Motojima K, Colman CD. (1991) RTX: a new ruthenium tetroxide fuming procedure. *J Forensic Ident* 41(6):429–436.
116. Mashiko K, Miyamoto T. (1998) Latent fingerprint processing by the ruthenium tetroxide method. *J Forensic Ident* 48(3):279–290.
117. Trapecar M, Balazic J. (2007) Fingerprint recovery from human skin surfaces. *Sci Justice* 47:136–140.
118. Flynn K, Maynard P, du Pasquier E, Lennard C, Stoilovic M, Roux C. (2004) Evaluation of iodine-benzoflavone and ruthenium tetroxide spray reagents for the detection of latent fingermarks at the crime scene. *J Forensic Sci* 49(4):707–715.
119. Medlin HO. (1967) The flame process. *Ident News* 17(12):4,11.
120. Vandiver JV. (1973) Comments on smoke technique. *Ident News* 23(6):12.
121. Corr JJ. (1975) Hot prints. *Ident News* 25(2):11.
122. Sturelle V, Cominotti C, Henrot D, Desbrosse X. (2006) The use of camphor in the development of latent prints on unfired cartridge casings. *J Forensic Ident* 56(5):694–705.
123. Waldoch TL.(1993) The flame method of soot deposition for the development of latent prints on non-porous surfaces. *J Forensic Ident* 43(5):463–465.
124. Spawn MA. (1994) Effects of fire in fingerprint evidence. *Fingerprint Whorld* 20(76):45–46.
125. Kelly PF, King RSP, Mortimer RJ. (2008) Fingerprint and inkjet-trace imaging using disulfur dinitride. *Chem Commun* 46:6111–6113.
126. Kelly PF, King RSP, Shah B, Mortimer RJ. (2009) The use of sulfur nitrides as fingerprint developers. Lewis C, ed. In: *Proceedings of the SPIE: Optics and Photonics for Counterterrorism and Crime Fighting V*, Vol. 7486, pp. 602–610.
127. Bleay SM, Kelly PF, King RSP. (2010) Polymerization of S_2N_2 to $(SN)_x$ as a tool for the rapid imaging of fingerprints removed from metal surfaces. *J Mater Chem* 20:10100–10102.

6

Blood Reagents

Robert S. Ramotowski

CONTENTS

6.1 Blood Chemistry

Hematology is the science that investigates blood-forming tissues, blood, and diseases associated with these tissues and fluids [1]. Blood has three essential functions: transportation (i.e., exchange of oxygen and carbon dioxide between cells and the lungs), regulation (e.g., pH and body temperature), and protection (e.g., clotting factors and antibodies against invading pathogens). The average temperature of blood is approximately 38°C (100.4°F) and it has a slightly alkaline pH of about 7.4 (a normal range is between 7.35 and 7.45). Blood constitutes about 8% of the total body weight. The average adult male has a total blood volume of 5–6 L (1.5 gal), compared to a volume of 4–5 L (1.2 gal) for adult females.

Blood is comprised of plasma and formed elements, constituting 55% and 45% of the total volume, respectively. Blood plasma is an aqueous solution of dissolved solutes that is composed of approximately 91% water. The majority of these solutes by weight are proteins, notably albumins (54%), globulins (38%), and fibrinogen (7%). Gamma globulins, also known as immunoglobulins (antibodies), are an essential part of the body's defense against antigens (pathogens). Most of these plasma proteins are produced in the liver. Additional solutes include inorganic salts (e.g., electrolytes that include ions like Na^+, K^+, Ca^{2+}, Cl^-, HCO_3^-, and HPO_4^{2-}), nutrients (e.g., amino acids, proteins, glucose, fatty acids, glycerol), enzymes, hormones, dissolved gases (e.g., O_2, CO_2, N_2), and wastes (e.g., urea, uric acid, creatine, creatinine, bilirubin, ammonia salts).

The formed elements (45% of the total blood volume) are composed of almost entirely (nearly 99%) red blood cells (erythrocytes). Platelets and white blood cells (leukocytes) make up the remaining 1% of the formed elements. Erythrocytes contain the oxygen-carrying protein hemoglobin, which is responsible for giving blood its red color. Hemoglobin is comprised of a globulin protein (with two α- and two β-polypeptide chains) and four heme moieties. Heme consists of iron molecule (in the reduced ferrous oxidation state) surrounded by a heterocyclic ring structure known as a porphyrin.

On average, healthy adults have between 4.8 and 5.4 million red blood cells per cubic millimeter of blood. For a single drop of blood (~50 mm^3), the number varies from 240 to 270 million. Each red blood cell contains about 280 million hemoglobin molecules. Quantitatively, the amounts of hemoglobin vary for adult males (13.5–18 g/100 mL blood) and adult females (12–16 g/100 mL blood). In the body, red blood cells last only about 120 days. To maintain normal levels throughout the body, more than 2 million need to be introduced into the circulatory system every second.

6.2 Blood Reagents

The reagents used to visualize latent (as well as patent or visible) blood prints can be generally classified into two distinct categories, protein stains and peroxidase reagents. Given that both plasma and formed elements contain protein reactive compounds, blood reagents based on protein stains (e.g., amido black, acid yellow 7) are likely to be more sensitive, but not very selective. On the other hand, peroxidase-reactive reagents (e.g., luminol, leucocrystal violet [LCV]) are likely to be more selective toward blood, but more than likely less sensitive. However, neither type of reagent can be considered to be blood specific. There is also a need to fix blood stains prior to the application of some of the blood reagents. The general purpose of a fixing solution is to denature the proteins and to render them less soluble (to prevent diffusing the print or washing it away). Recent advances in the optimization of blood reagents will be covered in more detail in a subsequent chapter of this book.

6.2.1 Protein Reagents

Generally, protein-reactive reagents are more sensitive than peroxidase-reactive ones because they react not only with proteins but also with the globular protein in hemoglobin. However, their reactions are nonspecific and cannot prove that blood is present upon a positive reaction.

6.2.1.1 Amido Black

Amido black (acid black 1) is an acid diazo dye that stains proteins, forming a dark blue-colored product. It is one of the more commonly used forensic reagents for trace blood detection and has been recommended for both nonporous and porous (significant background staining can limit application) surfaces. One of the earliest reports of the use of amido black to stain proteins was by Puchtler et al. in 1962 [2]. The authors reported that hemoglobin and methemoglobin (the form of hemoglobin where the iron is present in its oxidized ferric state, Fe^{3+}) were stained blue by the reagent while serum proteins (e.g., fibrinogen, gelatin) were stained yellow. It could not distinguish between hemoglobin and methemoglobin (despite the difference in oxidation states), thus indicating that the reagent was selective toward proteins rather than the heme group. In 1957, Oden mentions in a patent application that the compound amido black "is especially suited as a protein indicator" [3]. Its use as a latent blood enhancement method (in a methanol–acetic acid mixed solvent) was first reported in the early 1970s. A water-based version of the reagent was introduced by Hussain et al. in 1989 [4].

The original Home Office Manual of Fingerprint Detection Techniques recommended a methanol-based formulation [5]. In a subsequent update, a water-based formulation was added. In the late 1990s, the Home Office Police Scientific Development Branch engaged in a comprehensive effort to review all blood reagents, including the optimization of amido black [6]. They also looked at factors such as the time required to fix blood deposits based on the amount present (i.e., light or heavy) as well as the effect of print age. With heavy deposits, increased soaking times were required in the fixative; however, if the deposit were left in the solution too long, leaching could occur that might destroy ridge detail as well as damage the substrate (e.g., paints, varnishes, plastics). Ethanol and methanol were found to be equally effective in destaining porous surfaces. Multiple rinsing steps may be required when background staining is significant.

Several identifiable prints were successfully recovered from a sheet used to cover up a homicide victim [7]. Since the crime had been committed 18 days prior to processing for latent prints, no fixative solution was used. Pure methanol was used as the primary rinsing solution and distilled water was used as the final rinse. Digital enhancement was required to improve the contrast between the ridge detail and the weave pattern background from the fabric.

In general, processing of items with cyanoacrylate ester fumes prior to the application of amido black was not found to adversely affect the success of the protein reagent, as long as post-cyanoacrylate dye stains were not used [8]. However, metal and glass surfaces were found to be exceptions. The authors suggest that the texture of the surface may be a factor. For amido black, preprocessing textured surfaces with cyanoacrylate ester fumes resulted in poorer development compared to using the protein stain alone. The methanol-based reagent was reported to have successfully visualized a latent print on the skin of a dead body [9].

Reagent preparation

Methanol-based amido black [10]

Staining solution

Amido black	2 g
Acetic acid	100 mL
Methanol	900 mL

1. The items should be mixed in the order given until the amido black has completely dissolved.
2. Store this solution in a dark glass bottle away from light.
3. The appropriate information (e.g., chemical contents, preparer's initials, date, reliability test result) should be recorded on the container's label.

Rinsing solution

Acetic acid	100 mL
Methanol	900 mL

1. These solvents should be mixed until the solution appears to be homogeneous.
2. Store this solution in a glass bottle.
3. The appropriate information (e.g., chemical contents, preparer's initials, date, reliability test result) should be recorded on the container's label.

Water-based amido black (Fischer) [10]

Staining solution

Amido black	3 g
5-Sulfosalicylic acid	20 g
Sodium carbonate	3 g
Glacial acetic acid	50 mL
Formic acid	50 mL
Kodak Photo-Flo 600	12.5 mL
Distilled water	500 mL

1. This formula involves a one-step fixing and staining solution and was reported by John Fischer in 1998.
2. The solid materials should be added to the distilled water first and then the remaining chemicals should be added in the order given and mixed thoroughly.
3. This solution should then be diluted to a final volume of 1000 mL with distilled water.
4. Although the reagent is ready to use after mixing, best results were obtained when the solution was left to stand for several days prior to use.
5. The appropriate information (e.g., chemical contents, preparer's initials, date, reliability test result) should be recorded on the container's label.

Water-based Amido black (HOSDB) [11]

Fixing solution

5-Sulfosalicylic acid	23 g
Distilled water	1 L

1. The solution should be stirred until all of the 5-sulfosalicylic acid has dissolved.
2. Store this solution in a glass or plastic bottle.
3. The appropriate information (e.g., chemical contents, preparer's initials, date, reliability test result) should be recorded on the container's label.

Staining solution

Amido black	1 g
Ethanol	250 mL
Acetic acid	50 mL
Distilled water	700 mL

1. The chemicals should be added in the order given and the solution should be stirred for at least 5 min to ensure that all of the amido black has dissolved.
2. The solution should be stored in a dark glass bottle.
3. The appropriate information (e.g., chemical contents, preparer's initials, date, reliability test result) should be recorded on the container's label.

Destaining solution

Ethanol	250 mL
Acetic acid	50 mL
Distilled water	700 mL

1. These three solvents should be stirred until they appear to create a homogeneous solution.
2. Store this solution in a glass or plastic bottle.
3. The appropriate information (e.g., chemical contents, preparer's initials, date, reliability test result) should be recorded on the container's label.

Reagent application

Methanol-based formulation

1. All appropriate personal protective equipment should be used when preparing and using this reagent.
2. Run the appropriate positive and negative controls to ensure that the reagent solution is working properly.
3. Items should be placed into the fixing solution (5-sulfosalicylic acid) for approximately 5 min.* For fresh samples, the color of the blood will change from dark red to dark brown. Methanol can also be used as the fixative for this process.† Reagents that fix and stain in a single step were found to not be as effective as ones that employed separate solutions [12].
4. Items should then be transferred to the staining solution and processed for approximately 3 min. The solution should be agitated during the staining process.
5. Once the desired level of development has been achieved, the items should be placed into the destaining solution. The items should be agitated in this solution for approximately 1 min or until the proper contrast has been achieved.‡
6. If necessary, items can be reprocessed to achieve better development.
7. When processing has been completed, all chemicals should be disposed of properly according to the appropriate federal, state, and local environmental laws.

* Heavier deposits may require additional time. Caution should be taken not to soak the item for too long in the fixing solution because leaching of the blood could occur.

† It is important to note that the use of a 5-sulfosalicylic fixing solution prior to immersing an item into the methanol-based reagent produced significantly poor results. Methanol itself can be used as a fixing solution. Only the HOSDB water-based reagent requires the 5-sulfosalicylic fixing solution.

‡ An additional destaining solution can be used to remove heavier or persistent background staining. It is prepared by mixing 950 mL of distilled water and 50 mL of acetic acid.

Water-based formulations (Fischer)

1. All appropriate personal protective equipment should be used when preparing and using this reagent.
2. Run the appropriate positive and negative controls to ensure that the reagent solution is working properly.
3. There is no fixing solution used with this reagent. Items should be placed directly into the staining solution.
4. Items should be processed in the staining solution for approximately 3–5 min. The solution should be agitated during the staining process.
5. Once the desired level of development has been achieved, the items should be destained using tap water until the proper contrast has been achieved.
6. If necessary, items can be reprocessed to achieve better development.
7. When processing has been completed, all chemicals should be disposed of properly according to the appropriate federal, state, and local environmental laws.

Water-based formulations (HOSDB)

1. All appropriate personal protective equipment should be used when preparing and using this reagent.
2. Run the appropriate positive and negative controls to ensure that the reagent solution is working properly.
3. Items should be placed into the fixing solution for approximately 5 min.* Reagents that fix and stain in a single step were found to not be as effective as the ones that employed separate solutions [12].
4. Items should then be transferred to the staining solution and processed for approximately 3 min. The solution should be agitated during the staining process.
5. Once the desired level of development has been achieved, the items should be placed into the destaining solution. The items should be agitated in this solution for approximately 1 min or until the proper contrast has been achieved. If necessary, items can be reprocessed to achieve better development.
6. When processing has been completed, all chemicals should be disposed of properly according to the appropriate federal, state, and local environmental laws.

6.2.1.2 Coomassie Blue

The compound Coomassie Brilliant Blue R250 is a triarylmethine dye (these dyes have traditionally been referred to as "triarylmethanes", but this nomenclature is incorrect since the central carbon is actually sp^2 hybridized) commonly used to stain proteins blue that have been separated by electrophoresis. The "R" in the compound's name refers to red (the dye has a reddish tint) and the "250" originally referred to the dye's purity. It differs from its analog, Coomassie Brilliant Blue G250, by the removal of two methyl groups. Its common name was derived from Levinstein Ltd, a nineteenth-century dye

* Heavier deposits may require additional time. Caution should be taken not to soak the item for too long in the fixing solution because leaching of the blood could occur.

manufacturer.* Coomassie (now called Kumasi) was the town in Ghana used by the British to land their expeditionary forces during the fourth Anglo-Ashanti War in 1896. The term "Coomassie" is now used in more than 20 different dyes [13]. Its first reported use to stain proteins was in 1963 by Fazekas de St. Groth et al. [14], who fixed protein bands using 5-sulfosalicylic acid. A dye stain solution based on glacial acetic acid, methanol, and distilled water was proposed by Meyer et al. in 1965 [15].

Coomassie Brilliant Blue R250 has been reported to be a more effective protein stain than crystal violet [16]. Coomassie was able to stain serial blood dilutions up to 1:30,000, compared to 1:10,000 for crystal violet. No fixing procedure (e.g., heat, aging/drying) is required for this reagent. Coomassie also was reported to be superior to crystal violet for nonblood prints on the adhesive side of tape. Prints were developed with virtually no background staining. Hunter reported that a 25 year old latent blood print was developed on the inside of a glove using Coomassie Blue [17]. Previous treatment with powder, specialized lighting techniques, and laser illumination had failed to produce any usable prints on that surface.

Reagent preparation [16]

Stain solution

Coomassie Brilliant Blue R250	0.44 g
Glacial acetic acid	40 mL
Methanol	200 mL
Distilled water	200 mL

1. The dye should be mixed into the acetic acid and methanol until it is completely dissolved.
2. Add the water and stir the mixture until the solution appears homogeneous.
3. This solution should be stored in a glass or plastic bottle.
4. The appropriate information (e.g., chemical contents, preparer's initials, date, reliability test result) should be recorded on the container's label.

Destaining solution

Glacial acetic acid	40 mL
Methanol	200 mL
Distilled water	200 mL

1. These three solvents should be stirred until they appear to create a homogeneous solution.
2. Store this solution in a glass or plastic bottle.
3. The appropriate information (e.g., chemical contents, preparer's initials, date, reliability test result) should be recorded on the container's label.

Reagent application

1. All appropriate personal protective equipment should be used when preparing and using this reagent.
2. Run the appropriate positive and negative controls to ensure that the reagent solution is working properly.

---

* This information was derived from http://en.wikipedia.org/wiki/Coomassie_Brilliant_Blue (accessed on March 5, 2011).

3. Items to be processed should be placed into a tray containing the staining solution. The solution should be continually agitated during the entire development time.
4. Depending on the surface type, prints can begin to appear after 2–30 min.
5. To clear the background, the items should be placed into a separate tray containing the destaining solution and agitated for approximately 1 min (or until the background clears). Items can be re-stained multiple times to improve the color intensity of the developed print.
6. When processing has been completed, all chemicals should be disposed of properly according to the appropriate federal, state, and local environmental laws.

6.2.1.3 Crowles Double Stain

Crowles Double Stain is a combination of Coomassie Brilliant Blue R250 and Crocein Scarlet 7B (Acid Red 71) [16]. Phillips reported the visualization of a latent blood print on knife with a plastic facing that had paper applied to the back side [18]. Crowles Double Stain was able to successfully develop an identifiable print on the underlying paper. Becraft et al. reported that Crowles Double Stain was able to develop good print detail on glass, photo paper, envelopes, tape, plastic bags, and painted surfaces [19].

Reagent preparation [16]

Staining solution

Crocein Scarlet 7B	2.5 g
Coomassie Brilliant Blue R250	150 mg
Glacial acetic acid	50 mL
Trichloroacetic acid	30 mL
Distilled water	920 mL

1. The two dyes should be mixed into the acetic and trichloroacetic acids until completely dissolved.
2. The solution should then be diluted up to a final volume of 1000 mL with distilled water.
3. This solution should be stored in a glass or plastic bottle.
4. The appropriate information (e.g., chemical contents, preparer's initials, date, reliability test result) should be recorded on the container's label.

Destaining solution

Glacial acetic acid	3 mL
Deionized water	1 L

1. These two solvents should be stirred until they appear to create a homogeneous solution.
2. Store this solution in a glass or plastic bottle.
3. The appropriate information (e.g., chemical contents, preparer's initials, date, reliability test result) should be recorded on the container's label.

Reagent application

1. All appropriate personal protective equipment should be used when preparing and using this reagent.
2. Run the appropriate positive and negative controls to ensure that the reagent solution is working properly.
3. Items to be processed should be placed into a tray containing the staining solution. The solution should be continually agitated during the entire development time.
4. Depending on the surface type, prints can begin to appear after 2–30 min.
5. To clear the background, the items should be placed into a separate tray containing the destaining solution and agitated for approximately 1 min (or until the background clears).
6. Items can be re-stained multiple times to improve the color intensity of the developed print.
7. When processing has been completed, all chemicals should be disposed of properly according to the appropriate federal, state, and local environmental laws.

6.2.1.4 Acid Violet 17

The compound Acid Violet 17 (AV 17) is a triarylmethine dye. It was first proposed as a blood enhancement method by the HOSDB in 2001 [20]. After staining proteins, AV 17 produces a dark purple–colored product, similar to LCV. It has also been noted that AV 17 exhibits some fluorescence in the red region of the spectrum. On porous surfaces, AV 17 performed better than both methanol and water-based amido black solutions and Crowles Double Stain. On nonporous surfaces that were not damaged by methanol, the methanol-based amido black was superior to AV 17. The addition of methanol to the AV 17 formulation was not found to improve the performance of the reagent.

Reagent preparation [11]

Fixing solution

5-Sulfosalicylic acid	20 g
Distilled water	1 L

1. The solution should be stirred until all of the 5-sulfosalicylic acid has dissolved.
2. Store the solution in a glass or plastic bottle.
3. The appropriate information (e.g., chemical contents, preparer's initials, date, reliability test result) should be recorded on the container's label.

Staining solution

Acid violet 17	1 g
Ethanol	250 mL
Acetic acid	50 mL
Distilled water	700 mL

1. The solution should be stirred for at least 5 min to ensure that all of the Acid Violet 17 has dissolved.
2. Store the solution in a glass or plastic bottle.
3. The appropriate information (e.g., chemical contents, preparer's initials, date, reliability test result) should be recorded on the container's label.

Destaining solution

Ethanol	250 mL
Acetic acid	50 mL
Distilled water	700 mL

1. These three solvents should be stirred until the solution appears to be homogeneous.
2. Store the solution in a glass or plastic bottle.
3. The appropriate information (e.g., chemical contents, preparer's initials, date, reliability test result) should be recorded on the container's label.

Reagent application

1. All appropriate personal protective equipment should be used when preparing and using this reagent.
2. Run the appropriate positive and negative controls to ensure that the reagent solution is working properly.
3. Items should be placed into the fixing solution for approximately 5 min.
4. Items should then be transferred to the staining solution and processed for a minimum of 3 min. The solution should be agitated during the staining process.
5. Once the desired level of development has been achieved, the items should be placed into the destaining solution. The items should be agitated in this solution for approximately 1 min or until the proper contrast has been achieved.
6. If necessary, items can be reprocessed to achieve better development.
7. When processing has been completed, all chemicals should be disposed of properly according to the appropriate federal, state, and local environmental laws.

6.2.1.5 Acid Yellow 7

The compound Acid Yellow 7 (AY 7) is an acid dye. It was first proposed as a blood enhancement method for nonporous surfaces by the HOSDB in 2001 [20]. After staining proteins, AY 7 produces a faint yellow-colored product that is intensely fluorescent. This reagent is particularly sensitive for very faint blood prints. In fact, heavier blood deposits can lead to fluorescence quenching (significantly diminishing the fluorescence). This compound's fluorescence intensity was found to be inferior to that produced by benzoxanthene yellow; however, the latter compound is unfortunately no longer commercially available. Excitation can be achieved using blue and blue-green light (approximately 400–490 nm) and fluorescence emission can be viewed using an orange filter (e.g., OG540 long pass filter). Preprocessing with cyanoacrylate ester fumes was not found to inhibit subsequent AY 7 development [21]. Sears et al. found that AY 7 was superior to a variety of different heme reactive and protein staining reagents [22].

Reagent preparation [11]

Fixing solution

5-Sulfosalicylic acid	20 g
Distilled water	1 L

1. The solution should be stirred until all of the 5-sulfosalicylic acid has dissolved.
2. Store this solution in a glass or plastic bottle.
3. The appropriate information (e.g., chemical contents, preparer's initials, date, reliability test result) should be recorded on the container's label.

Staining solution

Acid Yellow 7	1 g
Ethanol	250 mL
Acetic acid	50 mL
Distilled water	700 mL

1. The solution should be stirred for at least 5 min to ensure that all of the Acid Yellow 7 has dissolved.
2. Store this solution in a glass or plastic bottle.
3. The appropriate information (e.g., chemical contents, preparer's initials, date, reliability test result) should be recorded on the container's label.

Destaining solution

Ethanol	250 mL
Acetic acid	50 mL
Distilled water	700 mL

1. These three solvents are stirred until the solution appears to be homogeneous.
2. Store this solution in a glass or plastic bottle.
3. The appropriate information (e.g., chemical contents, preparer's initials, date, reliability test result) should be recorded on the container's label.

Reagent application

1. All appropriate personal protective equipment should be used when preparing and using this reagent.
2. Run the appropriate positive and negative controls to ensure that the reagent solution is working properly.
3. Items should be placed into the fixing solution for approximately 5 min.*

* An alternate procedure for fixing blood prints (primarily for crime scene work) was suggested by BVDA. The company suggests placing a piece of filter paper slightly above the area of interest. One edge of the paper is dropped onto the surface and it should be moistened thoroughly by using a wash bottle containing the fixing solution. The rest of the paper should also be moistened and then pressed onto the entire surface area of interest. For normal deposits, the paper should be left in place for 5 min. For heavier deposits, 5 min or more may be required [23].

4. Items should then be transferred to the staining solution and processed for a minimum of 3 min. The solution should be agitated during the staining process.
5. Alternatively, the staining solution can be applied to nonporous surfaces using a spray or wash bottle. Allow the stain to react for 3 min after spraying.
6. Once the desired level of development has been achieved, the items should be placed into the destaining solution. The items should be agitated in this solution for approximately 1 min or until the proper contrast has been achieved.
7. Alternatively, the destaining solution can be applied using a wash or spray bottle for nonporous surfaces. Excess destaining solution can be removed with towels or special vacuums that can handle liquids.
8. If necessary, items can be reprocessed to achieve better development.
9. When processing has been completed, all chemicals should be disposed of properly according to the appropriate federal, state, and local environmental laws.

6.2.1.6 Hungarian Red

The commercially available staining solution Hungarian red (Fuchsin Acid) contains the triarylmethine dye Acid Violet 19. This compound is a trisulfonated derivative of pararosanilin (an analog of methyl and crystal violet). The reaction of Hungarian red with proteins produces a light red-colored product, which also fluoresces. The reagent is primarily used on nonporous substrates. The water-based HOSDB amido black reagent and Acid Violet 17 were reported to produce better print development than the Hungarian red solution [20].

Reagent preparation*

Fixing solution

5-Sulfosalicylic acid	20 g
Distilled water	1 L

1. The solution should be stirred until all of the 5-sulfosalicylic acid has dissolved.
2. Store this solution in a glass or plastic bottle.
3. The appropriate information (e.g., chemical contents, preparer's initials, date, reliability test result) should be recorded on the container's label.

Staining solution

The staining solution is commercially available from BVDA.

Destaining solution

Acetic acid	50 mL
Distilled water	950 mL

1. These two solvents should be stirred until the solution appears to be homogeneous.
2. This solution should be stored in a glass or plastic bottle.
3. The appropriate information (e.g., chemical contents, preparer's initials, date, reliability test result) should be recorded on the container's label.

* The preparation and application of this reagent was obtained from http://www.bvda.com/EN/prdctinf/en_hu_red.html

Reagent application

1. All appropriate personal protective equipment should be used when preparing and using this reagent.
2. Run the appropriate positive and negative controls to ensure that the reagent solution is working properly.
3. Items should be placed into the fixing solution for approximately 5 min. For fresh samples, the color of the blood will change from dark red to dark brown. An alternative method for fixing can be found in the Acid Yellow 7 reagent application procedure [24].
4. The staining solution can be applied to non-porous surfaces using a spray or wash bottle. Allow the stain to react for approximately 1 min after spraying. This reagent is not recommended for porous surfaces.
5. The destaining solution can be applied using a wash or spray bottle for nonporous surfaces. Excess destaining solution can be removed with towels or special vacuums that can handle liquids.
6. Hungarian red–stained prints can be lifted using gelatin lifters. The area of interest must be completely dry prior to lifting. Place the gelatin lifter on the surface (taking care to avoid air bubbles) and leave it in place for 15–30 min. Record the lifted image as soon as possible as it will continue to diffuse into the gelatin and blur any print detail.
7. The lifted print is fluorescent. The prints can be excited using green light (515–560 nm) and fluorescence emission can be viewed through a red filter (e.g., Kodak Wratten 25 filter).
8. If necessary, items can be reprocessed and lifted numerous times to achieve better development.
9. When processing has been completed, all chemicals should be disposed of properly according to the appropriate federal, state, and local environmental laws.

6.2.1.7 Amino Acid Reagents

Amino acid reagents can be very sensitive blood reagents, particularly on porous surfaces. Reagents like ninhydrin, 1,8-diazafluoren-9-one, 1,2-indanedione/zinc can react with blood proteins and produce either colored or fluorescent ridge detail. They are typically used prior to the aforementioned protein stains because they will detect nonblood prints (which may be destroyed in protein stains are used first). Basic procedures for preparing and applying these reagents can be found in Chapter 2.

6.2.2 Peroxidase Reagents

Shortly after the discovery of the peroxidase-like activity of blood by Schonbein in 1857 [25], the guaiacum test was described by van Deen in 1861 [26]. This test reacted with heme from blood to create a colored product in the presence of hydrogen peroxide. The reaction between horseradish peroxidase and guaiacum was first reported in 1810 by Planche [27]. The reagent was found to work erratically and was largely replaced with benzidine by the early twentieth century. Most of the original peroxidase reagents for visualizing blood have been abandoned, mostly due to health concerns. For this reason, formulations will not be provided but can be obtained from the references cited.

6.2.2.1 Benzidine

Benzidine was first synthesized in 1904 [28]. It was initially considered a specific test for blood; however, in 1964 Culliford and Nickolls reported that the reagent produced false positives with blood contamination, chemical oxidants, catalysts, and vegetable peroxidases [29]. Benzidine was reported to be a potent carcinogen in 1964 [29], but its use and manufacture were not restricted until 1974 [30]. As late as 1986, the benzidine test was still recommended by Olsen as the most sensitive for blood [31]. In 1974, a tetramethyl analog of benzidine was reported by Holland et al. to be at least as sensitive as its parent compound but less toxic [32]. 3,3′,5,5′-Tetramethylbenzidine (TMB) was evaluated by Garner et al. and found to work as well as the traditional benzidine reagent [33]. The detection limit was reported to be 1 ppm, but the analog was not as soluble in glacial acetic acid as benzidine. Upon reaction with blood, TMB changes from a colorless form to a green-blue color in the presence of hydrogen peroxide. The use of heat was reported to reverse this coloration, thus allowing for the possibility of recovering overdeveloped prints [34].

6.2.2.2 o-Tolidine

Another suggested replacement for benzidine was *o*-tolidine. This reagent appears to have first been used in 1912 by Ruttan et al. for the detection of occult blood (i.e., blood that is in such small quantities that it requires chemicals to visualize) [35]. Trudeau reported that *o*-tolidine developed blood prints could be successfully lifted from skin [36,37]. Compared to other peroxidase reagents, *o*-tolidine produced mixed results. Cox found that *o*-tolidine was more sensitive than phenolphthalein [38]; however, Nutt reported that TMB was more sensitive [39]. The reagent's use has diminished significantly because of health concerns. *o*-Tolidine has been classified by the U.S. Environmental Protection Agency as a group 2B probable human carcinogen [40].

6.2.2.3 Diaminobenzidine

3,3′-Diaminobenzidine (DAB) is another catalytic blood reagent. It reacts with blood and hydrogen peroxide to form a dark brown-colored product. This dark brown color can make it difficult to discern the product from dried blood. One effort to improve contrast involved the addition of MBD (i.e., 7-(*p*-methoxybenzylamino)-4-nitrobenze-2-oxa-1,3-diazole) to the sulfosalicylic fixative solution to produce fluorescent prints [41]. Latent blood prints did fluoresce at 450 nm, but that was quenched upon the subsequent application of DAB. Another variation of the reagent involved the use of metal toning [42]. Addition of nickel chloride changed the color of the reaction product to a purplish-blue while cobalt chloride produced a dark blue-black color. The use of DAB has now diminished due to its listing as a suspect carcinogen.

6.2.2.4 Luminol

Luminol (5-amino-2,3-dihydrophthalazine-1,4-dione or 3-aminophthalhydrazide) was first synthesized in 1853 [43]. The chemiluminescent properties of luminol were first reported by Albrecht in 1928 [44]. Chemiluminescence is a special form of luminescence that involves emission of light via chemical reaction rather than by absorption of radiation and photon emission (i.e., luminescence). Its first use to detect blood stains at crime scenes was reported by Specht in 1937 [45]. The most commonly used formulation for the luminol reagent was first introduced by Grodsky et al. in 1951 [46]. It was based on the use of sodium carbonate (pH adjustment) and sodium perborate (oxidizing agent). Although not used as often, an alternate formulation was introduced by Weber in 1966. This reagent was based on sodium or potassium hydroxide (pH adjustment) and hydrogen peroxide (oxidizing agent).

The reaction involves activation of luminol with an oxidizing agent, most often hydrogen peroxide. Since the solution has an optimal pH in the basic range (10.5–13) [47], luminol can react with hydroxide ions to form a di-anion compound. In the presence of the iron catalyst (from the four heme groups found in hemoglobin), hydrogen peroxide decomposes to form oxygen and water. The oxygen reacts with luminol to form an unstable peroxide, which decomposes to 3-aminophthalic acid in the excited state with the loss of nitrogen. As the excited state, 3-aminophthalic acid, converts back to the more stable ground state configuration, a photon of light is produced. This is the characteristic blue glow that lasts for approximately 30 s.

Experiments using the Grodsky luminol formula found that it reacted to levels of blood as low as 10^{-1} ppm [48]. Luminol was also reported to react with blood from a 72 day old crime scene where there had been 23 days of measureable precipitation [49]. The surface that produced the positive results was old and pitted asphalt, a surface where blood may have been protected in microfissures.

One of the difficulties encountered when working with luminol was that the chemiluminescent reaction typically lasts for less than 1 min and requires almost total darkness. These issues make recording the luminol patterns difficult. A film overlay method was recommended by Niebauer et al. [50]. It involved combining the negative from an image of the scene captured using ambient light with a negative from an image of the luminol reaction captured in total darkness. The final combined image shows the luminol reactions in the proper context with the object and materials at the scene. Night vision technology has also been advocated for recording luminol chemiluminescence [51]. A camera with low-light capability was used to record video images in the near infrared of the positive luminol reaction areas throughout the crime scene. The use of sensitized thermal detectors for the detection of blood on fabrics has also been reported [52].

There are a number of different materials that will interfere with the luminol reaction (and thus most other peroxidase reagents as well). False-positive test results have been reported for peroxidases (e.g., horseradish peroxidase, turnip isoperoxidase), metal ions (e.g., copper, cobalt, chromium, nickel, manganese), or other oxidants (e.g., hypochlorite, iodine, potassium permanganate). Creamer et al. investigated 250 potentially interfering substances and found that nine produced significant false-positive chemiluminescent reactions [53]. Substances that can suppress the luminol reaction and possibly lead to false-negative results include ligands with a high affinity for ferrous or ferryl ions (e.g., cyanide, sulfide), chemiluminescence quenchers (e.g., heme, oxygen, tertiary amino acids), and antioxidants (e.g., ascorbate, phenolics, anilines, thiols) [54].

The presence of bleach at a scene can often be differentiated from blood as it has been reported to produce brighter flashes of chemiluminescence as opposed to the more gradual development from the reaction with blood. Creamer et al. reported that the interference caused by the presence of bleach diminished significantly if the blood was allowed to dry for at least 8 h, due to the breakdown and volatility of hypochlorite [55]. Household cleaners based on sodium percarbonate have been reported to destroy heme so effectively that heme-reactive reagents do not detect the presence of blood (false negative) [56]. It appears that such cleaners completely oxidize the heme, making it unreactive to heme-reactive blood reagents.

The use of amines to compete with luminol for hypochlorite in order to decrease its interference was reported by Kent et al. [57]. Up to 90% inhibition of the hypochlorite-luminol reaction was reported when 0.08 mol/L of 1,2-diaminoethane was added. The amine molecules reacted rapidly with the hypochlorite ions to form chloramines, which do not produce a chemiluminescent product with luminol. The search for less toxic amines resulted in a variation of the Grodsky reagent by addition of 0.05 mol/L glycine [58]. The addition of glycine as well as an increase in reagent pH to 12 was reported to increase the specificity of the blood-luminol chemiluminescence 11-fold. Allowing the materials to dry for several days (preferably outdoors rather than in a small confined room) can also significantly reduce interference reaction [57,59].

The effect of luminol on subsequent DNA analysis has been reported by Cresap et al. [60]. No measurable adverse effects were observed on DNA stability and extraction or polymerase chain reaction (PCR) chemistry. Fregeau et al. reported that DNA yields from luminol-treated bloody fingerprints were diminished by a factor of 2–12 [61]. However, this would have an impact only on the smallest of blood stain samples.

In 2000, work began on an effort to develop an improved luminol reagent.* Professor Loic J. Blum produced a new blood reagent based on luminol chemistry and introduced it commercially in 2001. A comparison of this new product to commercially available luminol kits was reported in 2006 [62]. Measured light intensities of the reaction between blood and Grodsky luminol formulation were measured (143,500 au). The value obtained for Bluestar (344,600 au) was found to be nearly two-and-a-half times more intense. In addition, the duration of the chemiluminescent reaction was monitored for both reagents. After 1 min, the Grodsky luminol chemiluminescence had reached zero. In contrast, the values reported for Bluestar after 7 min were 10% of the original intensity and 1% after 10 min. In comparative testing, Bluestar Forensic was found to outperform classic luminol reagent formulations [63].

Concerns about the health and safety of the luminol process have limited its use in some parts of the world. Larkin et al. presented a good overview of these issues [64]. Some have labeled luminol as a mutagen,† but the studies are not all in agreement. The U.K. Department of Health reported that "…there are no concerns regarding the mutagenicity profile of this compound." The LD50‡ has been reported to be greater than 500 mg/kg. Sanders et al. reported that if luminol were to react in humans as it does rats it would have little potential for dermal absorption, bioaccumulation in tissues, or chronic toxicity [29]. In the body, luminol would be rapidly absorbed from the gastrointestinal tract, quickly metabolized, and then removed by excretion primarily in urine. Neither luminol nor its metabolites would accumulate in body tissues. The primary concerns can be addressed by using the proper protective equipment. When spraying aerosols, chemical vapors can remain suspended in poorly ventilated rooms for up to 30 min before returning to the recommended exposure limits.

In general, luminol is not recommended for detecting latent prints because of the blurring effect from the chemiluminescence, which can diffuse the ridge detail. It is often used as a

* This information was obtained from product literature found at the following website: http://www.bluestar-forensic.com/gb/bluestar-chemistry.php

† A mutagen is a compound that can cause genetic mutations.

‡ The LD50 refers to the amount of material required to kill half of a test population.

screening method to find blood at crime scenes (e.g., blood spatter, shoe prints). Other reagents are more suitable for developing the fine details associated with friction ridge impressions.

Reagent preparation

Grodsky formula [46]

Sodium perborate	3.5 g
Deionized water	0.5 L
Luminol	0.5 g
Sodium carbonate	25 g

1. The sodium perborate and water should be mixed first until completely dissolved.
2. The luminol and sodium carbonate should then be added in sequence and the solution should be mixed until all components have completely dissolved.
3. This solution should be decanted into a vaporizer or sprayer immediately after mixing.
4. The appropriate information (e.g., chemical contents, preparer's initials, date, reliability test result) should be recorded on the container's label.

Weber formula [65]

Stock solution A

Sodium hydroxide	8 g
Deionized water	0.5 L

Stock solution B

30% Hydrogen peroxide	10 mL
Deionized water	0.49 L

Stock solution C

Luminol	0.354 g
Solution A	62.5 mL
Deionized water	0.48 L

1. The sodium hydroxide should be mixed with water until it has completely dissolved. This will create a 0.4 N solution.
2. The 30% hydrogen peroxide should then be mixed with the water. This will create a 0.176 M solution.
3. The luminol should then be completely dissolved in 62.5 mL of solution A (0.4 N sodium hydroxide) and then diluted up to a final volume of 0.5 L with deionized water. This will create a 0.004 M solution.
4. These stock solutions can be stored in glass or plastic containers at 4°C and away from direct sunlight.
5. The working solution can be prepared by mixing 0.01 L of each stock solution and adding 0.07 L of deionized water to obtain a final volume of 0.1 L.
6. This solution should be decanted into a vaporizer or sprayer immediately after mixing.
7. The appropriate information (e.g., chemical contents, preparer's initials, date, reliability test result) should be recorded on the container's label.

Bluestar forensic*

Forensic kit

Completely dissolve 3 Bluestar Forensic tablets into 500 mL of the reagent solution provided with the kit. The appropriate information (e.g., chemical contents, preparer's initials, date, reliability test result) should be recorded on the container's label.

Tablets

To prepare 125 mL of the reagent, completely dissolve a pair of tablets (one white the other beige) into 125 mL of distilled water. Four pairs of tablets can be used to prepare 500 mL of the reagent. The appropriate information (e.g., chemical contents, preparer's initials, date, reliability test result) should be recorded on the container's label.

Reagent application

1. All appropriate personal protective equipment should be used when preparing and using this reagent.
2. Run the appropriate positive and negative controls to ensure that the reagent solution is working properly.
3. The luminol solution should be used as soon as possible after being prepared. The most effective method for applying luminol is by spraying the surfaces suspected of containing blood.†
4. The area must be as dark as possible to maximize the ability to detect the reagent's chemiluminescence.
5. Chemiluminescence can be recorded either by digital or video camera.
6. Areas exhibiting the luminol reaction should be marked since the chemiluminescence is short-lived (typically on the order of 1 min).
7. All proper personal protective equipment should be used when preparing and using this reagent.
8. When processing has been completed, all chemicals should be disposed of properly according to the appropriate federal, state, and local environmental laws.

6.2.2.5 ABTS

The search for a safer alternative to DAB lead to the discovery of 2,2′-Azino-di-[3-ethylbenzthiazoline sulfonate] diammonium salt (ABTS). This compound oxidizes in the presence of hydrogen peroxide and blood to its green-colored form [66]. The study indicated that excess amounts of hydrogen peroxide inhibited color development, possibly due to oxidative degradation of the ABTS compound. Overall, ABTS was found to produce development comparable to that of DAB on porous and nonporous surfaces, but without the health and safety risks. In addition to ABTS, *o*-phenylenediamine (OPD) and *p*-phenylenediamine (PPD) were suggested to expand the range of possible colors from the oxidized form of these reagents (in the presence of blood and hydrogen peroxide) [67]. In their oxidized forms, OPD is orange and PPD is purple.

---

* Information was obtained from the following website: http://www.bluestar-forensic.com/gb/bluestar.php (accessed on March 19, 2011).

† Some authors have recommended that a 2% hydrochloric acid solution be used on surfaces as a pretreatment. Subsequent evaluation of this procedure found that the hydrochloric acid decreased the intensity of the luminol reaction, increased the background chemiluminescence level, and was found to have detrimental effects on subsequent DNA analysis. This pretreatment is not recommended.

Reagent preparation [66]

Fixing solution

5-Sulfosalicylic acid	20 g
Distilled water	1 L

1. Combine the 5-sulfosalicylic acid and water and mix vigorously until it has completely dissolved.
2. Transfer to a dark glass bottle and store in the dark at room temperature.
3. The appropriate information (e.g., chemical contents, preparer's initials, date, reliability test result) should be recorded on the container's label.

Citric acid/phosphate buffer solution

Sodium phosphate (dibasic)	71.64 g
Citric acid monohydrate	21.01 g
Distilled water	2 L

1. Combine the sodium phosphate and 1 L of distilled water in a volumetric flask and mix thoroughly. This will produce a 0.2 M solution.
2. Transfer the solution to a glass reagent bottle.
3. Combine the citric acid and distilled water in a 1 L volumetric flask and mix thoroughly. This will produce a 0.1 M solution.
4. Transfer the solution to a glass reagent bottle.
5. In a separate reagent bottle, combine 223 mL of the sodium phosphate solution with 177 mL of the citric acid solution and mix thoroughly. This will produce a buffer solution with a pH of 5.4.
6. The appropriate information (e.g., chemical contents, preparer's initials, date, reliability test result) should be recorded on the container's label.

ABTS staining solution

ABTS	1.25 g
Buffer solution	250 mL

1. Combine the ABTS and buffer solution and mix vigorously until it has dissolved completely.
2. Transfer to a dark glass bottle and store in the in a refrigerator.
3. The appropriate information (e.g., chemical contents, preparer's initials, date, reliability test result) should be recorded on the container's label.

Reagent application

Immersion method

1. All appropriate personal protective equipment should be used when preparing and using this reagent.
2. Run the appropriate positive and negative controls to ensure that the reagent solution is working properly.

3. Place a sufficient amount of the fixative solution into a glass tray to completely cover all of the items.
4. Soak the items in the solution for 3 min and then rinse with distilled water.
5. Place the items into a clean glass tray.
6. Transfer 50 mL of the ABTS reagent solution into a glass reagent bottle and combine with 0.5 mL of 27% hydrogen peroxide. Shake the contents thoroughly to ensure complete mixing.
7. Allow the items to remain in the activated ABTS working solution for 5 min.
8. Rinse items with distilled water and allow them to air dry.
9. When processing has been completed, all chemicals should be disposed of properly according to the appropriate federal, state, and local environmental laws.

Reservoir method

1. All appropriate personal protective equipment should be used when preparing and using this reagent.
2. Run the appropriate positive and negative controls to ensure that the reagent solution is working properly.
3. Place a piece of clean, dry filter paper over the area suspected to contain latent blood prints.
4. Saturate the filter paper with the fixative solution using a pipette and maintain saturation for 3 min.
5. Remove the filter paper and rinse the area underneath with distilled water.
6. Place a new clean, dry piece of filter paper over the processing area.
7. Saturate the filter paper with the ABTS working solution (with the hydrogen peroxide added) and maintain saturation for 5 min.
8. Remove the filter paper and rinse the area underneath with distilled water.
9. Allow items to air dry.
10. When processing has been completed, all chemicals should be disposed of properly according to the appropriate federal, state, and local environmental laws.

6.2.2.6 Leucocrystal Violet

LCV is the reduced and colorless form of crystal violet (Basic violet 3). Crystal violet was first prepared as a mixture with methyl violet in 1861 by Lauth. It was first synthesized in its pure form by Kern in 1883. It reacts to form a violet-colored print that is also luminescent in the near-infrared. Bodziak described an LCV reagent based on one reported by Fischer [68]. This reagent differed from Fischer's by incorporation of a fixative (5-sulfosalicylic acid) into the working solution. Amido black (methanol based) was reported to work in sequence after LCV treatment. Czarnecki reported the successful recovery of latent blood impressions on animal horns [69]. Michaud et al. reported on the use of 0.4 μm neutral nylon 66 membranes impregnated with LCV to develop and lift blood impressions [70]. Print detail was successfully lifted from surfaces like skin, tile, untreated wood, and cardboard. Gorn et al. reported the successful recovery of footwear impressions at a smoldering fire crime scene using LCV [71]. The toxicity of this reagent has been recently considered as potentially dangerous and caution should be exercised when using it, especially at crime scenes. LCV has been reported to be biohazardous due to its ability to damage chromosomes [72].

Reagent preparation [68]

Working solution

5-Sulfosalicylic acid	10 g
3% Hydrogen peroxide	500 mL
Sodium acetate	3.7 g
LCV	1 g

1. If the LCV crystals have turned yellow (instead of white), find a new supply.
2. Combine the 5-sulfosalicylic acid, hydrogen peroxide, sodium acetate, and LCV and mix thoroughly until it has dissolved completely.
3. Transfer to a dark glass bottle and store in the dark in a refrigerator.
4. The appropriate information (e.g., chemical contents, preparer's initials, date, reliability test result) should be recorded on the container's label.
5. The shelf life has been reported to be several months under these conditions.

Reagent application

1. All appropriate personal protective equipment should be used when preparing and using this reagent.
2. Run the appropriate positive and negative controls to ensure that the reagent solution is working properly.
3. The working solution can be applied by lightly spraying (e.g., hand spray bottle, pressurized aerosol pump sprayer) the area of interest or by immersing smaller items into the solution.
4. When LCV makes contact with blood traces, the impression will turn a purple color.
5. If necessary for certain processed items, rinse items with distilled water and allow them to air dry. Care must be exercised with rinsing since it can compromise developed stains on some surfaces.
6. When processing has been completed, all chemicals should be disposed of properly according to the appropriate federal, state, and local environmental laws.

6.2.2.7 Leucomalachite Green

Leucomlachite green (LMG) is the colorless form of the dye malachite green (Basic green 4). It is a triarylmethine dye, which turns a deep-green color upon reaction with blood and hydrogen peroxide. LMG was used to develop blood spatter patterns on a suicide victim [73]. These results were used to corroborate a witness's testimony that suicide was the cause of death. Jaret et al. reported that LMG prints could be lifted from surfaces using black and white fixed photographic paper [74]. Both the leuco and colored forms of malachite green have been reported to be suspected carcinogens and have been banned as food additives by both the Food and Drug Administration and the European Union [75]. These compounds are often used as inexpensive fungicides; however, quantities of these materials have been known to bioaccumulate in the fatty tissues of fish.

Reagent preparation [74]

Working solution

5-Sulfosalicylic acid	2.2 g
Distilled water	100 mL
Leucomalachite green	0.16 g
30% Hydrogen peroxide	10 mL

1. Combine the 5-sulfosalicylic acid and water and mix vigorously until it has completely dissolved.
2. Add LMG to the solution and mix thoroughly until it has completely dissolved.
3. Carefully add the hydrogen peroxide to the solution and mix completely to ensure that the reagent has been activated.
4. Transfer to a dark glass bottle. The solution should be used as soon as possible after mixing.
5. The appropriate information (e.g., chemical contents, preparer's initials, date, reliability test result) should be recorded on the container's label.

Reagent application

1. All appropriate personal protective equipment should be used when preparing and using this reagent.
2. Run the appropriate positive and negative controls to ensure that the reagent solution is working properly.
3. Small items can be immersed into a solution of the working solution (approximately 3–5 min with a distilled water rinse) while larger areas can be sprayed.
4. If necessary, carefully rinse items/surfaces with distilled water and allow them to air dry.
5. When processing has been completed, all chemicals should be disposed of properly according to the appropriate federal, state, and local environmental laws.

6.2.2.8 Fluorescein

Fluorescein (Acid Yellow 73 or D&C Yellow no. 7) was first synthesized by von Baeyer in 1871 [76]. It is a xanthene derivative of phenolphthalein and is the colored form of fluorescin [77]. Fluorescein was reported to be a safer alternative to luminol [78]. The fluorescent reaction product (upon contact with hydrogen peroxide and blood) was found to degrade rapidly and develop background interference after only a few minutes. It has also been used successfully to visualize latent bloody foot trails [79].

Reagent preparation [78]

Working solution

Sodium hydroxide	10 g
Deionized water	100 mL
Fluorescein	1 g
Zinc powder	10 g
Ketrol RD	4.75 g

1. Combine the sodium hydroxide and deionized water and mix until it has completely dissolved.
2. Add the fluorescein to the solution and mix thoroughly until it has completely dissolved. Gently heat the solution while stirring continuously.
3. Carefully add the zinc powder to the solution and continue to mix. Not all of the zinc powder will dissolve.
4. Bring the solution to a gentle boil.
5. The solution will lose most of its color by this time and it should be allowed to cool.
6. Carefully decant the solution while leaving the remaining zinc behind.
7. Mix the thickening agent, Ketrol RD, with 950 mL of deionized water. Ketrol RD requires a significant amount of time to dissolve (this can be done in advance).
8. The working solution is prepared by mixing the solution prepared earlier with deionized water in a 1:20 ratio (i.e., 50 mL fluorescein solution with 950 mL of the thickening agent-deionized water solution).*
9. Transfer to a spray bottle. The solution should be used as soon as possible after mixing.
10. The appropriate information (e.g., chemical contents, preparer's initials, date, reliability test result) should be recorded on the container's label.

Hydrogen peroxide solution

30% Hydrogen peroxide	100 mL
Deionized water	200 mL

1. Carefully combine the water and hydrogen peroxide and mix until the solution is homogeneous.
2. Place the solution into a spray bottle.
3. The appropriate information (e.g., chemical contents, preparer's initials, date) should be recorded on the container's label.

Reagent application

1. All appropriate personal protective equipment should be used when preparing and using this reagent.
2. Run the appropriate positive and negative controls to ensure that the reagent solution is working properly.
3. The fluorescin working solution is first sprayed on the area of interest from a distance of 12–18 in.
4. No more than two applications should be made to reduce running on vertical surfaces. A slight yellow color will appear within a few seconds.
5. The hydrogen peroxide solution spray should be applied next in a similar manner as described earlier. This application can help reduce background interference.

* Note that this is a fluorescin (or leuco fluorescein) solution. Only upon reaction with hydrogen peroxide and blood will the fluorescent product, fluorescein, be formed.

6. Illumination of the treated surfaces should be done using 450nm wavelength of light and emission should be viewed using orange filters (e.g., OG535).
7. When processing has been completed, all chemicals should be disposed of properly according to the appropriate federal, state, and local environmental laws.

6.2.2.9 Phenolphthalein

Like fluorescein, phenolphthalein was also first synthesized by von Baeyer in 1871. In 1903, the compound became the basis for the Kastle-Meyer presumptive blood test [80]. A positive test for blood results in the formation of a pink color. Cox reported that phenolphthalein was the best single presumptive blood test when compared to leucomalachite green, tetramethylbenzidine, and *o*-tolidine [81].

Reagent preparation

Stock solution

Phenolphthalein	2 g
Potassium hydroxide	20 g
Distilled water	100 mL
Zinc powder	20 g

1. Combine the phenolphthalein, potassium hydroxide, zinc powder, and distilled water and reflux for 2h until the solution becomes colorless.
2. Transfer to a dark glass bottle and store in a refrigerator. Excess zinc can be added to keep the phenolphthalein in its reduced, colorless form (phenolphthalein).
3. The appropriate information (e.g., chemical contents, preparer's initials, date, reliability test result) should be recorded on the container's label.

Working solution

Phenolphthalein stock solution	20 mL
Ethanol	80 mL
3% Hydrogen peroxide	5 drops

1. Combine the phenolphthalein stock solution and ethanol and mix thoroughly.
2. Add approximately 5 drops of the hydrogen peroxide solution into the mixture.
3. Transfer the solution to a spray bottle.
4. The appropriate information (e.g., chemical contents, preparer's initials, date, reliability test result) should be recorded on the container's label.

Reagent application

1. All appropriate personal protective equipment should be used when preparing and using this reagent.
2. Run the appropriate positive and negative controls to ensure that the reagent solution is working properly.
3. The working solution should be sprayed on the area of interest from a distance of 12–18 in.

4. No more than two applications should be made to reduce running on vertical surfaces. A pink color will appear within a few seconds and indicate a positive result.
5. Allow items to air dry.
6. When processing has been completed, all chemicals should be disposed of properly according to the appropriate federal, state, and local environmental laws.

References

1. Tortora GJ, Grabowski SR. (1996) *Principles of Anatomy and Physiology*, 8th edn. HarperCollins, New York.
2. Puchtler H, Sweat F. (1962) Amido black as a stain for hemoglobin. *Arch Pathol* 73:245–249.
3. Oden S. (1957) Process of developing fingerprints. *Ident News* 7(1):1–2.
4. Hussain JI, Pounds CA. (1989) The enhancement of marks in blood. Part II. A modified amido black staining technique. CRSE Report No. 685.
5. Kent T, ed. (1986) *Manual of Fingerprint Development Techniques*, 1st edn. U.K. Home Office, Police Scientific Development Branch, Sandridge, U.K.
6. Sears V, Prizeman TM. (2000) Enhancement of fingerprints in blood—Part 1: The optimization of amido black. *J Forensic Ident* 50(5):470–480.
7. Warrick P. (2000) Identification of blood prints on fabric using amido black and digital enhancement. *J Forensic Ident* 50(1):20–32.
8. McCarthy MM, Grieve DL. (1989) Preprocessing with cyanoacrylate ester fuming for fingerprint impressions in blood. *J Forensic Ident* 39(1):23–32.
9. Anon. (1993) Amido black treatment of a murder victim. *Fingerprint Whorld* 19(73):55.
10. Trozzi TA, Schwartz RL, Hollars ML. (2001) Processing guide for developing latent prints. U.S. Department of Justice, Federal Bureau of Investigation, Washington, DC.
11. Bowman V, Ed. (2009) *Manual of Fingerprint Development Techniques*, 2nd edn. Home Office, Police Scientific Development Branch: Sandridge, U.K.
12. Barnett KG, Bone RG, Hall PW, Ide RH. (1988) The use of water soluble protein dye for the enhancement of footwear impressions in blood on non-porous surfaces, Part 1. Tech Note No. 629.
13. Society of Dyers and Colourists with acknowledgement to the American Association of Textile Chemists and Colorists. (1982) *Colour Index*, 3rd edn. (second revision). Huddersfield , U.K.: H. Charlesworth & Co. Ltd. 5:5435.
14. Fazekas de St Groth S, Webster RG, Datyner A. (1963) Two new staining procedures for quantitative estimation of proteins on electrophoretic strips. *Biochim Biophys Acta* 71:377–391.
15. Meyer TS, Lambert BL. (1965) Use of Coomassie Brilliant Blue R250 for the electrophoresis of microgram quantities of parotid saliva proteins on acrylamide-gel strips. *Biochim Biophys Acta* 107:144–145.
16. Norkus P, Noppinger K. (1986) New reagent for the enhancement of blood prints. *Fingerprint Whorld* 12(45):15–16.
17. Hunter JL. (1994) Fingerprint evidence with Coomassie Blue—after 25 years. *J Forensic Ident* 44(6):619–622.
18. Phillips JD. (1988) The Dexter murder—a protein stain success. *Fingerprint Whorld* 13(52):71–72.
19. Becraft M, Heintzman M. (1987) Application of Crowle's stain in the enhancement of bloody fingerprints. *Fingerprint Whorld* 12(47):65–66.
20. Sears VG, Butcher CPG, Prizeman TM. (2001) Enhancement of fingerprints in blood—Part 2: Protein dyes. *J Forensic Ident* 51(1):28–38.

21. Atkins AL. (2007) Development of bloody latent prints on dark surfaces. United States Army Criminal Investigation Command Laboratory, presented at the International Association for Identification Annual Conference, San Diego, CA (July 27).
22. Sears VG, Butcher CPG, Fitzgerald LA. (2005) Enhancement of fingerprints in blood part 3: Reactive techniques, Acid Yellow 7, and process sequences. *J Forensic Ident* 55(6):741–763.
23. Anon. (2006) *Acid Yellow 7*. BVDA Product Information. Haarlem, the Netherlands. January 2006.
24. Anon. *How to Use Hungarian Red*. BVDA Product Information. Haarlem, the Netherlands.
25. Schonbein CF. (1857) Ueber chemische berührungswirkungen. *Verhand Naturforsch Gesellsch Basel* 1:467–482.
26. Ross G, Gray CH, de Silva S, Newman J. (1964) Assessment of routine tests for occult blood in faeces. *Br Med J* 1:1351–1354.
27. Azevedo AM, Martins VC, Prazeres DMF, Vojinovic V, Cabral JMS, Fonseca LP. (2003) Horseradish peroxidase: a valuable tool in biotechnology. *Biotechnol Annu Rev* 9:199–247.
28. Alder O, Alder R. (1904) Über das verhalten gewisser organisher verbindungen gegenüber blut mit besonderer berücksichtigung das nachweises von blut. *Hoppe-Seyler's Z Physiol Chem* 41:59–67.
29. Culliford BJ, Nickolls LC. (1964) The benzidine test. *J Forensic Sci* 9(1):175–191.
30. Occupational Safety and Health Administration. (1974) OSHA Regulation H002, 29 January 1974.
31. Olsen RD. (1986) Sensitivity comparison of blood enhancement techniques. *Ident News* 36(8):5–8.
32. Holland VR, Saunders BC, Rose FL, Walpole AL. (1974) A safer substitute for benzidine in the detection of blood. *Tetrahedron* 30:3299.
33. Garner DD, Cano KM, Peimer RS, Yeshion TE. (1976) An evaluation of tetramethylbenzidine as a presumptive test for blood. *J Forensic Sci* 21(4):816–821.
34. Lee HC, Hazen R, Nutt J. (1984) TMB as an enhancement reagent for bloody prints. *Ident News* 34(3):10–11.
35. Ruttan R, Hardisty R. (1912) A new reagent for detecting occult blood. *Can Med Assoc J* 41:995–998.
36. Trudeau D. (1996) Ortho-tolidine: an "explosive" mixture that can yield tremendous results. *RCMP Gazette* 58(6):14–17.
37. Lauth C. (1867) On the new aniline dye, "violet de Paris." *Laboratory* 1:138–139.
38. Cox M. (1990) Effect of fabric washing on the presumptive identification of bloodstains. *J Forensic Sci* 35(6):1335–1341.
39. Nutt J. (1984) Don't touch the body. *Ident News* 34:2,13.
40. Anon. (1987) U.S. environmental protection agency. Health and environmental effects profile for 2-methylaniline and 2-methylaniline hydrochloride. Environmental Criteria and Assessment Office, Office of Health and Environmental Assessment, Office of Research and Development, Cincinnati, OH.
41. Sahs PT. (1992) DAB: an advancement in blood print detection. *J Forensic Ident* 42(5):412–420.
42. Hsu SM, Soban E. (1982) Color modification of diaminobenzidine (DAB) precipitation by metallic ions and its application for double immunohistochemistry. *J Histochem Cytochem* 30(10):1079–1082.
43. James SH, Kish PE, Sutton TP. (2005) *Principles of Bloodstain Pattern Analysis: Theory and Practice*. CRC Press, Boca Raton, FL.
44. Albrecht HO. (1928) Uber die chemiluminescenz des amonophthalsaurehydrazids. *Z Phys Chem* 136:321–330.
45. Specht W. (1937) Die chemiluminescenz des hamins, ein hilfsmittel zur auffindung und erkennung forensisch wichtiger blutspuren. *Angew Chem* 50:155–157.
46. Grodsky M, Wright K, Kirk PL. (1951) Simplified preliminary blood testing: an improved technique and a comparative study of methods. *J Crim Law Criminol Pol Sci* 42:95–104.
47. Roswell DF, White EH. (1979) The chemiluminescence of luminol and related hydrazides. *Methods Enzymol* 57:409–423.

48. Lytle LT, Hedgecock DG. (1978) Chemiluminescence in the visualization of forensic bloodstains. *J Forensic Sci* 23(3):550–562.
49. Waldoch TL. (1996) Chemical detection of blood after dilution by rain over a 72 day period. *J Forensic Ident* 46(2):173–178.
50. Niebauer JC, Booth JB, Brewer BL. (1990) Recording luminol luminescence in its context using a film overlay method. *J Forensic Ident* 40(5):271–278.
51. Shirk SA. (1995) Night vision video and luminol. *J Forensic Ident* 45(5):513–514.
52. Morgan SL, Myrick ML, Brooke H, Baranowski MR, McCutcheon JN. (2011) Design of a prototype mid-IR imaging system for visualizing blood at crime scenes. Presented at the American Academy of Forensic Sciences Annual Meeting, Chicago, IL, 26 February.
53. Creamer JI, Quickenden TI, Apanah MV, Kerr KA, Robertson P. (2003) A comprehensive experimental study of industrial, domestic and environmental interferences with the forensic luminol test for blood. *Luminescence* 18:193–198.
54. Barni F, Lewis SW, Berti A, Miskelly GM, Lago G. (2007) Forensic application of the luminol reaction as a presumptive test for latent blood detection. *Talanta* 72:896–913.
55. Creamer JI, Quickenden TI, Chrichton LB, Robertson P, Ruhayel RA. (2005) Attempted cleaning of bloodstains and its effect on the forensic luminol test. *Luminescence* 20:411–413.
56. Ehrenberg R. (2008) Household cleaners using oxygen may make blood removal too simple. *Sci News* 174(12):12.
57. Kent EJM, Elliot DA, Miskelly GM. (2003) Inhibition of bleach-induced luminol chemiluminescence. *J Forensic Sci* 48(1):64–67.
58. King R, Miskelly GM. (2005) The inhibition by amines and amino acids of bleach-induced luminol chemiluminescence during forensic screening for blood. *Talanta* 67:345–353.
59. Castelló A, Francés F, Verdú F. (2009) Bleach interference in forensic luminol tests on porous surfaces: more about the drying time effect. *Talanta* 77:1555–1557.
60. Cresap TR, Pecko JL, Zeliff DJ, Fristoe VL, Moses MA, Ricciardone MD et al. (1995) The effects of luminol and Coomassie Blue on DNA typing by PCR. Presented at 47th Annual American Academy of Forensic Sciences Meeting, Seattle, WA.
61. Frégeau CJ, Germain O, Fourney RM. (2000) Fingerprint enhancement revisited and the effects of blood enhancement chemicals on subsequent *Profiler Plus*™ fluorescent short tandem repeat DNA analysis of fresh and aged bloody fingerprints. *J Forensic Sci* 45(2):354–380.
62. Blum LJ, Esperanca P, Rocquefelte S. (2006) A new high-performance reagent and procedure for latent bloodstain detection based on luminol chemiluminescence. *Can Soc Forensic Sci J* 39(3):81–100.
63. Dilbeck L. (2006) Use of Bluestar Forensic in lieu of luminol at crime scenes. *J Forensic Ident* 56(5):706–720.
64. Larkin T, Gannicliffe C. (2008) Illuminating the health and safety of luminol. *Sci Justice* 48:71–75.
65. Weber K. (1966) Die andwendung der chemiluminescenz des luminols in der gerichtlichen medizin und toxicologie. I. Der nachweis von blutspuren. *Dtsch Z Gesamte Gerichtl Med* 57:410–423.
66. Caldwell JP, Henderson W, Kim ND. (2000) ABTS: a safe alternative to DAB for the enhancement of blood fingerprints. *J Forensic Sci* 45(4):785–794.
67. Caldwell JP, Kim ND. (2002) Extension of the color suite available for chemical enhancement of fingerprints in blood. *J Forensic Sci* 47(2):332–340.
68. Bodziak WJ. (1996) Use of leuco crystal violet to enhance shoe prints in blood. *Forensic Sci Int* 82:45–52.
69. Czarnecki ER. (2002) Development of prints on antlers and horns. *J Forensic Sci* 52(4):433–437.
70. Michaud AL, Brun-Conti L. (2004) A method for impregnating nylon transfer membranes with leucocrystal violet for enhancing and lifting bloody impressions. *J Forensic Sci* 49(3):511–516.
71. Gorn M, Stafford-Allen P, Stevenson J, White P. (2007) The recovery of footwear marks in blood at a homicide scene involving a smoldering fire. *J Forensic Ident* 57(5):706–716.
72. Au W, Pathak S, Collie CJ, Hsu TC. (1978) Cytogenetic toxicity of gentian violet and crystal violet on mammalian cells in vitro. *Mutat Res* 58(2–3):269–276.

73. Hansen TA. (1994) Presumptive blood test used for statement corroboration. *J Forensic Ident* 44(5):517–520.
74. Jaret Y, Heriau M, Donche A. (1997) Transfer of bloody fingerprints. *J Forensic Ident* 47(1):38–41.
75. Ding T, Xu J, Wu B, Chen H, Shen C, Liu F, Wang K. (2008) LC-MS-MS determination of malachite green and leucomalachite green in fish products. *Curr Trends Mass Spectrom* 8:18–21.
76. Duan Y, Liu M, Sun W, Wang M, Liu S, Li QX. (2009) Recent progress on synthesis of fluorescein probes. *Rev Org Chem* 6:35–43.
77. Zollinger H. (2003) *Color Chemistry. Syntheses, Properties, and Applications of Organic Dyes and Pigments*, 3rd revised edn. Verlag Helvetica Chimica Acta, Zurich, Switzerland.
78. Cheeseman R, DiMeo LA. (1995) Fluorescein as a field-worthy latent bloodstain detection system. *J Forensic Ident* 45(6):631–646.
79. Cheeseman R, Tomboc R. (2001) Fluorescein technique performance study on bloody foot trails. *J Forensic Ident* 51(1):16–27.
80. Gaensslen RE. (1989) *Sourcebook in Forensic Serology, Immunology, and Biochemistry,* National Institutes of Justice, U.S. Department of Justice, Washington, DC, pp. 103–105.
81. Cox M. (1991) A study of the sensitivity and specificity of four presumptive tests for blood. *J Forensic Sci* 36(5):1503–1511.

7

Miscellaneous Methods and Challenging Surfaces

Robert S. Ramotowski

CONTENTS

7.1 Miscellaneous Methods

7.1.1 Radioactive Techniques

Radiographic techniques have been used for fingerprint development since the 1950s. A good overview of these techniques was provided by Knowles [1]. One of the earliest methods was described by Takeuchi et al. in 1958 [2]. The process involved the use of ^{14}C-labeled stearic acid, which is selectively absorbed by fats present in latent print deposits. Successful results were obtained on substrates like paper, glass, and metal foil. Gel'fman et al. described the use of ^{14}C-labeled formaldehyde to develop latent prints [3]. The process was first described and patented by Takeuchi in 1960 [4]. The labeled formaldehyde was thought to react with the amino acids or fatty materials in the print, which could then be imaged using contact radiography.

In 1963, Grant et al. described the use of ^{35}S-labeled sulfur dioxide to develop latent prints on paper [5]. The method was further refined by Spedding for application to a wider variety of papers and fabrics [6]. Sulfur dioxide is thought to either react with unsaturated lipids in the latent print or interact in such a way that it is fixed within the print as a sulfate [1]. After exposure to the $^{35}SO_2$ gas, the latent print material was selectively labeled and subsequently imaged using autoradiography. The typical exposure time required to produce a satisfactory print was approximately 40 h. Lipid breakdown and competition with atmospheric SO_2 limited the effectiveness of the technique on fabric to samples only a few hours old. Ganson described some successful operational applications of the method to casework [7]. One such case involved the unsuccessful recovery of latent prints by traditional means (i.e., iodine, ninhydrin, and silver nitrate) on counterfeit £5 notes. No trace of friction ridge detail was visualized. After processing four notes with $^{35}SO_2$, a total of three identifiable prints were developed.

In 1974, Morgan et al. reported on the use of radioactive halogens, such as bromine (^{82}Br) and iodine monochloride (^{133}ICl), to develop latent prints [8]. The iodine monochloride procedure was noted to be simpler and safer than using ^{128}I or ^{131}I (these two isotopes emit γ-radiation as well as high-energy β-rays). The radioactive halogens are thought to enter the latent print residue by exchange with chloride ions. Prints treated with ^{131}I-labeled iodine monochloride produced radiographs that were inferior to $^{35}SO_2$ treatment; however, prints treated with ^{82}Br-labeled bromine produced nearly the same quality radiographs as those from $^{35}SO_2$. The successful use of these techniques was limited by the degradation of the unsaturated components of the latent print, especially with items exposed to outside environments.

In 1976, Knowles et al. reported on the use of a ^{35}S-labeled thiourea solution to image physically developed prints on patterned backgrounds [9]. The silver PD prints were first converted to silver bromide and then tagged with ^{35}S by reaction with ^{35}S-labeled thiourea. Radiolabeled silver sulfide is formed and subsequently imaged by autoradiography. Radioactive silver (^{110}Ag) was reported by Akerman [10] and Stverak et al. [11] to react with latent print residue. A radiolabeled silver nitrate solution reacted with chlorides in the latent print to produce radioactive silver chloride. Subsequent imaging with autoradiography was reported to produce good results on several papers types, polyethylene, and ungrained leather.

The use of radionucleotides of sodium and chlorine, generated by neutron activation, was suggested as far back as 1956 [1,12]. This process converted the sodium chloride present in the latent print *in situ* to ^{24}Na and ^{38}Cl. In addition to requiring access to a nuclear reactor, the process had two significant limitations. The process was limited to substrates that did not contain elements with high neutron cross sections (e.g., sodium). Also, chloride ions are known to migrate, especially in humid environments. This could lead to diffuse print detail in the autoradiograph.

7.1.2 Biological Techniques

The use of enzymes to enhance development of latent prints using amino acid reagents was first described by McLaughlin in 1961 [13]. Everse et al. investigated trypsin and pronase as candidates for sequential treatment of prints both before and after ninhydrin [14]. The technique worked for relatively fresh prints, but not older ones. A subsequent study found that the enzyme particle size was a significant factor [15]. Finely powdered, lyophylized Sigma Type III trypsin produced the most significant contrast improvement. Almost no background interference was observed.

The use of bacteria to develop latent prints was first reported by O'Neill in 1941 [16]. Several different approaches have been described since that time, but these techniques are not in use today. Development of latent prints using the gram-negative bacterium *Acinetobacter calciacaticus* was reported by Mason in 1987 [17]. The bacteria were contained within a nutrient gel, which was then directly applied to the substrate surface. Growth occurred preferentially along the latent friction ridges, after incubating for approximately 24 h. Harper et al. reported good results with this technique on polyethylene surfaces after 48 h of incubation and subsequent staining with amido black [18].

Lectin, isolated from seeds of the gorse plant *Ulex europeus*, is known to bind to sugars located on the surface of red blood cells [19]. In addition, the use of antibodies to react with the three red blood cell antigens (i.e., A, B, H) could also visualize latent prints. The latter technique was first reported by Ishiyama et al. in 1977 [20]. Ridge detail was developed by agglutination of the red blood cells bound to the latent print residue only when prints were donated by secretors whose blood was type A or type B. To improve the print's contrast, a wash step was required to remove unbound red blood cells. Subsequent testing of monoclonal antibodies against A, B, and H antigens determined that prints from nonsecretors and those with type O blood could be developed. Nonspecific binding was found to be a problem, although the addition of Tween 80 to the lectin and monoclonal anti-H solutions essentially eliminated background staining. Antibody-coated latex particles could be used to develop fluorescent, colored, or radioactive print detail. The best surfaces for recovering prints with this technique were found to be polyethylene, polyvinyl chloride (PVC), adhesive tapes, metal foils, and cellulose acetate.

Drapel et al. have reported success in visualizing prints using protein antibodies [21]. A quantitative assay of proteins in latent print residue yielded approximately 133 μg for eccrine prints (composed of mostly sweat) and approximately 384 μg for mixed residues (composed of eccrine and sebaceous material). Prints were placed on both paper and polyvinylidene difluoride (PVDF) membranes and aged up to 1 week. Good ridge quality was obtained on PVDF when anti-keratin 1 and 10 antibodies were used. These proteins are typically derived from skin cell desquamation rather than excretion from pores. The anti-cathepsin-D and anti-dermcidin antibodies produced more spotty development, perhaps due to the fact that these proteins are derived mostly from the pores of the skin. The results for paper were generally weaker than the ones on PVDF, possibly due to diffusion of the developed prints into the paper. Spindler et al. have also reported on the use of antigens for latent print development [22]. Anti-L-amino acid antibodies conjugated with gold nanoparticles were used to visualize prints. The antibodies had been labeled with Fluorescent Red 610, which made the resulting prints fluoresce (590 nm excitation with a 650 nm band-pass filter). However, the quality of the developed prints was not as good as those fumed with cyanoacrylate and stained with rhodamine 6G. As prints aged (up to several months), the quality of the developed prints were comparable to dry powder processing.

Recently, antibody functionalized nanoparticles have been used to target drug metabolites in latent print resides. Anti-cotinine antibodies functionalized with magnetic nanoparticles have been used to detect cotinine in sweat deposited from smokers [23–25]. A similar approach was used to detect morphine (metabolite of heroin) and benzoylecgonine (a metabolite of cocaine) simultaneously from a single latent print residue [26]. In addition to providing intelligence information about drug usage, these two approaches produced good quality prints.

7.1.3 Reflected Ultraviolet Imaging Systems

The ultraviolet portion of the electromagnetic spectrum is often divided into three distinct regions. The first region, UVA, is also known as "black light" and spans the wavelength range of 320–400 nm. Long-wave UV lamps operate in this region (~365 nm). This is the least energetic region and is sometimes referred to as the "tanning UV." The second region, UVB, is referred to as the "burning UV" and covers wavelengths between 290 and 320 nm. The third region, UVC, covers wavelengths between 190 and 290 nm and is where short-wave UV lamps operate (~254 nm). This highly energetic region can be used to sterilize surfaces. This region of the spectrum does not reach the Earth's surface as it is absorbed by the planet's protective ozone layer. Standard glass lenses or plastic filters will not transmit this wavelength range, as their transmission begins above 300 nm. As a result, imaging devices operating in this range must use optics made from materials like quartz, calcium fluoride, magnesium fluoride, or a combination of these substances (their transmission begins above 200 nm). The vacuum UV region covers wavelengths below 190 nm. These wavelengths are absorbed by air molecules and can only be used within a vacuum environment.

Physicist R.W. Wood was one of the pioneers in the use of ultraviolet radiation for covert signaling purposes during the First World War [27]. He created a long-wave ultraviolet illumination device that eventually came to be known as a Woods lamp. The first photographs of human skin using an ultraviolet radiation source were reported in 1935 [28]. Bite marks were imaged using ultraviolet photography in the 1970s [29]. Ultraviolet photography historically used UV-sensitive film, specialized optics, and took advantage of a unique property of human skin. As the illumination wavelength decreases, human skin becomes more reflective and can reveal details not present in the visible portion of the spectrum. The percentage of radiation reflected or scattered by human skin at 400 nm (20%) increases dramatically at 300 nm (66%) and 250 nm (81%) [27]. Skin illuminated in the short-wave region of the ultraviolet can take on a shiny, metallic appearance when viewed in the short-wave UV region. With this shorter wavelength comes better resolution. Imaging of latent prints in this region takes advantage of this phenomenon.

The first reported successful detection of a latent print in the ultraviolet was by Ohki in 1970 [30]. Both long- and short-wave radiation was used to image prints on paper and plastic. Ishiwata and Nakamura of the National Police Agency of Japan began experimenting with short-wave, UV-sensitive image intensifiers in the mid-1980s [31]. Zhou reported on the photographic detection of latent prints using short-wave ultraviolet radiation in 1987 [32]. In 1987, the use of a short-wave, UV-sensitive imaging device was reported [33].

This device, referred to as a reflected (sometimes referred to as "reflective") ultraviolet imaging system (RUVIS) was first manufactured by the Hamamatsu Corporation [34]. This device was portable and could be used to search for latent prints at crime scenes. A major advantage of this system was the viewing capability that allowed for real-time optimization of both illuminant and imaging conditions to produce maximum contrast. The impact of most complex or patterned surfaces, which interfered with imaging in the visible spectrum, was found to be significantly diminished in the short-wave ultraviolet.

Qiang provides a good overview of the optical phenomena involved in reflective UV imaging [35]. When radiation is reflected from a surface it can do so in either a specular or diffuse manner. Specular reflection occurs when radiation is reflected at an angle equal to the angle of incidence. Diffuse reflection occurs at angles independent of the original angle of incidence. A combination of these two phenomena is called intermediate reflection. The latter type of reflection is what is encountered when using a RUVIS. The strongest reflection of the short-wave ultraviolet radiation occurs at the angle of incidence and decreases as the angle changes. When viewing latent or processed prints on a UV-absorbing surface with a RUVIS, light ridges are observed on a dark background. Changing the angle of illumination can result in improved contrast between the specular reflection from the smooth surface and intermediate reflection from the raised surfaces of the friction ridges. For smooth, UV-absorbent surfaces, an incident angle between 10° and 30° is recommended. Dark fingerprint ridges on a lighter background can occur on non-UV-absorbing and matte surfaces. Diffuse reflection results from the difference in UV-absorption properties of the surface and ridge detail. On such surfaces, changing the illumination angle does not produce significant changes in contrast between the surface and ridge detail. For such surfaces, an incident angle of 45° is recommended.

One reason that RUVIS works so well in enhancing faint prints on smooth surfaces is that the raised surfaces of the friction ridges are more pronounced in the ultraviolet than in the visible region of the spectrum (due to the shorter wavelength). Surface roughness becomes more pronounced, particularly if the average height of the ridges is larger than the wavelength of the illuminating radiation [36].

A RUVIS examination can be conducted prior to the use of latent print techniques as well as after. Superglue fuming has been noted to increase the contrast of ridge detail viewed with a RUVIS. In addition, high-noise backgrounds like magazine paper and color photographs, which are UV-absorbent and turn dark when illuminated with short-wave radiation, can yield high-contrast prints [37]. Footwear impressions in floor wax have also been recovered with a RUVIS. The impact of the surface type and age of the latent print deposit has also been investigated [38]. On ideal surfaces like ceramic tiles and glass, prints could be visualized with a RUVIS up to 6 weeks with no noticeable degradation. Latent prints on other surfaces like plastics bowls, varnished wood, polished stainless steel, and china, could be observed only hours or days after deposition. No prints could be detected on porous surfaces. Recently, a study was published that examined the efficacy of using a RUVIS to examine postblast material for latent prints [39]. The technique was successfully able to recover a print on a postblast piece of plastic that had not been subjected to any prior fingerprint detection technique.

7.1.4 Scanning Electron Microscopy/X-Ray Fluorescence

Scanning electron microscopy (SEM) has been used to image latent prints on a variety of different surfaces [40]. In this particular effort, the method was attempted prior to any conventional chemical processes being used. The SEM technique has the advantage of having a depth-of-field nearly 300 times greater than that of a conventional light microscope. Samples were coated with a trace amount of gold to increase surface conductivity. Good results were reported with this technique on both conductive and nonconductive surfaces that had been heated and aged. However, samples exposed to the sun and rain developed a coating that obscured viewing with the SEM.

Worley et al. tried micro-x-ray fluorescence as a technique for visualizing untreated latent prints using elemental mapping [41]. This nondestructive method allowed for the specific targeting of elements (e.g., potassium, chloride, calcium, silicon) that would be present in latent print residue. Images of uncontaminated and contaminated (e.g., lotion, saliva) latent prints were successfully acquired. However, some drawbacks of this technique include the requirement to have a general knowledge where the print is located on the substrate and the sample size limitations imposed by the chamber of the instrument.

7.1.5 Chemical Imaging

Chemical imaging is a relatively new approach to latent print visualization and it involves a combination of molecular spectroscopy and digital imaging [42]. The method involves the collection of high spatial/spectral resolution data as well as quantitative and qualitative information for both organic and inorganic compounds. The combination of both techniques allows for the collection of data as a function of wavelength (spectroscopy) and location (imaging) [43]. The result is an image at each wavelength and a full spectrum at each pixel. Data analysis involves the use of principal component analysis, which is used to produce a least squares fit to model variability in the spectral data. Each spectrum in an image is represented as a linear combination of the most important principle components.

Chemical imaging acquires data at many different wavelengths (multispectral) or up to potentially dozens of wavelengths (hyperspectral). This technique takes advantage of liquid crystal tunable filters (instead of acousto-optic tunable filters), which have no moving parts, allow for simultaneous wavelength selection, wavelength tuning, high resolution, and decreased sample analysis times. Chemical imaging can be based on a wide variety of spectroscopic methods, including visible absorption [44], fluorescent emission, Raman scattering, and infrared absorption. Other types of chemical imaging have also been reported. Desorption electrospray ionization mass spectrometry was used to chemically image latent fingerprints [45]. This technique has also been applied to the detection of trace drug and explosive residues within the untreated print residue.

Chemical imaging in the infrared portion of the spectrum has been used in a number of forensic science disciplines. In addition to targeting fingerprints, infrared chemical imaging has been used to determine the sequence of writing strokes [46] and to detect counterfeit pharmaceuticals [47]. Attenuated total reflection Fourier transform infrared spectroscopy has also been used to image chemical components of latent prints under controlled temperature and humidity conditions [48]. Tahtouh et al. report the use of infrared chemical imaging to successfully visualize latent prints on Australian polymer banknotes [49]. They subsequently reported on improvements for detecting prints on nonporous surfaces, but noted difficulties with porous surfaces due to background interference from cellulose [50]. Crane et al. also used infrared chemical imaging to detect latent prints as well as trace evidence contained within the residue [51]. Chemical imaging will be addressed in greater detail in a subsequent chapter.

7.2 Challenging Surfaces

7.2.1 Thermal Paper

Thermal paper is typically comprised of a series of layers or coatings on the glossy, emulsion-side of the paper [52]. However, it is possible for both sides to be coated, as NCR Corporation has recently introduced a two-sided thermal paper [53]. Although thermal paper can contain lignin, alum, and rosin (which should make the pH of the paper acidic), the overall pH is around 8.5, perhaps due to additives contained in the coating [54]. The coating typically contains a fluoran-leuco dye that reacts with an acid (e.g., octadecylphosphonic acid). Thermal papers can often contain up to 0.8%–3.0% (8–17 g/kg) by weight bisphenol A, which is an endocrine disruptor (with estrogenic activity) [55]. Upon contact with a heated printer head, a shift from the uncolored form to a colored one occurs [56]. The coating matrix then stabilizes the final colored form. Exposure to certain solvents used in fingerprint reagents can cause these reactions to occur as well, which leads to unwanted discoloration (or darkening) of the emulsion-side of the thermal paper. Thermal papers are known to degrade over time. Even when stored under recommended conditions (20°C, 50% RH, and dark conditions), thermal papers have been reported to last only up to 5 years [54].

7.2.1.1 Solvent Treatments

Solvents can be used as either pretreatments or posttreatments to clear away the active layer of the thermal paper. However, some have observed that some solvents, like acetone, can diminish the quality of the developed ridge detail [57]. The Home Office Scientific Development Branch advocated the use of an ethanol prewash to remove the active coating from the thermal paper before using conventional reagents (e.g., 1,8-diazafluoren-9-one (DFO), ninhydrin) [58]. The items were dipped into the ethanol for 5–10 s to remove any thermal printing present, resulting in a clear background (no darkening) even after amino acid reagents are used. This prewash, done prior to DFO or ninhydrin, was reported to be more effective than pDMAC fuming [59].

Solvent posttreatments are also possible. Schwarz and Klenke recommended the use of a post-ninhydrin clearing solution (the authors referred to this as a "whitening" solution) called G3 [57]. The G3 solution was composed of an equimolar (12.5 mmol) mixture of 4-pyrrolidino-pyridine, oenantholactam, 1-octyl-2-pyrrolidone, and 1-cyclohexyl-pyrrolidone in ethanol and petroleum ether. Interestingly, upon processing ninhydrin-treated prints on thermal paper with the G3 solution, the developed prints turned blue and there was no damage to any ballpoint inks present on the item. While effective, it is important to note that these solvent prewash processes remove all of the printed material from the thermal paper. Because of the volatile nature of the compounds used in this mixture, the decolorization can also fade over time [60]. In instances where there is a need to preserve the printed material on the receipt, alternative methods need to be employed (e.g., PDMAC, ThermaNin).

7.2.1.2 Amino Acid/Protein Reagents

The use of *p*-dimethylaminocinnamaldehyde (pDMAC or DMAC) has been suggested for processing thermal papers. The material can be either directly heated [61] or exposed to vapor by "sandwiching" the item between two pDMAC impregnated pieces of paper [62].* The use of humidification (heating water at 85°C for 30 min in a chamber) has been noted to speed the development process [63]. One study found that pDMAC performance dropped off more rapidly compared to DFO and ninhydrin formulations [64]. Results from this study indicated that the HOSDB DFO formulation performed better than ninhydrin or pDMAC.

Modifications to the formulations for DFO and ninhydrin have been made in an effort to minimize background darkening. One approach involved increasing the amount of ethanol in the ninhydrin reagent solution to approximately 10% v/v and doubling the amount of methanol in the DFO formula [65]. Extra-processing time might be required to completely remove the coating from the paper [66]. Another approach used a combination of HFE-711PA and HFE 7100, which required refluxing to completely dissolve the ninhydrin crystals [52].

Schwarz and Klenke described a modified ninhydrin formulation that used polyvinylpyrrolidones (PVPs) [60]. Previous attempts to integrate ninhydrin into the G3 "whitening" solution proved to be unsuccessful. Since PVPs have higher masses, the resulting decolorization would be more stable due to the decreased volatility. Ultimately, Kolloidon® 12 PF was chosen because of its greater solubility in the ninhydrin solution. For the working solution (which the authors referred to as "NinK12"), 1-propanol was chosen as the polar solvent and a 2:1 mixture of pentane and cyclohexane was chosen for the nonpolar component. The final mixture contained 3.0 g/L ninhydrin and 4.0 g/L of the Kolloidon 12 PF with a solvent ratio of 1:9 for the polar and nonpolar solvents, respectively. Latent prints developed with this reagent were bluish-violet in color.

The sublimation of ninhydrin in a vacuum has also been evaluated [67–69]. The optimized conditions involved hanging the thermal paper 15 cm above the heat source (set at 150°C) with dispersed ninhydrin crystals (50 mg) in the vacuum chamber at 2–5 mbar for 30 min.

BVDA developed a product called ThermaNin, which uses a ninhydrin hemiketal dissolved in a nonpolar solvent (e.g., HFE 7100, petroleum ether, heptane) [70].† Exposure of the reagent solution to moisture in the paper causes the compound to revert to ninhydrin and the parent alcohol molecule. The minimal amount of polar cosolvents (2% v/v) prevents darkening of the background. The German Bundeskriminalamt reported good results on thermal papers with a similar reagent, isononylninhydrin (INON) [69].

Several dry contact methods have been suggested as alternatives to solvent-based reagents to avoid damaging the printing on thermal receipts. Dry ninhydrin was introduced by Ludas in 1992 [71] and evaluated on thermal fax papers by McMahon in 1996 [72]. The original method involved preparing a concentrated ninhydrin solution in acetone (2%–3% w/v) and using it to soak blotter papers. As with the dry PDMAC procedure [62], the items were placed between the blotters and allowed to interact for 3–7 days.

* The reagent can be prepared by mixing equal volumes of two solutions. The first is prepared by mixing 0.25 g of *p*-dimethylaminocinnamaldehyde into 50 mL of ethanol. The second is prepared by mixing 1 g of 5-sulfosalicylic acid into 50 mL of ethanol. The final mixture should be filtered if it does not appear homogeneous. The paper blotters should then be dipped into this reagent and allowed to dry. Items can then be placed between the sheets for at least 24 h before a fluorescence examination. When excited with ~515 nm light, the prints should exhibit a yellow fluorescence.

† This reagent is prepared by mixing 4 g of ThermaNin into 980 mL of either heptane, petroleum ether, or HFE 7100. This mixture is shaken vigorously for 5–10 min to dissolve the ThermaNin. Warming the solution to 30°C–40°C will improve the dissolution process. In particular, if HFE 7100 is to be used, 5 mL of isopropanol and 15 mL of ethyl acetate will be needed, as the ThermaNin is not very soluble in HFE 7100. These co-solvents are optional when using heptane or petroleum ether.

Patton et al. reported a dry contact method for treating thermal papers with 1,2-indanedione-zinc [73]. The best results were obtained when contact sheets were treated with a nonacidified, HFE 7100-based indanedione solution. The sheets had to remain in contact with the item(s) for at least 48 h. A similar technique was reported by Parasram [74]. Items were placed between circular sheets of Whatman filter paper (twice predipped into an 1,2-indanedione/zinc solution and dried), placed into a Ziploc™ bag, and then heated in a laboratory oven for 15 min at 60°C. Latent print fluorescence was viewed using a green TracER™ laser (532 nm) and orange filters.

A modified formulation for 1,2-indanedione has also been reported [75].* Recovery of DNA after treatment of thermal paper with this 1,2-indanedione reagent has been reported [76]. Recovery rates were rather low (4 out of 100), but the poor results were attributed to the surface characteristics of the thermal paper rather than the 1,2-indanedione reagent itself.

Schwarz and Hermanowski reported that 1,2-indanedione/zinc, heat and the G3 "whitening" solution produced good results [77]. As expected, the use of the 1,2-indanedione/zinc solution (and heat—supplied by a heat press set at 160°C for 10 s) caused the active layer of the thermal paper to darken significantly. This discoloration was removed within seconds after application of the G3 "whitening" solution. Fluorescent prints were observed using an excitation wavelength of 490 nm and an orange-red filter. Overall, this sequence was able to produce good quality fluorescent prints in less than 10 min.

The use of fumes from alkaline substances (e.g., ammonia, pyrollidone) has been suggested to force the leuco-dye back to the colorless form. However, the effect was found to be short-lived, as the darkening returned to the paper shortly after removing it from the basic fumes. Covering the latent prints on thermal paper (after treatment with acetone and petroleum ether based solutions) with certain brands of cellophane tape has been reported to decolorize the darkened background within as little as 2 h [78].

Another approach involved the use of light sources and filters to recover prints from ninhydrin-treated thermal papers [79]. This technique was applied to items that had been processed with ninhydrin (in accordance with the U.K. Home Office Manual of Fingerprint Detection Techniques) and had turned dark gray. The recommended procedure involved the use of a Polilight alternate light source set at wavelengths of either 350 or 415 nm, in conjunction with various filters at different wavelengths.

7.2.1.3 Fuming Methods

Several fuming techniques have been recommended for visualizing prints on thermal paper. These methods develop prints only on the emulsion side of the paper. The use of muriatic acid (i.e., hydrochloric acid, HCl) fuming [80,81] has been reported. Prints developed with HCl vapor tended to fade with time and exposing the nonemulsion side of the paper to the acid fumes was reported to have a detrimental effect on subsequent processing with DFO. The final sequence recommended first treating the item with the HCl vapor, followed by DFO, and then dry ninhydrin [80].

Another experiment reported on the comparative success of fuming with nine different organic chemicals [82]. Five of the nine (acetic acid, acetone, ethanol, ethyl acetate, and methanol) were found to develop prints; however, acetic acid was found to work the best.

* This reagent is prepared by thoroughly mixing 2 g of 1,2-indanedione into 70 mL of ethyl acetate. Once the 1,2-indanedione has completely dissolved, the HFE 7100 can be added. Processed prints should be left to develop in the dark for 24 h. Any print detail should be viewed with an orange filter and excited with wavelengths below 530 nm.

The results indicated that polarity of the solvent may not be the best criteria for clearing the blackened emulsion, since it was observed that isopropyl alcohol (which is more polar) caused less darkening than acetone. Cyanoacrylate fuming has also been used for visualizing latent prints on thermal papers, although without much success [61].

7.2.1.4 Miscellaneous Reagents

The use of Oil Red O has been proposed for developing prints on thermal paper [83]. Oil Red O was found to be superior to PD on seven different types of thermal paper. The item was then removed, rinsed with deionized water, and finally left to air dry [84]. Vacuum metal deposition treatment of thermal papers has also been attempted [61]. No print detail was visualized in those trials. Another study proposed the use of dihydroxytetraphenyl-porphyrinatotin(IV) (abbreviated as (TPP)Sn$(OH)_2$) [85]. The recommended procedure involved a 2 min soak in a 2.5×10^{-3} M solution of the reagent (0.191 g (TPP)Sn$(OH)_2$ in 100 mL ethanol). The optimum excitation wavelength for viewing prints was found to be 405 nm when viewed through the appropriate filter (e.g., Kodak CC20Y color compensating filter).

Low-temperature heating has been suggested as a method for developing prints on the coated-side of the thermal papers [86,87]. Extreme caution should be exercised when using heating techniques because the paper can darken very rapidly. Heat from a portable hair dryer was passed over the substrates for 45 s. Initially, if no prints were developed, the paper was allowed to cool and then the same heating regimen was applied again. An approximately 30°C difference was observed between the temperature required for the print to develop (45°C–47°C) and the temperature at which darkening of the background (i.e., discoloration) occurred (71°C–76°C). Development conditions and times were found to vary by the brand of hair dryer. Using this method, friction ridge detail was obtained only on the coated-side of the thermal paper. Interestingly, Scott found that increasing the relative humidity (by heating the thermal paper over a beaker of hot water) resulted in a significant improvement of results [88].

7.2.2 Metallic Surfaces

Many different methods have been suggested for processing metal surfaces and specifically cartridge casings. However, given the differences in metallic content and caliber, there is rarely one method that has been found to work in all situations. The metallic content of cartridges can vary, including copper, steel, lacquered steel, brass, nickel, and alloys of aluminum (which may also vary in composition). Typical civilian rifle and handgun calibers can range from 0.17 (as used in weapons like Remington's 700 series bolt action rifles) to 0.50 (as used in handguns like the IMI Desert Eagle) [89]. Larger caliber bullets have been used for military purposes. The smaller the caliber, the less likely it is that a significant amount of latent print residue will transfer onto its highly curved surface. However, Wertheim reported that a print was successfully recovered from a .22 casing and identified to a suspect [90].

To determine why recovery rates are so low for fired cartridge casings, a study was commissioned by the Israel National Police [91]. The aim of the study was to determine which issue was more significant, the damage to latent prints caused during shooting process or that the commonly employed chemical reagents fail to develop ridge detail. Since it is possible to recover latent prints from metallic surfaces in general, the study focused on the former hypothesis. Although the conclusion was that all aspects of the firing process can lead to some latent print degradation, the main cause was due to the widening of the cartridge diameter caused by the pressure created during the firing process. The expanded cartridge then has a tendency to experience friction between itself and the gun's chamber. This friction can lead to smearing of the print prior to the ejection process.

Despite their widespread use in violent crimes, handguns seldom yield usable quantities of latent prints. Between 1992 and 1995, the Bureau of Alcohol, Tobacco, and Firearms examined 1000 weapons for latent prints [92].* A total of 114 identifiable latent prints were recovered from only 93 firearms (approximately a 10% recovery rate). Some of the identified prints were linked to the individuals responsible for collecting the evidence. A latent print recovery rate of 32% on firearms was reported by the Boston Police Department in 2007 [93]. This higher recovery rate included more than just identifiable prints.

7.2.2.1 Gun Blueing Reagents

Prints can develop on metallic surfaces on their own without subsequent processing in some cases. Sweat can be quite acidic, as low as 5.0 pH units at low sweat rates [94]. The pH will rise with increasing sweat rate and become more neutral, indicating that the sweat gland duct itself acidifies the sweat (presumably by reabsorbing bicarbonate and/or secreting H^+ in exchange for a Na^+ ion) [95]. People who suffer from a condition known as hyperhidrosis, a condition characterized by abnormally high sweat rate, have been known to etch their prints onto metallic surfaces. These individuals are colloquially known as "rusters" and have difficulty not leaving sweat behind, even when wearing gloves [96]. Similar observations were made for a group of women working on an assembly line making cadmium-plated parts for aircraft [97]. Hamm reported that an identifiable print on a weapon was obliterated when the metallic surface beneath the print rusted. The author attributed this result to moisture from breathing on the print, as well as the warm and humid storage environment maintained prior to photographing the print [98].

The use of gun blueing solutions has led to some level of success in the recovery of latent prints from cartridge casings. Gun blueing is a passivation process used to make steel surfaces (e.g., guns) more resistant to rust. These solutions typically contain copper and selenium compounds in an acidic solution, although the composition may vary depending on the composition of the surface (see Table 7.1). Developed prints tend to appear light colored (i.e., the color of the surface of the cartridge) against a dark blue-black background. The copper and selenium present in these solutions are reduced (i.e., deposited) on the cartridge's metal surface, while the latent print acts as a resist (i.e., protects the surface and prevents metal deposition) [99].

One study found that the type of metal used in the cartridge was important for choosing the best gun blueing solution (see Table 7.2) [100]. A slow fuming superglue process seemed to work best before applying the gun blueing solution. A similar processing sequence has been recommended by Bentsen et al. [101]. They found that a sequence of vacuum cyanoacrylate fuming followed by gun blueing and staining with Basic Yellow 40 worked best.

* The procedure used in this study for processing the weapons involved the following sequence: atmospheric pressure cyanoacrylate fuming, staining with rhodamine 6G, and light source examination (Omnichrome 1000). Other methods used included 20 W argon ion laser, ultraviolet radiation, Polaroid high contrast photography, Ardrox, standard and magnetic fluorescent powders, standard and magnetic black and silver powders, and crystal violet.

TABLE 7.1

Summary of Recommended Protocols for Treating Cartridge Casings

Cartridge Type	Suggested Treatment after Superglue	Gun Blue (GB) Dilution	Comments
Nickel-plated brass	Brass black	1 mL GB in 40 mL distilled or RO-DI water	Other solutions also worked well on these casings
Brass	Formula 44/40 instant gun blue	0.5 mL GB in 40 mL distilled or RO-DI water	Other solutions also worked well on these casings
Lacquered steel	Superglue only	N/A	None of the gun blueing solutions worked
Aluminum	Aluminum black	0.5 mL GB in 40 mL distilled or RO-DI water	This is the only GB solution that worked for this metal

Source: Leben, D.A. and Ramotowski, R.S., *Chesapeake Examiner*, October, 8,10, 1996.

TABLE 7.2

Chemical Composition of Different Gun Blueing Solutions

	Outers	Aluminum Black	Perma Blue (Liquid)	Brass Black	Perma Blue (Paste)	Super Blue	44/40
Selenious acid		<4%	<3%	<3%	<2%	<5%	<6%
Selenious dioxide	<3%						
Amido sulfonic acid							<12%
Nitric acid			<3%			<4%	
Cupric chloride					<3%		
Cupric nitrate						<4%	
Cupric sulfate	<2%	<8%	<3%	<4%			<8%
Nickel sulfate		<1%					
Zinc sulfate				<5%			
Phosphoric acid		<3%		<8%	<4%	<4%	
Fluoboric acid		<2%					
Ammonium molybdate				<4%			
Ammonium bifluoride					<1%		
Polyoxyethylene stearyl ether					<15%		
Hydrochloric acid	<2%						
Octylphenoxypolyethoxyethanol						>1%	
Water	>93%	>82%	>91%	>76%	>75%	>82%	>74%
pH of solution	3.3	2.3	2.3	2.3	1.5	2.3	1.8

7.2.2.2 Miscellaneous Oxidation–Reduction Methods

Historically, quite a few methods have been suggested for developing ridge detail on cartridge casings. A considerable number of these utilize oxidation/reduction (also known as redox) methods. One early method employed involved the use nitric acid fumes to etch the bullet casings and the subsequent application of fingerprint powder (via a fiberglass brush) to enhance contrast [102]. The technique worked better on cartridges made of brass than nickel. Similar results were obtained when black powder was applied with a camel hair brush and lifted with commercial brand tapes [103]. Remarkably, this study indicated that good results could be obtained on brass cartridges aged up to 3 weeks. Poor results were obtained on nickel cartridges. A combination of silver nitrate and sulfuric acid was also recommended* [104]. Good results on brass casings were reported. Heating stainless steel and aluminum cartridge casings also was reported to produce dark ridge detail on a slightly less dark background [105].

The use of potassium permanganate solution for 30–60 s has been reported to develop ridge detail on steel casings with a thin coating of brass or copper [106]. A 3% aqueous silver nitrate solution was used on brass coin slugs and was reported to produce ridge detail when cyanoacrylate fuming and powdering did not [107].

Acidified hydrogen peroxide has also been recommended as a good etching technique for developing prints on cartridges [108]. The solution involved the mixing of 14.1 mL of 5% vinegar and 20 mL of 3% hydrogen peroxide. Solutions were freshly made for each application and should not be reused. This solution is strong enough to remove excess copper and selenium deposited on casings that have been overprocessed with gun blueing solutions.

The use of metal deposition techniques has been reported. Saunders detailed results in which MMD treatment led to a rapid deposition of a dark layer that covered both print and background [104]. Another reference indicated that it was the physical developer portion of the process that produced the print detail [109]. This was also confirmed by Saunders, who recommended a modified physical developer redox solution [104]. A palladium metal deposition technique was used to attempt to develop prints on fired and unfired casings. Initial studies showed good results on unfired cartridges but not on fired ones [110]. The use of iodine or sulfuric acid pretreatments did improve the developed detail slightly. A follow-up study in which the palladium developed prints were analyzed by Auger electron spectroscopy, scanning electron microscopy, and electron probe microanalysis, found that the deposition process was quite complex [111].

Additional work by this group found that latent print residue does survive the firing process, and that sebaceous-laden prints offer a better chance for visualization than eccrine-laden ones [112]. One proposed hypothesis for why fired prints are difficult to visualize involved the migration of sebaceous material into the valleys between ridges. This migration could be due to either a sudden increase in temperature during firing, friction of the expended case with the barrel, or both. Thus, these techniques will either coat the entire print or not react at all in such situations. Donche reported that cyanoacrylate fuming works best on dry casings while colloidal gold followed by a modified physical developer produced the best detail on wetted cartridges [113].

7.2.2.3 Other Electrochemical/Corrosion Methods

There have been some different approaches to visualizing prints on metallic surfaces recently. In one instance, a scanning Kelvin microprobe was used to image an untreated print on a metal surface [114]. Latent print residue induces localized Volta potential variations that may be directly imaged by using such a probe. These potential variations are most likely caused by an electrochemical depassivation of the metal surface by chloride ions and can last at least 1 month from the time of print deposition. Contamination of the surface postprint deposition (e.g., spray paint or polymer coating) did not appear to affect the Volta potentials; however, the print residue must be in direct contact with the metal surface to produce these potentials. The use of an

* This reagent was created by mixing 9 mL of a 0.1 N sulfuric acid solution with 1 mL of a 0.1% w/v solution of silver nitrate.

electropolymerization process has been proposed for selective metallic surfaces [115]. Fingerprint legibility was found to depend on the morphological properties of the film (i.e., surface roughness). These properties are in turn determined by the polymerization conditions (e.g., monomer concentration, potential scan rate, and supporting electrolyte). Print detail could be imaged on the metallic surface of certain weapons made from Ergal (a metallic aluminum alloy commonly used in Italy, which contains zinc and often magnesium).

Another electrochemical approach was reported by Hillman et al. [116]. A monomer (e.g., aniline) was dissolved in a dilute aqueous electrolyte, a 1 M sulfuric acid solution. The monomer was then irreversibly oxidized (to polyaniline [PANI]) and subsequently deposited as a thin film on metallic surfaces. The latent print residue would act as a resist; thus, the polymer thin film would deposit only on the background and in the furrows of the print. Another polymer thin film material, poly(3,4-ethylenedioxythiophene [PEDOT]), was also used to successfully develop prints on metallic surfaces. The latter material was found to perform better than PANI.

A recent study examined the corrosive effects of heating latent print residue on metallic surfaces [117]. Prints were deposited and aged over a range of periods, from as short as 5 min to as long as 1 week. Heating temperatures ranged from 200°C to 600°C. Results indicate that the ridge detail developed was independent of the age of the samples. Humidity was a significant factor. At room temperature, prints could develop without heating if the relative humidity was sufficiently high.

An electrostatic enhancement method was also described [117]. This involved charging the metal surface and then developing prints by applying black conductive powder (similar to the one used with an electrostatic detection device (ESDA) to visualize indented writing on documents). This study was extended by looking at the thermodynamic effects of latent print corrosion on metals and alloys [118]. As a result, a fingerprint corrosion series was developed for 10 pure metals and ten metal alloys. This method was used to develop ridge detail on a 14 year old fired shell casing, which had been processed unsuccessfully using cyanoacrylate fuming [119].

7.2.2.4 Fuming Methods

Sampson reported that cyanoacrylate fuming produced ridge detail on nickel but not for brass casings. One hour of fuming at low humidity along with dry sodium hydroxide and an encapsulated fuming agent did produce detail on brass casings. However, no casings yielded results after a period of 66 h [120]. Saunders processed approximately 180 casings with cyanoacrylate (Loctite® Hard Evidence™) [104]. Cartridge casings were aged for 3 weeks prior to being fumed for up to 75 min. Sixty-four of the casings had at least some ridge detail, although few were of value for identification. Sequential processing was also investigated. Results indicated that the best sequence involved the use of cyanoacrylate fuming prior to immersion in a gun blueing solution. More recently, positive results were achieved when cartridge casings were fumed with disulfur dinitride [121]. Sturelle et al. suggested the use of camphor fuming to develop 1 week old latent prints on a wide range of unfired cartridge casings (e.g., copper, aluminum, brass, nickel-plated brass, lacquered brass, varnished steel) [122]. Sufficient black soot was generated within 1 min of igniting the camphor. Traditional gel lifters and silicone casting material were used to transfer ridge detail from the curved shell casing surface. Good results were obtained from all cartridge types except for varnished steel, which responded better to cyanoacrylate fuming.

7.2.3 Gloves

Both the interior and exterior surfaces of gloves can be difficult substrates from which to visualize latent prints. There are many types of gloves (in addition to cloth and leather gloves) that can be worn including rubber, neoprene, vinyl, nitrile, latex, butyl, polyvinyl chloride, and polyvinyl alcohol. These surfaces can react differently when the same reagent is used.

7.2.3.1 Deposition of Latent Prints While Wearing Gloves

There have been a number of reports of people wearing gloves and leaving latent prints on surfaces. Depending on the thickness and type of glove, it is possible for transfer of friction ridge detail to occur. It was hypothesized that thin latex gloves could conform to the surface structure of the finger and (along with contaminants on the glove surface), could lead to clear friction ridge detail when processed with certain reagents [123]. It has also been observed to occur even when two gloves are worn on the same hand. Interestingly, not all brands of gloves were equally effective. In one study, only one brand of gloves successfully prevented the transfer of friction ridge detail [124]. In one particular case, a series of latent prints was left behind by a suspect who had been assumed to be wearing gloves [125]. The developed ridge detail was for the most part identifiable. Another study found that subjects wearing a variety of different types of gloves could leave friction ridge detail in as little as 20 min [126].

Lounsbury and Thompson found that vinyl gloves do not successfully prevent the deposition of latent ridge detail on surfaces [127]; however, latex and nitrile gloves were found not to leave latent ridge detail behind. Gloves also have the potential to accumulate and transfer DNA to different surfaces [128]. Primary, secondary, and even tertiary transfers of DNA can be avoided by changing gloves frequently. In some cases, the impression pattern of the glove material can be used to match to a questioned item [129]. Using characteristics like grain, seams, and unique damage patterns, several identifications in different cases were affected.

There is even a new class of gloves known as "liquid gloves." One example of this relatively new technology is a product called Marly Skin® [130]. The material is composed of stearate, propylene glycol, glycerol, sorbitol, dimethicone (polydimethylsiloxane), and propane/butane. Liquid gloves are typically sprayed onto the skin surface and provide temporary resistance for a short period of time (typically about 4 h). Once applied, the nontoxic liquid glove provides protection from a wide variety of chemicals and biological fluids, while allowing for a considerable level of dexterity. These products also have application in instances where the wearer is allergic to the glove material (e.g., latex). Interestingly, application of these liquid glove products does not necessarily inhibit the deposition of latent prints on a surface. A study showed no differences between prints deposited before and after application of the liquid glove product [131]. However, another product, New Skin from Germolene, has been reported to inhibit the transfer of friction ridge detail to surfaces [132]. A group of criminals in the United Kingdom used the product to successfully pass thousands of pounds sterling worth of fraudulent checks without leaving any print detail behind.

Some prosthetic hands have friction ridge skin patterns incorporated into them. These prosthetics can potentially leave latent prints behind on surfaces. Custom-designed vinyl-based gloves that have friction ridge patterns can be made to fit over prosthetic hands. These can also leave impressions on surfaces, due to the fact that the vinyl material can secrete oils that were used during the manufacturing process [133].

7.2.3.2 Developing Latent Prints on Gloves

A number of different approaches have been used to develop prints on or inside gloves. Historically, ninhydrin, gentian violet, Sudan black, gel lifters, cyanoacrylate fuming, small particle reagent, regular and magnetic powders, fluorescent powders, powder suspension methods, multimetal deposition, and dye stains have produced low recovery rates.

7.2.3.2.1 Powder Suspension Methods

When using powder suspensions, the type of glove material can have a drastic impact on the recovery rate. One study reported a high success rate (77%) with latex and nitrile gloves using Wetwop™ [134]. Interestingly, during the study, a different brand of latex gloves (Tronex) produced poor results. Most importantly, prior cyanoacrylate fuming was found to inhibit the Wetwop™ process. No significant difference in the quality of the friction ridge detail was noted between gloves processed within minutes of wearing them and gloves processed 1 year after being worn. The most significant variable in the successful recovery of prints was found to be the donor, rather than the glove material type. Some donors had recovery rates near 90% while others were as low as 20%.

7.2.3.2.2 Amino Acid/Protein Methods

Ninhydrin has been used to successfully develop prints on gloves as far back as 1966 [135]. A heptane-based ninhydrin solution was used to successfully develop a print on the inside of a latex glove recovered from an armed robbery site [136].* The inside surface of the glove was dipped in the reagent solution and then allowed to develop without acceleration with heat or humidity. Friction ridge detail became visible after about 1 h at ambient laboratory conditions. Ninhydrin was also reported to develop ridge detail on the inside of gloves in two different cases [137]. In the first instance, clear ridge detail was visualized on the interior portion of a latex glove within 1 h after processing with the aforementioned heptane-based ninhydrin solution. In the second case, ridge detail was developed at two locations on the interior of a household rubber glove (that had been fumed with cyanoacrylate without success) within a period of 3–5 h with the heptane-based ninhydrin solution. In both instances, the ridge detail began to fade after the time of maximum contrast.

Another case involved the use of the protein stain Coomassie Blue to develop a 25 year old print on the inside of a rubber glove used by a suspect who was eventually convicted of multiple homicides [138]. The gloves had initially been processed unsuccessfully with powder after they had been collected from the crime scene. After a 2 min application of Coomassie Blue (done twice), sufficient ridge detail was visualized to effect a comparison and ultimately an identification with the suspect.

7.2.3.2.3 Lifting Methods

Recently, the use of gelatin lifters has been reported to successfully recover prints from the inside surfaces of laboratory gloves [139]. The author of that publication successfully recovered a print from the interior portion of a glove only once during his 30 year career. Powders, ninhydrin, and cyanoacrylate fuming had been used but had been unsuccessful. The use of black gelatin lifters without any prior chemical or physical processing appeared to produce the best results. Once the glove had been carefully turned inside out, it was placed on an individual piece of PVC tubing of variable diameter and then each finger

* The reagent was prepared by dissolving 33 g of ninhydrin into 220 mL of ethyl alcohol. After the ninhydrin dissolved completely, 3.78 L (approximately one gallon) of heptane was carefully added and then stirred until the resulting solution was homogeneous.

was rolled onto the surface of the gelatin lifter (as if taking a person's inked fingerprints). Prints were visible when enhanced with side-lighting. Prints were recovered up to 10 days after the glove's use. Although not specified in the reference, it was possible to process the prints on the gelatin lifter with conventional chemical and/or physical methods to further enhance contrast.

7.2.4 Adhesive Tapes

Adhesive tapes can pose a problem when processing for latent prints, as many different varieties are available on the market. In most cases the tapes need to be separated from a substrate (e.g., paper, cardboard, plastics), or itself, prior to processing. Generally, the nonadhesive side is processed first while protecting the adhesive side from any damage. Separation of the tape from either itself or a substrate can be done either before or after processing the nonadhesive side (depending on the particular circumstances involved).

For the adhesive side, different reagents are typically required for rubber-based (e.g., styrene, butadiene) and acrylic-based (e.g., ethyl-, butyl-, ethylhexyl acrylates) adhesives [140]. Determining the adhesive type cannot be achieved simply by visual inspection. Instrumental methods, like Fourier transfer infrared spectroscopy, are required to confirm the chemical composition of the adhesive. However, a spot test can be done on the adhesive to determine whether or not the reagent will produce significant background interference. In addition, some specialized tapes, like masking or fabric, also require careful selection of processing techniques as they can have either rubber or acrylic-based adhesives.

7.2.4.1 Tape Separation Methods

A number of different methods have been suggested for separating tapes. Peeling the tape apart can work in some situations; however, this can lead to serious distortions of the adhesive material, which can significantly damage print detail [141]. Freezing (either in a conventional freezer or with freezer sprays) followed by separation with tweezers has been recommended. This method is generally limited to removing tapes from plastic.

Liquid nitrogen has also been recommended. A good review of the relative successes and failures of this technique to separate certain brands and types of tape was reported by Bergeron [142]. Successful separation was even achieved when the tape was stuck adhesive side to adhesive side. Bailey and Crane reported on the use of a cryogun to facilitate the separation of duct tape [143]. Caution should be taken when using liquid nitrogen since its extremely cold temperature (approximately –195.79°C) can cause frostbite and burns within seconds of contact with skin.

Heating has also been suggested, but this technique can damage the adhesive layer of the tape and significantly damage any potential latent prints. Campbell reported on the use of heat supplied by a portable hair dryer to separate a variety of different tapes [144]. The heat was applied to the point of softening the adhesive and then the tape was slowly separated with tweezers. Good results were obtained for all tapes as well as with tapes attached to cardboard.

Different chemical solvents have been suggested for separating tapes. A slow, drop-wise application of Shandon solvent (a blend of aliphatic and halogenated hydrocarbons) mixed with 5% chloroform was reported to cause the least damage to print detail [145]. The Shandon solvent was a replacement for xylene, which was reported to potentially damage plastics [146]. A similar application of a 1:2 mixture of cyclohexane and isopropanol was demonstrated in Turkey and allowed tapes to be separated from each other, as well as paper, with minimal damage to latent prints on the adhesive side [147].

Un-du® was invented by Chuck Foley (a prolific inventor who, along with Neil Rabens, invented the game Twister in 1966) and first introduced into commercial marketplace in 1996. It is a hydrocarbon-based (primarily *n*-heptane) adhesive remover. Stimac reported on the use of un-du to separate rubber and acrylic-based adhesive tapes from paper envelopes [148]. The material has also been used to separate tapes stuck together, adhesive-side to adhesive-side [149,150].

The effect of the use of un-du on subsequent latent print development techniques was reported by Schwartz et al. [151]. Self-adhesive stamps and labels on envelopes were removed with un-du and then processed with either gentian violet (GV) or alternate black powder (ABP), a powder suspension reagent made with black powder and Liqui-Nox™ detergent. The envelopes were then processed with ninhydrin and physical developer. When processing with GV, 24% of the stamps or labels had ridge detail, while ABP produced detail on 64%. Overall, the use of un-du was not found to inhibit subsequent processing of the envelopes with ninhydrin or physical developer. However, when ninhydrin processing was done prior to removing the label or stamp, it was found to have an adverse effect on the success of ABP to develop ridge detail. The authors recommended removing adhesive items prior to processing the envelopes with ninhydrin.

When tapes and stamps were stuck on paper substrates, Maceo et al. recommended processing the item with ninhydrin prior to attempts to remove the items [152]. With tapes stuck to cardboard, the authors recommended separation with ethyl acetate and separate processing of the tape and cardboard. They also noted that prints could transfer from the tape adhesive to the porous surface of the paper, with the exception of cardboard (these prints will be reversed images). They observed that eccrine prints easily transferred while sebaceous ones tended to remain on the adhesive surface.

The handling and storage of tapes is critical to recovering latent prints. Once tape has been separated, it can be placed onto a low adhesion surface, like silicon release paper [153]. This can protect the adhesive side of the tape during storage and processing of the nonadhesive side. Another option involved the use of a special, cast-aluminum apparatus for handling and holding adhesive tapes [154]. The frame could hold numerous tapes simultaneously, totaling up to two meters in length.

7.2.4.2 Processing the Adhesive Side of Tapes

7.2.4.2.1 Dye Stain Methods

The first reported use of gentian violet to develop prints on the adhesive side of tapes was reported by the Italian police in the late 1960s [155]. Members of the Southwest Criminal Records Office also discussed its usage at a forensic conference in 1969. A variation of the reagent formulation that included phenol (also known as carbolic acid) was reported to work effectively on the adhesive side of tapes [156]. A 10% hydrochloric acid solution could be used to reduce overdevelopment and background staining caused by excess amounts of gentian violet [157]. However, the presence of phenol in the formulation raised significant health and safety concerns [158]. Gentian violet has also been reported to be a possible mutagen and carcinogen. The use of gentian violet on dark-colored tapes, followed by lifting with photographic paper, was reported by Kent [155] and Wilson et al. [157] in the early 1980s. Gentian violet was also reported to exhibit fluorescence in the near infrared, when excited with light from the blue-green region of the electromagnetic spectrum (~400–600 nm) [159,160].

A fluorescent variation of the gentian violet reagent was described by Jumper in the mid-1990s [161]. This reagent involved mixing gentian violet with rhodamine 6G to produce fluorescent prints. The use of basic fuchsin (rosanaline chloride) to produce fluorescent prints was reported by Menzel [162,163] and Howard [164].* The chemical structure of basic fuchsin is very similar to that of gentian violet, but the compound was considered toxic and a potential carcinogen. Arima recommended the use of a UV-excited, fluorescent brightening agent, Mikephor BS (C.I. fluorescent brightening agent 90), for colored tapes [165]. Wilson found that the dye stain RAY (a combination of rhodamine 6G, Ardrox, Basic Yellow 40) outperformed gentian violet and alternate black powder (a powder suspension technique) on the adhesive side of tape after cyanoacrylate fuming [166].

Aqueous fabric dye stain solutions have been reported to have produced good results on tapes [167]. Rit® Neon Green and Tintex® Brown produced development on the adhesive side of paper labels, but had more limited success with duct tape. Steele et al. described the use of heat to sublime disperse dyes, which would then preferentially stain the cyanoacrylate polymer on the adhesive side of tapes [168]. Cyanoacrylate fuming followed by the use of Disperse Yellow 211 dye produced the best results. Sodhi reported on the use of an aqueous reagent containing Rose Bengal and a phase transfer catalyst (a quaternary ammonium salt) [169]. Good results were reported on a variety of different tapes, including fabric and brown packaging tapes. In addition, the developed prints fluoresced purple when excited with short-wave ultraviolet radiation.

7.2.4.2.2 Powder Suspension Methods

Powder suspension techniques are now becoming a more common approach to processing the adhesive side of tapes. Sticky-side Powder™ was reported to be significantly better at developing prints on duct tape than gentian violet [170,171]. Acceptable prints were developed with gentian violet in 42% of samples, while Sticky-side Powder produced development in 81% of the samples [171]. A similar trend was observed for aged prints. However, it should be noted that these results were obtained using a nonphenol-based gentian violet reagent, whose concentration was approximately five times weaker than the standard formula [172]. Another commercially available powder suspension reagent, Wetwop™, has been reported to produce better latent print development on the adhesive side of tapes, compared to Sticky-side Powder™ [149].

Bratton et al. described a modified version of Sticky-side Powder™ that contained tap water, Liqui-Nox glassware detergent, and black powder (Lightning Powder) [173]. This reagent was found to produce the best results on adhesive tape surfaces when compared to gentian violet, ninhydrin, Sticky-side Powder™, cyanoacrylate fuming, and cyanoacrylate fuming with a fluorescent dye stain [174]. Sneddon described a modified powder suspension reagent, designed specifically for developing prints on duct tape [170].

The use of metallic powders with water and a cleaning agent was reported by Freeman [175]. The powder film remained on the surface and would coat the adhesive rather than the latent print residue. An additional rinse with the detergent solution significantly improved the developed ridge detail. Kimble reported on the use of regular, metallic, and fluorescent powder suspensions to develop prints on clear tape [176]. White powders, like titanium dioxide, have been recommended for dark-colored tapes [177,178].

* Basic fuchsin can be prepared by dissolving 0.02 g of the dye into 400 mL of either methanol or distilled water. Basic fuchsin dissolves readily in methanol but can take considerably longer to dissolve in water. The item is placed into the dye solution for up to 60 s and can be rinsed under running tap water.

Martin reported on the use of ash grey and white powders to develop an identifiable print on black electrical tape used to bind a homicide victim [179]. Hollars et al. recommended the use of Liqui-Drox, a combination of Liqui-Nox and Ardrox, to produce fluorescent prints on dark-colored tapes [180]. Long-wave ultraviolet radiation was required to excite the processed prints. Prints developed with this reagent will tend to fade into the adhesive background within 24–48 h.

Variations in the types of adhesive materials used can cause dramatic differences in the effectiveness of processing methods [153]. The HOSDB noted that rubber-based adhesives responded well to powder suspension methods. However, this is not the case with acrylic-based adhesives, where the powder material adheres to both the print detail and background, providing little or no contrast. The HOSDB recommended that a nonphenol-based gentian violet solution be used to process these types of adhesive tapes. For masking tapes, the HOSDB recommended black powder suspensions for rubber-based adhesives and physical developer for acrylic-based ones.

7.2.4.2.3 Fuming Methods

There has been debate as to whether or not cyanoacrylate fuming of items prior to the application of powder suspension solutions should be done. Sampson advocated prior cyanoacrylate fuming of items to stabilize latent prints on both the adhesive and nonadhesive sides [181]. However, others have reported that cyanoacrylate fuming significantly inhibits development of latent prints using powder suspension techniques [182]. Processing of the nonadhesive side could be done; however, care should be taken not to damage prints on the adhesive side.

A comprehensive review of numerous techniques for developing latent prints on five different brands of black electrical tape was reported by Schiemer et al. [183]. The overall recommendation for sequentially treating these tapes was for cyanoacrylate fuming, staining with a combined BY40/BR28 fluorescent dye stain, and finally application of a white powder suspension. Although toxic, gentian violet (with phenol) was found to work well when developed prints were transferred from the tape to photographic paper.

In the 1970s, the effectiveness of fuming iodine and osmic acid to develop prints on tapes was reported by Smith [184]. A subsequent evaluation of iodine fuming by Midkiff et al. found that good results were achieved with fresh prints on clear and light-colored tapes [185]. Poor results were obtained with cloth, paper, or plastic tapes. Darker and more stable prints were obtained when iodine fuming was followed by application of a 7,8-benzoflavone staining solution.

7.2.4.2.4 Miscellaneous Methods

A modified silver staining method, described by Taylor and Mankevich in 1984, was reported to react with proteins present in the latent print deposit [186]. This method was observed to be significantly more sensitive than the traditional silver nitrate reagent.

Physical developer was found to produce good development on double-sided and mustard-colored plastic tapes [187]. However, the best overall results were observed when cyanoacrylate fuming was done in conjunction with either rhodamine 6G or MBD fluorescent dye stains (it is important to note that powder suspensions were not evaluated in this study). Fluorescent nanoparticles (quantum dots) have also been used to develop prints on black electrical tape [188]. Cadmium sulfide nanocrystals capped with dioctyl sulfosuccinate were dissolved in either heptane or hexane and applied to the surface of the item in the same way as traditional dye stains. The items could be prefumed with cyanoacrylate without affecting the efficacy of the quantum dots.

7.2.4.3 Processing the Nonadhesive Side of Tapes

One of the more commonly used methods for visualizing prints on the backing of tapes is cyanoacrylate fuming followed by the use of a fluorescent dye stain [183]. Berg reported that the use of cyanoacrylate fuming followed by the drop-wise addition of a solution of rhodamine 6G in methanol produced fluorescent print detail on the nonadhesive side of duct tape [189]. However, caution must be exercised when processing the nonadhesive side of tape with cyanoacrylate fumes. The adhesive side needs to be protected (e.g., placement onto silicon release paper) while the fuming process is being conducted. However, cyanoacrylate fumes can still seep under the tape and potentially inhibit the success of subsequent powder suspension methods on the adhesive side of the tape [140]. The HOSDB also noted that carbon-based powder suspensions are more effective on the nonadhesive side of tapes than iron-based powder suspension formulas. Sticky-side Powder™ was also reported to occasionally develop prints on the nonadhesive side of tape.

The HOSDB recommended the use of vacuum metal deposition for the nonadhesive side of masking tapes [153]. A silver-only variation of the vacuum metal technique was reported to successfully develop prints on both sides of adhesive tapes [190]. For other types of tapes, the HOSDB recommend the use of cyanoacrylate fuming followed by dye staining and powder suspensions for items that have not been wet. For tapes that have been exposed to water, powder suspension reagents should be used.

7.2.5 Skin

Visualizing latent prints from live or dead skin is one of the most difficult tasks facing forensic scientists. It was once estimated that the chances of recovering an identifiable print on human skin is 15,000,000 to one [191]. Prior to the 1960s, there were no documented examples of operational successes. To date, the majority of published work has focused on prints obtained under laboratory conditions. However, a report based on the work of William and Karen Sampson described 67 cases in which latent prints were developed (as of 2004) [192]. Sixty of these cases occurred in 19 states within the United States, with the remainder taking place in the United Kingdom (3), Canada (2), Japan (1), and Thailand (1). Within the United States, Florida reported 22 successful examples. Of these, three came from living victims and the remainder from deceased persons. Details of 14 of these cases were published by Sampson et al. in 1997 [193]. While these statistics are at least somewhat encouraging, the vast majority of cases yield no latent prints of value at all.

A number of different methods have been suggested over the past half-century for visualizing prints on skin. The inherent difficulty in achieving success is due to the fact that, even after death, the surface of the victim's body exudes the same chemicals present in the perpetrator's latent print. Prints left on a warm victim's body soon after death will quickly diffuse into the sweat and sebum present on the skin surface. Environmental conditions (e.g., ambient relative humidity, temperature) play a crucial role in this process. Optimum conditions favor a temperature range of 21°C–30°C (70°F–86°F) [191,194]. The author recommended that under those conditions, the lifting medium temperature should differ by ~7°C (~20°F) from than the skin (in this case approximately 32°C, or 90°F). The temperature of the victim's body and storage conditions (i.e., cold storage at a morgue) also play an important role. Newitt and Green noted that multiple factors affect the cooling rate of a cadaver, including ambient temperature, evaporation of skin moisture, variation in body surface area, and amounts of clothing [195].

There have been a number of articles that have given a good overview of existing techniques for visualizing latent prints on skin [193,196–199]. In particular, one reference [200] has perhaps the most comprehensive list of prints recovered from skin from actual cases. However, it is important to note that prior to attempting any visualization process on either live or dead skin, the appropriate medico-legal professionals must be consulted.

7.2.5.1 Iodine-Silver Plate Transfer

Dr. John McMorris introduced the iodine fuming-silver plate transfer method for developing latent prints at a meeting of the California Division of the International Association for Identification in 1936 [196]. He first published the technique in 1937 [201]. Foley suggested the use of this technique for developing and lifting prints from skin [202]. The process involved fuming an area of skin with iodine vapor until an impression was visible. After waiting 10–20 s, a polished silver plate was placed in contact with the impression for 15 s. This contact produces ridge detail that is composed of silver iodide. The plate was then exposed to an intense light source to break down the silver iodide, converting it to a dark silver, reverse-image impression. Mooney found that the plate must have pure silver on its outer surface [203]. The author also noted that although the method worked well under laboratory test conditions, the best results obtained were from a strangulation victim that had been dead for 12 h. Three-finger impressions were developed, but none had ridge detail. Under test conditions, the method worked up to 8 h on live skin and up to 108 h on cadavers.

Adcock was able to redevelop an iodine-fumed test latent print deposited on a cadaver's wrist that had been soaked in water for 24 h [204]. After soaking, the print was fumed again and a suitable image was obtained. Feldman et al. reported on the use of iodine fuming followed by lifting the impression with a strip of leuco crystal violet–infused 35 mm film [205]. Good results were obtained with test prints on live skin up to 1 h after deposition. Gray reported less successful results on live skin, noting that 76.5% of impressions were developed immediately after deposition, but only 31.3% after 10 min and 2.9% after 15 min.

7.2.5.2 Electronography

Graham and Gray first reported the use of electronography and auto-electronography to recover latent prints from skin in 1966 [206]. The technique first involved carefully dusting the skin surface with a metallic powder. Lead is typically chosen because of the large number of highly energetic electrons ejected after exposure to hard x-rays in the 5–30 kV range [207]. Although iron has a lower electron emission density, it has the advantage of producing lower background interferences. Cunn reported that bismuth powder and a mixture of lead and iron powders could also be used but found the results to be poor [208].

Emission of radiation from the lead powder can be captured on a photographic film emulsion. The silver halides present in the film are darkened by the radiation and can produce an image of ridge detail present on the skin surface. In order to obtain a proper image, the emitted radiation must be filtered to remove longer wavelengths that can fog the photographic emulsion. This is accomplished by using separate copper and aluminum filters. A Thoraeus filter (composed of separate tin, copper, and aluminum filters) acts to absorb any emitted or scattered radiation from extraneous sources.

For irregularly shaped objects, like a human limb, Graham recommended using a sphygmomanometer (i.e., the cuff from a blood pressure meter) to form a light-tight seal around the limb, filters, and recording film. The x-ray beam is sufficiently strong enough to pass through the cuff and image the print detail. Print-bearing skin can also be removed and imaged in the conventional manner. Prints on cadaver skin were obtained up to 48 h after deposition, when the body remained at room temperature. The author also reported the recovery of a print after 41 h of exposure to rain and sunshine. However, there are significant practical limitations to using this technique. The primary issue is the health and safety issues associated with using finely powdered lead and x-ray radiation. As described by Graham, the technique requires bulky equipment in a laboratory environment. However, Winstanley described the use of portable x-ray generating equipment and a specially designed film cassette that could be used at a crime scene [209]. Several authors report varying results using this technique.

7.2.5.3 Powder Methods

The use of magnetic powder to dust for latent prints on live subjects was reported by Gutierrez in 1976 [210]. Compressed air was used to remove excess powder from the skin surface. Hammer recommended the use of magnetic powder followed by lifting with a white plastic/foil-like material called Dakty foil [211]. The initial application removed excess powder and sweat. Subsequent lifts were often of superior quality. Detection limits of up to 30 min on live skin and 6 h on cadaver skin were reported.

Melis described the use of direct dusting with magnetic powder to obtain three prints on a female victim after the Kromekote lifting technique failed to produce any ridge detail [212]. The prints were photographed and lifted. There was sufficient ridge detail to make an identification to a suspect in the case. A similar result was reported in Ontario, Canada, by Haslett [213]. Two impressions were developed on the victim's inner knee and thigh area by direct dusting with magnetic powder. Black and white photographs of the impressions were unsuitable for comparison purposes. However, color photographs taken of the impressions contained sufficient detail to make an identification of a suspect.

A report issued in 2001 by the German Bundeskriminalamt recommended the use of magnetic powder [214]. Approximately 30% of test prints placed on 20 cadavers were recovered using this method. Iodine fuming was used to locate prints, but the method did not produce useful ridge detail. The best method found for lifting the magnetic powder-developed prints was the use of a silicone-based casting material called Isomark®. It was found to lift more powder than gelatin sheets. The skin temperature was maintained at or below 22°C while the ambient temperature did not exceed 27°C. Best results were achieved when the skin surface temperature ranged from 10°C to 15°C. Färber et al. compared the effectiveness of standard and magnetic black powders [215]. In the study, 18.4% of prints developed with magnetic powder were classified as elimination or identification, compared to 13.6% of prints developed with standard powder. The authors recommended a combination of magnetic powder and Isomark for visualizing and lifting prints from skin. Trapecar reported on the use of Swedish Soot powder to successfully recover latent prints (1–4 h old) from live skin [216]. Several different lifting methods were able to record the powder-developed prints (e.g., black and white gel lifters, silicone, transparent adhesive tape).

Menzel reported on the use of fluorescent powders followed by laser examination to reveal prints on skin [217]. Although no inherent fluorescent prints were observed, dusting with Mars Red and rhodamine 6G did produce ridge detail. Direct heating of rhodamine 6G to form a vapor was also found to develop prints.

7.2.5.4 Cyanoacrylate Fuming

Hamilton and DiBattista described the use of cyanoacrylate, accelerated by using sodium hydroxide, to successfully recover an identifiable print from the skin surface of a 5 year old victim [218]. Gray magnetic powder was used after fuming and the print was subsequently transferred using frosted lifting tape. Ridge detail on the lifted impression was only visible when a light source was placed at a 50° angle. Delmas described a sequence involving the use of a laser (for inherent fluorescence), followed by cyanoacrylate fuming, and black magnetic powder mixed with rhodamine 6G [219]. A 5W argon ion laser was used to illuminate the powder-developed prints. A modified cyanoacrylate method was reported by Jian and Dao-An [220]. The technique involved coating neutral filter paper with a cyanoacrylate-ether solution. After drying, the filter paper sheets were placed onto the skin surface for 5–60 min. Test prints on live skin were developed up to 36 h and up to several days on cadavers. Hebrard and Donche noted that cyanoacrylate fuming results were better on a warm skin compared to a body that had been in a cold room [221].

Misner et al. reported on the use of a technique based on cyanoacrylate fuming followed by staining with thenoyl europium chelate (TEC) [222]. The cyanoacrylate fuming was done at room temperature at the lowest effective relative humidity level (in this case 66% was recommended). The TEC solution was poured over the developed cyanoacrylate polymer, allowed to dry, and then rinsed. The presence of methyl ethyl ketone in the stain solution was found to be critical, as it aids the incorporation of TEC into the polymer fibers. The dye stain was excited with long-wave ultraviolet radiation and the maximum emission occurred at 614 nm (no filter is required).

7.2.5.5 Iodine-Naphthoflavone

Wilkinson et al. investigated the use of iodine followed by α-naphthoflavone (also known as 7,8-benzoflavone) for developing prints on skin [223]. The technique was compared to cyanoacrylate fuming-TEC staining, RTX fuming, magnetic powder, and iodine-silver plate transfer. The α-naphthoflavone was dissolved in a 1:9 mixture of chloroform and cyclohexane and applied using either a wash bottle or an aerosol sprayer. The iodine/α-naphthoflavone technique was found to produce the most consistent results, although the prints developed by this method were relatively fresh (up to several hours). The skin temperature measured at the time of latent print deposition ranged from 14.5°C to 32°C. In one instance, a body at 30°C produced excellent quality ridge detail after cyanoacrylate fuming and TEC dye staining; however, in another instance where the body temperature ranged from 16°C to 30°C, test prints were not recovered using the same procedure.

7.2.5.6 Direct Lifting Methods

The application of various substrates to the untreated skin surface as a lifting medium has been reported. Silva reported on the use of index cards wrapped around an ink roller as a transfer method [224]. The author had reported previous difficulty in using exposed photographic paper for the same purpose. The index card was subsequently removed from the roller and processed with magnetic powder. The method was able to develop identifiable detail from test prints aged up to 30 min.

In 1978, Reichardt et al. recommended the use of the Kromekote lifting technique as an alternative to iodine-silver plate processing [225]. The technique had been created by one of his colleagues, E. G. Stone, who worked at the Dade County Public Safety Department in Miami, FL. The method involved the use of Kromekote cards (made from 80# paper with a high-gloss, cast-coated surface) to lift prints from areas of the skin surface after a few seconds of firm pressure. The card was then processed with standard fingerprint powders. Additional lifts could be taken and often produced superior detail, possibly due to the previous lift removing excess oils from the skin. After lifting, the skin surface can be dusted with standard or magnetic powders as well. This method was used to successfully recover a palm print from a deceased victim's calf. However, caution must be exercised when interpreting results from a Kromekote lift (or any other type of lifting medium). Hamm reported a case in which a print recovered from a Kromekote lift from a murder victim's skin turned out to have belonged to a crime scene analyst who had prepared the lift cards more than a year before using it [226]. Although the lift had been processed with black powder, the ridge detail appeared to be white in color instead of black.

Guo and Xing recommended the use of polyethylene terephthalate (PET) to directly lift prints from skin [227]. The PET sheet was coated on one side with dark printing ink, primarily to improve contrast. After warming, the sheet was placed onto the skin surface and pressed with the hands or an insulation plate for a few seconds. After removing the sheet, latent prints could become visible on the dark background with ordinary light. The sheet could then be processed with traditional nonporous visualization techniques. Imamura and Asahida reported the lifting of a plastic impression on the neck of a strangulation victim using silicone rubber [228]. The impression contained 12 points and was subsequently linked to a suspect.

Sampson reported on the use of glass as a transfer medium [200]. While using this method, a test latent print placed on live skin was lifted using a glass plate. The glass plates were then fumed with cyanoacrylate, dusted with magnetic powder, and then transferred using lifting tape onto a suitable background. The best results were observed when the glass plates were maintained at approximately 21°C (70°F). A similar technique that involved the use of a sheet of Kodak Roller Transport Cleanup Film to transfer latent prints from skin was reported by Hoyser [229]. The lifted prints were subsequently processed with cyanoacrylate and standard powders.

7.2.5.7 Miscellaneous Methods

For faint blood prints on skin, the use of benzidine [203], *o*-tolidine [230] and amido black [231,232] have been reported. Lawley [231] was able to recover latent ridge detail (although insufficient for comparison) from the right inner thigh of a murder victim using a methanol-based amido black formulation. Previous use of an alternate light source, cyanoacrylate fuming, and fluorescent powder did not develop any suitable ridge detail. A similar experience was reported by Jernigan [232]. A methanol-based amido black solution was used to develop a print on the right inner thigh of a murder victim. Multiple applications of the reagent produced sufficient detail to identify a suspect in the case. Trapecar and Balazic found that prints developed on cadavers using RTX fuming were superior to those developed by cyanoacrylate fuming followed by Swedish Black or Magnetic Jet Black powders [233]. Others have reported more limited success using RTX fuming on skin [221,223].

References

1. Knowles AM. (1978) Aspects of physicochemical methods for the detection of latent fingerprints. *J Phys E Sci Instrum* 11:713–721.
2. Takeuchi T, Sakaguchi M, Nakamoto Y. (1958) Detection of latent finger-print by autoradiography. *Naturwissenschaften* 45:36.

3. Gel'fman AY, Granovskii GL, Kheifets LY. (1964) A simple radiographic technique in fingerprint studies. *Atom Energ* 17(1):71.
4. Takeuchi T. (1960) Application of radioactive ^{14}C formaldehyde to the detection of latent fingerprints. Japanese Patent 9150 (60).
5. Grant RL, Lyth HF, Hockey JA. (1963) A new method for detecting fingerprints on paper. *J Forensic Sci Soc* 4:85–86.
6. Spedding DJ. (1971) Detection of latent fingerprints with $^{35}SO_2$. *Nature* 229:123–124.
7. Ganson A. (1973) Latent fingerprints on paper and fabrics. *Ident News* 23(2):3–5.
8. Morgan A, Walsh M, Black A. (1974) AERE Progress Report EMS1 (London, U.K.: HMSO).
9. Knowles AM, Jones RJ, Clark LS. (1976) Development of latent fingerprints on patterned papers and on papers subjected to wetting. PSDB Home Office Technical Memorandum 6/76.
10. Akerman K. (1966) Application of silver nitrate labeled with $Ag^{110}m$ for autoradiographic detection of fingerprints. *Int J Appl Radiat Isotopes* 17:657–661.
11. Stverak B, Kopejtko J, Chodora F, Chyska J. (1974) Radiotracer method for the detection of latent fingerprints. *Radioisotopy* 15:805–817.
12. Yamamoto D. (1956) *Kagaku* 29:208.
13. McLaughlin AR. (1961) Developing latent prints on absorbent surfaces. *Fingerprint Ident Mag* 42(8):3–16.
14. Everse K, Menzel ER. (1986) Sensitivity enhancement of ninhydrin-treated latent fingerprints by enzymes and metal salts. *J Forensic Sci* 31(2):446–454.
15. Menzel ER, Everse J, Everse KE, Sinor TW, Burt JA. (1984) Room light and laser development of latent fingerprints with enzymes. *J Forensic Sci* 29(1):99–109.
16. O'Neill ME. (1941) Bacterial fingerprints. *J Crim Law Criminol Pol Sci* 32:482.
17. Mason I. (1987) Bacteria fool the light-fingered thief. *New Sci* 1563:40.
18. Harper DR, Clare CM, Heaps CD, Brennan J, Hussain J. (1987) A bacteriological technique for the development of latent fingerprints. *Forensic Sci Int* 33(3):209–214.
19. Pounds CA, Hussain JI. (1987) Biologic and chemical aspects of latent fingerprint detection. In: *Proceedings of the International Forensic Symposium on Latent Prints*, U.S. Department of Justice, U.S. Government Printing Office, July 1987, pp. 9–13.
20. Ishiyama I, Orui M, Ogawa K, Kimura T. (1977) The determination of isoantigenic activity from latent fingerprints: mixed cell agglutination reaction in forensic serology. *J Forensic Sci* 22(2):365–375.
21. Drapel V, Becue A, Champod C, Margot P. (2009) Identification of promising antigenic components in latent fingermark residues. *Forensic Sci Int* 184:47–53.
22. Spindler X, Hofstetter O, McDonagh AM, Roux C, Lennard C. (2011) Enhancement of latent fingermarks on non-porous surfaces using anti-L-amino acid antibodies conjugated to gold nanoparticles. *Chem Commun* 47:5602–5604.
23. Leggett R, Lee-Smith EE, Jickells SM, Russell DA. (2007) "Intelligent" fingerprinting: simultaneous identification of drug metabolites and individuals by using antibody-functionalized nanoparticles. *Angew Chem Int Ed* 46:4100–4103.
24. Hazarika P, Jickells SM, Russell DA. (2009) Rapid detection of drug metabolites in latent fingermarks. *Analyst* 134:93–96.
25. Boddis AM, Russel DA. (2011) Simultaneous development and detection of drug metabolites in latent fingermarks using antibody-magnetic particle conjugates. *Anal Methods* 11:519–523.
26. Hazarika P, Jickells SM, Wolff K, Russel DA. (2010) Multiplexed detection of metabolites of narcotic drugs from a single latent fingermark. *Anal Chem* 82:9150–9154.
27. West M, Barsley RE, Frair J, Stewart W. (1992) Ultraviolet radiation and its role in wound pattern documentation. *J Forensic Sci* 37(6):1466–1479.
28. Davidson AM, Boyd SA, Haltalin CP. (1935) An improved source of ultraviolet light for the diagnosis of the scalp. *Can Med Assoc J* 33:534–536.
29. Ruddick RF. (1974) A technique for recording bite marks in forensic studies. *Med Biol Illu* 24(3):128–129.

30. Ohki H. (1970) Physico-chemical study of latent fingerprint. *Rep Nat Res Inst Pol Sci* 23(1):33–40.
31. German ER. (1996) Reflected ultraviolet imaging system applications. In: Almog J, Springer E, Eds., *Proceedings of the International Symposium on Fingerprint Detection and Identification*, Hemed Press, Jerusalem, Israel, pp. 99–108.
32. Zhou YB, Qin MW, Cao ZH. (1987) TXZ technique of photographing fingerprint. *J Forensic Tech* 1987:2.
33. German ER. (1987) Computer image enhancement of latent prints and hard copy output devices. In: *Proceedings of the International Forensic Symposium on Latent Prints*, Laboratory & Identification Divisions, Federal Bureau of Investigation, FSRTC FBI Academy, Quantico, VA, U.S. Government Printing Office, Washington, DC, pp. 151–152.
34. Anon. (1987) Fingerprint detection and recording with Hamamatsu intensified ultraviolet viewer. *Hamamatsu Appl Bull* (November).
35. Qiang WG. (1996) Detecting and enhancing latent fingerprints with short wave UV reflection photography. In: Almog J, Springer E, Eds., *Proceedings of the International Symposium on Fingerprint Detection and Identification*. Hemed Press, Jerusalem, Israel, pp. 37–49.
36. Hapke B. (1993) *Theory of Reflectance and Emittance Spectroscopy*. Cambridge University Press, Cambridge, U.K.
37. Keith LV, Runion W. (1998) Short-wave UV imaging casework applications. *J Forensic Ident* 48(5):563–569.
38. Saferstein R, Graf SL. (2001) Evaluation of a reflected ultraviolet imaging system for fingerprint detection. *J Forensic Ident* 51(4):385–393.
39. Gardner E. (2010) Using a reflected ultraviolet imaging system to recover friction ridge impressions on post-blast material. *J Forensic Ident* 60(1):104–118.
40. Garner GE, Fontan CR, Hobson DW. (1975) Visualization of fingerprints in the scanning electron microscope. *J Forensic Sci Soc* 15:281–288.
41. Worley CG, Wiltshire SS, Miller TC, Havrilla GJ, Majidi V. (2006) Detection of visible and latent fingerprints using micro-X-ray fluorescence elemental imaging. *J Forensic Sci* 51(1):57–63.
42. Exline DL, Wallace C, Roux C, Lennard C, Nelson MP, Treado PJ. (2003) Forensic applications of chemical imaging: latent fingerprint detection using visible absorption and luminescence. *J Forensic Sci* 48(5):1047–1053.
43. Payne G, Reedy B, Lennard C, Comber B, Exline D, Roux C. (2005) A further study to investigate the detection and enhancement of latent fingerprints using visible absorption and luminescence chemical imaging. *Forensic Sci Int* 150:33–51.
44. Plese CA, Exline DL, Stewart SD. (2010) Improved methods of visible hyperspectral imaging provide enhanced visualization of untreated latent fingerprints. *J Forensic Ident* 60(6):603–618.
45. Ifa DR, Manicke NE, Dill AL, Cooks RG. (2008) Latent fingerprint chemical imaging by mass spectrometry. *Science* 321:805.
46. Bojko K, Roux C, Reedy BJ. (2008) An examination of the sequence of intersecting lines using attenuated total reflectance-Fourier transform infrared spectral imaging. *J Forensic Sci* 53(6):1458–1467.
47. Alsberg BK, Loke T, Baarstad I. (2011) PryJector: a device for in situ visualization of chemical and physical property distributions on surfaces using projection and hyperspectral imaging. *J Forensic Sci* 56(4):976–983.
48. Ricci C, Phiriyavityopas P, Curum N, Chan KLA, Jickells S, Kazarian SG. (2007) Chemical imaging of latent fingerprint residues. *Appl Spectrosc* 61(5):514–522.
49. Tahtouh M, Kalman JR, Roux C, Lennard C, Reedy BJ. (2005) The detection and enhancement of latent fingermarks using infrared chemical imaging. *J Forensic Sci* 50(1):64–72.
50. Tahtouh M, Despland P, Shimmon R, Kalman JR, Reedy BJ. (2007) The application of infrared chemical imaging to the detection and enhancement of latent fingerprints: method optimization and further findings. *J Forensic Sci* 52(5):1089–1096.
51. Crane NJ, Bartick EG, Perlman RS, Huffman S. (2007) Infrared spectroscopic imaging for noninvasive detection of latent fingerprints. *J Forensic Sci* 52(1):48–53.

52. Stimac JT. (2003) Thermal and carbonless papers: a fundamental understanding for latent friction ridge development. *J Forensic Ident* 53(2):185–197.
53. http://www.ncr.com/solutions/printer_consumables_solutions/2st_two_sided_thermal_printing/index.jsp (accessed on 9-3-11).
54. Jackson C. (1989) A short research project into the permanence of thermal fax papers. *AICCM Newsletter*, June, pp. 10, 11. http://palimpsest.stanford.edu/byorg/abbey/an/an13/an13-8/an13-802.html (accessed on 9-3-11).
55. Biedermann S, Tschudin P, Grob K. (2010) Transfer of bisphenol A from thermal printer paper to the skin. *Anal Bioanal Chem* 398(1):571–576.
56. http://en.wikipedia.org/wiki/Thermal_paper (accessed on 9-3-11).
57. Schwarz L, Klenke I. (2007) Enhancement of ninhydrin- or DFO-treated latent fingerprints on thermal paper. *J Forensic Sci* 52(3):649–655.
58. Anon. (2006) Use of DMAC on thermal papers. *Fingerprint and Footwear Forensics Newsletter*, HOSDB Publication No. 58/06.
59. Lee JL, Bleay SM, Sears VG, Mehmet S, Croxton R. (2009) Evaluation of dimethylaminocinnemaldehyde [sic] contact transfer process and its application to fingerprint development on thermal papers. *J Forensic Ident* 59(5):545–568.
60. Schwarz L, Klenke I. (2010) Improvement in latent fingerprint detection on thermal paper using a one-step treatment with polyvinylpyrrolidones. *J Forensic Sci* 55(4):1076–1079.
61. Brennan JS. (1996) The development of fingerprints by fuming with dimethylaminocinnamaldehyde (DMAC). In: Almog J, Springer E, Eds., *Proceedings of the International Symposium on Fingerprint Detection and Identification*. Hemed Press, Jerusalem, Israel, pp. 85–90.
62. Ramotowski R. (1996) Fluorescence visualization of latent fingerprints on paper using *p*-dimethylaminocinnamaldehyde (PDMAC). In: Almog J, Springer E, Eds., *Proceedings of the International Symposium on Fingerprint Detection and Identification*. Hemed Press, Jerusalem, Israel, pp. 91–94.
63. Theeuven A, Rodriguez C, Limborgh J. (2003) Dimethylaminocinnamaldehyde (DMAC) experiments on thermal paper (preliminary results). Presented at the International Fingerprint Research Group Meeting, St. Albans, Hertfordshire, U.K., May.
64. Bleay S. (2007) Evaluation of DMAC for thermal papers. Presented at the International Fingerprint Research Group Meeting, Canberra, ACT, Australia, March.
65. Bowman V, Ed. (2009) *Manual of Fingerprint Development Techniques*, 2nd edn. Home Office Police Scientific Development Branch, Sandridge, U.K.
66. Fitzgerald L, Sears V. (2003) Ninhydrin and DFO on thermal coated papers. Presented at the International Fingerprint Research Group Meeting, St. Albans, Hertfordshire, U.K., May.
67. Schwarz L, Frerichs I. (2002) Advanced solvent-free application of ninhydrin for detection of latent fingerprints on thermal paper and other surfaces. *J Forensic Sci* 47(6):1274–1277.
68. Nobel A. (2003) Detection of latent fingerprints on thermal paper. Presented at the International Fingerprint Research Group Meeting, St. Albans, Hertfordshire, U.K., May.
69. Schwarz L, Beisel M. (2007) Research, development, testing of fingerprint detection methods. Presented at the International Fingerprint Research Group Meeting, Canberra, Australian Capital Territory, Australia, March.
70. http://www.bvda.com/EN/prdctinf/en_thermanin.html (accessed on 9-3-11).
71. Ludas M. (1992) Nin dry: a non-destructive ninhydrin application for bank robbery demand notes and check forgery cases. In: *77th International Association for Identification Annual Educational Conference*, Atlantic City, NJ.
72. McMahon P. (1996) Procedure to develop latent prints on thermal papers. *Ident Canada* 19(3):4.
73. Patton ELT, Brown DH, Lewis SW. (2010) Detection of latent fingermarks on thermal printer paper by dry contact with 1,2-indanedione. *Anal Methods* 2:631–637.
74. Parasram L. (2011) Processing thermal paper with 1,2-indanedione/zinc chloride—a novel technique. *Ident Canada* 34(1):15–22.
75. Stimac JT. (2003) Thermal paper: latent friction ridge development via 1,2-indanedione. *J Forensic Ident* 53(3):265–271.

76. Yu P-H, Wallace MM. (2007) Effect of 1,2-indanedione on PCR-STR typing of fingerprints deposited on thermal and carbonless papers. *Forensic Sci Int* 168:112–118.
77. Schwarz L, Hermanowski ML. (2011) Using indanedione-zinc, heat, and G3 solution sequentially to detect latent fingerprints on thermal paper. *J Forensic Ident* 61(1):30–37.
78. Siegel SD. (2007) The use of cellophane tape to overcome the background discoloration on thermal paper. *J Forensic Ident* 57(2):240–243.
79. Humphries M. (2007) Thermal paper and ninhydrin. Presented at the International Fingerprint Research Group Meeting, Canberra, Australian Capital Territory, Australia, March.
80. Tsourounakis N, Howard S, Bertucca F. (2004) Latent fingerprint development on thermal paper using muriatic acid: a comparative analysis. *Ident Canada* 27(1):4–13.
81. Broniek B, Knaap W. (2002) Latent fingerprint development on thermal paper using muriatic (hydrochloric) acid. *J Forensic Ident* 52(4):427–432.
82. Ma R, Wei Q. (2006) Chemical fuming: a practical method for fingerprint development on thermal paper. *J Forensic Ident* 56(3):364–373.
83. Rawji A, Beaudoin A. (2007) Oil red O versus physical developer for wet substrates: a comparative study. *Ident Canada* 30(1):4–18.
84. Beaudoin A. (2004) New technique for revealing latent fingerprints on wet, porous surfaces: oil red O. *J Forensic Ident* 54(4):413–421.
85. Murphy KA, Cartner AM, Henderson W, Kim ND. (1999) Appraisal of the porphyrin compound, $(TTP)Sn(OH)_2$, as a latent fingerprint reagent. *J Forensic Ident* 49(3):269–282.
86. http://www.clpex.com, Weekly Detail 097 dated 06/16/03 (accessed on 9-3-11).
87. Wakefield M, Armitage S. (2005) The development of latent fingerprints on thermal paper using a novel, solvent-free method. *J Forensic Ident* 55(2):202–213.
88. Scott M. (2008) Improved results in the development of latent fingerprints on thermal paper. *J Forensic Ident* 58(4):424–428.
89. Barnes FC. (1993) *Cartridges of the World*, 7th edn. Vol 15, DBI Books, Northbrook, IL, 225pp.
90. Anon. (2009) SWGFAST training to competency. www.clpex.com, August 9, 2009 (accessed on 9-3-11).
91. Wiesner S, Springer E, Argaman U. (1996) A closer look at the effects of the shooting process on fingerprint development on fired cartridge cases. In: Almog J, Springer E, Eds., *Proceedings of the International Symposium on Fingerprint Detection and Identification*. Hemed Press, Jerusalem, Israel, pp. 161–178.
92. Barnum CA, Klasey DR. (1997) Factors affecting the recovery of latent prints on firearms. *J Forensic Ident* 47(2):141–149.
93. O'Brien K. (2007) Thumbs up. *Boston Globe*, May 13, online at http://www.boston.com/news/globe/magazi… thumbs_up/ (accessed on 9-3-11).
94. Ramotowski RS. (2001) Composition of latent print residue. In: Lee HC, Gaensslen RE, Eds. *Advances in Fingerprint Technology*, 2nd edn. CRC Press, Boca Raton, FL, pp. 63–104.
95. Kaiser D, Drack E. (1974) Diminished excretion of bicarbonate from the single sweat gland of patients with cystic fibrosis of the pancreas. *Eur J Clin Invest* 4:261–265.
96. Jensen O, Nielsen E. (1979) "Rusters." The corrosive action of palmar sweat: II. Physical and chemical factors in palmar hyperhidrosis. *Acta Derm Venereol* 59:139–143.
97. Merston T. (1984) The mensural factor. *Fingerprint Whorld* 10(38):51.
98. Hamm ED. (1987) The rust of the story. *Fingerprint Whorld* 13(49):105.
99. Angier RH. (1936) *Firearm Blueing and Browning*. Arms & Armour Press, London, U.K.
100. Leben DA, Ramotowski RS. (1996) Evaluation of gun blueing solutions and their ability to develop latent fingerprints on cartridge casings. *Chesapeake Examiner* (October):8, 10.
101. Bentsen RK, Brown JK, Dinsmore A, Harvey KK, Kee TG. (1996) Post firing visualisation of fingerprints on spent cartridge cases. *Sci Justice* 36:3–8.
102. Vandiver JV. (1976) Fingerprints on cartridges. *Ident News* 26(6):5.
103. Given BW. (1976) Latent fingerprints on cartridges and expended cartridge casings. *J Forensic Sci* 21(3):587–594.

104. Saunders GC, Cantu AA. (1996) Evaluation of several techniques for developing latent fingerprints on unfired and fired cartridge casings. In: Almog J, Springer E, Eds., *Proceedings of the International Symposium on Fingerprint Detection and Identification*. Hemed Press, Jerusalem, Israel, pp. 155–160.
105. Belcher GL. (1978) Latent recovery methods. *Fingerprint Whorld* 4(14):51–52.
106. Belcher GL. (1980) Developing latents on copper coated casings. *Fingerprint Whorld* 6(22):39.
107. Reed R. (1985) Development of latent prints on brass with silver nitrate. *Ident News* 35(7):11.
108. Cantu AA, Leben DA, Ramotowski R, Kopera J, Simms JR. (1998) Use of acidified hydrogen peroxide to remove excess gun blue from gun blue-treated cartridge cases and to develop latent prints on untreated cartridge cases. *J Forensic Sci* 43(2):294–298.
109. Schutz F, Bonfanti M, Champod C. (2000) La révélation des traces papillaires sur les douilles par les techniques de etching et de blueing et comparaison avec la déposition multimétallique. *Can Soc Forensic Sci J* 33(2):65–81.
110. Migron Y, Mandler D, Frank A, Springer E, Almog J. (1996) Is a fingerprint left on a fired cartridge? The development of latent fingerprints on metallic surfaces by palladium deposition. In: Almog J, Springer E, Eds., *Proceedings of the International Symposium on Fingerprint Detection and Identification*. Hemed Press, Jerusalem, Israel, pp. 217–225.
111. Migron Y, Mandler D. (1997) Development of latent fingerprints on unfired cartridges by palladium deposition: a surface study. *J Forensic Sci* 42(6):982–992.
112. Migron Y, Hocherman G, Springer E, Almog J, Mandler D. (1998) Visualization of sebaceous fingerprints on fired cartridge cases: a laboratory study. *J Forensic Sci* 43(3):543–548.
113. Donche A. (1994) Development of latent fingerprints on cartridge casings. *Fingerprint Whorld* 20 (75):13–19.
114. Williams G, McMurray N, Worsley DA. (2001) Latent fingerprint detection using a scanning Kelvin microprobe. *J Forensic Sci* 46(5):1085–1092.
115. Bersellini C, Garofano L, Giannetto M, Lusardi F, Mori G. (2001) Development of latent fingerprints on metallic surfaces using electropolymerization processes. *J Forensic Sci* 46(4):871–877.
116. Hillman R, Goddard A, Beresford A, Brown R, Levesley J, Pirashvili M, Bond J. (2011) Electrochemical enhancement of latent fingerprints. Presented at the International Fingerprint Research Group Meeting, Linköping, Sweden, June.
117. Bond J. (2008) Visualization of latent fingerprint corrosion of metallic surfaces. *J Forensic Sci* 53(4):812–822.
118. Bond J. (2008) The thermodynamics of latent fingerprint corrosion of metal elements and alloys. *J Forensic Sci* 53(6):1344–1352.
119. Bond JW, Heidel C. (2009) Visualization of latent fingerprint corrosion on a discharged brass shell casing. *J Forensic Sci* 54(4):892–894.
120. Sampson WC. (1993) An inquiry into the methodology of preserving and developing latent prints on expended cartridge casings. *J Forensic Ident* 43(1):4–12.
121. Bleay SM, Kelly PF, King RSP. (2010) Polymerisation of S_2N_2 to $(SN)_x$ as a tool for the rapid imaging of fingerprints removed from metal surfaces. *J Mater Chem* 20(45):10100–10102.
122. Sturelle V, Cominotti C, Henrot D, Desbrosse X. (2006) The use of camphor in the development of latent prints on unfired cartridge casings. *J Forensic Ident* 56(5):694–705.
123. Hall MM. (1991) Ridge detail through latex gloves. *J Forensic Ident* 41(6):415–416.
124. St. Amand F. (1994) True facts about latex gloves. *RCMP Gazette* 56:6.
125. Comber B. (1997) Fingerprints through gloves. *Fingerprint Whorld* 23(90):125–128.
126. Willinski G. (1980) Permeation of fingerprints through laboratory gloves. *J Forensic Sci* 25(3):682–685.
127. Lounsbury DA, Thompson LF. (2006) Concerns when using examination gloves at the crime scene. *J Forensic Ident* 56(2):179–185.
128. Poy AL, van Oorschot RAH. (2006) Trace DNA presence, origin, and transfer within a forensic biology laboratory and its potential effect on casework. *J Forensic Ident* 56(4):558–576.
129. Lambourne G. (1988) Glove print identification. *J Forensic Ident* 38(1):7–24.
130. http://www.marly-skin.de/index.html (accessed 9-3-11).

131. Grimoldi G, Lennard CJ, Margot, PA. (1990) "Liquid gloves" and latent fingerprint detection. *J Forensic Ident* 40(1):23–27.
132. Anon. (1982) Tricksters used beauty aid to hide fingerprints. *Fingerprint Whorld* 8(30):32.
133. Mock JP. (1986) Prosthetic fingerprints. *Ident News* 36(1):3–5,13.
134. Pleckaitis J. (2007) Developing friction ridge detail on the interior of latex and nitrile gloves. *J Forensic Ident* 57(2):230–239.
135. Speaks HA. (1966) Ninhydrin prints from rubber gloves. *Fingerprint Ident Mag* 47(9):3–5.
136. Pressly J. (1999) Ninhydrin on latex gloves: an alternative use for an old technique. *J Forensic Ident* 49(3):257–260.
137. Rinehart DJ. (2000) Developing and identifying a latent print recovered from a piece of latex glove using ninhydrin–heptane carrier (case 1). Developing latent prints on household rubber gloves using ninhydrin-heptane carrier after superglue fuming (case 2). *J Forensic Ident* 50(5):443–446.
138. Hunter JL. (1994) Fingerprint evidence with coomassie blue—after 25 years. *J Forensic Ident* 44(6):619–622.
139. Velders MJM. (2004) Visualization of latent fingerprints on used vinyl and latex gloves using gel-lifters. Presented at the 89th International Association for Identification Conference, St. Louis, MO, August. See also: http://usa.bvda.com/productinfo.php?file=fp_latex_gloves (accessed on 9-3-11).
140. Bleay S, Sears V. (2007) Powder suspensions: magnificent or myth? Presented at the International Fingerprint Research Group Meeting, Canberra, Australian Capital Territory, Australia, August.
141. Midkiff CR. (1994) Development of latent prints on tape. *Fingerprint Whorld* 20(75):5–7.
142. Bergeron JW. (2009) Use of liquid nitrogen to separate adhesive tapes. *J Forensic Ident* 59(1):7–25.
143. Bailey JA, Crane JS. (2011) Use of nitrogen cryogun for separating duct tape and recovery of latent fingerprints with a powder suspension method. *Forensic Sci Int* 210:170–173.
144. Campbell BM. (1991) Separation of adhesive tapes. *J Forensic Ident* 41(2):102–106.
145. Choudhry MY, Whritenour RD. (1990) A new approach to unraveling tangled adhesive tape for potential detection of latent prints and recovery of trace evidence. *J Forensic Sci* 35(6):1373–1383.
146. McMahon P. (1992) Preservation of latents on adhesive tapes. *RCMP Gazette* 54(1):22–23.
147. Mevissen M. (2003) "Turkish solution" for detaching tapes. Presented at the International Fingerprint Research Group Meeting, St. Albans, Hertfordshire, U.K., May.
148. Stimac JT. (2000) Adhesive tape separation with un-du. *Fingerprint Whorld* 26(102):153–157.
149. Molina D. (2007) The use of un-du to separate adhesive materials. *J Forensic Ident* 57(5):688–696.
150. Watkins MD, Brown KC. (2004) Using un-du adhesive remover. *Evidence Tech Mag* (September–October):12–13.
151. Schwartz RL, Higginbotham LC, Smith DR. (2003) The effect of un-du on latent print development. *Fingerprint Whorld* 29(112):66–73.
152. Maceo AV, Wertheim K. (2000) Use of ninhydrin in the recovery of latent prints on evidence involving adhesive surfaces attached to porous surfaces. *J Forensic Ident* 50(6):581–594.
153. Hart A, Sears V, Bowman V, Wheeler E. (2006) Additional fingerprint development techniques for adhesive tapes. Home Office Scientific Development Branch Publication No. 23/06.
154. Geller B, Springer E. (1996) A special frame for easing the handling of adhesive tapes in fingerprint development. *J Forensic Ident* 46(3):281–285.
155. Kent T. (1980) A modified gentian violet development technique for fingerprints on black adhesive tape. PSDB Technical Memorandum No 1/80.
156. Haylock SE. (1979) Carbolic gentian violet solution. *Fingerprint Whorld* 4(15):82–83.
157. Wilson BL, McCloud VD. (1982) Development of latent prints on black plastic tape using crystal violet dye and photographic paper. *Ident News* 32(3):3–4.
158. Richtarcik EG. (1981) Hazards of phenol. *Ident News* 31(8):13.
159. Bramble SK, Cantu AA, Ramotowski RS, Brennan JS. (2000) Deep red to near infrared (NIR) fluorescence of gentian violet-treated latent prints. *J Forensic Ident* 50(1):33–49.

160. Creer KE, Brennan JS. (1987) The work of the serious crimes unit. In: *Proceedings of the International Forensic Symposium on Latent Prints*, Laboratory & Identification Divisions, Federal Bureau of Investigation, FSRTC FBI Academy, Quantico, VA, U.S. Government Printing Office, Washington, DC, pp. 91–99.
161. Jumper AJ. (1996) Fluorescent gentian violet. *The Print* 12(4):10.
162. Menzel ER. (1989) Pretreatment of latent prints for laser development. *Forensic Sci Rev* 1(1):43–66.
163. Menzel ER. (2001) Application of laser technology in latent fingerprint enhancement. In: Lee HC, Gaensslen RE, Eds., *Advances in Fingerprint Technology*, 2nd edn. CRC Press, Boca Raton, FL, pp. 135–162.
164. Howard S. (1993) Basic fuchsin—a guide to a one-step processing technique for black electrical tape. *J Forensic Sci* 38(6):1391–1403.
165. Arima T. (1981) Development of latent fingerprints on sticky surfaces by dye staining of fluorescent brightening. *Ident News* 31(2):9–10.
166. Wilson HD. (2010) RAY dye stain versus gentian violet and alternate powder for development of latent prints on the adhesive side of tape. *J Forensic Ident* 60(5):510–523.
167. Midkiff CR, Codell DE. (1994) Development of latent prints on tape (part II). *Fingerprint Whorld* 21(79):21–26.
168. Steele CA, Ball MS. (2003) Enhancing contrast of fingerprints on plastic tape. *J Forensic Sci* 48(6):1314–1317.
169. Sodhi GS. (2005) Detection of latent fingerprints on adhesive tapes. Presented at the International Fingerprint Research Group Meeting, The Hague, the Netherlands, April.
170. Sneddon N. (1999) Black powder method to process duct tape. *J Forensic Ident* 49(4):347–356.
171. Gray ML. (1996) Sticky-side powder versus gentian violet: the search for the superior method for processing the sticky side of adhesive tape. *J Forensic Ident* 46(3):268–272.
172. Tuthill H. (1997) Re: Sticky-side powder versus gentian violet: the search for the superior method for processing the sticky-side of adhesive tape [letter to the editor]. *J Forensic Ident* 47(1):4–10.
173. Bratton R, Gregus J. (1996) A black powder method to process adhesive tapes. In: Almog J, Springer E, Eds., *Proceedings of the International Symposium on Fingerprint Detection and Identification*. Hemed Press, Jerusalem, Israel, pp. 143–147.
174. Bratton R, Gregus J. (1997) Development of a black powder method to process adhesive tapes. *Fingerprint Whorld* 23(87):21–23.
175. Freeman HN. (1991) The use of fingerprint powders to develop latent prints on electrical or plastic tapes. *J Forensic Ident* 41(6):417–420.
176. Kimble GW. (1996) Powder suspension processing. *J Forensic Ident* 46(3):273–280.
177. Frank A, Almog J. (1993) Modified SPR for latent fingerprint development on wet, dark objects. *J Forensic Ident* 43(3):240–244.
178. Wade DC. (2002) Development of latent prints with titanium dioxide (TiO_2). *J Forensic Ident* 52(5):551–559.
179. Martin BL. (1999) Developing latent prints on the adhesive surface of black electrical tape. *J Forensic Ident* 49(2):127–129.
180. Hollars ML, Trozzi TA, Barron BL. (2000) Development of latent fingerprints on dark colored sticky surfaces using liqui-drox. *J Forensic Ident* 50(4):357–362.
181. Sampson WC. (1997) Letter to the editor. *J Forensic Ident* 47(2):252–253.
182. Scott M. (2009) Does CA Fuming interfere with powder suspension processing? *J Forensic Ident* 59(2):144–151.
183. Schiemer C, Lennard C, Maynard P, Roux C. (2005) Evaluation of techniques for the detection and enhancement of latent fingermarks on black electrical tape. *J Forensic Ident* 55(2):214–238.
184. Smith DW. (1977) A practical method for the recovery of latent impressions on adhesive surfaces. *Ident News* 27(10):3–4.
185. Midkiff CR, Codell D, Chapman J. (1994) Development of latent prints on tape—part III. *Fingerprint Whorld* 23(89):83–86.

186. Taylor EM, Mankevich A. (1984) A new latent print developing method for use on tape. *Ident News* 34(7):4–5,13.
187. Lo IKL. (1993) A review on detection of latent prints on self-adhesive tapes. *Fingerprint Whorld* 19(74):89–96.
188. Menzel ER, Savoy SM, Ulvick SJ, Cheng KH, Murdock RH, Sudduth MR. (2000) Photoluminescent semiconductor nanocrystals for fingerprint detection. *J Forensic Sci* 45(3):545–551.
189. Berg EC. (1992) Latent prints from duct tape. *J Forensic Ident* 42(5):401–403.
190. Hart A. (2005) Adhesive tapes. Presented at the International Fingerprint Research Group Meeting, The Hague, the Netherlands, April.
191. Sampson WC. (1996) Latent fingerprint evidence on human skin (part 1). *J Forensic Ident* 46(2):188–195.
192. Anon. (2004) Statistics. Latent prints that have been recovered from human skin nationally—internationally. *Evidence Tech Mag* July–August:10–11.
193. Sampson WC, Sampson KL, Shonberger MF. (1997) Recovery of latent fingerprint evidence from human skin: causation, isolation and processing techniques. KLS Forensics, Inc. (published by Lightning Powder, Inc.).
194. Sampson WC. (1997) Sequential applications in the development and recovery of latent fingerprint evidence from human skin. *Fingerprint Whorld* 23(89):94–97.
195. Newitt C, Green MA. (1979) A thermographic study of surface cooling of cadavers. *J Forensic Sci Soc* 19:179–181.
196. Allman DS, Pounds CA. (1991) Detection of fingerprints on skin. *Forensic Sci Rev* 3(2):84–89.
197. Sampson WC, Sampson KL. (2005) Recovery of latent prints from human skin. *J Forensic Ident* 55(3):362–385.
198. Bettencourt DS. (1991) A compilation of techniques for processing deceased human skin for latent prints. *J Forensic Ident* 41(2):111–120.
199. Wilkinson D. (2011) A review of fingerprints from human skin. *Ident Canada* 34(2):48–60.
200. Sampson WC. (1992) Glass recovery investigative technique: G.R.I.T. *J Forensic Ident* 42(2):96–100.
201. McMorris J. (1937) The iodine-silver transfer method for the detection of latent fingerprints. *Fingerprint Ident Mag* 18(9):6.
202. Foley JF. (1971) Development of latent fingerprints—silver transfer method. *Ontario Prov Pol Rev* 6:7.
203. Mooney DJ. (1977) Fingerprints on human skin. *Ident News* 27(2):5–8.
204. Adcock JM. (1977) The development of latent fingerprints on human skin: the iodine-silver plate transfer method. *J Forensic Sci* 22(3):599–605.
205. Feldman MA, Meloan CE, Lambert JL. (1982) A new method for recovering latent fingerprints from skin. *J Forensic Sci* 27(4):806–811.
206. Graham D, Gray HC. (1966) The use of X-ray electronography and autoelectronography in forensic investigation. *J Forensic Sci* 11:124–143.
207. Graham D. (1969) Some technical aspects of the demonstration and visualization of fingerprints on human skin. *J Forensic Sci* 14(1):1–12.
208. Cunn AL. (1969) Use of X-ray and other techniques to visualize and reproduce fingerprints from living human skin. *Ident News* 19(8):4,8.
209. Winstanley R. (1977) Recovery of latent fingerprints from difficult surfaces by an X-ray method. *J Forensic Sci Soc* 17(2):121–125.
210. Gutierrez CH. (1976) Developing and photographing latent prints found on human skin. *Fingerprint Ident Mag* 57:10.
211. Hammer HJ. (1980) Über methoden zur darstellung von latenten fingerabdrücken auf der menschlichen haut. *Forensic Sci Int* 16:35–41.
212. Melis A. (1981) The spa murders. Identification of a lift from human skin. *Fingerprint Whorld* 6(23):55–57.
213. Haslett M. (1983) Fingerprints from skin using the MagnaBrush technique. *Fingerprint Whorld* 8(32):118–119.

214. Anon. (2001) Final report on the 1st series of experiments: latent fingerprints on human skin. Bundeskriminalamt, unpublished report.
215. Färber D, Seul A, Weisser H-J, Bohnert M. (2010) Recovery of latent fingerprints and DNA on human skin. *J Forensic Sci* 55(6):1457–1461.
216. Trapecar M. (2009) Lifting techniques for finger marks on human skin previous enhancement by Swedish Black powder—a preliminary study. *Sci Justice* 49:292–295.
217. Menzel ER. (1982) Laser detection of latent fingerprints on skin. *J Forensic Sci* 27(4):918–922.
218. Hamilton J, DiBattista J. (1985) Cyanoacrylate ester-latent print from murdered body. *Fingerprint Whorld* 11(41):18–19.
219. Delmas BJ. (1988) Postmortem latent print recovery from skin surfaces. *J Forensic Ident* 38(2):49–56.
220. Jian Z, Dao-An G. (1991) A modified cyanoacrylate technique utilizing treated neutral filter paper for developing latent fingerprints. *Forensic Sci Int* 52:31–34.
221. Hebrard J, Donche A. (1994) Fingerprint detection methods on skin: experimental study on 16 live subjects and 23 cadavers. *J Forensic Ident* 44(6):623–631.
222. Misner A, Wilkinson D, Watkin J. (1993) Thenoyl europium chelate: a new fluorescent dye with a narrow emission band to detect cyanoacrylate developed fingerprints on non-porous substrates and cadavers. *J Forensic Ident* 43(2):154–165.
223. Wilkinson DA, Watkin JE, Misner AH. (1996) A comparison of techniques for the visualization of fingerprints on human skin including the application of iodine and α-naphthoflavone. *J Forensic Ident* 46(4):432–453.
224. Silva J. (1978) Skin latents. *Fingerprint Whorld* 4(14):53–55.
225. Reichardt GJ, Carr JC, Stone EG. (1978) A conventional method for lifting latent fingerprints from human skin surfaces. *J Forensic Sci* 23(1):135–141.
226. Hamm ED. (1988) A latent from human skin or is it? *Fingerprint Whorld* 14(54):56–58.
227. Guo Y-C, Xing L-P. (1992) Visualization method for fingerprints on skin by impression on a polyethylene terephthalate (PET) semirigid sheet. *J Forensic Sci* 37(2):604–611.
228. Imamura M, Asahida M. (1981) Fingerprint lifted from cadaver skin surface. *Ident News* 31(7):13–14.
229. Hoyser RL. (1992) An alternative G.R.I.T. technique. *J Forensic Ident* 42(3):19–20.
230. Clements WW. (1983) Blood print on human skin. *Ident News* 33(8):4,6.
231. Lawley R. (2003) Application of amido black mixture for the development of blood-based fingerprints on human skin. *J Forensic Ident* 53(4):404–408.
232. Jernigan M. (1993) Amido black treatment of a murder victim. *Fingerprint Whorld* 19(73):55–56.
233. Trapecar M, Balazic J. (2007) Fingerprint recovery from human skin surfaces. *Sci Justice* 47:136–140.

8

Powders for Fingerprint Development

Helen L. Bandey, Stephen M. Bleay, and Andrew P. Gibson

CONTENTS

8.1 History of the Technique

The use of powders is one of the oldest reported techniques for development of latent fingerprints. Faulds, in his publication *Dactyloscopy* in 1912 [1], refers to the experiments conducted by Forgeot in the late nineteenth century as the first studies into the powdering technique, and also comments on subsequent experiments of his own [2]. By 1912 Faulds [1] was able to describe formulations and application techniques for both black and white powders, and by 1920 many more types of powders had been reported for development of fingerprints, including mercury–chalk (hydrargyrum-cum-creta), graphite, lamp black, ferric oxide, magnesium carbonate, aniline dye stuffs, lycopodium powder–Sudan red mixture, red lead oxide, lead carbonate, lead iodide, and lead acetate [3]. By the end of the decade, a further selection of fingerprint development powders had been reported, including the first references to the use of aluminum powder. The purpose of many of these materials was to provide investigators with a range of different colored powders that could be used to both develop a crime scene mark and provide contrast with colored backgrounds. Some of these early powders persisted in use for many years. Mercury–chalk was still in use in the United Kingdom in the 1970s, and carbon black–based powders remain in use worldwide to the current day.

Another technique for providing contrast between the developed mark and the substrate and considered relatively early in the history of fingerprint development was fluorescence. Zinc sulfide and anthracene were proposed as fluorescent dusting powders in the 1930s [4], with the developed marks being illuminated with long-wave ultraviolet radiation to promote phosphorescence and fluorescence, respectively. Variants of these powders were still being recommended for development of latent fingerprints on multicolored surfaces in 1954 [5].

The range of powders that have been formulated and marketed for fingerprint development in the intervening years far exceeds the number of chemical development techniques, and more enter the market every year. Some examples of powder "recipes" that have been used by police forces in the past [6,7] but are now predominantly obsolete are given in Table 8.1.

These early powder formulations do not appear to have been devised by any standardized testing system nor were any recorded comparative trials carried out to establish which formulations were most effective. Their use was often according to the personal preferences of the person treating the marks at the crime scene rather than any scientific assessment of which powder was most appropriate for a particular type of surface. As a consequence, no single type of powder predominated and many local variations in practice arose worldwide.

Some of the constituents used in early fingerprint powder formulations were toxic or carcinogenic and their prolonged use could cause health problems. The best documented of these problems is the occurrence of mercury poisoning among officers in United Kingdom police forces [8,9], initially reported in the late 1940s and caused by the use of mercury–chalk powder. Although most of these powder formulations have since been withdrawn, it is still recommended that users consult material safety data sheets before employing any new type of powder.

Many powders used for fingerprint development in the first half of the twentieth century were also granular in nature, typically applied with animal hair brushes. Photography of the marks developed by powdering was almost exclusively carried out *in situ*. Developments in the 1960s meant that alternative types of powders began to become more widely used. The first of these developments was the "Magna brush" in the early 1960s [10], consisting of a retractable bar magnet within a nonmagnetic cover material. When dipped into a pot of magnetic powder, a brush-like head of powder became attracted to the magnet which could then be drawn across the surface like a hair brush. A range of magnetic powders were soon developed for use with this brush. The second development was the increasing recognition that aluminum flake powder, already in operational use in the 1950s, had a combination of properties that made it ideally suited for use with lifting media, thus overcoming the need for photography *in situ* and enabling the separation of the developed mark from backgrounds that may have made photography difficult.

TABLE 8.1

Published Formulations for Various Types of Early Fingerprint Powders

Color of Powder	Constituents	Wt% of Constituent
Black	Lamp black	70
	Graphite	20
	Gum acacia	10
	Black magnetic ferric oxide	50
	Rosin	25
	Lamp black	25
White	Titanium dioxide	67
	Kaolin	16.5
	French chalk	16.5
	Titanium dioxide	33.3
	Basic lead carbonate	33.3
	Gum Arabic	33.3
Grey	Mercury	25
	Chalk	50
	Aluminum powder	25
	Basic lead carbonate	87.5
	Gum Arabic	12.5
	Aluminum powder	trace
	Lamp black	trace to give color
Red/orange	Red lead oxide	33
	Rosin	67
	Lycopodium	90
	Sudan Red III	10
Fluorescent	Anthracene	50
	White tempera	50

Since then, aluminum flake and magnetic powders have been increasingly used in place of granular powders and the types of powder currently in widespread use can be grouped into four main classes, namely:

- Metal flake powder (e.g., aluminum and bronze)
- Granular powder (black and white)
- Magnetic powders
- Fluorescent powders

The categories given earlier represent a general classification; the actual number of powder formulations that are available on the world market can be numbered in the hundreds, and some formulations actually fall into more than one category. Each of these different powder types have particular types of surface to which they are most suited—there is no one powder that will consistently develop marks of optimal quality on all surfaces. However, despite this recognized performance variation there is very little reported evidence of large-scale comparative studies to demonstrate the relative effectiveness of powders other than the experiments carried out by the Home Office Scientific Development Branch of the United Kingdom [11–13]. These comparisons were limited to a small number of powders identified as being representative of the general categories by a survey of police force scene of crime units and by preliminary evaluations. By tracing the commercial powders back to the source it was established that many differently labeled products were in effect the same powder, and some other less-used powders performed poorly in early trials and were therefore eliminated from subsequent studies. This enabled the large-scale trials to focus on powders that were effective and/or widely used. A methodology is presented [11] that allows researchers to carry out similar comparative assessments for any new powder system.

Powdered marks probably account for the largest number of fingerprint identifications worldwide, in the United Kingdom alone approximately 50% of the ~60,000 fingerprint identifications per annum arise from marks developed using this process. It is therefore evident that even the small percentage improvements that can be achieved by selection of the optimum powder and brush combination for a particular surface have the potential to provide significant operational benefits, and further study of this area may be required.

8.2 Theory

The development of fingermarks by powdering occurs by preferential adhesion of powder particles to the ridges, with the background material having less affinity for the particles. This means that powders should not be used where surfaces are sticky or heavily contaminated because the particles will not be able to discriminate between the constituents in the fingerprint residues and the contaminant and will adhere across the entire surface.

The factors that are thought to play a role in promoting powder particles to adhere to fingerprint ridges are as follows:

- Particle shape
- Surface chemistry of the powder particle
- Electrostatic charge on the particle
- Adhesion to grease or liquid
- Low(er) adhesion to substrate

The overall adhesive effect of a particle to a fingerprint ridge is likely to be a combination of all these factors and therefore no one dominant mechanism can easily be identified.

In terms of particle shape, it has been suggested that flake powders are more sensitive than granular powders because their shape gives them a higher surface area and hence better contact with the fingerprint deposits.

With regard to surface chemistry, it is known that the adhesion of a powder particle to a solid surface in air or a gaseous medium is partly due to molecular forces [14]. It is therefore anticipated that changing the molecules on the surface of the powder particle will have an effect on the interaction between that particle and the medium it adheres to. It has been demonstrated that surface coatings do play a role in the effectiveness of metallic flake powders for fingerprint development. Experiments conducted by James et al. [15,16] demonstrated that flake powders without stearic acid coatings were poor for fingerprint development, irrespective of flake diameter. Further investigation of stearic acid coating thickness showed that optimum results were obtained for a coating thickness of 70 nm.

Electrostatic charge can potentially make large contributions to adhesion. It has been stated [14] that if particles are highly charged, the value of the attractive Coulomb forces exceeds that of other contributions to adhesion. Researchers have investigated various ways of utilizing this effect for enhancing fingerprint development using powders but it is not the major mechanism used in any of the types of powder widely used at crime scenes.

The presence of liquid or grease in a fingerprint deposit will promote adhesion of the particle to it for two principal reasons. The first is that the liquid is able to wet the surfaces, thus giving a greater contact area for the powder particles. The second is the capillary force of the liquid caused by surface tension. In atmospheres where the relative humidity is in excess of 70%, the increase observed in the adhesion of microscopic particles is due to capillary forces. It has been suggested that in dry climates or for fingerprints that have dried out, "huffing" (blowing warm, hot air or breath over the mark) or rehumidification prior to powdering may improve the quality of the developed print [17].

Once the initial layer of powder particles has adhered to the fingerprint ridge, the process of autoadhesion (the interaction between individual powder particles) becomes important. In the case of aluminum powders, it is suggested that repeated passes of the brush are used to "build up" the mark, indicating that strong autoadhesive bonds do exist between aluminum powder particles. For powdering with magnetic flake powders, a single sweep of the applicator is suggested, with further passes thought to "fill in" or reduce the quality of the fingerprint. This indicates that autoadhesive forces between magnetic flake particles are weak, and there is a possibility that the magnetized particles may repel each other.

8.3 Applications of the Technique

The principal application of powders is the development of fingerprints on nonporous surfaces at crime scenes. The brush application method allows large areas such as windows, doors and door frames to be speculatively treated without recourse to more destructive or time-consuming chemical treatments. The speed, effectiveness, and low cost of the technique make powders well-suited to volume crime applications and the fact that other chemical treatments (such as blood dyes, powder suspensions, and superglue) can be used sequentially after it also makes it an important first treatment at serious crime scenes.

In the laboratory, powders can be used on nonporous exhibits where it is suspected that there may be a mixture of latent prints and marks in blood, because they may develop both types of mark and have no detrimental impact of subsequent treatment with blood dyes (unlike the other treatment option, superglue).

As stated previously, powders should not be used if it is suspected a surface is contaminated with any sticky residues (e.g., foodstuffs, oils) because powder will adhere to the entire surface and marks will not be resolved.

8.4 Equipment

8.4.1 Powders

The general classes of fingerprint powder available on the market have been outlined earlier. This section provides further detail on each of these generic powder types. Some electron microscopy studies have been carried out on powders and powdered marks [18,19] and micrographs are included to show the powder microstructures and the interactions of the powders with fingerprint deposits.

8.4.1.1 Flake Powders

Aluminum flake is probably the most widely used powder in the United Kingdom, although it is less widely utilized in other countries worldwide. This is a metal flake powder, with smooth surfaces and jagged edges. The diameter of the particles falls within the range 1–12 µm and the thickness is ~0.5 µm. The flakes are coated with stearic acid during the milling process to prevent clumping. The microstructure of a typical aluminum powder is shown in Figure 8.1.

The powder preferentially adheres to fingerprint ridges, but does not form a continuous layer across the entirety of the ridge area. Some powder deposition may also take place on the background (Figure 8.2). The powder lies flat on the surface in layers (Figure 8.3),

FIGURE 8.1
Scanning electron micrograph of a typical aluminum flake powder.

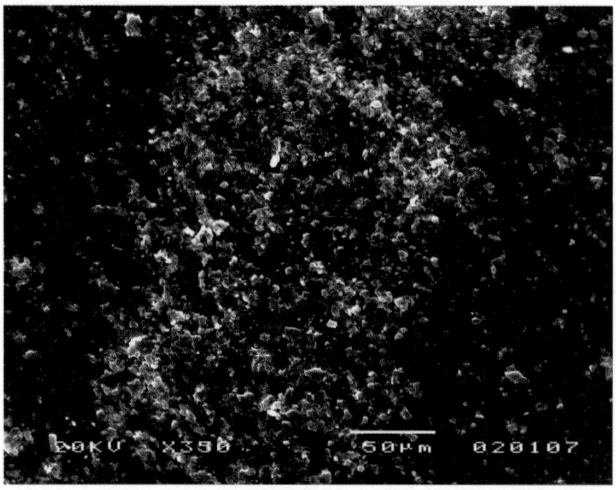

FIGURE 8.2
Scanning electron micrograph of fingerprint ridges treated with aluminum powder, imaged perpendicular to the ridge direction.

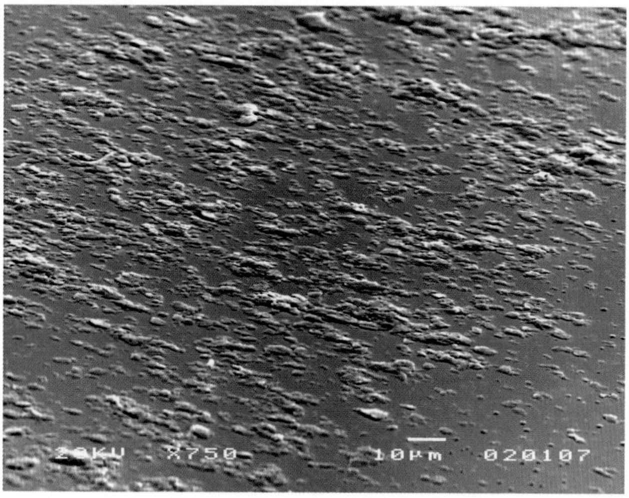

FIGURE 8.3
Scanning electron micrograph of fingerprint ridges treated with aluminum powder, imaged obliquely to the ridge direction.

enabling it to be easily lifted by removal of the surface layers of powder, although the bottom layers stay tightly bound to the fingerprint ridges and will usually remain *in situ*.

Aluminum is a powder best suited to smooth surfaces because surface irregularities will trap the fine flakes and result in heavy retention of the powder by the background with a correspondingly poor definition of fingerprint ridges. The way in which the powder is applied can also play a role, with incorrect brush selection and poor powdering technique also contributing to high background retention of the powder.

Bronze (sometimes described as brass or gold) flake powders may be used to give increased contrast where the nature of the surface makes marks developed using aluminum difficult to see, for example, "silver metallic" vehicle bodywork. The powder is essentially similar in morphology and means of application to aluminum (Figure 8.4).

FIGURE 8.4
Scanning electron micrograph of a typical bronze flake powder.

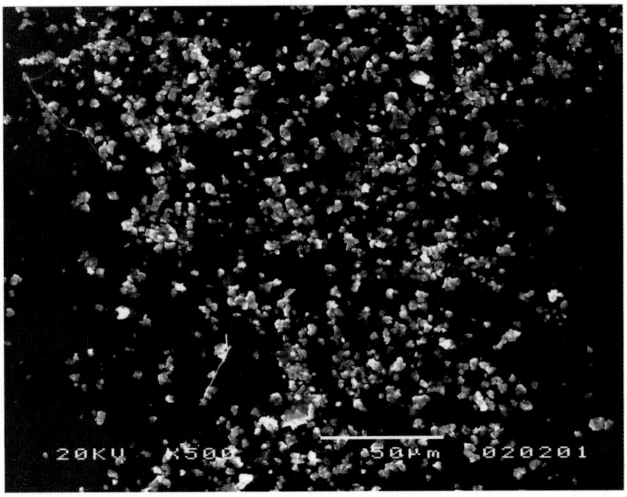

FIGURE 8.5
Scanning electron micrograph of fingerprint ridges treated with bronze powder, imaged perpendicular to the ridge direction.

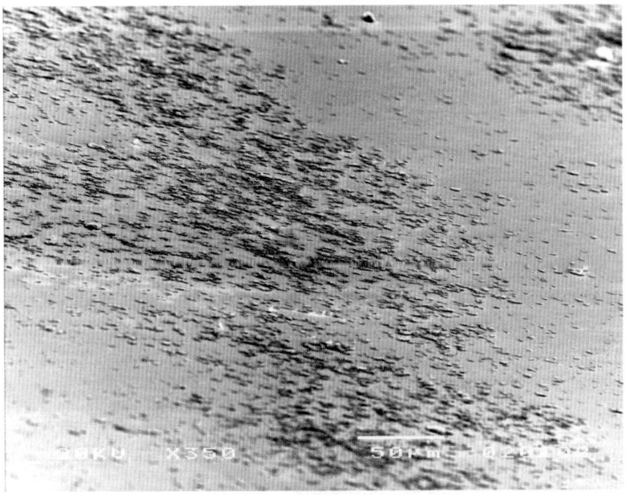

FIGURE 8.6
Scanning electron micrograph of fingerprint ridges treated with bronze powder, imaged obliquely to the ridge direction.

Powdered marks are microscopically similar to those developed using aluminum (Figures 8.5 and 8.6).

Bronze powder has a lower working exposure limit (WEL) than aluminum due to the copper content, and the use of face masks is recommended for users of this powder.

8.4.1.2 Granular Powders

Most black granular powders are carbon-based. A typical grade of carbon black used for powder formulations is Elftex 415, provided by Cabot Carbon, the microstructure of which is shown in Figure 8.7. This is an amorphous, elemental carbon with a particle size in the

FIGURE 8.7
Scanning electron micrograph of a typical black granular powder.

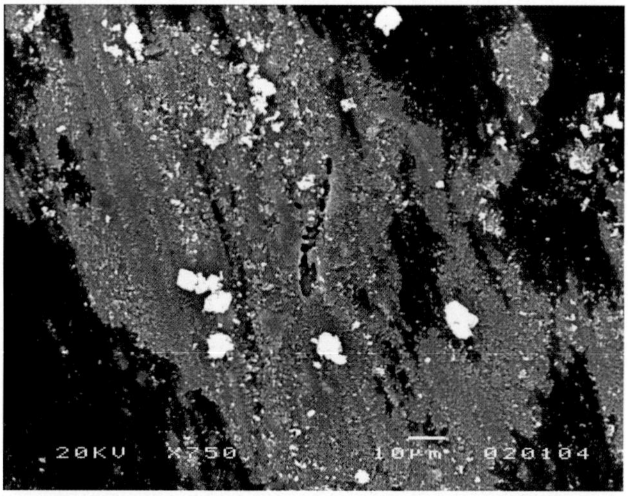

FIGURE 8.8
Scanning electron micrograph of fingerprint ridges treated with black granular powder, imaged perpendicular to the ridge direction.

range 5–10 μm and a textured, irregular (but smooth) shape. Other types of carbon black are used in numerous alternative black granular powder formulations.

Powdered marks exhibit a continuous, dense covering of the finer (~1 μm) particulates across the entire area of the fingerprint ridge. Some evidence of the brush direction used to apply the powder may also be evident (Figures 8.8 and 8.9).

White granular powders often contain more than one particle type. The example shown in Figure 8.10 consists of large flakes of magnesium silicate (20–100 μm in size) with small granules of titanium dioxide (mostly <1 μm). The small granules coat the surface of the larger flakes, suggesting that the flakes act as the carrier for the fine titanium dioxide granules.

Similarly to the black granular powder, it is generally the finer particulates that eventually adhere to the fingerprint ridges and provide the development, although larger clumps may also be visible (Figures 8.11 and 8.12).

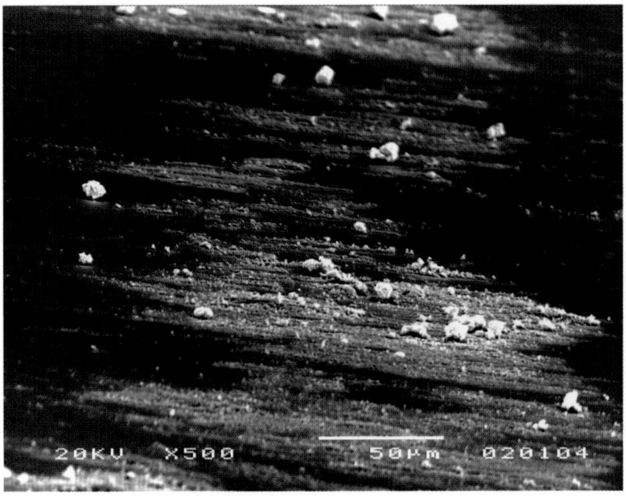

FIGURE 8.9
Scanning electron micrograph of fingerprint ridges treated with black granular powder, imaged obliquely to the ridge direction.

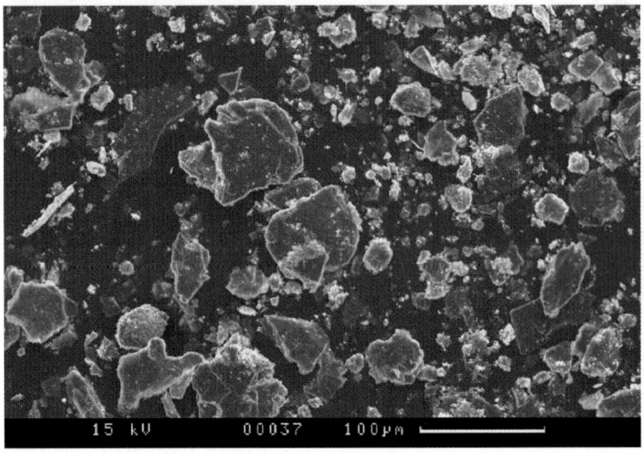

FIGURE 8.10
Scanning electron micrograph of a typical white granular powder.

Granular powders are not well suited for subsequent lifting with adhesive tapes, but give reasonable performance on a wide range of surfaces although they are rarely the best option. They may also give appreciable amounts of powder retention by the background, making marks more difficult to resolve.

8.4.1.3 Magnetic Powders

There are two distinct types of magnetic powder, the "Magneta Flake" type of powder and standard magnetic powders. Magneta Flake (CSI Equipment Ltd, U.K.) was developed as part of a joint project between the U.K. Home Office and the University of Swansea in the early 1990s [15,16]. It is produced by milling spherical carbonyl iron with 3%–5% stearic acid in an appropriate solvent to produce a smooth edged flake with particle sizes in the range 10–60 μm (Figure 8.13).

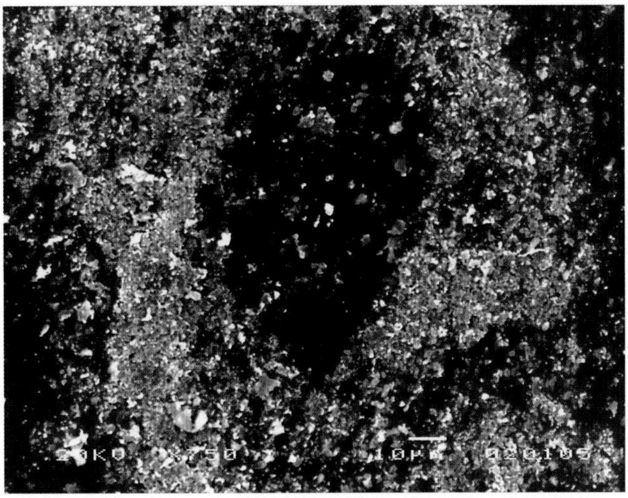

FIGURE 8.11
Scanning electron micrograph of fingerprint ridges treated with white granular powder, imaged perpendicular to the ridge direction.

FIGURE 8.12
Scanning electron micrograph of fingerprint ridges treated with white granular powder, imaged obliquely to the ridge direction.

In effect, Magneta Flake possesses both magnetic properties and the large surface area of a flake powder. Powdered marks consist of discrete particles adhering to the ridges, not necessarily giving a continuous coating, and there may also be some flakes adhering to the adjacent background (Figures 8.14 and 8.15). More than one layer of particles may build up on the ridge, making lifting possible.

Most standard magnetic powders have a substantially different microstructure, the image shown in Figure 8.16 for a typical black magnetic powder shows large magnetic carrier particles of elemental iron (20–200 μm) and smaller nonmagnetic particles of iron oxide (Fe_3O_4) with a particle size in the range 3–12 μm. The larger particles act as a carrier medium

FIGURE 8.13
Scanning electron micrograph of "Magneta Flake" powder.

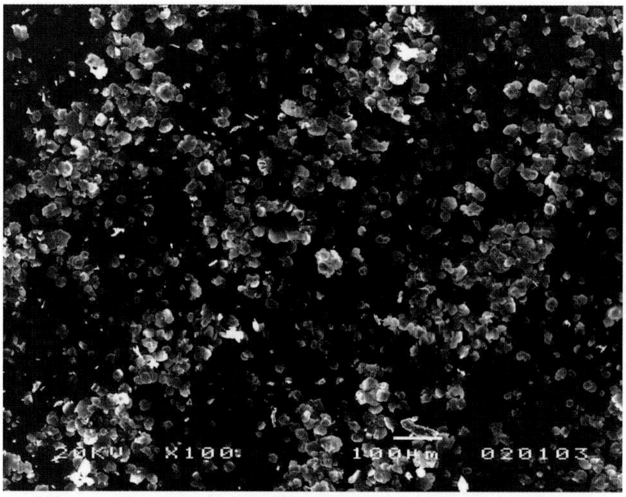

FIGURE 8.14
Scanning electron micrograph of fingerprint ridges treated with "Magneta Flake" powder, imaged perpendicular to the ridge direction.

for the smaller particles, which adhere to the fingerprint ridges and develop the mark. The small particles give a dense coverage of the fingerprint ridge (Figures 8.17 and 8.18).

Both types of magnetic powder have been found to give better results than flake or granular powders on textured surfaces, with more particles adhering to the fingerprint deposit than are trapped by the surface features.

8.4.1.4 Fluorescent Powders

Fluorescent powders have been proposed for use on surfaces where either the background color or texture would make it difficult to visualize marks developed by other powders, in particular on multi-colored surfaces. Although a range of fluorescent dyes and pigments have been proposed for use in this application, most commercially available fluorescent

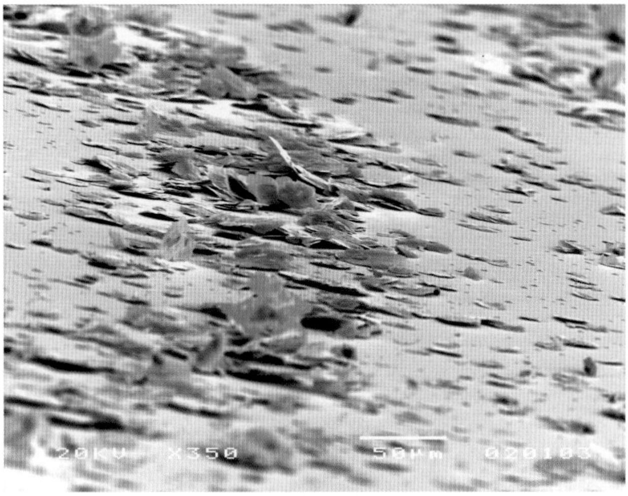

FIGURE 8.15
Scanning electron micrograph of fingerprint ridges treated with "Magneta Flake" powder, imaged obliquely to the ridge direction.

FIGURE 8.16
Scanning electron micrograph of a typical black magnetic powder.

powder formulations incorporate large organic particles such as cornstarch to act as carriers for the fine fluorescent particles (Figure 8.19). Different fluorescent powder colors (e.g., red, green, yellow) can be obtained by varying the dye used in the formulation.

8.4.1.5 Miscellaneous Powders

Historically, several other substances have been proposed and used as fingerprint powders, including organic substances such as lycopodium powder (Figure 8.20). In this case, the regular size of the spores allows dense packing of the powder on the surface and the surface texture of the powder gives a large surface area to interact with the fingerprint deposit.

FIGURE 8.17
Scanning electron micrograph of fingerprint ridges treated with black magnetic powder, imaged perpendicular to the ridge direction.

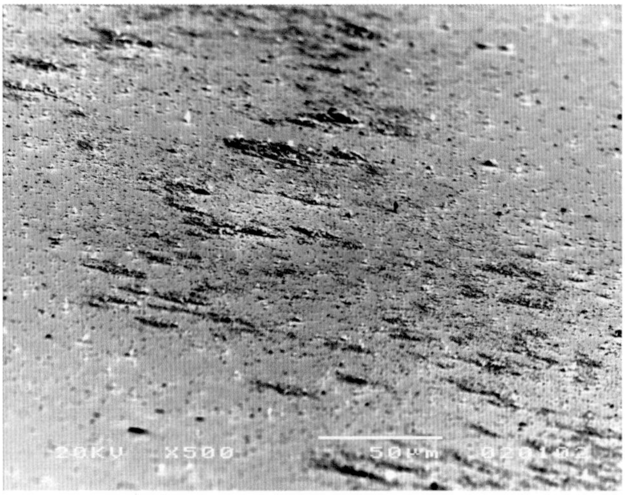

FIGURE 8.18
Scanning electron micrograph of fingerprint ridges treated with black magnetic powder, imaged obliquely to the ridge direction.

Other powders proposed for specific applications included lead, for the development of fingerprints on skin [20,21]. The high atomic density of the powder meant that the developed marks could easily be detected by x-ray electronography, although the toxicity of the powder and the health and safety issues and complexity associated with the subsequent x-ray imaging process have led to this practice being discontinued.

8.4.2 Brushes

Powders cannot be considered in isolation, operator skill, and the means by which powders are applied are equally important to the success in developing a mark. There is a wide

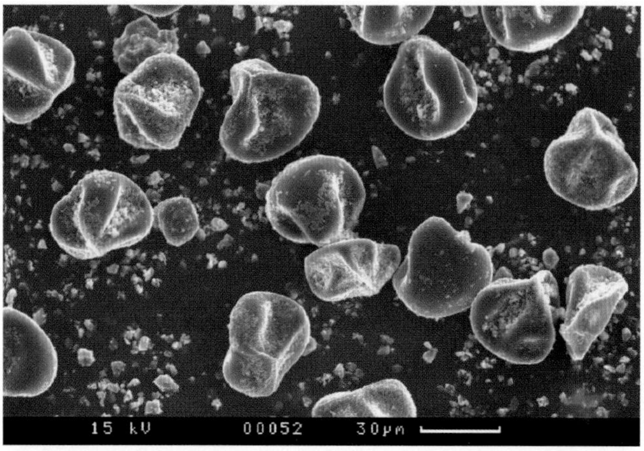

FIGURE 8.19
Scanning electron micrograph of a typical fluorescent powder.

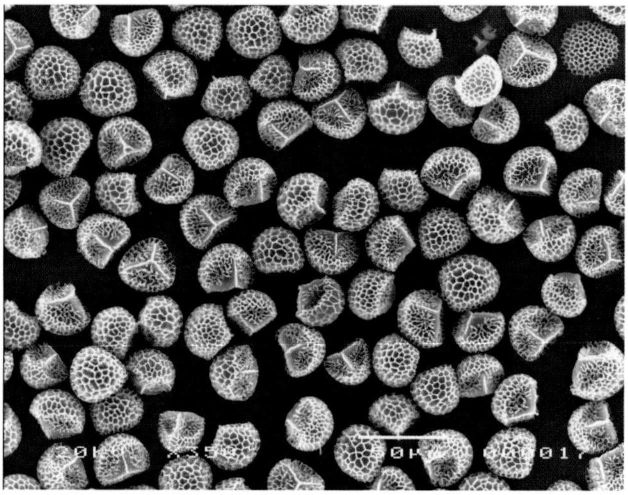

FIGURE 8.20
Scanning electron micrograph of lycopodium powder.

range of different brushes that can be considered for this purpose, some of which are illustrated in Figure 8.21. Brushes are the most commonly used application route for powders, although aerosol and electrostatic application techniques have been considered in the past but have not found widespread acceptance.

The observation that the type of brush used to apply the powder has an effect on the quality of the developed mark was reported by Faulds in 1912 [1], with the comment that sable hairbrushes were not as effective as camel hair brushes when developing marks using black powder. The impact of incorrect brush selection for a particular powder is not confined to a reduction in the amount of ridge detail developed, and it can also lead to damage to the mark and permanent destruction of the ridges. The potential of brushes to cause damage to marks whilst powdering has been recognized and highlighted by James et al. [22].

FIGURE 8.21
Photograph showing a range of different brush types used to apply powders to fingermarks.

Similarly to powders, the types of brush available can be divided into several generic types, these being the following:

- Glass fiber brushes
- Polyester fiber brushes
- Animal hair brushes
- Feather brushes
- Magnetic applicators

Nylon and carbon fiber brushes have also been evaluated, but have not been found to be as effective as those listed earlier. Not every type of brush is suitable for use with the full range of powders and some work has been carried out to identify optimum brush and powder combinations. Further information on each generic type of brush is given in the following.

A general observation for selection of fiber brushes is that the brush must be soft, flexible, and retain powder well if it is to be effective for fingerprint development.

8.4.2.1 Glass Fiber Brushes

Glass fiber brushes consist of bundles of several thousand glass fibers, ~12 μm in diameter (Figure 8.22). The most common geometry for the glass fiber brush is the "Zephyr," a square cut conical fiber arrangement. Both starched and unstarched brushes are available; however trials indicate that the starch has little effect on performance.

Studies have shown that Zephyr-style glass fiber brushes are particularly effective when used with aluminum flake powder on smooth surfaces [11,23].

8.4.2.2 Polyester Fiber Brushes

Polyester fiber brushes are available in very similar styles to glass fiber brushes, although in some cases the fibers used in the brush may have tapered ends (Figure 8.23). The fiber diameter is substantially larger than for glass fiber brushes, being in the region of 100 μm.

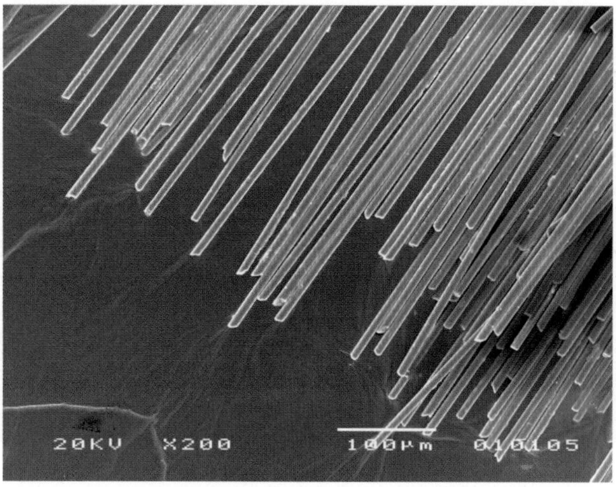

FIGURE 8.22
Scanning electron micrograph of a glass fiber fingerprint brush.

FIGURE 8.23
Scanning electron micrograph of a tapered polyester fiber fingerprint brush.

Polyester brushes are heavier than glass fiber brushes and have the potential to cause more damage to the mark. Polyester brushes have been found to be much more variable in performance than glass fiber brushes. The performance of good polyester fiber brushes is marginally worse than the equivalent glass fiber brush when used to apply aluminum powder, but washable variants of polyester fiber brushes are also available that may reduce the need to replace brushes when they become clogged with powder.

8.4.2.3 Animal Hair Brushes

Animal hair brushes are available from a range of animals, including pony, squirrel, and camel, and in a range of styles, including mop, flat, and zephyr. The natural source of the fibers means that they are less consistent and rougher when examined microscopically (Figures 8.24 and 8.25).

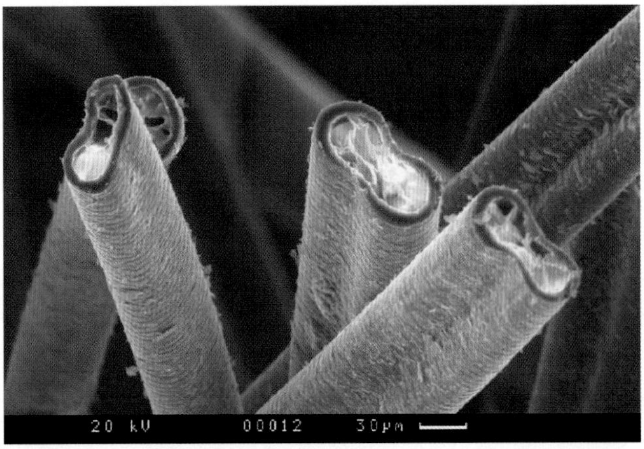

FIGURE 8.24
Scanning electron micrograph of a squirrel hair fingerprint brush.

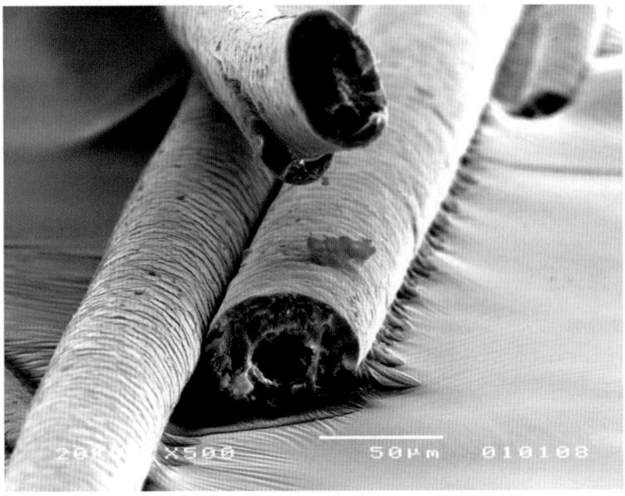

FIGURE 8.25
Scanning electron micrograph of a camel hair fingerprint brush.

This type of brush is not the optimum for application of aluminum powder, but has been shown to give good performance when used with granular or magnetic powders. One disadvantage of animal hair brushes is that they do not retain powder very well and the brush has to be regularly recharged when powdering large areas.

8.4.2.4 Feather Brushes

Similarly to animal hair brushes, feather brushes originate from a natural source and may vary from brush to brush. Microscopically they consist of many fine tendrils that pick up and apply the powder (Figure 8.26).

Tests have indicated that they are not the optimum brush for application of aluminum powder, but have not been extensively investigated for application of other powder types.

FIGURE 8.26
Scanning electron micrograph of a maribou feather fingerprint brush.

Some feather brushes are trimmed to shape, and this may lead to problems with the coarse, cut ends of the feathers when powdering.

8.4.2.5 Magnetic Applicators

Magnetic powders are applied using magnetic wand applicators such as the Magna Brush [10], where a small magnet in the tip of the wand picks up a "brush" of powder when dipped into the powder container. This powder "brush" is then applied to the surface, thus avoiding any direct contact between the applicator and the surface. Although such powders are relatively easy to apply to horizontal surfaces, application to vertical surfaces is less straightforward and powder may drop off. Difficulties may also be encountered when powdering magnetizable metal surfaces.

A range of different magnetic applicators are available, all based on the same basic concept but differing in the size of the applicator and the strength of the magnet used. In general, applicators with strong magnets are preferred because they pick up larger powder "brushes," increasing the distance between the surface and the applicator and reducing the risk that damage will be caused by scraping the applicator across the surface.

Another consideration is the differences in the type of "brush" formed on the applicator head by different powder types. The "brush" formed by black magnetic powder is fine and even in shape (Figure 8.27a), whereas Magneta Flake forms a much more clumpy "brush" (Figure 8.27b). Some powders form "brushes" that become permanently flattened on initial contact with the surface, again causing potential issues with scraping of the applicator on the surface. An example of this occurring for a grey magnetic powder is shown in Figure 8.27c.

8.4.3 Lifting Materials

Lifting of powdered marks from surfaces is not a recent concept. It was first proposed in 1913 for the lifting of latent marks dusted with lead acetate and subsequently treated with hydrogen sulfide. In this case, the lifting medium used was a paper coated with a gelatine/glycerol mix [24]. With the identification of more suitable powders and a growing acceptance of the practice, the "lifting" of powdered marks has gradually become standard practice worldwide; however, there are advantages and disadvantages associated with the lifting process.

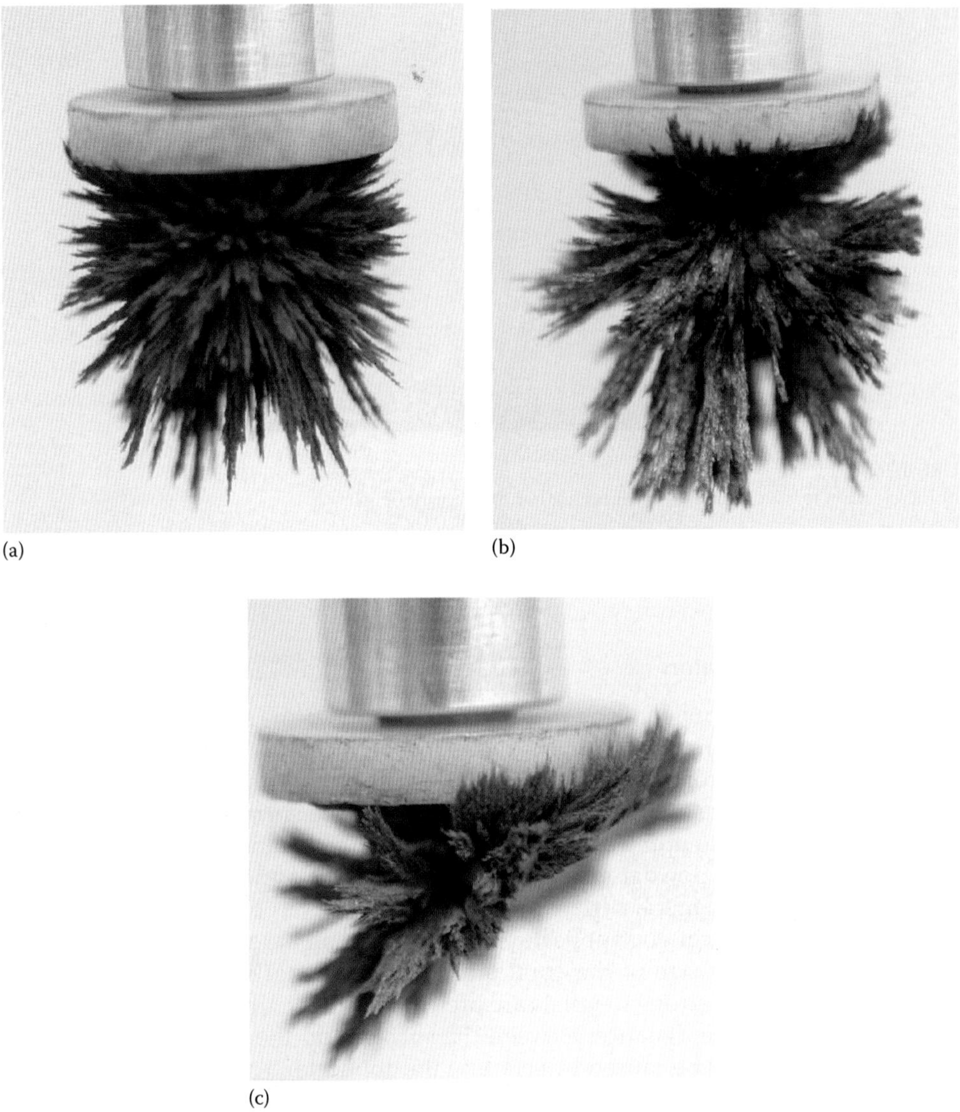

(a) (b) (c)

FIGURE 8.27
Photographs showing the "brush" of powder formed by a Magna Brush for (a) black magnetic powder, (b) Magneta Flake powder, and (c) gray magnetic powder.

Advantages include the fact that it enables a large number of marks developed using powder to be rapidly collected from a scene, removes the powdered mark from the background environment it has been developed on and thus makes imaging of the marks in isolation easier, and removes many issues associated with the level of skill of the crime scene photographer in capturing a good quality image.

To counter this, some disadvantages are that lifting may remove contextual information about the environment the mark was found in, and the quality of the lifted mark is potentially degraded from the mark developed *in situ* because some powder remains on the surface while the remainder adheres to the lifting medium. Lifting is most compatible with flake powders but it is less appropriate for granular and magnetic powders and may cause greater degradation to the quality of the lifted mark for these powder types. If it has been decided that the developed mark is to be lifted, there are several types of material that can be used as lifting media, including

- Adhesive tapes and sheets
- Gelatine lifts
- Casting compounds

In common with powders and brushes, selection of the optimum lifting medium for a particular type of mark may improve the quantity and quality of the marks recovered. However, there are few extensive published studies in this area.

8.4.3.1 Adhesive Tapes and Sheets

Adhesive tapes (and precut, clear, polymer sheets with adhesive backing) are the most widely used form of lifting media. They are best suited to lifting flake powders from smooth surfaces, and the tape used should have a high degree of clarity to enable the lifted mark to be visualized. The type of lifting tape used does have an effect on the quality of the mark, and some studies have been carried out to assess this [25]. However, in practice there are few, if any, adhesive tapes produced solely for forensic use and it is difficult to ensure that any particular tape type will perform consistently from roll to roll.

8.4.3.2 Gelatine Lifts

Gelatine lifts are available in black, white and clear forms, and because they are flexible and can be compressed against a surface on application they are better suited to lifting of marks from textured surfaces. Gelatine lifts are also highly effective for marks on smooth surfaces, but their greater cost precludes their regular use for this purpose. The color of the lift can be selected to give optimum contrast with the powder used, and the lifts are better suited for lifting and subsequent imaging of marks powdered with granular and magnetic powders [26].

8.4.3.3 Casting Compounds

For marks developed on highly textured surfaces, even the greater formability of gelatine lifts may not make contact with every point of the textured surface and thus not all of the mark will be lifted. Silicone rubber casting compounds traditionally used for casting of tool marks may be used in these cases, allowing the liquid to flow over the mark, solidify *in situ* and then be peeled off to remove the mark from the surface. These materials are generally available in a range of colors (black, white, gray) and the most appropriate color for giving contrast with the powder can be selected. Reference has also been made to the use of dental casting compounds and adhesives of various colors for this application [27–29].

8.5 Imaging of Powdered Marks

A variety of imaging techniques have been used to capture images of marks developed using powders, some of which have been specialized pieces of equipment optimized either for imaging the mark *in situ* or obtaining an image of the lift. Some of these techniques are described in the section that follows.

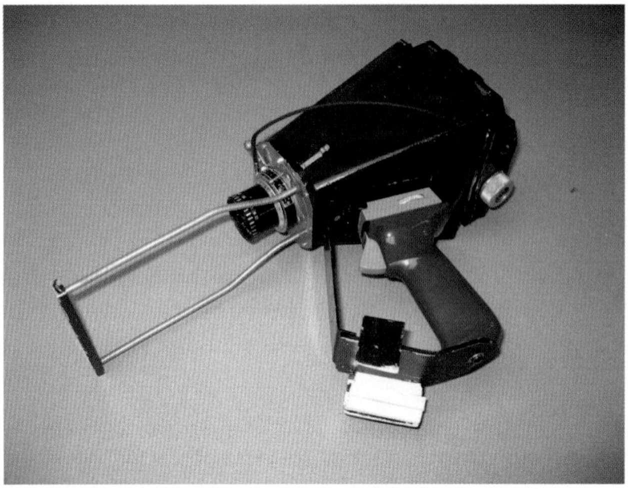

FIGURE 8.28
Photograph of a fixed focus camera used for photographing powdered marks.

Prior to the widespread adoption of lifting, the majority of powdered marks were imaged *in situ* using conventional film techniques. For comparison purposes, these marks needed to be rescaled during printing so that the resultant print was at a 1:1 scale. To overcome the potential variability in scale that could arise during photography at the scene, fixed focus cameras were developed in some countries that consisted of a rigid frame that could be used to maintain a constant distance between mark and camera (Figure 8.28), thus ensuring that all marks were captured at the same scale and were 1:1 when printed out on standard photographic paper. However, this camera was only suitable for fingermarks developed on flat surfaces and marks on other surfaces still required specialist photography.

With the increasing adoption of lifting, in particular for marks developed using aluminum powder, imaging techniques and equipment began to be developed for the "lifts" rather than the marks *in situ*. The contrast between the reflective aluminum powder and the transparent tape and acetate of the lift can be utilized to capture images of the lifted mark, for example using a "black box" to enhance the contrast (Figure 8.29).

Prior to the introduction of digital imaging, equipment was developed specifically for the automated, rapid production of photographic images from aluminum lifts, an example of this being the "Camtac 121" machine [30]. This operated by rapidly feeding in lifted marks and placing each acetate lift over a rectangular aperture above a light absorbing black surface, known as the "black void." The lift was illuminated by two obliquely angled lights, with light passing through the clear regions of the lift being absorbed and light scattered back from the reflective aluminum powder being focused onto photographic paper by a lens (in a similar manner to the arrangement illustrated earlier). After the required exposure, the photographic paper was rapidly passed through a developing unit to provide a negative (black ridges, light background) image of the lift. The ease and speed of obtaining the lift and the final image for comparison meant that aluminum powder became the predominant system in use in the United Kingdom from the 1970s onward.

With the development of digital photography and scanning, a range of products are now becoming available for the rapid scanning and image optimization of lifted marks, and wet photography is becoming less common.

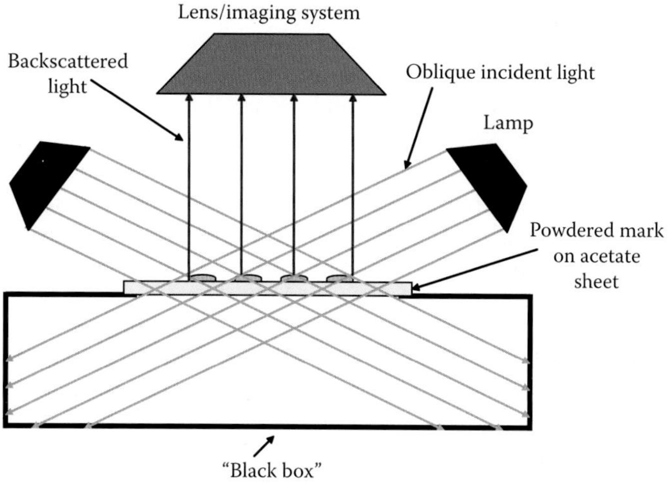

FIGURE 8.29
"Black box" imaging arrangement used to enhance contrast of aluminum lifts.

Other recent developments associated with the powdering process include the introduction of wireless transmission of the fingerprint image from the crime scene to the fingerprint bureau. One approach [31] uses a flat bed scanner with a gloss black backing paper to scan the aluminum lift and image compression software to reduce the file size to a level that can transmitted over a general packet radio service (GPRS) mobile phone network in ~30 s, this time being reduced further for 3G mobile phone networks.

8.6 Powder Selection

In contrast to chemical development techniques, where comparative trials are often carried out and reported, there is less evidence to indicate which type of powder is most appropriate for use on a particular surface and which type of application technique is likely to give the best results. Some testing has been conducted [11–13], but this is constrained to a limited range of powders, albeit over a wide range of representative surfaces. Conclusions from these studies have been published [32], and can be summarized as follows:

Aluminum flake powder is the most effective powder on glass, but shows similar performance to several alternative powders on other smooth, nonporous surfaces. For these surfaces, aluminum may still be the powder of choice as it is easy to apply and develops marks with good contrast on most smooth surfaces. The most effective brush for use with aluminum powder is the glass fiber, Zephyr-style [11].

Brass/bronze flake powders perform similarly to aluminum flake powder but should only be used on smooth, silver-colored surfaces where aluminum would give low contrast. An appropriate dust mask must be worn when using this type of powder because of lower safe occupational exposure limits.

Black granular powder may be used on some smooth surfaces only and can be considered as an alternative to brass/bronze flake powder on silver-colored surfaces. Dust masks should be worn when using this powder.

Black magnetic powder is the most effective powder on textured surfaces and unplasticized polyvinyl chloride (u-PVC). Similar results were obtained with "jet black" magnetic powder, but others (grey, silver, etc.) were found to be considerably less sensitive. White magnetic powder, although less sensitive, may be used on dark, textured surfaces when contrast is an issue.

Magneta Flake powder is slightly less sensitive than black magnetic powder on textured surfaces, but may offer an alternative on dark textured surfaces. It may also be used on most smooth surfaces, although application can be difficult and inconsistent.

A schematic chart for the selection of the optimum powder type for a particular surface has been proposed and is reproduced in Figure 8.30.

There are many different types of powder being sold for fingerprint development applications and it is not possible to evaluate every product on the market. As a consequence, the advice given refers to generic powder types only and not to specific manufacturers' products.

If the use of a product not currently within the generic powder types outlined earlier is proposed, it should be extensively evaluated against the existing powder types in laboratory trials on representative surfaces before being used operationally. The guidance given by HOSDB [11–13,32] originates from tests utilizing thousands of developed marks and a number of different surfaces, and any trials likely to result in changes to existing guidance should ideally incorporate an equivalent number of marks and surfaces.

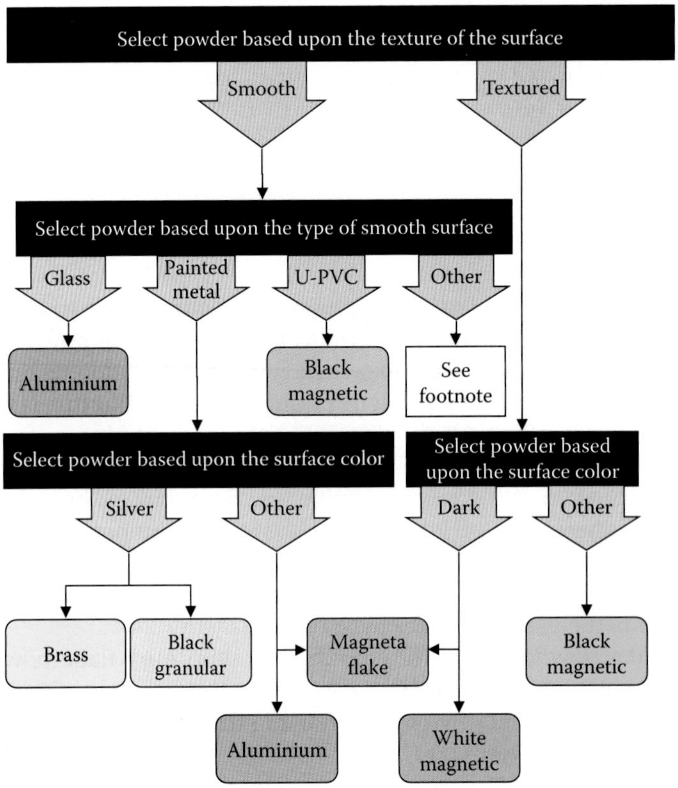

FIGURE 8.30
Powder selection chart. (Reproduced with the permission of Home Office Scientific Development Branch.)

It may also be possible to apply powders in a sequential manner, with the use of a second powder sometimes enhancing ridge detail and developing additional marks that have not been detected by the first powder. This has not been extensively investigated, but observations by the authors indicate that black granular powder can develop additional marks when used sequentially after both aluminum and black magnetic powder. Further studies are required before guidelines can be provided for sequential powdering routes.

8.7 Nanoparticles

Reference should also be made to the increasing number of research papers associated with the use of nanoparticles for fingerprint development, both as dusting powders and in liquid suspensions. Potential advantages quoted for of the use of nanoparticles include better definition of developed ridge detail due to the smaller particle size in the powder, and the use of the properties of the nanoparticles to amplify the response of the fingerprint residues to subsequent analytical techniques. Many of the researchers are investigating adding functionality to the nanoparticles by doping them with fluorescent [33–35], metallic, and magnetic [34,36] molecules and substances. It is too early to comment on the operational advantages of such powders at the current time, because few studies have been carried out on operational material or even realistic marks. However, it is anticipated that nanoparticulate powder formulations will become increasingly available for fingerprint development in the coming years.

Acknowledgments

The authors would like to acknowledge the extensive amount of work on powder development instigated and conducted by previous members of staff and placement students at the Home Office Scientific Development Branch, including Terry Kent, Sheila Hardwick, Simon Walker, Stephen Lau, Andrea Wiggett, Edward Quinn, Laura Woods, and Tom Hardy. Without the information obtained from their studies, this chapter could not have been compiled. The electron micrographs used to illustrate the chapter were obtained using the facilities at Imperial College, London, and the University of Hertfordshire.

Authors

Helen L. Bandey, PhD, obtained a first class BSc (Hons) in chemistry from the University of Leicester, United Kingdom, in 1994. In 1998, she completed her PhD studies, again at the University of Leicester, in physical chemistry—in particular, using acoustic sensor platforms to study electroactive polymer films. She then worked at Sandia National Laboratories, Albuquerque, New Mexico, as a postdoctoral appointee in the Microsensors R&D group for 2 years. Since January 2001, she has worked at the U.K.'s Home Office on developing and evaluating fingerprint, footwear, and blood enhancement methods. Her current work involves overseeing the production of the *3rd Edition Manual of Fingerprint Development Techniques*.

Steve M. Bleay, PhD, obtained a BSc in materials science from the University of Bath, Bath, United Kingdom, in 1988 and remained at the University of Bath carrying out postgraduate research in electron microscopy of composite materials until 1993. He was awarded a PhD in 1991. He joined the Defence Research Agency (later QinetiQ) in 1993 and spent 10 years developing stealth materials and carrying out research into the production of novel fiber systems. Dr. Bleay joined the Home Office in May 2003 and has worked on novel vacuum metal deposition techniques, recovery of fingerprints from arson scenes, development and production of a digital imaging workstation, and digital imaging.

Andrew P. Gibson obtained an MEng in materials science and engineering from the University of Manchester Institute of Science and Technology, Manchester, United Kingdom, in 2000. He then worked for Thermofibertek U.K. Ltd, developing composite components for use in the paper industry. In 2002, Andrew joined the U.K. Home Office and has worked on fingerprint powders, physical developer enhancement, digital imaging, and UV-C imaging. In 2010, he became a professional member of the Institute of Materials Minerals and Mining and a chartered engineer. Recently, he has been investigating the effect on fingerprint quality that jp2000 compression and the printing and scanning of fingerprint images have.

References

1. Faulds H. (1912) *Dactylography, or the Study of Fingerprints*. London, U.K.: Halifax.
2. Faulds H. (1905) *Guide to Fingerprint Identification*. Hanley, U.K.: Wood, Mitchell and Co.
3. Mitchell CA. (1920) The detection of fingerprints on documents. *Analyst* 45:122–129.
4. Brose HL. (1934) Finger-print detection. *Analyst* 59:25–27.
5. Cherrill FR. (1954) *The Finger Print System at Scotland Yard*. London, U.K.: HMSO.
6. Goode GC, Morris JR. (1983) Latent fingerprints: a review of their origin, composition and methods of detection. AWRE Report No. 22/83.
7. Olsen RD. (1978) *Scott's Fingerprint Mechanics*. Springfield, IL: Charles C Thomas.
8. Blench TH, Brindle H. (1951) Fingerprint detection and mercury poisoning. *Lancet* 1(6651):378–380.
9. Agate JN, Buckell M. (1949) Mercury poisoning from fingerprint photography, an occupational hazard of policemen. *Ind Hyg Newsl* 9(12):6.
10. MacDonell HL. (1962) Recent developments in processing latent finger prints. *Ident News* (August):3–18.
11. Bandey HL. (2004) The powders process, study 1: evaluation of fingerprint brushes for use with aluminium powder. *Fingerprint Development and Imaging Newsletter*, Special Edition, PSDB Publication No. 54/04.
12. Bandey HL, Gibson AP. (2006) The powders process, study 2: evaluation of fingerprint powders on smooth surfaces. *Fingerprint Development and Imaging Newsletter*, Special Edition, HOSDB Publication No. 08/06.
13. Bandey HL, Hardy T. (2006) The powders process, study 3: evaluation of fingerprint powders on textured surfaces and u-pvc. *Fingerprint and Footwear Forensics Newsletter*, Special Edition, HOSDB Publication No. 67/06.
14. Zimon AD. (1969) *Adhesion of Dust and Powder*. New York: Plenum Press.

15. James JD, Pounds CA, Wilshire B. (1991) Flake metal powders for revealing latent fingerprints. *J Forensic Sci* 36(5):1368–1375.
16. James JD, Pounds CA, Wilshire B. (1991) Production and characterisation of flake metal powders for fingerprint detection. *Powder Metall* 34(1):39–43.
17. Wertheim PA. (1997) Magnetic powder. *Minutiae*, The Lightning Powder Co. Newsletter, July–August, p. 43.
18. Quinn EJ. (2003) Alternative fingerprint powders. PSDB Student Placement Report.
19. Lau SMF. (1999) Evaluation of fingerprint powders project. Imperial College of Science and Technology, London/PSDB joint project report.
20. Graham D, Gray HC. (1965) X-rays reveal fingerprints. *New Sci* (October):35.
21. Graham D. (1969) Some technical aspects of the demonstration and visualisation of fingerprints on human skin. *J Forensic Sci* 14(1):1–12.
22. James JD, Pounds CA, Wilshire B. (1991) Obliteration of latent fingerprints. *J Forensic Sci* 36(5):1376–1386.
23. Wiggett AE. (2002) The performance of aluminium powder with a series of fingerprint brushes on surfaces commonly encountered at scenes of crime. PSDB placement report.
24. Crispo D. (1913) *Bull Soc Chim Belg* 26:190–193.
25. Swinge P. (2005) Review of the quality of developed finger marks when lifted with different types of lifting tapes. MSc thesis, Kings College, University of London, London, U.K.
26. Gellifter brochure. (2008) BVDA International. http://www.bvda.com/EN/download/Gellifter_brochure.pdf (accessed April 3, 2009).
27. Hamm ED. (1987) The custom-made rubber lifter. *Ident News* 37(7):7,10,12.
28. Menke J. (1987) Lifting method for latent prints on curved surfaces. *Ident News* 37(12):4–5.
29. Guerrero MB. (1992) The transparent, liquid adhesive, latent print lifter. *J Forensic Ident* 42(2):101–105.
30. Berry AM. (1972) Fingerprint lift reproduction equipment. *Pol J* (January):61–65.
31. Allinson NM, Sivirajah J, Gledhill I, Carling M, Allinson LJ. (2007) Robust wireless transmission of compressed latent fingerprint images. *IEEE Trans Inform Forensics Security* 2(3):331–340.
32. Bandey HL. (2007) Fingerprint powders guidelines. HOSDB Publication No. 09/07.
33. Choi MJ, Smoother T, Martin, AA. et al. (2007) Fluorescent TiO_2 powders prepared using a new perylene diimide dye: applications in latent fingermark detection. *Forensic Sci Int* 173(2–3):154–160.
34. Theaker BJ, Hudson KE, Rowell FJ. (2008) Doped hydrophobic silica nano- and micro-particles as novel agents for developing latent fingerprints. *Forensic Sci Int* 174(1):26–34.
35. Liu L, Gill SK, Gao YP, Hope-Weeks LJ, Cheng KH. (2008) Exploration of the use of novel SiO_2 nanocomposites with fluorescent Eu^{3+}/sensitizer complex for latent fingerprint detection. *Forensic Sci Int* 176(2–3):163–172.
36. Choi MJ, McDonagh AM, Maynard P, Roux C. (2008) Metal-containing nanoparticles and nanostructured particles in fingerprint detection. *Forensic Sci Int* 179(2–3):87–97.

9

Enhancement Techniques for Fingerprints in Blood

Vaughn G. Sears

CONTENTS

9.1 History

9.1.1 Introduction

Blood is the most commonly observed known contaminant found at scenes of crime, which is possibly because, when present even in small quantities, it is easily seen as it strongly absorbs light throughout the visible spectrum. However, when present in minute amounts or in the dark, patterned, or multicolored confusing backgrounds, the blood may require enhancement to make it more useful for evidential purposes. Additionally, proof that a stain is actually blood rather than an innocuous substance may be important in assessing guilt or innocence and may even be a matter of life or death in some cases.

The history of proving the presence of blood evidence in forensic investigations dates back over 150 years using chemical means and further still when microscopical methods are considered. Anton van Leeuwenhoek was said to be the first person to describe and illustrate blood cells in the latter part of the seventeenth century, although this is disputed.

However, the earliest record of blood testing may be considerably older as it would appear from a translation by Rosner in 1973 [1] of the *Talmud*, which was written in the second century AD. The translation details a chemical method to differentiate blood from a dye stain on a garment using a series of seven different substances, although the exact nature of some of the substances is disputed in various translations.

Other tests for blood are referred to in the Middle Ages. In 1973, Kiel [2] published a paper discussing traditional and contemporary Chinese forensic science in which he notes that around 1250 AD, a treatise on legal medicine, known as Hsi Yuan Lu, or *"Instructions to Coroners"* was compiled. It says that an old bloodstain could be detected on a knife by heating the stain and treating it with vinegar, after which a brown stain would appear. This would appear to be an early form of the test later used by Teichmann.

In October 1849, at the Old Bailey in London, during the trial of Fredrick George Manning and Maria Manning, who were indicted for the willful murder of Patrick O'Conner [3], chemical tests for albumen, a constituent of blood, were described. William Odding, a practical chemist, says, "I cut out the stained portion of the dress and cut it into several slips, which I suspended one after another in a small quantity of distilled water; they imparted their colour to the water. It was a smoky red colour, from which I afterwards obtained a precipitate indicating albumen, one of the constituents of the blood." It was a crucial piece of evidence linking the defendants to the murder and they were found guilty and hanged.

Even in detective fiction, authors through their characters see the value in proving that a stain is blood as a way to give more realism to their tale. Sir Arthur Conan Doyle writes in his first novel in 1887 *A Study in Scarlet* [4,5] that the first thing Sherlock Holmes says to Dr. Watson, even before being formally introduced, "I have found a re-agent which is precipitated by haemoglobin, and by nothing else." He then goes on to say, "It is the most practical medico-legal discovery for years. Don't you see that it gives us an infallible test for blood stains?" Unfortunately, this wonder test, which works at a maximum dilution of one in a million, is never named, although described, "… he threw into the vessel a few white crystals, and then added some drops of a transparent fluid. In an instant, the contents assumed a dull mahogany color and brownish dust was precipitated to the bottom of the glass jar." He then goes on to condemn a popular test at the time, saying, "The old guaiacum test was very clumsy and uncertain."

9.1.2 Use and Development of Techniques for the Proof and Enhancement of Blood

The earliest chemical tests for the proof and enhancement of blood that actually utilized a fundamental component of blood relied on the presence of the heme group in the hemoglobin molecule and were of two types: those that produced crystals and those that relied on its catalytic nature.

The crystal or confirmatory tests were formulated by Teichmann in 1853 [6], producing crystals of hematin, and by Takayama in 1912 [7], producing crystals of hemochromogen. However, these tests require that the blood be scraped from the surface, therefore they are only able to be used where blood was easily observed and cannot be used speculatively. Having to scrape blood also gives no regard to the forms of physical evidence that may be present, such as fingerprints, footwear impressions, or splash patterns.

Catalytic or presumptive tests that attempted to keep much of the physical evidence intact were produced by Van Deen and Day in 1862 based on guaiacum [8], Schönbein in 1863 using hydrogen peroxide [9], and by Adler and Adler in 1904 using benzidine [10]. The use of leuco-malachite green was also pioneered by Adler and Adler in 1904 [10]; their method was later modified by Medinger in 1933 [11] to make it more sensitive.

In 1901, Kastle and Sheed [12] developed another catalytic test using phenolphthalein, which Meyer in 1903 [13] modified to detect blood. Further investigation by Kastle and Amos in 1906 [14] proved the phenolphthalein to be reacting with hemoglobin present in blood. This is the test we now know as the Kastle–Meyer test.

Other presumptive tests for blood were developed for forensic use by Ruttan and Hardisty in 1912 using *o*-tolidine [15], by Specht in 1937 using luminol (3-amino-phthalhydrazide) [16] and by Gershenfeld in 1939 using *o*-toluidine [17].

In 1911, Abderhalden and Schmidt [18] reported the development of latent fingerprints on the bottle label of triketohydrindene hydrate (ninhydrin). This discovery was not exploited for the detection of fingerprints until 1954 when Oden [19] produced his ninhydrin formulation based on acetone. It is not clear who or when it was noticed that ninhydrin reacted quickly with blood to give the strongly colored "Ruhemann's purple" but this observation revolutionized thinking in this area of forensic investigation. This discovery then opened up a completely different approach to the detection of blood by producing intensely colored products that were more easily observed although they did not prove the mark was in blood. These techniques were easier to use and generally more sensitive than the presumptive tests for heme, which generally required expert opinion to interpret the test results correctly.

It is believed that the introduction of the protein dye amido black (acid black 1) quickly became popular with forensic investigators. Its use by the Metropolitan Police Laboratory, in a solvent base of methanol and acetic acid, was discussed at a forensic science symposium in October 1961 by Godsell [20]. It was not specified where this formulation originated, but it appears to be related to the work being carried out by Puchtler and Sweat [21,22].

This formulation continued to be the basis of that recommended for the enhancement of fingerprints in blood by the U.K. Home Office until 2004 [23,24], although in the interim period various refinements were made. The use of heat to fix blood was superseded by immersion in methanol in 1981 [25] and an alternative water-based version was introduced by Hussain and Pounds in 1989 [26]. In 2004, both the methanol- and water-based formulations were replaced by one based on water, ethanol, and acetic acid recommended by Sears and Prizeman [27].

Many other protein stains have also been proposed for the enhancement of both fingerprints and footwear impressions in blood: Coomassie blue (acid blue 83) and Crowle's double stain (acid blue 83 and acid red 71) by Norkus and Noppinger in1986 [28]; fuchsin acid (acid violet 19, Hungarian Red); patent blue V (acid blue 1) and tartrazine (acid yellow 23) by Barnett et al. in 1988 [29]; benzoxanthene yellow and acid violet 17 by Sears et al. in 2001 [30]; and acid yellow 7 by Sears et al. in 2005 [31].

Although protein dyes became the most popular techniques for enhancing fingerprints in blood, research on presumptive enhancement methods continued and in 1976 Garner et al. [32] proposed the use of tetramethylbenzidene (TMB) as a safer and more effective technique than benzidine. Suggestions for other presumptive tests continued including tetra aminobiphenyl (TAB) and diaminobenzidine (DAB) in 1989 by Hussain and Pounds [33]; fluorescein in 1995 by Cheeseman and DiMeo [34]; and leucocrystal violet (LCV) in 1996 by Bodziak [35].

In addition, there have been many modifications made to the ninhydrin formulation to increase its effectiveness and safety by Crown in 1969 [36] and Morris and Goode in 1974 [37]. Further changes were forced on the fingerprint community because of the worldwide adoption of The Montreal Protocol on Substances That Deplete the Ozone Layer and new formulations were proposed by Watling and Smith in 1993 [38] and Hewlett et al. in 1997 [39]. The use of transition metal toners to change the color or make the reaction product between amines and ninhydrin fluoresce have also been proposed by Morris in 1978 [40], Everse and Menzel 1986 [41], and Stoilovic et al. in 1986 [42].

It was also suggested that the use of one of several ninhydrin analogues would improve sensitivity and many have been proposed, most notably benzo[f]ninhydrin in 1982 by Almog et al. [43], 5-methoxyninhydrin by Almog and Hirshfield in 1988 [44], DFO (1,8-diazafluen-9-one) in 1990 by Grigg et al. [45], and indandione by Ramotowski et al. in 1997 [46]. All of these techniques, although primarily intended to target with amino acids in latent fingerprints on porous surfaces, will react strongly with the proteins present in blood to produce colored and/or fluorescent products.

Most recently in 1999, Hochmeister et al. [47] validated a one-step immunochromatographic test using anti-human Hb antibodies to prove the presence of human blood. However, this method requires removal of blood from the surface, so it cannot be used to enhance the physical evidence *in situ*, although if this test could be carried out after application of the more sensitive protein dyes this would then cover all issues. In 2008, Johnston et al. [48] compared several of these tests with luminol and concluded the latter was more sensitive.

It was observed from the earliest times that blood strongly absorbed light and a number of researchers in the mid- to late nineteenth century tried to use this as a way to identify that a stain was blood. Among them were Hoppe in 1862 [49], who investigated the spectral properties of the coloring matter in blood, Stokes in 1864 [50], who was able to recognize the difference between hemoglobin and oxy-hemoglobin and Soret in 1883 [51], who characterized the absorption bands of hemoglobin in the violet and ultraviolet regions of the spectrum. In 1865, Sorby [52] studied the spectra of various hemoglobin derivatives and proposed these as a means of identification for blood stains.

However, it was not until the late 1970s and early 1980s that this property was utilized on blood *in situ* by those developing high-intensity light sources. They found that one of the most useful properties of typical surfaces (wood, paper, plastic, etc.) was that the shorter wavelengths of light in the ultraviolet and violet cause them to fluoresce strongly and this could give extra detail if a fingerprint was in a strongly light-absorbing material such as blood [53–55].

All these developments meant that by the late 1990s, there were so many reagents and formulations in existence for the enhancement of blood-contaminated fingerprints and footwear impressions, with little or no comparative data on their effectiveness, that there was immense confusion amongst practitioners. Also the emergence of DNA profiling heaped even more uncertainty over which techniques could or should be used for the enhancement of blood, and concern that vital evidence could be lost by the wrong choices. Therefore the U.K. Home Office set out to clarify the situation and began a program of work to review and compare the most commonly used of these techniques [27,30,31]. Resulting from this large task, there were a number of key findings including the most effective dyes and the sequencing of techniques to gain most evidence, which were incorporated in a comprehensive update to *The Manual of Fingerprint Development Techniques* in 2004 [24].

9.2 Theory

9.2.1 Introduction

Blood consists of red cells (erythrocytes), white cells (leukocytes), and platelets (thrombocytes) in a proteinaceous fluid called plasma, which makes up roughly 55% of the whole blood volume. The red cells principally contain the hemoglobin protein but also have specific surface proteins (agglutinogens) that determine blood group. The white cells, which form part of the immune system, have a nucleus that contains DNA.

Hemoglobin makes up roughly 95% of red blood cells' protein content and is made of four protein subunits each containing a heme group. The heme group is made of a flat porphyrin ring and a conjugated ferrous ion.

As mentioned earlier, chemical blood enhancement methods fall broadly into two types: those react with the heme grouping and those that interact with proteins or their breakdown products. The last type are not at all specific for blood; however, because of the high percentage of protein and its products present in blood, and the fact that they do not rely on the effectiveness of cell lysation (as do the heme-specific type), the techniques that interact with proteinous material are the most sensitive available to the forensic investigator [31].

Many researchers measure the sensitivity of their techniques by diluting blood with water [31,34,56–58]. This method favors techniques that utilize the heme as all the red cells would be lysed because of osmotic pressure during dilution, something that will not happen when these techniques are used operationally. Dilution with a buffer at the same osmotic pressure as blood serum would give clearer indication of ultimate technique sensitivity.

There is also one other major advantage of the protein staining techniques, in that they generally incorporate a stage that either denatures or fixes proteins to the surface. Most proteins, including hemoglobin, are water soluble, so that the blood contaminated fingerprint is not then diffused during treatment.

9.2.2 Heme Techniques

There are three kinds of tests that use the heme group in hemoglobin; crystal tests, catalytic tests, and antibody tests. The sensitivity of these techniques is limited by their effectiveness to lyse blood cells, which releases the heme-containing proteins that are only present within the red blood cells.

Crystal tests are specific or confirmatory for the presence of heme, as they specifically form products that incorporate part or all of the heme group, but do not prove whether the blood is human or not. The two most well-known crystal tests were those formulated by Teichmann and Takayama. The Teichmann test [6] results in the formation of brown, rhombohedral crystals of hematin and the Takayama test [7] in red-pink crystals of pyridine hemochromogen. Both of these tests have to be carried out ex situ, so are of no use for fingerprint enhancement as the ridge detail is inevitably destroyed as the blood is removed unless an area containing no ridge detail, such as a smear, alongside the fingermark is used.

There are a number of advantages to the Takayama test, as compared with the Teichmann test. Heating is not required to obtain results within a reasonable amount of time in the Takayama test; and even if heat is applied, the test is not subject to being ruined by overheating. The test also yields positive results under some of the circumstances where the Teichmann test fails.

The catalytic tests are only presumptive or infer the presence of heme as they only use the heme to facilitate another reaction and are subject to both false-positive and false-negative reactions caused by a variety of nonblood substances. Consequently, individual results require careful interpretation by experts.

These tests all rely on the peroxidase activity of the heme group. Enzymes that catalyze the peroxide-mediated oxidation of organic compounds in vivo are called peroxidases; hemoglobin and the other compounds that show this catalytic property are thus said to have peroxidase activity. This peroxidase activity may be utilized to cause the oxidation of colorless reduced dyes, such as phenolphthalein, leuco-crystal violet, tetramethylbenzidine, and fluorescein, which when oxidized form their colored, or in the case of the latter fluorescent, counterparts.

$$\begin{aligned} &H_2O_2 + \text{colorless reduced dye (in the presence of blood)} \\ &\quad \rightarrow H_2O + \text{colored oxidized dye [59]} \end{aligned}$$

The luminol test also relies on the peroxidase activity of the heme group but can be used with either hydrogen peroxide [60] or sodium perborate [61]. Then in the presence of blood, a product that chemiluminescence is produced. The bluish-white chemiluminescence is faint and must be viewed in the dark by an operator who is fully dark-adapted to gain the best evidence from this test. However, even with careful application of luminol, it is extremely easy to damage the fine detail of blood-contaminated fingerprint ridges on both porous and nonporous surfaces. Therefore this technique should only be used when fine detail is not required and when other techniques might be compromised by surface type or impracticality, such as dark or patterned carpets [31].

The major concern with the catalytic tests for blood is that they can produce false-positive results in the presence of chemical oxidants and catalysts, salts of heavy metals such as copper, nickel, and iron and plant peroxidases such as those found in horseradish, citrus fruits, and numerous root vegetables [62]. A two-stage test can help to stop false positives from true peroxidases. The reduced colorless dye is applied initially and if no color change is observed then the hydrogen peroxide is added. A color change at this point is more likely to indicate the presence of blood rather than a peroxidase, although contamination by metal salts is not distinguished.

It is generally accepted that a negative result with a catalytic test proves the absence of blood; however, strong reducing agents such as ascorbic acid [63] and active oxygen cleaning products [64] may inhibit such tests.

The antibody tests [47,48] like the crystal tests are confirmatory for blood, but as they use anti-human Hb antibodies, they are also specific for human blood. Currently, they have to be used ex situ so are of no use for fingerprint enhancement, and it remains to be seen whether these tests can be used after the more effective enhancement techniques [48] to prove that what is being enhanced is human blood.

9.2.3 Protein Staining Blood Enhancement Techniques

There are two types of techniques for proteins: those that stain proteinous material and those that react with amines. Blood contains more protein than any other material and as they do not rely on the lysing of red cells, these techniques are more sensitive than those that utilize the heme molecule, although they are not at all specific for blood.

9.2.3.1 Protein Staining Techniques

Enhancing blood using protein dyes is a three-stage process: fixing, staining, and destaining. The fixing stage denatures or fixes blood proteins to the surface so that ridge detail is not diffused or washed away during the subsequent staining and destaining stages. The staining and destaining solutions should be designed so that the fixed blood is not resolubilized and the deep coloration is retained in the dyed blood.

A number of different fixing agents have been used, but the most effective are 5-sulphosalicylic acid and methanol [27]. Which one is used depends upon the major solvent used in the staining process. If water is the main solvent, then a solution of 5-sulphosalicylic acid is most effective; but if the main solvent in the staining solution is methanol, then methanol is the best fixing agent [27]. These fixing agents act in different ways: 5-sulphosalicylic acid precipitates basic proteins and methanol dehydrates the blood.

It was found that all-in-one formulations that contain the fixative and stain in one solution are generally not stable for more than a day or two and are much less effective than a two-stage process, both in fixing and staining [27].

The use of solutions based on methanol has waned for a number of reasons including its toxicity, flammability, and damage to surfaces, such as paints, varnishes, and some plastics, which then has a negative effect on fingerprint development [27].

The most effective dyes for the enhancement of fingerprints in blood are a group known as acid dyes. They stain the proteins present in blood but are not at all specific for blood.

A great number of acid dyes have been investigated over the years, some of which are listed in Section 9.3.3.3; but, the U.K. Home Office has found three to be more effective than others: acid black 1, acid violet 17, and acid yellow 7 [27,30,31].

Acid dyes are often characterized by the presence of one or more sulfonate $\left(-SO_3^-\right)$ groups, usually the sodium (Na^+) salt. These groups function in two ways: firstly to provide solubility in water or alcohol (the favored major solvents from which to apply these dyes) and secondly by virtue of their negative charge (anionic). If acidic conditions are used, acetic acid being the favored option, the blood protein molecules acquire a positive charge (cationic) and this attracts the acid dye anions. Also hydrogen bonding and other physical forces such as van der Waals may play a part in the affinity of acid dyes to protein molecules [65]. It was found that concentrations of dye less 0.1% w/v resulted in less effective staining with acid black 1, acid violet 17, and acid yellow 7 [27].

In addition to being a solvent for the dye, the presence of a short chain alcohol in the staining solution helps to prevent the blood from diffusing during the staining stage [27]. Ethanol is preferred as this offers lower toxicity and flammability than methanol. The use of water as the major solvent in the solution helps to raise the flash point to around 30°C, enabling this formulation, containing water, ethanol, and acetic acid, to be used at scenes of crime with a few simple precautions [24].

A washing or destaining stage is required poststaining. On nonporous surfaces, this just removes excess dye; however, on porous surfaces, this also acts as a destainer, removing dye that has been absorbed by the background surface.

Just like the staining solution, the wash or destaining solution has to be carefully constructed so that it solubilizes the excess dye, but does not either diffuse or wash away the dyed fingerprint and retains the intensity of color of the dye in the fingerprint. For this reason, the same solvent mix as that used for the dyeing process or some small variation of it is generally most effective [27].

9.2.3.2 Amino Acid Techniques

Ninhydrin and DFO react with amino acids and amines and are the two most widely used techniques to develop latent fingerprints on porous surfaces. They are also very effective for the enhancement of blood [31]. They both react with amino acids by similar mechanisms to form products that contain two deoxygenated molecules of the starting product bridged by a nitrogen atom, which is donated from the amine [66,67] (Figure 9.1).

While the reaction mechanisms and products have similarities, the method of their visualization is entirely different. Ninhydrin, under the right conditions, produces an intensely colored product called Ruhemann's purple, after the discoverer, and DFO a pale pink, extremely fluorescent product, although this cannot be seen on marks with heavy blood contamination as the fluorescence is reabsorbed by the heme group. Ruhemann's purple can be made to fluoresce by complexing it with metal salts but the product that results from this additional process is still not as sensitive as DFO [68]. However, DFO requires heat for the reaction to proceed [69], while ninhydrin will react at room temperature provided moisture is available, although the process proceeds much faster at elevated temperatures and humidities.

However, if it is required to prove the presence of blood for evidential purposes, then a presumptive test or DNA profiling must also be carried out on the fingerprints.

9.2.3.3 Powder Suspension Techniques

Powder suspensions are a relatively new technique and little is currently known of their mechanism of action. This is currently being investigated in the U.K. and papers will be forthcoming. However, it appears that some formulations of powder suspensions may have an affinity for some component in blood [70,71]. Faint fingerprints on nonporous surfaces may give some enhancement, although the current methods will disastrously diffuse heavy deposits of blood. Powder suspensions have the advantage in that they can be successfully used after all the other processes.

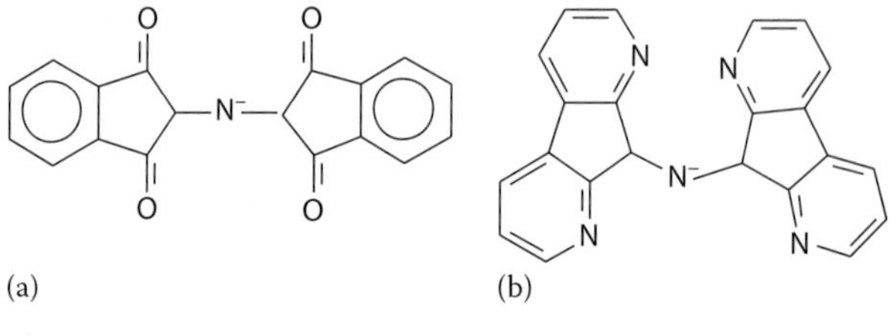

FIGURE 9.1
The reaction products with ninhydrin (a) and DFO (b) and amines.

9.2.4 Spectrophotometric and Spectrofluorimetric Methods

There are many ways of identifying blood using spectroscopic methods [51,52], but they are all carried out ex situ, so are of no use in the enhancement of blood-contaminated fingerprints.

Hemoglobin strongly absorbs light throughout the ultraviolet, visible, and near-infrared parts of spectrum and this property can be utilized to detect and enhance blood. Where deposits of blood are heavy or are present on light-colored surfaces, a good white light may suffice to enable enough detail to be observed. However, for pale or insubstantial deposits, it may be necessary to use high-intensity light sources to enhance contrast between the blood and the surface.

The use of fluorescence to enhance fingerprints in blood can be extremely effective in these circumstances. There are two ways this may be achieved, either by exciting fluorescence of the background surface on which the blood is deposited or by treatment with a process that either breaks the heme group, or turns the blood into a fluorescent species, or does both of these.

Many materials fluoresce when excited by high-intensity light in the ultraviolet and violet regions of the spectrum. This is coincidently where the heme group is most absorbent, with a peak around 421 nm (known as the Soret Band) [51,54,55], and why blood-contaminated fingerprints will appear dark against a light background. Fluorescence examination may be used before any other fingerprint enhancement techniques as it is nondestructive and if long-wave ultraviolet or violet/blue light (350–450 nm) [53] is used, then DNA typing is also unaffected [24]. The use of ninhydrin, acid black 1, or acid violet 17 can further intensify the contrast between fingerprint and background by increasing the light absorption properties of the blood.

The use of a strong organic acid in conjunction with hydrogen peroxide [31,72] breaks up the heme group so that it is no longer effective at absorbing light. After such treatment, blood will fluoresce orange when excited by green light (500–550 nm). This effect has also been noted as blood ages.

DFO and acid yellow 7 both produce fluorescent species with blood, which can be excited by green (510–570 nm) and blue (420–485 nm) light, respectively. Both can be less effective on heavy deposits of blood as the heme group retains its ability to absorb both the excitation light and that emitted as fluorescence.

It has been observed that acid violet 17 has weak fluorescence in the deep red and near infrared wavelengths when excited with green/yellow and yellow wavelengths and it may be possible to use this property to visualize marks on some fluorescent and/or patterned backgrounds.

9.3 Application of Enhancement Techniques

9.3.1 Introduction

The U.K. Home Office recommends the use of a comprehensive array of fingerprint development and blood enhancement processes for use on fingerprints in blood, depending on the surface characteristics [24]. Three acid dyes (acid black 1 [naphthlene black, naphthol blue black, CI 20470], acid violet 17 [Coomassie brilliant violet R150, CI 42650], and acid yellow 7 [brilliant sulphoflavine, CI 56205]) are recommended only for use on blood. DFO and ninhydrin will also develop fingerprints contaminated with blood, but are also the recommended techniques for latent fingerprints on porous surfaces [27,30,31].

A holistic approach has been adopted where the formulations for fixing, staining, and destaining have been very carefully constructed so that the blood is fixed effectively, then kept from diffusing during the staining and destaining stages, and that the strong coloration from the dye is retained during destaining [27].

Therefore the most effective formulation for the three recommended acid dyes is as follows [31]:

Fixing solution – 23 g 5-sulphosalicylic acid dihydrate dissolved in 1 L water.

Staining solution – 1 g acid dye (acid black 1 {AB1}, acid violet 17 {AV17}, and acid yellow 7 {AY7}) dissolved in 700 mL distilled water, 250 mL ethanol, and 50 mL acetic acid.

Washing solution – 700 mL water, 250 mL ethanol, and 50 mL acetic acid.

The staining and washing solutions are flammable. Safety precautions must be taken if these solutions are used outside a fume cupboard and with ambient temperatures above 28°C [24].

9.3.2 Application

The most appropriate techniques to use, either individually or in order in a sequence, for maximum effectiveness, depends on the porosity of the surface to be treated. The techniques currently recommended for enhancement of blood-contaminated fingerprints include white light followed by a fluorescence examination, two amino acid reagents, three acid dyes, and powder suspensions. These are the most effective means of enhancing fingerprints in blood [31].

A thorough white light search should be carried out before anything else. Both direct and diffuse lighting should be used. Subsequent to this, high-intensity light sources with outputs between 350 and 450 nm should be used to make background surfaces fluoresce [53,55]. This can be a very effective way of increasing contrast between blood and the surface.

DFO and ninhydrin working solutions should be applied by dipping or with a soft brush on larger articles or surfaces. It is recommended that DFO is heated to 100°C for 20 min; however, where this is not possible, temperatures as low as 50°C may be used but the rate of reaction is much slower [69]. It is recommended that ninhydrin-treated articles or surfaces be heated to 80°C and humidified to 65% RH. However, the reaction will proceed at room temperature and humidity, although more slowly.

High-intensity light sources capable of outputting wavelengths between 510 and 570 nm must be used to excite fluorescence from blood reacted with DFO. The fluorescence emitted is between 550 and 650 nm. Benefit may also be gained by using shorter wavelengths, between 350 and 450 nm, to excite background fluorescence after ninhydrin treatment.

Application of three recommended acid dyes, acid black 1, acid violet 17, and acid yellow 7, is most effective by immersion, firstly in a fixing solution of 5-sulphosalicylic acid for at least 5 min. This is followed by immersion in a staining solution for at least 3 min for acid black 1 and acid violet 17, whereas acid yellow 7 requires immersion for at least 5 min. Areas heavily contaminated with blood require longer fixing and dyeing times. Articles should then be destained until excess dye is removed (see Figures 9.2 and 9.3).

FIGURE 9.2
Blood contaminated fingerprints before staining with acid yellow 7.

FIGURE 9.3
Blood contaminated fingerprints after staining with acid yellow 7.

On horizontal surfaces, it may be possible to construct a well around areas of interest that may be flooded and drained with the solutions as appropriate. However, if it is not possible to fully immerse the areas bearing the blood-contaminated fingerprints, such as on large horizontal or vertical surfaces at scenes of crime, another approach must be taken.

5-Sulphosalicylic acid fixing solution may be sprayed onto areas of interest so that they are kept damp for at least 30 min. The staining solution may then be liberally applied to thick tissue or fine cloth so that it is kept damp and in contact with the surface for at least 5 min for acid black 1 and acid violet 17 and 10 min for acid yellow 7. The destaining can be performed using the same method as that for staining, but finally a dry tissue or fine cloth should be applied very carefully to mop up excess solution [73]. Staining or destaining solutions must never be sprayed as this atomizes the flammable solvents, which allows them to be ignited by a less energetic ignition source [74].

High-intensity light sources capable of emanating wavelengths between 420 and 485nm must be used to excite fluorescence from blood dyed with acid yellow 7. The fluorescence emitted is between 480 and 550nm. The use of shorter wavelengths between 350 and 450nm to excite background fluorescence after acid black 1 or acid violet 17 treatment may be beneficial.

Work carried out by the U.K. Home Office has demonstrated that positive DNA identifications may be made after fluorescence examination and any single chemical treatment provided simple guidelines are followed. If more than one fingerprint development technique is used in sequence prior to DNA recovery, then the chances of successfully carrying out DNA identification are much reduced [24].

9.3.3 Alternative Formulations

There are a large number of blood reagents, only some of which have been mentioned earlier, and there can be many different formulations of each of those reagents to consider. However, the water-based formulation of the acid dyes are probably the most practical as they can be used at all times, although methanol-based solutions might prove beneficial under some specialized circumstances when taking appropriate precautions (Table 9.1).

Originally these formulations were developed for use with acid black1 dye, but both can be used equally effectively with acid violet 17 and acid yellow 7.

9.3.3.1 Advantages of Water-Based and Methanol-Based Acid Dye Formulations [27]

The water-based formula does not use flammable or toxic solvents and can therefore be used safely whatever the temperature at the scene of a crime as well as in a laboratory. It is a simple process to use and inexpensive to carry out.

The methanol-based formula is very effective and simple to use for enhancing fingerprints in blood. It gives good ridge definition and little background staining and produces dark blue-black fingerprints.

TABLE 9.1
Methanol-Based and Water-Based Acid Dye Formulations

	Water-Based Method	Methanol-Based Method
Fixing solution	23g 5-Sulphosalicylic acid (dihydrate) 1000mL distilled water	Methanol (99%+)
Staining solution	2g acid dye (AB1, AV17 or AY7) 20g citric acid or 5% v/v acetic acid 1000mL distilled water	2g acid dye (AB1, AV17 or AY7) 900mL methanol 100mL acetic acid
Destaining solution 1	Distilled water (5% v/v acetic acid helps to retain coloration)	900mL methanol 100mL acetic acid
Destaining solution 2	Distilled water (5% v/v acetic acid helps to retain coloration)	950mL distilled water 50mL acetic acid

9.3.3.2 Disadvantages of Water-Based and Methanol-Based Acid Dye Formulations [27]

The water-based formula does not always produce optimum results as it may give diffuse fingerprint ridges and lower contrast coloration, especially on porous surfaces. Deeper coloration may be retained by the inclusion of 5% v/v acetic acid in the destaining solutions. Also on porous surfaces, the contrast between fingerprint and background can sometimes be less good than that achieved when using the methanol-based formulation, because of relatively high levels of background staining and the reduced color intensity of the developed ridges.

The methanol-based solutions are toxic by ingestion and skin absorption. Methanol is also a highly flammable solvent. Although this formulation can be used safely in a laboratory inside a fume cupboard, its use at scenes of crime is not recommended due to potential ignition or the possibility of absorption of methanol through the skin. Leaching of blood from heavy deposits also occurs with this formulation unless much longer fixing times are used. The methanol-based formulation may also soften or destroy some surfaces including paints, varnishes, and some plastics, damaging or obliterating ridge detail.

9.3.3.3 Rejected Dyes and Techniques

The U.K. Home Office's blood enhancement project investigated many dyes and reactive techniques that proved less effective than others. Effectiveness of techniques were measured by numbers of developed fingerprints and blood dilution spots [30,31]. Also many techniques detailed in the literature were rejected and not studied because of health and safety concerns (Table 9.2).

9.3.4 Posttreatments

Fluorescence examination is the most notable posttreatment process and this has been discussed fully above. Also mentioned earlier are the powder suspensions, which may be used to good effect after other blood enhancement techniques on nonporous surfaces.

9.4 Sequencing of Techniques to Maximize Enhancement of Fingerprints

9.4.1 Introduction

There are two strategies that can be adopted to maximize the number of fingerprints developed on articles where there is blood contamination. The first is to use all compatible techniques in a sequence so that development of latent fingerprints as well as those that are contaminated with blood are maximized and the second is to only use techniques that will target the blood. The latter strategy should be selected only after careful consideration of all circumstances, as some of the blood-targeting techniques will destroy latent fingerprints, perhaps only to be used where suspects have legitimate access so that latent fingerprints will be irrelevant. However in that case any developed fingerprints will certainly need subsequent proof that they are in blood and DNA profiling must be carried out as soon after treatment as possible [24].

TABLE 9.2

The Less Effective Dyes and Techniques in Categories

Protein Dyes [30]	Heme-Specific Reactive Techniques [31]	Amine and Protein Reactive Techniques [31]
Acid blue 74 (indigo carmine)	ABTS (azino-di-benzthiazoline sulphonic acid)	ATTO-TAG™ CBQCA
Acid blue 83 (Coomassie brilliant blue R250)	DAB (3,3′-diaminobenzidine, TAB, 3,3′,4,4′-tetraamino-biphenyl)	ATTO-TAG™ FQ
Acid blue 90 (Coomassie brilliant blue G250)	Guaiacol	Fluorescamine
Acid blue 92 (Coomassie blue R)	LCV (leuco-crystal violet)	Lucifer yellow VS (VS = vinyl sulphone)
Acid blue 147 (xylene cyanol FF)	LMG (leuco-malachite green)	SYPRO® Ruby Protein Blot Stain
Acid red 1 (amido naphthol red G)	Luminol (5-Amino-2,3-dihydro-1,4-phthalazinedione)	
Acid red 71 (Crocein scarlet 7B)	Organic acid (formic or acetic) and hydrogen peroxide (hematoporphyrin)	
Acid red 87 (eosin y)	Fluorescein	
Acid red 88 (roccellin)		
Acid red 112 (Ponceau S)		
Acid violet 19 (fuchsin acid, Hungarian red)		
Acid yellow 23 (tartrazine)		
Benzoxanthene yellow (Hœchst 2495)		
Brilliant sulphaflavine		
Crowles double-stain *(acid blue 83 and acid red 71)*		
Direct yellow 12 (chrysophenine)		
MBD (7-(*p*-methoxybenylamino)-4-nitro-2,1,3-benzoxadiazole)		

9.4.2 Sequencing Techniques to Maximize the Number of Fingerprints

When both latent and blood-contaminated fingerprints are considered important, the following sequences of techniques have been found to be most effective (Figure 9.4).

Porous surfaces: DFO, ninhydrin, either acid black 1 or acid violet 17 (after carrying out a spot test to see which is most suitable), and then finally physical developer [31].

Nonporous surfaces: Vacuum metal deposition (VMD), powders, acid yellow 7, acid violet 17, powder suspensions, and then finally basic violet 3 (crystal violet) or solvent black 3 (Sudan black). Acid violet 17 is preferred to acid black 1 after acid yellow 7 as the color of these two dyes in combination gives greater contrast.

It is unsafe to consider the use of superglue instead of VMD or powders to develop latent fingerprints, as the glue covers the blood, forming a barrier that hinders the dye from reaching the blood, inhibiting the staining process [31] and rendering the blood enhancement less or even noneffective.

Semiporous surfaces, such as glossy papers and cards, should be treated with a combination of non-porous and porous techniques.

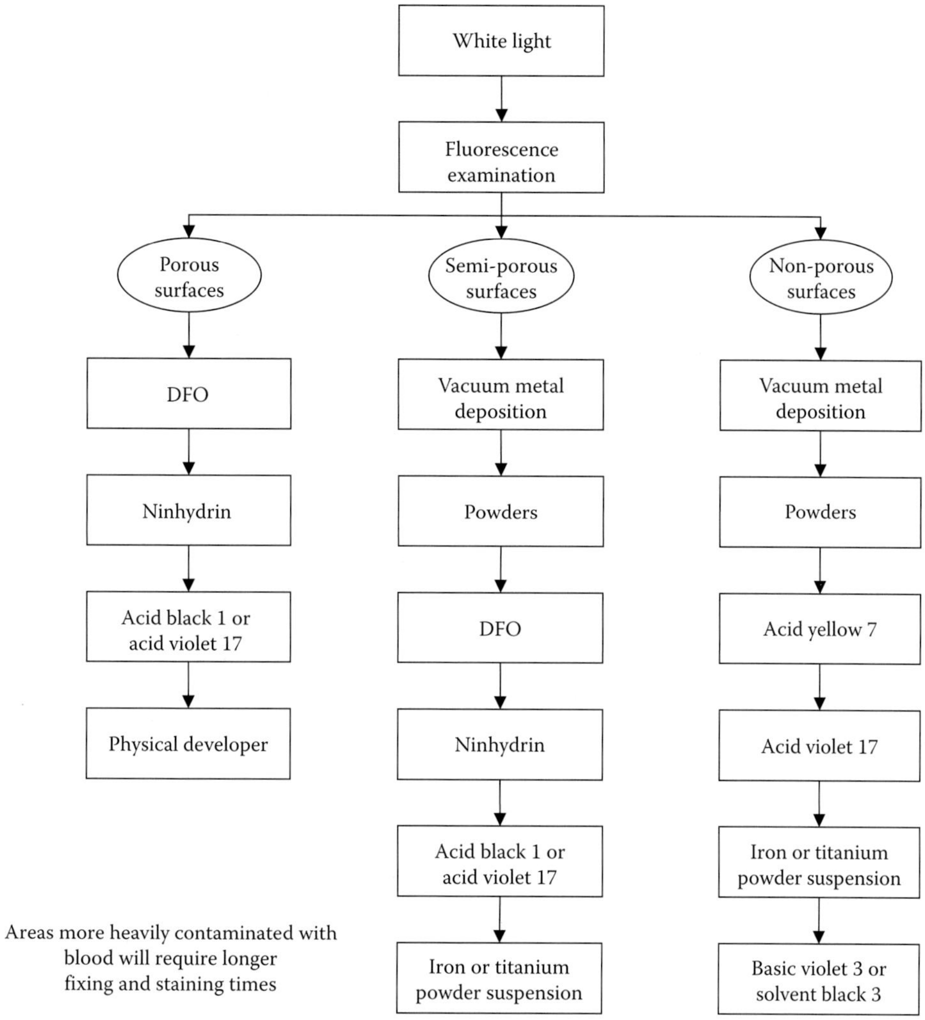

FIGURE 9.4
Maximizing the number of latent and blood contaminated fingerprints.

9.4.3 Sequencing Techniques That Target Blood

When only blood-contaminated fingerprints are considered important, the techniques that have been discussed should be used in the following sequences (Figure 9.5).

9.5 Which Came First: Blood or Latent Fingerprint

It has been claimed by a few defendants that had legitimate access to the scene of a crime that the blood from the victim must have developed one or more of their latent fingerprints that had been previously deposited on a surface, giving the appearance of a mark deposited by a blood-contaminated finger. In 1997, Creighton [75] conducted experiments where blood was allowed to flow or splash over latent fingerprints and found that there

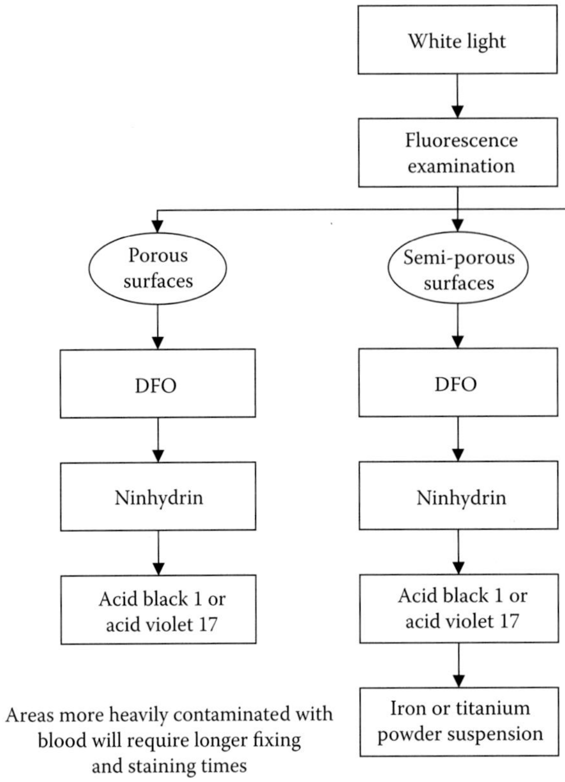

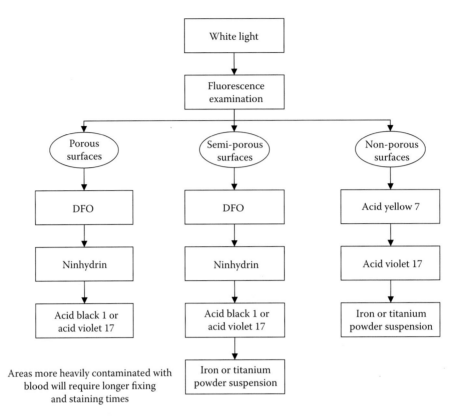

FIGURE 9.5
Blood enhancement techniques.

was no development. It was observed that it was more likely that the blood was repelled by the latent fingerprint. Huss et al. in 2000 [76] continued work in this area, confirming that blood will not develop latent fingerprints; however, they did find that a heavy sebaceous fingerprint may be revealed by the blood flowing around and between some of the ridges.

Langenburg [77] conducted research in a related area: the dynamics of deposition of bloody fingerprints. He investigated the effects of pressure, the volume-loading of blood on fingertips, the angle of the surface (horizontal or vertical), and various times blood had been on the finger so that it was in various states of drying. There were a number of important conclusions including that blood dries reasonably quickly on the finger, from 30 s for the lowest volumes to 3–4 min at the highest loadings, and that reversed fingerprints were not always observed with greater deposition pressure as had been expected.

9.6 Age of Blood

Aging bloodstains have been said to undergo characteristic changes, and there have been many attempts to devise methods for estimating the time between the deposition of blood and its analysis in the laboratory. This information could prove valuable in some instances, if it could be reliably quantified, but there are many difficulties with all the methods.

The major factor, regardless of the method, is that a variety of different environmental features, including heat, light, humidity, precipitation, and the presence of contaminants all influence the rate at which the changes occur.

However recent work by Ballantyne in 2008 [78] showed a previously unidentified hypsochromic shift (shift to shorter wavelengths) of the hemoglobin Soret band that demonstrated a high correlation to the time since deposition of dried bloodstains, permitting a distinction to be made between stains that were deposited minutes, hours, days, and months prior to analysis. In future, a method based on this information may help crime scene investigators determine the time of the crime if that information is crucial.

9.7 Conclusion

Generally, protein stains are the most effective enhancement techniques for blood. However, they have two major disadvantages in that they will not develop latent fingerprints and they are not specific for blood. If latent fingerprints could be important to the case, then the first disadvantage may be overcome by careful selection and ordering of techniques for latent fingerprint components and the second disadvantage may be overcome by obtaining a DNA profile.

There are many questions still left unanswered and future investigations might include the sequencing of protein stains and presumptive or antibody tests as this would deliver both effective enhancement and the presence of blood. This may also be accomplished by the development of a single reagent with the enhancement abilities of protein stains but with added specificity for blood. Basic fixative solutions, in combination with basic dyes for protein staining, could be explored as could other colored and more intense chemiluminescers than luminol, which might also be used in combination with any basic fixative to overcome the ridge diffusion caused by these reagents.

Acknowledgments

The author would like to acknowledge the extensive amount of work on blood enhancement techniques conducted around the world and especially by previous members of staff and placement students at the Centre for Applied Science and Technology (CAST) Home Office U.K., including Terry Kent, Lesley Fitzgerald, Helen Bandey, Tomasz Ciuksza, Marion Mutch, Tania Prizeman, Colin Butcher, and Laura Powell. Without the information obtained from their studies, this chapter could not have been compiled.

Author

Vaughn Sears, BSc, AIS, ARPS, received his BSc in biochemistry in 1981 from the University of Sussex. He joined the U.K. Home Office to work in the Fingerprint Development Group. Since then he has carried out research and development on almost all the Home

Office–recommended fingerprint development processes. More specifically, Sears was responsible for the development of the HFE-based ninhydrin and DFO formulations, the blood enhancement dyes—acid black 1, acid violet 17, and acid yellow 7—and the iron-based powder suspension. Sears has also carried out many studies of the image capture of fingerprints, including equipment and capture media. He has published more than 20 scientific papers on various fingerprint related topics. In 2005 he was awarded the title of Accredited Imaging Scientist and Associate of the Society by the Royal Photographic Society for his work on fingerprint imaging techniques.

References

1. Rosner F. (1973) Bloodstain identification as described in the Talmud. *Isr J Med Sci* 9:1077–1079.
2. Kiel FW. (1970) Forensic science in China—traditional and contemporary aspects. *J Forensic Sci* 15:201.
3. http://www.oldbaileyonline.org/; Reference Number t18491029–1890 (accessed September 6, 2011) Fredrick George Manning and Maria Manning were indicted for the wilful murder of Patrick O'Connor in 1849.
4. Conan-Doyle A. (1887) *Sherlock Holmes: A Study in Scarlet*.
5. Snyder L. (2004) Sherlock Holmes: scientific detective. *Endeavour* 28(3):104.
6. Teichmann L. (1853) Ueber die krystallisation des orpnischen be-standtheile des blutes. *Z Ration Med* 3:375.
7. Takayama M. (1912) A method for identifying blood by hemochromogen crystallization. *Kokka Igakkai Zasshi* 306:463.
8. Van Deen J. (1862) Tinctura guajaci und ein ozontrager, als reagens auf schrgeringe blutmenge; namentlich in medico-forensischen; fallen arch, hollend. *Beitr Natur Heilk* 3(2):228.
9. Schönbein CF. (1863) Ueber das verhalten des blutes zum sauerstoff. *Verh Naturforsch Ges Basel* 3:516.
10. Adler O, Adler R. (1904) Über das verhalten gewisscr organischer verindungen gegenüber blut mit besonderer berücksichtipng des nachweises von blut. *Z Physiol Chem* 41:59.
11. Medinger P. (1933) Zum nachweis minimalster blutspuren. *Dtsch Z Gesamte Gerichtl Med* 20:74.
12. Kastle JH, Shedd OM. (1901) Phenolphthalin as a reagent for the oxidizing ferments. *Am Chem J* 26:526.
13. Meyer E. (1903) Beiträge zur leukocytenfrage. *Muench Med Wochenshr* 50(35):1489.
14. Kastle JH, Amoss HL. (1906) Variations in the peroxidase activity of the blood in health and disease. US Hygienic Laboratory Bull (31) U.S. Public Health and Marine Hospital Service, U.S. Government Printing Office, Washington, DC.
15. Ruttan RF, Hardisty RHM. (1912) A new reagent for detecting occult blood. *Can Med Assoc J* 41(2):995.
16. Specht W. (1937) Die chemiluminescenz des hämins, ein hilfsmittel zur auffindung und erkennung forensisch wichtiger blutspunn. *Angew Chem* 50:155.
17. Gershenfeld L. (1939) Orthotolidine and orthotoluidine tests for occult blood. *Am J Pharm* 111:17.
18. Abderhalden E, Schmidt H. (1911) Utilization of triketohydrindene hydrate for the detection of proteins and their cleavage products. *Z Physiol Chem* 72:37.
19. Oden S. (1954) Detection of fingerprints by the ninhydrin reaction. *Nature* 173:449.
20. Godsell J. (1963) Fingerprint techniques. *J Forensic Sci Soc* 3(2):79. (From a paper presented at the Fourth Symposium of the Forensic Science Society on Saturday, October 28, 1961).

21. Puchtler H, Sweat F. (1962) Amido black as a stain for haemoglobin. *Arch Pathol* 73:245.
22. Puchtler H, Rosenthal SI, Sweat F. (1964) Revision of the amido black stain for haemoglobin. *Arch Pathol* 78:76.
23. Kent T (Ed.) (1986) *Manual of Fingerprint Development Techniques*, 1st edn. Home Office Police Scientific Development Branch. U.K. Home Office, London, U.K. (ISBN 0 86252 230 7).
24. Bowman V (Ed.) (2004) *Manual of Fingerprint Development Techniques*, 2nd edn. Home Office Police Scientific Development Branch. U.K. Home Office, London, U.K. (ISBN 1 85893 972 0).
25. Faragher A, Summerscales L. (1981) Fingerprint enhancement using the amido black technique after chemical fixation. Forensic Science Service U.K.; Technical Note 240.
26. Hussain JI, Pounds CA. (1989) The enhancement of fingerprints in blood part ii: a modified amido black staining technique. Forensic Science Service U.K., Home Office Central Research Establishment Report 649 (June).
27. Sears VG, Prizeman TM. (2000) The enhancement of fingerprints in blood—part 1: the optimization of amido black. *J Forensic Ident* 50(5):470.
28. Norkus P, Noppinger K. (1986) New reagents for the enhancement of fingerprints in blood. *Ident News* 26(4):5.
29. Barnett KG, Bone RG, Hall PW, Ide RH. (1988) The use of water soluble protein dye for the enhancement of footwear impressions in blood on non-porous surfaces part 1. Forensic Science Service U.K., Tech Note 629 (July).
30. Sears VG, Butcher CPG, Prizeman TM. (2001) The enhancement of fingerprints in blood—part 2: protein dyes. *J Forensic Ident* 51(1):28.
31. Sears V, Butcher C, Fitzgerald L. (2005) Enhancement of fingerprints in blood—part 3 reactive techniques, acid yellow 7 and process sequences. *J Forensic Ident* 55(6):741.
32. Garner DD, Cano KM, Peimer RS, Yeshion TE. (1976) An evaluation of tetramethylbenzidine as a presumptive test for blood. *J Forensic Sci* 21(4):816.
33. Hussain JI, Pounds CA. (1989) The enhancement of marks made in blood with 3,3′,4,4′-tetraaminobiphenyl. Forensic Science Service U.K., CRSE Report 653.
34. Cheeseman R, DiMeo LA. (1995) Fluorescein as a field-worthy latent bloodstain detection system. *J Forensic Ident* 45(6):631.
35. Bodziak WJ. (1996) Use of leuco-crystal violet to enhance shoeprints in blood. *Forensic Sci Int* 82:45.
36. Crown DA. (1969) The development of latent fingerprints with ninhydrin. *J Crim Law Criminal Pol Sci* 60(2):258.
37. Morris JR, Goode GC. (1974) NFN an improved ninhydrin reagent for the detection of latent fingerprints. *Pol Res Bull* 24:45.
38. Watling WJ, Smith KO. (1993) Heptane an alternative to the freon ninhydrin mixture. *J Forensic Ident* 43(2):131.
39. Hewlett DF, Sears VG, Suzuki S. (1997) Replacements for cfc113 in the ninhydrin process part 2. *J Forensic Ident* 47(3):300.
40. Morris JR. (1978) Extensions to the nfn reagent for the development of latent fingerprints. AWRE Report (February).
41. Everse KE, Menzel ER. (1986) Sensitivity enhancement of ninhydrin treated latent fingerprints by enzymes and metal salts. *J Forensic Sci* 31(2):446.
42. Stoilovic M, Kobus HJ, Margot PA, Warrener RN. (1986) Improved enhancement of ninhydrin developed fingerprints by cadmium complexation using low temperature. *J Forensic Sci* 31(2):432.
43. Almog J, Hirshfield A, Klug JT. (1982) Reagents for the chemical development of latent fingerprints: synthesis and properties of some ninhydrin analogues. *J Forensic Sci* 27(4):912.
44. Almog J, Hirshfield A. (1988) 5-methoxyninhydrin: a reagent for the chemical development of latent fingerprints that is compatible with the copper vapour laser. *J Forensic Sci* 33(4):1027.
45. Grigg R, Mongkolaussavaratana T, Pounds CA, Sivagnanam S. (1990) 1,8-Diazafluorenone and related compounds. a new reagent for the detection of α-amino acids and latent fingerprints. *Tetrahedron Lett* 31(49):7215.

46. Ramatowski R, Cantu AA, Joullie J, Petrovskaia O. (1997) 1,2 Indandiones: a preliminary evaluation of a new class of amino acid visualizing compounds. *Fingerprint Whorld* 23(90):131.
47. Hochmeister MN, Budowle B, Sparkes R, Rudin O, Gehrig C, Thali M, Schmidt L, Cordier A, Dirnhofer R. (1999) Validation studies of an immunochromatographic 1-step test for the forensic identification of human blood. *J Forensic Sci* 44(3):597.
48. Johnston E, Ames CE, Dagnell KE, Foster J, Daniel BE. (2008) Comparison of presumptive blood test kits including hexagon obti. *J Forensic Sci* 53(3):687.
49. Hoppe F. (1862) Ueber das verhalten des blutfarbstoffes in spectrum des sonnenlichtes. 1862; *Arch Pathol Anat Physiol Klin Med* 23(4):446.
50. Stokes GG. (1864) On the reduction and oxidation of the colouring matter of the blood. *Proc Royal Soc Lond* 13:355.
51. Soret JL. (1883) Anallyse spectrale: sur le spectre d'absorption du sang dans la partie violette et ultra-violette. *Comp Rend Acad Sci* 97:1269.
52. Sorby HC. (1865) On the application of spectrum analysis to microscopical investigations, and especially to the detection of bloodstains. *Q J Sci* 865(2):198.
53. Hardwick SA, Kent T, Sears VG. (1990) *Fingerprint Detection by Fluorescence Examination; A Guide to Operational Implementation*. U.K. Home Office, London, U.K. (ISBN 0 86252 554 3).
54. Kotowski TM, Grieve MC. (1986) The use of microspectrophotometry to characterize microscopic amounts of blood. *J Forensic Sci* 31(3):1079.
55. Stoilovic M. (1991) Detection of semen and blood stains using polilight as a light source. *Forensic Sci Int* 51:289.
56. Olsen RD. (1985) Sensitivity comparison of blood enhancement techniques. *Ident News* 35(8):10.
57. Cheeseman R. (1999) Direct sensitivity comparison of the fluorescein and luminol bloodstain enhancement techniques. *J Forensic Ident* 49(3):261.
58. Theeuwen ABE, van Barneveld S, Drok JW, Keereweer I, Limborgh JCM, Naber WM, Velders T. (1998) Enhancement of footwear impressions in blood. *Forensic Sci Int* 95:133.
59. Seigel J. (Ed-in-chief) (2000) *Encyclopedia of Forensic Sciences*. Academic Press, London, U.K., p. 1333 (ISBN 0-12-227215-3).
60. Weber K. (1966) Die anwendung der chemiluminescenz des luminols in der gerichtlichen medizin und toxikologie. *Deut Z Gericht Med* 57:10.
61. Grodsky M, Wright K, Kirk P. (1951) Simplified preliminary blood testing. *J Criminol Pol Sci* 42:95.
62. Seigel J. (Ed-in-chief) (2000) Encyclopedia of Forensic Sciences. Academic Press, London, U.K., p. 1334 (ISBN 0-12-227215-3).
63. Eckert WG, James SH. (1989) *Interpretation of Bloodstain Evidence at Crime Scenes*. Elsevier Science Publishing, New York, p. 121.
64. Castelló A, Francés F, Corella D, Verdú F. (2009) Active oxygen doctors the evidence. *Die Naturwissenschaften* 96(2):303.
65. Christie RM, Mather RR, Wardman RH. (2000) *The Chemistry of Colour Application*. Blackwell Science Ltd, Oxford, U.K., p. 19 (ISBN 0-632-04782-8).
66. McCaldin DJ. (1960) The chemistry of ninhydrin. *Chem Rev* 60:39.
67. Wilkinson D. (2000) Study of the reaction mechanism of 1,8-diazafluoren-9-one with the amino-acid l-alanine. *Forensic Sci Int* 109:87.
68. Stoilovic M. (1993) Improved method for DFO development of latent fingerprints. *Forensic Sci Int* 60:141.
69. Hardwick S, Kent T, Sears V, Winfield P. (1993) Improvements to the formulation of DFO and the effects of heat on the reaction with latent fingerprints. *Fingerprint Whorld* 19(73):65.
70. Bergeron J. (2003) Development of bloody prints on dark surfaces with titanium dioxide and methanol. *J Forensic Ident* 53(2):149.

71. Au C, Jackson-Smith H, Quinones I, Jones BJ, Daniel B. (2001) Wet powder suspensions as an additional technique for the enhancement of bloodied marks. *Forensic Sci Int* 204:13–18.
72. Fischer JF, Miller WG. (1984) The enhancement of blood prints by chemical methods and laser induced fluorescence. *Ident News* 34(7):2.
73. Bandey H. (2008) *Fingerprint and Footwear Forensics Newsletter.* Publication No 24/08, May, p. 11.
74. von Pidoll U. (2001) The ignition of clouds of sprays, powders and fibers by flames and electric sparks. *J Loss Prevent Process Ind* 14(2):103.
75. Creighton JT. (1997) Visualization of latent impressions after incidental or direct with human blood. *J Forensic Ident* 47(5):534.
76. Huss K, Clark J, Chisum WJ. (2000) What was first—fingerprint or blood. *J Forensic Ident* 50(4):344.
77. Langenburg G. (2008) Deposition of bloody friction ridge impressions. *J Forensic Ident* 58(3):355.
78. Ballantyne J. (2009) Determination of the age (time since deposition) of a biological stain; National Institute of Justice Award 2005-MU-BX-K071, Document No. 226811 (May).

10

Vacuum Metal Deposition

Milutin Stoilovic, Naomi Speers, and Chris Lennard

CONTENTS

10.1 Introduction

Vacuum metal deposition (VMD) is an extremely sensitive technique for the development of latent fingermarks on nonporous and semiporous surfaces. VMD is generally recognized as being more sensitive than cyanoacrylate fuming, which is the most common routine development technique for nonporous surfaces [1–3]. The increased sensitivity achieved with VMD is particularly evident in instances where marks are old, have been exposed to adverse environmental conditions, or are present on otherwise difficult surfaces [4,5]. A further advantage of VMD is that, with normal development, the substrate is covered with a layer of metallic zinc that can assist in overcoming background interference such as heavy printing or multicolored patterns. VMD is generally not considered a routine method for fingermark development due to the expense of the equipment (Figure 10.1), the time required for application of the technique, and the need for experienced operators to obtain optimum results.

The VMD development of latent marks traditionally involves the evaporation and deposition, under vacuum, of gold and then zinc. Zinc will not deposit onto a nonmetallic surface under vacuum unless the surface is very cold or if the surface contains nucleating sites of another metal, such as gold. This property is exploited in VMD to develop latent fingermarks. The clusters (agglomerates) of gold atoms formed during the first evaporation step create nucleation sites to which the zinc can bond, enabling the deposition of a zinc film during the second evaporation step. Fingermark residue, and any other surface contaminants, will generally inhibit zinc deposition. As a result, the zinc film that forms will generally cover the whole surface except where fingermark residue is present, resulting in transparent ridges and a metallic (zinc-coated) background (Figure 10.2).

10.1.1 History

Vacuum deposition of metals has been used extensively for many purposes, such as the production of evaporated metal films used in the electrical industry [6] and in sample preparation for scanning electron microscopy (SEM) [7].

FIGURE 10.1
Vacuum metal deposition unit used by the Australian Federal Police (Canberra, Australia) for fingermark detection on nonporous and semiporous surfaces.

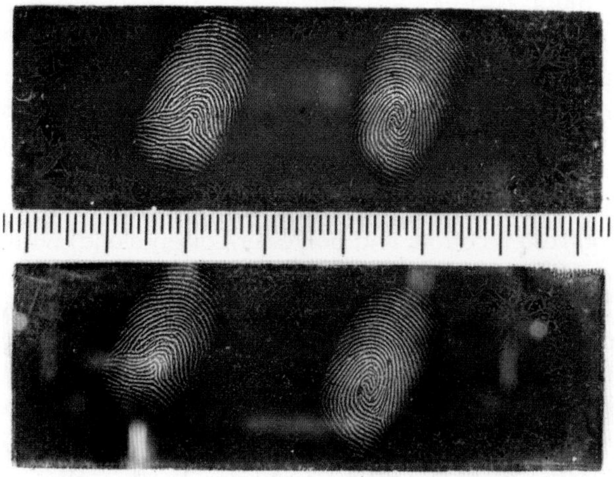

FIGURE 10.2
Three year old fingermarks on glass microscope slides developed by VMD.

VMD was first applied to fingermark detection by Theys and coworkers in 1968 [8]. They reported the development of prints on paper by volatizing a mixture of zinc, antimony, and copper powder. The technique worked well for fresh marks on paper but, as the deposit aged, poorer results were obtained due to the fingermark material being absorbed into the surface. Hambley and coworkers (as cited by Thomas [9]) further developed the technique for use on paper and fabric. VMD was subsequently applied to polyethylene substrates and first used operationally by Kent and coworkers in the mid-1970s [10].

Kent and coworkers experimented with a number of metals and metal combinations [10]. Single metals that may give visible marks in some cases are gold, silver, copper, zinc, cadmium, aluminum, bismuth, chromium, magnesium, platinum, lead, antimony, and tin. The combinations of copper, gold, or silver with cadmium or zinc also develop visible marks. The best results were seen using lead alone and gold or silver in combination with cadmium or zinc, with the combinations showing advantages over lead alone.

The combination of gold followed by zinc is generally used for latent fingermark development. Cadmium is not used due to its toxicity [11]. Silver was reported to attack fingermark constituents, causing diffusion of the fingermark over time; hence gold, which is less chemically active than silver, is generally used [12].

Philipson and Bleay [13] investigated the deposition of single metals as an alternative to the standard gold and zinc combination. Trials were conducted with copper, silver, gold, indium, and tin. Silver was found to be the most suitable metal. Silver deposition was found to develop extra detail compared to standard gold and zinc deposition. This was particularly the case where gold and zinc deposition resulted in "empty" or "halo" prints, which is where metal deposition has occurred around the fingermark area but with no visible ridge detail. In these situations, silver deposition was able to reveal ridge detail in the fingermarks.

Gunaratne and coworkers [14] compared conventional gold/zinc vacuum metal deposition (Au/Zn VMD) with a new one-step aluminum process (Al VMD). The sensitivity was compared for latent fingermark detection on a variety of common plastic substrates. The results indicated that Al VMD could produce significantly more usable marks than Au/Zn VMD for fresh samples (<48 h), but not for aged samples (>90 days), where a drop in efficiency was noted for both processes. The authors concluded that Al VMD is an effective alternative to the conventional VMD method for fingermark detection on such surfaces.

Yu and colleagues [15] described a simplified vacuum deposition process utilizing pure zinc oxide (ZnO) rather than sequential Au and Zn depositions. The direct deposition of ZnO, thermally evaporated under vacuum, was found to develop fingermarks on the polyethylene terephthalate (PET) substrate tested. The technique was found to be less effective on aged samples; however, some fingermark detail was obtained even after 45 days.

Conventional Au/Zn VMD has been shown to be effective for the visualization of fingermarks and grab impressions on fabrics [16]. In the reported study, four different fabrics were tested (nylon, polyester, cotton, and polyester/cotton blend) with latent fingermarks from 15 donors. These fingermarks were aged for up to 28 days prior to VMD treatment. Greater ridge detail was observed on the smoother, nonporous fabrics (e.g., nylon), while the rougher, more porous fabrics (cotton) only produced empty marks and impressions. However, touch marks were developed by VMD on all of the fabrics tested and this can assist in targeting any DNA that may have been deposited with the latent impressions.

10.1.2 Comparison with Other Detection Techniques

VMD is effective for developing fingermarks on nonporous and semiporous surfaces. VMD is more time intensive than most other fingermark development techniques so it is not commonly used for the routine treatment of exhibits. In situations where routine techniques such as cyanoacrylate fuming and fluorescent staining are effective, the time and expense related to VMD processing makes it an uneconomical option. VMD's usefulness is in developing marks that are too weak to be detected by routine techniques or where fingermarks are present on problematic surfaces.

Numerous studies have shown that VMD is generally more sensitive than other development techniques. On nonporous surfaces, VMD has been reported to be more sensitive than

- Powdering [2,17]
- Small particle reagent [1,18]
- Cyanoacrylate fuming [1,2]
- Cyanoacrylate fuming followed by fluorescent staining [1,3]

VMD's greater sensitivity is even more evident for older fingermarks [2,3] and those subject to adverse environmental conditions [1]. The sensitivity of VMD for weaker marks has also been demonstrated in casework. Batey and coworkers [4] reported a number of casework examples involving the use of VMD. Three of these examples were the development of prints, which were

1. Sixteen years old
2. Located on a plastic bag used to contain a human torso that was placed inside a suitcase and believed to have been in a river for 18 h before being discovered
3. Located on a plastic bag wrapped around a murder victim which had been in an outdoor location for at least 5 days before being discovered

VMD was critical to the case of "The Last Call Killer" [19]. In the early 1990s, the dismembered remains of 5 males were found wrapped in multiple layers of plastic bags and dumped on major roadways in Pennsylvania, New York, and New Jersey. No usable marks were located on the bags used to wrap the remains until, 7 years after the last murder, the bags were treated by VMD. Numerous fingermarks were developed on a number of the bags. Identification of some of these marks led police to Richard Rogers, Jr. Over 30 fingermarks were subsequently confirmed as belonging to Rogers who was found guilty of two of the murders and remains a suspect in other three murders [19].

Research into the development of fingermarks from arson scenes has also highlighted the power of VMD to develop degraded prints. VMD was able to detect latent marks on ceramic tiles that had been exposed to high temperatures (600°C) and was able to detect areas where fingermarks in blood had been deposited after exposure to even higher temperatures (900°C) [20,21].

Polymer banknotes are an example of a problematic surface for which VMD is the recommended development technique. Polymer banknotes, in use in 18 countries, including Australia and New Zealand, are composed of a polyethylene base that is coated with an opacifier that enables printing on the surface [22]. Notes are printed using a variety of printing techniques then coated with a clear primer and "mattcoat" (matte coating). The resulting semiporous surface is problematic with respect to latent fingermark development. Under laboratory conditions, the development of latent marks on unused banknotes with cyanoacrylate fuming and staining is limited to prints under 7 days old, while VMD is able to develop marks aged for up to 18 months [5,23]. VMD has the added advantage of masking the heavy printing of the banknote, which otherwise make the location and examination of developed fingermarks difficult.

VMD has also been shown to be more sensitive than routine techniques for the development of latent fingermarks on ferromagnetic-coated surfaces (used for train tickets in Japan) [24]. While Suzuki and coworkers found VMD to be superior to routine techniques on styrofoam substrates [25], other research found that multimetal deposition II (MMDII) was superior to VMD on the same surface type [25].

VMD and white powder suspension have been compared in terms of their ability to develop latent fingermarks on wetted, nonporous dark substrates [26]. The performance of the powder suspension was found to be comparable with VMD across the nonporous surfaces tested. The authors concluded that powder suspension was an effective, straightforward, cost-effective, and rapid method for fingermark detection under these circumstances. If VMD development fails on a particular nonporous surface, then a powder suspension can be used in an attempt to develop any latent fingermarks that may be present.

It has been observed that, in recent years, conventional Au/Zn VMD processing has shown a reduction in performance with respect to fingermark detection on plastic substrates [14]. This may be due to the changing nature of the polymer substrates being encountered in operational casework. Manufacturers are now using a wider range of base polymers, in addition to recycled materials and various additives such as antimicrobial treatments and plasticizers (which tend to congregate at the surface of the polymer). In terms of fingermark development, the resulting changes in surface characteristics may have resulted in a drop in sensitivity of the traditional VMD process.

10.2 General Operation of a VMD Unit

10.2.1 Metal Evaporation and Deposition at Reduced Pressure

Some substances such as the noble metals can be evaporated and deposited at atmospheric pressure, but air or water molecules are often trapped in the deposited layer and such coatings therefore lack homogeneity and smoothness. Other materials may chemically react with air molecules, resulting in the deposition of a different compound. A typical example is zinc. During the evaporation of zinc at atmospheric pressure, the zinc atoms react with oxygen, resulting in the deposition of zinc oxide rather than metallic zinc.

In order to achieve a smooth, uniform layer, to have better control over the deposition process, and to reduce chemical reactions with air/water molecules, a technique known as evaporation under vacuum was developed and perfected over many years. By reducing the pressure in the coating chamber, evaporated molecules have less chance to collide with air molecules, resulting in increased evaporation and deposition rates.

10.2.2 Pressure

Pressure represents a measure of force per unit area:

$$\text{Pressure} = \frac{\text{Force}}{\text{Area}}$$

In the International System of Units (SI), the unit for pressure is the pascal (Pa):

$$\text{Pascal (Pa)} = \frac{\text{Newton}}{\text{Square meter}} = \frac{1\,\text{kg}\cdot\text{m s}^{-2}}{\text{m}^2} = \frac{1\,\text{kg}}{\text{m s}^2}$$

Two other units, atmosphere and bar, are also acceptable as units for pressure:

$$1\ \text{atmosphere (atm)} = 760\ \text{mm Hg} = 760\ \text{torr} = 101{,}325\ \text{Pa} = 101.3\ \text{kPa}$$

$$1\ \text{bar} = 1{,}000\ \text{mbar} = 100{,}000\ \text{Pa} = 100\ \text{kPa} = 0.987\ \text{atm} = 750\ \text{torr}$$

10.2.3 Mean Free Path

According to the kinetic theory of gases, an air molecule moves in a straight-line path until it collides with another molecule (or with a wall of the confining vessel). We may assume that, under normal conditions, such collisions are elastic (i.e., kinetic energy is preserved and can be transferred from one molecule to another). As a result of these encounters, any molecule in a gas follows a zigzag path. At atmospheric pressure, the density of molecules in air is high and the average traversed distance between two collisions is very small. The average traversed distance between two collisions is known as the "mean free path." When the vacuum coating chamber starts to evacuate, the gas pressure in the chamber is lowered and the mean free path increases. For example, at a pressure of 1.3×10^{-4} mbar, the mean free path of air molecules is about 50 cm. We would ideally like to achieve a condition whereby evaporated atoms travel from the evaporation boat to the target without experiencing any collisions with residual air molecules in the chamber. Therefore, we have to achieve a reduced pressure—before we commence evaporation—that results in a mean free path that is larger than the boat-to-target distance.

For example, if the distance between the boats and the target is 44 cm, then the equivalent pressure to achieve a mean free path of this magnitude is approximately 1.5×10^{-4} mbar. Therefore the "fire ready" threshold that needs to be achieved prior to the commencement of the evaporation step should be set at 1.5×10^{-4} mbar (or greater vacuum).

10.2.4 Components of a Vacuum Metal Deposition Unit

A typical vacuum metal deposition unit consists of a large vacuum (coating) chamber, a diffusion pump with a large baffle valve, two sets of vacuum valves, and a rotary pump (Figure 10.3). Various commercial VMD units are available, of various sizes and various configurations. The description provided in the following is for a configuration and operating protocols that have been optimized for latent fingermark detection.

10.2.4.1 Coating Chamber

This is a large vacuum compartment, cylindrical in shape, fitted with tungsten boats, a crystal (thickness) monitor, a sample holder, and a shutter (located between the evaporation boats and the sample holder; Figure 10.4). Some VMD units may not be fitted with a shutter and crystal (thickness) monitor. The value of these components is discussed later.

The evaporation and deposition processes, under vacuum, occur in this chamber. Samples to be treated need to be affixed to the sample holder with the surface to be treated facing down (toward the tungsten boats). Depending on the chamber size, there may be two to four tungsten boats for zinc evaporation and the same number for gold. A large current (over 100 A) is used to heat the tungsten boats and to evaporate the metals. Gold is evaporated in minute quantities, requiring very high temperature well above 1000°C (white-hot). Therefore, the gold evaporation boats must be smaller to achieve this high temperature. Zinc requires larger evaporated quantities and a lower temperature, around 400°C (dark red-hot); therefore, larger tungsten boats are required for this metal.

10.2.4.2 Thickness Monitor

A thin quartz crystal, approximately 8–10 mm in diameter, is coated with gold on both sides. The resonance frequency of the crystal depends on its size and mass. An electronic

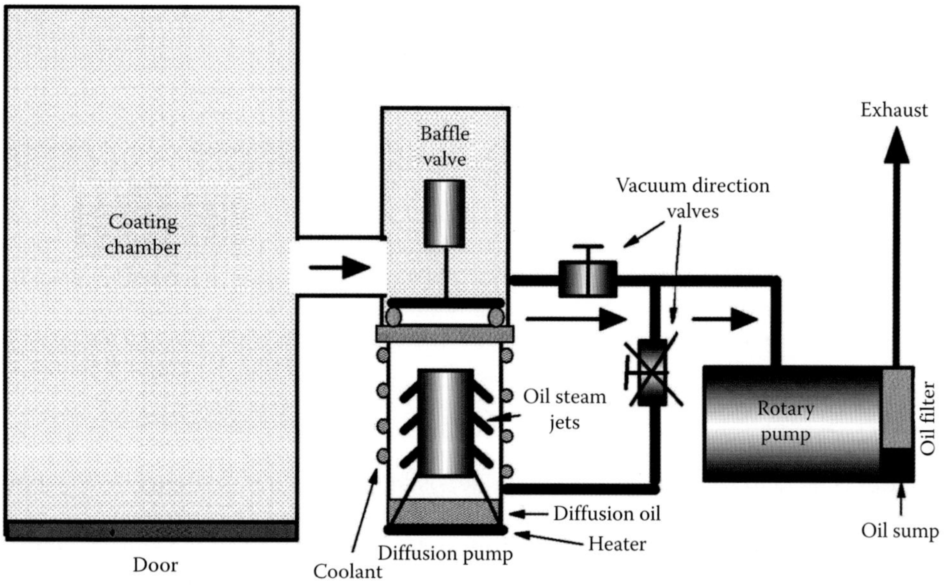

FIGURE 10.3
Schematic representation of a typical vacuum metal deposition unit.

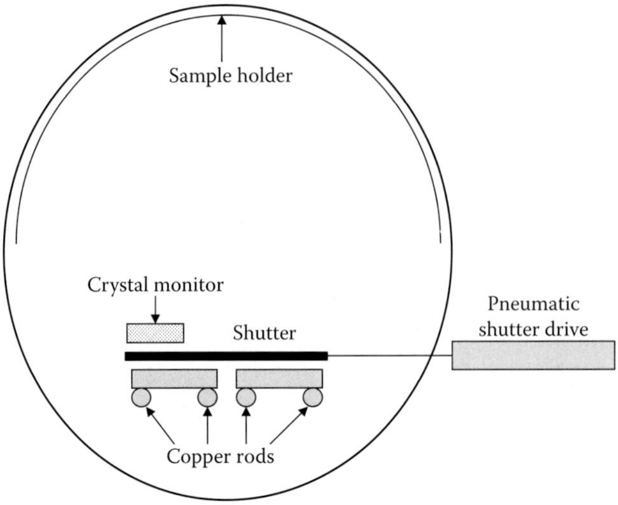

FIGURE 10.4
Cross-section of a typical VMD chamber showing various chamber components.

circuit continuously monitors the resonance frequency of the quartz crystal. During the evaporation process, gold deposits on one side of the quartz crystal changing its mass; therefore, the resonance frequency changes. When the correct parameters for the evaporant being monitored (gold) are entered, the monitor can calculate the deposited mass and display it in arbitrary units, known as "counts."

In this way, the monitor can calculate and display the following:

- Evaporation rate (counts per second)
- Total number of counts (for the time that that the shutter has been opened, which corresponds to the time that the samples have been exposed to the evaporated metal)

For the VMD development of latent fingermarks, the monitor is used to check the evaporation rate and the total number of counts for the gold evaporation step only, not for zinc. Given that the amount of gold deposited on the exhibit is a critical factor for optimum VMD development, a thickness monitor is a valuable component of the VMD unit. Without a thickness monitor, other measures have to be taken to control the quantity of evaporated gold (e.g., evaporation of a fixed quantity of gold or evaporation over a specified timeframe). Such measures are not accurate and a wide variability in fingermark development may be observed as a result.

10.2.4.3 Shutter

The shutter is used to control the amount of deposited gold and is operated by a fast pneumatic drive. When the gold current is switched on, the shutter is kept closed for around 30 s to allow for the gold boats to reach optimum temperature. Then the shutter is opened for a certain period of time so that the evaporated gold atoms can bombard the target. The shutter can be operated automatically in conjunction with the thickness monitor. The system can be programmed to open the shutter 30 s after the gold current is switched on.

FIGURE 10.5
VMD unit depicted in Figure 10.1, with the door opened and the sample holder removed. Small magnets can be used to affix exhibits (e.g., plastic bags) to the sample holder.

Deposition is then allowed to proceed until a predetermined number of counts is reached, and then the shutter closed (with the current to the gold boat switched off at this point). The shutter is not used for the zinc deposition step.

10.2.4.4 Sample Holder

The sample holder is in the form of a large semi-cylinder covering the top half of the VMD chamber. The sample holder can be taken out of the chamber and rotated to a vertical and/or horizontal position for easy sample loading (Figure 10.5). Exhibits can be held in place using small magnets.

10.2.4.5 Baffle Valve

The baffle valve is a large heavy steel plate that is pneumatically operated and sits directly above the diffusion pump. The baffle valve is closed at all times except when the pressure in the chamber is below a preset threshold pressure (e.g., 8×10^{-2} mbar, achieved using the rotary pump). In this way, the diffusion pump is always kept under vacuum and the expensive diffusion pump oil protected from degradation by oxidation.

10.2.4.6 Vacuum Direction Valves

There are two vacuum direction valves that operate alternatively.

10.2.4.7 Rotary Pump

A two-stage rotary pump is used to evacuate the chamber until a pressure threshold is reached within the coating chamber (Figure 10.3). (This initial vacuum threshold must be achieved by the rotary pump before the diffusion pump is employed to achieve the final vacuum required for metal evaporation/deposition.) Once the threshold is reached, the baffle valve opens and the vacuum direction valves change the evacuation direction (Figure 10.6). In this way, the rotary pump acts as a backing pump for the diffusion pump.

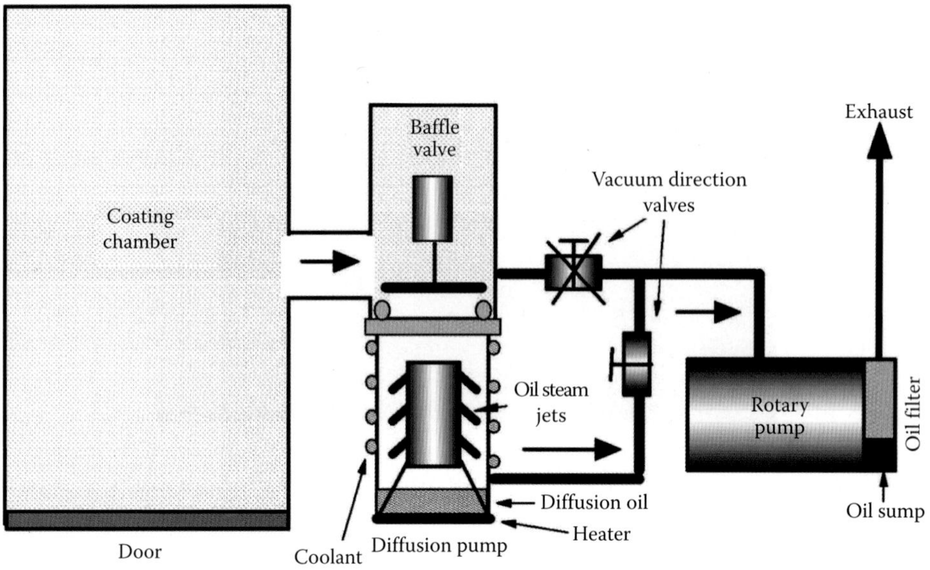

FIGURE 10.6
Evacuation direction when the threshold pressure is reached. The baffle valve is opened and evacuation is directed through the diffusion pump.

10.2.4.8 Diffusion Pump

The diffusion pump does not have moving parts and is very simple in construction. At the bottom of the pump, there is a specified amount of a special-purpose silicone oil (e.g., a large Edwards diffusion pump takes 600 mL of DC-704 Dow Corning silicone oil). Diffusion pump oils are designed according to the pressure to be achieved in the coating chamber, so the correct oil should always be used in a particular system. Above the oil there is a large cylinder that is closed at the top. On the side of the cylinder there are a number of jets. The oil is heated to its boiling point and kept boiling while the pump operates. Oil steam fills the cylinder and is forced, at very high speed, through the jets. The fast oil molecules capture air molecules, concentrating them toward the bottom of the pump. The coolant through the coil around the diffusion pump condenses the oil that then travels down to the sump. The rotary pump (acting as a backing pump) then removes free air molecules from the condensed diffusion pump oil.

10.2.5 Evaporation of Gold

Gold is a soft noble metal with a density of 18.9 g/cm^3. The melting point of gold is 1064°C, and the boiling point is 3080°C at atmospheric pressure. The boiling point is significantly lowered at reduced pressure, to around 1600°C at 10^{-4} mbar. Gold used for the VMD process is typically 99% pure and in the form of 0.5 mm thick wire.

When utilizing a VMD unit with a thickness monitor and shutter, pieces of wire of 5 mm in length can be used for evaporation. Initially, each tungsten boat is loaded with three or four pieces; thereafter, the tungsten boats are reloaded with gold wire as needed (i.e., when the quantity of gold remaining in the boats has diminished). The shutter/monitor system precisely controls the amount of evaporated gold; therefore, there is no requirement to completely evaporate the available gold from the tungsten boats.

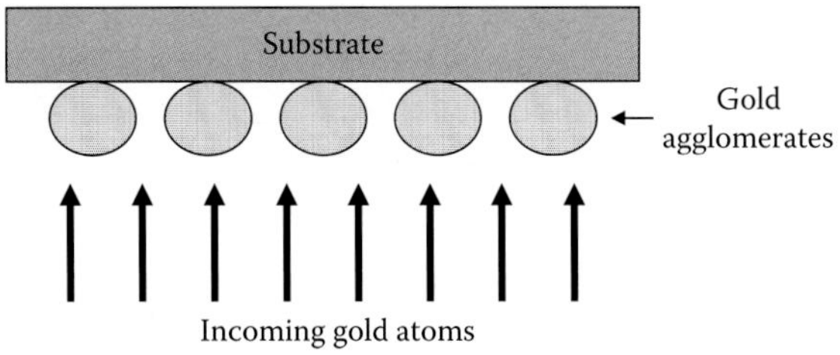

FIGURE 10.7
Schematic representation of gold cluster formation on an exposed substrate.

If a VMD unit without a thickness monitor and shutter is used, then the amount of gold employed for each treatment must be measured as accurately as possible. The consistent use of the same amount of gold (for the same substrate type) will make gold deposition as reproducible as is possible in the absence of a thickness monitor. However, the problem with this approach is that different substrates may require different amounts of gold to be deposited if optimum results are to be achieved.

When the "fire ready" pressure is reached, a high current is directed through the tungsten boats to heat them up. This may take some time before the optimum temperature is reached (around 30 s, depending on the nature of the tungsten boats). Gold atoms start to evaporate before the melting point is reached, but this is not significant at temperatures below the melting point. The kinetic energy of the evaporated gold atoms is directly related to the temperature of the boat. Initially, the evaporated heavy gold atoms do not have sufficient energy to reach the target. An optimum temperature has to be reached where most of the evaporated atoms bombard the target. These high-energy gold atoms traverse the coating chamber in straight lines.

When gold atoms approach the target surface, they do not immediately deposit on the surface at the arrival point but continue to move around the surface, experiencing collisions with other gold atoms. The attraction force between gold atoms is stronger than the attraction force between gold atoms and the substrate. This results in the formation of gold clusters (agglomerates) instead of a uniform gold layer across the surface (Figure 10.7). Dai and coworkers confirmed the formation of these agglomerates using transmission electron microscopic (TEM) imaging (Figure 10.8) [27].

The thin gold layer required for zinc to deposit under vacuum is therefore discontinuous rather than continuous. It has been demonstrated that the size and shape of the gold clusters are critical for subsequent zinc deposition [28]. It is therefore important that careful control is exercised during the gold deposition step (i.e., monitoring of the quantity of evaporated gold) if optimum results are to be obtained from the two-step VMD process. This careful control and monitoring of gold evaporation is far more easily achieved in a VMD unit fitted with a thickness monitor.

10.2.6 Evaporation of Zinc

Compared to gold, zinc is a much lighter metal with a density of 7.1 g/cm^3. It has a melting point of 420°C and a boiling point of 907°C at atmospheric pressure. The boiling point is significantly lowered at reduced pressure (to around 700°C at 10^{-4} mbar). Zinc starts to sublime (evaporate from a solid state) well before the melting point is reached. Once the boiling point is reached, zinc starts to "dance" on top of the tungsten boat, resulting in intense evaporation. An unusual property of zinc is that, in the gas phase, its atoms can travel via both straight and curved trajectories (depending on the presence of any obstacles).

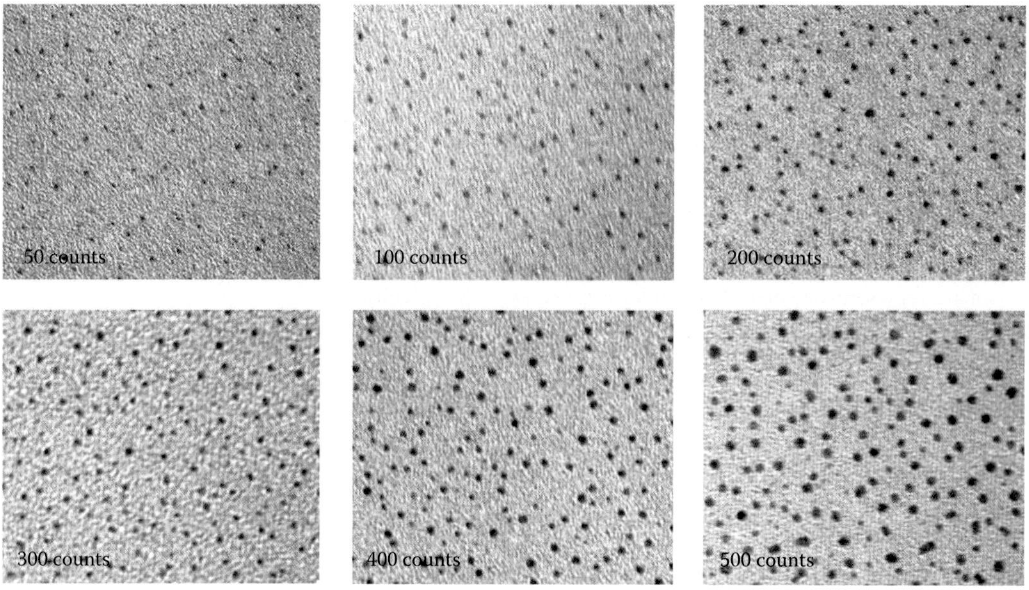

FIGURE 10.8
Gold agglomerates, formed by the VMD process, visualized by TEM imaging (for gold counts from 50 to 500; 500K magnification). (From Dai, X. et al., Vacuum metal deposition: Visualisation of gold agglomerates using TEM imaging, *Forensic Sci. Int.*, 168(2–3), 219, 2007. With permission from Elsevier.)

As a result, zinc deposition will occur even with the shutter closed; therefore, the shutter is not employed for the zinc evaporation step (i.e., it is left in the "open" position during the zinc treatment). Another unusual property of zinc is that its atoms do not deposit on non-metallic surfaces unless nucleation sites of another metal exist on the surface (or unless the surface is very cold). Therefore, creation of the correct size and shape for the gold nucleation sites (agglomerates) is of critical importance if optimum zinc deposition is to be obtained.

While the quantity of evaporated gold needs to be carefully controlled, the zinc deposition is allowed to proceed until good fingermark development is observed (in the case where fingermarks are present). The operator will generally monitor the surface during the course of the zinc treatment, with zinc evaporation halted when good development has been achieved. The quantity of zinc that needs to be evaporated will vary depending on the nature of the substrate.

10.3 VMD Development of Latent Fingermarks

10.3.1 General Principle

The VMD technique for the development of latent fingermarks on nonporous and semiporous surfaces involves evaporation and deposition, under high vacuum, of a small amount of gold and then a relatively large amount of zinc. The thin discontinuous gold layer that is formed during the first step acts as a catalyst, resulting in nucleation sites upon which zinc atoms can subsequently deposit, to build up a much thicker metallic layer during the second step. The discontinuous gold layer is only several atoms thick and is believed to penetrate the latent fingermark ridges. The zinc then deposits preferentially on the exposed gold but does

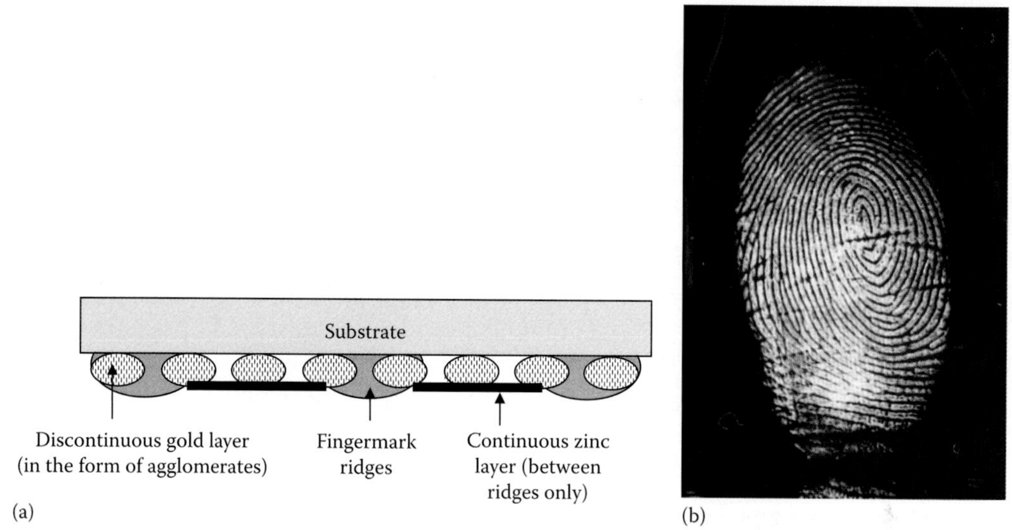

FIGURE 10.9
(a) Schematic representation and (b) example of "normal" VMD development.

not penetrate the fingerprint deposit—the ridges are therefore left transparent while the background becomes plated with a layer of metallic zinc that is silvery-grey in color (Figure 10.9). This is referred to as the "normal" fingermark development achieved by VMD treatment.

10.3.2 Types of Fingermark Development Achieved by VMD Treatment

Depending on the type of substrate and the amount of deposited gold, the following developments are possible: normal, reverse, overdevelopment, and empty prints. Each of these is described in the following.

10.3.2.1 Normal Development

A thick zinc layer covers the whole surface except for the fingermark ridges (Figure 10.9). The ridges are therefore transparent against a metallized (zinc) background. This occurs when the correct amount of gold is deposited for that type of surface. This is the type of fingermark development that is generally preferred where possible.

10.3.2.2 Overdevelopment

This may occur on certain types of surfaces (e.g., high-density polyethylene) when an excess amount of gold is deposited. The gold clusters over-grow the ridges and a continuous zinc layer is formed across the whole surface, covering both the substrate and the fingermark ridges (Figure 10.10). It is not possible to recover the fingermark once this has occurred.

10.3.2.3 Reverse Development

On some surface types (e.g., low-density polyethylene), a reduced attraction between the incoming gold atoms and the substrate results in the formation of a low concentration of large gold clusters (agglomerates) rather than a relatively high concentration of small gold

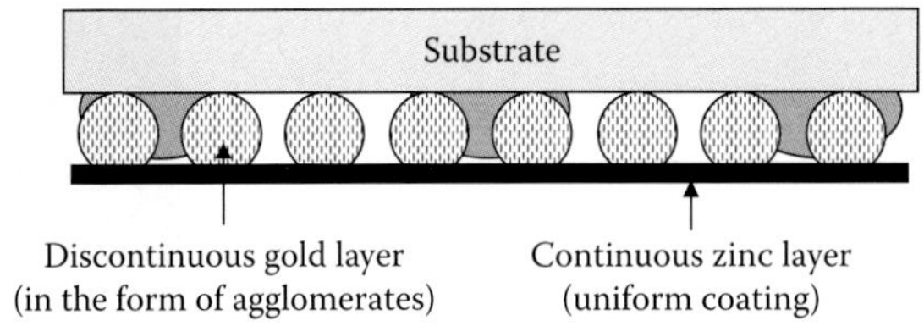

FIGURE 10.10
Schematic representation of VMD overdevelopment.

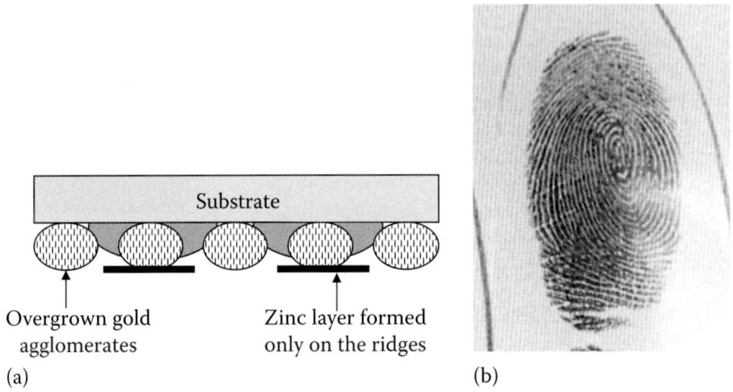

FIGURE 10.11
(a) Schematic representation and (b) example of "reverse" VMD development.

clusters. The larger clusters no longer have the morphology required to act as nucleating sites for zinc deposition and therefore zinc deposition is inhibited.

Reverse development occurs when these clusters overgrow the latent fingermark deposits to the extent that they can act as nucleating sites for zinc deposition along the ridges. The clusters on the substrate, however, are of a size and shape that prevent effective zinc deposition so no significant deposition occurs on the substrate itself (Figure 10.11).

Although reverse development results in ridge detail being revealed, this type of development should be avoided where possible. The main reason for this is that, with reverse development, the advantage of VMD with respect to covering background interference (such as heavy printing on polymer banknotes) with a layer of zinc is lost. In addition, if reverse development occurs after cyanoacrylate fuming, developed fingermarks can no longer be treated with a luminescent stain due to the zinc coating on the ridges.

10.3.2.4 Empty Prints

With fresh, heavy fingermark deposits, the VMD technique may fail to reveal any ridge detail. In these cases, zinc may deposit around the fingermark but not between the ridges (Figure 10.12). This results in an "empty" print (or "halo" effect). Recent research has indicated that, in such cases, fingermark detail may be revealed by subsequent vacuum deposition of silver metal [13].

10.3.3 VMD Development on Polyethylene Substrates

Polyethylene (or polythene) is a common, low-cost thermoplastic that is widely used in consumer products, particularly for the manufacture of plastic shopping bags. As such,

FIGURE 10.12
An example of "empty" fingermarks after VMD treatment.

polyethylene (PE) is frequently encountered as a substrate for the application for fingermark detection techniques. PE exists in various forms, with the most common being high-density polyethylene (HDPE) and low-density polyethylene (LDPE). In some cases, the type of polyethylene used to manufacture an item is specified (e.g., stamped or printed) on the item itself. Otherwise, it is possible to differentiate the two common forms of PE by infrared spectroscopy. The results obtained by VMD can vary significantly depending on the type of PE making up the item being treated [28].

10.3.3.1 High-Density Polyethylene

HDPE is composed of essentially linear PE polymers, with a low degree of branching. This results in a higher polymer density, with stronger intermolecular forces and increased tensile strength. Manufacturing applications include plastic film, water pipes, and rigid containers such as plastic bottles, garbage containers, and margarine tubs.

Jones and coworkers determined that, depending on the amount of deposited gold, there are three possibilities for latent fingermark development on HDPE by VMD: (i) normal development, (ii) overdevelopment, and (iii) weak development [28]. Using the VMD configuration and thickness monitor specified in their study, the three stages of development were encountered for the gold counts specified in Figure 10.13. For other configurations, experiments need to be conducted to determine these values.

It is critical that the initial gold treatment results in an amount of deposited gold that falls within the first region (normal development). If excess gold is deposited, then inferior fingermark development will result that cannot be recovered.

10.3.3.2 Low-Density Polyethylene

LDPE has a high degree of branching in the polymer structure. This results in lower density packing in the crystal structure, reduced intermolecular forces, a lower tensile strength, and increased ductility. Manufacturing applications include rigid containers and plastic film used for shopping and garbage bags, and film wrap.

It has been determined that, depending on the amount of deposited gold, there are three possibilities with respect to latent fingermark development on LDPE

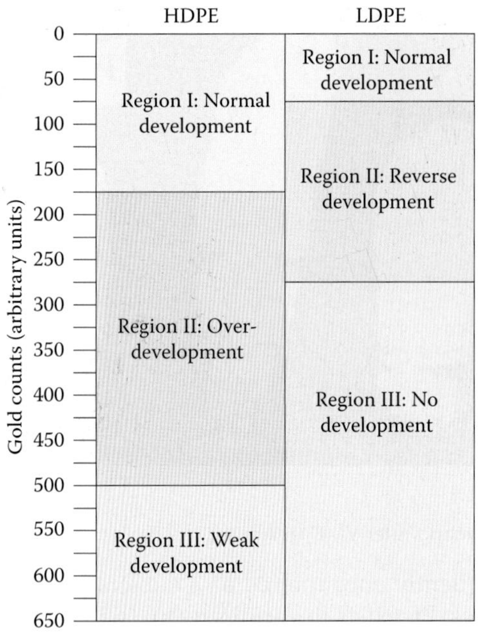

FIGURE 10.13
Variations in VMD development on HDPE and LDPE substrates according to the amount of evaporated gold (as measured in arbitrary gold counts).

by VMD: (i) normal development, (ii) reverse development, and (iii) no development [28]. For the VMD configuration and thickness monitor specified in the study, the three stages of development were encountered for the gold counts specified in Figure 10.13. If other instrument configurations are employed, experiments would need to be undertaken to determine the associated gold values.

Initial gold treatment should be designed to produce normal development (region I). If a slight excess of gold is deposited then this may result in reverse development (region II). This situation cannot be corrected but good fingermark detail may still result. If the amount of deposited gold is excessive, then no zinc deposition will occur in the second evaporation step (region III). In this case, the exhibit should be exposed to air. It has been shown that this deactivates the gold clusters created by the initial treatment [29]. The exhibit can then be retreated by VMD using the correct amount of gold for normal development.

10.3.4 Application of VMD on Various Polymer Substrates

The conditions employed for VMD development, particularly the amount of evaporated gold, should be selected based on the nature of the substrate. For plastic materials, it has been determined that the polymer type is the critical factor with respect to the type of VMD development that results [28,30]. In some cases, it may be necessary to determine the polymer type by infrared spectroscopy prior to undertaking the VMD treatment. Once the polymer type is known, the VMD conditions specific to that polymer can be selected to achieve optimum VMD development for any latent fingermarks that may be present.

The recommended initial "gold counts" (arbitrary units) specified in Table 10.1 are based on a particular VMD configuration and thickness monitor [28]. For other VMD systems, experiments should be conducted to determine these values. The values specified in this

TABLE 10.1

VMD Treatment on Various Polymer Substrates with Recommended Initial Gold Counts (Arbitrary Units) for Optimum Fingermark Development

Polymer Substrate	Applications (Examples Only)	Recommended Initial Gold Counts (Arbitrary Units)	Expected Types of Development (with Increasing Gold Counts)	Comments
Low-density polyethylene (LDPE)	Rigid containers and plastic film used for shopping and garbage bags, and film wrap	30	Normal development Reverse development No development	If high gold counts have been used (>500) and no development occurs, then this can be corrected by opening the chamber. The VMD treatment is then repeated using a gold count of 45
High-density polyethylene (HDPE)	Plastic film, water pipes, and rigid containers such as plastic bottles, garbage containers, and margarine tubs	5–50	Normal development (may be weak at low gold counts) Overdevelopment Weak development	Different forms of HDPE have been found to produce normal development with different gold counts. Some forms (generally thin, clear samples) develop well with low gold counts, while others (generally thick, colored samples) require higher gold counts. The initial gold count can be set to five but if no zinc deposits then the amount of deposited gold should be increased
Polypropylene (PP)	Packaging materials, plastic parts, and reusable containers of various types	10	Empty prints Normal development Overdevelopment	The occurrence of empty prints may be minimized by the use of cyanoacrylate fuming prior to VMD treatment
Polyvinyl chloride (PVC)	Upholstery, hoses, tubing, flooring, and electrical cable insulation (e.g., electrical tape)	500 (after CA fuming)	Empty prints Normal development	The occurrence of empty prints may be minimized by the use of cyanoacrylate fuming prior to VMD treatment
Polyethylene terephthalate (PET)	Plastic containers for food, beverages and other liquids (e.g., plastic water and soft drink bottles)	250 (after CA fuming)	Empty prints Normal development	The occurrence of empty prints may be minimized by the use of cyanoacrylate fuming prior to VMD treatment
Polymer banknotes (PP base)	In use in 18 countries including Australia and New Zealand	100 (after CA fuming)	Normal development	It is recommended that the banknotes are fumed with cyanoacrylate, stained (Basic Yellow 40) and examined prior to VMD treatment

table are for the initial gold treatment. If, during the zinc evaporation step, a zinc layer does not form on the substrate (or an acceptable "reverse" development is not obtained), then the item should be retreated with gold. This second gold treatment should be 1.5 times the initial treatment if the chamber has not been opened and twice the initial recommended gold count if the items have been exposed to air. This is further explained in the following section.

10.3.5 Multiple VMD Treatments

Even if the correct amount of gold has been deposited on the substrate during the first stage of the treatment, this does not necessarily guarantee optimum fingermark development. Poor zinc deposition generally means that the gold agglomerates that have formed on the substrate are not of an appropriate size and shape to be effective in trapping the zinc atoms. In such instances, multiple VMD treatments are recommended. However, it must be recognized that the zinc treatment, whether effective or not, will have an impact on subsequent gold deposition [29]. Some zinc deposition will occur, which covers and inactivates the gold layer. For this reason, it is recommended that any subsequent VMD treatment—provided that the chamber has not been opened—uses gold counts that are 1.5 times that of the previous treatment.

If, after VMD treatment, the chamber is opened and the exhibits exposed to air, then other factors need to be taken into consideration. At least some of the zinc deposited on the substrate will be oxidized to zinc oxide, and moisture will also deposit on the surface (due to ambient humidity). These two effects deactivate the gold clusters that are already present. Any subsequent gold treatment then generally results in the formation of new gold clusters rather than adding to existing ones [29]. As a result of this phenomenon, the gold counts in any subsequent VMD treatment have to be twice that of the previous treatment.

10.3.6 Impact of Prior Cyanoacrylate Fuming and Staining

VMD is sensitive to all surface contamination, not just to fingermarks, and so any treatment applied to an exhibit prior to VMD can have some impact on the development. Cyanoacrylate (CA) fuming and staining are routine techniques that are commonly used on nonporous surfaces and so are likely to be applied prior to VMD. Both of these treatments (CA fuming and staining) can dramatically change the VMD conditions required for optimum fingermark development.

Cyanoacrylate fuming generally results in at least some cyanoacrylate polymer being formed on the general surface of a treated item (e.g., due to surface moisture) as well as on the fingermark ridges themselves. There is a strong indication that this cyanoacrylate polymer behaves in a similar fashion to a LDPE surface. Therefore, the required VMD conditions after cyanoacrylate fuming may be totally different to those recommended for the original polymer substrate. Similarly, the application of a cyanoacrylate stain (or any other surface treatment) prior to VMD processing may impact on the results obtained. In some cases, experiments may need to be conducted on a similar surface to determine the best treatment sequence and the VMD conditions required for optimum development.

10.3.7 Impact of Surface Contamination

Exhibits are sometimes submitted for VMD treatment that are contaminated with substances such as soil, salt (e.g., from seawater), illicit drugs (e.g., powder coating on plastic bags), fingerprint powder, or body fluids such as blood. It is recommended that these exhibits are gently soaked in fresh, cold water for several hours, with the water changed frequently. The exhibits should then be rinsed in distilled or deionized water and then allowed to dry at room temperature for at least 24h.

Note that exhibits heavily contaminated with blood or other body fluids may exude methane gas that may prevent the achievement of an adequate vacuum in the deposition chamber of the VMD. Methane gas is not detected by the vacuum gauges; the vacuum gauges may therefore indicate that a satisfactory vacuum has been achieved when this is actually not the case (and therefore metal deposition is inhibited). It is therefore recommended, with such exhibits, that

- A test latent fingermark is deposited on a similar surface and placed next to the exhibit so that it can be monitored for satisfactory VMD development
- The exhibit is allowed to de-gas in the vacuum chamber for at least 24h before commencement of the metal deposition process

10.3.8 Impact of Fingermark Quality and Age

The "strength" of the fingermark deposit will also have an impact on the development achieved by VMD. With heavy fingermark deposits (e.g., high sebaceous content), particularly when fresh, inadequate fingermark detail may result from initial VMD treatment (with "empty" prints observed in some cases, due to residues being present in the fingermark valleys as well as along the ridges). Higher gold counts are required in these instances to achieve good development. In contrast, weaker or older fingermarks will consist of a thinner deposit that may lead to overdevelopment during the VMD process. If the fingermarks being sought are likely to have been aged over a significant period of time, then it is recommended that the initial VMD treatment is undertaken using a lower gold count than might otherwise be applied. Multiple VMD treatments can then be employed as required.

10.4 Conclusions

There is no doubt that VMD, when applied correctly, is probably the most sensitive fingermark detection technique currently available for nonporous surfaces, such as plastic substrates. Optimum development by this method, however, requires an appropriately configured VMD chamber (with a thickness monitor and shutter highly recommended), and an operator experienced in applying the technique on a range of different surfaces. Research conducted over the last 10 years has confirmed that the results obtained by VMD treatment on polymer substrates is highly dependent on the polymer type and on the amount of gold deposited during the first step of the process (i.e., prior to subsequent zinc deposition). Optimum results can therefore only be obtained if the polymer type is identified and if the amount of deposited gold is carefully monitored to ensure that it is appropriate for the substrate being treated.

For operational reasons, VMD users may choose to employ a "standard" set of conditions for the treatment of exhibits. This may achieve satisfactory results in most cases, but may also lead to reverse development, "empty" prints, over-development, or no development depending on the exact nature of the evidential item.

The high capital costs and labor-intensive nature of the VMD treatment generally negate its use for routine casework. As a result, and where the technique is available, it is generally reserved for high-profile casework.

Authors

Milutin Stoilovic obtained his bachelor's and master's degrees at the University of Belgrade, Belgrade, Serbia. In 1980, he migrated to Australia. From 1980 to 1989, Milutin was involved in fingerprint research at the Australian National University, Canberra, Australian Capital Territory, Australia. This research led to the development of a forensic light source that was subsequently commercialized by Rofin Australia as the Polilight. In 1990, Milutin joined the Australian Federal Police (AFP) where, among other duties, he continued his fingerprint research. This included designing a vacuum metal deposition (VMD) unit for the AFP that was built in Melbourne by the company Dynavac Milutin is now retired from AFP.

Naomi Speers completed a doctor of philosophy in science at the University of Technology Sydney in 2002. Her thesis focused on metal deposition techniques for the development of latent fingerprints on semiporous surfaces. Since completing her PhD, Naomi has worked within the Chemical Criminalistics team, Forensic and Data Centres, Australian Federal Police, where she is currently the team leader.

Chris Lennard has a PhD in chemistry from the Australian National University (1986) for research on the chemical detection of fingermarks. After completing his PhD, he undertook postdoctoral work at the School of Forensic Science, University of Lausanne (Switzerland), where he gained the position of associate professor in criminalistics in 1989. He returned to Australia in 1994 to take up a position with Forensic Services, Australian Federal Police (AFP). Chris left the AFP in October 2006 to take up his current position as professor of forensic studies at the University of Canberra, where he is head of the forensic studies discipline.

References

1. Kent T. (1990) Recent research on superglue, vacuum metal deposition and fluorescence examination. Home Office Police Scientific Development Branch, Sandridge, U.K.
2. Masters NE, DeHaan JD. (1996) Vacuum metal deposition and cyanoacrylate detection of older latent prints. *J Forensic Ident* 46(1):32–45.
3. Misner AH. (1992) Latent fingerprint detection on low density polyethylene comparing vacuum metal deposition to cyanoacrylate fuming and fluorescence. *J Forensic Ident* 42(1):26–33.
4. Batey GW, Copeland J, Donnelly DL, Hill CL, Laturnus PL, McDiarmid CH, Miller KL, Misner AH, Tario A, Yamashita AB. (1998) Metal deposition for latent print development. *J Forensic Ident* 48(2):165–175.
5. Jones N, Kelly M, Stoilovic M, Lennard C, Roux C. (2003) The development of latent fingerprints on polymer banknotes. *J Forensic Ident* 53(1):50–77.

6. Holland L. (1956) *Vacuum Deposition of Thin Films*. Chapman & Hall Ltd., London, U.K.
7. Wells O. (1974) *Scanning Electron Microscopy*. McGraw-Hill, New York.
8. Theys P, Turgis Y, Lepareux A, Chevet G, Ceccaldi P. (1968) New technique for bringing out latent fingerprints on paper: Vacuum metallisation. *Int Criminal Pol Rev* 217:106–108.
9. Thomas G. (1978) The physics of fingerprints and their detection. *J Phys E Sci Instrum* 11:722–731.
10. Kent T, Thomas GL, Reynoldson TE, East HW. (1976) A vacuum coating technique for the development of latent fingerprints on polyethylene. *J Forensic Sci Soc* 16:93–100.
11. Kent T. (1981) Latent fingerprints and their detection. *J Forensic Sci Soc* 21:15–22.
12. Godsell J. (1972) Fingermarks—use of radio-active gas and vacuum metal deposition for the development of latent fingermarks on paper and fabric. *Pol Res Bull* 19:16–21.
13. Philipson D, Bleay S. (2007) Alternative metal processes for vacuum metal deposition. *J Forensic Ident* 57(2):252–273.
14. Gunaratne A, Knaggs C, Stansbury D. (2007) Vacuum metal deposition: Comparing conventional gold/zinc VMD to aluminium VMD. *Ident Canada* 30(2):40–62.
15. Yu I-H, Jou S, Chen C-M, Wang K-C, Pang L-J, Liao JS. (2011) Development of latent fingerprint by ZnO deposition. *Forensic Sci Int* 207(1–3):14–18.
16. Fraser J, Sturrock K, Deacon P, Bleay S, Bremner DH. (2011) Visualisation of fingermarks and grab impressions on fabrics. Part 1: Gold–zinc vacuum metal deposition. *Forensic Sci Int* 208(1–3):74–78.
17. Kent T, Gillett P, Lee D. (1978) A comparative study of three techniques; aluminium powdering, lead powdering and metal deposition for the development of latent fingerprints on polythene. Technical Memorandum 6/78. Home Office Police Scientific Development Branch, Sandridge, U.K.
18. Reynoldson TE, Reed FA. (1979) Operational trial comparing metal deposition with small particle reagent for the development of latent fingerprints on polythene. Technical Memorandum 16/79. Home Office Police Scientific Development Branch, Sandridge, U.K.
19. Ramsland K. (2007). *Inside the Minds of Healthcare Serial Killers: Why They Kill*. Praeger Publishing, Westport, CT.
20. Bradshaw G, Bleay S, Deans J, Nic Daéid N. (2008) Recovery of fingerprints from arson scenes: Part 1—latent fingerprints. *J Forensic Ident* 58(1):54–82.
21. Moore J, Bleay S, Deans J, Nic Daéid N. (2008) Recovery of fingerprints from arson scenes: Part 2—fingermarks in blood. *J Forensic Ident* 58(1):83–108.
22. http://www.noteprinting.com/banknotes.html (accessed October 5, 2011).
23. Flynn J, Stoilovic M, Lennard C. (1999) The detection and enhancement of latent fingerprints on polymer banknotes: A preliminary study. *J Forensic Ident* 49(6):594–613.
24. Suzuki S, Suzuki Y, Ohta H. (2002) Detection of latent fingerprints on newly developed substances using the vacuum metal deposition method. *J Forensic Ident* 52(5):573–578.
25. Jones N, Lennard C, Stoilovic M, Roux C. (2003) An evaluation of multimetal deposition II. *J Forensic Ident* 53(4):444–488.
26. Nic Daéid N, Carter S, Laing K. (2008) Comparison of vacuum metal deposition and powder suspension for recovery of fingerprints on wetted nonporous surfaces. *J Forensic Ident* 58(5):600–613.
27. Dai X, Stoilovic M, Lennard C, Speers N. (2007) Vacuum metal deposition: Visualisation of gold agglomerates using TEM imaging. *Forensic Sci Int* 168(2–3):219–222.
28. Jones N, Stoilovic M, Lennard C, Roux C. (2001) Vacuum metal deposition: Factors affecting normal and reverse development of latent fingerprints on polyethylene substrates. *Forensic Sci Int* 115(1–2):73–88.
29. Jones N, Stoilovic M, Lennard C, Roux C. (2001) Vacuum metal deposition: Developing latent fingerprints on polyethylene substrates after the deposition of excess gold. *Forensic Sci Int* 123(1):5–12.
30. Jones N, Mansour D, Stoilovic M, Lennard C, Roux C. (2001) The influence of polymer type, print donor and age on the quality of fingerprints developed on plastic substrates using vacuum metal deposition. *Forensic Sci Int* 124(2–3):167–177.

11

Cyanoacrylate Fuming Method

Linda A. Lewis

CONTENTS

11.1 Introduction

Since the initial reporting of the cyanoacrylate (Super Glue) fuming method (CFM) in the United States in 1982, the method has become the prominent means of detecting latent fingerprints on nonporous surfaces. Over the years, the technique has performed well; however, under various conditions, latent fingerprints could not be detected on items that were known to contain fingerprints. Specifically, nonporous items such as ammunition, guns, knives, and other metallic weapons were known to be more difficult to develop latent fingerprints using the CFM. Additionally, items aged under various conditions, such as solar-exposed or arid environments, proved difficult to yield latent fingerprints with this method. The specifics associated with protocols for developing latent fingerprints by CFM have been thoroughly detailed in *Advances in Fingerprint Technology*, 2nd edition [1]. Since the publication of this edition, several studies have been conducted with the aim of understanding the chemical polymerization mechanism, developing methods for improving fingerprint quality, and understanding shortfalls associated with the cyanoacrylate fuming method [2–5]. In this chapter, the current understanding of the chemistry associated with CFM, as well as the chemical nature of fingerprints in relation to the fuming technique, will be emphasized. The overall goal is to convey the technique from a chemical perspective with the aspiration of inspiring future research aimed at further understanding and optimizing the method with respect to high detection efficiency and print quality.

11.2 Origin of the Cyanoacrylates and the Cyanoacrylate Fuming Method for Latent Fingerprint Detection

Cyanoacrylate esters were first synthesized by Dr. Harry Coover in 1949, while working for Kodak Laboratories in an initiative to develop an optically clear plastic to support the production of precision gunsights [6]. Coover was frustrated by the fact that cyanoacrylates stuck to everything, but did not fully recognize its adhesive potential until 1951, when he was overseeing research to identify a stronger, heat-resistant acrylate polymer for jet-plane canopies. During this initiative, one of his research students synthesized ethyl cyanoacrylate, and was soon faced with a dilemma when unable to separate the two very expensive prisms used to make a refractive index measurement on the material. At this point, Coover realized that they had produced a very powerful adhesive, commonly referred to today as Super Glue or superglue. Apparently, the term "Super Glue" was not accepted as a trademark due to the general use of the name to describe any strong adhesive.

The CFM for latent fingerprint detection has been reported to have been almost simultaneously discovered in the late 1970s by independent researchers in the United Kingdom, Japan, and Canada. Shortly thereafter, two latent fingerprint examiners from the U.S. Army Criminal Investigation Laboratory (USACIL) and a laser expert from the Bureau of Alcohol, Tobacco, and Firearms (ATF) transitioned the method to the United States [7,8].

Masato Soba, an employee of the Saga Prefectural Crime Laboratory (SPCL) of the National Police Agency (NPA) of Japan, was the first latent print examiner to intentionally use the CFM to detect fingerprints. The glue application was learned from a SPCL hair and fiber expert, Fuseo Matsumura, who initially discovered his own fingerprints being developed on microscope slides while mounting hairs with cyanoacrylate [7].

In September 1979, two U.S. Army Crime Lab fingerprint experts, Paul Norkus and Ed German, assigned to work American military cases while stationed at Kanagawa-ken in the western suburbs of Tokyo, were introduced to the CFM at NPA. During a U.S. Air Force murder trial, Norkus and German visited the Identification Division Research Office of the NPA. During their visit, they observed a fuming method (cyanoacrylate) demonstration for latent fingerprint development on nonporous surfaces. The Japanese hosts would not give Norkus and German the name of the chemical used to develop the fingerprints. However, unknown to the host, German was able to read the Katakana writing on the bottle, note the words, and soon after discover that the name referred to a superglue product. While in Japan, Norkus and German experimented with developing latent fingerprints using this method, and in 1980 upon their return to USACIL near Atlanta, Georgia, continued their superglue fuming experiments. At that time, the USACIL had the only laser in the Georgia area, and Frank Kendall at the Atlanta ATF Laboratory routinely used the laser to examined evidence. When Kendall learned about the CFM at the Army Crime Lab, it was conducted on small items without heat or other acceleration. After understanding the basic approach, Kendall continued optimizing the procedure and soon published his findings on the CFM [8]. Initially, latent prints were developed at ambient temperature and pressure through exposure to low concentrations of the cyanoacrylate vapors within an enclosure, such as a fish tank. Print development using this technique required long exposure times, and often produced a high background of polymer. Several research articles aimed at reducing exposure times followed [9–13]. Kendall and Rehn published an article detailing a rapid method of superglue fuming using absorbent cotton and sodium hydroxide as a means to accelerate the fuming process and reduce the development time to approximately 1 h [10]. Around the same time, several reports described the use of heat as a means of accelerating the fuming process [12,13]. To date, heat fuming of the cyanoacrylate ester, in an aluminum container, which also acts as a polymerization retardant [14], remains a widely used method for developing latent prints. When using this method, a lower amount of time is actually required to develop a latent print without the buildup of a polymer background. Latent fingerprints developed by the Federal Bureau of Investigation's (FBI) Latent Print Unit have been processed using the "microburst method." When using this technique, the cyanoacrylate ester is heated in a small chamber at a hot temperature (approximately 400°C) to quickly produce a high concentration of the cyanoacrylate vapor [15]. A piece of evidence is repeatedly placed in the fuming chamber and developed for 30 s periods, for a maximum time of 2 min, until the prints are developed. The "microburst method" allows the ridges of the latent print to be developed at a maximum rate, while maintaining a low background of polymer.

Vacuum deposition is an alternative method for developing latent prints with the cyanoacrylate ester in the absence of heat [16,17]. When using vacuum deposition, the cyanoacrylate ester is placed inside of a vacuum chamber along with the item to be fumed. With a vacuum pump, the pressure inside of the closed system is reduced to approximately 1 torr. Once the desired pressure is achieved, the container is sealed, allowing the cyanoacrylate ester to vaporize at room temperature under reduced pressure. Prints developed by vacuum deposition tend to be translucent, requiring a secondary treatment, such as fluorescent-dye staining for print visualization [17].

Since the CFM was first reported, it has become one of the main techniques used to develop latent fingerprints on nonporous evidence including glass, metal, coated papers, and many types of plastics (predominately using the methyl or ethyl cyanoacrylates). Until recently, the underlying chemistry of how the CFM actually worked for the development of latent fingerprints was not well understood and the refinement of the CFM, such as understanding humidity requirements, acceleration methods, etc., was discovered empirically. While these empirical improvements helped mature the technology to support forensic investigations, a purely empirical development approach limits technical advancements. In order to optimize the method to the true potential, one must possess a molecular-level understanding of the chemistry, with regard to the polymerization process, latent fingerprint composition, and reaction kinetics, as well as physical properties such as vapor transport, temperature, and deposition surface. Since around 2001, several research efforts have been made with the aim of understanding the underlying chemistry and physical processes involved in the successful development latent fingerprints by the CFM [2–5]. A better understanding of these parameters is emerging, with the goal of optimizing the CFM into an even more robust method that consistently yields good quality prints in support of fingerprint biometric examinations.

11.3 Polymerization Mechanism of Cyanoacrylate Esters

Prior to moving on to an assessment of parameters that affect CFM developed latent print quality and quantity, it is essential to first evaluate the superglue polymerization steps and mechanisms. During a polymerization process, three major steps are involved: (1) initiation, (2) propagation, and (3) termination. Prior to going into the detail of these three steps, the terms nucleophile and electrophile will be briefly covered. In chemistry, a nucleophile is an electron-rich reagent that is attracted to and forms a chemical bond with a second reagent that is electron-deficient (the electrophile). The nucleophile donates both bonding electrons to the electrophile, and the two reagents form a strong covalent bond [18]. Since a nucleophile donates both bonding electrons, it is by definition a Lewis base. All molecules or ions with a free pair of electrons, including alcohol and water, can act as a nucleophile. The degree of nucleophile/electrophile or Lewis base/Lewis acid strength can be classified from hard to soft, with hard representing a much stronger electronegative reagent for a nucleophile/base or electropositive reagent for an electrophile/acid than that of soft or weakly charged reagent. From this perspective, soft nucleophiles include I^-, RS^-, RSH, alkenes; hard nucleophiles include H_2O, OH^-, Cl^-; and medium-hard nucleophiles include RNH_2, Br^-, as well as anions of amino acids, fatty acids, proteins, and small acids such as lactic acid [19].

In the case of CFM, the cyanoacrylate is an electrophile due to the presence of a carbon double bond, and is subjected to attack by a nucleophile (Lewis base). In a cyanoacrylate mechanism proposed by de Puit et al., the nucleophilic attack is not a 1,2-addition found in the mechanism of hard nucleophiles, nor the 1,4-conjugate addition found in the mechanism of soft nucleophiles, due to steric hindrance issues. The reaction is thus *initiated* by a medium-hard nucleophile, in which the nucleophile attacks the first carbon containing the double bond, with an electron transferring to the double-bonded oxygen as illustrated in Figure 11.1. The negative charge is then held at the second carbon and distributed between the cyano and ester groups [19].

Water is classified as a hard nucleophile, and is actually more of an acid or a base then a nucleophile as illustrated in Figure 11.2 [19]. In the proposed mechanism, water actually serves as a catalyst for the polymerization process, and as such is not consumed, with the

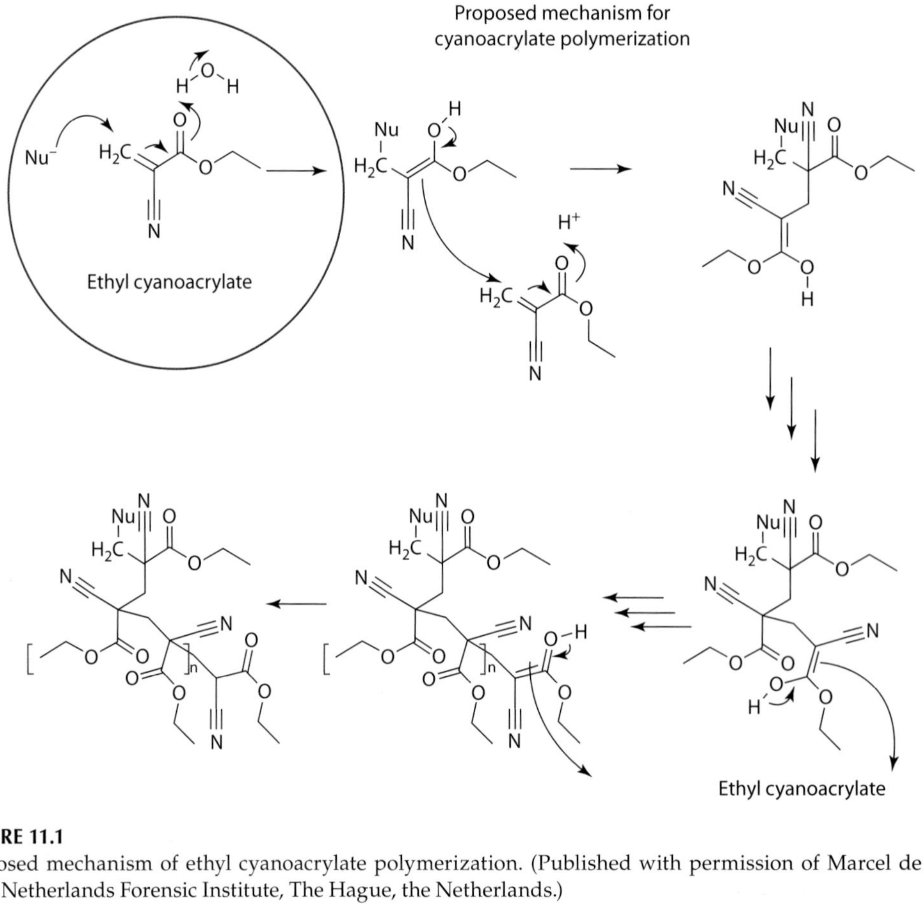

FIGURE 11.1
Proposed mechanism of ethyl cyanoacrylate polymerization. (Published with permission of Marcel de Puit, PhD, Netherlands Forensic Institute, The Hague, the Netherlands.)

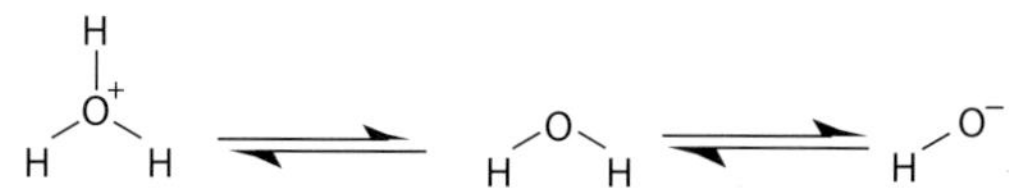

FIGURE 11.2
Illustration of the acidic and basic forms of water.

amount of water present at the reaction onset being equal to the amount present at the end of the reaction. The growing cyanoacrylate polymer in turn serves as the nucleophile, and continues to *propagate* the polymerization by attacking the cyanoacrylate monomer, until the reaction is *terminated* when one of two conditions occur. Either the monomer supply is exhausted or the propagating anion collides with a terminating agent, such as a positively charged hydrogen ion.

The exact mechanism for the vapor-phase CFM has not been confirmed to date, but research is ongoing to provide a definitive description of the overall process, to include fingerprint components capable of initiating the cyanoacrylate polymerization. The topic of nucleophiles capable of initiating the cyanoacrylate polymerization will be further discussed within the context of this chapter. Although the vapor-phase mechanism has not yet been fully identified, a thorough study of solution-based polymerization of cyanoacrylates has been reported in the literature [20–26]. While the cyanoacrylates polymerize anionically, the unique chemical structure, with the cyano and acrylate group adjacent to the vinyl group, produces a very stable anion postinitiation, stable to the point that the polymer is considered "living" in that the negative charge can be held for extensive periods of time [21,23,27]. It is known that the presence of acids affects the polymerization, where strong acids are used as stabilizers to prevent cyanoacrylate polymerization; however, cyanoacrylates in the presence of protons or weaker acids lead to the formation of lower molecular weight oligomers or polymers without completely stopping the polymerization process [24,27–29].

11.4 Parameters Relevant to Cyanoacrylate Fuming

Although cyanoacrylate fuming has proven to be an extremely successful method for developing latent fingerprints, problems continued to be encountered with the application of the CFM on evidence due to several factors, including (1) the original composition of the latent fingerprint not being optimum for the CFM after aging, (2) the print being exposed to environmental conditions leading to an inability to detect the presence of a latent print, and (3) nonideal chemical and physical parameters set during the CFM. For these reasons, several research efforts have been conducted with the aim of understanding latent print composition and decomposition processes, molecular level mechanisms, critical CFM development parameters that affect the ability to successfully detect the presence of a latent fingerprint, and the quality of the developed print.

11.4.1 Fingerprint Composition in Relation to the CFM

Two fingerprint composition extremes have been reported: clean and oily prints [2]. Clean prints represent the latent material deposited by a child or an individual with freshly cleaned hands, and oily prints represent the latent material deposited by an individual with sebum-coated fingers. Ideally, clean prints contain components of eccrine sweat, where oily prints contain sebaceous sweat mixed with the eccrine secretions on the finger/

palm. The morphologies of fresh and aged CFM developed clean and oily latent prints have proven to be vastly different, as illustrated in the scanning electron microscopic (SEM) images given in Figures 11.3 and 11.4. Fumed fresh prints, clean and oily, yield a visible, grainy-white polymer on the ridges of the print. The polymerized print ridges are high in contrast, especially when developed on a dark surface, compared to the furrow

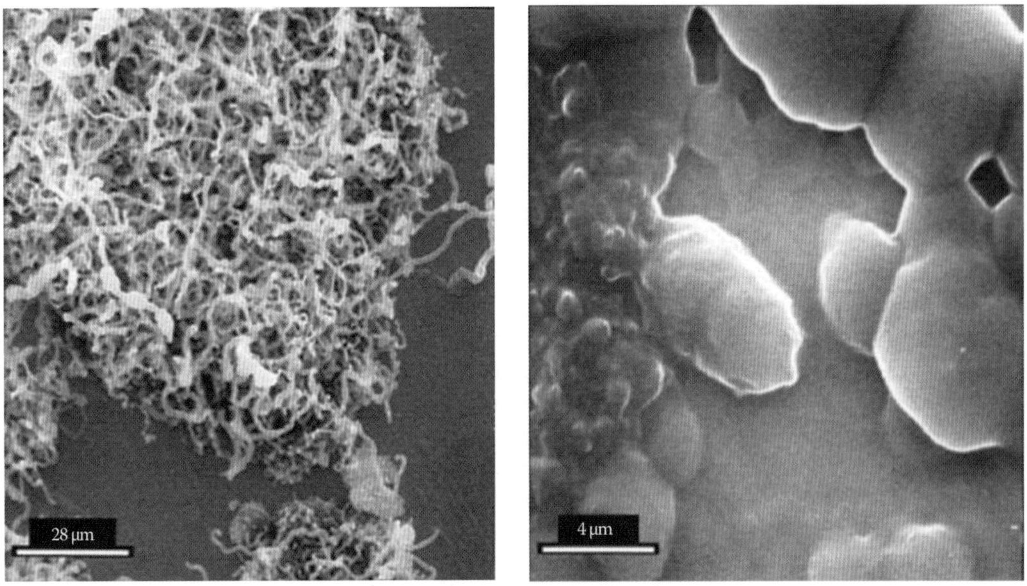

(a) (b)

FIGURE 11.3
SEM images of (a) freshly deposited and (b) 2 day old clean (eccrine) prints prior to development by CFM. (Reprinted from Lewis, L.A. et al., *J. Forensic Sci.*, 46(2), 243, 2001.)

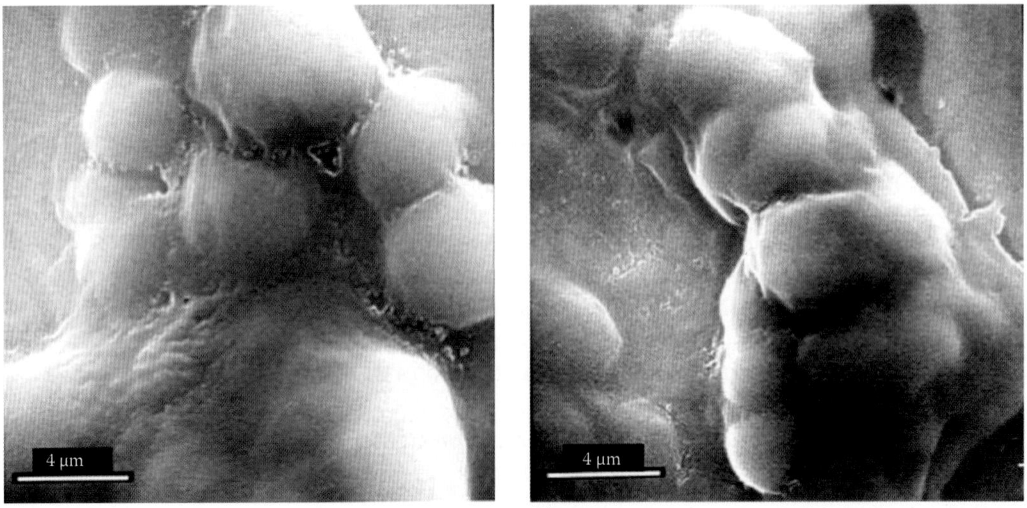

(a) (b)

FIGURE 11.4
SEM images of (a) freshly deposited and (b) 2 day old oily (sebaceous) prints prior to development by CFM. (Reprinted from Lewis, L.A. et al., *J. Forensic Sci.*, 46(2), 243, 2001.)

and background regions. Aged prints tend to lose the grainy-white appearance (especially aged clean prints), and become more translucent, which greatly reduces the visible contrast between the ridge and background areas.

In the case of the clean print, a noodle-like structure is consistently obtained from a freshly deposited and developed print. Such a structure is very effective in scattering light, thus making the print visible. SEM images of how the clean-print noodle structures are formed and developed were captured for fuming intervals of 20–120 s. The polymer formations are first initiated within a 20 s. period, as can be seen in Figure 11.5a. Once the base of the polymer structure is formed, the noodle-type structure grows very rapidly. After polymer initiation, Figure 11.5b through 11.5d suggests that the process is completed within 45–120 s.

Gel permeation chromatography (GPC) analysis of the clean-print polymer structures, dissolved in THF, revealed three distinct molecular weight ranges including a 2,000, 100,000, and >100,000 distribution [2]. The 100,000 and >100,000 distributions would be consistent with the long noodle-type structure illustrated in Figure 11.5 whereas, the 2,000

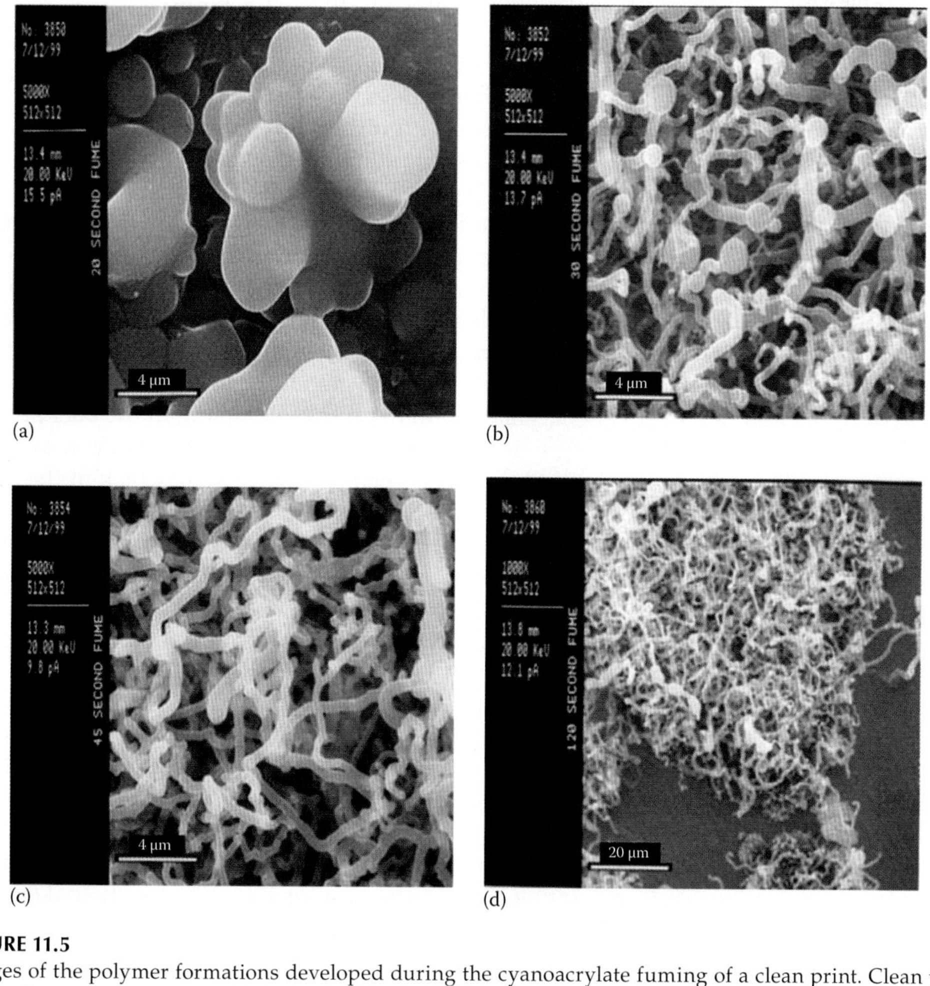

FIGURE 11.5
Images of the polymer formations developed during the cyanoacrylate fuming of a clean print. Clean print exposed to cyanoacrylate vapors for (a) 20 s, (b) 30 s, (c) 45 s, and (d) 120 s. (Reprinted from Lewis, L.A. et al., *J. Forensic Sci.*, 46(2), 243, 2001.)

distribution may be attributed to the spherical structures that are carried by the developing polymers in Figure 11.5b, as well as by a smaller portion of the structures in Figure 11.5d. Figure 11.5 appears to give some insight into how the polymers formed on clean prints progress in the vapor phase. In the case where the clean prints were aged 48 h in the laboratory prior to development, the polymer morphology changes as can be seen in Figure 11.3b, in a manner that results in the absence of the noodle structure, leading to a visibly translucent ridge.

In the case of the oily print, nodules are the representative structure obtained from CFM developed prints. In Figure 11.4, the nodule size in the fresh print ranges from 3 to 6 μm, and the 2 day old sphere size ranges from 2 to 4 μm. GPC results were consistent with the 100,000 and >100,000 molecular weight distributions of the clean-print noodle structure (excluding the 2000 molecular weight distribution thought to correlate with the spherical structure at the visible end of the noodle) [2]. Due to the high solubility of the cyanoacrylate monomer in sebum, the consistent nodule formation for oily prints, as opposed to noodles in fresh clean prints, may be a result of the monomer collecting in the sebaceous deposit prior to polymer initiation, thus leading to a solution-based polymerization.

Upon oily print aging prior to development, the structures in the Figure 11.4b SEM image remain, but some ridge/polymer shrinkage can be detected. Aged, oily prints were found to be distinguishable for prints 6 months and older when aged prior to fuming. The ability to develop good quality oily prints, older than 2 days, may be attributed to the presence of fatty acids and mono- and diacyl glycerols within the sebaceous material of the print [2]. These components have the potential to hold moisture within the print residue and to prevent dehydration. A mechanism has been proposed in which free fatty acids and mono- and diacyl glycerols, from the surface sebum, help retain moisture in skin through the formation of thin-film barriers, thus delaying evaporation. In addition, the presence of mono- and diacyl glycerols, as well as glycerol, released during hydrolysis of the triacyl glycerols helps to retain moisture in skin due to their hygroscopic nature. The presence of hygroscopic material within the oily latent print could explain the improved quality of cyanoacrylate developed aged oily prints fumed at elevated humidity levels.

The first indication that the cyanoacrylate monomer was condensing in the background regions during cyanoacrylate fuming was noted in Figure 11.6. The planchet containing a fresh oily print was etched prior to SEM analysis. The etching caused a crack in the clear, groove area on the opposite side of the disk. Apparently, the cyanoacrylate vapor condensed on the cooler background regions during fuming, accumulating at a rate slower than that of the propagating polymer on the print ridge. Figure 11.6 is a good illustration of the fact that overexposure to the cyanoacrylate vapor will only lead to the background being developed to a point in which the latent print may become obscured.

In early experiments designed to understand the cyanoacrylate polymerization initiators, it was determined that an oily fingerprint could be soaked in either water or chloroform, dried prior to CFM development, and developed to yield a firm polymer print from the chloroform-soaked print and a nonrigid liquid mixture from the water-soaked print [2]. At that time, it was established that the water leached out the polymerization initiators from the oily fingerprint, inhibiting polymerization. A large amount of the cyanoacrylate monomer did accumulate in the remaining sebaceous components, indicating a high monomer solubility in sebum, but did not polymerize. In the case of the chloroform-soaked oily print, a very good firm polymer ridge was formed; thus, the initiating species were not extracted from the print ridge during the chloroform soaking. During the early experiments, numerous water soluble eccrine-based, single-constituent solutions were exposed to cyanoacrylate vapors to determine what chemical classes were capable of initiating the

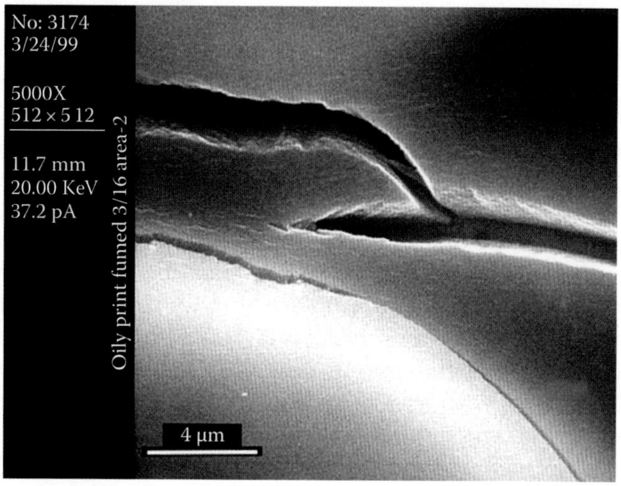

FIGURE 11.6
Oily print developed by the CFM. A crack in the print furrow indicates that the cyanoacrylate ester was also deposited on the background regions. The ridges of the latent print are polymerized at a faster rate than the background due to the polymer growth process during fuming. (Reprinted from Lewis, L.A. et al., *J. Forensic Sci.*, 46(2), 243, 2001.)

cyaloacrylate polymer. For some of the materials that did form polymers, the molecular weights were analyzed by GPC and SEM imaging. During these experiments, it was confirmed that lactate and amino acids are two chemical classes capable of initiating polymerization. This fact supports the medium-hard nucleophilic initiation of the cyanoacrylates proposed by de Puit et al. [19].

Significant differences have also been noted between clean and oily fingerprint compositions [2,30–37]. Only eccrine glands are located on the palm and finger regions. Eccrine sweat is largely comprised of water with traces of salts, free amino acids, sodium lactate, urea, mucoproteins (mucin-type glycoproteins) [34–36], and ammonia, but does not contain a significant quantity of lipid material [37]. Most of the lipids on the skin surface come from sebaceous glands [33]. Surface lipids are reported to contain squalene (10%), sterol esters (2.5%), sterols (1.5%), wax esters (22%), triacyl glycerols (25%), di- and monoacyl glycerols (10%), unesterified fatty acids (25%), and 4% unidentified constituents. Sebaceous glands are not located within the finger/palm regions of the hands; however, sebaceous material is a typical composition of a latent fingerprint [31,33]. Most likely, sebum is transferred to the hand and fingers from contact with other sebum-producing regions of the body, such as the face, hair, and neck.

Significant differences have been identified in the sebum composition between children and adults [30]. A difference in the ability to detect children prints as opposed to adult fingerprints, especially after a 24–48 h period, has also been identified by a Knoxville criminologist, Art Bohanan [32]. As a result of his observations, research was initiated at Oak Ridge National Laboratory under the direction of Dr. Michelle Buchanan to chemically profile the fingerprint residue from adults and children. Findings from this research were in agreement with the research of Stewart's et al. on the sebaceous gland activity and serum dehydroepiandrosterone sulfate levels in boys and girls [32,38]. Very low quantities of sebum are secreted in young children prior to the production of adrenal androgens. Production of these androgens typically occurs between the ages of 7 and 10. The materials secreted, before generating adrenal androgens, consist largely of volatile components, such as free fatty acids [32] and cholesterol esters derived from the recycling of cholesterol released when sebaceous cell membranes break down [39]. After the age of 7–10 years, the sebaceous glands begin to excrete sebum, an oily material.

Reported differences in detecting aged children versus adult fingerprints and a potential acetic acid regeneration discovery reported in a National Institute of Justice (NIJ)-sponsored research effort inspired a research initiative to assess the ability to regenerate aged/dehydrated children's fingerprints and adult clean fingerprints [40]. Unlike oily prints, clean (eccrine) prints do not contain hygroscopic materials such a di- and monoacyl glycerols and glycerol. As a result, clean prints are not able to maintain a hydrated print composition. Thus, clean prints become dehydrated with time, leaving the print in a condition that is not amenable to polymer initiation. As previously stated, clean prints, older than 48 h prior to fuming, degrade severely in print quality when developed. Simple rehydration of aged, clean prints with water vapor was found to be unsuccessful in regenerating prints. Prior research results indicated that acids, such as acetic and propionic, were capable of regenerating clean prints. As illustrated in Figure 11.7, early tests proved that a clean print regeneration method could successfully develop latent prints deposited by pre-pubescent children for prints aged over 48 h prior to fuming. The regeneration method was designed to regenerate clean fingerprints for subsequent cyanoacrylate fuming, while not degrading the quality of any oily fingerprints present. During these experiments, oily and clean prints were deposited upon 2 in. × 2 in. glass slides and allowed to age over 48 h. The following agents were evaluated with regard to regeneration efficiency: water, formic acid, propionic acid, isobutyric acid, valeric acid, vinegar, and glacial acetic acid.

The prints were exposed to these agents by heating the material on a hotplate, within a laboratory fume hood, at approximately 150°C, while holding the prints in the vapors. Only a fine mist was allowed to deposit on the prints, analogous to fogging a cold mirror with warm breath [40]. The prints were subsequently fumed after drying. The drying time was evaluated given intervals between 5 and 60 s. The treatment results were compared with nontreated, aged clean prints, which consistently failed to be developed upon fuming. Glacial acetic acid was found to perform far superior to the other chemicals. Glacial acidic

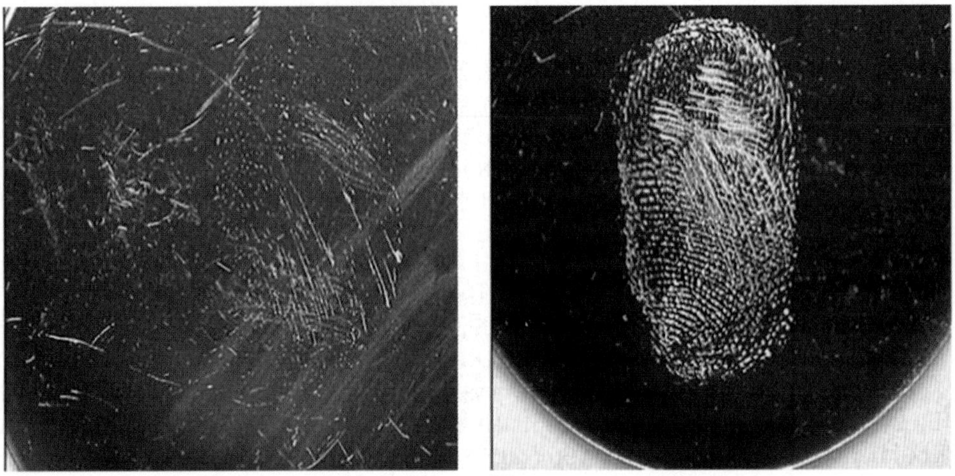

(a) (b)

FIGURE 11.7
Two different fingerprints deposited by a 2 year old boy developed by the CFM after aging the prints 13 days prior to fuming, with (a) no treatment prior to fuming and (b) exposure to hot 75% acetic acid prior to fuming.

acid could not be heated in the humidifier used for these experiments. For this reason, a study was conducted in order to determine the best acid–water mixture for print treatment. Using the humidifier, a hot (65°C) fine-vapor mist of 75% acetic acid–25% water was found to be optimum for clean-print regeneration. It was found that the mist should not coat or bead (form droplets) on the sample in order to prevent a high background or smearing of print-ridge detail. The samples were slightly fogged three times, while allowing the fog to dissipate between each exposure. After the acid treatment, the samples were dried for 30 s prior to fuming. The developed method consistently regenerated adult-clean prints that were aged up to 5 months prior to fuming. The quality of these regenerated and developed clean prints was found to be equivalent to fresh-fumed clean prints.

In order to evaluate the regeneration method performance and confirm its effectiveness on children's prints, a total of 660 prints were collected before and after hand washing [40]. These prints were collected from 33 children between the ages of 2 and 5 years. During this study, it was found that the regeneration treatment did not increase the quality score for treated prints over nontreated prints. However, during the regeneration optimization experiments (performed in the spring), the humidity during fuming was on average 75%. During the actual study on the children prints (performed in the winter), the humidity averaged below 30%. A significant decrease in performance was noted during the study at the lower humidity level. Attempts to increase the humidity in the fuming hood were unsuccessful in the open air configuration utilized in the study. The cause for the decrease in regeneration performance in low-humidity conditions is an area that needs to be better understood. In an effort to demonstrate the effect of humidity on the performance of the regeneration method, a pair of children's prints collected during the NIJ study was allowed to age 8 months prior to conducting the CFM. Once the daily humidity rose to an acceptable level, one of the prints was developed with regeneration and the other was developed without treatment. A comparison of the print quality is depicted in Figure 11.8.

Dr. Charles Guttman of the NIST Polymer Division analyzed the polymers produced by the acidic acid regeneration method using matrix assisted laser desorption ionization–mass spectrometry (MALDI–MS). The polymers produced by the regeneration method

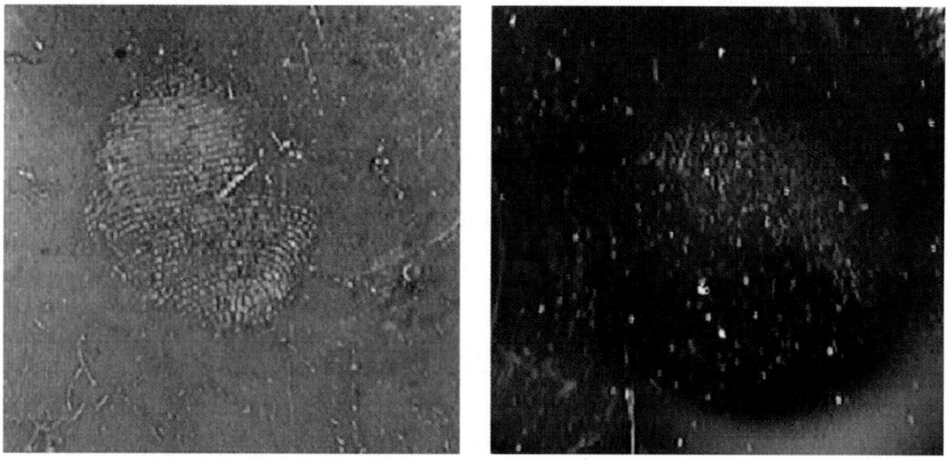

(a) (b)

FIGURE 11.8
Clean fingerprints deposited by a prepubescent child 8 months prior to conducting the CFM. The print images illustrate the effects of (a) treatment and (b) nontreatment with a hot mist of acetic acid prior to fuming in a 75% humidity environment.

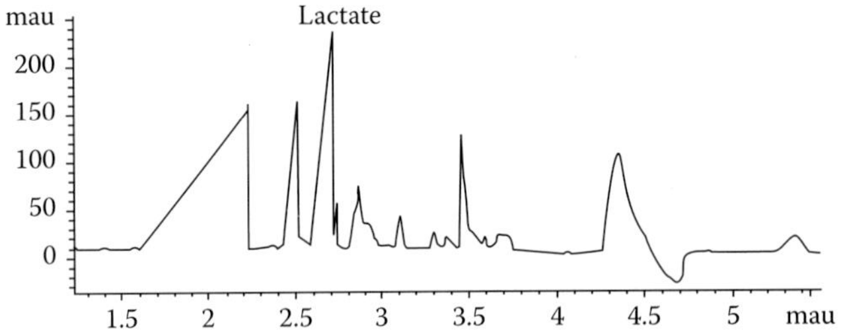

FIGURE 11.9
Capillary electrophoretic separation of the artificial eccrine fingerprint solution. Separation conducted using 2 mM CTAC, 50 mM borate, 5 mM Ca, and 6% MeOH. Operating conditions included potential −17 keV, temp. 25°C, and 50 cm column with 75 μm id.

were found to be lower in molecular weight (molecular weight of 2,000 for acid treated compared to 100,000 and greater for fresh prints) [40].

Another very important discovery identified during the NIJ effort was the effect of light exposure on the effectiveness of the acetic acid regeneration method. Components in the eccrine material known to initiate the cyanoacrylate polymerization were found to degrade in the presence of fluorescent lighting. This problem was first noted during print regeneration optimization studies [40]. Sodium lactate had been identified as one of the major CFM polymerization initiators in clean prints [2]. A literature search on lactate photodegradation led to an article using Fe(III) as a means of photochemically determining lactate [41]. It was found that the rate of lactate degradation was higher on stainless steel in comparison to glass disks. The level of Fe(III) was expected to be higher in the steel. In order to confirm the degradation of lactate in the presence of Fe(III), a capillary electrophoretic (CE) method (Figure 11.9), developed to detect constituents of eccrine prints, was employed to analyze an artificial clean print solution as well as actual clean prints, with and without Fe(III) under different lighting conditions.

Artificial-print solutions were developed with and without the addition of lactate. Three solutions were prepared for the first experiment: lactate with Fe(III), lactate without Fe(III), and Fe(III) without lactate. All these solutions were exposed to 254 nm UV in a dark area. Samples of these solutions were collected and analyzed for lactate at time intervals provided in Table 11.1.

Subsequent experiments showed that lactate in real fingerprints degraded at a faster rate in sunlight with Fe(III) added. However, even without added Fe(III), lactate degraded, but at a slower rate. Degradation of lactate in real fingerprints was also noted under fluorescent lighting with and without the addition of Fe(III). Fe(III) is known to be excreted from the eccrine glands. Thus, photodegradation could occur without the presence of surface-derived Fe(III).

During previous research, lactate was found to a major superglue initiator [2,4]. Since the regeneration method failed to be effective on fingerprints exposed to UV radiation for a given amount of time, the study indicates that prints deposited on metal evidence (such as firearms, ammunition, fragments from metal pipe-bombs, etc.) may actually be present, but not detected using the CFM. Additionally, this data confirmed that lactate is a major cyanoacrylate polymerization initiator, since degradation led to the inability to regenerate the print.

In order to better understand the CFM chemistry, Wargacki et al. studied a lactate and alanine system as models to better understand ethyl cyanoacrylate polymer growth from the vapor phase [4]. The lactate ion represents the second most abundant compound in eccrine sweat and contains a carboxylate functionality found to effectively polymerize cyanoacrylates in solution. The amino acid alanine contains both a carboxylate and amine

TABLE 11.1
Lactate Anion Degradation in the Presence of Iron(III) with Exposure to 254 nm UV Light

Exposure Time	Loss of Lactate with Fe(III) (%)	Loss of Lactate, No Fe(III) (%)	Fe(III), No Lactate
30 min	32	0	—
1 h 15 min	38	0	—
3 h 0 min	66	0	—
3 h 45 min	73	0	—
4 h 45 min	76	0	—
5 h 15 min	78	0	—

Note: 38% excess of lactate was added to the lactate/Fe(III) solutions.

functionality capable of initiating polymerization. The influence of the pH of the two systems on their ability to polymerize ethyl cyanoacrylate from the vapor was examined. The pH was altered since pH has a direct effect on the electronic structure of the initiators. In the lactate system, the variation in pH dictates the counterion at the carboxylate group, either a sodium or hydrogen atom. In the alanine system, the carboxylate group is altered in much the same way as in the lactate system; however, pH adjustment also impacts the protonation of the amine, as well as the zwitterionic nature of amino acids. Amino acids display zwitterionic behavior around the isoelectric (neutral) point (6.02 for alanine).

Figure 11.10 shows the mass accumulation of cyanoacrylate for the lactate system as a function of time for various pH values, as well as for planchets that contained distilled water only. When the lactate system was both acidic and neutral, the mass accumulation was found to be comparable to the water. Increasing the pH led to an increase in mass accumulation, and an increase was noted on all systems, especially at long exposure times.

Adjusting the pH of the alanine samples provided similar results to those observed for the lactate system (Figure 11.11) [4]. Lowering the pH appears to have little effect on the mass accumulation rate, while an increase in pH yields higher mass accumulation at long exposure times. Thus, both initiators consume more ethyl cyanoacrylate monomer from the vapor with an increase in pH. Furthermore, the mass uptake in both systems is

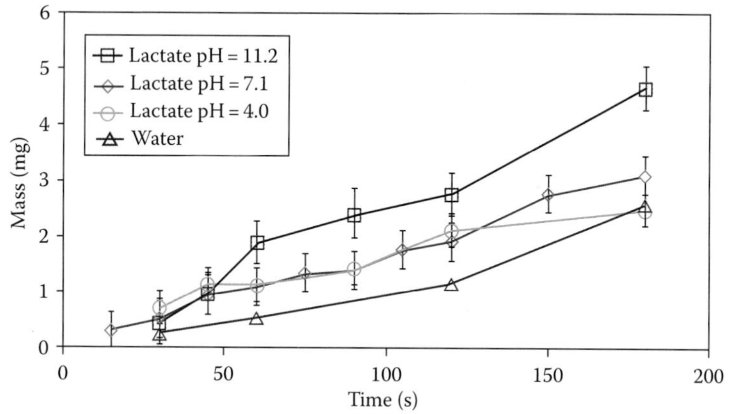

FIGURE 11.10
Mass accumulation of ethyl cyanoacrylate in lactate-initiated systems during exposure to the monomer vapor. (Reprinted from Wargacki, S.P. et al., *J. Forensic Sci.*, 52(5), 1057, 2007.)

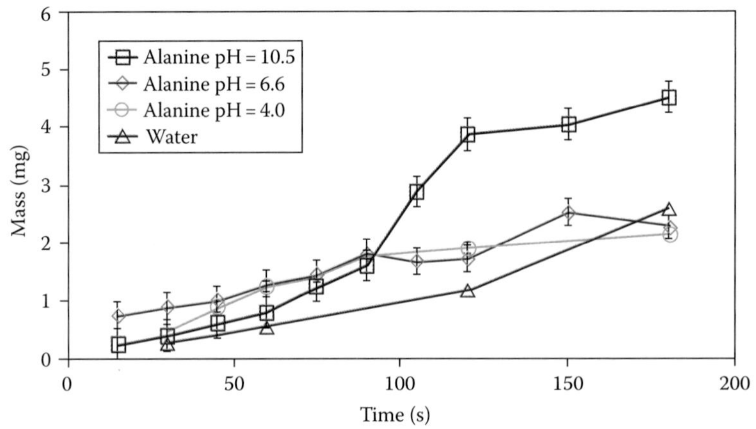

FIGURE 11.11
Mass accumulation of ethyl cyanoacrylate in alanine-initiated systems during exposure to the monomer vapor. (Reprinted from Wargacki, S.P. et al., *J. Forensic Sci.*, 52(5), 1057, 2007.)

nearly identical, suggesting that the alanine system predominately initiates by the carboxylate functionality.

The mass accumulation data provides insight into the uptake of the amount of monomer, but not into the actual polymerization process. To better understand the polymerization processes, the molecular weights of the accumulated material were assessed [4]. Figures 11.12 and 11.13 show the average molecular weight of the accumulated for the lactate and alanine systems, respectively, as a function of fuming time. A significant difference was noted between the samples accumulated on the neutral lactate and alanine systems compared to distilled water.

Although pure water was shown to accumulate similar mass to the neutral systems, the water grew only very few chains of any significant length, essentially producing

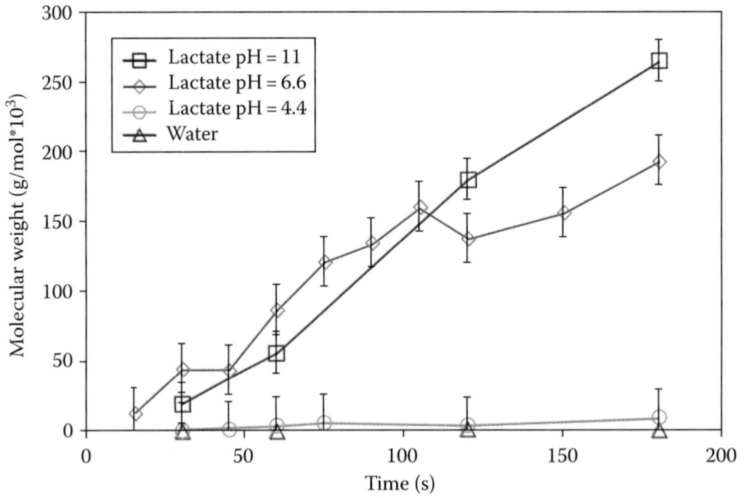

FIGURE 11.12
Molecular weights of ethyl cyanoacrylate in lactate-initiated systems as a function of exposure time at various pH values. (Reprinted from Wargacki, S.P. et al., *J. Forensic Sci.*, 52(5), 1057, 2007.)

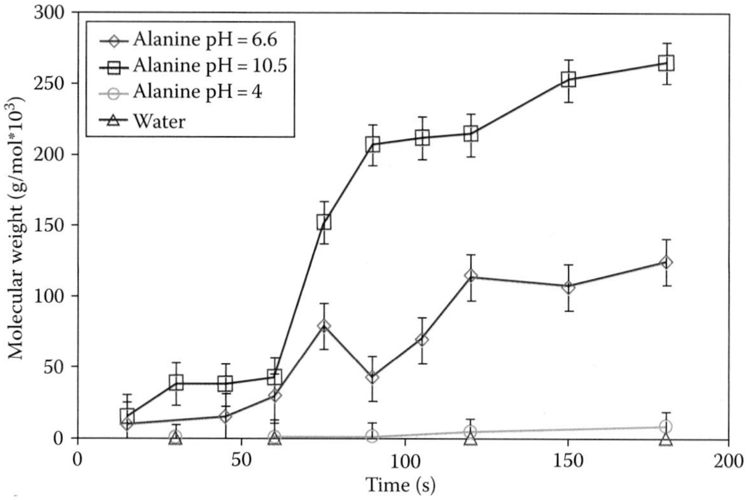

FIGURE 11.13
Molecular weights of ethyl cyanoacrylate in alanine-initiated systems as a function of exposure time at various pH values. (Reprinted from Wargacki, S.P. et al., *J. Forensic Sci.*, 52(5), 1057, 2007.)

oligomers of no significant molecular weight. This very clearly supports the concept that lactate and alanine ions, not water, are responsible for the initiation of the cyanoacrylates during the fuming process. However, water does play a major role in the form of moisture within the print (critical for clean print development) and/or humidity during fuming (beneficial for hydrated clean and sebum-ontaining prints). In the case of clean prints, hydration is essential in order for the initiators to be solvated. Additionally, according to the mechanism proposed by de Puit et al., water is required as a catalyst for the polymerization process. Such a requirement would explain the need for moisture or humidity during the fuming process.

11.4.2 Environmental Effects on the CFM

As previously noted, the success rate for developing prints with cyanoacrylate esters under low-humidity conditions is much lower than the development in a more humid environment. Additionally, in the case of clean prints, dehydration of the print prior to fuming, even when fuming under high humidity conditions, leads to ineffective print development. In order to understand the aging processes that cause these changes in polymer formations, the effect of atmospheric conditions on clean latent fingerprints was studied [2]. Pairs of clean prints, on stainless-steel planchets, were exposed to one of the following conditions for a period of 1–4 days prior to fuming: normal conditions (blank), high humidity (90+%), low humidity (~7%), enriched O_2, enriched N_2, and enriched CO_2. Results indicated that high levels O_2, N_2, and CO_2 made very little difference in visible quality of the print upon development compared to the blank. The prints aged 1–2 days under high humidity tended to have slightly better visible quality than the blank upon fuming, but the quality tended to merge toward that of the blank on days 3 and 4. The low-humidity conditions yielded a major difference in developed print quality compared to the blank. Prints aged 1 through 4 days in low humidity did not develop when exposed to the cyanoacrylate vapor. In fact, when the low-humidity experiment was repeated with the print exposure evaluated on an hour-by-hour basis, no print was developed after being exposed to approximately 7% humidity for 4 h or longer. In the case of oily prints, dehydration was not found to have such a severe effect, where whiter, more easily visualized prints were typically formed when fumed at high humidity levels. Thus, aging of prints containing low levels of sebum prior to fuming could result in reduced detection efficiency.

Print dehydration, particularly in the case of clean prints, is one of two processes that lead to lower detection effectiveness with the CFM. The second process is the environmental degradation of cyanoacrylate initiators within the print. In order to better understand the effects of light and temperature on the fingerprint composition, a study was conducted by de Paoli et al. to characterize these effects on eccrine components under controlled laboratory conditions [31]. During the effort, extraction, separation, and mass spectral detection protocols were developed for two different groups: amino acids and lactic acid/urea, deposited on either stainless steel or Teflon®. The photo-degradation was conducted using a 200–500 W Xe/HgXe arc lamp intense light source for periods equivalent to 0, 2, 5, 7, 14, 28, and 56 days. The light source emitted UV-A, UV-B, UV-C, visible and IR wavelengths, simulating 365 days of sunlight exposure in a 24 h period. The photodegradation studies showed no light effect on the amino acid stability. However, in the case of lactic acid, an apparent effect was detected. When a lactic acid solution at a concentration of 100 times more than the concentration present in a single fingerprint was deposited on galvanized steel and Teflon disks, which were exposed to light between 0 and 56 days, the degradation of lactic acid was noted with a subsequent in growth of pyruvic acid. After exposure, the disks were extracted and analyzed by direct infusion atmospheric pressure chemical ionization–mass spectrometry (APCI–MS) in the negative mode. Two sets of samples were analyzed for each single exposure time. The final number of steel and Teflon disks analyzed was 28 (14 each). At the end of the analyses, M^+ ions at m/z 89, 87, and 128 (respectively for lactic acid, pyruvic acid, and cyanuric acid) were detected. The aim of these experiments was to verify the degree of degradation of lactic acid exposed to light at different periods of time and then to investigate the presence of degradation products.

The ingrowth of pyruvic acid was found to correlate with lactic acid photodegradation [31]. Light in fact, in presence of iron ions, appeared to play a fundamental role in the production of pyruvic acid as the oxidation product. The final amount of lactic acid recovered for samples on Teflon and steel was calculated and plotted in the graphs along with the area ratio obtained from pyruvic acid and internal standard (Figures 11.14 through 11.17). At the conclusion of these experiments, it was observed that lactic acid was affected by the action of light, even for short exposure times in different types of materials. Comparing the slope of the curves, decay on steel is faster than on Teflon. After monitoring the pyruvic acid peak, it was observed that along with the lactic acid decomposition, pyruvic acid also degraded on exposure to light.

In a subsequent effort, de Paoli et al. conducted a thermal degradation study on the same two amino acids and urea/lactic acid groups [31]. The samples were thermally exposed using a commercially available 120 V, 1200 W heat gun that was turned on to the "high" setting for at least 3 min prior to suspending a stainless steel coupon containing the component of interest directly over the heat source, with the nondeposited side facing the source. A thermocouple in contact with the steel coupon measured the temperature experienced by the side spotted with the fingerprint sample. Once the desired temperature of 50°C, 100°C, or 150°C was achieved, the steel coupon was immediately removed from the heat source and allowed to cool.

Serine and glycine data yielded a large-scale reduction in detected amino acid for the sample heated to 150°C, and no peak was present for threonine at that temperature. Ornithine, aspartic acid, histidine, and glutamic acid all experienced a similar

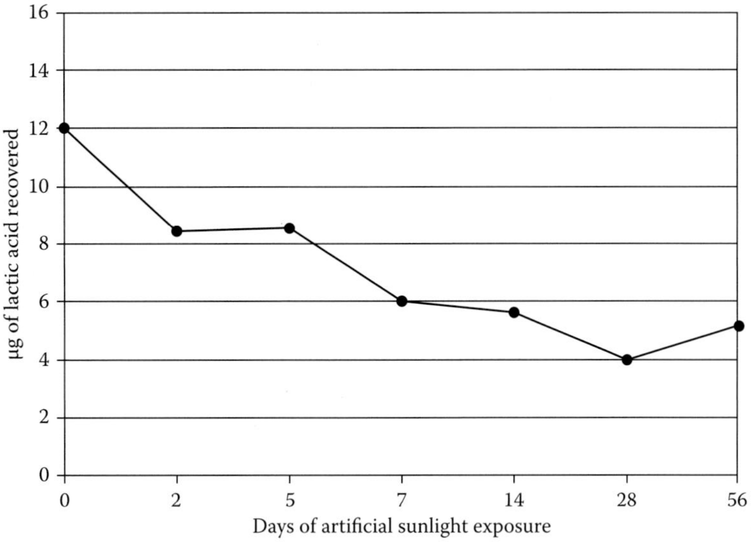

FIGURE 11.14
Lactic acid photodegradation on steel. (Reprinted from De Paoli, G. et al., *J. Forensic Sci.*, 55(4), 962, 2010.)

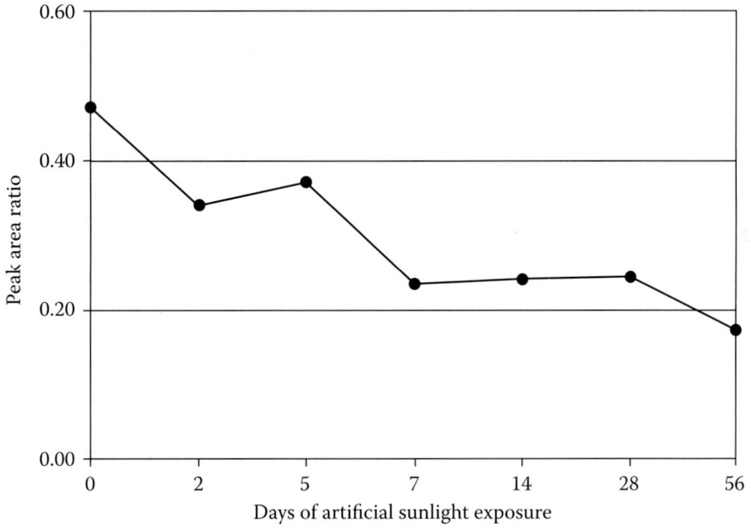

FIGURE 11.15
Pyruvic acid photodegradation on steel. (Reprinted from De Paoli, G. et al., *J. Forensic Sci.*, 55(4), 962, 2010.)

degradation pattern: substantial amino acid loss was incurred at the 100°C temperature point and additional loss at the 150°C sample. Unfortunately, when the chromatograms were analyzed for ingrowth products, none could be found. Additionally, the fact that thermal decomposition of urea was initiated around 150°C was confirmed in the reported results illustrated in Figure 11.18.

In the de Paoli et al. study, a lactic acid solution at a concentration of 100 times more than the concentration present in a single fingerprint was deposited on galvanized steel disks. The disks were arranged on a hot plate and warmed up at different temperatures (0°C, 50°C, 100°C, 150°C) [31]. Two samples were analyzed for each single temperature exposure.

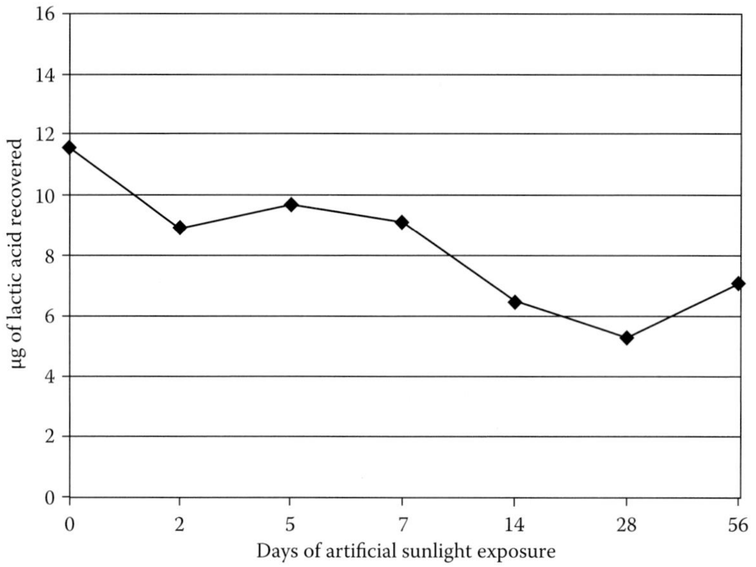

FIGURE 11.16
Lactic acid photodegradation on Teflon. (Reprinted from De Paoli, G. et al., *J. Forensic Sci.*, 55(4), 962, 2010.)

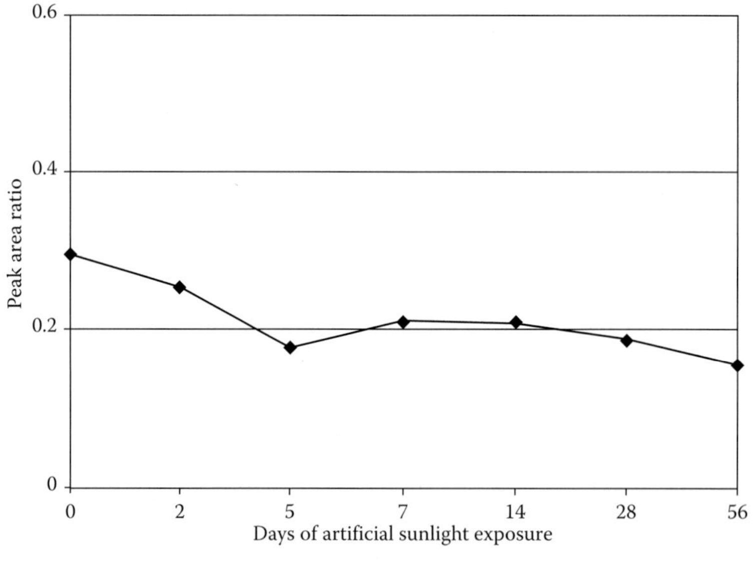

FIGURE 11.17
Pyruvic acid photodegradation on Teflon. (Reprinted from De Paoli, G. et al., *J. Forensic Sci.*, 55(4), 962, 2010.)

The final number of steel disks analyzed was 8 (4 each). Sample extraction and preparation were the same as described for the photodegradation study. The goal of these experiments was (1) to verify the degree of degradation when exposed to heat at different temperatures and (2) to investigate the presence of degradation products. Lactic acid M^+ ion (m/z 89) and pyruvic acid M^+ ion (m/z 87) were monitored for these samples. Figures 11.19 and 11.20 summarize lactic acid degradation resulting from heat exposure up to 150°C.

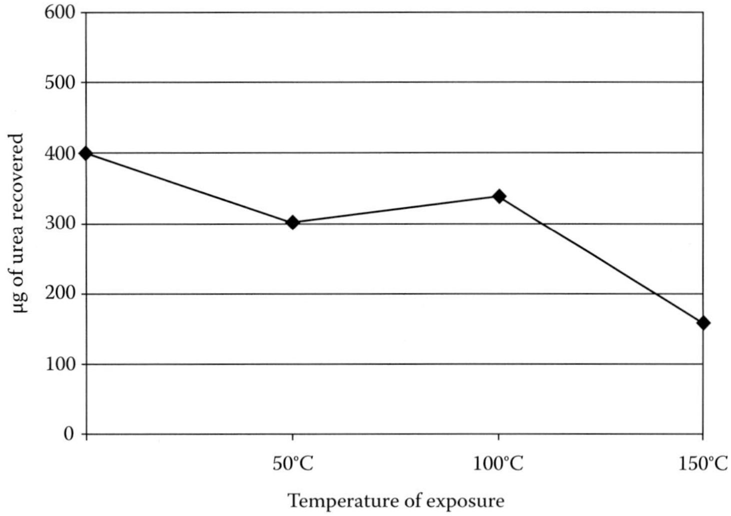

FIGURE 11.18
Urea thermal degradation experiment on steel. (Reprinted from De Paoli, G. et al., *J. Forensic Sci.*, 55(4), 962, 2010.)

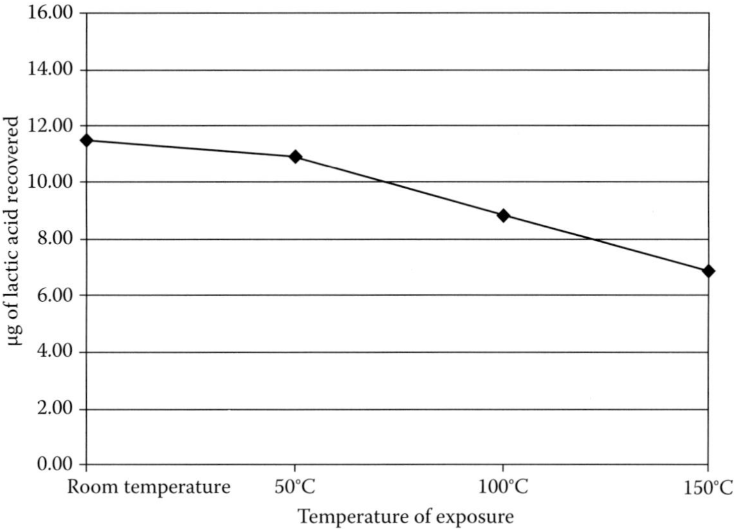

FIGURE 11.19
Lactic acid thermal degradation on steel. (Reprinted from De Paoli, G. et al., *J. Forensic Sci.*, 55(4), 962, 2010.)

The lactic acid thermal degradation process was initiated between 50°C and 100°C along with pyruvic acid generation and subsequent degradation. These experiments were useful to clarify the stability of lactic acid, and explain why the CFM for prints exposed to light and/or heat are not as effectively detected after one of the major initiators degrades.

11.4.3 Chemical and Physical Influences on the CFM

Two studies were recently reported in NIJ final reports covering the chemical and physical influences important to CFM developed prints. Dr. M. Dadmun of the University of Tennessee, Knoxville, reported on his research, which was aimed to

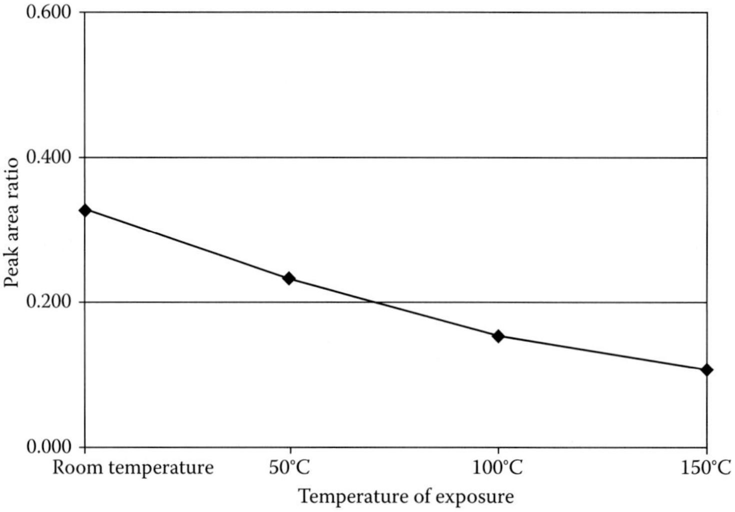

FIGURE 11.20
Pyruvic acid thermal degradation on steel. (Reprinted from De Paoli, G. et al., *J. Forensic Sci.*, 55(4), 962, 2010.)

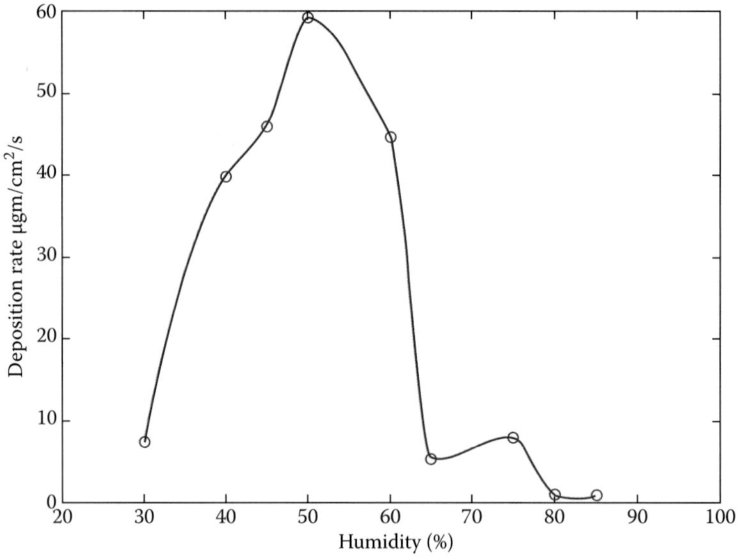

FIGURE 11.21
Change in deposition rate of PECA on latent fingerprints as a function of humidity.

understand molecular-level processes that impact the CFM in order to gain insight into how to optimize the process [41]. Experiments were designed to understand the role of water and temperature during the fuming process. In one of the reported experiments, the growth of poly(ethyl cyanoacrylate) (PECA) on controlled latent print depositions, as well as monolayered carboxylic acid and amine groups, was monitored using a quartz crystal microbalance. The results of this study are illustrated in Figures 11.21 and 11.22 for latent fingerprints and carboxylic acid/amine monolayers, respectively. As can be seen in Figure 11.21, it is apparent that a maximum in polymer growth occurs at approximately 48% humidity, which correlates

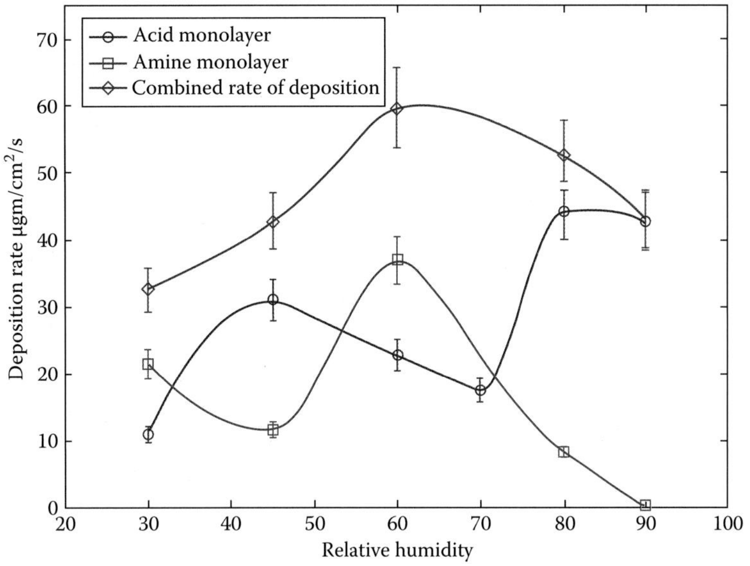

FIGURE 11.22
Change in deposition rate of PECA on carboxylic acid and amine monolayers as a function of humidity.

well with the first maximum for the carboxylic acid monolayer. The overall humidity level for optimum polymer growth on the real fingerprint correlates fairly well for the combined deposition rate of the carboxylic acid and amine monolayers given in Figure 11.22, with an exception at the low and high humidity extremes. With the effect of humidity on the amount of polymer growth demonstrated, Dadmun reported experiments designed to illustrate the importance of atmospheric moisture on solvating the initiating ions, specifically lactate, prior to fuming as opposed to initiating the polymerization with constituents in a salt form [41]. Thus, another parameter, ion-pair dissociation, relating to the importance of moisture was disclosed.

A second parameter studied by Dadmun involved the importance of temperature during the fuming process [41]. Results indicated that the polymer mass grown from a latent print increases dramatically at lower temperatures as illustrated in Figure 11.23.

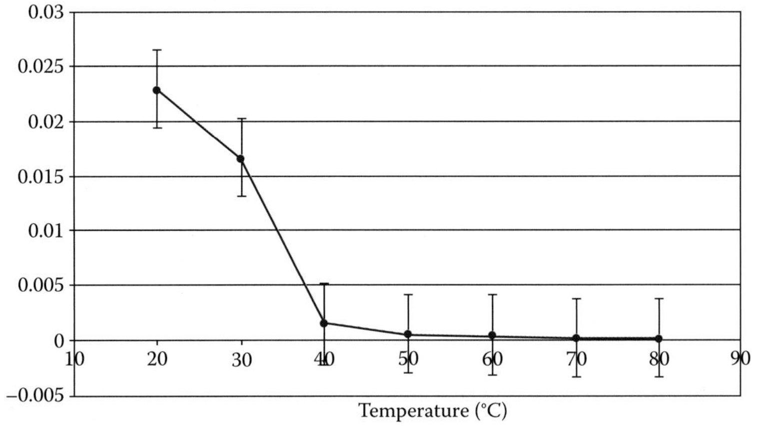

FIGURE 11.23
Mass of ethyl cyanoacrylate that polymerizes from latent prints as a function of temperature.

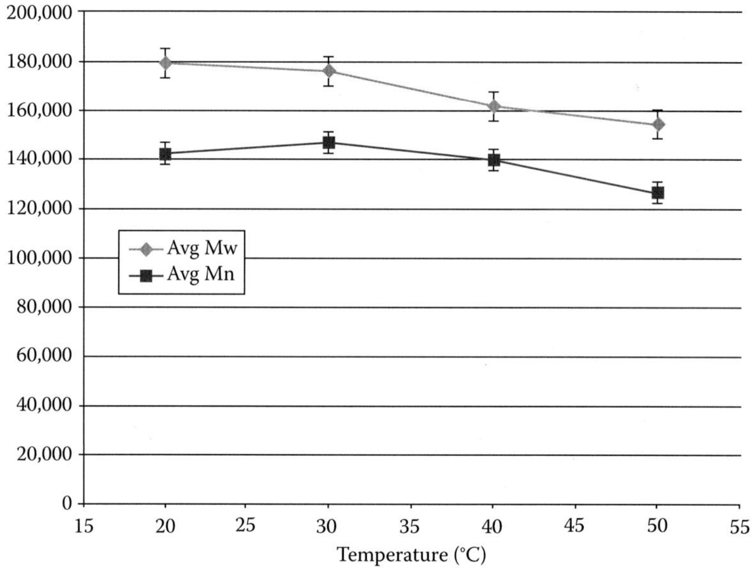

FIGURE 11.24
Molecular weight of ethyl cyanoacrylate that polymerizes from latent prints as a function of temperature.

However, the molecular weight of the polymer was not noted to be related to temperature during fuming (Figure 11.24).

Dadmun stated that the trend toward increased weight with decreased temperature without affecting the molecular weight was indicative that the change in temperature results in an increase in initiation and propagation. This finding was correlated to solution chemistry reaction rates, in which lower reaction temperatures of anionic polymerizations increase the availability of an ion pair that resides at the end of the growing polymer, thus increasing the rate of initiation and propagation.

The second NIJ study, conducted by Weaver et al., assessed the importance of the surface temperature of an item containing a latent print when fuming in relation to the effectiveness of print development by the CFM [42]. The experiments were designed to evaluate the influence of specific heat (heat required to increase the temperature of 1 g of material by 1°C) and thermal conductivity (the property of a material that indicates its ability to conduct heat) of the substrate, and to potentially use these parameters as a guide for setting the optimum surface temperature for print development. From a purely physical perspective, the premise was that monomer condensation from the vapor phase to a liquid phase on the surface plays an important role in the CFM. Condensation occurs when vapor molecules encounter a cooler surface and transfers sufficient heat energy to undergo a phase transition in which the vapor turns into a liquid at the surface. The amount of heat a surface can absorb is related to the specific heat capacity, thermal conductivity, and temperature difference between vapor and surface. The research aim was to understand which of these parameters dominates in the cyanoacrylate vapor condensation when developing latent prints. By selecting materials used for print deposition possessing significant differences in the specific heat and thermal conductivity and evaluating the amount of polymer deposited onto the surface, Weaver et al. concluded that the increase in heat on a surface affected polymer deposition greater than the ability to dissipate heat. Not only did they report that cooler surfaces yielded an increase in polymer deposition, but the larger the difference between the ambient and surface temperature (with 20°F being the transition point), the greater the polymer deposition. Weaver et al. pointed out that overcooling results in a reduced reaction rate, but positive results were obtained with up to a 25°F delta and a surface temperature of 48°F or higher; however, optimum values must be set as a function of material type, in relation to specific heat capacity, upon which a latent print is deposited.

11.5 Recently Reported Enhancement Methods for Cyanoacrylate Developed Fingerprints

Once conditions that hinder the effectiveness of the CFM were identified, a method to reverse the effect was of great interest. Methods to regenerate these prints by rehydrating or replenishing the initiator on the print ridge without increasing the background by exposing prints to small molecule vapors were reported [40,43,44]. The use of a hot mist of 75% acetic acid as a clean print regeneration technique has already been detailed with respect to print composition requirements for successful development. Additionally, a method of adding ammonia to latent prints as a means of increasing polymer deposition and print quality has been reported by Burns et al. [43]. In order to better understand these enhancement methods aimed to improve the quality of aged latent prints developed using the CFM from a polymerization perspective, Wargacki et al. studied the exposure of fresh and aged clean prints exposed to the fumes of ammonia (amine functionality) and glacial acetic acid (carboxylic acid functionality) [44].

To explore the enhancement potential, latent prints that had been degraded for 1 week in the presence of light and airflow were exposed to the vapor of either concentrated ammonia or glacial acidic acid for either 5–10 min immediately prior to development by the CFM [44]. The influence of exposure to either ammonia or acidic acid vapor on print quality is shown in Figures 11.25 and 11.26, respectively. Additionally, the growth of the cyanoacrylate polymer in the form of deposition rate onto the fingerprint surface is displayed for the base- and acid-exposed prints in Figures 11.27 and 11.28, respectively, as a function of fuming time for both the enhanced prints as well as prints that received no enhancement. Exposing the prints to the either basic or acidic vapor prior to development with the CFM does lead to an increase in the amount of observed polymer growth as shown in Table 11.2.

(a) (b) (c)

FIGURE 11.25
Photographic images of latent prints aged for 1 week, then receiving (a) no enhancement, (b) 5 min enhancement with ammonia, and (c) 10 min enhancement with ammonia prior to development with the CFM.

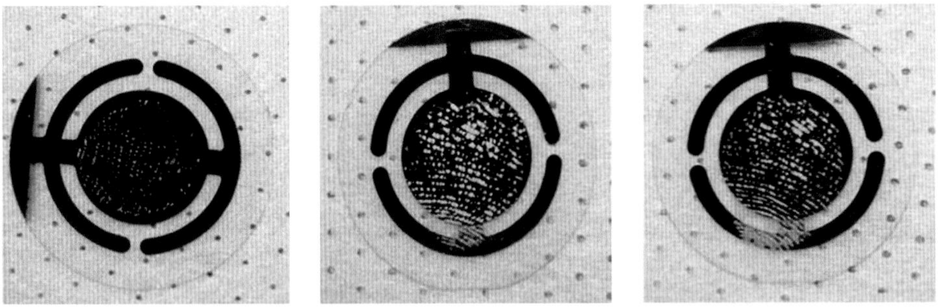

(a) (b) (c)

FIGURE 11.26
Photographic images of latent prints aged for 1 week, then receiving (a) no enhancement, (b) 5 min enhancement with acetic acid, and (c) 10 min enhancement with acetic acid prior to development with the CFM. (Reprinted from Wargacki, S.P. et al., *J. Forensic Sci.*, 53(5), 1138, 2007.)

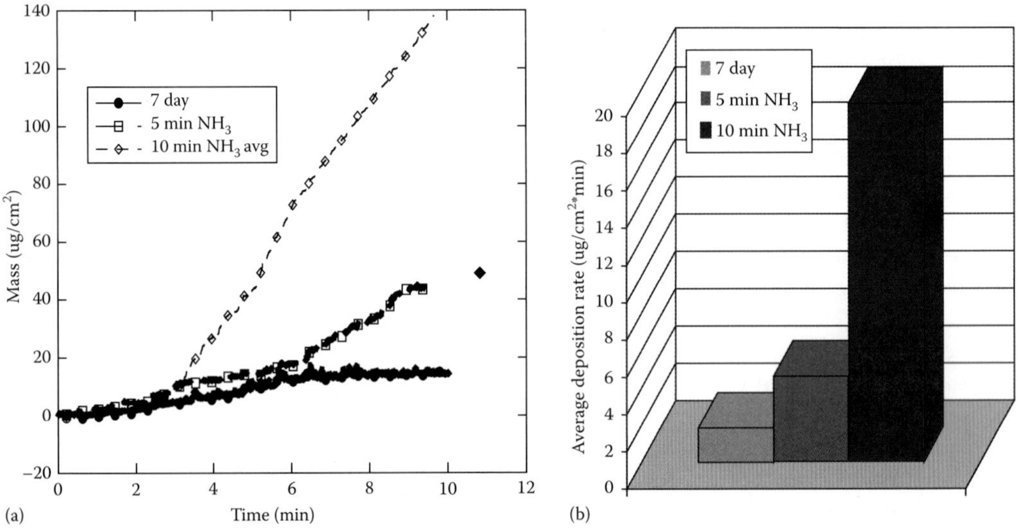

FIGURE 11.27
(a) A comparison of the mass of ethyl cyanoacrylate accumulating on the quartz crystal microbalance crystal platform containing week-old latent prints that either received no enhancement, enhancement from 5 min exposure to ammonia vapor, or enhancement by 10 min exposure to ammonia vapor prior to development by the CFM. (b) A direct comparison of the effect of exposure to ammonia vapor on the average deposition rate of ethyl cyanoacrylate onto week-old latent prints. (Reprinted from Wargacki, S.P. et al., *J. Forensic Sci.*, 53(5), 1138, 2007.)

A quantitative measure of this observed enhancement can be obtained from the average deposition rate extracted from each curve [44]. The 10 min exposed prints showed clear enhancement, leading to a deposition rate that is an order of magnitude higher than that of the unaltered aged print. Additionally, if the images of the developed prints are examined (Figures 11.25 and 11.26), the increase in polymer growth indeed occurs along the fingerprint ridges and improves ridge definition over that of the unaltered print. If the enhancement produced by the ammonia is compared to that produced by the acetic acid, insight into the nature of the enhancement can be extrapolated. A data comparison from Table 11.2 on the two enhancement agents at a 10 min exposure indicates that acetic acid produced a significantly higher amount of polymer growth over ammonia. This statement supports

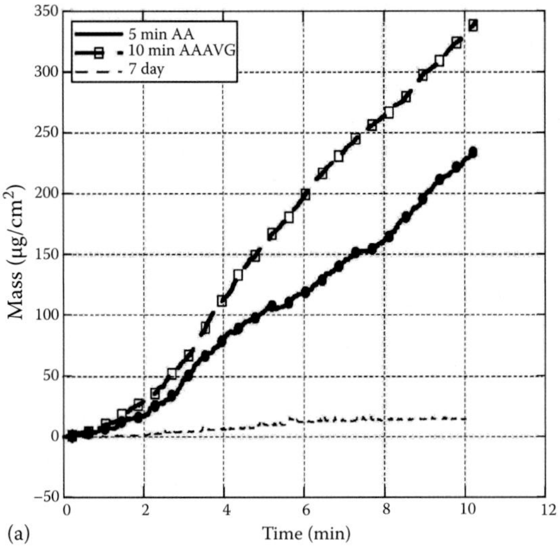

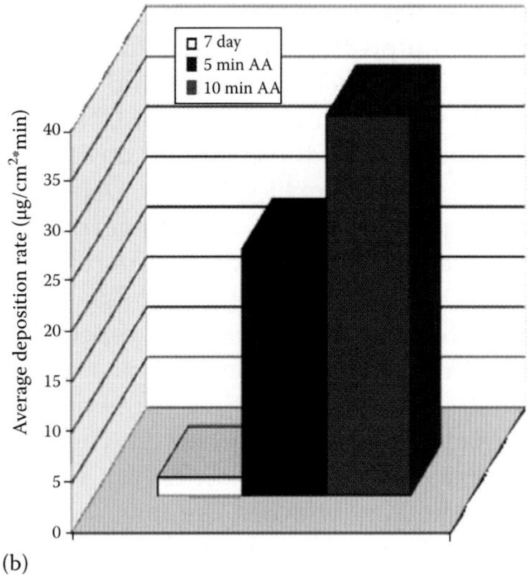

FIGURE 11.28
(a) A comparison of the mass of ethyl cyanoacrylate accumulating on the quartz crystal microbalance platform containing week-old latent prints that either received no enhancement, enhancement from 5 min exposure to glacial acetic acid vapor, or enhancement by 10 min exposure to glacial acidic acid vapor prior to development by the CFM. (b) A direct comparison of the effect of exposure to glacial acidic acid vapor on the average deposition rate of ethyl cyanoacrylate onto week-old latent prints. (Reprinted from Wargacki, S.P. et al., *J. Forensic Sci.*, 53(5), 1138, 2007.)

TABLE 11.2
A Comparison of the Effectiveness of the Two Enhancement Agents Studied (Acetic Acid and Ammonia) to Increase the Average Deposition Rate of Ethyl Cyanoacrylate onto the Print Surface during Development with the CFM

Type of Enhancement Week-Old "Clean" Prints	Average Deposition Rate ($\mu g/cm^2$ min)	% Increase
None	1.85	—
5 min NH_3	4.62 ± 1.15	250
10 min NH_3	19.28 ± 4.82	1042
5 min AA	24.58 ± 6.14	1329
10 min AA	37.88 ± 9.46	2048

the observation that carboxylic acid appears to be more effective at polymerizing cyanoacrylate vapor than an amine [4]. If the nature of the enhancement were a result of altering surface composition with vapor treatment, ammonia would be expected to produce greater enhancement due to an increase in pH [44].

11.6 Cyanoacrylate Fuming and Subsequent DNA Analysis

Often evidence processed for the presence of fingerprints by the CFM is subsequently submitted for DNA analysis. In order to understand the effect of cyanoacrylates on DNA analysis, several articles have been published covering DNA recovery as a function of time, extraction method and efficiency, quality, typing, PCR amplification, and survivability on postblast improvised explosive device (IED) fragments [45–48]. In a majority of the cases, these articles found no significant effect of DNA exposure to the cyanoacrylate vapor on the analysis of DNA compared to untreated samples. Initially, Shipp et al. reported that the CFM had no effect on either the amount or patterning of DNA isolated from human bloodstains. DNA typing and amplification of fumed biological stains subsequently treated with fingerprint visualization agents, for example, Rhodamine 6G, was found to yield no difference in results from that of untreated samples from metal, plastic, glass, and paper [46]. A reduction in the amounts of specific PCR products from fumed biological stains, especially from Chelex extracted aged/degraded biological materials or very small stains, was reported by von Wurub et al. [47]. For older or small samples, the Invitek extraction or similar method was preferred. A decrease in PCR efficacy was also observed when amplifying control DNA in cyanoacrylate exposed samples. However, no difference was identified in the actual extraction of DNA from control stains between the fast, inexpensive Chelex method, and the more expensive, labor-intensive Invitek method [47]. In the case of postblast pipe bomb fragments, cyanoacrylate fuming showed no protective quality for the preservation of DNA on aged, postblast materials, nor did it appear to have a detrimental effect on DNA analysis regardless of the time since detonation [48].

11.7 Future Research Needs

Through an understanding of the basic chemical properties related to the CFM, the hope is to facilitate optimization of the method in a manner that supports high detection efficiency and developed print quality. The chemistry relating to the CFM is complex, and many variables affect the success of print development (print hydration, humidity, print degradation, physical parameters affecting monomer transport and condensation, etc.) as outlined in this chapter. With the reporting of important print-development parameters, the current need is to comprehensively understand these variables with respect to the polymer development on latent prints, facilitating an optimized method that leads to a reduction in the number of latent prints rendered undetected or possessing too little information to support an identification.

Author

Linda A. Lewis, PhD, is a senior research staff member, Chemical Sciences Division, Oak Ridge National Laboratory, Oak Ridge, Tennessee, with 24 years of experience as an analytical chemist in the Oak Ridge area. Currently, Dr. Lewis serves as the principal investigator for multiple Department of Defense (DOD) and Department of Justice (DOJ) sponsored forensic science projects. Dr. Lewis and her team have conducted research in the fundamental mechanisms that led to the development of latent fingerprints using the cyanoacrylate fuming method, developed fingerprint regeneration protocol, and assisted in the development of novel chemical and instrumental macro-Raman and fluorescence imaging methods of detecting latent fingerprints on very difficult evidence (e.g., detonated IED fragments).

References

1. Lee HC, Gaensslen RE. (2001) Methods of latent fingerprint development. In *Advances in Fingerprint Technology*, 2nd edn., eds. H.C. Lee and R.E Gaensslen, CRC Press, Boca Raton, FL, pp. 117–127.
2. Lewis LA, Smithwick RW, Devault GL, Bolinger B, Lewis SA. (2001) Processes involved in the development of latent fingerprints using the cyanoacrylate fuming method. *J Forensic Sci* 46(2):241–246.
3. Czekanski P, Fasola M, Allison J. (2006) A mechanistic model for the superglue fuming of latent fingerprints. *J Forensic Sci* 51(6):1323–1328.
4. Wargacki SP, Lewis LA, Dadmun MD. (2007) Understanding the chemistry of the development of latent fingerprints by superglue fuming. *J Forensic Sci* 52(5):1057–1062.
5. Wargacki SP. (2005) Understanding and controlling the molecular level processes involved in the development of latent fingerprints using the cyanoacrylate fuming method. PhD dissertation, University of Tennessee, Knoxville, TN.
6. Coover HW. (2000) Discovery of superglue shows the power of pursuing the unexplained. *Res Technol Manage* (September–October):36–39.
7. German ER. (2005) Cyanoacrylate (superglue) fuming tips. http://www.onin.com/fp (accessed November 21, 2010).
8. Kendall FG. (1982) Super glue fuming application for the development of latent fingerprints. *Ident News* 32(5):3–5.
9. Jueneman FB. (1982) Stick it to'em. *Ident News* 32(6):5–15.
10. Kendall FG, Rehn BW. (1983) Rapid method of super glue fuming application for the development of latent fingerprints. *J Forensic Sci* 28(3):777–780.
11. Besonen JA. (1982) Heat acceleration of the super glue fuming method for development of latent fingerprints. *Ident News* 33(2):3–4.
12. Olenik JH. (1983) Super glue—a rapid method. *Ident News* 33(1):9–10.
13. Olenik JH. (1984) Super glue, a modified technique for the development of latent fingerprints. *J Forensic Sci* 29(3):881–884.
14. Kotzev DL. (1999) Heat sterilization of cyanoacrylate. US Patent 5,874,044.
15. Trozzi TA, Schwartz RL, Hollars ML. (2001) Processing Guide for Developing Latent Prints. U.S. Department of Justice, Federal Bureau of Investigation, Washington, DC.
16. Yamashita AB. (1994) Use of a benchtop desiccator for vacuum cyanoacrylate treatment of latent prints. *J Forensic Ident* 44(2):149–158.
17. Watkin JE, Wilkinson DA, Misner AH, Yamashita AB. (1994) Cyanoacrylate fuming of latent prints: vacuum versus heat/humidity. *J Forensic Ident* 44(5):545–556.
18. IUPAC. (1997) *Compendium of Chemical Terminology*, 2nd edn. (the "Gold Book"). Compiled by A. D. McNaught, and A. Wilkinson. Blackwell Scientific Publications, Oxford, U.K. XML online corrected version: http://goldbook.iupac.org (2006) created by M. Nic, J. Jirat, B. Kosata; updates compiled by A. Jenkins. ISBN 0-9678550-9-8.
19. de Puit M, Velthuis S. (2009). Latent fingerprint detection and organic chemistry. International Fingerprint Research Group meeting presentation, Lausanne, Switzerland.

20. Eromosele IC, Peppper DC. (1989) Anionic polymerization of butyl cyanoacrylate by tetrabutylammonium salts. 1. Initiation processes. *Makromol Chem* 190:3085–3094.
21. Coover HH, McInyire JM. (1976) *Handbook of Adhesives*. Van Nostrand Reinhold Company, New York.
22. Pepper DC. (1978) Anionic and zwitterionic polymerization of α-cyanoacrylates. *J Polym Sci Polym Symp* 62:65–77.
23. Brinkman NR, Schaefer HF, Sanderson CT, Kutal C. (2002) Can the radical anion of alkyl-2-cyanoacrylates initiate anionic polymerization of these instant adhesive monomers? *J Phys Chem A* 106:847–853.
24. Pepper DC, Ryan B. (1983) Initiation processes in polymerization of alkyl cyanoacrylates by tertiary amine: inhibition by strong acids. *Makromol Chem* 184:383–394.
25. Eromosele IC, Peppper DC. (1989) Anionic polymerization of butyl cyanoacrylate by tetrabutylammonium salts, 2. Propagation rate constants. *Makromol Chem* 190:3095–3103.
26. Ficht K, Eisenbach CD. (1993) The isolation of a zwitterionic initiating species for ethyl cyanoacrylate (ECA) polymerization and the identification of the reaction products between 1°, 2°, and 3° amines with ECA. *Makromol Chem Rapid Commun* 14:669–676.
27. Comyn J. (1998) Moisture cure of adhesives and sealants. *Int J Adhes* 18:247–253.
28. Eromosele IC. (1991) Effect of acetic acid on polymerization of buytlcyanoacrylate by tetrabutylammonium acetate in tetrahydrofuran. *J Makromol Sci* 28:347–358.
29. Pepper DC. (1987) Transfer by weak acids in the slow-initiation-no-termination (SINT) polymerization of butyl cyanoacrylate. *Makromol Chem* 188:527–536.
30. Ramotowski RS. (2001) Composition of latent print residue. In: *Advances in Fingerprint Technology*, 2nd edn., eds. H.C. Lee and R.E Gaensslen, CRC Press, Boca Raton, FL, pp. 63–95.
31. De Paoli G, Lewis SA, Schuette EL, Lewis LA, Connatser RM, Farkas T. (2010) Photo- and thermal-degradation studies of select eccrine fingerprint constituents. *J Forensic Sci* 55(4):962–969.
32. Noble D. (1995) Vanished into thin air: the search for children's fingerprints. *Anal Chem* 67(13):435A–438A.
33. Nicolaides N. (1974) Skin lipids: their biochemical uniqueness. *Science* 186:19–26.
34. Jirka M, Kotas J. (1957) The occurrence of mucoproteins in human sweat. *Clin Chim Acta* 2:292–296.
35. Dupuy P, LePendu J, Jothy S, Wilkinson RD. (1990) Characterization of a monoclonal antibody against a mucin-type glycoprotein in human sweat. *Hybridoma* 9(6):589–596.
36. Metze D, Bhardwaj R, Amann U, Eades-Perner AM, Neumaier M, Wagener C, Jantscheff P, Grunert F, Luger TA. (1996) Glycoproteins of the carcinoembryonic antigen (cea) family are expressed in sweat and sebaceous glands of human fetal and adult skin. *J Invest Dermatol* 106(1):64–69.
37. Diem K, Lentner C, eds. (1970) *Geigy Scientific Tables*, 7th edn. Geigy Pharmaceuticals, New York, pp. 679–681.
38. Stewart ME, Downing DT, Cook JS, Hansen JR, Strauss JS. (1992) Sebaceous gland activity and serum dehydroepiandrosterone sulfate levels in boys and girls. *Arch Dermatol* 128:1345–1348.
39. Stewart ME. (1992) Sebaceous gland lipids. *Semin Dermatol* 11:100–105.
40. Lewis LA, Smithwick RW, Devault GL. (2004) Technology development, enhanced latent fingerprint detection in missing and exploited children investigations. Oak Ridge National Laboratory. NIJ Final Report No. 2001-LT-R-082.
41. Dadmun M. (2010) Cultivating methods to enhance the quality of aged fingerprints developed by cyanoacrylate fuming. University of Tennessee Knoxville. NIJ Final Report No. 2006-DN-BX-K031.
42. Weaver DE, Steele CA, Wheeler A, Pokharel G, Hines MA, Farmer S, Basher J. (2009) Specific heat capacity thermal function of the cyanoacrylate fingerprint development process. NIJ Final Report No. 2007-DN-BX-K242.

43. Burns DT, Brown JK, Dinsmore A, Harvey KK. (1998) Base-activated latent fingerprints fumed with a cyanoacrylate monomer. A quantitative study using Fourier-transform infra-red spectroscopy. *Anal Chim Acta* 362:171–176.
44. Wargacki SP, Lewis LA, Dadmun MD. (2007) Enhancing the quality of aged latent fingerprints developed by superglue fuming: loss and replenishment of initiator. *J Forensic Sci* 53(5):1138–1144.
45. Shipp E, Roelofs R, Togneri E, Wright R, Atkinson D, Henry B. (1993) Effects of argon laser light, alternate source light, and cyanoacrylate fuming on DNA typing of human bloodstains. *J Forensic Sci* 38(1):184–191.
46. Stein C, Kyeck SH, Henssge C. (1996) DNA typing of fingerprint reagent treated biological stains. *J Forensic Sci* 41(6):1012–1017.
47. Von Wurmb N, Meissner D, Wegener R. (2001) Influence of cyanoacrylate on the efficiency of forensics PCRs. *Forensic Sci Int* 124:11–16.
48. Bille TW, Cromartie C, Farr M. (2009) Effects of cyanoacrylate fuming, time after recovery, and location of biological material on the recovery and analysis of DNA from post-blast pipe bomb fragments. *J Forensic Sci* 54(5):1059–1067.

12

Ninhydrin and Ninhydrin Analogues: Recent Developments

Joseph Almog

CONTENTS

12.1 Introduction

This chapter surveys developments in the area of ninhydrin and its analogues since the appearance of the second edition of Lee and Gaensslen's *Advances in Fingerprint Technology* in 2001 [1].

Several reviews covering the chemistry, applications, and mechanistic aspects of ninhydrin appeared during this period, some of them specifically addressing forensic uses of ninhydrin and its analogues. In 2001, Hark et al. published an article on the synthesis of ninhydrin analogues [2]. A comprehensive review on ninhydrin, also addressing fingermark visualization by M. Friedmann, appeared in 2004 [3]. A comprehensive chapter on ninhydrin and its analogues for fingerprint detection appeared in *Fingerprint and Other Ridge Skin Impressions* by Champod, Lennard, Margot, and Stoilovic [4]. A year later, Hansen and Joullié published a review on novel ninhydrin analogues, also addressing the visualization of latent fingermarks [5]. Another comprehensive review by Lewis et al., summarizing the development and use of amino acid reagents for the detection of latent fingermarks on porous surfaces, appeared recently [6]. It includes a historical background, forensic significance, and a general approach to the development of latent fingermarks on porous surfaces.

The main topics pertaining to the title of this chapter that were reported and discussed in the literature during this period are as follows:

- Premixed metal–ninhydrin formulations as "dual fingerprint reagents"
- Synthesis and evaluation of ninhydrin analogues bearing oxygen, sulfur, and selenium-containing substituents
- The preparation and evaluation of two more analogues, nitrophenylninhydrin and benzofuroninhydrin
- Computational design of ninhydrins with potentially improved reactivity
- Synthesis of thiohemiketal derivatives of ninhydrin as potential stabilizers of gold nanoparticles

The dispute over the advantages and disadvantages of 1,2-indanedione seems to have subsided recently. Despite some questions that are still open in several law enforcement agencies, the indanedione–zinc chloride formulation is gradually replacing DFO as the major fluorogenic fingermark reagent.

Two natural substances, genipin and lawsone, have also been reported as potential fingermark reagents. Both of them produce with amino acids a dual effect, color, and fluorescence. The mechanisms of their reactions have not been fully elucidated, but the authors suggest that at least the latter reacts with amino acids in a similar manner to ninhydrin. Several compounds having the naphthoquinone skeleton, like lawsone, have also been shown to be potential dual fingermark reagents.

Finally, substituted benzimidazole-carboxaldehydes were found to react with latent fingermarks, producing stable, fluorescent impressions.

12.2 Ninhydrin

Several articles describing modified formulations of ninhydrin, or performance comparisons of other reagents with ninhydrin (see Figure 12.1), have appeared in the literature since 2001. An international survey on fingerprint reagents revealed a high degree of variability between the laboratories (16 different ninhydrin formulations), mainly for cost issues [7].

A ninhydrin formulation, which works on regular paper as well as thermal paper with short contact times, appeared in a Japanese patent in 2008. Besides ninhydrin and water, the new solution contains 1-(2,2,2-trifluoroethoxy)-1,1,2,2,-tetrafluoroethane as the carrier [8]. In a German patent, a fingerprint technique and device are described by which a nebulized ninhydrin derivative follows iodine fuming [9].

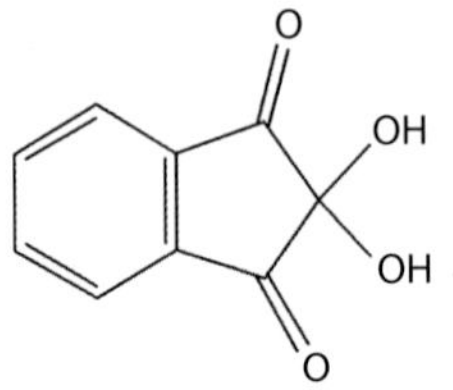

FIGURE 12.1
Ninhydrin.

A technique for enhancing ninhydrin and DFO-treated latent fingermarks on thermal paper was reported by Schwarz and Klenke [10,11]. The new method reduces the dark staining, which normally occurs on thermosensitive papers, by adding polivinylpyrrolidone to the ninhydrin solution.

The use of ninhydrin under conditions simulating crime scenes was suggested as an educational technique for chemistry students by Boucher and Spect [12] and by Anastasios and Limperopoulou-Karaliota [13].

Roux et al. studied the effect of formaldehyde gas on fingermark development by ninhydrin (and other techniques), as well as on evidence suspected to be contaminated with biological warfare agents [14]. A protocol for formaldehyde gas decontamination was developed, which allowed the destruction of viable spores and the successful recovery of latent marks, all within a rapid response time of less than 1 h.

Bialek et al. compared several fingermark techniques, including ninhydrin, for revealing latent fingermarks on Polish currency. They found that sebum-rich marks developed better with ninhydrin, while DFO produced better impressions on eccrine marks [15].

12.3 New Ninhydrin Analogues

In an unpublished manuscript that was prepared in 2000, Hark presented 87 ninhydrin analogues that have been prepared and described in the scientific literature [16], most of them as potential fingermark reagents. Some, particularly the two "indirect" analogues, DFO and 1,2-indanedione, have been studied in great detail by fingerprint researchers. DFO has become a "first line" fingermark reagent for many forensic laboratories; however, and indanedione is making steady progress as its replacement. In view of the limited advantage of most of the new analogues over ninhydrin, many of them have been abandoned right after initial experiments, particularly since they are not commercially available and their syntheses are tedious and complicated [2,4,17]. This view was corroborated by the theoretical findings of Elber et al., stating that simple ninhydrin analogues are not supposed to produce significantly better (visible) impressions than ninhydrin itself. Their computational studies indicated that better results are expected with ninhydrin analogues bearing divalent sulfur atoms instead of the carbonyl oxygens (thiono-ninhydrin) [17]. Subsequently, only a handful of new analogues have been synthesized and reported since the publication of Elber's report.

The only new addition to this list was reported by Della, Kobus, and their coworkers [18,19], who prepared six novel ninhydrin analogues bearing oxygen-, sulfur-, and selenium-containing substituents at the C-5 position (see Figure 12.2). Two more analogues,

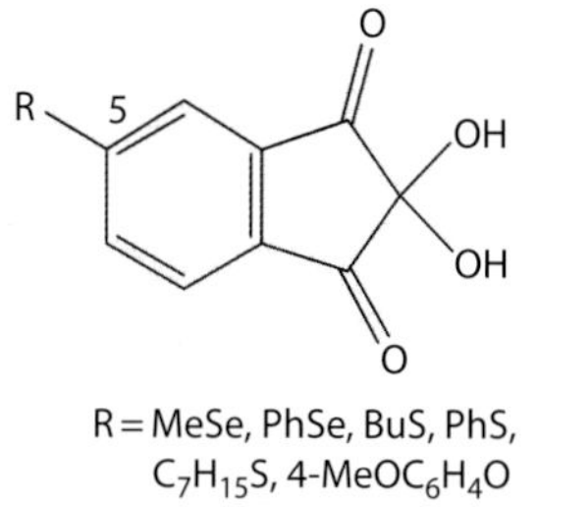

FIGURE 12.2
Ninhydrin analogues bearing oxygen-, sulfur-, and selenium-containing substituents at the C-5 position.

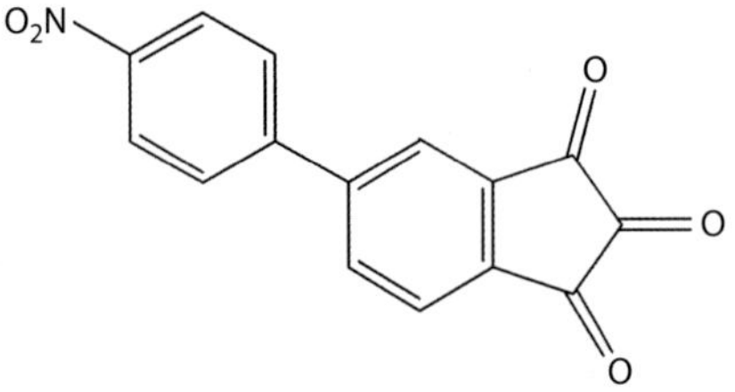

FIGURE 12.3
Nitrophenylninhydrin.

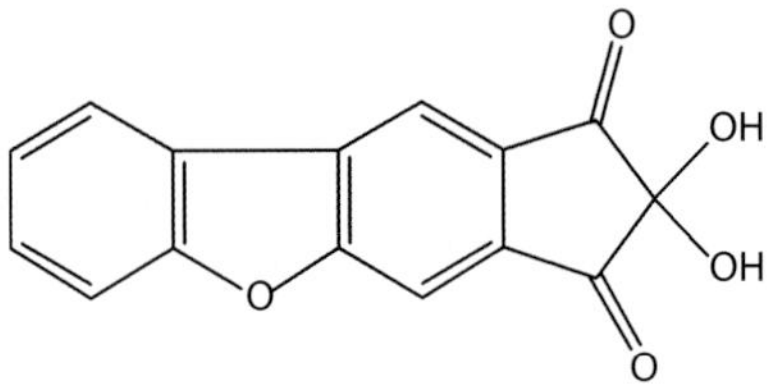

FIGURE 12.4
Benzofuroninhydrin.

nitrophenylninhydrin (see Figure 12.3) and benzofuroninhydrin (see Figure 12.4), were also prepared by the same group [18,19]. The new compounds showed good fingerprint color development, but were not superior to ninhydrin in this respect. The benzofuro derivative (see Figure 12.4) developed latent fingermarks at room temperature as intensely luminescing impressions, after secondary treatment with zinc salts. The nitrophenyl derivative (see Figure 12.3) required cooling to –196°C to produce optimum luminescence. Another group of novel compounds related to ninhydrin, which are not "analogues," ninhydrin thiohemiketals, is surveyed later on in this chapter.

12.4 Dual Fingermark Reagents

The term "dual fingermark reagents" (formerly "dual fingerprint reagent") was suggested in 2007 for chemical reagents that produce in a single step latent fingermark impressions that are both colored and fluorescent [20]. Premixed solutions containing ninhydrin and group IIb metal salts were found to be true dual reagents. Application of these formulations to latent fingermarks on paper was reported to be as efficient as the two-step process, beginning with ninhydrin and followed by treatment with metal salt. In the color mode, fingerprint detectability with the two ninhydrin–metal salt reagents (one with zinc chloride and the other with cadmium chloride) was comparable to that of ninhydrin itself, in spite of the difference in color. The sensitivity was significantly higher in the fluorescence mode. To view the latent impressions, the exhibits were treated with ninhydrin–metal salt reagents and observed under white light illumination and under fluorescence conditions. Cooling to liquid nitrogen temperature enhanced the fluorescence considerably. In the shorter wavelength domain, ninhydrin–metal salt reagents exhibited higher sensitivity than genipin (see Section 12.8). However, the latter gave better results in the longer wavelength domain, on paper items with strong self-fluorescence, such as brown wrapping paper or paper printed with fluorescent ink. The authors reported that upon reducing the ninhydrin concentration by 10-fold, ninhydrin–metal salt formulations became purely fluorogenic reagents; no color was noticed, but the fluorescence was as intense as with concentrated solutions. Working at lower concentrations is an advantage from ecological and economical viewpoints. A mechanism was suggested for both pathways, the one-stage and two-stage reactions [20]. In a subsequent article, the same authors reported that premixed solutions of the two commercially available ninhydrin analogues, 5-methoxyninhydrin (MN, see Figure 12.5) and 5-methylthioninhydrin (MTN, see Figure 12.6) with zinc or cadmium salts, are not only true dual reagents, but they are also much more sensitive than the parent dual reagent, ninhydrin/$ZnCl_2$ [21]. The main advantage of the new formulations is that they can be used at room temperature, with no need to cool the sample to liquid nitrogen temperature. At 0.05% concentration, which is 10-fold lower than the common ninhydrin working solution, MTN/$ZnCl_2$ was found to be as sensitive as DFO in the fluorescence mode and considerably more sensitive in the color mode. The authors mentioned that MTN is also slightly cheaper than DFO. The premixed solution of 1,2-indanedione (see Figure 12.7) and zinc chloride was reported recently by three groups in the United States, United Kingdom, and Australia as an efficient fingerprint reagent with dual effect, color, and fluorescence, although the authors did not use this definition [22–24]. Due to its dual reactivity, combined with high sensitivity and reasonable cost, 1,2-indanedione/$ZnCl_2$ may gradually become the successor of DFO as the leading fluorogenic reagent, and perhaps also ninhydrin, as a fingermark color reagent, both in a single step. Genipin (see Figure 12.8), and later lawsone (see Figure 12.9), were also found to be efficient dual reagents (see Section 12.8).

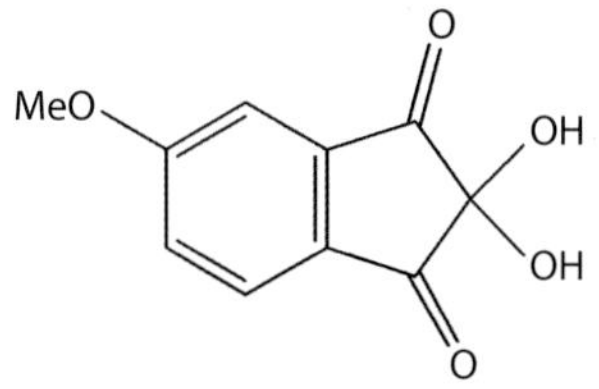

FIGURE 12.5
5-methoxyninhydrin.

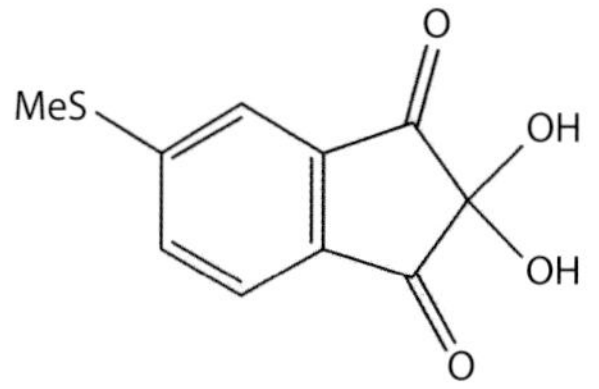

FIGURE 12.6
5-methylthioninhydrin.

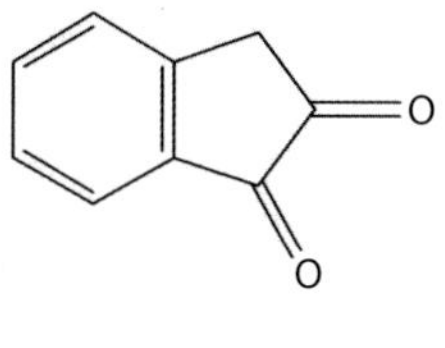

FIGURE 12.7
1,2-indanedione.

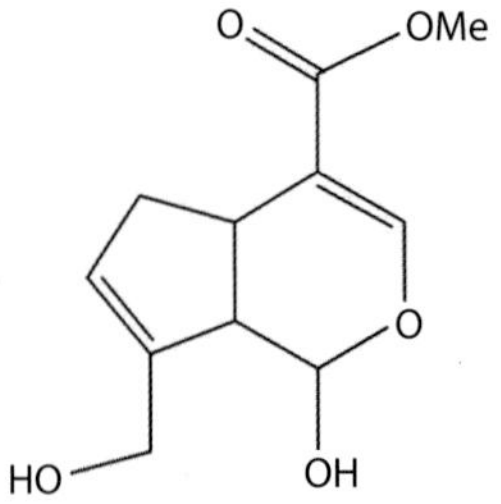

FIGURE 12.8
Genipin.

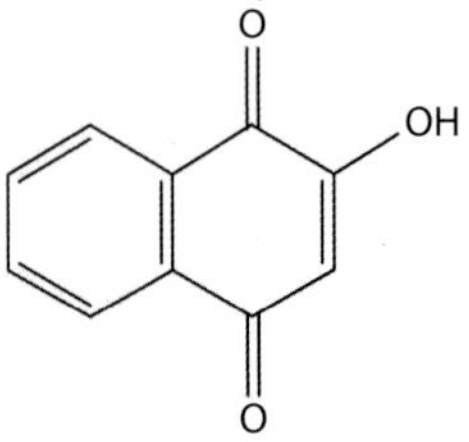

FIGURE 12.9
Lawsone.

12.5 Computational Design of Improved Ninhydrin Analogues

Elber et al. explored the design of more potent ninhydrin analogues computationally for the development of latent fingermarks. They were able to show why past attempts to improve the widely used ninhydrin provided relatively small improvements (referring to color only). According to their findings, the optical transition in the product between the ninhydrin analogue and amino acid is connected with a "transition core" and, therefore, is only little influenced by the substitution on the ninhydrin aromatic rings. Based on their findings, they

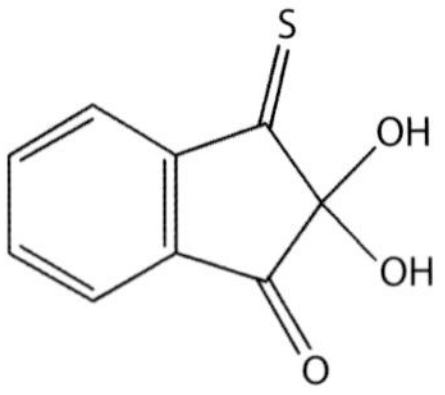

FIGURE 12.10
Thiono derivative.

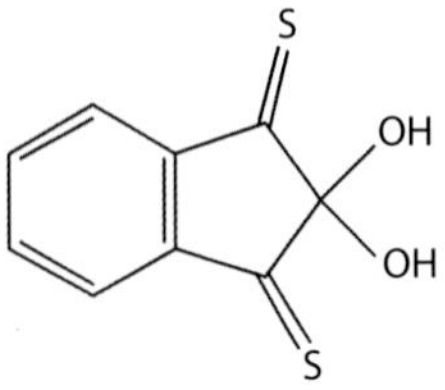

FIGURE 12.11
Dithiono derivative.

proposed two new ninhydrin derivatives with significant potential, such as thiono derivatives (see Figures 12.10 and 12.11). Unfortunately, due to inherent synthetic difficulties, they were unable to prepare these compounds [17]. More recently Sapse and Petraco suggested that based on net energetics of the reactions in the formation of substituted Ruhemann's purples, fluoro derivatives of ninhydrin could become more efficient fingermark reagents [25].

12.6 Ninhydrin Thiohemiketals

In an attempt to improve the application of nanotechnology to fingerprint visualization, Almog and Glasner investigated the possibility of a more selective binding of gold nanoparticles to fingerprint material. They synthesized thiohemiketals of ninhydrin, which are characterized by loosely bound thiol groups attached to the central carbon atom (see Figure 12.12). Ninhydrin thiohemiketals reacted with amino acids to produce the expected Ruhemann's purple, and they also developed latent fingermarks on paper in a similar manner to that of ninhydrin [26]. In the second part of the research, they intend to use the thiols, which are released on the ridges by the reaction with amino acids, as stabilizers for gold nanoparticles. The latter will become covalently bound to the fingerprint ridges and, according to their plan, will catalyze the precipitation of metallic silver by the multimetal deposition technique [27,28].

12.7 1,2-Indanedione/Zinc Chloride: Settling the Dispute?

Perhaps the decade's most significant development in the field of fingerprint amino acid reagents is the premixed formulation of 1,2-indanedione (see Figure 12.7) with zinc salt.

Since Joullie and coworkers introduced indanedione as a fingermark reagent in the late 1990s [29,30], researchers in Israel [31–34], Australia [35–37], United States [22,38,39], United Kingdom [23,40,41], Morocco [42], and Canada [43,44] have conducted research to thoroughly evaluate its potential as a possible substitute for ninhydrin and DFO. Preliminary experiments performed in Israel indicated that 1,2-indanedione is in no way inferior to DFO [31,32]. Encouraging results were reported also by Roux et al. in 2000 [35]. Roux and his coworkers tested the parent compound, 1,2-indanedione and its 5,6-dimethoxy derivative, and concluded that fingermarks developed by the new reagents displayed superior luminescence to those developed with DFO. They also compared various carrier solvents

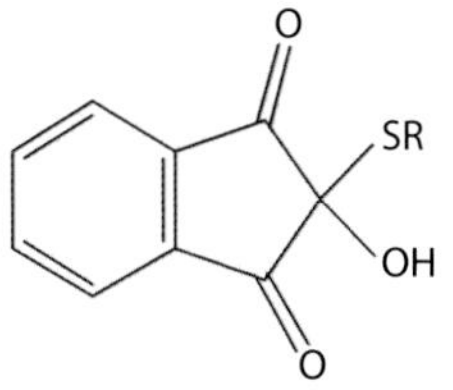

R = $(CH_3)_2CH$, $CH_3(CH_2)_{11}$, $CH_3(CH_2)_{17}$, cyclohexyl, Ph, 4-MeC_6H_4

FIGURE 12.12
Loosely bound thiol groups attached to the central carbon atom.

for the indanedione reagent and found that HFE 7100 produced the best results. The researchers compared 1,2-indanedione and DFO in actual casework with 46% more fingermarks reportedly developed by 1,2-indanedione. However, one problem was the limited availability of the compound. In 2002, 1,2-indanedione became commercially available through the Netherlands-based company, BVDA International; later on, the Casali Institute of Applied Chemistry at the Hebrew University of Jerusalem started to manufacture 99.7% pure 1,2-indanedione for fingermark visualization (for further information, contact Tom Koevary at koevary@vms.huji.ac.il).

Research by Wiesner and coworkers in 2001 led to 1,2-indanedione being approved for use in casework in Israel [32]. In that year, indanedione had its first spectacular success by enabling the identification of the assassin of the Israeli Minister of Tourism, through his latent fingermark, which was developed on a newspaper found in the suspect's hotel room [45]. A validation study on 1,2-indanedione, in response to the Daubert requirement that all scientific processes be validated and subjected to peer review before being used as evidence in courts of law, was reported by the Florida Department of Law Enforcement in 2002 [46]. Along with the encouraging results, contradicting findings started to appear. In 2002, the United Kingdom Home Office Scientific Development Branch (U.K. HOSDB) reported that 1,2-indanedione was the least effective reagent in a comparison with ozone-friendly DFO reagents based on HFC 4310mee and HFE 7100 formulations [41]. A possible reason for the discrepancy was that while HOSDB experimented with an optimum formulation of 0.025%, all other formulations had a significantly higher concentration of indanedione varying between 0.05 and 0.3% w/v [36]. Disappointing results were reported also by Wilkinson [44], who also studied NMR spectroscopy and mass spectrometry of indanedione [43]. The wide distribution of indanedione results was attributed to the differences in paper composition in different countries, or to the effect of local climatic conditions, particularly temperature and humidity. The dispute has subsided lately in a positive way, through the comprehensive works of Wallace-Kunkel, Stoilovic, and coworkers in Australia [24,36] and Bicknell and Ramotowski in the United States [22] (still, with contradicting results by Sears et al. in the United Kingdom [23]). The authors identified optimal sets of working conditions, which provided results equal to those or better than the ones obtained with DFO. All three groups recommended using a premixed solution of indanedione with zinc chloride. The premixed formulations are much more resilient to environmental fluctuations than the separate solutions. The recommended working solutions are slightly different; they contain 0.1%–0.025% indanedione, and the main carrier is HFE 7100. The Australian development conditions, for instance, involve using a heat press set at 160°C for 10 s [36]. Consequently, several law enforcement agencies have adapted indanedione as their major fluorogenic fingermark reagent instead of DFO [47].

Dry contact with indanedione was found lately as an efficient technique for fingermark development on thermal paper [37].

12.8 Genipin and Lawsone

In their search for potentially safer and wider scope reagents, Almog and coworkers suggested the natural product genipin (see Figure 12.8) as an operationally safer and environmentally benign fingermark reagent, exhibiting both color and photoluminescence [48,49].

The potential of genipin, a hydrolytic product of geniposide extracted from gardenia fruit, was thoroughly studied as a fingermark reagent, and optimal conditions for fingerprint development have been determined. Latent fingerprints on paper items that have been treated with a nonink-running formulation containing 0.17% of the reagent, showed up as both colored (blue) and fluorescent impressions. On brown wrapping paper and on papers with highly luminescent backgrounds, genipin developed more visible and clearer prints than did classical reagents such as ninhydrin or DFO. Another potential advantage of genipin is that it is totally harmless and an environmentally friendly reagent. In a more recent study, Almog and Dalrymple obtained less exciting results with genipin, but the experiments were carried out under totally different environmental conditions than the previous ones. The authors assumed that like the dispute over indanedione, many factors governing the quality of the developed marks are environmentally dependent and that the potential of genipin is still far from optimization [50]. Furthermore, the reaction mechanism has not been elucidated yet, and the blue product is probably a mixture of several colored compounds [51,52].

Traditionally, genipin had been used as a fabric and skin dye, and this led Lewis et al. to investigate the potential of other natural products, which have been used in this fashion as fingermark reagents. Henna, a natural product extracted from the leaves of *Lawsonia inermis*, in a similar manner to genipin, has been used as a skin and hair dye for millennia, with reports of its use dating back to 1400 BC. Lawsone (2-hydroxy-1,4-naphthoquinone [see Figure 12.9]) is the compound thought to be responsible for the staining properties of henna. This compound was thus selected to be investigated for its ability to develop latent fingermarks on paper surfaces. As expected, lawsone reacted with latent fingermark deposits on paper to yield purple-brown impressions of ridge details that were also photoluminescent. The authors proposed a ninhydrin-like mechanism for the lawsone reaction [53]. Following that work, other compounds possessing the naphthoquinone structure were also tried, and some developed latent fingermarks in a similar fashion [54]. Further research is required to investigate the reaction mechanism involved and to optimize the development conditions. In addition, there is the possibility that a wider application of lawsone could be found as a fluorogenic reagent for amino acids; however, additional studies are required in order to determine the optimum reaction conditions in solution and the sensitivity compared to existing reagents.

12.9 Benzimidazole-2-Carboxaldehydes

The recent discovery of a fluorogenic reaction between benzimidazole-2-carboxaldehydes and latent fingermarks is presented only briefly, since the reagent is not exactly a "ninhydrin analogue." It was decided, however, to include this information in this chapter since the initial stage of the chemical reaction between the reagent and amino acids produces a "Schiff base" in a similar manner to the reaction with ninhydrin and ninhydrin analogues. In 2009, Plater and his coworkers, from the University of Aberdeen, reported that *N*-alkyl and *N*-aryl substituted benzimidazole-2-carboxaldehydes (see Figure 12.13), upon reaction with latent fingermarks, produce stable fluorescent impressions [55]. Development was achieved in 2 min at 60°C–100°C and the impressions fluoresced strongly under a UV lamp at 254 and 366 nm. The authors stated that compound 13 showed promise as a reagent for the development of latent fingerprints, and that it should be commercially available and inexpensive [55].

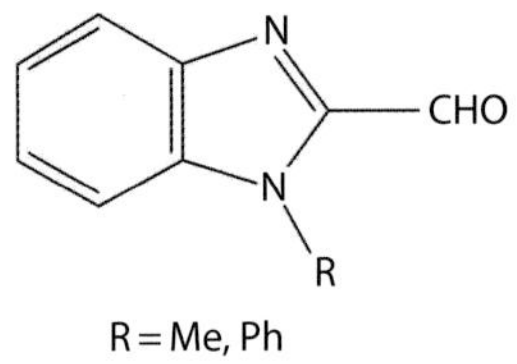

FIGURE 12.13
N-alkyl and *N*-aryl substituted benzimidazole-2-carboxaldehydes.

12.10 Conclusions

In spite of a great variety of existing fingermark techniques, research continues aiming at developing new, more sensitive reagents. It is assumed that ninhydrin and DFO will continue to be the main reagents for paper surfaces in the near future, but 1,2-indanedione/zinc chloride is making steady progress toward replacing DFO. The potential of the naturally occurring "dual fingermark reagents" genipin and lawsone and their analogues will be further investigated.

Author

Joseph Almog received his PhD in organic chemistry in 1972 from the Hebrew University of Jerusalem. Between 1972 and 1974, he conducted postdoctoral studies at the Imperial College in London and Massachusetts Institute of Technology in Cambridge, Massachusetts. He joined the Israel National Police in 1974. From 1984 to 2000, he was the director of the Division of Identification and Forensic Science. After retiring from police service, he became a professor of forensic chemistry at the Hebrew University of Jerusalem in 2000. In 2005, he received the Lucas Medal from the American Academy of Forensic Sciences "for outstanding achievements in forensic science." His fields of interest include fingerprints, explosives analysis, field tests, and forensic science as a tool against terrorism.

References

1. Almog J. (2001) Fingerprint development by ninhydrin and its analogues. In: Lee HC, Gaensslen RE. Eds. *Advances in Fingerprint Technology*, 2nd edn., Boca Raton, FL: CRC Press.
2. Hark RR, Hauze DB, Petrovskaia O, Joulliè MM. (2001) Synthetic studies of novel ninhydrin analogues. *Can J Chem* 79(11):1632–1654.
3. Friedman M. (2004) Applications of the ninhydrin reaction for analysis of amino acids, peptides, and proteins to agricultural and biomedical sciences. *J Agric Food Chem* 52:385–406.
4. Champod C, Lennard C, Margot P, Stoilovic M. (2004) *Fingerprints and Other Ridge Skin Impressions*. International Forensic Science and Investigation Series, Robertson J, Ed. Boca Raton, FL: CRC Press.
5. Hansen DB, Joullié MM. (2005) The development of novel ninhydrin analogues. *Chem Soc Rev* 34(5):408–417.

6. Jelly R, Patton ELT, Lennard C. (2009) The detection of latent fingermarks on porous surfaces using amino acid sensitive reagents: a review. *Anal Chim Acta* 652(1–2):128–142.
7. Wallace-Kunkel C, Roux C, Lennard C, Stoilovic M. (2004) The detection and enhancement of latent fingermarks on porous surfaces—a survey. *J Forensic Ident* 54(6):687–705.
8. Haruyuki K. (2008) Fingerprint detection solution, its production method, and fingerprint detection method using it. Japanese Patent JP 2008307195 A 20081225.
9. Appel K, Binder S. (2006) Method and device for the development of latent fingerprints on a fingerprint carrier. Ger: DE 102004063745 B3 20060928.
10. Schwarz L, Klenke I. (2007) Enhancement of ninhydrin- or DFO-treated latent fingerprints on thermal paper. *J Forensic Sci* 52(3):649–655.
11. Schwarz L, Klenke I. (2010) Improvement in latent fingerprint detection on thermal paper using a one-step ninhydrin treatment with polyvinylpyrrolidones (PVP). *J Forensic Sci* 55(4):1076–1079.
12. Boucher MA, Specht KM. (2007) Was it a murder? A case study for an organic chemistry laboratory. Abstracts of papers, 234th ACS National Meeting, Boston, MA, August 19–23, 2007.
13. Anastasios N, Limperopoulou-Karaliota A. (2007) Chemical methods for identification of fingerprints and cross-curricular links in teaching of chemistry (in Greek). *Chem Chron Genike Ekdose* 69(7):16–18.
14. Hoile R, Walsh SJ, Roux C. Bioterrorism: processing contaminated evidence, the effects of formaldehyde gas on the recovery of latent fingermarks. *J Forensic Sci* 52(5):1097–1102.
15. Bialek I, Zajak A, Brozowski J. (2006) Developing latent fingerprints on banknotes issued by the national bank of Poland (in English). *Z Zagadnien Nauk Sadowiych* 68:339–350.
16. Hark RR. Personal communication.
17. Elber R, Frank A, Almog J. (2000) Chemical development of latent fingerprints: computational design of ninhydrin analogues. *J Forensic Sci* 45(4):757–760.
18. Della EW, Janowski WK, Pigou PE, Taylor BM. (1999) Synthesis of fingerprint reagents: aromatic nucleophilic substitution as a route to 5-substituted ninhydrins. *Synthesis* 12:2119–2123.
19. Kobus HJ, Pigou PE, Jahangiri S. (2002) Evaluation of some oxygen, sulfur, and selenium substituted ninhydrin analogues, nitrophenylninhydrin and benzo[f]furoninhydrin. *J Forensic Sci* 47(2):254–259.
20. Almog J, Levinton-Shamuilov G, Cohen Y, Azoury M. (2007) Fingerprint reagents with dual action: color and fluorescence. *J Forensic Sci* 52(2):330–334.
21. Almog J, Klein A, Davidi I, Cohen Y, Azoury M, Levin-Elad M. (2008) Dual fingerprint reagents with enhanced sensitivity: 5-methoxy- and 5-methylthioninhydrin. *J Forensic Sci* 53(2):364–368.
22. Bicknell DE, Ramotowski RS. (2008) Use of an optimized 1,2-indanedione process for the development of latent prints. *J Forensic Sci* 53(5):1108–1116.
23. Sears V, Batham R, Bleay S. (2009) The effectiveness of 1,2-indandione-zinc formulations and comparison with HFE-based 1,8-diazafluoren-9-one for fingerprint development. *J Forensic Ident* 59(6):654–678.
24. Stoilovic M, Lennard C, Wallace-Kunkel C, Roux C. (2007) Evaluation of a 1,2-indanedione formulation containing zinc chloride for improved fingermark detection on paper. *J Forensic Ident* 57(1):4–18.
25. Sapse D, Petraco NDK. (2007) A step on the path in the discovery of new latent fingerprint development reagents: substituted Ruhemann's purples and implications for the law. *J Mol Model* 13:943–948.
26. Almog J, Glasner H. (2010) Ninhydrin thiohemiketals: basic research towards improved fingerprint techniques employing nano-technology. *J Forensic Sci* 55(1):215–220.
27. Saunders GC. (1989) Multimetal deposition technique for latent fingerprint development. In: *74th IAI Educational Conference Proceedings*, Pensacola, FL, June 1989.
28. Schnetz B, Margot P. (2001) Latent fingermarks, colloidal gold and multimetal deposition (MMD)—optimisation of the method. *Forensic Sci Int* 118(1):21–28.

29. Ramotowski RS, Cantu AA, Joullié MM, Petrovskaia O. (1997) 1,2-Indanediones: a preliminary evaluation of a new class of amino acid visualizing compounds. *Fingerprint Whorld* 23:131–140.
30. Hauze DB, Petrovskaia O, Taylor B, Joullié MM, Ramotowski RS, Cantu AA. (1998) 1,2-indanediones: new reagents for visualizing the amino acid components of latent prints. *J Forensic Sci* 43(4):744–747, 1998.
31. Almog J, Springer E, Wiesner S, Frank A, Khodzhaev O, Lidor R, Bahar E, Varkony H, Dayan S, Rozen S. (1999) Latent fingerprint visualization by 1,2-indanedione and related compounds: preliminary results. *J Forensic Sci* 44(1):114–118.
32. Wiesner S, Springer E, Sasson Y, Almog J. (2001) Chemical development of latent fingerprints: 1,2-indanedione has come of age. *J Forensic Sci* 46(5):1082–1084.
33. Azoury M, Zamir A, Oz, C. (2002) The effect of 1,2-indanedione, a latent fingerprint reagent on subsequent DNA profiling. *J Forensic Sci* 47(3):586–588.
34. Azoury M, Gabbay R, Cohen D, Almog J. (2003) ESDA processing and latent fingerprint development: the humidity effect. *J Forensic Sci* 48(3):564–570.
35. Roux C, Jones N, Lennard C. (2000) Evaluation of 1,2-indanedione and 5,8-dimethoxy-1,2-indanedione for the detection of latent fingerprints on porous surfaces. *J Forensic Sci* 45(4):761–769.
36. Wallace-Kunkel C, Lennard C, Stoilovic M. (2007) Optimisation and evaluation of 1,2-indanedione for use as a fingermark reagent and its application to real samples. *J Forensic Sci* 168(1):14–26.
37. Patton ELT, Brown DH, Lewis SW. (2010) Detection of latent fingermarks on thermal printer paper by dry contact with 1,2-indanedione. *Anal Methods* 2(6):631–637.
38. Alaoui IM, Menzel ER, Farag M. (2005) Mass spectra and time-resolved fluorescence spectroscopy of the reaction product of glycine with 1,2-indanedione in methanol. *Forensic Sci Int* 152(2–3):215–219.
39. Yu PH, Wallace MM. (2007) Effect of 1,2-indanedione on PCR-STR typing of fingerprints deposited on thermal and carbonless paper. *Forensic Sci Int* 168(2–3):112–118.
40. Gardner SJ, Hewlett DF. (2003) Optimization and initial evaluation of 1,2-indandione as a reagent for fingerprint detection. *J Forensic Sci* 48(6):1288–1292.
41. Merrick S, Gardner SJ, Sears VG, Hewlett D. (2002) An operational trial of ozone-friendly DFO and 1,2-indandione formulations for latent fingerprint detection. *J Forensic Ident* 52(50):595–605.
42. Alaoui IM. (2007) Photodegradation studies by laser-induced fluorescence of the reaction product of 1,2-indanedione and glycine. *Spectrosc Lett* 40(5):715–721.
43. Wilkinson D. (2000) Spectroscopic study of 1,2-indanedione. *Forensic Sci Int* 114:123–132.
44. Wilkinson D, McKenzie E, Leech C, Mayowski D, Bertrand S, Walker T. (2003) The results from a Canadian national field trial comparing two formulations of DFO with 1,2-indanedione. *Ident Canada* 26(2):8–18.
45. Almog, J. (2003) Forensic science as a strategic tool for combating terrorism, Presented at the AAFS Annual Conference, Chicago, IL, February.
46. Kasper S, Minnillo D, Rockhold A. (2002) Validating ind (1,2-indanedione), *Forensic Sci Commun* 4(4).
47. C. Lennard [Australia], J. Cheng [Taiwan], Personal communications.
48. Almog J, Cohen Y, Azoury M, Hahn T-R. (2004) Genipin, a novel fingerprint reagent with colorimetric and fluorogenic activity. *J Forensic Sci* 49(2):255–257.
49. Levinton-Shamuilov G, Cohen Y, Azoury M, Chaikovsky A, Almog J. (2005) Genipin, a novel fingerprint reagent with colorimetric and fluorogenic activity. Part II: optimization, scope and limitations. *J Forensic Sci* 50(6):1367–1371.
50. Almog J, Dalrymple B. (2010) Assessment of one new laser and two new amino acid reagents for visualizing latent fingermarks. Presented at the IAI annual educational conference, Spokane Washington (July).

51. Inouye H, Takeda Y, Inoue K, Kawamura I, Yatsuzuka M, Touyama R, Ikumoto T, Shingu T, Yokoi T. (1984) Structure of blue pseudoazulene-skeleton pigment derived from genipin and amino acids. *Tennen Yuki Kagobutsu Toronkai Koen Yoshishu* 26:577–584. CODEN: TYKYDS Journal, written in Japanese. CAN 100:99895, AN 1984:99895.
52. Fujikawa S, Fukui Y, Koga K, Kumada J-I. (1987) Brilliant skyblue pigment formation from gardenia fruits. *J Ferment Technol* 65(4):419–424.
53. Jelly R, Lewis SW, Lennard C, Lim KF, Almog J. (2008) Lawsone: a novel reagent for the detection of latent fingermarks on paper surfaces. *Chem Commun* 3513–3515.
54. Jelly R, Lewis SW, Lennard C, Lim KF, Almog J. (2008) Substituted naphthoquinones as novel amino acid sensitive reagents for the detection of latent fingermarks on paper surfaces, *Talanta* 82:1717–1724.
55. Plater MJ, Barnes P, McDonald LK, Wallace S, Archer N, Gelbrich T, Horton PN, Hursthouse MB. (2009) Hidden signatures: new reagents for developing latent fingerprints. *Org Biomol Chem* 7:1633–1641.

13

Fingermark Detection Using Nanoparticles

Andy Bécue and Antonio A. Cantú

CONTENTS

13.1 Introduction

The terminology that is used in this chapter clearly differentiates a "fingerprint" from a "fingermark," by following the definitions proposed by Champod and Chamberlain in a recent publication [1]. A fingerprint is defined as "a reference impression from a known sample taken with cooperation and under controlled conditions using either an inking process or an optical device [...] Because of their pristine acquisition conditions, prints are a near perfect representation of the friction ridge skin" (from Ref. [1]). A fingermark is defined as an impression, generally composed of sweat residues, that is "left adventitiously when one touches an object without gloves or foot wear. By the uncontrolled nature of the deposition, marks are often of varying quality compared to the prints" (from Ref. [1]). It should be noted that the distinction between fingerprint and fingermarks was already mentioned in another book [2], with a fingerprint defined as "a record or comparison print taken for identification, exclusion, or database purposes," and fingermarks as "traces left (unknowingly) by a person on an object."

A fingermark constitutes one of the most powerful traces that can be exploited as evidence of identity of source, since it constitutes a partial representation of the ridge skin pattern of an individual's finger. Three kinds of fingermarks may be found during an investigation (being at a crime scene or on a related item): visible, plastic, and latent (invisible). The first two kinds are directly visible to the investigators and require only a camera and optical skills to record them. The last kind is the most common form encountered and corresponds to invisible marks, which require the application of detection techniques to allow their visualization. Their detection constitutes a major and continuous challenge for forensic scientists and investigators. As a consequence, numerous efficient techniques have been developed over several years to detect latent fingermarks on various substrates [3,4]. The books by Champod et al. and by Lee and Gaensslen offer two thorough and complete summaries about fingerprints, the composition of the secretion residue, and the existing fingermark detection techniques [2,5]. It should also be noted that most of the techniques able to detect fingermarks are also suitable to detect marks that emerge from the contact of a surface with other parts of the body presenting papillary ridges (e.g., palms and foot).

Detection techniques are generally classified according to the type and state of substrate and secretion that are targeted. For example, latent fingermarks on porous surfaces may be detected using 1,2-indanedione or ninhydrin (non-exhaustive list); on nonporous surfaces, cyanoacrylate fuming (followed by a staining step) or vacuum metal deposition gives excellent results; physical developer (Ag-PD) or Oil Red O is applied in case of wet fingermarks; and blood-contaminated marks require the use of specific blood reagents (e.g., Acid Yellow 7 or Acid Violet 17), just to cite a few of several situations encountered. However, a more practical way of classifying the methods, especially when working on the improvement of existing ones or the development of new ones, is to do it by their mode of interaction with the secretion components. If we exclude optical methods from this classification, we can distinguish the methods driven by (1) chemical reactions (e.g., 1,2-indanedione, ninhydrin, and blood reagents), (2) physicochemical mechanisms (e.g., Ag-PD, multimetal deposition [MMD], and cyanoacrylate fuming), and (3) physical processes (e.g., powder dusting and powder suspensions). Each interaction mode possesses its advantages and drawbacks in terms of efficiency and sensitivity according to the latent secretions, the nature of the substrate, and various other parameters.

Despite the dozens of techniques currently available to the investigators, some serious issues remain: for example, some surfaces are considered as "problematic," with no or few possibilities to detect fingermarks on them; very faint marks may not be detected using conventional techniques; and environmental conditions (humidity, heat, light) may have a detrimental effect on the latent residue, decreasing the efficiency of the existing methods. The last 20 years have shown the need to develop new techniques, and to improve existing ones, by widening the application fields and increasing the global sensitivity and success rate of detection. Among the existing improvement possibilities, a promising alternative to conventional techniques exploits nanoparticles or nanostructured materials, which have recently made great strides within forensic research laboratories (see Section 13.4) [3,6–8].

The following definitions from the field of nanotechnology (e.g., see Refs. [9–12]) will be applied throughout this chapter:

- Materials with morphological features smaller than 100 nm, in at least one of their dimensions, are referred to as nanomaterials. Nanoparticles constitute a category of nanomaterials that are nanoscale in three dimensions. Nanostructures are nanoscale structures on the surface of materials (not necessarily nanomaterials).
- Nanoscience, or nanotechnology, is that part of science (or a technique) concerned with how nanostructures and nanomaterials are designed, fabricated, and applied to specific and well-defined uses. Given such a wide definition, nanotechnology is to be found at the interface between chemistry, biology, physics, as well as material science, since it combines synthetic steps and chemical assemblies, solubility and stability issues, optical and spectroscopic properties, as well as biocompatibility issues.
- Nanoparticles are subsets of colloidal particles whose spherical enclosure can range up to 1000 nm (1 μm) in diameter. The terms "nanoparticles" and "colloidal particles" will thus be used preferentially, and interchangeably, according to the context in the following sections. Since colloidal particles include nanoparticles, what is said about colloidal particles will also be true for nanoparticles, unless otherwise stated.
- A dispersion of colloidal-size particles in a medium whether a gas, a liquid, or a solid is called a colloid (sometimes also a colloidal system, a colloidal dispersion, or a colloidal suspension). Current developments covered here are confined

to systems of solid colloidal particles in liquids, also called "sols" (colloidal solutions). Such colloids are usually divided into two types: lyophilic (strong attraction between the colloid medium and the dispersion medium of a colloidal system) and lyophobic (lack of attraction between the colloid medium and the dispersion medium of a colloidal system), depending on how well the system can be redispersed (peptized) after it has dried out [9]. When the solvent is water, these systems are called hydrophilic or hydrophobic, respectively.

- A gel is defined as a porous three-dimensional interconnected solid network that expands throughout a liquid medium. If the solid network is made of colloidal sol particles, the gel is said to be colloidal.

Nanoparticles in the nano-size range exhibit size-dependent properties that differ from those observed in the bulk materials or in atoms (e.g., melting points, magnetic properties, and hardness). This phenomenon is referred to as the "quantum size effect" [13–15]. The optical properties exhibited by quantum dots (QDs), which are commonly characterized as "zero-dimension" species, are good examples of the "quantum size effect" (QDs are discussed further in Sections 13.2.1.2 and 13.2.3.2). The confinement of electrons in all three dimensions leads to discrete electronic states, giving QDs' specific optical properties such as a strong luminescence, which is not encountered in the bulk material. Another important characteristic of nanoparticles is their very large "relative surface area." In other words, nanoparticles have a much greater surface area per unit mass compared to larger particles or bulk materials (this subject is further treated in Section 13.2.2.1). This constitutes an advantage in terms of catalytic activity and functionalization possibilities. Indeed, since catalytic chemical reactions occur at the surface, a given mass of nanoparticles will be much more reactive than the same mass of material made up of larger particles or as a unique bulk. For example, gold in its bulk state does not present significant catalytic properties whereas gold nanocrystals are known to be good low temperature heterogeneous catalysts [16–18]. The origin of this effect is to be found in the fact that the fraction of atoms at the surface of a particle (compared with the ones embedded in its core) increases as the mean particle size decreases.

The properties emerging from the nanometer scale promote research and development of new methods that will benefit from nanomaterials, in various scientific domains. Scientists have recently developed the ability to visualize, engineer, and manipulate nanometer-scaled materials. Modern synthetic chemistry permits the creation of particles of almost any structure, either through direct synthesis or through molecular assembly (especially useful when dealing with molecular recognition). The smart combination of all these elements leads to nanostructured materials possessing their own specificities in terms of composition, solubility, optical properties, and targeting abilities. Common application fields for nanoparticles cover domains like biomedical, optical, and electronic devices, for which the nanoscale size, optical properties, and chemical versatility are of prime interest compared to classical (organic) molecules [19–23]. The manipulation and engineering of nanomaterials seem to be a recent activity, but the use of nanoparticles for their specific properties is not new. Numerous historical examples have shown that men were already using nanoparticles centuries ago, mainly as stains. A good example is the Lycurgus Cup, a fourth century AD glass cup illustrating a mythological scene [24]. The main particularity of this cup is its dichroism (this means that the cup changes its color when it is held up to the light) due to the presence of gold and silver colloidal particles in the glass.

The interest of forensic science research in nanoparticles can be found in the intimate characteristics they feature: the nanoscale particles should guarantee a good resolution in terms of ridge details; the specific optical properties—such as luminescence—should constitute a strong advantage in terms of contrast between the mark and the substrate; and the chemical versatility offered by the surface modifications should provide an increased selectivity for very faint latent fingermarks. All of these properties should combine to lead to an increased success rate of detection compared to conventional existing methods. As to their size, the advantages of using such small elements for fingermark detection can be illustrated by representing an average nanoparticle of ~40 nm by a green pea. At this scale, the width of an average ridge measures almost the width of an American football field. This gives an idea of the great potential of nanoparticles in terms of ridge resolution and representation, when targeting and detecting latent secretions. Of course, this has meaning only if nanoparticles show specificity toward the secretions rather than their surroundings (i.e., inter-ridge regions or furrows). This issue can be addressed by chemically modifying the particle surface in order to increase the specific affinity of the nanoparticles for the ridges (i.e., the secretions) instead of the underlying substrate. Moreover, nanoparticles can be dried and used as powders to detect fingermarks. But a more interesting and safer way of using them is to develop a detection technique based on the use of nanoparticles in solution, in which case they can be modified to increase the selectivity. To reach this goal, it is necessary to understand the way nanoparticles are being formed, how they behave in solution, and how it is possible to tune their chemical and optical properties. All these points are covered in Section 13.2. These are crucial points to assimilate, since they greatly influence the interaction mechanisms between nanoparticles and the secretion residues.

Finally, the development of a new fingermark detection technique based on the use of nanoparticles involves two distinct stages: first, the choice of the "marker" that will be optically detected (i.e., the atomic composition and the optical properties of the nanoparticle of interest), and second, once the marker is defined, a surface engineering step is usually necessary to tune its behavior so that it will specifically target secretion residues. These two stages may be considered independently. Indeed, markers of different kinds (e.g., QDs, silica nanoparticles, or colloidal gold) can share the same targeting strategy if they bear the same outer-surface ligands. The resulting nanomaterials will then target the latent secretions in the same ways, even if they are different in terms of composition of the markers. Similarly, a nanoparticle can be modified so that it will interact differently with the secretions according to the ligand that is added to its surface (the targets can be lipids, amino acids, or other chemical species). By smartly combining these two aspects (i.e., "marker" and "functionalization"), one could offer forensic investigators new, powerful tools for detection. For all of these reasons, this field of research certainly opens a new era in the development of new, original, and efficient techniques to detect fingermarks.

Another parameter that plays a major role is the choice of the solvent in which the nanoparticles are synthesized or redispersed (peptized after precipitation). Indeed, aqueous solutions are generally preferred for their lower toxicity and the possibility of being used without the need for working under a fume hood, or applied as a spray at crime scenes, for example. This is the case for colloidal gold in the MMD process [25–28]. Given the high number of synthesis protocols that can be found in the literature, it is often possible to synthesize the "same" nanocomposites (if we exclude the nature of the capping ligands, which ensures the stability of the nanoparticles in their medium) either in organic solvents or in water. However, some chemical modifications, such as the addition of hydrophobic ligands on the surface of the nanoparticles, may force their transfer to organic solvents since the resulting nanocomposites are no longer soluble in water [29,30]. The chosen application protocols (e.g., spray at the crime scene, powder dusting, or immersion without the need for a fume hood) will mainly drive the choice for one synthesis route or another.

Besides their application to detect latent fingermarks, nanoparticles can also be used to add security to official documents (e.g., passports), jewelry, and the like, to assure the owner of its authenticity or to decrease the possibility of counterfeits. In Oliver's presentation titled *Digital Security Printing Inks and Toners: Recent Developments in Nano-and Smart-Materials* [31], several examples are provided about the use of QDs and other nanoparticles in security and anti-counterfeiting. Other applications of nanoparticles in forensic science include their use in biomedical examinations where visualizing specific bioorganic components in forensic toxicology or pathology is important, and in the fight against terrorism in terms of decontamination of contaminated sites. These applications are beyond the strict context of this chapter and will therefore not be developed further. The readers are invited to refer to the article of Cantú for further information [32].

The following sections give a global overview of commonly encountered nanoparticles, that is, their synthesis and structural/optical properties (Section 13.2), how they could be used to detect fingermarks, with the issues that should be answered (Section 13.3), and a review of the existing techniques using nanoparticles to detect latent fingermarks (Section 13.4).

13.2 Nanoparticles: Structure and Properties

Numerous books or publications are currently dealing with nanoparticles and nanoscale materials, in terms of detailed fundamental and theoretical approaches, synthesis, and applications. The reader is strongly encouraged to refer to them if more detailed information about nanoparticles is required. The aim of this section is not to constitute a thorough review of this field since it would certainly be outside of our primary objective. We managed to concentrate our attention on the principal characteristics of interest in fingermark detection techniques based on nanoparticles. The following topics will be covered:

- Synthesis of monodisperse spherical nanoparticles (Section 13.2.1)
- Stability of nanoparticles in solution (Section 13.2.2)
- Optical properties of nanoparticles (Section 13.2.3)
- Surface functionalization (Section 13.2.4)
- Health and safety issues (Section 13.2.5)

13.2.1 Synthesis of Monodisperse Spherical Nanoparticles

Nanoparticles can be synthesized from a variety of different materials, in aqueous or organic solutions, leading to versatile compositions, shapes, and properties. All these synthetic procedures can be classified according to only two major approaches: "top-down" and "bottom-up." The "top-down" approach consists in starting with a larger existing structure down-sized by attrition or milling. These physical mechanisms lead to particles of tens to several hundreds of nanometers in size, but generally characterized by a broad size distribution and several surface defects. This approach is not favored when nanometer-scale structures are to be obtained. The "bottom-up" approach consists in building nanoparticles by following a chemical process (element-by-element) through solution-phase colloidal chemistry. More homogeneous particles with few surface imperfections result from this approach. It is thus preferred in the context of nanoparticles of small size. It encompasses two different synthetic processes, namely, thermodynamic and kinetic [33]:

1. In the thermodynamic approach, precursor species are placed in a supersaturation state. By doing this, the formation of a second phase (e.g., solid in liquid) occurs to allow the reduction of the system's overall Gibbs free energy [34] (i.e., the system's available energy to do work). This is called the "nucleation step." Once a thermodynamically stable nucleus is created (i.e., when it reaches the critical size at which it will not dissolve again in the surrounding medium), it will start to grow in size by the addition of growth species on its surface. This is called the "growth step," during which the monomers (i.e., the building blocks or atoms) are transported toward the surface of the nucleus and react with it. It should be noted that both nucleation and growth steps can occur simultaneously (if the concentration of precursors is above the supersaturation state), but at different speeds. When the quantity of precursors is no longer sufficient to allow the creation of new nuclei, only the growth will continue (Figure 13.1). Ideally, the nucleation process should be terminated before the system enters into the growth process, so that a uniform (i.e., monodisperse) size distribution is obtained. Nevertheless, according to the nucleation and growth rates, one can obtain monodisperse or polydisperse solutions. A typical example of such an approach is the synthesis of QDs in organic solvents, during which reactants are quickly injected in an organic solvent at high temperature [13], leading to an instantaneous burst in the nucleation process which lasts only a very short time due to the sharp decrease in monomer concentration and the fast cooling of the reaction mixture [35]. Only the growth process remains, and the nanoparticles grow homogeneously in size.
2. In the kinetic approach, a limited amount of precursors is available for the growth, or the process is confined in a limited space (e.g., microemulsion or micelles). The growth of the nanoparticles is constrained since it stops when the limited amount

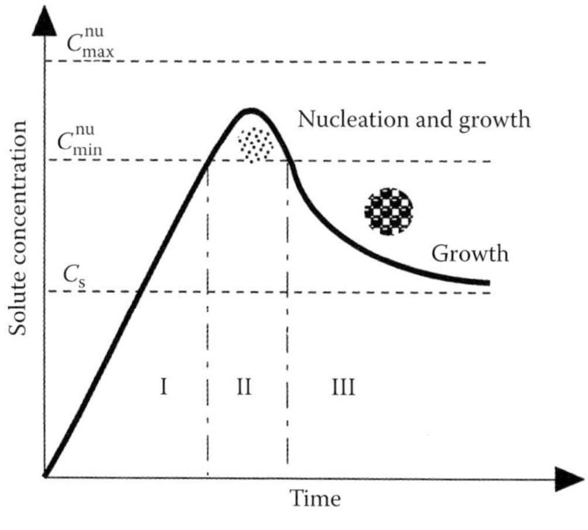

FIGURE 13.1
Illustration of the evolution of the precursor concentration with time in the case of a homogeneous growth of nanoparticles. Nucleation begins once a critical concentration value is reached. When the concentration of solute falls below this limit, only growth keeps proceeding. (Image source from Pierre AC. (1998) *Introduction to Sol–Gel Processing*. Boston, USA: Kluwer Academic Publishers, 1–9 (introduction on sol–gel); 103 (Figure); 124–146 (electrostatic interactions). With permission from Springer.)

of precursors has been consumed or if the space has been filled up with the particle. A typical example of such an approach is the synthesis of nanoparticles (e.g., silica or silver) inside small droplets of water suspended in oil, which is also known as reverse microemulsion [36–38]. Briefly, water nanodroplets are formed in an oil phase (bulk), stabilized by surrounding surfactant molecules, and act as nanoreactors for the formation of nanoparticles. The formation of silica nanoparticles inside the water droplets takes place by hydrolysis of silica precursor molecules using ammonium hydroxide as a catalyst [39]. This process is widely used to obtain nanoparticles with a perfect spherical shape and a very narrow size distribution, with the size of the droplets being controlled by the water-to-surfactant molar ratio.

In forensic science, we can observe that the "bottom-up" approach, and more particularly the thermodynamic process, is encountered for the MMD technique (gold colloids) [25], during the Ag-PD process (silver nanoparticles) [40], or in recently developed techniques using QDs [41–43], silica nanoparticles [44], or zinc oxide nanoparticles [45] (see Section 13.4 for further details).

The scope of this chapter will be limited to the description of three representative nanoparticles:

1. Synthesis of gold colloids using reduction agents (Section 13.2.1.1)
2. Synthesis of semiconductor nanocrystals by thermal decomposition (Section 13.2.1.2)
3. Synthesis of silica nanospheres following a sol–gel process (Section 13.2.1.3)

Two reasons have led to this choice: (1) from a chemical point of view, they are characterized by different nucleation and growth processes, and (2) from a forensic point of view, these nanoparticles are currently focusing research toward the development of new fingermark detection techniques, as it can be seen in Section 13.4.

For further information about the synthesis of other kinds of nanomaterials (e.g., various metal or magnetic nanocrystals), or other mechanisms, the reader is referred to existing thorough reviews on this subject [46–48].

13.2.1.1 Synthesis of Gold Colloids Using Reduction Agents

The conventional method to synthesize gold nanoparticles in aqueous solution consists of reducing gold (III) derivatives (soluble in water) using reduction agents (e.g., tetrachloroauric acid—$HAuCl_4$—reduced by sodium citrate). The reduction of the metallic salt leads to the formation of insoluble metallic gold entities that further aggregate to form discrete particles with sizes ranging from a few to hundreds of nanometers. The widely accepted mechanism is a LaMer nucleation-growth model, based on the concept of "burst nucleation" [46,49]. Gold chloride ions are first reduced to atomic Au, up to the supersaturation level of concentration. At a certain moment, many nuclei are being formed at the same time (nucleation step) and most of the other gold atoms begin to get attached to the particles in solution (growth step). During the synthesis, the color of the solution changes from pale yellow ($AuCl_4^-$) to colorless (gold atoms), dark blue, and finally ruby red (~20 nm gold nanoparticles). However, a recent study suggests that this nucleation-growth mechanism (according to which each nucleus progressively increases its size until the final colloidal particles are formed) is not compatible with the range of colors that is observed during the synthesis, in particular the transient dark coloration [50]. Pong et al. revisited the growth mechanism

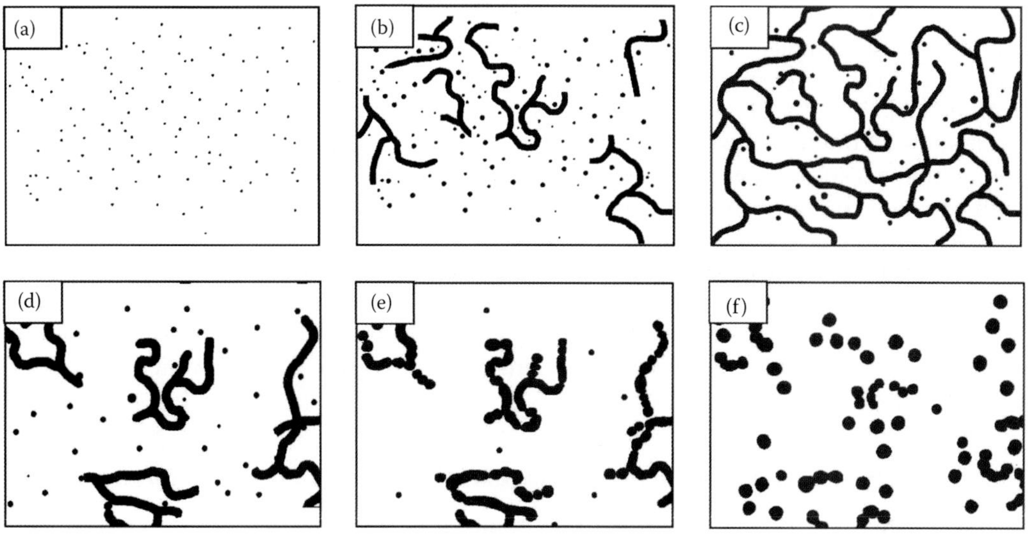

FIGURE 13.2
Formation mechanism of gold colloids in the citrate reduction process, as proposed by Pong et al. Early in the process, gold aggregates (step a) self-assemble to form an extensive network of nanowires (steps b–d), explaining the dark-blue transient color. At a certain point, the network undergoes fragmentation into small segments to finally form individual, and spherical, gold nanoparticles (steps e and f). (Image source from Pong, B.-K. et al., *J. Phys. Chem. C*, 111, 6281, 2007.)

of gold nanoparticles. They kept the idea of burst nucleation with formation of individual gold nuclei, but they showed that gold nanoclusters of about 5 nm diameter self-assemble during the initial stage of the reaction to form an extensive network of nanowires of ~5 nm diameter (which explains the dark blue intermediate color). The nanowire network grows in size, through addition of gold atoms, until it reaches ~10 nm of diameter. At this point, the structure starts to break up into well-defined spherical particles of diameter ~13–15 nm, due to the adsorption of negatively charged citrate ions, which induce repulsion between the linked gold nanospheres (Figure 13.2).

The reduction of gold chloride in aqueous solution was first observed by Faraday, in 1857, using phosphorus as reduction agent [51], and has been further applied, modified, and optimized [52–57]. The reduction of $HAuCl_4$ by sodium citrate in boiling water is one of the most currently used procedures for obtaining monodisperse spherical gold nanoparticles of generally ~10–20 nm diameter, with excellent time stability (several months to years) [55]. The process of gold nanoparticle formation by citrate reduction has been investigated in detail by Kimling et al., who found a general relation between the gold-to-reductant molar ratio and the final size of the particles [58]. By following the earlier work of Turkevich, they also showed that gold nanoparticles can be synthesized in a wide range of sizes, from 9 to 120 nm, with varying size distributions. The time stability of colloidal gold can be explained by the formation of an ionic shell around each gold nanoparticle, due to the adsorption of negatively charged ions coming from the reaction mixture (mainly from citrate ions). Thus the sodium citrate ions play a double role: the first one as reducing agents and the second one as capping agents, preventing gold nanoparticles in solution from aggregating, through electrostatic repulsion (see Section 13.2.2.2).

For nanoparticles with diameters below 10 nm, an alternative to the sodium citrate route exists: the sodium borohydride ($NaBH_4$) reduction of gold chloride in a two-phase process (water/toluene) [29]. The nanoparticles synthesized according to this method are capped with thiolated ligands (e.g., alkanethiols R–SH). These colloids can be repeatedly isolated and redissolved in common organic solvents without irreversible aggregation or decomposition [30]. Recently, Hussain et al. proposed a way to prepare a near-monodisperse gold hydrosol with diameter size below 5 nm, in a single-step reduction process using $NaBH_4$ and a thioether-terminated polymeric stabilizer [59]. These particles are readily soluble in both aqueous and nonaqueous solvents. Moreover, the particle size can be controlled by varying the ratio of Au to the capping ligand.

Once synthesized, gold colloids can be used to detect fingermarks (like in the MMD) or can be subsequently surface-functionalized if needed (see Section 13.4.4). For further information about colloidal gold (structure, properties, and applications), the reader is strongly invited to refer to the two following excellent reviews on the subject: Daniel and Astruc [60] and Ghosh and Pal [61].

13.2.1.2 Synthesis of Semiconductor Nanocrystals by Thermal Decomposition

Semiconductor nanocrystals are composed of hundreds to a few thousands of atoms only, corresponding to a size range of 1–10 nm. These are so-called "QDs" or "zero-dimension particles" due to the nanometer confinement exerted in all three dimensions. Such nanoparticles are of a first interest in imaging applications due to their specific photoluminescence abilities, which are directly related to their quantum confinement (see Section 13.2.3.1), and the fact that they can be synthesized from a variety of different materials (e.g., CdSe, CdTe, ZnS, HgTe, InP, GaAs, or InAs). During the last decade, various reviews were published on the subject [23,35,46,62–68], as a proof of the strong interest of the scientific community for such nanoparticles.

Two main synthetic routes exist, which differ by the media into which the QDs are synthesized, organic solvent or aqueous solution. For both routes, the general growth model of the nanocrystals is based on the same principles as previously described, which is a "bottom-up" process initiated by a supersaturation-induced nucleation step followed by a growth step [34]. The choice for one route instead of another has to be made according to the specificities of each one and to the subsequent application of the QDs:

- The synthesis in organic media was first proposed in 1993 [13] and is certainly the most popular and the most exhaustively studied route for synthesizing QDs [34,35,62,69,70]. From a synthetic point of view, the decomposition of molecular precursors (i.e., the molecule that will bring the atomic species) is performed by injecting them quickly in a hot coordinating solvent (e.g., 200°C–360°C). This is the "hot injection" step [13]. As a consequence, the nucleation step will readily start. The high temperature is required to form nuclei because the activation energy for nucleation is much higher than that for the growth of nanocrystals. The role of the organic solvent during the synthesis is twofold, solubilizing the reactive species and controlling the growth of the nanocrystals by playing the role of surface ligands. Indeed, at high temperature, solvent molecules will continuously bind and unbind from the surface of the nucleus, allowing new atomic species to bind to it and make the nanocrystal grow according to the dynamic induced by the solvent. Currently, trioctylphosphine oxide (TOPO) and trioctylphosphine (TOP) are frequently used to play the role of surface ligands, but the possible combinations of precursor, stabilizer, and solvent are numerous (see Table 2 from [35]). The QDs that are obtained are soluble in organic solvents such as toluene, chloroform, or hexane. Among the advantages of this synthetic route, we can cite: a narrow size distribution, a high degree of crystallinity, and a high photoluminescence quantum yield—up to 65%. Among the disadvantages of this synthetic route, we can cite: the need for high reaction temperature (i.e., 200°C–360°C) and the low compatibility of the resulting particles with aqueous solutions. This last point may be problematic in the context of the development of a user- or environment-friendly fingermark detection technique based on water instead of flammable organic solvents. It is somewhat possible to transfer QDs synthesized according to the organometallic approach into water, principally through encapsulation, surface modifications, or ligand exchange [20,71–75]. However, these processes require additional synthetic steps, which are time-consuming. The solubility of the resulting nanocrystals may not be excellent since the colloidal solutions may be unstable and the quantum yields may be low.

- The synthesis in water is historically the first successful preparation method for semiconductor nanocrystals [76]. However, the first syntheses in water led to QDs with low quantum yields, typically 5%–10%, which explains why the organometallic route was preferred once discovered. Nevertheless, recent advances in the domain of aqueous synthesis make it a promising alternative to the traditional organometallic one [66,77–81]. It is indeed possible to increase the quantum yield up to 40%–65% through optimization of different parameters involved in the synthesis, for example, the ratio of cadmium to ligand [80,82,83], the surface ligands [66], or the pH [77,80]. Some authors also report obtaining aqueous soluble QDs with quantum yields of ~80% using glutathione as capping reagent [84]. The aqueous route is more user-friendly because it is performed at 100°C, compared to ~300°C for the organometallic route, and does not require dangerous materials or solvents. The size distribution is somewhat broader than the one obtained by following the organometallic route, but it can be sharpened through a size-selective precipitation process.

This discussion demonstrates that the synthesis of semiconductor nanocrystals, either in organic or aqueous solution, is well documented and constantly being optimized. Such nanoparticles are stable in solution, similar to gold colloids, mainly due to the ligand capping that occurs during the synthesis. They can be used as synthesized or they can be further functionalized, if needed. These kinds of particles are promising for use in the field of fingermark detection.

13.2.1.3 Synthesis of Silica Nanospheres Following a Sol–Gel Process

The sol–gel process is certainly one of the most popular routes for the synthesis of various oxide materials [85], like silica oxide (SiO_2) nanoparticles. The concept of sol–gel consists of creating an oxide network by polymerization reactions of chemical precursors dissolved in a liquid medium [86]. As stated in Section 13.1, a sol is defined as a stable suspension of colloidal solid particles within a liquid. Since the particles are generally denser than the surrounding liquid, a stable sol can only be obtained if the dispersion forces are greater than the gravity.

Silica nanoparticles are inorganic oxide particles or organic–inorganic hybrids that can be put in suspension either in aqueous solution or in organic solvents. Their synthesis generally consists of a wet chemical mechanism into which reactive precursors (generally silicon alkoxides in alcohol, Si–O–R) are first hydrolyzed, resulting in the corresponding hydroxide species (Si–O–H). The hydrolysis is followed by a (poly)condensation process between the species in solution through elimination of water, leading to the formation of a network of silicon oxide (Si–O–Si), to finally form a colloidal suspension. The rates of the hydrolysis and condensation steps are important since they will affect the properties of the final product. For example, a slower and more controlled hydrolysis leads to smaller particle sizes. For alkoxides that have low rates of hydrolysis, it is possible to use acids or bases as catalysts to enhance the process. The acids protonate the relatively negative alkoxide molecules, creating a better leaving group and eliminating the need for proton transfer. The bases provide better nucleophiles for hydrolysis [87].

The synthesis of SiO_2 nanoparticles follows either of two major synthetic routes: the "Stöber" or the "reverse microemulsion" method, which differ by the media into which the nanoparticles are synthesized (bulk water or water-in-oil emulsion, respectively):

1. The Stöber method is a wet chemical technique used in materials science and ceramic engineering (metal oxides) to synthesize pure silica nanoparticles or hydrophobic/organic dye-doped nanoparticles [88–91]. This process requires the hydrolysis and the condensation of silica precursors in an alkaline solution of ethanol, water, and ammonia. The role of ammonia as a catalyst is to bring the mixture under basic conditions so that three-dimensional structures are formed instead of linear ones. Commonly used silica precursors are silicon alkoxides bearing four alkyl ligands, like tetraethoxysilane (TEOS)—$Si(OCH_2CH_3)_4$. Functionalized precursors may also be used to confer new capabilities to the particles. For example, Johnston et al. proposed to synthesize silica nanoparticles starting from 3-mercaptopropyl trimethoxysilane monomers, $Si(OCH_3)_3$–$CH_2CH_2CH_2SH$, to obtain fully functionalized particles of 1–100 μm in diameter, into which fluorescent dyes can be covalently incorporated post-synthesis [91]. The Stöber method is simple, cheap, and can be carried out in only a few minutes or hours. The silica oxide nanoparticles are characterized by diameter sizes ranging from 50 nm to 2 μm, according to the amount of reagents and catalyst, the nature of the solvent, and the temperature [90]. This synthesis presents the following advantages: a one-pot synthesis carried out at room temperature; the use of ethanol:water mixtures under alkaline conditions, thus avoiding the use of organic solvents; and the possibility to physically trap fluorescent organic compounds in the inorganic network to obtain fluorescent nanoparticles (see Section 13.2.3.3). This synthesis suffers from the following disadvantages: the necessity for further filtration and separation steps if monodispersity is required.
2. The reverse microemulsion process, also known as "water-in-oil microemulsion (W/O)," is commonly used to synthesize dye-doped or magnetic nanoparticles with a narrow size distribution. It consists of a single-phase system, isotropic, and thermodynamically stable, composed of three primary components: water, oil, and surfactant (sometimes, a cosurfactant can be added into the system). The principle is based on the solubilization of surfactants in organic solvents to form spheroidal aggregates, called reversed micelles. In the presence of water, the polar head groups of the surfactant organize themselves around the small water pools, leading to dispersion of the aqueous phase in the continuous oil phase. Those water nanodroplets act as nanoreactors for the formation of nanoparticles. The formation of silica nanoparticles inside the W/O microemulsion takes place by hydrolysis of precursor molecules using NH_4OH as a catalyst. The formation of

nanoparticles is performed in four steps: (1) association of the silicon precursors (e.g., alkoxides) with the W/O microemulsion, (2) hydrolysis and formation of the monomers, (3) nucleation, and (4) particle growth. Ammonium hydroxide acts as a catalyst, by providing the OH^- ions necessary for the hydrolysis of the silicon precursor. In order for hydrolysis to take place, the precursor molecules need to diffuse from the surrounding organic phase into the W/O microemulsion, where NH_4OH is concentrated (due to its polarity). The size of the droplets is mainly controlled by the water-to-surfactant molar ratio (W_0). For example, a W_0 ratio of 10, combined with Triton X-100 as surfactant, can lead to the formation of nanoparticles with diameters of 60–70 nm [92]. An increase in the water-to-surfactant ratio changes three parameters: (1) it increases the size of the water pool of the reverse micelles; (2) it increases the number of monomers per microemulsion droplet; and (3) it increases the intermicellar exchange rate due to a decrease in the rigidity of the surfactant film. As a consequence, the size of the obtained nanoparticles decreases [93]. A disadvantage of the reverse microemulsion route is that it requires several thorough washing steps to remove the oil phase and surfactants before being able to recover silica nanoparticles for further applications.

Silica nanoparticles, being synthesized according to the Stöber or to the W/O microemulsion methods, are not readily useful on their own since they are chemically inert and optically transparent and do not possess a natural affinity for finger secretions. It is thus necessary to combine them with a dye (see Section 13.2.3.3) and to functionalize their outer surface (see Section 13.2.4.3) before being used to detect fingermarks.

13.2.2 Stability of Nanoparticles in Solution

In this section, each of the energetic contributions implicated in the stabilization (or destabilization) of colloidal particles in solution will be detailed. This section is thus not directly linked with the use of nanoparticles to detect fingermarks, but could constitute a precious tool for those willing to develop a detection technique based on nanoparticles in solution and facing colloidal instability problems.

13.2.2.1 van der Waals Interactions

Colloidal particles have an extremely large specific surface area (i.e., ratio of the area divided by the mass of an array of particles) due to their small size. To illustrate this, consider the example of a spherical particle of radius R. Its surface area is $4\pi R^2$; its volume is $(4/3)\pi R^3$; its mass is density × volume; and, therefore, the ratio of its surface area to its mass is $3/(R \times \text{density})$. As R decreases, this ratio increases. It means that a collection of colloidal particles has an enormous surface area compared to the single macro-sized particle consisting of all the colloidal particles collapsed into a single unit. The left side of Table 13.1 shows this for the case of dividing a 1 cm^3 cube into smaller ones. Similarly, if a macro-sized particle is finely divided into tiny colloidal particles of equal size, the overall surface area of the collection of particles is enormous. Consequently, when colloidal particles are dispersed in solution, the collection as a whole has a very pronounced ability to adsorb substances from its surroundings. Such substances include atoms, molecules, ions, and other colloidal particles (whether similar or foreign). In the latter case, when colloidal particles adhere to each other, they coalesce (agglomerate) and no longer remain dispersed (i.e., they become unstable).

TABLE 13.1

Variation of Particle Parameters (Mass, Volume, Edge Length, Areas, and Energies) with Particle Size

Given: A 1.0 g cube of NaCl (density = 2.2 g/cc) is successively divided into smaller cubes

Assume that the surface energy for NaCl is 2.0×10^{-5} J/cm^2 (independent of the particle size or configuration)

Each parameter is expressed with two significant figures

Cubes Generated by Dividing a 1.0 cc Cube into Smaller Cubes		Particle Parameters per Cube Generated						
					Areas		Energies	
Total Number of Cubes Generated from a 1.0 cc Cube	**Sum of Surface Areas of All Cubes Generated from a 1.0 cc Cube (cm^2)**	**Mass of Each Cube (g)**	**Volume of Each Cube (cc)**	**Side Length of Each Cube (cm)**	**Surface Area of Each Cube (cm^2)**	**Specific Surface Area of Each Cube (cm^2/g)**	**Surface Energy of Each Cube (J)**	**Specific Surface Energy of Each Cube (J/g)**
Column 1	**Column 2**	**Column 3**	**Column 4**	**Column 5**	**Column 6**	**Column 7**	**Column 8**	**Column 9**
—	—	**1.0 (initial cube)**	**0.45**	**0.77 (calc)**	**3.6**	**3.6**	**7.0×10^{-5}**	**7.2×10^{-5}**
1	6.0	2.2 (a 1 cc cube)	1.0	1.0 (10 mm)	6.0	2.7	1.2×10^{-4}	5.4×10^{-5}
10^3	60	2.2×10^{-3}	1.0×10^{-3}	0.1 (1 mm)	0.060	27	1.2×10^{-6}	5.4×10^{-4}
10^6	600	2.2×10^{-6}	1.0×10^{-6}	0.01 (100 μm)	6.0×10^{-4}	270	1.2×10^{-8}	5.4×10^{-3}
10^9	6.0×10^3	2.2×10^{-9}	1.0×10^{-9}	0.001 (10 μm)	6.0×10^{-6}	2.7×10^3	1.2×10^{-10}	5.4×10^{-2}
10^{12}	6.0×10^4	2.2×10^{-12}	1.0×10^{-12}	10^{-4} (1 μm)	6.0×10^{-8}	2.7×10^4	1.2×10^{-12}	0.54
10^{15}	6.0×10^5	2.2×10^{-15}	1.0×10^{-15}	10^{-5} (100 nm)	6.0×10^{-10}	2.7×10^5	1.2×10^{-14}	5.4
10^{18}	6.0×10^6	2.2×10^{-18}	1.0×10^{-18}	10^{-6} (10 nm)	6.0×10^{-12}	2.7×10^6	1.2×10^{-16}	54
10^{21}	6.0×10^7	2.2×10^{-21}	1.0×10^{-21}	10^{-7} (1 nm)	6.0×10^{-14}	2.7×10^7	1.2×10^{-18}	540 (130 cal)

Explanation	Summary
Column 1: Number of cubes = (volume of original cube)/(volume each cube)	col. 1 = (1.0 cc)/(col. 4).
Column 2: Surface area (cm^2) of total number of cubes = (surface area of each cube in cm^2) × (number of cubes)	col. 2 = (col. 6) × (col. 1).
Column 3: Mass (g) per cube = (density in g/cc) × (volume per cube in cc) = (2.2 g/cc) × (volume per cube in cc)	col. 3 = (2.2 g/cc) × (col. 4).
Column 4: Volume (cc) per cube = (side length per cube in cm)^3; the first (0.45 cc) is calculated as volume = (1 g)/density = 1/2.2 = 0.45 cc	col. 4 = (col. 5)^3.
Column 5: Side length (cm) per cube – the first (0.77 cm) is calculated as [(1 g)/density]$^{1/3}$ = 0.77 cm. The rest are given.	col. 5 = given (first is calculated).
Column 6: Surface area (cm^2) per cube = [face area per cube in cm^2/side] × (6 sides) = (side length in cm)^2 × 6	col. 6 = (col. 5)^2 × 6.
Column 7: Specific surface area (cm^2/g) per cube = (surface area per cube in cm^2)/(mass per cube in g)	col. 7 = (col. 6)/(col. 3).
Column 8: Surface energy (J) per cube = (surface energy in J/cm^2) × (surface area per cube in cm^2) = (2.0×10^{-5} J/cm^2) × (col. 6)	col. 8 = (2.0×10^{-5} J/cm^2) (col. 6).
Column 9: Specific surface energy (J/g) per cube can be defined in at least three equivalent ways:	
1. (surface energy in J per cube)/(mass in g per cube)	col. 9 = (col. 8)/(col. 3).
2. (surface energy in J/cm^2) × (specific surface area in cm^2/g per cube) = (2.0×10^{-5}J/cm^2) × (col. 7)	col. 9 = (2.0×10^{-5} J/cm^2) (col. 7).
3. [(surface energy in J per cube) × (total number of such cubes formed from a 1.0 cc cube)]/(mass of original cube)	col. 9 = [(col. 8) × (col. 1)]/(2.2 g).

How well a substance gets attracted to the surface of a colloidal particle depends on the size of both. How well the adsorbed substance adheres to the surface of the particle depends on the surface energy of the particle:

1. The attractive forces between a colloidal particle and surrounding substances are associated with interatomic–molecular dipole interactions (induced or permanent polarities created in atoms or molecules by the electric fields of neighboring atoms or molecules). Such forces include permanent dipole–permanent dipole interactions (Keesom), permanent dipole–induced dipole interactions (Debye), and induced dipole–induced dipole interactions (London). Collectively, these forces are known as van der Waals interactions [94].
2. For two particles of atomic or molecular size separated by a distance R, these interactions are of short range (their energy of attraction has a $1/R^6$ dependence). As with particles getting larger (approaching a plane relative to the smaller particle), the interactions become longer range (their attraction energy goes from a $1/R^6$ dependence to a $1/R^3$ dependence) [9,10,12,33,95]. As a consequence, the attractive force of a colloidal particle may extend to distances of several nanometers [33], a range comparable or superior to the electrostatic force caused by the interaction of the electrostatic double layers around charged particles (see Section 13.2.2.2). This explains why it is sometimes referred to as the "long-range van der Waals force," or "Hamacker force" [9].
3. The particle surface energy dictates how well a substance adheres to its surface. Because surface atoms are bonded only to inner atoms (i.e., there are no atoms above them with which to bond), atom-to-atom bond distances involving surface atoms are shorter than those involving interior atoms. The energy that causes this tightening (tension) is the surface (free) energy and is expressed as energy per area (J/cm^2). It can be defined as the excess energy at the surface of a material compared to the bulk. This contribution is important in the case of nanoparticles, since the ratio of surface atoms to interior ones increases rapidly as the size of the particle decreases and reaches the nanometer scale. For example, a 3 nm iron particle has 50% of its atoms on the surface, whereas a 10 nm particle has just 20% and a 30 nm particle only 5% [11]. The surface energy value can be reduced by adsorption (and adhesion) of substances from the surroundings.
4. For an isolated colloidal-sized particle, the surface area is extremely small, as well as the energy of its surface (surface energy [J/cm^2] × surface area [cm^2]). However, for an entire collection of colloidal particles collectively weighing M grams, the sum of all the surface areas divided by M and the sum of the energy of all the surfaces divided by M are enormous. The adjective "specific" is given to such terms as specific surface area (cm^2/g) and specific surface energy (J/g) (see the right side of Table 13.1). This information is taken in part from Adamson's Table VII-3 [95]. The differences between his table and Table 13.1 are as follows: his energy values are in ergs (ours are in Joules), he treats edge energy (we do not), and some of his specific surface area values differ slightly from ours due to the rounding-off process. The vast amount of adsorption and adhesion that occurs among the collection of colloidal particles lowers this overall excess surface free energy (giving the system thermodynamic stability).

When compiling all these contributions, it can be concluded that the nanoparticles have a thermodynamically natural tendency to adhere to each other, so that the resulting size is higher and the specific surface energy lower. This phenomenon is mainly due to the van der Waals attraction forces that play an increasing role as the size of the particle decreases. This aggregation process is logically to be avoided in order to obtain colloidal dispersions that are stable in time. To reach this goal, it is necessary to oppose the van der Waals attraction with other energetic contributions whose role is to repel colloidal particles from each other. This can be done through electrostatic repulsion or steric hindrance.

13.2.2.2 Electrostatic Repulsion

Let us consider colloidal particles of inorganic crystals in aqueous solution. The crystal lattice consists of anions and cations positioned according to their crystal structure. Though such crystals are neutral, they contain localized centers of positive and negative charges on their surface. Such centers include the atoms in the faces, edges, and corners of the crystal. These act as points for surface interaction. For sols of inorganic crystals, there are at least four factors that govern which ions are preferentially adsorbed. These factors are the Paneth–Fajans–Hahn Law, concentration effect, ion charge effect, and size of the ion [96]. When all the other factors are equal:

1. The Paneth–Fajans–Hahn Law states that if two or more types of ions are available for adsorption, then the ions which form a compound with the lowest solubility with one of the lattice ions will be preferentially adsorbed.
2. The concentration effect states that the ions present in greater concentration will be adsorbed preferentially. Furthermore, the quantity of any ions that is adsorbed varies directly with its concentration.
3. The ionic charge effect states that a multi-charged ion will be adsorbed more readily than a singly charged ion since the strength of adsorption is governed in part by van der Waals attractions which include the electrostatic attraction between the ion and the partial oppositely charged centers on the crystal surface (the van der Waals–Keesom forces).
4. The size-of-ion effect states that the ion that is more nearly the same size as the lattice ion which it replaces will be adsorbed preferentially.

Consequently, once a nanoparticle is placed in water or in a solvent characterized by high dielectric value, an "electrical double layer" structure will appear. This structure is composed of two parallel layers of ions (Figure 13.3): the first one is the surface charge (either positive or negative) and the other one is formed in the liquid to electrically screen the first layer. The surface charge can arise from the adsorption of the surrounding ions, from the dissociation of surface atoms or groups (e.g., protons or hydroxyl groups), from electron transfer, or from other phenomena [33]. The second layer of charge will form because of the electrostatic neutrality of the sol. Counterions will accumulate near the surface to balance the surface charge by an equal, but opposite, charge [86,97]. This second layer is diffuse, because it is composed of non-adsorbed ions, free in the liquid, and moving by Brownian motion. The ion concentration decreases progressively as the distance to the particle increases, up to the average concentration in the medium. This causes the

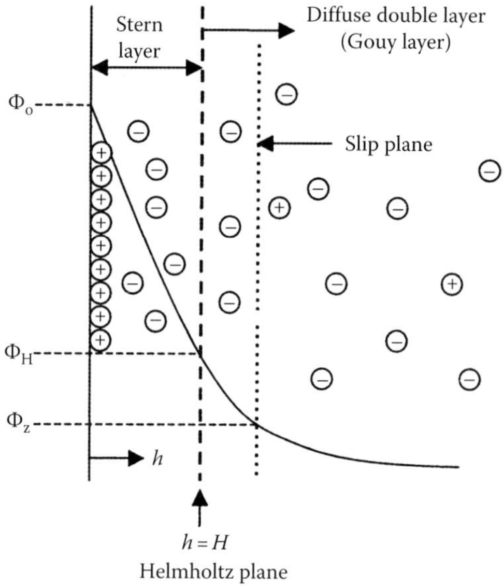

FIGURE 13.3
Illustration of the "electric double layer" of a colloidal particle (positively charged) in aqueous suspension. The double layer is composed of the Stern (or Helmholtz) layer, which contains the strongly adsorbed counterions, and the Gouy layer, which is more diffuse than the first one in terms of ion and counterion concentrations. (Image source from Cao, G., *Nanostructures & Nanomaterials: Synthesis, Properties & Applications*, Imperial College Press, London, U.K.)

electric potential to slowly decay to zero (when moving away from the particle surface). As illustrated in Figure 13.3, some ions may somewhat adsorb strongly near the surface and build an inner sublayer (i.e., the Stern layer). The outer part of the screening layer is called the diffuse layer. The double layer may extend up to 10 nm and act like a capacitor (condenser) [94].

It is also important to introduce the concept of "shearing surface," which can be imagined as an envelope lying close to the solid surface and within which the fluid is stationary. When an electric field is applied to a sol, the colloidal particles carrying an electric charge move in the direction of the electrode with the opposite charge. Simultaneously, a certain quantity of the surrounding shearing surface and the counterions contained in it move jointly with the particles. A measure of the electrophoretic mobility of the particle and its closely stationary counterions could thus give an idea of the apparent surface charge on the solid particle, as it would be seen by a closely approaching neighboring particle. This leads to a definition of zeta potential (ζ), which is the electrostatic potential at the shearing surface of a particle [98,99]. In general, the zeta potential is smaller than the potential at the surface of a particle, due to the screening effect of the counterions contained in the shearing surface.

The electrostatic interactions between two spherical particles will be influenced by the electric charges adsorbed on the particles according to the electrical double layer structure. As the particles come sufficiently close to each other, the counterion layers start to overlap. It means that the local counterion concentration is higher than it should be for a single particle. Consequently, an osmotic solvent flow is created and the particles undergo some kind of "repulsion force" [86]. This phenomenon directly competes with the van der Waals attraction, which tends to make particles in solution aggregate. The electrical double layer thus plays a role in the stability of the nanoparticles, with respect to coagulation into larger aggregates.

According to the D.L.V.O. theory (from the names of the persons who developed the theory [100,101]), when the attractive forces between two approaching particles (i.e., van der Waals attraction) are balanced with the repulsive forces that could also be experienced by these particles (i.e., electrostatic double layer overlapping), a "repulsion barrier" appears (i.e., a maximum in the potential energy of the interacting particles) and has to be overcome by the two colliding particles to aggregate (Figure 13.4). If this barrier is not reached, the two particles remain separated in solution. In other words, the combination of the attractive and repulsive forces will determine the stability of a lyophobic colloidal sol. In this context, the zeta potential is generally used as an index of the magnitude of repulsive forces that could be experienced between two particles [99], and in the same way, as an index of a colloidal stability. It is, for example, widely accepted that if a sol has a zeta potential greater than +30 mV or lower than −30 mV, then the electrostatic stability among the particles is sufficient to keep the sol stable [98,102,103]. Moreover, when considering two systems with two different zeta potential values (all other factors being considered equal), the one with the higher zeta potential value (being toward positive or negative values) is expected to be the more stable with respect to aggregation compared to the other.

However, the repulsion barrier is strongly dependent on the surrounding conditions, for example, ionic strength or pH [94]. For some species in aqueous solutions, the surface charge can be modified according to the pH, whose value is directly related with the quantity of protons or hydroxyl groups in solution. It is the case for oxide species, whose charge is mainly derived from adsorbed protons and hydroxyl groups [86]. In such conditions, it is possible to find a pH value at which a particle exhibits a neutral state (zero charge) or, in other words, conditions for which the electric charge density on a surface is zero. This is called a "point of zero charge" (p.z.c.). At the p.z.c., the particle exhibits a neutral zeta potential (the particle remains stationary under an electric field) and is generally

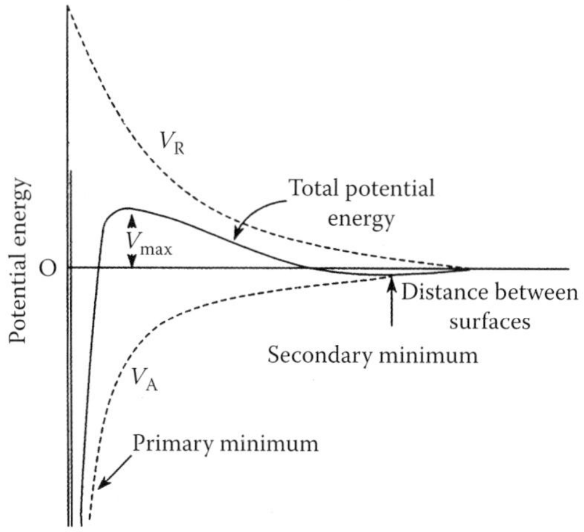

FIGURE 13.4
Schematic representation of a D.L.V.O. potential between two surfaces or particles [100,101]. According to this model, a "repulsion barrier" is created when combining the attractive van der Waals potential (V_A) and the repulsive electrostatic potential (V_R). This potential barrier has to be overcome before the aggregation of two colliding particles can occur. (Image source from Cao, G., *Nanostructures & Nanomaterials: Synthesis, Properties & Applications*, Imperial College Press, London, U.K.)

accompanied by a rather low stability of the sol and a strong tendency for nanoparticles to flocculate or aggregate (due to insufficiently balanced van der Waals attraction forces). If the pH is set above the p.z.c., the particles will be negatively charged. If the pH is set below the p.z.c., the particles will be positively charged. The reader is referred to the extensive compilation of values published by Kosmulski on this subject for several metal oxides [104]. As an example, p.z.c. values for SiO_2 in water are comprised in the range 2–3.7, and around 6.0 for TiO_2 [99]. This information is crucial to ensure that a solution is stable in time, but also when developing a technique based on the electrostatic attraction between nanoparticles and finger secretions (see Section 13.3.2.1).

Another good example of the pH dependence of the stability of a sol is colloidal gold. When gold colloids are synthesized via the sodium citrate metal reduction route, the sols obtained generally remain stable for months. This long-time stability is due to the adsorption of tri-negatively charged citrate ions which preferentially adhere to the metal nanoparticle (via van der Waals attractive forces). As a consequence, the nanoparticles are characterized by a negative charge and are prevented from aggregating through electrostatic repulsion [57]. Faraday, in his experiments, showed that the addition of salts to colloidal gold turned the solution from ruby red to blue, a sign of the formation of bigger nanoparticles through aggregation of smaller ones as a result of the increase of the ionic strength of the solution [51]. This can be explained by the fact that an increase in the ionic strength significantly decreases the thickness of the double layer (since the amount of counterions required to balance the surface charge is available in a smaller volume surrounding the particle). As the ionic strength is increased, the double layer is reduced to a point at which the interparticle potential is attractive, leading to a coagulation of the colloids. For example, it is said that, at ionic strengths greater than 10^{-1} M, the thickness of the double layer is less than 1 nm, which causes the electrostatic repulsion to be insufficient to outweigh the van der Waals attraction [105]. Similarly for gold sols, when the pH is lowered below a limit value (e.g., 1.70), the electrostatic repulsion is no longer sufficient to counterbalance the van der Waals attraction and the sol is irreversibly destroyed by precipitation of large gold aggregates. The origin of this phenomenon is to be found in the neutralization (by protonation) of the citrate ions. As a consequence, the colloidal particles lose their citrate cap; the zeta potential falls below the ± 30 mV limit; and the resulting sol becomes unstable (Figure 13.5). The same phenomenon is observed if citrate ions are replaced by uncharged species [106].

Electrostatic repulsion also plays a role in aqueous solution of CdTe QDs. The nanocrystals are generally capped by using thioglycolic acid (TGA). This results in an electrostatic repulsion, caused by the negative charge induced by the carboxylic groups, and prevents the nanocrystals from aggregating. It explains why such colloidal particles are known to be among the most stable (typically, for years) [66].

13.2.2.3 Steric Hindrance

The stabilization through steric interactions consists of placing bulky or long-chained molecules around the nanoparticles to create a physical barrier preventing them from aggregating [33,105]. In colloidal chemistry, dispersions of such macromolecules are called protective colloids [107]. This can be done through the adsorption of polymers that bind through weak physical forces to the surface, or through a chemisorption process, which requires the formation of a chemical bond between the particle and the surrounding molecule. This is typically the case with thiolated molecules which covalently bind around gold nanoparticles to prevent them from coalescing upon drying or after centrifugation cycles [108].

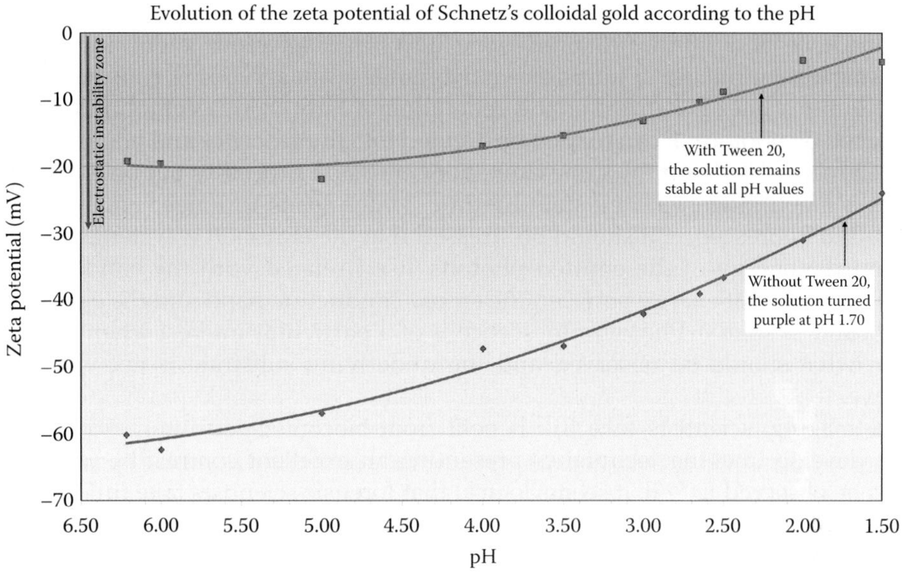

FIGURE 13.5
The zeta potential progression of Schnetz's colloidal gold solution according to a decrease of the pH (blue curve), and stabilization role played by the addition of Tween 20 into the solution (orange curve). Caution: the *X*-axis is inverted, with the aqueous solution being more acidic as the axis progresses on the right. Colloidal gold has been synthesized according to Schnetz and Margot (From Schnetz, B. and Margot, P., *Forensic Sci. Int.*, 118, 21, 2001.), and the pH is decreased by adding 0.1 M citric acid. At some point, the zeta potential falls inside the ±30 mV instability zone. Without Tween 20, the sol turns purple, due to the aggregation of gold nanoparticles, at a pH of 1.70. With Tween 20, the sol remains stable even if its zeta values are located within the electrostatic instability zone across the whole pH range.

Early literature on colloids describes the conversion of hydrophobic sols to hydrophilic sols by adding to the former macromolecules like gelatin, glue, casein, or gum Arabic so that these get adsorbed by the colloidal particles giving them lyophilic character [109]. Compared to electrostatic stabilization, steric stabilization offers some nonnegligible advantages: insensitivity to electrolytes (in the case of nonionic polymers), equal effectiveness for both aqueous and nonaqueous dispersions, and effectiveness at low and high nanoparticle concentrations. It has to be noted that the steric stabilization plays a major role in nonaqueous solvents, into which electrostatic stabilization is generally ineffective.

The steric hindrance can be combined with the electrostatic repulsion to form what is called an "electrosteric stabilization" [105]. The electrostatic contribution may originate from the surface itself (net surface charge) or from the polymer that is attached to the surface. It is typically the case when charged particles are surrounded by nonionic molecules, as in the MMD-II process [25]. In this method, Tween 20, a nonionic surfactant, is added to prevent unwanted background staining, but it also plays a role in the stabilization of the colloidal gold when pH begins to reach low values (Figure 13.5). This aspect will be detailed in Section 13.3.2.2.

13.2.3 Optical Properties

In forensic science, techniques leading to photoluminescent fingermarks are generally preferred compared to the ones leading to nonluminescent ones, especially when dealing with dark or complex, multicolored printed backgrounds. This explains the success of 1,2-indanedione and 1,8-diazafluoren-9-one (DFO) for detecting latent fingermarks on porous surfaces, or the use of luminescent dyes after cyanoacrylate fuming [2,3,110,111].

Photoluminescence is defined as the generation of light from a compound after it has been excited by photons. It can further be divided into fluorescence and phosphorescence. Both are broadly based on the same excitation–emission processes but phosphorescence presents a much longer excited-state lifetime, which leads to longer emission of light compared to fluorescence. It should be stressed that the emission wavelength is directly related to the energy of the emitted photons, itself related with the band gap energy (i.e., the difference of energy between the empty conduction band and the electron-filled valence band in solids). Photoluminescence is of a particular interest when the contrast between what should be observed and the underlying substrate is not visible to the naked eye.

In bio-imaging, scientists take full benefit from bioconjugated luminescent nanoparticles to develop imaging techniques presenting an excellent contrast between the elements to be observed [20,22]. It seems logical that forensic scientists take full benefit from luminescent nanoparticles in the development of new fingermark detection techniques. Among the wide variety of existing nanoparticles, some are luminescent by nature (e.g., QDs), and others become luminescent after physical entrapment of organic fluorophores in their structure (e.g., silica nanoparticles).

The following sections will focus only on a limited number of nanoparticles of interest.

13.2.3.1 Gold Nanoclusters

Gold nanoparticles are not commonly known for their luminescence properties, but more for their strong surface plasmon absorption associated with the most commonly used colloidal gold solutions (with diameter >5nm). Nevertheless, it has been shown that gold nanoclusters of very small sizes (few tens of gold atoms per cluster only), stabilized in aqueous solution by organic ligands or polymers, could behave as molecules and present some photoluminescence behavior in the infrared (IR) and visible range. Link et al. reported the observation of visible to IR luminescence for a 28-atom gold cluster stabilized by glutathione [112]. Wilcoxon et al. reported a visible luminescence (i.e., 440nm) of small gold nanoclusters (diameter 5nm) formed in water by sodium citrate reduction [113], once excited with a 230nm light source. Only the smallest-sized nanoclusters showed significant photoluminescence quantum yield, with the photoluminescence totally disappearing for gold nanoparticles of bigger sizes. Nevertheless, the associated quantum yields were extremely low (i.e., 3.5×10^{-3} [112] and 10^{-4} to 10^{-5} [113], respectively). More recently, some researchers reported strong fluorescence behavior of small gold nanodots (diameter <2nm) encapsulated in a dendrimer [114]. A blue emission at 450nm has been recorded when illuminating the solution at 384nm, with measured quantum yield of ~0.4, which is much higher than previously observed luminescence intensities. Bao et al. reported the synthesis of gold nanoclusters utilizing a hydroxyl-terminated poly(amidoamine) or PAMAM dendrimer as a template and ascorbic acid as a reductant [115]. The nanoclusters were characterized by blue, green, and red emissions, with quantum yields ranging from 0.09 to 0.38.

As a conclusion, the low quantum yields initially observed for gold nanoclusters prevented them from becoming good fluorophores. Some recent observations showed that higher quantum yields (up to 0.4) could be obtained when stabilizing gold nanodots with dendrimers. Nevertheless, the necessity to synthesize, purify, and stabilize gold nanoclusters of very small size considerably limits their application in the field of fingermark detection. The luminescence of gold nanoclusters remains thus anecdotal and represents no particular appeal in this application, at the moment.

13.2.3.2 Quantum Dots

The size of the QDs directly influences their optical properties. The origin of this specificity is to be found in quantum chemistry and in the combination of atomic orbitals [116,117]. Briefly, when a particle reaches dimensions in the range of the nanometer scale, the energy levels (i.e., bonding and anti-bonding) do not exist anymore in terms of bands of energy but are quantized into discrete values. This phenomenon is accompanied with an increase in the effective band gap of the material with decreasing crystallite size and is called the "quantum size effect" [13–15]. For example, the quantum size effect can be observed with a CdS nanocrystal when its size is comparable or below 5–6nm (which corresponds to 3000–4000 atoms) [14]. As a result of this quantum confinement, a hypsochromic shift of the absorption and emission spectra can be observed as the particle size decreases [15,118]. In other words, for the same atomic composition, both the optical absorption and emission of QDs shift to the blue (higher energies) as the size of the dots gets smaller (Figure 13.6). When modifying the atomic composition of QDs and their size, it is possible to obtain spectral emissions ranging from UV blue (e.g., ZnS, ZnSe, and CdS) to the near-IR (e.g., PbSe, HgTe, and InAs), including the visible spectrum (e.g., CdSe, CdTe, and InP) (Figure 13.7). Moreover, overcoating nanocrystallites with higher band gap inorganic materials (to form the so-called core/shell structures) results in an improvement of the photoluminescence quantum yield [119]. On this subject, Lupton and Müller propose a thorough review of the recent progress made in studying the spectral characteristics of CdSe nanocrystals [120].

When compared with molecular organic dyes, QDs offer superior optical properties such as (1) the possibility to tune the fluorescence emission wavelength as a function of the nanoparticle diameter, (2) broad excitation spectra combined with narrow emission spectra, and (3) high fluorescence quantum yield [121]. The second point means that the excitation of a range of QDs of different sizes can be performed at a single excitation wavelength, with each QD emitting according to its specific narrow range of emission wavelengths. Despite the fact that the manipulation of nanocolloids in biological environments may be more complicated, the optical advantages of QDs over classical organic dyes explain their success in biological domains like cellular imaging and labeling [20,21,71,122–124], especially in multicolor imaging [125–127] or IR imaging [128]. As an illustration of the optical superiority of QDs to organic dyes, CdSe/ZnS QDs were described as being 20 times as bright, 100 times as stable against photobleaching (i.e., the total loss of fluorescence through destruction of fluorescent molecules), and one-third as wide in spectral linewidth in comparison with organic dyes such as rhodamine [129]. In addition to this, large Stokes shifts (>100nm) and high molar extinction coefficients (i.e., the measure of how strongly a chemical species can absorb light at a given wavelength) make QDs promising nanoparticles to be used in the context of fingermark detection.

It should be noted that anti-Stokes photoluminescence has been observed in some semiconductor nanocrystals. This means that the emission of light is observed at shorter wavelengths than that at which the material has been excited. This phenomenon is also called an "up-conversion process" and is reviewed by Rakovich and Donegan [130]. The up-conversion process can be of interest in the domain of fingermark detection by avoiding

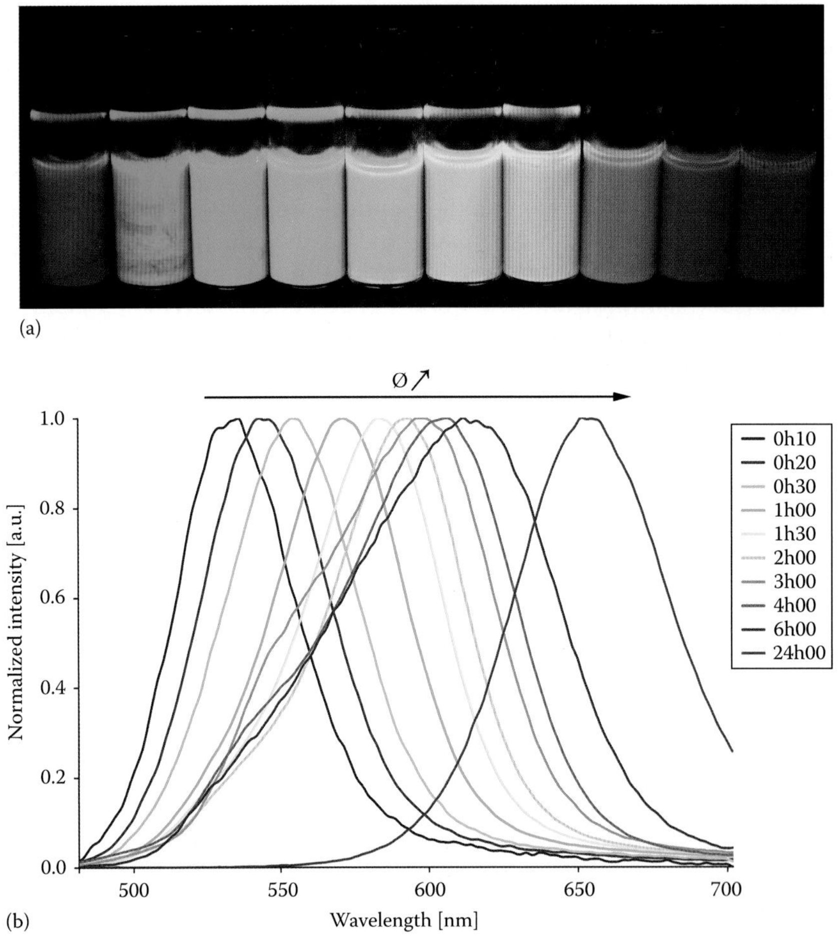

FIGURE 13.6
(a) Evolution of the luminescence emission for cadmium telluride quantum dots of increasing size (from left to right), illuminated under UV radiation (300–400 nm) using a Mini-Crimescope 400. (b) Emission spectra obtained for the samples shown using a Perkin Elmer LS-50B luminescence spectrophotometer. The spectra were normalized to 1.0 to illustrate the progression of the maxima of intensity to higher wavelengths as the quantum dots are growing in size (diameter ø). The samples were obtained by removing a small amount (2.5 mL) of concentrated quantum dots from the reaction mixture at different reaction times (in hrs and min, reported in the box at the side of the curves). (Image from Bécue, A, Moret S, Champod C, Margot P. (2009) Use of Quantum Dots in Aqueous Solution to Detect Blood Fingermarks on Non-Porous Surfaces. *Forensic Sci. Int.* 191: 36–41. With permisison from Elsevier.)

the background fluorescence of some substrates that considerably decreases the contrast between the mark and the substrate upon illumination [131].

13.2.3.3 Silica Nanospheres

Silica nanoparticles differ from QDs, or from other self-luminescent nanoparticles, in a sense that they are optically inert on their own. Nevertheless, one of the advantages of the sol–gel process is that the reactions are performed at low temperature, permitting organic and inorganic species to coexist within the same matrix. An organic dye molecule can thus be easily added to a sol–gel liquid solution, resulting in its encapsulation in the porous oxide matrix. Such entities are called "dye-doped silica nanoparticles."

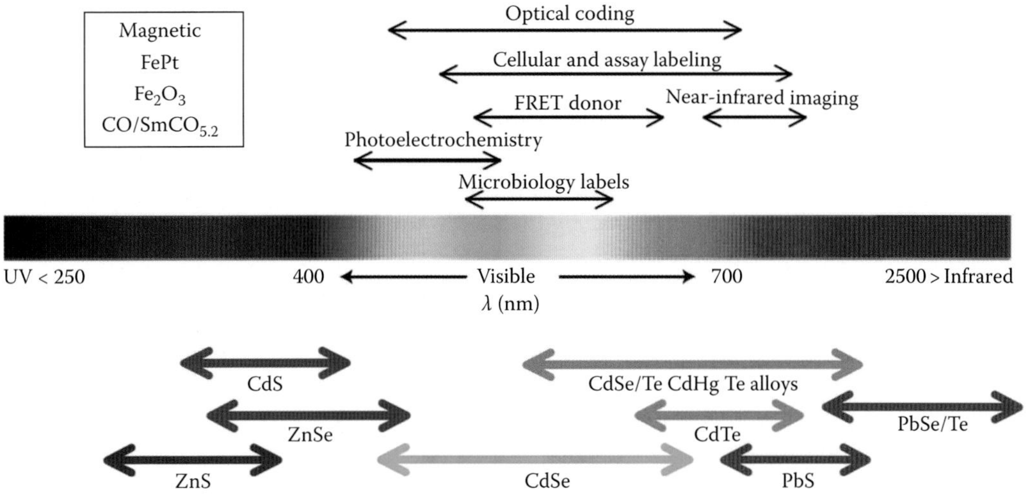

FIGURE 13.7
Illustration of the different emission wavelength ranges according to the atomic composition of the most commonly encountered quantum dots. On the top are also represented the areas of biological interest, mainly located in the visible–near-infrared regions of the spectrum. (Image source from Medintz IL, Uyeda HT, Goldman ER, Mattoussi H. (2005) Quantum Dot Bioconjugates for Imaging, Labelling and Sensing. *Nat. Mater.* 4(6): 435–446. With permission from Nature Publishing Group.)

Each nanoparticle is able to encapsulate tens of thousands of fluorescent dye molecules in their silica matrix, providing highly amplified and reproducible signal. This also allows the dyes to be isolated from the outside environment (oxygen and water), resulting in an increased photostability and emission quantum yield, and a decreased photobleaching phenomenon [92]. Consequently, the luminescence of dye-doped silica nanoparticles may be up to several tens of thousands of times more intense than those based on single organic fluorophore [132]. Organic dyes are generally preferred to inorganic ones due to a relatively higher quantum yield [133], for example, 60%–70% for inorganic compared to >90% for organic dyes [22]. In bio-imaging applications, silica has been identified as being more appropriate than polymers since it is not subject to microbial attack and there is no swelling or porosity change with a change of pH [134]. For all these reasons, and in addition to their excellent biocompatibility as well as the possibility of easily tuning their surface properties, dye-doped silica nanoparticles are hailed as highly promising biological markers [103,132,133].

Several possibilities are offered to scientists willing to encapsulate fluorescent dyes. This can be done during the nanoparticles' formation, using the Stöber synthesis [90,135,136] or the reverse microemulsion [92,133,137–142]. However, the incorporation of dyes into the silica matrix is challenging since the hydrophilic environment of silica does not favor the entrapment of hydrophobic molecules. Consequently, one of the major problems with fluorescent nanoparticles is the leakage of dye molecules from the silica nanoparticles after dispersion in an aqueous medium (e.g., while performing bioanalytical tests). Several possibilities exist to solve this issue:

1. The use of polar dyes so that the electrostatic interactions are maximized with the negatively charged silica matrix [90,133,137–140,142]
2. The use of dyes of a sufficiently large size, preventing them from leaking outside of the silica nanoparticle through the pores [133]

3. The combination of the organic dye with a hydrophilic moiety to make it water-soluble (e.g., dextran M_w 3000) [133]
4. The use of a hydrophobic silica precursor that would place itself inside the structure and promote hydrophobic interactions with the dye [44,143]
5. The covalent binding of the dye to the silica matrix [89,91,136], followed by the addition of a supplemental silica shell around the dye-doped core to increase the photostability of the organic dye (and, by the same way, the fluorescence of the whole nanoparticle) [144,145]

About the electrostatic interactions, Zhou and Yip studied the difference in behavior between a negatively charged dye (i.e., fluorescein) and a positively charged one (i.e., rhodamine 6G) once inserted in a silica hydrogel [146]. They observed that the strong Coulombic interactions between rhodamine 6G and the negatively charged silica surface render them immobile, permanently embedded inside the silica matrix as the particles (or the network) grow in size. On the contrary, the electrostatic repulsion between fluorescein and the silica matrix renders it extremely mobile in the hydrogel.

Some authors observed a slight shift of the emission spectra of the encapsulated dyes (from reverse emulsion synthesis) compared to the dyes in solution [93,137,138,140,142,147]. Additionally, it is possible that entrapped dyes exhibit an excimer-like emission in place of a monomeric optical behavior, especially in case where the dye concentration was high during the doping process [148].

13.2.4 Surface Functionalization

One of the biggest advantages that nanoparticles offer compared to organic fluorophores is that they can be functionalized (on their outer surface) almost without interfering with their optical properties. The addition of organic chains or molecular groups therefore modifies their physicochemical properties and offers new possibilities in terms of solubility in aqueous or organic solvents, affinity for some specific molecular target, or enhanced stability. This mechanism is widely used in biosensing or biomedical imaging, where nanoparticles should be biocompatible (i.e., stable and compatible with physiological conditions), a process also known as "biofunctionalization" [20,22,124,149–155]. Biofunctionalization is defined as the linkage of biomolecules to nanoparticles or designing appropriate biocompatible coatings. The coupling must be stable and the surface modification should not modify the photoluminescent properties of the nanoparticles. In the context of fingermark detection, the one trend consists in grafting biomolecules (e.g., proteins affording catalytic activity), with some publications referring to antibody–antigen recognition of latent fingermarks [156–163]. Nevertheless, most publications refer to the addition of organic chains to promote hydrophobicity (e.g., alkanes) or to add simple functional groups (e.g., carboxylic acid or amino group), as illustrated in Figure 13.8.

A great freedom is offered in terms of outer functionalization and the choice for a ligand or a biomolecule mainly depends on what goal is to be reached. As illustrated in Figure 13.8, the nature of the nanoparticle itself will also play a role, but less major in this case since it will be mostly related with the choice for a specific anchoring group (having little influence on the terminal functionalization and the optical properties). The same functionality can consequently be added to various nanoparticles (e.g., colloidal gold, QDs, and silica nanoparticles to keep with the examples chosen before), but the functionalization process will differ for each nanoparticle, due to its intrinsic nature, as discussed later.

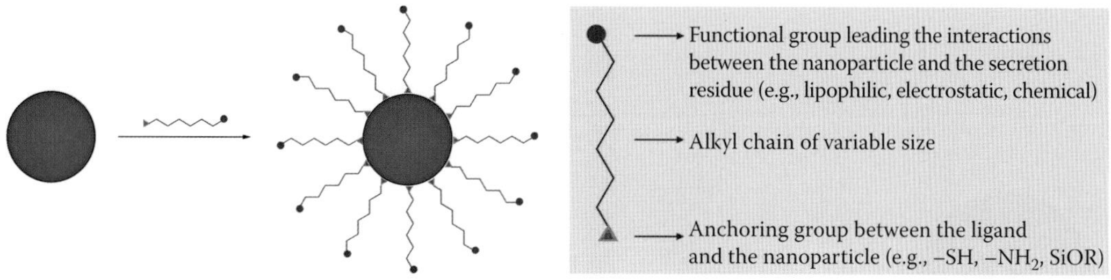

FIGURE 13.8
Illustration of the functionalization strategy, which involves functionalizing the outer surface of nanoparticles with ligands to increase their physicochemical properties (affinity) and chemical behavior toward secretion residue.

13.2.4.1 Functionalization of Gold Nanoparticles

In the case of gold nanoparticles (as well as for silver nanoparticles), gold atoms on the surface of the particle are coordinately unsaturated (i.e., unoccupied orbitals are available for nucleophiles to donate electrons). Thiol or amino groups do constitute good anchoring groups, given their nucleophilic behavior. This explains why the most common coatings for metal nanoparticles are ω-substituted alkanethiols, $HS–(CH_2)_n–R$. Such molecules spontaneously chemisorb on the metal surface to create an interface between the nanoparticles and the surrounding environment (Figure 13.9). Alkanethiols generally permit the creation of well-defined coverings in terms of composition and structure, as well as in terms of chemical and physicochemical properties through the terminal functional groups ("R").

The mixing of gold nanoparticles with molecules (or biomolecules) bearing thiol or amino groups leads to a spontaneous binding and formation of self-assembled monolayers onto the metal surface, without the need for harsh reaction conditions (temperature, pressure). Self-assembled monolayers were reported to be created within minutes of reaction [164]; however, it is generally accepted that a longer deposition period (e.g., several hours) facilitates a monolayer with a high degree of order by enabling surface rearrangement. Another aspect of the functionalized gold nanoparticles is the possibility of removing the solvent, drying the nanoparticles, and still keeping the ability to resolubilize them later (which is not the case with unmodified gold nanoparticles) [29].

The ligands of water-soluble, citrate-capped gold nanoparticles can be easily displaced and replaced by other ones [165]. The functionalization can also directly be performed during the reduction process leading to the formation of functionalized gold nanoparticles. This is the case in the procedure described by Brust et al. [29,166], which permits alkanethiol- or alkylamine-ended ligand-protected gold nanoparticles to be obtained that are mainly soluble in organic solvents. Similar to Brust et al., Templeton et al. described the obtaining of water-soluble, ligand-protected gold nanoparticles, using tiopronin [167,168]. The solubility of the ligand-capped gold nanoparticles is highly dependent on the choice of the capping ligand. Zheng and Huang distinguished three kinds of ligands according to their ionic behavior (i.e., strongly ionic, weakly ionic, and neutral), allowing one to determine in which mediums such capped gold nanoparticles will be soluble [150].

The created "metal–S" or "metal–N" bonds are quite strong, almost covalent, ensuring by the same way a good stability of the functionalization. Nevertheless, these bonds can still be broken through ligand exchange by the addition of a second one, presenting an increased affinity for the metal surface (e.g., another thiolated molecule). The replacement

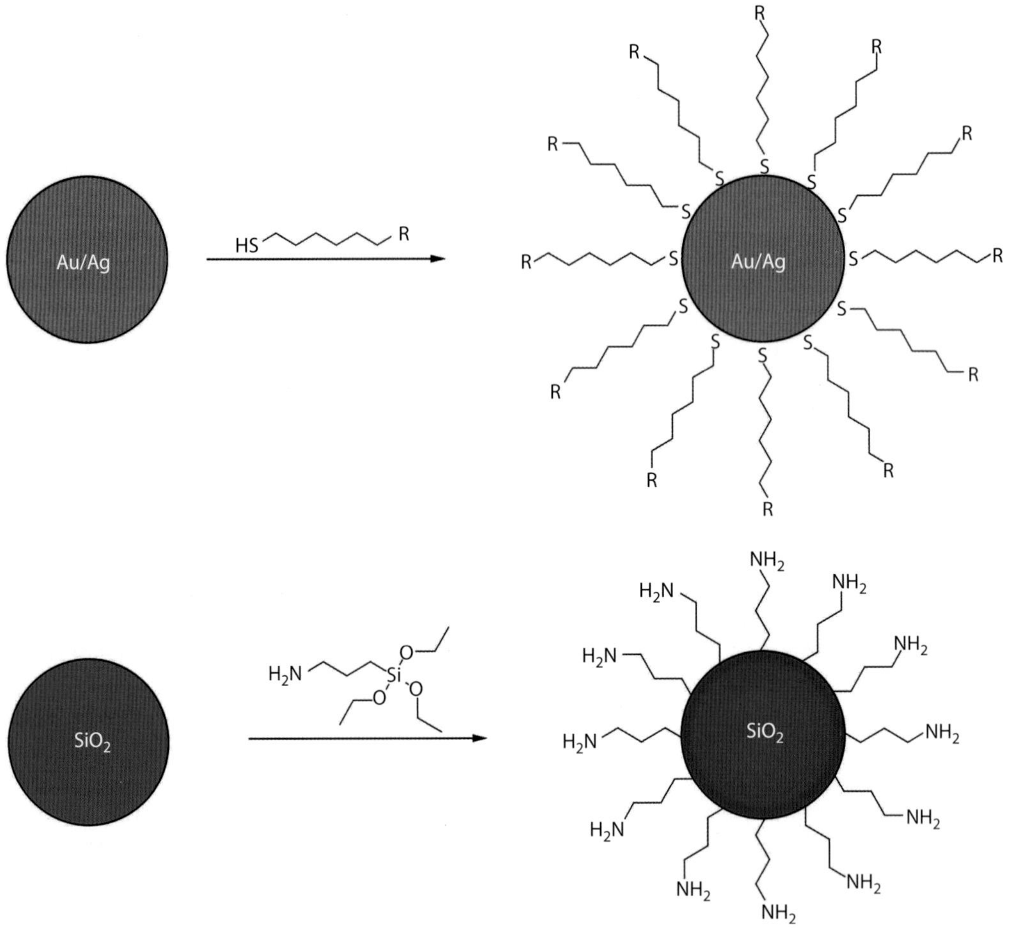

FIGURE 13.9
Illustration of how metal nanoparticles (up) and silica nanoparticles (down) can be functionalized using well-adapted ligands, namely, alkanethiol for gold and 3-amino-propyltriethoxylsilane for silica.

of existing Au-X (X = P, S, N) bonds with other ligands leads to homogeneous or heterogeneous monolayers [169]. Compared to direct synthesis, the ligand exchange reaction introduces a versatility aspect to the functionality of nanoparticles in solution. However, it also adds supplemental synthetic steps and it is sometimes difficult to control the composition of the final monolayers.

Since biomolecules bear outer amino and thiol groups, coming from amino acid side chains, they can also present a spontaneous affinity for gold nanoparticles [152,155]. For example, citrate-capped gold nanoparticles, which are water-soluble, can be bioconjugated by a ligand exchange process using thiolated proteins [170]. Lévy et al. have functionalized citrate-capped gold nanoparticles with pentapeptides to obtain stable, protein-like gold nanoparticles [171]. The same work has been performed using silver nanoparticles, to increase their stability in aqueous solution [172]. Similarly, thiol- or amino-containing amino acids can also spontaneously bind to the gold surface to form self-assembled monolayers, as shown for cysteine [173], lysine [174,175], or tryptophan [176]. Another possibility for immobilizing biomolecules on gold and silver substrates through covalent or non-covalent interactions involves using carboxylic acid thiol derivative coatings (e.g., HS−R−COOH, where "R" is a hydrocarbon linker). For example, 2-mercaptosuccinic acid (MSA) [108,177,178] or mercaptoproprionic acid (MPA) [179] can be successfully used as a biocompatible coating for protein's or enzyme's adsorption/immobilization.

The functionalization of gold nanoparticles by silica creates a shell that is chemically inert and optically transparent (e.g., for gold imaging) [180–182]. However, gold metal has very little affinity for silica because it does not form a passivating oxide film in solution. Moreover, the ions that stabilize the gold nanoparticles in solution (e.g., sodium citrate ions) are generally vitreophobic (silica has no affinity for them). To circumvent this problem, it is necessary to use silane-coupling agents as surface primers, that is, molecules bearing a Si atom and $-NH_2$ or −SH functions at their extremities to ensure gold binding (e.g., (3-aminopropyl)trimethoxysilane [APTMS]). Such silane-coupling agents are generally added during a post-functionalization process, but can also be introduced during gold nanoparticle synthesis [183]. It should be noted that if the silica layer formed in water is too thin, the van der Waals forces are still very strong and can induce flocculation [184].

Finally, isothiocyanate groups (S=C=N−) are also able to bind to gold nanoparticles, as it has been shown with fluorescein isothiocyanate (FITC) [182]. When FITC is added to gold sol, the suspension remains stable for months. The electrostatic repulsion between the negatively charged particles (anionic form of FITC at neutral and basic pH values) prevents the aggregation of the particles. As a proof of the functionalization, the FITC fluorescence band (518 nm) overlaps with the gold surface plasmon band (520 nm), leading to an effective energy transfer from the excited molecule to the gold surface (quenching). This transfer is effective, even at 1 nm from the gold surface.

13.2.4.2 Functionalization of Quantum Dots

A surface functionalization is already performed during the synthesis of QDs, due to the coordinating ligands (being in water or in organic solvents). This is the case with the use of TGA, leading to carboxylic acid–surrounded, water-soluble QDs (the anchoring group being a thiol) [77,81]. Nevertheless, this initial coating is not always adapted to the application for which the QDs are synthesized. For example, their use as biomarkers requires their combination with biomolecules, generally through the addition of functional groups or reactive sites on their outer surface [23,67,68,122]. This can be done through covalent coupling using amines or thiolated molecules, or by surrounding the QD core with a silica shell [185]. Thiolated biomolecules can also replace the thiolated ligands present on the QD surface, through a ligand exchange process. Another possibility involves grafting carboxylic groups to the QD surface and then to couple them with amine groups from proteins [129] or antibodies [186].

Non-covalent coupling, hydrophobically or electrostatically driven, is also possible. Some examples exist, like negatively charged CdTe QDs capped with 3-mercaptopropyl acid, then coupled at pH 7.3 with papain (an enzyme) which is positively charged at this pH value [187]. Positively charged protein domain (pentahistadine segment) can also bind with negatively charged alkyl−COOH-capped QDs. For example, Goldman et al. showed that avidin (a positively charged protein) can adsorb tightly to QDs modified with dihydrolipoic acid, since it gives a homogeneous negative charge on the QD surface [188].

13.2.4.3 Functionalization of Silica Nanoparticles

In the case of silica nanoparticles, one of the most popular strategies consists in taking benefit of the chemistry of their surface silanol (i.e., Si–OH) and siloxane (i.e., Si–O–Si) groups.

The addition of supplemental siloxane layers (bearing specific functional groups) around existing nanoparticles in solution is easily performed by using an organosilane, or a functionalized alkoxysilane bearing a non-hydrolyzable Si−C bond (e.g., $X-(CH_2)_n-Si-(OR)_3$, where X is the functionality to add). Similar to the formation of the nanoparticles, the combination of hydrolysis and condensation steps permits to create an additional silica layer around the existing nanoparticles. However, instead of bearing silanol groups (Si–OH), this new layer will exhibit organic chains bearing functionality on their other end. As an example, a common functionalized alkoxysilane is the (3-aminopropyl)-triethoxysilane (APTES) which leads to amino-functionalized silica nanoparticles, as illustrated in Figure 13.9. This kind of functionalization is extremely stable since numerous covalent bonds are formed between the ligands and the nanoparticle. It is a common way to modify bare silica nanoparticles with a huge variety of organic chemical functions [154], such as thiol [90–92,189], amine [89,137], or carboxylate groups [22,139,141], to only cite the three major chemical functions usually implicated in fingermark detection mechanisms.

Functionalization of silica nanoparticles can be done in the same mixture that was used to synthesize them (we talk about "one-pot synthesis") or after the nanoparticles have been synthesized (we talk about "post-functionalization," "post-grafting," or "two-step process"). Functionalization can also be performed through the covalent addition of ligands or precursors, or achieved by the (electrostatic) adsorption of (charged) ligands on the surface of the nanoparticles. According to the functional group that has been added on the nanoparticle surface, a variety of subsequent surface modifications and immobilization procedures can be used to couple the functionalized silica nanoparticle with (bio)molecular groups [139,154]. When linking a probe biomolecule, it becomes possible to target oligonucleotides, enzymes, antibodies, or other proteins of interest. For example, Qhobosheane et al. used an amino-terminated chain to initiate the bioconjugation of silica nanoparticles [141]. Santra et al. modified the surface of luminescent silica nanoparticles using TSPDT (a primary amine group with a long chain), and further with antibodies [138]. Hydrophobic chains can also be added on the surface of the silica nanoparticles, such as octadecanol [89] or lauroyl chloride [137], so that they can be dispersible in organic solvents (e.g., cyclohexane or chloroform). The use of amino-functionalized (dye-doped) silica nanoparticles has also allowed them to be coated with nano-sized metal colloids, to finally form a homogeneous gold [145,190] or a silver [135] shell around them.

These three sections were aimed at providing to the reader with an overview of the wide possibilities offered by the functionalization of nanoparticles. Combining optical properties with specific functionalization constitutes the main challenge in designing a new fingermark detection reagent. In addition, solubility and solution instability issues are parameters that need to be addressed when trying to set up an optimal application protocol.

13.2.5 Health and Safety Issues

It seemed necessary to introduce the potential risks, in terms of environmental and health and safety issues, which could arise when working with nanoparticles. Indeed, the increasing use of manmade nanomaterials may lead to possible health impacts [191] or environmental dangers [192], that were not considered or encountered until now. Recently, several studies and publications have dealt with these concerns, especially since commercial applications of nanoparticles has increased (e.g., cosmetics, clothes, medicine, water filtration, among others) and will certainly continue to increase in the upcoming years [193–198].

There is growing concern of the potential health hazards of nano-sized materials because they may interact adversely with biological systems at the cellular and subcellular level. Questions have been raised about their potential toxicity, their long-term secondary effects on human beings, or their biodegradability.

Due to their small size, nanoparticles may penetrate the body (through skin, ingestion, or inhalation) or cell membranes, and interact further with biological systems [195,199] and cell life cycle [197]. Rothen-Rutishauser et al. showed, for example, that size was the most important factor (compared to the charge or the nature of the nanoparticles) that influenced the ability of nanoparticles to penetrate inside red blood cells by mechanisms not related to phagocytosis or endocytosis [200]. Moreover, some engineered surface coatings may also enhance the ability for nanoparticles to penetrate natural organic barriers. The main worries expressed toward the penetration of nanoparticles in human bodies are related to their high surface-to-volume ratio, which makes of them very reactive or catalytic species. This may lead to the formation of reactive oxygen species, for example, which may induce pulmonary inflammation, oxidative injury, or cytotoxicity, even if the same material is inert in its bulk form [191,196,199]. It is also currently recognized that the potential toxicity of nanomaterials cannot be deduced from the toxicity of the corresponding bulk material, since new properties may emerge with nanoparticles compared to larger ones. For example, the toxicity of asbestos mainly comes from its shape (sharp needles), not from its elemental composition. This explains why carbon nanotubes are now compared to asbestos in terms of risks in inducing inflammations (e.g., reactive oxygen species generation, lipid peroxidation, oxidative stress, or lung inflammation) [196,201]. However, Nel et al. showed that no conclusive data indicating that toxic effects related to nanomaterials currently exist or that they may become a major problem that could not be addressed by a rational scientific approach [196]. Indeed, only a limited number of nanomaterials, at high doses, have shown to induce toxicity in tissue cultures and animal experiments [194]. However, potential health risks due to the use of nanoparticles cannot be neglected.

The issue of the risks related with the (industrial) synthesis of different nanomaterials (e.g., carbon nanotubes, ZnSe QDs, or TiO_2 nanoparticles) has also been thoroughly studied in terms of volatility, carcinogenicity, flammability, toxicity, and persistence of the used materials, and compared with the impact of other manufacturing processes (e.g., lead–acid batteries, aspirin, wine, or polyethylene production) [202]. The authors concluded that there does not appear to be any unusual risks related to the production of the studied nanomaterials compared to other common processes.

In the context of the development of new forensic applications based on nanoparticles or nanomaterials, a proactive approach is thus required from researchers. Choices have to be made when choosing the nature and chemical composition of the nanoparticles of interest, as well as in their application protocol, so that they are the least toxic possible for the users (investigators or laboratory workers). For example, applying nanoparticles in solution is certainly a safer technique than dusting with a nano-based powder at the crime scene, due to their dilution and the fact that in solution they are less likely to be released in the atmosphere (even if there is still a possibility to form aerosols). Forensic investigators should, in any event, wear proper protective equipment to prevent any further risk associated with a long-term exposure to these materials. However, these safety precautions are not limited to nanomaterials and are valid for all reagents and organic solvents that are currently used in commonly applied fingermark development techniques.

The following section provides details concerning the secretions contained in latent mark residues, since these substances will be the target of reagent containing nanoparticles.

13.3 Affinity for the Papillary Secretions

Given the physicochemical and optical properties described in Section 13.2, nanoparticles have great promise in the field of fingermark detection due to their high surface-to-volume ratio, their size-dependent qualities, their optical properties, and the fact that they can easily be chemically tuned. If all these elements are considered together, particles with high selectivity and sensitivity toward molecular or biological targets can be obtained. To use nanoparticles as fingermark sensors, one issue still remains to be answered: "how to maximize the affinity of nanoparticles (whatever their nature) toward the secretion residues."

Indeed, possessing a good "marker" (in terms of luminescence capabilities or solubility) is only half of the work that has to be done. To obtain well-defined ridges and a good contrast between the marks and the support, it is necessary for the markers (i.e., the nanoparticles) to be engineered so that they present a selective affinity for the secretion residue, and, on the contrary, less or no attraction for the underlying surface. On this subject, some nanoparticles possess a spontaneous affinity for secretion components as a consequence of their nature (e.g., TiO_2 with hemoglobin-containing marks [203]) or as a consequence of the synthetic protocol (e.g., colloidal gold particles surrounded by negatively charged citrate ions in aqueous solution [25]). However, most of the time, additional groups or functions (added by the outer-surface functionalization) are necessary for nanoparticles to be able to target latent secretions.

The choice of the added functional groups greatly influences the way nanoparticles behave when approaching the secretion components. To ensure an efficient targeting strategy, it is necessary to (1) be aware of the molecular composition of the secretion, (2) determine a list of promising targets, and finally (3) engineer nanoparticles with chemical groups or functions that are able to interact with the identified potential targets. In addition to this, the mode of application also plays a crucial role. Indeed, if the nanoparticles are applied in solution, full benefits can be taken from the various physicochemical and chemical interactions that take place between two chemical entities. On the contrary, the application of nanoparticles as a dry powder is generally not a very specific application mode since these particles are somewhat "forced" to be in contact with the secretions, to which they mechanically stick. This application mode is thus less sensitive compared to chemically oriented protocols. This explains why traditional powders are generally limited to fresh marks on nonporous surfaces, since dusting porous surfaces may lead to strong background staining. However, the application in solution is much more difficult to develop since a strong and specific affinity for secretions has to be introduced in the nanomaterials (otherwise, no fingermark will be detected or a strong background staining will be obtained).

When looking at the possible interactions that could take place between a nanoparticle and a latent fingermark, three kinds were identified: "electrostatic," "lipophilic," and "chemical." Most of the existing techniques are driven by the first two. The third one is less encountered but may constitute a serious and efficient alternative for future developments. The following sections will describe each mode of interaction more specifically, with illustrated examples for each one. It should be noted that a fourth mode of interaction could have been added, namely, "physical interaction." However, the role played by van der Waals forces only is not evident since, most of the time, they are generally combined with one of the three other interactions cited earlier. For example, even the dusting of a powder with a brush on a surface bearing fingermarks requires the addition of lipid or lipid-like material (e.g., stearic acid, other long-chain fatty acids, mineral oil, or rosin) to coat the microparticles so they can attach better to the papillary secretions. The use of uncoated particles is only of early historical value. For this reason, we decided not to include this fourth interaction mode, but it will be addressed in Section 13.3.3.

13.3.1 Glance on the Composition of Secretion Residue

The work of Knowles is the most cited reference on this topic [204]. However, Ramotowski's expansion of this work contains more recent information [205]. Basically, under the human skin, there are three types of glands: eccrine and apocrine glands, which produce sweat, and sebaceous glands, which produce sebum. These glands secrete chemicals that help moisturize, lubricate, and protect the skin.

Eccrine glands are found all over the body, but are most concentrated on the palms of the hands and soles of the feet. These areas contain only eccrine glands, which secrete an aqueous liquid through the pores on the skin. This liquid is over 98% water and contains salt, amino acids, urea, and proteins, and a small amount of lipids, among other chemicals. All are water-soluble except the lipids and proteins, which are dispersed as a colloidal suspension. Per liter, it generates about 0.02–0.22 mg of lipids (fatty acids and sterols), 0.3–2.59 mg of amino acids, and 150–250 mg of proteins [205]. When considering an average molecular weight of proteins between 10,000 and 100,000 g/mol, the concentration of proteins can be estimated between 1.5 and 25.0 nmol/mL. The same calculation can be made for the amino acid fraction, by considering an average molecular weight of 125 g/mol, leading to an amino acid concentration estimated to be between 2.4 and 20.7 nmol/mL. A given volume of eccrine sweat is thus slightly more concentrated (or at least equally concentrated) with proteins than amino acids.

Apocrine glands are mostly found in the arm pits, nipple areola, and genital area. These secrete an aqueous liquid through the base of hair roots. Its composition has not been accurately characterized, but is believed to be low in salt and amino acids and high in proteins.

Sebaceous glands secrete sebum, or what some may call the "fats and oils" of the skin. They are found all over the body, at the exception of the palm and sole area. These glands release their sebum also through the base of the hair root. Although the face and forehead appear to be hairless, they have a high concentration of tiny hair follicles that produce sebum. Sebum consists of lipids and the most commonly found are fatty acids, wax esters (fatty acids esterified with a fatty alcohol), and squalene (levels of squalene are higher in adults than in children).

It is important to note that the secretions on the skin of recently cleaned hands can only come from eccrine glands on the hands. If these hands touch hair or the face, they acquire sebaceous secretions. They can also acquire sebaceous secretions by handling certain food or cosmetic products such as oily foods or hand creams, respectively. Inevitably, this is the case with most fingermarks; it contains both secretions and exogenous contaminants. Furthermore, one normally encounters secretion residue after it has dried. This means that the lipid material, which oxidizes over time, can trap eccrine material. Also, suspended (dispersed) proteins, after they dry, do not easily redisperse in water (probably due to their aggregation). We shall therefore divide the components of dried fingermark residue into those that are water-soluble or dispersible (salts, amino acids, urea, and any redispersible proteins) and those that are water-insoluble (lipids, non- or low-dispersible proteins, and any trapped eccrine material). The silver PD (Ag-PD) is a good example of a technique whose aim is to visualize the water-insoluble components of latent fingermark residue on porous surfaces. Much of what is discussed in this section is taken from Cantú [206].

13.3.2 Electrostatic Interaction

The electrostatic attraction between charged nanoparticles and secretion components is a mechanism that takes place mostly in aqueous-based techniques, since ionic species can exist in solution. Just as Section 13.2.2.2 addressed aspects of the existence of charge and electrostatic interactions at the surface of nanoparticles, here we address those aspects at the level of the secretion components. This is followed by the description of two techniques that were identified as being mostly driven by electrostatic interactions, i.e., MMD (Section 13.3.2.2) and Ag-PD (Section 13.3.2.3).

13.3.2.1 General Principles: Origin and Nature of the Charge on Secretions

As stated in Section 13.3.1, when a finger touches an object it leaves some residue consisting of papillary glandular secretions and possibly exogenous material that may have been on the surface of the finger. This residue contains a multitude of chemicals among which are proteins and amino acids that are trapped in water-insoluble lipids. Recall that a protein is an organic compound made of amino acids arranged in a linear chain. Each protein is characterized by its own sequence of amino acids, among a library of 20 different L-α-amino acids. In solution, a protein does not remain linear since it immediately starts to fold into a unique three-dimensional structure. During the folding process, some part of the amino acid chain will link with other parts of the chain, first locally (this is the secondary structure) then at the scale of the whole polypeptide chain (this is the tertiary structure). The tertiary structure is stabilized by nonlocal interactions (e.g., hydrophobic core, salt bridges, hydrogen bonds, or covalent disulfide bonds), and gives to a protein its catalytic activity. More importantly, in our case, the three-dimensional configuration causes amino acids with ionizable side chains to be present on the outer surface of a protein, facing the aqueous surrounding and thus stabilizing the protein in solution, while neutral amino acids are tightly kept in the hydrophobic core. Among the 20 different amino acids, only a few contain ionizable groups on their side chains: lysine, arginine, and histidine possess basic amino groups; glutamic acid and aspartic acid possess terminal carboxylic acid groups. In addition to this, one has to consider the amino- and carboxyl-ending groups of a polypeptide chain or of each free amino acid. As a consequence, these groups may bear a charge (positive or negative) when they are in contact with an aqueous medium.

When the substrate bearing a fingermark is immersed in an aqueous solution, these chemicals (i.e., proteins and trapped amino acids) are no longer solubilized if they are trapped in the dried, hardened residue. Proteins also do not solubilize (i.e., disperse) well in water. The ionizable groups, in contact with the aqueous surrounding, will thus potentially bear an electronic charge according to their pK_a values (the negative log of the acid dissociation constant) and the pH value [207]. Before considering the behavior of the secretion residue as a whole, it is necessary to decompose the system according to the main ionizable functions in presence. In this context, we can distinguish two distinct ranges of pH corresponding to the appearance or disappearance of charges on the functional groups of amino acids (and, by the same way, on proteins through ionization of the external ionizable side chains):

1. In the pH range "2–4," negative charges appear (or disappear) if the pH rises (or decreases) from these values. These negative charges find their origin in the deprotonation of carboxyl groups (R–COOH) that are converted to carboxylate anions ($R-COO^-$). At pH ~ 2 and above, terminal carboxyl groups are predominantly deprotonated (the terminal carboxyl groups are the ones located at

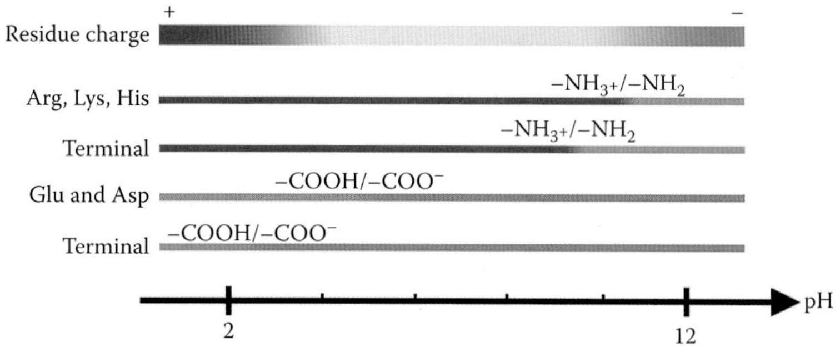

FIGURE 13.10
Illustration of the evolution of the charge on the residue according to the pH. Red, blue, and gray zones correspond to positive, negative, and neutral states, respectively. The "green–gray" zone corresponds to the pH region where the residue has the least charge, since there is a competition between the positively and the negatively charged components.

the extremity of a protein backbone or at one end of an amino acid), whereas the carboxyl groups of glutamic and aspartic acids (side chains) are converted to carboxylate anions at slightly higher pH (~4). See the behavior of "Glu" and "Asp" and also of "terminal" carbonyl group in Figure 13.10.

2. In the pH range "9–10," positive charges appear (or disappear) if the pH decreases (or rises) from these values. These positive charges find their origin in the protonation of amino groups ($R–NH_2$) to form ammonium groups $\left(R–NH_3^+\right)$. At pH ~ 9 and below, terminal amino groups are predominantly under the form of ammonium groups (the terminal ammonium groups are the ones located at the extremity of a protein backbone or at one end of an amino acid), whereas the basic groups of arginine, lysine, and histidine get deprotonated at pH > 10. See the behavior of "Arg," "Lys," and "His" and also of "terminal" amino groups in Figure 13.10.

If the pH of a solution increases, starting from highly acidic values, the positive charge of proteins and amino acids (due to protonated basic groups) progressively decreases (due to the appearance of negative charges from the carboxylate anions), up to reach a "no net charge" point (equilibrium between positive and negative charges), before it becomes negative (due to the deprotonation of basic groups, only the carboxylate anions remain). The "isoelectric point" (p*I*) is defined as the pH at which a protein has no net charge (considering the individual charges of all the amino acids that comprise it). At its p*I*, an amino acid is a neutral zwitterion. In other words, it bears simultaneously a negative charge (from its terminal $-COO^-$) and a positive charge (from its terminal $–NH_3^+$). When the pH > p*I*, a protein bears a net negative charge and when the pH < p*I*, a protein bears a net positive charge. The p*I* value also varies between proteins.

The protonation and deprotonation of proteins and amino acids certainly constitute the major contribution to the net charge of the fingermark residue, which varies according to the pH. It should be noted that lipids bearing carbon–carbon double bonds may behave as nucleophiles (Lewis bases) in polar reactions by donating a pair of electrons to an electrophile (Lewis acid) under low pH conditions. It may thus be supposed that positively charged protons or silver ions can be electrostatically attracted to the electron-rich double bond from mono- to polyunsaturated fatty acids [40].

Considering all these observations, it is possible to define three pH ranges, in relation with the charge of the residue as a whole (Figure 13.10):

1. The first pH range (pH ~2–3 and below) corresponds to positively charged fingermark residue. At these pH values, the amino groups are protonated ($-NH_3^+$), as well as the carboxylic acids (non-charged, $-COOH$; see gray region in the lower left of Figure 13.10).
2. The second pH range (intermediate pH value) corresponds to fingermark residue having the least charge. At these pH values, proteins and free amino acids are close to their isoelectric points. Since the residue contains several amino acids and proteins, not all are neutral at the same pH; thus, we speak of a range in which the residue has the least charge.
3. The third pH range (pH ~9 and more) corresponds to negatively charged fingermark residue. At these pH values, the carboxyl groups are deprotonated ($-COO^-$), as well as the amino groups (non-charged, $-NH_2$; see gray region in the upper right of Figure 13.10).

If one plans to develop a technique based on the electrostatic attraction between nanoparticles and latent secretions, one should set the pH within the first pH range (the acidic one) if the nanoparticles are negatively charged, and within the third pH range (the basic one) if the nanoparticles are positively charged. However, since the charge of the nanoparticles is also function of the pH values and could be neutralized if the pH reaches a certain value, it is sometimes necessary to set the pH in the intermediate pH range (the second one), until the Coulombic attraction between the latent mark and the charged nanoparticles is a maximum. To confirm this theory, we will now look more closely at two existing methods, based on negatively charged nanoparticles in aqueous solution.

13.3.2.2 Electric Charge Aspects of the Gold Sol (Description of the MMD in Terms of Zeta Potential, Size, and Charge)

In MMD, the colloidal gold solution must be set at a pH between 2.5 and 2.8 for the gold colloidal particles to attach to the latent fingermark residue [25]. Outside this range, the successful detection of latent fingermarks decreases drastically. The explanation for this may lie in the negatively charged citrate-capped gold particles that are used to detect fingermarks in the first step of this process.

Following the MMD-II protocol [25], the colloidal gold obtained consists of an aqueous monodisperse suspension of 14 nm (diameter) gold colloids, capped with citrate ions, and of a pH of ~6.2. In such conditions, the carboxylic acid groups of the citrate ions are mostly deprotonated. The gold nanoparticles are thus highly negatively charged and repel each other in solution, avoiding aggregation. This explains why such a colloidal solution is stable for months. In the context of a method based on electrostatic interactions, this constitutes ideal conditions for the gold colloids, since their negative charge is almost at its maximum. Nevertheless, at this pH, the secretion residues are the least charged and possess no specific affinity for the gold colloids. This explains why no fingermarks are detected when immersing a sample in a colloidal gold solution (synthesized according to the MMD-II recipe) whose pH has not been modified from its initial value.

The latent fingermarks should be positively charged to promote electrostatic attraction. As previously said, the latent residue contains water-indispersible proteins which become positively charged in an acidic environment (due to protonation of the amine groups).

With the decrease of the gold solution pH, the latent fingermark residue becomes more positively charged (protonated). However, a drawback occurs at the same time: the gold nanoparticles become less negatively charged with decreasing pH (due to the protonation of the carboxylate groups of the adsorbed citrate ions). This effect is empirically observed when decreasing the pH to 1.7 and below. The ruby red–colored gold colloid immediately turns dark purple, with the gold nanoparticles aggregating due to the neutralization of the citrate ions, resulting in an insufficient electrostatic repulsion compared to the van der Waals attraction. Figure 13.5 illustrates this effect in terms of zeta potential measurements. It is thus inadvisable to set the pH of the colloidal gold solution at a pH of 2 or below in order to maximize the positive charge of the fingermark residue, because it would result in a highly unstable colloidal gold solution and no detection of fingermarks.

To limit this effect, a neutral nonionic surfactant (i.e., Tween 20) is added to the colloidal gold before reducing the pH [25]. The stability of the sol at low pH is maintained by steric hindrance. However, the charge of the gold colloid is screened by a ligand replacement effect and the steric effect induced by the capping (Figure 13.5). Stability is thus obtained to the detriment of the negative charge. Nevertheless, this does not solve the problem of citrate neutralization at low pH values, resulting in uncharged gold colloids.

Consequently, it was necessary to find experimental conditions for which (1) the gold nanoparticles still possess a sufficiently high negative charge and (2) the fingermark residues are sufficiently positively charged to attract the nanoparticles. These experimental conditions have been empirically set at a very narrow pH range between 2.5 and 2.8. Figure 13.11 schematically illustrates this concept.

We can thus conclude that the MMD method is one based on electrostatic attraction between negatively charged nanoparticles and positively charged fingermark residues. However, due to the constraints imposed by the intrinsic nature of both, this process is taking place in nonideal physicochemical conditions in terms of charge (the gold nanoparticles and fingermark residue are not at their maximum charge). It also explains why this technique is so sensitive to pH modifications.

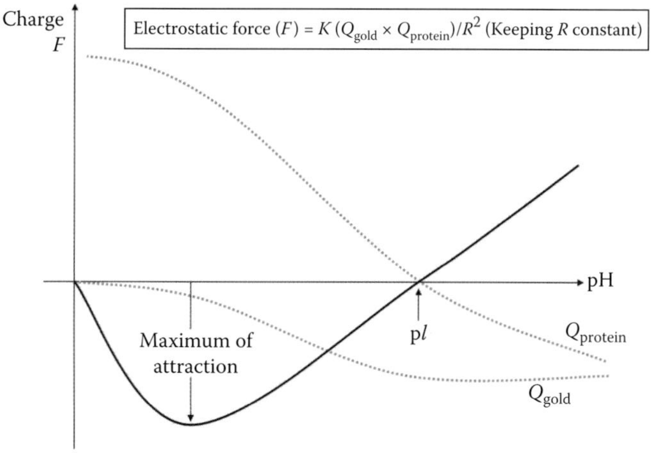

FIGURE 13.11
Evolution of the electrostatic force between gold colloids and proteins contained in the residue (in the context of multimetal deposition). The force is attractive (negative value) below the isoelectric point of proteins (p*I*), since gold nanoparticles are negatively charged (Q_{gold}) and proteins start to be positively charged (Q_{prot}). Conversely, the force is repulsive (positive value) above the p*I*, since gold colloids and proteins are negatively charged. In the equation, *K* is a constant whose value depends only on the permittivity of the medium into which the nanoparticles are dispersed.

13.3.2.3 Electrostatic Aspects of the Silver Physical Developer

Ag-PD is a process whereby silver ions get reduced to silver metal by a reducing agent present only at a catalytic site. Such nucleating (catalytic) sites include silver, gold, and silver sulfide (either in bulk or as particles). Since silver catalyzes Ag-PD, any silver deposited (reduced) on a catalytic site adds to the catalytic activity of this site and more silver is deposited. This explains why the process is referred to as autocatalytic. The use of the Ag-PD to detect fingermarks on porous surfaces thus consists of depositing silver nanoparticles on the secretion, so that they may constitute catalytic sites for further silver deposition. We now explain how this occurs.

The development of latent fingermarks on porous surfaces with a Ag-PD depends on the spontaneous formation of silver colloidal particles. Indeed, the Ag-PD is an aqueous solution containing silver ions, a reducing agent, and other components, all of which are carefully balanced so that the silver is not reduced by the reducing agent unless a nucleation site is present. These colloidal particles begin as single silver atoms, which grow to form silver nanocrystals with sizes ranging from 1 to 100 nm. Under some circumstances, these nanoparticles get electrostatically attracted to the latent fingermark residue and become nucleating sites for further physical development [40,208]. Here is a summary of the underlying processes driving the attraction of silver nanoparticles for papillary secretions:

1. The water-insoluble components of latent fingermark residue contain lipids (if the fingers touched skin areas bearing sebum or exogenous lipid-bearing material) and a significant amount of nondispersible proteins (from the eccrine secretions which contain circa 200 mg/L of proteins and just about 0.12 mg/L of lipids [205]). When latent fingermark residue on a surface dries, the proteins do not readily redisperse in water, they remain on the surface.
2. Similar to the colloidal gold treatment (Section 13.3.2.2), it can be assumed that the water-insoluble fraction of latent fingermark residue becomes positive, since the pH of the Ag-PD is acidic (pH evaluated at 1.38) [40]. The Forensic Science Service (FSS) developed test papers for latent fingermark visualizing reagents, including the Ag-PD [209]. The FSS used a solution of ethylenediaminetetraacetate (EDTA) in its sodium salt form (the four carboxylic acid groups are deprotonated) to print a test pattern on paper. In acid solution, EDTA gets protonated (the four carboxylate groups and the two amines as well), making the molecule acquire a positive charge. It also becomes insoluble. This was done to simulate the protonation of the nondispersible proteins contained in the latent fingermark residue.
3. No matter how stable the Ag-PD is, silver nanoparticles are formed spontaneously in the solution and grow with time. Their *rate of formation* is suppressed by keeping the possibility of silver ions getting reduced close to zero, but still positive. Hence, their formation is suppressed but not stopped. Their *rate of growth* is suppressed by introducing a cationic surfactant in the formulation. Note, the full electrochemical treatment of the Ag-PD and its stabilization is given by Jonker et al. [210], Cantú [40], and Cantú and Johnson [208].
4. Spontaneously formed silver nanoparticles, just like the gold nanoparticles, are capped with citrate ions and are thus negatively charged. The magnitude of their negative charge increases with their growth. Though the pH of the Ag-PD is 1.38 [40], the citrate ions are not completely neutralized. Each of these

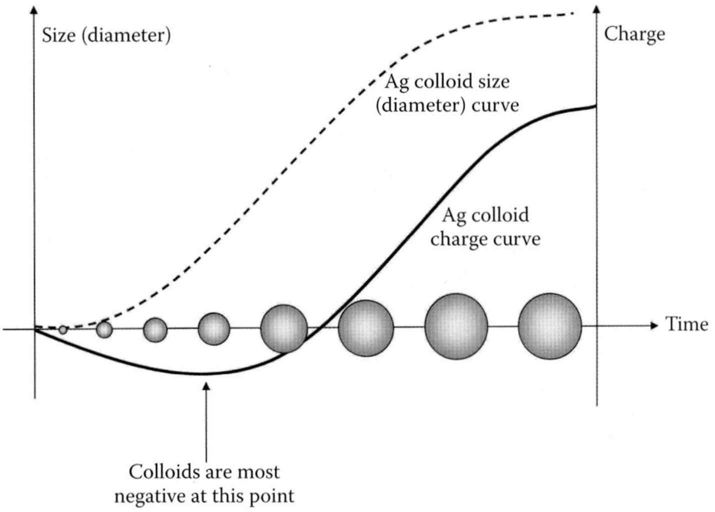

FIGURE 13.12
Evolution of the size and charge of silver colloids in the context of the physical developer. The colloids are first negatively charged (due to the adsorption of citrate ions), but as they grow in size, cationic surfactant molecules begin to surround the colloids so that the charge is reversed toward positive values.

negatively charged nanoparticles electrostatically attracts cationic surfactant molecules and is prone to get encased by them forming a positively charged micelle. But those near or on the fingermark residue are also electrostatically attracted to the positively charged residue. There is a point in their growth where the nanoparticles are mostly negative (they begin at zero, reach a maximum negative charge, and then take a turn toward a positive charge). A schematic representation of this is given in Figure 13.12. If these (mostly negative) nanoparticles are near or on the positive latent fingermark residue, they attach (electrostatically) to the residue; get neutralized (lose their charge); lose their citrate caps (and thus lose any adhered cationic surfactant molecules); and finally become bare nucleating (catalytic) sites for Ag-PD. Figure 13.13 is a scanning electron microscopic (SEM) image of a silver colloidal particle that has grown on fingermark residue on a paper fiber. It began as a small nanoparticle that grew into a colloidal particle several microns in diameter. The multitude of filaments that make up this particle trap light and thus make the particle appear dark rather than silver in color.

5. Latent fingermark residue is more exposed (i.e., it has more of its components exposed over a larger surface area) when it is on a porous surface than if it is on a nonporous surface. Since the exposed surface components carry a charge, it follows that the apparent positive charge of the residue is higher if it resides on porous surfaces than if it sits on nonporous surfaces. This may explain why the Ag-PD develops latent fingermarks on porous surfaces but not if it is on nonporous surfaces. If the negatively charged nanoparticles were not dynamically changing in size and charge, then they would gradually adhere to the (less positively charged) residue in sufficient number to act as nucleating sites. This happens with the colloidal gold system. The gold colloid particles, which do not change in size or charge, can take up to 2h to have a perceptible amount adhere to residue on nonporous surfaces.

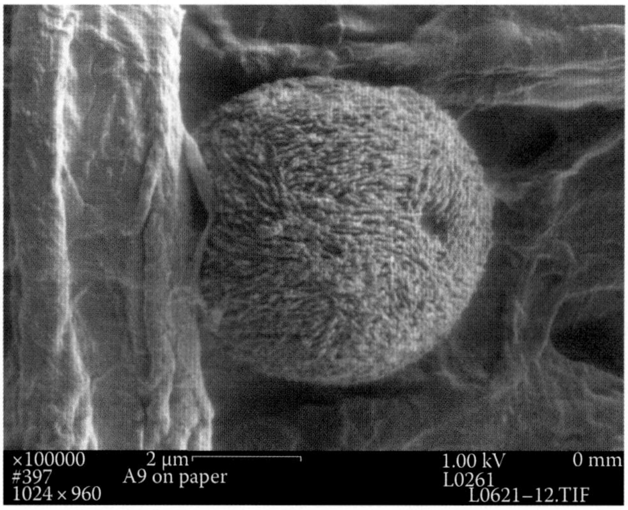

FIGURE 13.13
Scanning electron microscope image of a silver colloid particle on a paper fiber bearing fingermark residue.

13.3.3 Lipophilic Interaction

Lipophilic interactions with nanoparticles are mainly confined to the use of powders to detect fingermarks. Nanoparticles functionalized with lipophilic molecules are described in Section 13.4 [30,211]. This section focuses on powders and starts with a brief comment on traditional micro-sized powders, in particular about the role played by physical interaction and the need for coating molecules. This is followed by the new trend of using nano-sized powders with enhanced lipophilic abilities. Both approaches, traditional and nano-enhanced particles, are compared in the following section.

13.3.3.1 Traditional Fingermark Powders

Traditional fingermark powders consist of micron-sized particles, some with nanostructured surfaces [45]. Many of these particles are coated with lipid or lipid-like material (e.g., stearic acid, other long-chain fatty acids, or mineral oil) or blended in with lipid-like substances (e.g., starch or rosin/resins) for greater adhesion. But some are raw ("naked") uncoated particles, particularly those in earlier powders. Coated particles adhere to latent fingermark residue via lipophilic attraction while uncoated ones probably adhere via van der Waals attraction forces (which depend on both the nature of the particle and the residue) provided they are sufficiently near the surface (as when they are applied with a brush). These van der Waals attractive forces can attract (adsorb) atoms, molecules, or ions (as noted in Section 13.2.2.1) from the surroundings. The resulting particle can be charged if it adsorbs ions or remain neutral if it adsorbs neutral species. These capped particles further interact with the residue via van der Waals forces. Furthermore, since the surface roughness of the residue is in the micron range, the nano-sized particles can easily get lodged within the surface roughness.

Traditional fingermark powders are generally applied to nonporous surfaces, especially at crime scenes, to develop latent fingermarks up to months after their deposition if the substrate has been protected from external degradation. But when applied to porous surfaces, they develop marks that are only a few days old since the residue dries more quickly on these surfaces than on nonporous surfaces.

Another way of promoting lipophilic interaction with particles involves putting micron-sized particles in solution, namely those found in small particle reagents (SPRs). Such solutions contain surfactants and work best on wet or dry nonporous surfaces. The original SPR consisted of molybdenum disulfide and the resulting reagent is black. The particle size can be as small as 400 nm. Currently, SPRs exist that are white (based on titanium dioxide or zinc carbonate) and/or fluorescent (e.g., made by mixing zinc carbonate and fluorescent dyes).

Therefore, the coating of traditional micro-sized nanoparticles rapidly shows its limits, especially in terms of the age of the fingermarks and the background staining. One way to enhance the ability for powders to more selectively or more efficiently develop latent traces involves enhancing the lipophilic character of the particles to be powdered or applied as SPR. The use of nanoparticles that can be chemically modified offers an important opportunity in this domain. This evolution is described in the following section.

13.3.3.2 Powders Containing Enhanced Nanopowders

Nano-sized particles can be coated or non-coated, but they can also be functionalized whereby molecules are chemically bonded to the surface of the nanoparticles. Such chemically bonded functionalization can also be applied to micron-sized particles, but to our knowledge this has not been reported, particularly for visualizing latent fingermarks. Some powders made with nanoparticles visualize very weak latent fingermarks better than traditional powders do [8]. It should be emphasized that when such small particles are in powder form and become aerosolized, they could be hazardous to one's health as stated in Section 13.2.5.

13.3.3.3 Illustrated Example: Alkane-Modified Metal Nanoparticles

Functionalized nanoparticles can be obtained through covalent bonding of molecules on their outer surface, as indicated in Section 13.2.4. Groups such as thiol and amine readily bind to the gold surface. Amine groups also bind well covalently on the surface of QDs, such as those having a ZnS shell with a CdSe core.

Sametband et al. used these properties to develop two types of reagents for visualizing latent traces [30]: gold nanoparticles functionalized with *n*-alkanethiols and CdSe/ZnS QDs coated with *n*-alkaneamines (Figure 13.14). How well these reagents visualized latent marks depended on the size of the alkane chain, with a C_{18} chain working best for both reagents. In any case, the lipophobic interactions are promoted compared to "classical" powders, leading to more detailed fingermarks with less unwanted background staining, as noticed by Choi et al. [211]. These aspects are discussed in greater detail in Section 13.4.

13.3.4 Chemical Reaction

Some of the most efficient detection techniques are based on chemical reactions between an organic reagent and some components of the latent fingermarks, especially the amino acid reagents on porous surfaces (e.g., ninhydrin, 1,2-indanedione, or genipin). This mode of interaction can be highly selective (in terms of recognition of chemical groups or patterns) and is also highly effective since chemical bonds are formed between the reagent and the latent secretions. Nevertheless, this third interaction mode is still rarely encountered in the field of nanoparticles, where electrostatic and lipophilic interactions prevail. The pioneering

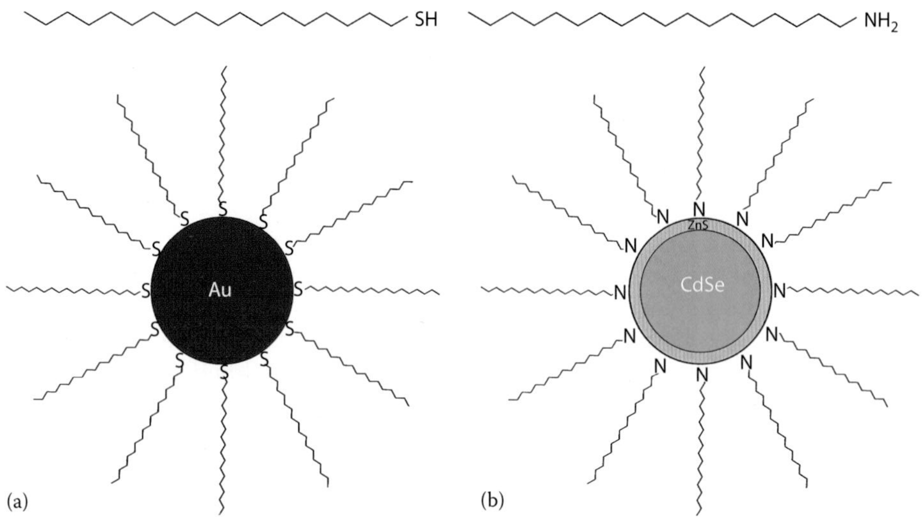

FIGURE 13.14
Illustration of *n*-octadecanethiol and the corresponding functionalized gold nanoparticle (a), and of *n*-octadecylamine and the corresponding functionalized CdSe/ZnS quantum dot (b), as used by Sametband et al. to promote lipophilic interactions with the lipid fraction of latent fingermarks. (From Sametband M, Shweky I, Banin U, Mandler D, Almog J. (2007) Application of Nanoparticles for the Enhancement of Latent Fingerprints. *Chem. Commun.*: 1142–1144. With permission from Royal Society of Chemistry.)

works of Menzel and coworkers somewhat opened the road to this mode of recognition and may constitute a serious and efficient alternative for future developments [212,213].

13.3.4.1 General Principles

We define a technique as being driven by "chemical reaction" if a covalent bond is actually created between the reagent and the fingermark residue. Only non-covalent interactions led to the detection of fingermarks in the techniques previously described (e.g., physical entrapment in lipids or electrostatic interactions). The formation of a chemical bond requires a molecule or a functional group to be present in most of the latent residues and able to undergo chemical reactions under ambient or mild conditions with other chemical groups. It is not necessary that the chemical reaction lead to some colored or luminescent product (like for amino acid reagents such as ninhydrin or 1,2-indanedione), since the goal is to form a covalent link between the particle (the "marker") and the residue. Once this is done, it is supposed that the particle will remain "stuck" to the residue at the location the reaction occurred. The use of dye-doped nanoparticles will permit detection of the nanoparticles and, in the same way, make the latent fingermark appear.

Two major limitations of this strategy may explain why it has not encountered the success it should meet:

1. The chemical reaction between the secretions (the target) and the functionalized nanoparticle (the sensor) has to be a fast process. Indeed, it seems useless to propose a fingermark detection technique requiring 24 h of immersion in order for the chemical reaction to occur. A solution could involve finding a way to speed up the kinetics of the reaction by using a catalyst or by activating one of the two reactive groups (e.g., by forming an unstable intermediate that will readily react

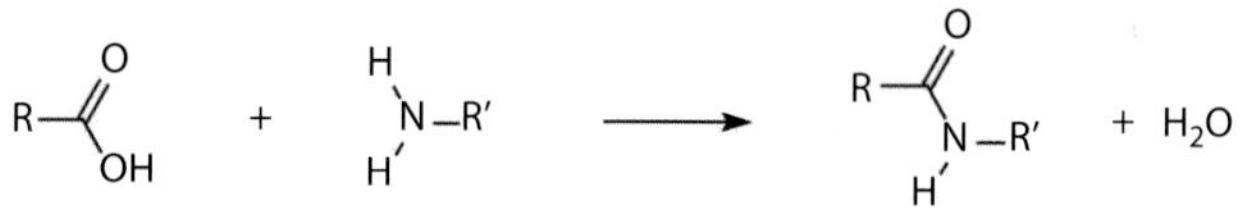

FIGURE 13.15
Formation of a peptide bond between a carboxylic acid and a primary amine. The reaction usually needs to be catalyzed through the activation of one of the two groups to occur quickly.

with another chemical group) prior to the immersion of the specimen in the working solution. However, it could considerably burden the application protocol and, simultaneously, reduce the forensic scientist's interest in this technique.

2. The chemical groups surrounding the nanoparticles must be specific to latent secretion residue and not to the underlying substrate. Since a major part of the latent residue components are of organic origin, it seems logical to try targeting amino or carboxylic groups that are very likely to be present in almost all latent fingermarks (e.g., in amino acids, proteins, or some lipids). However, since a great part of the substrates may also have an organic origin, they may also constitute targeting sites for the functionalized nanoparticles. In such a case, an unwanted background staining will occur, reducing the selectivity for fingermarks and the contrast.

13.3.4.2 *Illustrated Example: Amide Bond Formation*

Fingermark residue contains several chemicals, each of which has at least one carboxyl group. These include amino acids, fatty acids, and proteins. Menzel felt these molecules could be visualized by chemically reacting them with molecules containing amine groups at one end and a luminescent nanoparticle at the other [214]. Indeed, an amine can react with a carboxyl group to form a very strong amide (peptide) bond (Figure 13.15).

The reaction is referred to as dehydration synthesis or condensation. The bond C(=O)–NH is called an amide (peptide) bond, the group −(C=O)−NH− is called an amide group or peptide group (when in proteins), and the molecule R−(C=O)−NH–R′ is called an amide. Here the −NH group is a secondary amine.

The molecules with amine groups at one end and a QD at the other that Menzel considered are Cd-based QDs functionalized with polyamidoamine (PAMAM) dendrimers. These dendrimers (treelike structures) have amines at one end and amines covalently bonded with the QD at the other. This approach is described in greater detail in Section 13.4.2.

13.4 Visualizing Fingermarks Using Nanoparticles

Techniques that are based on the use of nanoparticles were first proposed in the 1970s, with the introduction of the Ag-PD by the Atomic Weapons Research Establishment (AWRE) [215,216]. Nevertheless, most of the efforts to take full advantage of nanoparticles, in terms of optical properties and surface engineering, only started in late 1990s and increased very rapidly since 2004. As an illustration of this increased interest, it can be observed that the number of publications related with the use of nanoparticles to detect fingermarks was of only 1 for the 2001–2004 year range (source: Interpol report) [217], 10 for 2004–2007 [218], and 27 for 2007–2010 [219]. The decision has been made to organize the following overview according to the chemical nature of the nanoparticles. Some kinds of nanoparticles have been obviously attracting more interest from researchers (i.e., gold- and cadmium-based nanoparticles) compared to others. Some other domains have also emerged and will certainly soon constitute highly promising alternatives to existing techniques (e.g., silica-based nanoparticles and antibody/antigen-driven techniques).

13.4.1 Aluminum-Based Nanoparticles

Sodhi and Kaur chose to coat aluminum oxide nanoparticles with two different molecules: eosin Y (a fluorescent dye) and a natural hydrophobic substance [220]. Their aim was to obtain a "nanopowder" to be dusted on substrates and characterized by an enhanced ability to detect fingermarks through lipophilic interactions. According to the authors, this nanopowder detects fingermarks on a wide range of surfaces such as porous and nonporous, as well as white and multicolored ones. It is particularly suitable for detecting fingermarks on glossy items, or on moist and sticky surfaces. The developed marks are luminescent (yellow–green color) when illuminated at 550 nm.

13.4.2 Cadmium-Based Nanoparticles

Cadmium is the most commonly used element to synthesize highly luminescent QDs, with numerous publications about their synthesis (see Section 13.2.1.2). This explains why the forensic use of QDs to detect fingermarks is limited to the use of cadmium sulfide (CdS) [42,213,214,221–225], cadmium selenide (CdSe) with or without a shell [30,43,212,226], and cadmium telluride (CdTe) [41,227,228]. All these nanocrystals were chosen for their remarkably high luminescent properties combined with the possibility of being chemically functionalized. Two trends are observed when considering QDs in the detection of fingermarks: those incorporating the nanocrystals in a more massive and bulky structure (typically a polymer) taking benefit only from the luminescence of the QDs [42,212,214,222,224,225], and those considering the nanocrystals not only as fluorescent markers but also especially as probes able to target latent residue by themselves [30,41,43,221,226–228]. In this latter case, a surface modification of the nanocrystals, using self-assembled monolayers of linear molecules, may be necessary.

Menzel et al. performed the pioneering work on the use of fluorescent semiconductor nanocrystals as fingermark labeling agents. Their first attempt consisted of solubilizing CdS nanocrystals capped with dioctyl sulfosuccinate (a two-branched molecule that exposed its aliphatic chains to the surroundings of the particle) in heptane or hexane (Figure 13.16) [221]. Such nanoparticles were applied on cyanoacrylate-fumed, and unfumed, fingermarks on aluminum and metallic soft-drink cans, as well as on the sticky side of unfumed adhesive tapes. The choice for QDs emerged from the desire to use phase-resolved detection to reduce the unwanted background fluorescence, since QDs are characterized by longer luminescence lifetimes than that of the background [212]. The application protocol consisted of immersing the substrates (previously fumed or not) for a few seconds to a few minutes in the nanocrystal solutions before rinsing them with an organic solvent. Examination using an argon-ion laser operating in the near-UV allowed for the observation of intensely fluorescent fingermarks on the cyanoacrylate-fumed aluminum and metallic soft-drink cans (Figure 13.16). Unfumed fingermarks on metal, glass, and plastics could not be developed by following this procedure, certainly due to a degradation of the

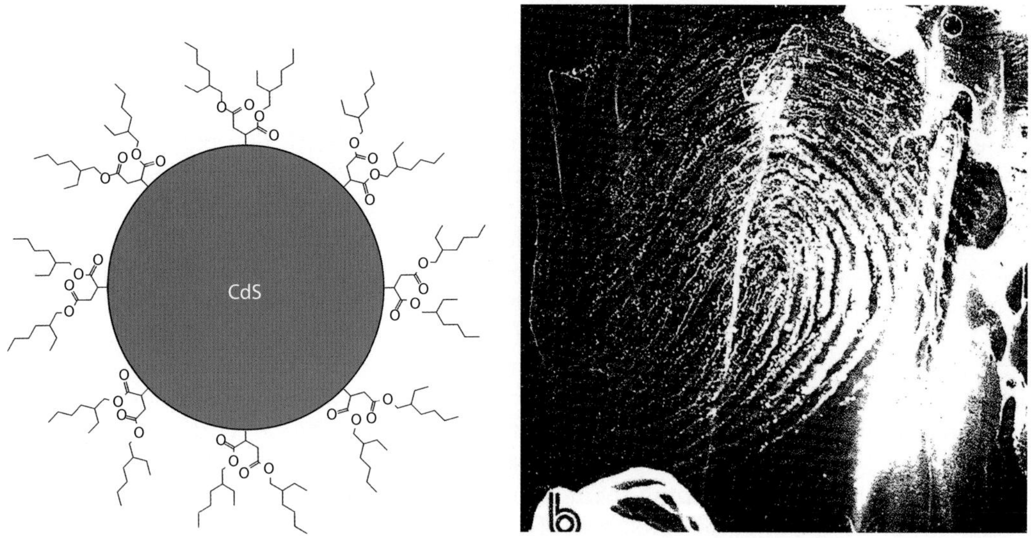

(a) (b)

FIGURE 13.16
(a) Schematic representation of the dioctyl sulfosuccinate–capped CdS quantum dot that has been used by Menzel et al. to detect fingermarks on nonporous surfaces. (b) The illustrated fingermark (From Menzel, E.R. et al., *J. Forensic Sci.*, 45, 545, 2000) has been developed by cyanoacrylate/CdS nanocrystal staining on a soft-drink can.

latent marks caused by the organic solvents. On the sticky side of unfumed adhesive tapes, the results were limited but encouraging, especially on black electrical tape.

Another attempt involved functionalizing CdSe/ZnS QDs with carboxylate groups to form amide bonds with amino acids in the secretions [212]. The detection of fingermarks on aluminum foil required an immersion time of 24 h, much too long for operational use. According to the authors, no ridge detail could be observed if unmodified QDs were used.

Recently, Gao et al. propose to functionalize CdTe QDs with ionizable groups allowing them to obtain negatively charged QDs (i.e., $-COO^-$) or positively charged ones (i.e., $-COONH_3-NH_3^+$), upon modification of the pH of the solution by using hydrazine (NH_2-NH_2) [228]. The detection protocol consisted in setting the pH of the QD solution between 7 and 11, pouring 1 mL of the solution on the latent fingermarks, allowing it to react for 30 min to 1 h, and then rinsing with water. The authors explain that the detection mechanism is based on the electrostatic interaction between the charged QDs and the amino acids from the secretion, at pH > 6.4, with an increased efficiency for positively charged QDs. However, a closer look of the illustrated fingermarks makes it clear that several of those fingermarks are "reversed" (meaning that the substrate has reacted, not the ridges). This point has not been raised by the authors, nor discussed. Several explanations may explain this: (1) contrary to what the authors claim, the amino acids are not sufficiently negatively charged at pH ~ 6.4 (as illustrated in Figure 13.10), (2) when the pH is sufficiently high for amino acids to be negatively charged (near pH 9), hydrazine is expected to be under its basic, uncharged form (since its pK_a is 8.1), and by the same way the QDs too, and (3) the formation of "$-COONH_3-NH_3^+$" groups is quite hard to understand from a chemical point of view since it stands on the double protonation of the hydrazine molecule. This attempt to develop an electrostatic attraction–based method is interesting, but it is more likely to believe that the detection is lead by other mechanisms, particularly an unwanted deposition of the QD on the substrates.

In further experiments, efforts were concentrated on the *in situ* synthesis of QDs inside a PAMAM dendrimer solubilized in methanol or in 1:9 methanol:water and used as cyanoacrylate staining dyes [42,212,214,222]. According to Menzel, the number of functional groups on the surface of the dendrimers (i.e., amino or carboxylate groups, depending on the kind of dendrimer that was used) may play a key role in the solubility of the reagent, in the interactions with latent secretions (physically and chemically), as well as in the reduction of unwanted background staining. Fresh fingermarks on aluminum foil and polyethylene bags were fumed and then immersed overnight in the nanocomposite solution before being observed for luminescence. It remained somewhat unclear to the authors whether or not the staining was due to physical interaction or chemical reaction (i.e., through the formation of actual peptidic bonds between the amino groups of the dendrimer and the carboxylic acids from the secretions). Further experiments were conducted to answer this question. First, fingermarks were "activated" by pretreating them in a 2.5% (w/v) diimide aqueous solution for 5–24 h at room temperature (shorter immersion times led to no observable fingermarks) before dipping them overnight in the amino-based nanocomposites [212,213]. A second attempt consisted of mixing stoichiometric amounts of diimide with carboxylate-based dendrimers (without QDs) to pre-activate them. The 1:9 methanol:water mixture containing the dendrimers was left overnight at 60°C. After this step, QDs were added and the fingermarks were finally immersed in the final mixture. Diimide compounds are known to activate the carboxylate groups to increase their reactivity toward amino groups. During their two experiments, Menzel et al. tried to promote the formation of peptide bonds between the nanocomposites and fingermarks by either activating the carboxylate groups contained in the latent secretions (first experiment) or by activating carboxylate-based dendrimers that could further react with amino groups contained in the latent secretions (second experiment). The formation of the CdS/dendrimer nanocomposite followed by diimide addition (prior to fingermark treatment) was not successful. Development attempts on porous surfaces were unsuccessful due to unwanted background staining.

Dilag et al. used CdS QDs, with an average size of ~6 nm, entrapped in chitosan (a biopolymer), leading to nanocomposites of ~20 nm of diameter [223]. The nanocomposites were freeze-dried and applied as a powder with a brush on both cyanoacrylate-fumed and unfumed fingermarks on aluminum foil. Successful results were obtained only when dusting unfumed fingermarks. The nanocomposites deposited on the secretions and permitted the visualization of ridges in the luminescent mode. When evaluating the performance of their nanocomposites, the authors admitted that conventional micron-sized powders gave finer results compared to theirs, explaining that the freeze-drying process certainly led to the formation of large aggregates, with a size greater than those contained in classical powders (~1–10 μm).

Sametband et al. synthesized core/shell CdSe/ZnS QDs with average size of ~3 nm and functionalized them with octadecaneamine (Figure 13.14). The nanocomposites were solubilized in petroleum ether to detect untreated latent fingermarks on silicon wafers and paper strips [30]. Their strategy was based on the lipophilic interactions that could take place between the *n*-alkane ligands covering the QD surface and the lipids from the latent mark secretions. Fluorescent fingermarks could be visualized immediately on the silicon wafers, when illuminated with UV radiation. However, it was impossible to observe fingermarks on the paper strips, due to a strong background luminescence caused by an unwanted deposition of QDs on the porous substrate itself. Further developments are thus required.

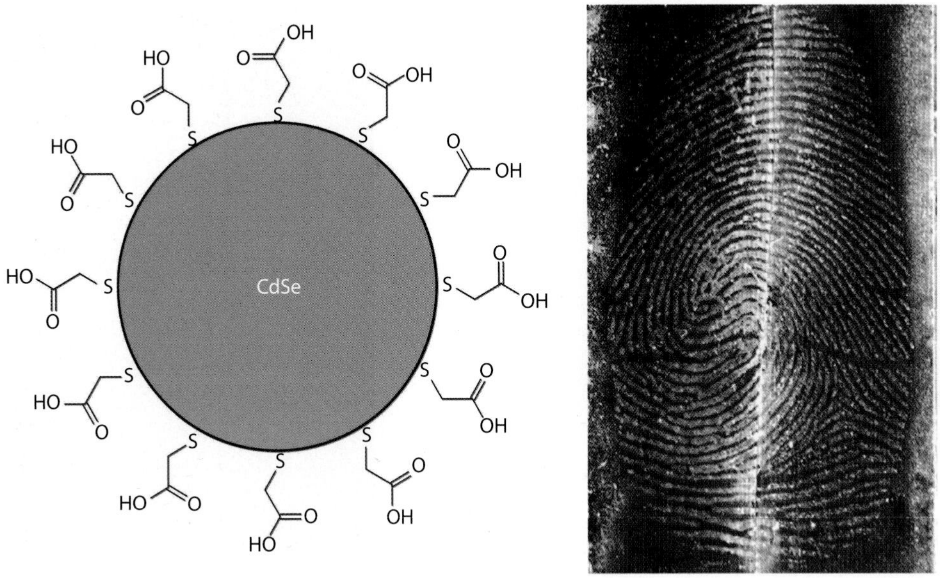

(a) (b)

FIGURE 13.17
(a) Schematic representation of the thioglycolic acid–capped CdSe quantum dot that has been used by Wang and coworkers to detect fingermarks on the sticky side of adhesives tapes. (b) The illustrated fingermark (From Wang YF, Yang RQ, Wang YJ, Shi ZX, Liu JJ. (2009) Application of CdSe Nanoparticle Suspension for Developing Latent Fingermarks on the Sticky Side of Adhesives. *Forensic Sci. Int.* 185: 96–99. With permission from Elsevier.) has been developed on the adhesive side of a black tape, at pH 8 for the left half and pH 11 for the right half.

More recently, publications referred to the use of TGA-stabilized QDs suspended in water to detect latent fingermarks [41,43,226,227]. TGA is a small molecule bearing a thiol group on one of its extremities, which allows its binding on the QD surface, and a carboxylic group on the other side, which allows its solubilization in aqueous solution. Wang et al. proposed the use of TGA-capped CdSe nanoparticles in aqueous solution to develop fingermarks on the sticky side of adhesives [43,226]. Sebaceous fingermarks were deposited on different kinds of colored adhesives and immersed in a basic solution of QDs for 15 min (pH 8–11). Clearly defined ridges were observed (Figure 13.17). The same strategy has been followed by Liu et al., who used TGA-capped CdTe QDs to detect latent fingermarks on nonporous substrates [227]. Bécue et al. proposed the use of CdTe nanoparticles in aqueous solution to detect bloody fingermarks on different nonporous surfaces [41]. The procedure consisted of immersing the substrates in an acidic solution of QDs (pH 3.5) for ~20 min. When comparing their results with those obtained using a conventional luminescent blood reagent (i.e., Acid Yellow 7), they concluded that QDs were equally sensitive on glass, polypropylene, and polyethylene sheets, but far more sensitive on aluminum foil, compared to Acid Yellow 7 (Figure 13.18). They additionally observed the fact that non-blood latent fingermarks (fresh sebaceous ones) were successfully detected by following the same procedure.

13.4.3 Europium-Based Nanoparticles

In the early 1990s, some authors reported the use of europium for the detection of fingermarks as a post-ninhydrin reagent [229], as a cyanoacrylate stain [230–233], or as a lipid reagent on untreated fingermarks [234–237]. One of the great advantages of using rare-earth elements, like europium, resides in the narrow emission band (~10 nm) located in the red region of the

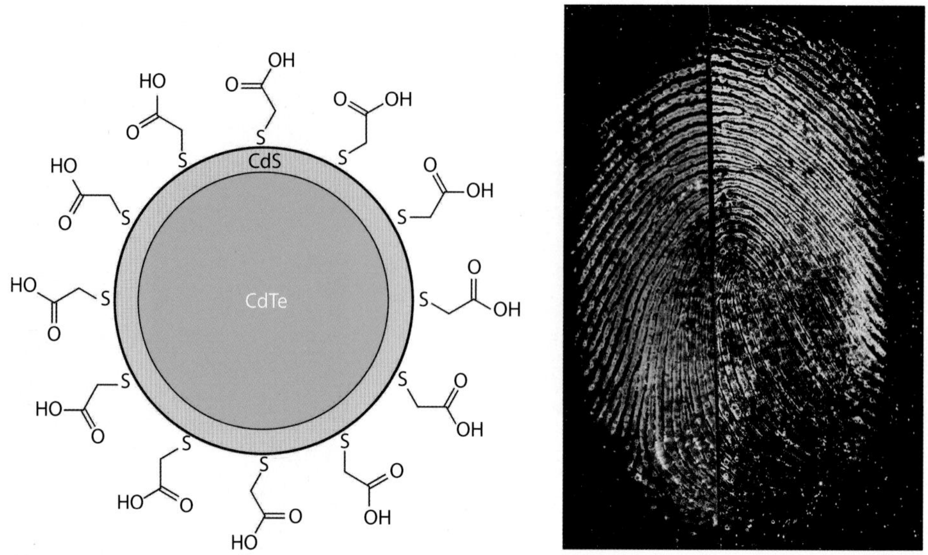

(a) (b)

FIGURE 13.18
(a) Schematic representation of the thioglycolic acid–capped CdTe/Cds quantum dot that has been used by Bécue et al. to detect blood fingermarks on nonporous surfaces. (b) The illustrated fingermark has been developed by CdTe/CdS nanocrystals (left half) and by Acid Yellow 7 (right half), which is a classical blood reagent. (After Bécue, A, Moret S, Champod C, Margot P. (2009) Use of Quantum Dots in Aqueous Solution to Detect Blood Fingermarks on Non-Porous Surfaces. *Forensic Sci. Int.* 191: 36–41. With permission from Elsevier.)

visible spectrum. Such a narrow band permits an efficient and precise filtering of unwanted backgrounds (especially when samples are excited with UV radiation). Moreover, europium is also characterized by a long excited-state lifetime compared to classical fluorophores, especially when it is chelated by organic ligands. The earlier-cited authors generally used chelating agents and detergent molecules to form a bulky structure around the europium ions, isolating them from the surrounding solvent molecules (e.g., water) [236]. Even if such structures do not fit exactly the definition of "nanoparticles" or "nanocomposites" in the way we defined them at the beginning of this section, the principle remains the same as if one would like to entrap europium ions into silicate nanospheres (see Section 13.4.6).

More recently, Menzel et al. used europium oxide (Eu_2O_3) nanoparticles to detect fingermarks [238]. Contrary to the earlier-cited works, actual Eu_2O_3 nanoparticles were amino-functionalized to target carboxylic acid groups contained in the latent secretions (Figure 13.19). Experimentally, the procedure required the immersion of the specimen in an aqueous solution containing the reactive compounds and heating it to 70°C–80°C for 30 min for optimal results. Without heating, no development was observed. It has to be noted that very fresh fingermarks (5 h) gave good results, whereas 1 week old marks gave poor ridge details.

13.4.4 Gold-Based Nanoparticles

One of the most common applications of gold nanoparticles in aqueous solution for the detection of latent fingermarks is certainly the MMD. Briefly, this technique is a two-step, wet chemical process consisting of the deposition of gold nanoparticles onto the latent residue under acidic conditions (pH 2.5–2.8), followed by an enhancement step to allow the visualization of the gold nanoparticles through an increase in their size (Figure 13.20).

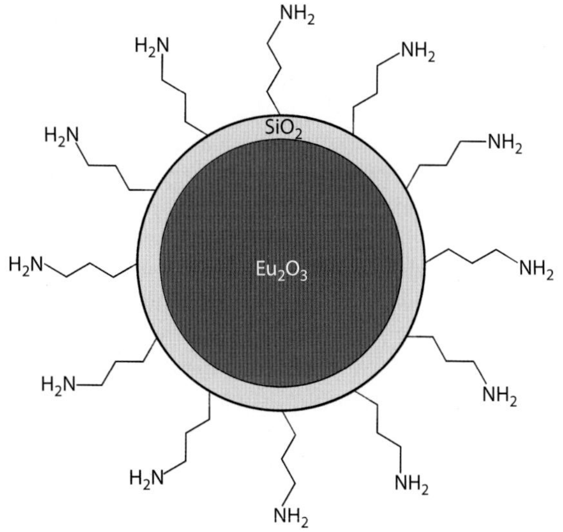

FIGURE 13.19
Schematic representation of the amino-functionalized Eu_2O_3 nanoparticle that has been used by Menzel and coworkers (From Menzel, E.R. et al., *J. For. Ident.*, 55, 189, 2005.) to detect fingermarks on nonporous surfaces. The europium-based core has been surrounded by a silica shell to permit the functionalization of the outer surface with amino groups.

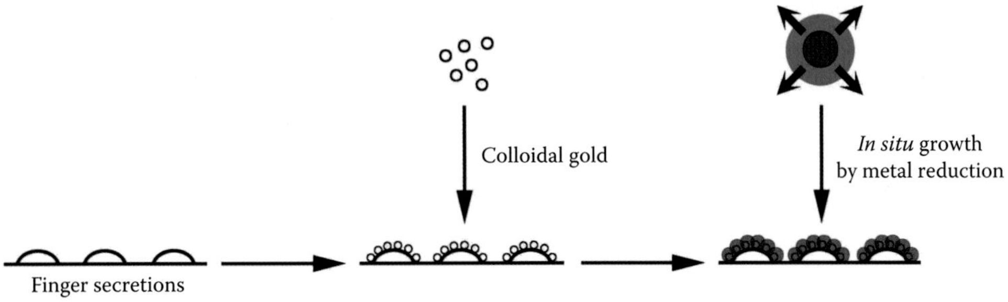

FIGURE 13.20
Schematic representation of the "two-step" process characteristic of the multimetal deposition (MMD) process for detection of latent fingermarks. In the case of the classical MMD method, metallic silver is used to coat the gold nanoparticles (NPs). For the single-metal deposition (SMD) method, gold NPs are grown by selective gold deposition. Finally, for the luminescent version of the MMD method, ZnO is deposited *in situ* on the gold NPs to obtain a luminescent structure. (Image source Bécue, A, Scoundrianos A, Champod C, Margot P. (2008) Fingermark Detection Based on the *in situ* Growth of Luminescent Nanoparticles-Towards a New Generation of Multimetal Deposition. *Forensic Sci. Int.* 179: 39–43. With permission from Elsevier.)

Initially developed by Saunders [239], the method has further been improved by Schnetz and Margot [25], who modified the procedure to increase the reproducibility of the results and the stability of the solutions. They also concluded that gold nanoparticles with a diameter of 14 nm were best suited for this method. This improved formulation is nowadays known as the "MMD-II" method and its effectiveness compared to the original formulation has been confirmed by Jones [240]. In 2006, Choi et al. observed marks treated with MMD-II using a SEM and confirmed the observations made by Schnetz [241], who visualized the gold nanoparticles on the secretions and their absence in the inter-ridge region. Recently, Zhang et al. showed that it was possible to chemically image MMD-enhanced fingermarks using a scanning electrochemical microscope (SECM) [242]. The principle of this method lies in the possibility of measuring the redox activity of a localized area due to the solubilization of the deposited silver. Since silver is preferentially reduced on the gold nanoparticles, which are themselves located on papillary ridges, it was possible to visualize the ridge details by scanning fingermarks detected by following the MMD protocol. This method could help visualizing classical MMD results on dark or patterned substrates. However, it needs to be optimized to enlarge the scanning area and to reduce the time required to perform a scan before it could be applied in practice.

The biggest advantage of MMD lies in its relative efficiency on various kinds of substrates (porous, nonporous, and "difficult" ones like polystyrene or Euro banknotes), as well as its ability to detect fresh as well as aged fingermarks, even if those have been previously wet. However, the technique is not routinely applied, mainly because it is labor-intensive (several baths, long immersion times) and because the quality of the results are highly sensitive to pH variations during the gold nanoparticles deposition. Indeed, a nonionic surfactant is required to stabilize the colloids in solution and the pH of the working solution has to be maintained between 2.5 and 3.0 during the deposition step. This is necessary for the gold colloidal particles to be attracted by the secretions (see Section 13.3.2.2). If those conditions are not met, gold nanoparticles do not ideally deposit well on the secretions. The resulting contrast will be poor or negative. This gold deposition step is thus crucial but the user has limited influence on it. For example, once immersed, some papers may induce a strong modification of the pH leading to no result at the end. Moreover, gold nanoparticles surrounded by silver appear as dark brown fingermarks, which is not ideal when dealing with dark or complex, multicolored printed substrates.

Further developments have been made to improve the initial MMD-II method. One attempt consisted of taking advantage of the ability for gold nanoparticles to be functionalized by thiolated molecules. Bécue et al. proposed a "one-bath" alternative for MMD by functionalizing the gold nanoparticles with thiolated cyclodextrins (doughnut-shaped molecular hosts) bearing a dye. The results were encouraging [26], but the technique was not ready for application to casework. Indeed, long and complicated synthetic steps (synthesis of the modified cyclodextrins, followed by colloidal gold modifications) were required before obtaining the working solution. Another attempt involved modifying the enhancement step. This step initially consisted of depositing silver onto the gold nanoparticles to allow their visualization [25]. Stauffer and coworkers replaced the silver-on-gold enhancement by a gold-on-gold treatment, using gold chloride and hydroxylamine [27,28]. This alternative to MMD-II was called "single metal deposition" (SMD), since only gold is used to detect fingermarks. According to the authors, SMD represents an advantageous alternative to MMD mainly due to lower costs, fewer solutions to prepare, and a shorter procedure since one bath has been removed. Finally, one of the latest evolutions of the method has involved obtaining luminescent fingermarks by replacing the silver (or gold) enhancement step by the formation of a ZnO shell around the gold nanoparticles [243]. The advantages that are offered by this modification are the use of the MMD method on black or complex, multicolored printed substrates, thanks to observation in the luminescence mode (Figure 13.21a). Moreover, ZnO nanoparticles are able to emit in the UV range, allowing the visualization of fingermarks on substrates that may present strong background fluorescence in the visible range, like illustrated in Figure 13.21b.

Recently, an original approach was proposed to enhance the selective binding of gold nanoparticles with the secretion residue as a pre-step to an MMD/SMD process [244]. As said before, the covalent binding of thiolated molecules with the surface of gold nanoparticles occurs spontaneously at room temperature. A way to exploit this affinity is proposed by Almog and Glasner who described a two-step process. First, a ninhydrin analog bearing

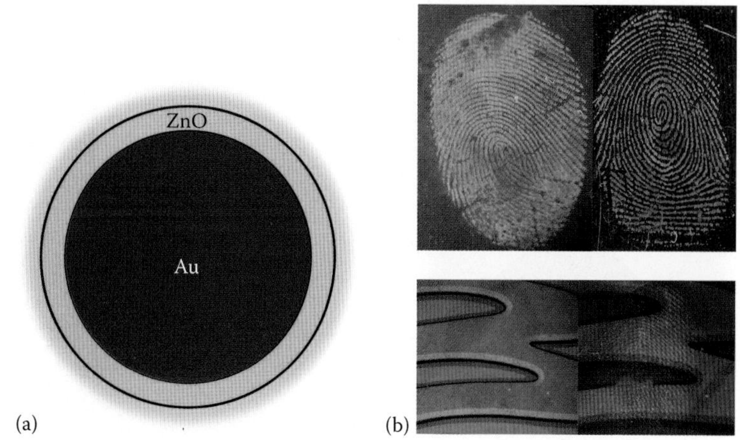

FIGURE 13.21
Schematic representation of the ZnO-capped gold nanoparticles that have been used by Bécue et al. to detect fingermarks on nonporous surfaces. (a) Fingermarks deposited on a black polyethylene bag (left mark) and on black polystyrene packaging (right mark), detected according to the MMD_{lumin} protocol. (From Bécue A, Scoundrianos A, Champod C, Margot P. (2008) Fingermark Detection Based on the *in situ* Growth of Luminescent Nanoparticles-Towards a New Generation of Multimetal Deposition. *Forensic Sci. Int.* 179: 39–43. With permission from Elsevier.) A 300–400 nm excitation light source has been used. (b) Fingermark deposited on commercial packaging and detected according to the MMD_{lumin} protocol. In visible luminescence mode (left), the substrate presents a strong luminescence, thus reducing the contrast with the mark. When observed in the UV range, the same mark is visible with good contrast due to the luminescence of ZnO in this range of the electromagnetic spectrum. The substrate presents no luminescence in this range of wavelengths.

a thiol function (i.e., a thiohemiketal [THK]) is used to detect fingermarks by reacting it with the amino acid fraction of the residue. This makes the fingermark visible by the formation of Ruhemann's purple, but it also locally enriches the secretions with insoluble long-chained aliphatic thiols, which are by-products of the reaction of THK with amino acids. The second step consists in processing the enriched fingermark with an MMD/SMD process. Gold nanoparticles are consequently expected to deposit more likely on the ridges due to the formation of thiol–gold bonds. The published article refers only to the synthesis and use of THK as amino acid reagent leading to the successful formation of Ruhemann's purple [244]. Another article is expected describing the second step, involving gold nanoparticles.

Gao et al. proposed a one-step MMD-like process to detect fingermarks, using glucose-capped gold nanoparticles and operating in a wider range of pH [245]. On the contrary to what the authors claim, the mechanism looks more like a "gold-based SPR," especially when it is said that it is working with bluish colloidal solution (this color being a consequence of nanoparticles aggregation). Another one-step "MMD-like" process was proposed based on the *in situ* reduction of tetrachloroauric acid ($HAuCl_4$) into visible gold nanoparticles by the secretion themselves [246]. The authors identified lecithin as one of the secretion components able to reduce the auric salt into gold nanoparticles, resulting in pink/purple fingermarks. Personal attempts to reproduce the published results failed and further investigations are consequently required to assess the actual efficiency of this technique.

Besides MMD, other methods use gold nanoparticles as intermediates for the detection of fingermarks in solution. Sametband et al. synthesized gold nanoparticles functionalized by *n*-alkanethiol (Figure 13.22), and solubilized them in petroleum ether [30]. The alkanethiol ligands strongly bind to the gold nanoparticle through covalent bonds with the thiol group, leaving the aliphatic chain in contact with the surrounding solvent. The authors

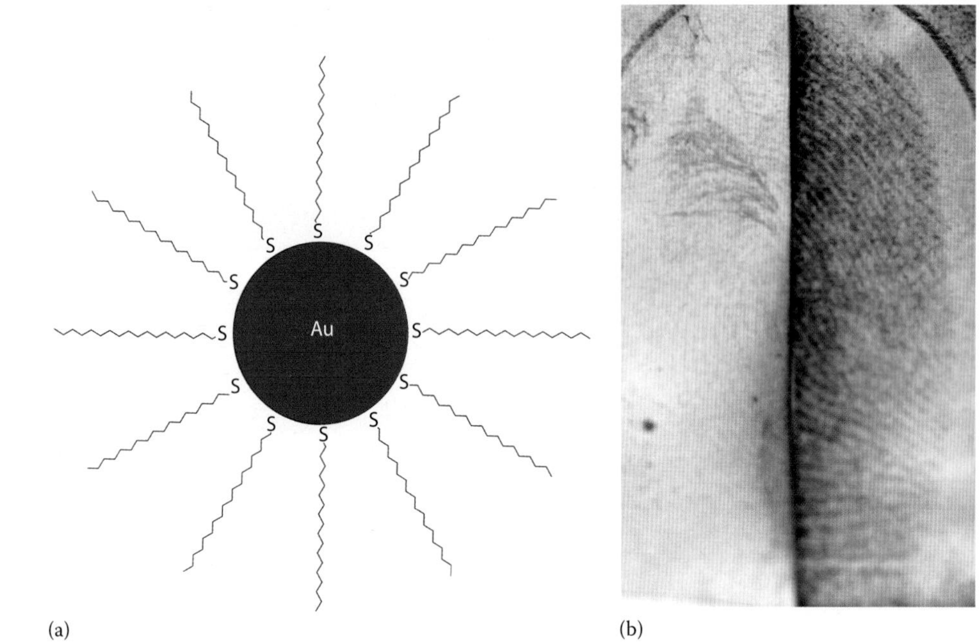

FIGURE 13.22
(a) Schematic representation of the alkanethiol-capped gold nanoparticles (Au-NP-C_{18}) that have been used by Sametband et al. to detect sebaceous fingermarks on porous and nonporous surfaces. (b) The illustrated fingermark (From Sametband M, Shweky I, Banin U, Mandler D, Almog J. (2007) Application of Nanoparticles for the Enhancement of Latent Fingerprints. *Chem. Commun.:* 1142–1144. With permission from Royal Society of Chemistry.) has been deposited on paper and developed with silver physical developer, Ag-PD, only (left half) and by Au-NP-C_{18} followed by Ag-PD (right half).

took advantage of the lipophilic interactions between the aliphatic chains and the fatty acids from the latent secretions. After an immersion time of ~3 min in the gold nanocomposites solutions, a Ag-PD was subsequently applied to allow the visualization of ridges as dark impressions. According to the authors, the hydrophobic capped gold nanoparticles improve the intensity and clarity of the developed marks compared to Ag-PD alone (Figure 13.22). Moreover, they found a relation between the chain length and the quality of the developed fingermarks, the results being better when using longer alkanes. This observation confirmed the role played by lipophilic interactions in the deposition process.

Leggett et al. presented a way to detect specific drug metabolites in secretion residue, to provide evidence of drug use (and not only by touching contaminated objects) [156]. Briefly, cotinine (a metabolite of nicotine present in the sweat of tobacco smokers) is targeted with anti-cotinine antibodies bound to gold nanoparticles and combined with a fluorescent marker. Highly detailed fingermarks, with third-level minutiae, were obtained on glass slides (Figure 13.23). In this case, gold nanoparticles play the role of antibody carrier and signal enhancer (given that approximately 50–60 antibody molecules may be bound to each nanoparticle).

Another trend related to the use of gold nanoparticles consists of developing new dusting powders (not to be used in solution) based on gold nanoparticles to which aliphatic chains are attached. Choi et al. coated gold (and silver) nanoparticles with oleylamine, a long-chain lipophilic molecule, so that the obtained nanopowders would preferentially be deposited on the lipid-containing components of the latent fingermarks (Figure 13.24) [211]. All of the nanopowders produced at least satisfactory performance on glass and painted

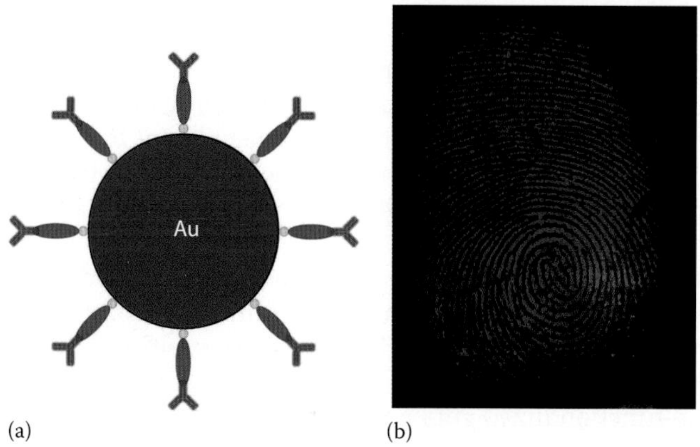

FIGURE 13.23
(a) Schematic representation of "protein A/antibody"-functionalized gold nanoparticles that have been used by Leggett et al. to detect fingermarks from smokers on glass. (b) The illustrated fingermark (From Leggett, R. et al., *Angew. Chem. Int. Ed. Engl.*, 46, 4100, 2007.) has been obtained from a male smoker after sweating for 40 min and detected using the antibody-functionalized nanoparticle and Alexa Fluor 546 as luminescent marker.

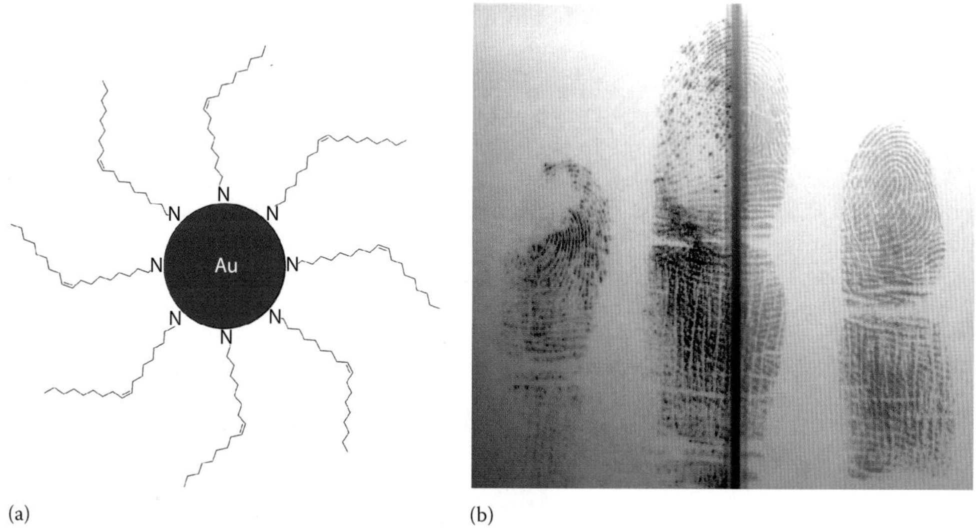

FIGURE 13.24
(a) Schematic representation of the oleylamine-functionalized gold nanoparticles that have been used by Choi et al. as a nanopowder to be dusted on fingermarks. (b) The illustrated fingermarks (From Choi, M.J. et al., *J. For. Ident.*, 56, 756, 2006.) are fresh ones that have been deposited on glass and dusted using a conventional black powder (left half) or using the gold nanopowder (right half).

wood, but the fingermarks on the plastic and aluminum surfaces were more difficult to develop, especially when they were not fresh. When compared with conventional micron-sized ones, the gold-based nanopowders produced sharper and clearer development of the latent fingermarks, without background staining, even if less contrast was generally observed compared to black classical powders (Figure 13.24). By comparison, classic (magnetic) powders are composed of flakes ranging from 5 to 25 μm in diameter [247,248], which is 500–2500 times larger than functionalized nanoparticles. Additionally, the authors successfully enhanced ridge detail by following the procedure with a Ag-PD.

13.4.5 Iron-Based Nanoparticles

Iron oxide (Fe_3O_4) powder is of a particular interest to detect fingermarks due to its intense black color. Since it is possible to obtain nano-sized iron oxide particles, it is worth citing its conventional use as suspended particles to detect latent fingermarks on nonporous surfaces [249] or, more recently, on the adhesive side of white- or light-colored tapes [250]. Iron oxide constitutes a really good alternative to conventional SPRs and it produced better sensitivity, ridge detail, and contrast.

Magnetic iron oxide nanoparticles were also used in an antibody-directed approach to detect a range of drugs (e.g., THC from marijuana and methadone) or drug metabolites (of methadone and cocaine) contained in the fingermarks, either through consumption or manipulation [158–162]. This approach is similar to Legget et al.'s, who targeted cotinine using anti-cotinine-functionalized gold nanoparticles [156], with the additional advantage offered by the magnetic core which facilitates the removal of unbound particles using a magnetic wand. The remaining nanoparticles (bound to the fingermarks) were fluorescently tagged before observation. Positive results were obtained for the drugs and metabolites tested, with visible third-level details such as pores.

13.4.6 Silica-Based Nanoparticles

Silica-based nanoparticles are initially nonluminescent, but they can be doped with organic dyes or rare-earth compounds to become extremely luminescent species (see Section 13.2.3.3). When used in biological imaging applications, uncoated silica nanoparticles suffer from a number of disadvantages, such as nonspecific adsorption of proteins [251]. Such phenomena could be an advantage in the case of fingermark detection since the secretion residue contains proteins. Despite this fact, the use of luminescent silica nanoparticles in forensic science still remains rare. Theaker et al. recently chose to enclose a variety of colored and fluorescent molecules (i.e., fluorescein, thiazole orange, oxazine perchlorate, methylene blue, Basic Yellow 40, Basic Red 28, rhodamine B, and rhodamine 6G) into silicate particles [44]. The resulting doped nanoparticles were used as aqueous suspensions to detect fingermarks. Micron-sized particles were also used as dusting agents. Both fresh (20 min) and aged fingermarks (40 days old) presented good definition after development (Figure 13.25).

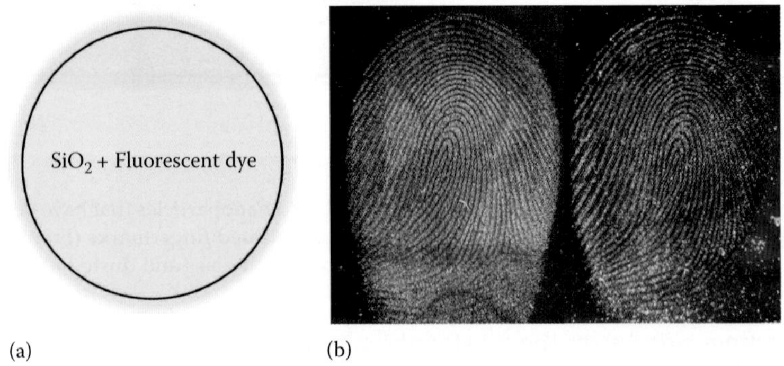

FIGURE 13.25
(a) Schematic representation of the dye-doped silica nanoparticles that have been used by Theaker et al. as a nanopowder to be dusted on fingermarks, or as a suspension in water. (b) The illustrated fingermarks (From Theaker BJ, Hudson KE, Rowell FJ. (2008) Doped Hydrophobic Silica Nano- and Micro-Particles as Novel Agents for Developing Latent Fingerprints. *Forensic Sci. Int.* 174: 26–34. With permission from Elsevier.) are on glass that have been detected using rhodamine 6G–doped silica nanoparticles in an aqueous suspension (left mark) or as a dusting powder (right mark).

Similarly, Chen et al. modified the surface of dye-doped clay with phenyltriethoxysilane, before grinding the material with a mortar and pestle [252]. The fluorescent powder obtained was used to detect very fresh fingermarks (few minutes) on glass. According to the authors, using amino-functional silanes instead of using dyed clay without surface modification does not give good results. Nevertheless, in this example, microparticles are likely to have been obtained instead of nanoparticles. Finally, functionalized silica nanoparticles were also used to help determining the molecular composition of fingermarks [253]. For this study, positively charged silica nanoparticles and hydrophobic ones were used to separate the polar components (i.e., amino acids) and nonpolar ones (i.e., squalene and fatty acid), respectively, of secretion residue left on a glass slide.

13.4.7 Silver-Based Nanoparticles

The Ag-PD is certainly the best-known technique based on the use of silver nanoparticles, which currently constitutes the reagent of choice to visualize the water-insoluble components of latent fingermark residue on porous surfaces. One of its latest formulations has been given in the Chapter 3.2 written by Ramotowski in this book. Figure 13.26 summarizes the procedure used for visualizing latent fingermarks on paper using the Ag-PD.

Historically, Ag-PD was first developed for photographic purposes. It thus had no initial link with the detection of latent fingermarks, mainly due to the fact that the existing formulations were highly unstable. Some enhancements were proposed to extend the stability of the solution by a few hours [254]. But the seminal work of Jonker et al. [210] from the Philips Research Laboratory (Einhoven, the Netherlands) can somehow be identified as the actual start of this technique with a formulation of a highly stable Ag-PD, which they referred to as FC1 (F for the ferrous/ferric redox couple and C for citric acid). Their application was not for use in classical photography, but for the photofabrication of printed circuit boards. Shortly after their formulation was published, scientists in the United Kingdom became aware of its use for visualizing latent fingermarks on porous surfaces. This formulation was further called "Philips physical developer" by researchers involved in its use in forensic science [255]. An excellent history of how the United Kingdom studied, modified, and implemented the use of the Ag-PD for visualizing latent fingermarks is given by Goode and Morris [216]. Cantú and Johnson also summarized the historical development in their chapters on Ag-PD [40,208]. Several modifications were made and eventually a recommended formulation was provided for use by police laboratories in the United Kingdom. A major one by the Police Scientific Development Branch

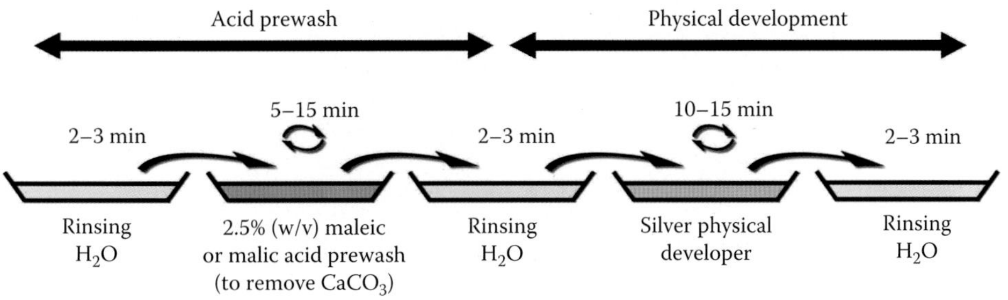

FIGURE 13.26
Schematic illustration of the application protocol for the U.K. silver physical developer (Ag-PD). The procedure begins with an acid prewash to remove the calcium carbonate contained in some substrates and is followed by the actual physical development step, which involves depositing silver colloids and amplifying them by reducing silver on their surface.

(Sandridge, United Kingdom) was the replacement of distilled water by the more pure reverse osmosis/deionized (RO/DI) water, which, in doing so, prompted a reduction of the amount of surfactants used. Burow et al. discuss this change [256]. Since then other modifications have been made, one of which was the change of the surfactant Synperonic N to Tween 20 due to the possible phasing out of the former [257]. Interestingly, this surfactant substitution gives greater stability to the Ag-PD [258].

If a silver or silver oxide fingermark is weak or if it has an interfering background, several methods exist to enhance such a mark, independently from the formulation that is used [40,208]. Three of them are detailed:

1. A mild hypochlorite solution (e.g., a dilute solution of household chlorine bleach) can be used to darken the fingermark and bleach the paper, resulting in an increase of the general contrast. The darkening of the fingermark is due to the reaction of hypochlorite ions with silver to form dark brown silver oxide.
2. One post-treatment involves using a reagent involving potassium iodide (KI). Initially developed by Dr. G. Saunders, this post-treatment has been detailed by Cantú et al. [259]. Briefly, a silver or silver oxide fingermark is converted to whitish yellow silver iodide fingermark due to the reaction between silver (or silver oxide) and the KI-based reagent. At the same time, the paper turns dark brown to black due to the reaction between tri-iodide ions in the KI-based reagent and starch, which is most current paper contain. Figure 13.27 is an example of how this method enhanced a Ag-PD fingermark on a counterfeit banknote.
3. One post-treatment involves transferring a silver or silver oxide fingermark onto a specially treated paper or film. The underlying idea is to transfer only the mark (not the background) onto such a white or clear surface. This treatment is actually based on a physical development process, requiring three things: (1) a brominating

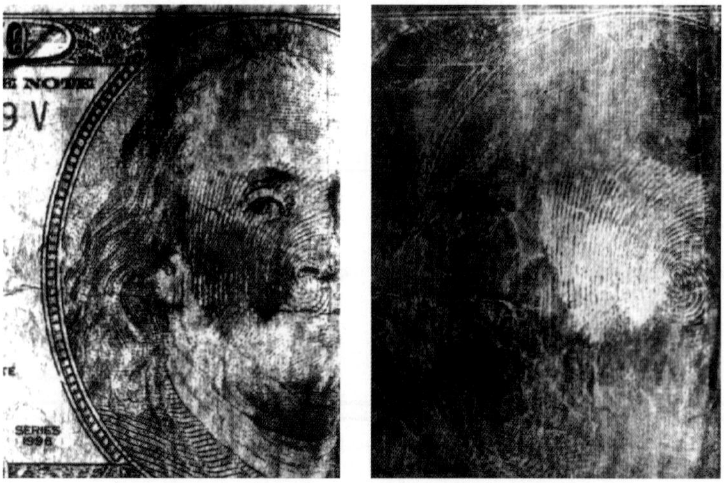

(a) (b)

FIGURE 13.27
Fingermark on a counterfeit U.S. banknote developed using a silver physical developer (and enhanced with a weak NaOCl bath) with interfering background (a) and enhanced by the KI method (b). (Image source from Cantú, A.A. et al., *Proceeding of SPIE—Sensors, and Command, Control, Communications, and Intelligence (C3I) Technologies for Homeland Defense and Law Enforcement II*, Orlando, FL, pp. 164–167, 2003.)

(bleaching) solution that converts the silver or silver oxide fingermark to a silver bromide fingermark; (2) a solution containing sodium thiosulfate ("hypo"), which converts the silver bromide to a soluble silver thiosulfate salt, and a photographic chemical developer; and (3) a gelatin-coated paper or film impregnated with colloidal gold particles, onto which the silver thiosulfate ions are reduced to silver by the chemical developer. This method is briefly described by Cantú and Johnson [208] and extensively treated by Land [260] and Levenson [261].

As a final comment, contrary to gold nanoparticles, not much work has been done in creating new detection techniques based on (functionalized) silver nanoparticles. We can however cite the work performed by Choi et al., who functionalized silver nanoparticles with oleylamine, a long-chained lipophilic molecule [211], as described in Section 13.4.4. However, the contrast that was obtained using silver-based nanopowder was less than the one obtained using gold-based nanopowder. For this reason, and due to a heavier and more time-consuming synthetic procedure, the use of silver-coated nanoparticles was not pursued.

13.4.8 Titanium-Based Nanoparticles

Titanium dioxide (TiO_2) is a well-known semiconductor material extensively used in optical, electrical, and photocatalytic applications starting from the second half of the twentieth century. TiO_2 has been used to detect latent fingermarks, mainly on nonporous substrates, as a powder or in suspension. Some authors also report its use to detect blood marks, discussed later. Commercially available TiO_2 particles are generally of a range of sizes near the submicron (0.2–0.3 μm, corresponding to 200–300 nm).

Due to its white color, its high refraction index, and its lack of absorption in the visible range of light, TiO_2 is extensively used as a white contrasting agent that can be useful on dark or transparent substrates. Given its extremely low solubility in water and organic solvents, the classical application modes that prevail are dusting powders, white SPR (SPR-w), and paste-like formulations (white powder suspension [WPS]). Micron-sized TiO_2 particles constitute a good alternative to zinc carbonate for the preparation of SPR-w to be used on nonporous surfaces or on the adhesive side of dark or transparent tapes, with excellent results obtained on such substrates [262–264]. Similarly, SPR-w can help in detecting fingermarks on substrates that were previously wet [265]. An experiment carried out on immersed plastic (vinyl acetate), glass, and painted metal surfaces (up to 1 month) showed no influence of the immersion time and of the substrate's nature in the quality of the results [266]. According to the authors, only the way the surface has been touched and the duration of contact played a role. Finally, TiO_2 is currently recommended by the Home Office (HOSDB, United Kingdom) to be used in their WPS formulation to detect fingermarks on the adhesive side of black or dark tapes, and it replaces the classical Sticky-Side Powder™ (SSP) [250].

Another field of application of TiO_2 is the detection of latent blood fingermarks on nonporous and semi-porous surfaces, when suspended in anhydrous methanol [203]. The application protocol involved spraying the methanol-based suspension (1 g TiO_2 in 10 mL methanol) onto the surface of interest, then rinsing it with pure anhydrous methanol. The results were excellent on nonporous surfaces, with fingermarks appearing in white and presenting third-level details. Bergeron observed no difference between fresh fingermarks and aged ones (>1 month). The results were less reproducible on semi-porous surfaces and they became poor on porous surfaces, with no observable ridge details. Bergeron also proposed to replace methanol with water, but the results were not as good as with methanol. Finally, he observed that TiO_2 spraying can be used in sequence if it is applied after the classical blood reagents. No other forensic science publications refer to the application of TiO_2 to detect blood marks.

The underlying mechanisms explaining the affinity of TiO_2 for blood were not described by Bergeron. However, some explanations may be found in the literature: Thurn et al. reported that the surface characteristics of nanometer-sized TiO_2 allow efficient conjugation to nucleic acids [19]. Moreover, larger TiO_2 particles can interact with the cellular membranes composed of phospholipid bilayers and adhere to them [267]. More specifically, authors reported some affinity between TiO_2 and blood [268] or between TiO_2 and proteins through electrostatic interactions [269]. Rothen-Rutishauser et al. also showed that ultrafine TiO_2 nanoparticles (diameter 32 nm) can penetrate the membrane of red blood cells, whereas aggregates larger than 200 nm were seen attached to the membrane but not within cells [200]. All of these observations may help in concluding that submicron TiO_2 particles may penetrate red blood cells and interact with hemoglobin, explaining their ability to detect blood marks.

Finally, Choi et al., following their global strategy to develop enhanced functionalized nanopowders, combined oleylamine with a fluorescent dye (perylene dianhydride) to form an entity that was then adsorbed onto TiO_2 nanoparticles to form a new powder exhibiting strong fluorescence at 650–700 nm, when excited at 505 nm [270]. Compared to conventional magnetic fluorescent powders, the nanopowder was slightly weaker in fluorescence intensity, but produced significantly less background development, resulting in good contrast between the fingermarks and the substrates.

In unpublished works, Saunders investigated the application to latent fingermark development of the TiO_2-based ITEK-RS process, which is a photographic process for obtaining silver images by Ag-PD using TiO_2 as a light-sensitive component [271]. Using plastic weighing boats with latent marks placed on them as test samples and diluted white paint (brought to a pH of about 3 with citric acid) as the source of TiO_2, the following sequence gave excellent fingermark development: add TiO_2 (in suspension) to the sample, remove the liquid, expose the sample to UV radiation, add a weak version of Ag-PD. It works as follows: TiO_2 adheres to the secretion residue and is then UV-activated (daylight works). This activated TiO_2 reduces the silver ions in the Ag-PD and thus creates nucleating sites for Ag-PD.

13.4.9 Zinc-Based Nanoparticles

Zinc oxide (ZnO) is generally used as a white pigment, but also for its photoluminescence properties, with emission peaks centered at 380 nm (UV) and 587 nm (visible). Similar to titanium dioxide, ZnO has extensively been used in SPR formulations to detect latent fingermarks on nonporous surfaces (wet powdering) due to its white color [265]. More recently, scientific works have considered the use of ZnO to detect fingermarks by taking advantage of its visible fluorescence. The first one consisted in the use of ZnO as a fluorescent pigment to be dry-dusted or applied as an SPR on nonporous surfaces [45]. The second one consisted in a modification of the classical MMD procedure to produce *in situ* luminescent fingermarks on nonporous substrates [243] (see Section 13.4.4).

Since the use of ZnO nanoparticles in the context of the MMD method has been previously described, this section will focus on the dusting powder application reported by Choi et al. [45]. Starting from published procedures for obtaining nanostructured ZnO particles, the authors finally obtained particles in the size range of 1–3 μm. Even if the synthesized

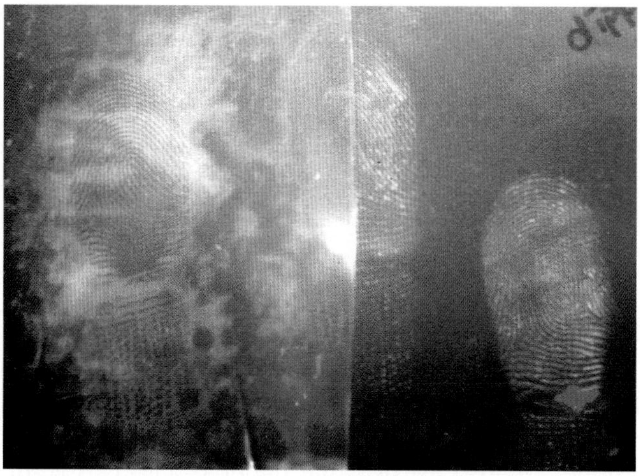

(a) (b)

FIGURE 13.28
Three week old fingermarks on polyethylene, developed using zinc oxide as a nanopowder (a) and as a small particle reagent (b). The samples were illuminated at 350 nm and observed using a 570 nm long pass filter. (Image source Choi MJ, McBean KE, Ng PHR, et al. (2008) An Evaluation of Nanostructured Zinc Oxide as a Fluorescent Powder for Fingerprint Detection. *J. Mater. Sci.* 43: 732–737. With permission from Springer.)

particles cannot be considered as nanoparticles, this application is worth being cited since a mechanical grinding took place before application, so that we can assume that submicron particles were finally obtained. ZnO particles were dusted and applied as SPRs. Detected fingermarks were characterized by a visible fluorescence when illuminated by long-range UV light source. ZnO-based SPR gave good results for all of the tested surfaces (glass, polyethylene, aluminum), while dry dusting led to some background staining on the polyethylene surface (Figure 13.28). When compared with conventional commercial powders, ZnO particles were less luminescent but showed excellent ridge detail, and with minimum background staining. The authors also tried to dope the powder using lithium ions, to enhance the visible luminescence, but this did not significantly improve the results.

13.5 Conclusions

The use of micron-sized particles for latent fingermark development has been around for over a century. Such particles include those in powder form and those suspended in solution. However, nano-sized particles, which are considerably smaller (their size ranging from a few nanometers to a few tens of nanometers) and whose small size provides them with some fascinating properties, are new to the fingerprint community. This chapter explored some of these properties, as well as some of the secretion residue properties, and showed how nanoparticles can be used to bind some components of secretion residue. This chapter may consequently provide the basis for developing new and original visualizing techniques.

About nanoparticles, we showed that some of the unique and important properties encompass their size, their optical properties, and their ability to have their surfaces modified. Photoluminescence can be an inner property, arising from the nature and composition of the nanoparticle, such as for QDs (a class of semiconducting nanoparticles luminescent by themselves and whose emission wavelength depends on the particle size), or can be introduced after a dye-doping process, such as for silica nanoparticles. Physicochemical properties generally arise once nanoparticles are put in aqueous solutions, with the presence of charges whose value varies according to the pH. However, the most significant property is certainly the ability of nanoparticle to get easily functionalized with molecules bearing specific functions. These molecules are generally chemically bonded to the particle surface and can be used to target numerous chemicals in latent residues during the detection process.

About the secretion residue, we learned in this chapter that the latent residue contains components that are not removed by water and that these water-insoluble components may become charged in solutions according to the pH. Thus, nanoparticles that are negatively charged at a low pH can potentially bind electrostatically to the positively charged residue. Two well-known techniques that rely on this property are the MMD technique and Ag-PD where colloidal gold and colloidal silver, respectively, are electrostatically attracted to the residue. We also learned that nanoparticles can be functionalized with lipophilic molecules so that, in a nonaqueous medium, they can get attracted to the lipid components of latent residue via hydrophobic interaction. Recent works involving gold nanoparticles functionalized with *n*-alkanethiols are an example of this.

About the development of new techniques, we showed that one should follow the usual three-step approach, which are (1) determining which components of latent fingermark residue to target for visualization, (2) determining how to target these components, through the use of functionalized nanoparticles, and (3) making sure these substances do not create background interference. Finally, the choice for adequate optical properties (linked with the inner core composition or doping) is to be dissociated from the targeting mechanism (linked with the outer functionalization).

This chapter finally presented a thorough review of the several techniques based on nanoparticles and used for visualizing latent fingermarks. Numerous novel techniques were developed over the last 10 years, with a sharp increase in interest since 2004. We showed that a large variety of atomic compositions exists, including silver (Ag), aluminum (Al), gold (Au), europium (Eu), cadmium (Cd), iron (Fe), titanium (Ti), and zinc (Zn). The newly developed techniques involve mainly nanoparticles dispersed in solution, but some report the dusting of dried nanoparticles. However, their use as powder carries a warning regarding the health hazards associated with their extremely small particle size. Nanoparticles were shown to be able to detect conventional latent fingermarks, as well as bloody ones or contaminated ones (e.g., by drugs), on a wide range of substrates. The immunodetection of some secretion components (or contaminants) is also of rising interest by the use of antibody-functionalized nanoparticles.

Despite their demonstrated efficiency (in terms of selectivity or sensitivity) to detect fingermarks, only few of the presented techniques are actually used for casework application. It is only possible to cite those involving gold (i.e., MMD) and silver (i.e., Ag-PD). On the contrary, the great majority of the newly developed techniques are still being investigated. Indeed, even if they are currently being successfully used for visualizing latent fingermarks on diverse surfaces under controlled conditions (using fresh or enriched marks sometimes), they still require making their proof on actual conditions by comparing with conventional reagents. For some of the published techniques, their intrinsic composition or application mode constitutes a major problem hampering their large-scale development (such as cadmium-containing QDs, or powdering of dried nanoparticles). This last step is required for the techniques based on nanoparticles to join the range of techniques commonly used by forensic scientists.

Acknowledgment

A. Bécue would like to thank the Swiss National Science Foundation (SNF) for supporting the research in the field of new fingermark detection reagents based on luminescent nanoparticles (Ambizione grants nos. PZ00P2_121907/1 and PZ00P2_139952).

Authors

Andy Bécue received his PhD in chemistry in 2004 and joined the Institut de Police Scientifique (IPS—Lausanne, Switzerland) as a postdoctoral researcher. His status evolved to a position of "maître assistant" from 2005 to 2009. During this time, he was in charge of the management of the practical teaching related to the "Identification Forensique I & II" courses for bachelor and master's degrees, and of the supervision of scientific projects related to the development of new fingermark detection techniques based on luminescent nanoparticles. In March 2009, his status evolved to a position of "maître assistant Ambizione," funded by the Swiss National Science Foundation (SNF). He is now working full time on the development of new detection techniques mainly based on the use of functionalized nanoparticules, as well as on the supervision of a PhD thesis aiming at using quantum dots as new fingermark sensors.

Antonio A. Cantú received his PhD in chemical physics from the University of Texas, Austin, Texas. His career spans more than 34 years in several areas of science and technology in law enforcement, particularly forensic science. When he retired in 2007, he was the chief scientist of the Forensic Services Division of the United States Secret Service. Prior to that, he spent some time with the FBI's research laboratory and 10 years with the Bureau of Alcohol, Tobacco, and Firearms. His key areas of expertise are in the chemical analysis of ink and paper and in the development of novel techniques for visualizing latent fingermarks.

References

1. Champod C, Chamberlain P. (2009) Fingerprints. In: *Handbook of Forensic Science*, eds. J Fraser and R Williams. Cullompton, U.K.: Willan Publishing, pp. 57–83.
2. Champod C, Lennard C, Margot P, Stoilovic M. (2004) *Fingerprints and Other Ridge Skin Impressions*. Boca Raton, FL: CRC Press.
3. Bécue A, Moret S, Champod C, Margot P. (2011) Use of stains to detect fingermarks. *Biotech. Histochem.* 86 (3): 140–160.
4. Lennard C. (2007) Fingerprint detection: Current capabilities. *Aust. J. Forensic Sci.* 39 (2): 55–71.
5. Lee HC, Gaensslen RE. (2001) Advances in fingerprint technology. In: *CRC Series in Forensic and Police Science*, 2nd edn., ed. by BAJ Fisher. Boca Raton, FL: CRC Press.
6. Bécue A. (2010) Les nanoparticules, une nouvelle arme contre le crime? *Acta Chim.* 342–343: 52–58.
7. Dilag J, Kobus HJ, Ellis AV. (2011) Nanotechnology as a new tool for fingermark detection: A review. *Curr. Nanosci.* 7 (2): 153–159.

8. Choi MJ, McDonagh AM, Maynard P, Roux C. (2008) Metal-containing nanoparticles and nanostructured particles in fingermark detection. *Forensic Sci. Int.* 179: 87–97.
9. Hunter RJ. (1993) *Introduction to Modern Colloid Science.* Oxford, U.K.: Oxford University Press, 5 (redispersion); 272 (van der Waals interactions); 269 (Hamacker forces).
10. Atkins PW. (1990) *Physical Chemistry,* 4th edn. New York: Freeman, p. 707 (van der Waals interactions).
11. Klabunde KJ. (2001) Introduction to nanotechnology. In: *Nanoscale Materials in Chemistry,* ed. KJ Klabunde. New York: Wiley Interscience, pp. 1–13.
12. Rogers B, Pennathur S, Adams J. (2008) *Nanotechnology: Understanding Small Systems.* Boca Raton, FL: CRC Press (Taylor & Francis), pp. 90–97 (van der Waals interactions); 123 (sphere–surface attractive interaction).
13. Murray CB, Norris DJ, Bawendi MG. (1993) Synthesis and characterization of nearly monodisperse CdE (E = S, Se, Te) semiconductor nanocrystallites. *J. Am. Chem. Soc.* 115: 8706–8715.
14. Wang Y, Herron N. (1991) Nanometer-sized semiconductor clusters: Materials synthesis, quantum size effects, and photophysical properties. *J. Phys. Chem.* 95 (2): 525–532.
15. Bawendi MG, Steigerwald ML, Brus LE. (1990) The quantum mechanics of larger semiconductor clusters ("quantum dots"). *Annu. Rev. Phys. Chem.* 41: 477–496.
16. Haruta M, Yamada N, Kobayashi T, Iijima S. (1989) Gold catalysts prepared by coprecipitation for low-temperature oxidation of hydrogen and of carbon monoxide. *J. Catal.* 115 (2): 301–309.
17. Bond GC, Louis C, Thompson DT. (2006) Catalysis by gold. In: *Catalytic Science Series,* ed. GJ Hutchings. London, U.K.: Imperial College Press.
18. Xu W, Kong JS, Yeh Y-TS, Chen P. (2008) Single-molecule nanocatalysis reveals heterogeneous reaction pathways and catalytic dynamics. *Nat. Mater.* 7: 992–996.
19. Thurn KT, Brown EMB, Wu A et al. (2007) Nanoparticles for applications in cellular imaging. *Nanoscale Res. Lett.* 2: 430–441.
20. Medintz IL, Uyeda HT, Goldman ER, Mattoussi H. (2005) Quantum dot bioconjugates for imaging, labelling and sensing. *Nat. Mater.* 4 (6): 435–446.
21. Parak WJ, Pellegrino T, Plank C. (2005) Topical review—Labelling of cells with quantum dots. *Nanotechnology* 16: R9–R29.
22. Bagwe RP, Zhao X, Tan W. (2003) Bioconjugated luminescent nanoparticles for biological applications. *J. Disp. Sci. Technol.* 24 (3&4): 453–464.
23. Smith AM, Duan H, Mohs AM, Nie S. (2008) Bioconjugated quantum dots for *in vivo* molecular and cellular imaging. *Adv. Drug Deliv. Rev.* 60: 1226–1240.
24. Freestone I, Meeks N, Sax M, Higgitt C. (2007) The Lycurgus Cup—A Roman nanotechnology. *Gold Bull.* 40 (4): 270–277.
25. Schnetz B, Margot P. (2001) Technical note: Latent fingermarks, colloidal gold and multimetal deposition (MMD)—Optimisation of the method. *Forensic Sci. Int.* 118: 21–28.
26. Bécue A, Champod C, Margot P. (2007) Use of gold nanoparticles as molecular intermediates for the detection of fingermarks. *Forensic Sci. Int.* 168: 169–176.
27. Stauffer E, Bécue A, Singh KV et al. (2007) Single-metal deposition (SMD) as a latent fingermark enhancement technique: An alternative to multimetal deposition (MMD). *Forensic Sci. Int.* 168: e5–e9.
28. Durussel P, Stauffer E, Bécue A, Champod C, Margot P. (2009) Single-metal deposition: Optimization of this fingermark enhancement technique. *J. Forensic Ident.* 59 (1): 80–96.
29. Brust M, Walker M, Bethell D, Schiffrin DJ, Whyman R. (1994) Synthesis of thiol-derivatised gold nanoparticles in a two-phase liquid–liquid system. *J. Chem. Soc. Chem. Commun.* 801–802.
30. Sametband M, Shweky I, Banin U, Mandler D, Almog J. (2007) Application of nanoparticles for the enhancement of latent fingerprints. *Chem. Commun.* 1142–1144.
31. Oliver J. (2004) Digital security printing inks and toners: Recent developments in nano- and smart-materials. Paper read at *Information Management Institute—1st Security Printing Conference,* April 28–30, St. Pete Beach, FL.
32. Cantú AA. (2008) Nanoparticles in forensic science. Paper read at *Proceeding of SPIE—Optics and Photonics for Counterterrorism and Crime Fighting IV,* October 3, Cardiff, U.K.

33. Cao G. (2004) *Nanostructures & Nanomaterials: Synthesis, Properties & Applications*. London, U.K.: Imperial College Press, pp. 7–10 (bottom-up approach); 32–42 (electrostatic stabilization); 36–38 (van der Waals interactions); 42–48 (steric stabilization).
34. Kudera S, Carbone L, Manna L, Parak WJ. (2008) Growth mechanism, shape and composition control of semiconductor nanocrystals. In: *Semiconductor Nanocrystal Quantum Dots—Synthesis, Assembly, Spectroscopy and Applications*, ed. AL Rogach. New York: Springer, pp. 1–34.
35. Reiss P. (2008) Synthesis of semiconductor nanocrystals in organic solvents. In: *Semiconductor Nanocrystal Quantum Dots—Synthesis, Assembly, Spectroscopy and Applications*, ed. AL Rogach. New York: Springer, 35–72.
36. Fendler JH. (1987) Atomic and molecular clusters in membrane mimetic chemistry. *Chem. Rev.* 87: 877–899.
37. Bagwe RP, Mishra BK, Khilar KC. (1999) Effect of chain length of oxyethylene group on particle size and absorption spectra of silver nanoparticles prepared in non-ionic water-in-oil micro emulsions. *J. Disp. Sci. Technol.* 20 (6): 1569–1579.
38. López-Quintela MA. (2003) Synthesis of nanomaterials in microemulsions: Formation mechanisms and growth control. *Curr. Opin. Colloid Interface Sci.* 8: 137–144.
39. Arriagada FJ, Osseo-Asare K. (1999) Controlled hydrolysis of tetraethoxysilane in a nonionic water-in-oil microemulsion: A statistical model of silica nucleation. *Colloids Surf. A* 154 (3): 311–326.
40. Cantú AA. (2001) Silver physical developers for the visualization of latent prints on paper. *Forensic Sci. Rev.* 13: 30–64.
41. Bécue A, Moret S, Champod C, Margot P. (2009) Use of quantum dots in aqueous solution to detect blood fingermarks on non-porous surfaces. *Forensic Sci. Int.* 191: 36–41.
42. Jin Y-J, Luo Y-J, Li G-P et al. (2008) Application of photoluminescent CdS/PAMAM nanocomposites in fingerprint detection. *Forensic Sci. Int.* 179: 34–38.
43. Wang YF, Yang RQ, Wang YJ, Shi ZX, Liu JJ. (2009) Application of CdSe nanoparticle suspension for developing latent fingermarks on the sticky side of adhesives. *Forensic Sci. Int.* 185: 96–99.
44. Theaker BJ, Hudson KE, Rowell FJ. (2008) Doped hydrophobic silica nano- and micro-particles as novel agents for developing latent fingerprints. *Forensic Sci. Int.* 174: 26–34.
45. Choi MJ, McBean KE, Ng PHR et al. (2008) An evaluation of nanostructured zinc oxide as a fluorescent powder for fingerprint detection. *J. Mater. Sci.* 43: 732–737.
46. Park J, Joo J, Kwon SG, Jang Y, Hyeon T. (2007) Synthesis of monodisperse spherical nanocrystals. *Angew. Chem. Int. Ed. Engl.* 46 (25): 4630–4660.
47. Hyeon T. (2003) Chemical synthesis of magnetic nanoparticles. *Chem. Commun.* 927–934.
48. Nath S, Jana S, Pradhan M, Pal T. (2010) Ligand stabilized metal nanoparticles in organic solvent. *J. Colloid Interface Sci.* 341 (2): 333–352.
49. LaMer VK, Dinegar RH. (1950) Theory, production and mechanism of formation of monodispersed hydrosols. *J. Am. Chem. Soc.* 72 (11): 4847–4854.
50. Pong B-K, Elim HI, Chong J-X et al. (2007) New insights on the nanoparticle growth mechanism in the citrate reduction of gold(III) salt: Formation of the Au nanowire intermediate and its nonlinear optical properties. *J. Phys. Chem. C* 111 (17): 6281–6287.
51. Faraday M. (1857) Experimental relations of gold (and other metals) to light. *Philos. Trans. Royal Soc. Lond.* 147: 145–181.
52. Turkevich J, Stevenson PC, Hillier J. (1951) A study of the nucleation and growth process in the synthesis of colloidal gold. *Discuss, Faraday Soc.* 11: 55–75.
53. Enüstün BV, Turkevich J. (1963) Coagulation of colloidal gold. *J. Am. Chem. Soc.* 85 (21): 3317–3328.
54. Frens G. (1973) Controlled nucleation for the regulation of the particle size in monodisperse gold suspensions. *Nat. Phys. Sci.* 241: 20–22.
55. Slot JW, Geuze HJ. (1981) Sizing of protein a—Colloidal gold probes for immunoelectron microscopy. *J. Cell Biol.* 90: 533–536.
56. Turkevich J. (1985) Colloidal gold—Part I. *Gold Bull.* 18 (3): 86–91.
57. Turkevich J. (1985) Colloidal gold—Part II. *Gold Bull.* 18 (4): 125–131.

58. Kimling J, Maier M, Okenve B et al. (2006) Turkevich method for gold nanoparticle synthesis revisited. *J. Phys. Chem. B* 110: 15700–15707.
59. Hussain I, Graham S, Wang Z et al. (2005) Size-controlled synthesis of near-monodisperse gold nanoparticles in the 1–4nm range using polymeric stabilizers. *J. Am. Chem. Soc.* 127: 16398–16399.
60. Daniel M-C, Astruc D. (2004) Gold nanoparticles: Assembly, supramolecular chemistry, quantum-size-related properties, and applications toward biology, catalysis, and nanotechnology. *Chem. Rev.* 104 (1): 293–346.
61. Ghosh SK, Pal T. (2007) Interparticle coupling effect on the surface plasmon resonance of gold nanoparticles: From theory to applications. *Chem. Rev.* 107: 4797–4862.
62. Murray CB, Kagan CR, Bawendi MG. (2000) Synthesis and characterization of monodisperse nanocrystals and close-packed nanocrystal assemblies. *Annu. Rev. Mater. Sci.* 30: 545–610.
63. Bukowski TJ, Simmons JH. (2002) Quantum dot research: Current state and future prospects. *Crit. Rev. Solid State Mater. Sci.* 27 (3): 119–142.
64. Yin Y, Alivisatos AP. (2005) Colloidal nanocrystal synthesis and the organic–inorganic interface. *Nature* 437 (7059): 664–670.
65. Green M. (2005) Organometallic based strategies for metal nanocrystal synthesis. *Chem. Commun.* (24): 3002–3011.
66. Gaponik N, Rogach AL. (2008) Aqueous synthesis of semiconductor nanocrystals. In: *Semiconductor Nanocrystal Quantum Dots—Synthesis, Assembly, Spectroscopy and Applications*, ed. AL Rogach. New York: Springer, pp. 73–99.
67. Hild WA, Breunig M, Goepferich A. (2008) Quantum dots—Nano-sized probes for the exploration of cellular and intracellular targeting. *Eur. J. Pharm. Biopharm.* 68: 153–168.
68. Jamieson T, Bakhshi R, Petrova D et al. (2007) Biological applications of quantum dots. *Biomaterials* 28: 4717–4732.
69. Peng ZA, Peng X. (2001) Formation of high-quality CdTe, CdSe, and CdS nanocrystals using CdO as precursor. *J. Am. Chem. Soc.* 123: 183–184.
70. Talapin DV, Rogach AL, Kornowski A, Haase M, Weller H. (2001) Highly luminescent monodisperse CdSe and CdSe/ZnS nanocrystals synthesized in a hexadecylamine–trioctylphosphine oxide–trioctylphospine mixture. *Nano Lett.* 1 (4): 207–211.
71. Bruchez M Jr, Moronne M, Gin P, Weiss S, Alivisatos AP. (1998) Semiconductor nanocrystals as fluorescent biological labels. *Science* 281: 2013–2016.
72. Mattoussi H, Mauro JM, Goldman ER et al. (2000) Self-assembly of CdSe–ZnS quantum dot bioconjugates using an engineered recombinant protein. *J. Am. Chem. Soc.* 122 (49): 12142–12150.
73. Dubertret B, Skourides P, Norris DJ et al. (2002) *In vivo* imaging of quantum dots encapsulated in phospholipid micelles. *Science* 298 (5599): 1759–1762.
74. Guo W, Li JJ, Wang YA, Peng X. (2003) Conjugation chemistry and bioapplications of semiconductor box nanocrystals prepared via dendrimer bridging. *Chem. Mater.* 15 (16): 3125–3133.
75. Zhang T, Ge J, Hu Y, Yin Y. (2007) A general approach for transferring hydrophobic nanocrystals into water. *Nano Lett.* 7 (10): 3203–3207.
76. Henglein A. (1982) Photodegradation and fluorescence of colloidal-cadmium sulphide in aqueous solution. *Ber. Bunsenges. Phys. Chem.* 86: 301–305.
77. Gaponik N, Talapin DV, Rogach AL et al. (2002) Thiol-capping of CdTe nanocrystals: An alternative to organometallic synthetic routes. *J. Phys. Chem. B* 106: 7177–7185.
78. Deng D-W, Qin Y-B, Yang X, Yu J-S, Pan Y. (2006) The selective synthesis of water-soluble highly luminescent CdTe nanoparticles and nanorods: The influence of the precursor Cd/Te molar ratio. *J. Cryst. Growth* 296: 141–149.
79. Deng D-W, Yu J-S, Pan Y. (2006) Water-soluble CdSe and CdSe/CdS nanocrystals: A greener synthetic route. *J. Colloid Interface Sci.* 299: 225–232.
80. Shavel A, Gaponik N, Eychmüller A. (2006) Factors governing the quality of aqueous CdTe nanocrystals: Calculations and experiment. *J. Phys. Chem. B* 110: 19280–19284.

81. Peng H, Zhang L, Soeller C, Travas-Sejdic J. (2007) Preparation of water-soluble CdTe/CdS core/shell quantum dots with enhanced photostability. *J. Lumin.* 127: 721–726.
82. Li C, Murase N. (2005) Surfactant-dependent photoluminescence of CdTe nanocrystals in aqueous solution. *Chem. Lett.* 34 (1): 92–93.
83. Rogach AL, Franzl T, Klar TA et al. (2007) Aqueous synthesis of thiol-capped CdTe nanocrystals: State-of-the-art. *J. Phys. Chem.* C 111: 14628–14637.
84. Liu Y-F, Yu J-S. (2009) Selective synthesis of CdTe and high luminescence CdTe/CdS quantum dots: The effect of ligands. *J. Colloid Interface Sci.* 333: 690–698.
85. Mackenzie JD, Bescher EP. (2007) Chemical routes in the synthesis of nanomaterials using the sol–gel process. *Acc. Chem. Res.* 40 (9): 810–818.
86. Pierre AC. (1998) *Introduction to Sol–Gel Processing*. Boston, MA: Kluwer Academic Publishers, pp. 1–9 (introduction on sol–gel); 103 (Figure); 124–146 (electrostatic interactions).
87. Khaleel A, Richards RM. (2001) Ceramics. In: *Nanoscale Materials in Chemistry*, ed. KJ Klabunde. New York: Wiley Interscience, pp. 85–120.
88. Stöber W, Fink A. (1968) Controlled growth of monodisperse silica spheres in the micron size range. *J. Colloid Interface Sci.* 26: 62–69.
89. van Blaaderen A, Vrij A. (1992) Synthesis and characterization of colloidal dispersions of fluorescent, monodisperse silica spheres. *Langmuir* 8: 2921–2931.
90. Rossi LM, Shi L, Quina FH, Rosenzweig Z. (2005) Stöber synthesis of monodispersed luminescent silica nanoparticles for bioanalytical assays. *Langmuir* 21: 4277–4280.
91. Johnston APR, Battersby BJ, Lawrie GA, Trau M. (2005) Porous functionalised silica particles: A potential platform for biomolecular screening. *Chem. Commun.* (7): 848–850.
92. Tan W, Wang K, He X et al. (2004) Bionanotechnology based on silica nanoparticles. *Med. Res. Rev.* 24 (5): 621–638.
93. Arriagada FJ, Osseo-Asare K. (1999) Synthesis of nanosize silica in a nonionic water-in-oil microemulsion: Effects of the water/surfactant molar ratio and ammonia concentration. *J. Colloid Interface Sci.* 211 (2): 210–220.
94. Hiemenz PC, Rajagopalan R. (1997) *Principles of Colloid and Surface Chemistry*, 3rd edn. New York: CRC Press, pp. 462–495 (van der Waals interactions); 538–550 (zeta potential), 585–592 (D.L.V.O. theory and colloid stability).
95. Adamson AW. (1990) *Physical Chemistry of Surfaces*, 5th edn. New York: Wiley-Interscience, pp. 265–268 (van der Waals interactions); 307 (Table VII-3).
96. Peters DG, Hayes JM, Hieftje GM. (1974) *Chemical Separations and Measurements*. Philadelphia, PA: W.B. Saunders Company, p. 215 (ion adsorption).
97. Mulvaney P. (2001) Metal nanoparticles: Double layers, optical properties, and electrochemistry. In: *Nanoscale Materials in Chemistry*, ed. KJ Klabunde. New York: Wiley Interscience, pp. 121–167.
98. Brinker CJ, Scherer GW. (1990) *Sol–Gel Science: The Physics and Chemistry of Sol–Gel Processing*. San Diego, CA: Academic Press, pp. 239–250 (zeta potential and stability of sols).
99. Hunter RJ. (1981) *Zeta Potential in Colloidal Science—Principles and Applications*, eds. RH Ottewill and RL Rowell. London, U.K.: Academic Press, pp. 4–7 (introduction to zeta potential); 224–229 (point of zero charge); 239–246 (zeta potential and colloidal stability).
100. Derjaguin BV, Landau L. (1941) Theory of the stability of strongly charged lyophobic sols and of the adhesion of strongly charged particles in solutions of electrolytes. *Acta Physicochim. URSS* 14: 633–662.
101. Verwey EJW, Overbeek JTG. (1948) *Theory of the Stability of Lyophobic Colloids—The Interaction of Sol Particles Having an Electric Double Layer*. Amsterdam, the Netherlands: Elsevier.
102. DeLuca T, Kaszuba M, Mattison K. (2006) Optimizing silicone emulsion stability using zeta potential. *Am. Lab. News* 38 (13): 14–15.
103. Wang L, Wang K, Santra S et al. (2006) Watching silica nanoparticles glow in the biological world. *Anal. Chem.* 78 (3): 646–654.
104. Kosmulski M. (2002) The pH-dependent surface charging and the points of zero charge. *J. Colloid Interface Sci.* 253: 77–87.

105. Napper DH. (1983) Polymeric stabilization of colloidal dispersions, eds. RH Ottewill and RL Rowell. London, U.K.: Academic Press, pp. 8–17 (colloid stabilization); 18–30 (stabilization by attached polymer).
106. Kim T, Lee C-H, Joo S-W, Lee K. (2008) Kinetics of gold nanoparticle aggregation: Experiments and modeling. *J. Colloid Interface Sci.* 318: 238–243.
107. Weiser HB. (1949) *A Textbook of Colloidal Chemistry*, 2nd edn. New York: Wiley & Sons, p. 141 (steric stabilization).
108. Zhu T, Vasilev K, Kreiter M, Mittler S, Knoll W. (2003) Surface modification of citrate-reduced colloidal gold nanoparticles with 2-mercaptosuccinic acid. *Langmuir* 19: 9518–9525.
109. Maron SH, Prutton CF. (1958) *Principles of Physical Chemistry*, 3rd edn. New York: MacMillan, p. 234 (steric stabilization).
110. Stoilovic M, Lennard C, Wallace-Kunkel C, Roux C. (2007) Evaluation of a 1,2-indanedione formulation containing zinc chloride for improved fingermark detection on paper. *J. Forensic Ident.* 57: 4–18.
111. Wallace-Kunkel C, Lennard C, Stoilovic M, Roux C. (2007) Optimisation and evaluation of 1,2-indanedione for use as a fingermark reagent and its application to real samples. *Forensic Sci. Int.* 168: 14–26.
112. Link S, Beeby A, Fitzgerald S et al. (2002) Visible to infrared luminescence from a 28-atom gold cluster. *J. Phys. Chem. B* 106 (13): 3410–3415.
113. Wilcoxon JP, Martin JE, Parsapour F, Wiedenman B, Kelley DF. (1998) Photoluminescence from nanosize gold clusters. *J. Chem. Phys.* 108 (21): 9137–9143.
114. Zheng J, Petty JT, Dickson RM. (2003) High quantum yield blue emission from water-soluble Au_8 nanodots. *J. Am. Chem. Soc.* 125: 7780–7781.
115. Bao Y, Zhong C, Vu DM et al. (2007) Nanoparticle-free synthesis of fluorescent gold nanoclusters at physiological temperature. *J. Phys. Chem. C* 111: 12194–12198.
116. Alivisatos AP. (1996) Semiconductor clusters, nanocrystals, and quantum dots. *Science* 271 (5251): 933–937.
117. Parak WJ, Manna L, Simmel FC, Gerion D, Alivisatos AP. (2004) Quantum dots. In: *Nanoparticles: From Theory to Application*, ed. G Schmid. Weinheim, Germany: Wiley-VCH, pp. 4–49.
118. Woggon U. (1997) *Optical Properties of Semiconductor Quantum Dots*. New York: Springer-Verlag.
119. Dabbousi BO, Rodriguez-Viejo J, Mikulec FV et al. (1997) (CdSe)ZnS core-shell quantum dots: Synthesis and characterization of a size series of highly luminescent nanocrystallites. *J. Phys. Chem. B* 101: 9463–9475.
120. Lupton JM, Müller J. (2008) Fluorescence spectroscopy of single CdSe nanocrystals. In: *Semiconductor Nanocrystal Quantum Dots—Synthesis, Assembly, Spectroscopy and Applications*, ed. AL Rogach. New York: Springer, pp. 311–347.
121. Resch-Genger U, Grabolle M, Cavaliere-Jaricot S, Nitschke R, Nann T. (2008) Quantum dots versus organic dyes as fluorescent labels. *Nat. Methods* 5 (9): 763–775.
122. Michalet X, Pinaud FF, Bentolila LA et al. (2005) Quantum dots for live cells, *in vivo* imaging, and diagnostics. *Science* 307 (5709): 538–544.
123. Choi AO, Maysinger D. (2008) Applications of quantum dots in biomedicine. In: *Semiconductor Nanocrystal Quantum Dots—Synthesis, Assembly, Spectroscopy and Applications*, ed. AL Rogach. New York: Springer, pp. 349–365.
124. Alivisatos AP. (2004) The use of nanocrystals in biological detection. *Nat. Biotechnol.* 22 (1): 47–52.
125. Jaiswal JK, Mattoussi H, Mauro JM, Simon SM. (2003) Long-term multiple color imaging of live cells using quantum dot bioconjugates. *Nat. Biotechnol.* 21 (1): 47–51.
126. Sukhanova A, Devy J, Venteo L et al. (2004) Biocompatible fluorescent nanocrystals for immunolabeling of membrane proteins and cells. *Anal. Biochem.* 324: 60–67.
127. Chan WCW, Maxwell DJ, Gao X et al. (2002) Luminescent quantum dots for multiplexed biological detection and imaging. *Curr. Opin. Biotechnol.* 13 (1): 40–46.
128. Sargent EH. (2005) Infrared quantum dots. *Adv. Mater.* 17 (5): 515–522.

129. Chan WCW, Nie S. (1998) Quantum dot bioconjugates for ultrasensitive nonisotopic detection. *Science* 281 (5385): 2016–2018.
130. Rakovich YP, Donegan JF. (2008) Anti-stokes photoluminescence in semiconductor nanocrystal quantum dots. In: *Semiconductor Nanocrystal Quantum Dots—Synthesis, Assembly, Spectroscopy and Applications*, ed. AL Rogach. New York: Springer, pp. 257–275.
131. Ma R, Bullock E, Maynard P et al. (2011) Fingermark detection on non-porous and semi-porous surfaces using $Nayf_4$:Er,Yb up-converter particles. *Forensic Sci. Int*. 207: 145–149.
132. Nagl S, Schaerferling M, Wolfbeis OS. (2005) Fluorescence analysis in microarray technology. *Microchim. Acta* 151: 1–21.
133. Zhao X, Bagwe RP, Tan W. (2004) Development of organic-dye-doped silica nanoparticles in a reverse microemulsion. *Adv. Mater*. 16 (2): 173–176.
134. Jain TK, Roy I, De TK, Maitra A. (1998) Nanometer silica particles encapsulating active compounds: A novel ceramic drug carrier. *J. Am. Chem. Soc.* 120: 11092–11095.
135. Zhang J, Gryczynski I, Gryczynski Z, Lakowicz JR. (2006) Dye-labeled silver nanoshell-bright particle. *J. Phys. Chem. B* 110: 8986–8991.
136. Wu C, Zheng J, Huang C et al. (2007) Hybrid silica–nanocrystal–organic dye superstructures as post-encoding fluorescent probes. *Angew. Chem. Int. Ed. Engl*. 46: 5393–5396.
137. Santra S, Wang K, Tapec R, Tan W. (2001) Development of novel dye-doped silica nanoparticles for biomarker application. *J. Biomed. Opt*. 6 (2): 160–166.
138. Santra S, Zhang P, Wang K, Tapec R, Tan W. (2001) Conjugation of biomolecules with luminophore-doped silica nanoparticles for photostable biomarkers. *Anal. Chem*. 73 (20): 4988–4993.
139. Lian W, Litherland SA, Badrane H et al. (2004) Ultrasensitive detection of biomolecules with fluorescent dye-doped nanoparticles. *Anal. Biochem*. 334: 135–144.
140. Senarath-Yapa MD, Phimphivong S, Coym JW et al. (2007) Preparation and characterization of poly(lipid)-coated, fluorophore-doped silica nanoparticles for biolabeling and cellular imaging. *Langmuir* 23 (25): 12624–12633.
141. Qhobosheane M, Santra S, Zhang P, Tan W. (2001) Biochemically functionalized silica nanoparticles. *Analyst* 126: 1274–1278.
142. Bagwe RP, Yang C, Hilliard LR, Tan W. (2004) Optimization of dye-doped silica nanoparticles prepared using a reverse microemulsion method. *Langmuir* 20: 8336–8342.
143. Tapec R, Zhao XJ, Tan W. (2002) Development of organic dye-doped silica nanoparticles for bioanalysis and biosensors. *J. Nanosci. Nanotechnol*. 2 (3–4): 405–409.
144. Ow H, Larson DR, Srivastava M et al. (2005) Bright and stable core-shell fluorescent silica nanoparticles. *Nano Lett*. 5 (1): 113–117.
145. Burns A, Ow H, Wiesner U. (2006) Fluorescent core-shell silica nanoparticles: Towards "lab on a particle" architectures for nanobiotechnology. *Chem. Soc. Rev*. 35: 1028–1042.
146. Zhou Y, Yip WT. (2009) Balance between Coulombic interactions and physical confinement in silica hydrogel encapsulation. *J. Phys. Chem. B* 113: 5720–5727.
147. Liu L, Gill SK, Gao Y, Hope-Weeks LJ, Cheng KH. (2008) Exploration of the use of novel SiO_2 nanocomposites doped with fluorescent Eu^{3+}/sensitizer complex for latent fingerprint detection. *Forensic Sci. Int*. 176: 163–172.
148. Rampazzo E, Bonacchi S, Montalti M, Prodi L, Zaccheroni N. (2007) Self-organizing core-shell nanostructures: Spontaneous accumulation of dye in the core of doped silica nanoparticles. *J. Am. Chem. Soc*. 129 (46): 14251–14256.
149. Murcia MJ, Naumann CA. (2005) Biofunctionalization of fluorescent nanoparticles. In: *Biofunctionalization of Nanomaterials*, ed. CSSR Kumar. Weinheim, Germany: Wiley-VCH Verlag GmbH & Co. KGaA, pp. 1–40.
150. Zheng M, Huang X. (2005) Biofunctionalization of gold nanoparticles. In: *Biofunctionalization of Nanomaterials*, ed. CSSR Kumar. Weinheim, Germany: Wiley-VCH Verlag GmbH & Co. KGaA, pp. 99–124.
151. Meziani MJ, Lin Y, Sun Y-P. (2005) Conjugation of nanomaterials with proteins. In: *Biofunctionalization of Nanomaterials*, ed. CSSR Kumar. Weinheim, Germany: Wiley-VCH Verlag GmbH & Co. KGaA, pp. 183–234.

152. Mandal S, Phadtare S, Sastry M. (2005) Interfacing biology with nanoparticles. *Curr. Appl. Phys.* 5 (2): 118–127.
153. Parak WJ, Gerion D, Pellegrino T et al. (2003) Biological applications of colloidal nanocrystals. *Nanotechnology* 14: R15–R27.
154. Smith JE, Wang L, Tan W. (2006) Bioconjugated silica-coated nanoparticles for bioseparation and bioanalysis. *Trends Anal. Chem.* 25 (9): 848–855.
155. Mahmoudi M, Lynch I, Ejtehadi MR et al. (2011) Protein–nanoparticle interactions: Opportunities and challenges. *Chem. Rev.* 111 (9): 5610–5637.
156. Leggett R, Lee-Smith EE, Jickells SM, Russell DA. (2007) "Intelligent" fingerprinting: Simultaneous identification of drug metabolites and individuals by using antibody-functionalized nanoparticles. *Angew. Chem. Int. Ed. Engl.* 46: 4100–4103.
157. Drapel V, Bécue A, Champod C, Margot P. (2009) Identification of promising antigenic components in latent fingermark residues. *Forensic Sci. Int.* 184: 47–53.
158. Hazarika P, Jickells SM, Wolff K, Russel DA. (2008) Imaging of latent fingerprints through the detection of drugs and metabolites. *Angew. Chem. Int. Ed. Engl.* 47: 10167–10170.
159. Hazarika P, Jickells SM, Russell DA. (2009) Rapid detection of drug metabolites in latent fingermarks. *Analyst* 134: 93–96.
160. Wolfbeis OS. (2009) Nanoparticle-enhanced fluorescence imaging of latent fingerprints reveals drug abuse. *Angew. Chem. Int. Ed. Engl.* 48: 2268–2269.
161. Hazarika P, Jickells SM, Wolff K, Russel DA. (2010) Multiplexed detection of metabolites of narcotic drugs from a single latent fingermark. *Anal. Chem.* 82: 9150–9154.
162. Boddis AM, Russel DA. (2011) Simultaneous development and detection of drug metabolites in latent fingermarks using antibody–magnetic particle conjugates. *Anal. Methods* 11: 519–523.
163. Spindler X, Hofstetter O, McDonagh AM, Roux C, Lennard C. (2011) Enhancement of latent fingermarks on non-porous surfaces using anti-L-amino acid antibodies conjugated to gold nanoparticles. *Chem. Commun.* 47: 5602–5604.
164. Ulman A. (1996) Formation and structure of self-assembled monolayers. *Chem. Rev.* 96 (4): 1533–1554.
165. Lévy R, Doty RC. (2005) Stabilization and functionalization of metallic nanoparticles: The peptide route. In: *Biofunctionalization of Nanomaterials*, ed. CSSR Kumar. Weinheim, Germany: Wiley-VCH Verlag GmbH & Co. KGaA, pp. 235–269.
166. Brust M, Fink J, Bethell D, Schiffrin DJ, Kiely C. (1995) Synthesis and reactions of functionalised gold nanoparticles. *J. Chem. Soc. Chem. Commun.* 1655–1656.
167. Templeton AC, Chen S, Gross SM, Murray RW. (1999) Water-soluble, isolable gold clusters protected by tiopronin and coenzyme a monolayers. *Langmuir* 15 (1): 66–76.
168. Templeton AC, Cliffel DE, Murray RW. (1999) Redox and fluorophore functionalization of water-soluble, tiopronin-protected gold clusters. *J. Am. Chem. Soc.* 121: 7081–7089.
169. Hostetler MJ, Green SJ, Stokes JJ, Murray RW. (1996) Monolayers in three dimensions: Synthesis and electrochemistry of Ω-functionalized alkanethiolate-stabilized gold cluster compounds. *J. Am. Chem. Soc.* 118 (17): 4212–4213.
170. Shenton W, Davis SA, Mann S. (1999) Directed self-assembly of nanoparticles into macroscopic materials using antibody–antigen recognition. *Adv. Mater.* 11 (6): 449–452.
171. Lévy R, Thanh NTK, Doty RC et al. (2004) Rational and combinatorial design of peptide capping ligands for gold nanoparticles. *J. Am. Chem. Soc.* 126: 10076–10084.
172. Doty RC, Tshikhudo TR, Brust M, Fernig DG. (2005) Extremely stable water-soluble Ag nanoparticles. *Chem. Mater.* 17: 4630–4635.
173. Zhang J, Chi Q, Nielsen JU et al. (2000) Two-dimensional cysteine and cystine cluster networks on Au(111) disclosed by voltammetry and *in situ* scanning tunneling microscopy. *Langmuir* 16 (18): 7229–7237.
174. Selvakannan PR, Mandal S, Phadtare S, Pasricha R, Sastry M. (2003) Capping of gold nanoparticles by the amino acid lysine renders them water-dispersible. *Langmuir* 19 (8): 3545–3549.
175. Xu L, Guo Y, Xie R et al. (2002) Three-dimensional assembly of Au nanoparticles using dipeptides. *Nanotechnology* 13 (6): 725–728.

176. Selvakannan PR, Mandal S, Phadtare S et al. (2004) Water-dispersible tryptophan-protected gold nanoparticles prepared by the spontaneous reduction of aqueous chloroaurate ions by the amino acid. *J. Colloid Interface Sci.* 269: 97–102.
177. Królikowska A, Bukowska J. (2007) Self-assembled monolayers of mercaptosuccinic acid on silver and gold surfaces designed for protein binding. Part I: Structure of the monolayer. *J. Raman Spectrosc.* 38: 936–942.
178. Chen S, Kimura K. (1999) Synthesis and characterization of carboxylate-modified gold nanoparticle powders dispersible in water. *Langmuir* 15: 1075–1082.
179. Sawaguchi T, Sato Y, Mizutani F. (2001) Ordered structures of self-assembled monolayers of 3-mercaptopropionic acid on Au(111): *In situ* scanning tunneling microscopy study. *Phys. Chem. Chem. Phys.* 3: 3399–3404.
180. Schroedter A, Weller H. (2002) Ligand design and bioconjugation of colloidal gold nanoparticles. *Angew. Chem. Int. Ed. Engl.* 41 (17): 3218–3221.
181. Liz-Marzán LM, Giersig M, Mulvaney P. (1996) Synthesis of nanosized gold-silica core-shell particles. *Langmuir* 12: 4329–4335.
182. Makarova OV, Ostafin AE, Miyoshi H, Norris JR Jr. (1999) Adsorption and encapsulation of fluorescent probes in nanoparticles. *J. Phys. Chem. B* 103: 9080–9084.
183. Buining PA, Humbel BM, Philipse AP, Verkleij AJ. (1997) Preparation of functional silane-stabilized gold colloids in the (sub)nanometer size range. *Langmuir* 13: 3921–3926.
184. Biggs S, Mulvaney P. (1994) Measurement of the forces between gold surfaces in water by atomic force microscopy. *J. Chem. Phys.* 100 (11): 8501–8505.
185. Darbandi M, Thomann R, Nann T. (2005) Single quantum dots in silica spheres by microemulsion synthesis. *Chem. Mater.* 17: 5720–5725.
186. Wang S, Mamedova N, Kotov NA, Chen W, Studer J. (2002) Antigen/antibody immunocomplex from CdTe nanoparticle bioconjugates. *Nano Lett.* 2 (8): 817–822.
187. Lin Z, Cui S, Zhang H et al. (2003) Studies on quantum dots synthesized in aqueous solution for biological labeling via electrostatic interaction. *Anal. Chem.* 319 (2): 239–243.
188. Goldman ER, Balighian ED, Mattoussi H et al. (2002) Avidin: A natural bridge for quantum dot–antibody conjugates. *J. Am. Chem. Soc.* 124: 6378–6382.
189. Hilliard LR, Zhao X, Tan W. (2002) Immobilization of oligonucleotides onto silica nanoparticles for DNA hybridization studies. *Anal. Chim. Acta* 470 (1): 51–56.
190. Pham T, Jackson JB, Halas NJ, Lee TR. (2002) Preparation and characterization of gold nanoshells coated with self-assembled monolayers. *Langmuir* 18: 4915–4920.
191. Hoet PHM, Brüske-Hohlfeld I, Salata OV. (2006) Possible health impact of nanomaterials. In: *Nanotechnologies for the Life Science—Volume 5: Nanomaterials—Toxicity, Health and Environmental Issues*, ed. C Kumar. Weinheim, Germany: Wiley-VCH, pp. 53–80.
192. Oberdörster E, McClellan-Green P, Haasch M. (2006) Ecotoxicity of engineered nanomaterials. In: *Nanotechnologies for the Life Science—Volume 5: Nanomaterials—Toxicity, Health and Environmental Issues*, ed. C Kumar. Weinheim, Germany: Wiley-VCH, pp. 35–49.
193. Colvin VL. (2003) The potential environmental impact of engineered nanomaterials. *Nat. Biotechnol.* 21 (10): 1166–1170.
194. Oberdörster G, Oberdörster E, Oberdörster J. (2005) Nanotoxicology: An emerging discipline evolving from studies of ultrafine particles. *Environ. Health Perspect.* 113 (7): 823–839.
195. Fond AM, Meyer GJ. (2006) Biotoxicity of metal oxide nanoparticles. In: *Nanotechnologies for the Life Science—Volume 5: Nanomaterials—Toxicity, Health and Environmental Issues*, ed. C Kumar. Weinheim, Germany: Wiley-VCH, pp. 3–34.
196. Nel A, Xia T, Mädler L, Li N. (2006) Toxic potential of materials at the nanolevel. *Science* 311: 622–627.
197. Mahmoudi M, Azadmanesh K, Shokrgozar MA, Journeay WS, Laurent S. (2011) Effect of nanoparticles on the cell life cycle. *Chem. Rev.* 111: 3407–3432.
198. Wolf LK. (2011) Scrutinizing sunscreens. *Chem. Eng. News* 89 (32): 44–46.
199. Li N, Sioutas C, Cho A et al. (2003) Ultrafine particulate pollutants induce oxidative stress and mitochondrial damage. *Environ. Health Perspect.* 111 (4): 455–460.

200. Rothen-Rutishauser BM, Schürch S, Haenni B, Kapp N, Gehr P. (2006) Interaction of fine particles and nanoparticles with red blood cells visualized with advanced microscopic techniques. *Environ. Sci. Technol.* 40 (14): 4353–4359.
201. Lam C-W, James JT, McCluskey R, Holian A, Hunter RL. (2006) Toxicity of carbon nanotubes and its implications for occupational and environmental health. In: *Nanotechnologies for the Life Science—Volume 5: Nanomaterials—Toxicity, Health and Environmental Issues*, ed. C Kumar. Weinheim, Germany: Wiley-VCH, pp. 130–152.
202. Robichaud C, Tanzil D, Weilenmann U, Wiesner MR. (2005) Relative risk analysis of several manufactured nanomaterials: An insurance industry context. *Environ. Sci. Technol.* 39: 8985–8994.
203. Bergeron J. (2003) Development of bloody prints on dark surfaces with titanium dioxide and methanol. *J. Forensic Ident.* 53: 149–161.
204. Knowles AM. (1978) Aspects of physicochemical methods for the detection of latent fingerprints. *J. Phys. E Sci. Instrum.* 11 (8): 713–721.
205. Ramotowski RS. (2001) Composition of latent print residue. In: *Advances in Fingerprint Technology*, 2nd edn, eds. HC Lee and RE Gaensslen. Boca Raton, FL: CRC Press, pp. 63–104.
206. Cantú AA. (2013) The chemistry of fingerprint science and document examination. In: *Forensic Chemistry*, eds. JR Almirall and JD Winefordner. New York: John Wiley & Sons.
207. Cantor CR, Schimmel PR. (1980) *Biophysical Chemistry—Part I: The Conformation of Biological Macromolecules*. San Francisco, CA: W.H. Freeman.
208. Cantú AA, Johnson JL. (2001) Silver physical development of latent prints. In: *Advances in Fingerprint Technology*, 2nd edn., eds. HC Lee and RE Gaensslen. Boca Raton, FL: CRC Press, pp. 242–247 (photographic chemistry); 254 (charge of latent print residue).
209. Archer N. (2005) Standardized evaluation of latent print developers. Paper read at *International Fingerprint Research Group Meeting—5th Biennial Meeting*, The Hague, the Netherlands.
210. Jonker H, Molenaar A, Dippel CJ. (1969) Physical development recording system: III. Physical development. *Photo. Sci. Eng.* 13: 38–44.
211. Choi MJ, McDonagh AM, Maynard PJ et al. (2006) Preparation and evaluation of metal nanopowders for the detection of fingermarks on nonporous surfaces. *J. Forensic Ident.* 56 (5): 756–768.
212. Menzel ER. (2000) Photoluminescence detection of latent fingerprints with quantum dots for time-resolved imaging. *Fingerprint Whorld* 26 (101): 119–123.
213. Bouldin KK, Menzel RE, Takatsu M, Murdock RH. (2000) Diimide-enhanced fingerprint detection with photoluminescent CdS/dendrimer nanocomposites. *J. Forensic Sci.* 45: 1239–1242.
214. Menzel ER. (2001) Fingerprint detection with photoluminescent nanoparticles. In: *Advances in Fingerprint Technology*, 2nd edn., eds. HC Lee and RE Gaensslen. Boca Raton, FL: CRC Press, pp. 216–276.
215. Hardwick SA. (1981) *User Guide to Physical Developer—A Reagent for Detecting Latent Fingerprints*, User Guide No. 14/81. London, U.K.: Home Office Police Scientific Development Branch.
216. Goode GC, Morris JR. (1983) Latent fingerprints: A review of their origin, composition and methods for detection. Atomic Weapons Research Establishment Report No. 022/83. Aldermaston, U.K.
217. Champod C, Egli N, Margot P. (2004) Fingermarks, shoesole, and footprint impressions, tire impressions, ear impressions, toolmarks, lipmarks, bitmarks—A review (September 2001–August 2004). Paper read at *14th Interpol Forensic Science Symposium*, October 19–22, Lyon, France.
218. Bécue A, Champod C, Margot P. (2007) Fingermarks, bitemarks and other impressions (barefoot, ears, lips)—A review (September 2004–July 2007). Paper read at *15th Interpol Forensic Science Symposium*, October 23–26, Lyon, France.
219. Bécue A, Egli N, Champod C, Margot P. (2010) Fingermarks and other impressions left by the human body—A review (August 2007–July 2010). Paper read at *16th Interpol Forensic Science Symposium*, October 5–8, Lyon, France.
220. Sodhi GS, Kaur J. (2006) Nanoparticle size fingerprint dusting composition based on fluorescent eosin Y dye. *Fingerprint Whorld* 32: 146–147.

221. Menzel ER, Savoy SM, Ulvick SJ et al. (2000) Photoluminescent semiconductor nanocrystals for fingerprint detection. *J. Forensic Sci.* 45: 545–551.
222. Menzel ER, Takatsu M, Murdock RH, Bouldin K, Cheng KH. (2000) Photoluminescent CdS/dendrimer nanocomposites for fingerprint detection. *J. Forensic Sci.* 45: 770–773.
223. Dilag J, Kobus H, Ellis AV. (2009) Cadmium sulfide quantum dot/chitosan nanocomposites for latent fingermark detection. *Forensic Sci. Int.* 187: 97–102.
224. Wang Y-F, Wang Y-J, Yang R-Q, Jin Y-J. (2008) Study on amidation reaction between CdS/PAMAM and amino acid and its application to latent fingerprint development. *Spectrosc. Spectral Anal.* 28 (12): 2843–2846.
225. Algarra M, Jiménez-Jiménez J, Moreno-Tost R, Campos BB, Esteves da Silva JCG. (2011) CdS Nanocomposites assembled in porous phosphate heterostructures for fingerprint detection. *Opt. Mater.* 33: 893–898.
226. Wang YF, Yang RQ, Shi ZX et al. (2011) The effectiveness of CdSe nanoparticle suspension for developing latent fingermarks. *J. Saudi Chem. Soc.*, doi: 10.1016/j.jscs.2011.05.007.
227. Liu JJ, Shi ZX, Yu Y, Yang RQ, Zuo S. (2010) Water-soluble multicolored fluorescent CdTe quantum dots: Synthesis and application for fingerprint developing. *J. Colloid Interface Sci.* 342 (2): 278–282.
228. Gao F, Han J, Zhang J et al. (2011) The synthesis of newly modified CdTe quantum dots and their application for improvement of latent fingerprint detection. *Nanotechnology* 22: Art. No. 075705.
229. Menzel RE, Mitchell KE. (1990) Intramolecular energy transfer in the europium–Ruhemann's purple complex: Application to latent fingerprint detection. *J. Forensic Sci.* 35: 35–45.
230. Misner A, Watkin JE. (1993) Thenoyl europium chelate: A new fluorescent dye with a narrow emission band to detect cyanoacrylate developed fingerprints on non-porous substrates and cadavers. *J. Forensic Ident.* 43: 154–165.
231. Wilkinson DA, Misner AH. (1993) A comparison of thenoyl europium chelate with Ardrox and rhodamine 6G for the fluorescent detection of cyanoacrylate prints. *J. Forensic Ident.* 44: 387–401.
232. Wilkinson DA, Watkin JE. (1993) Europium aryl-β-diketone complexes as fluorescent dyes for the detection of cyanoacrylate developed fingerprints on human skin. *Forensic Sci. Int.* 60: 67–79.
233. Lock ER, Mazzella WD, Margot P. (1995) A new europium chelate as a fluorescent dye for cyanoacrylate pretreated fingerprints—EuTTAPhen: Europium thenoyltrifluoroacetone ortho-phenanthroline. *J. Forensic Sci.* 40: 654–658.
234. Allred CE, Menzel RE. (1997) A novel europium-bioconjugate method for latent fingerprint detection. *Forensic Sci. Int.* 85: 83–94.
235. Allred CE, Murdock RH, Menzel RE. (1997) New lipid-specific, rare earth-based chemical fingerprint detection method. *J. Forensic Ident.* 446: 542–556.
236. Wilkinson D. (1999) A one-step fluorescent detection method for lipid fingerprints—$Eu(TTA)_3$.2TOPO. *Forensic Sci. Int.* 99: 5–23.
237. Li C, Li B, Yu S, Gao J, Yao P. (2004) Study on the direct developing of a latent fingerprint using a new fluorescent developer. *J. Forensic Ident.* 54: 653–659.
238. Menzel ER, Schwierking JR, Menzel LW. (2005) Functionalized europium oxide nanoparticles for fingerprint detection: A preliminary study. *J. Forensic Ident.* 55 (2): 189–195.
239. Saunders G. (1989) Multimetal deposition method for latent fingerprint development. Paper read at *74th Annual Educational Conference of the International Association for Identification*, Pensacola, FL.
240. Jones N. (2002) *Metal Deposition Techniques for the Detection and Enhancement of Latent Fingerprints on Semi-Porous Surfaces*. Sydney, New South Wales, Australia: University of Technology.
241. Choi MJ, McBean KE, Wuhrer R et al. (2006) Investigation into binding of gold nanoparticles to fingermarks using scanning electron microscopy. *J. Forensic Ident.* 56 (1): 24–32.
242. Zhang M, Bécue A, Prudent M, Champod C, Girault HH. (2007) SECM imaging of MMD-enhanced latent fingermarks. *Chem. Commun.* 38: 3948–3950.

243. Bécue A, Scoundrianos A, Champod C, Margot P. (2008) Fingermark detection based on the *in situ* growth of luminescent nanoparticles—Towards a new generation of multimetal deposition. *Forensic Sci. Int.* 179: 39–43.
244. Almog J, Glasner H. (2010) Ninhydrin thiohemiketals: Basic research towards improved fingermark detection techniques employing nano-technology. *J. Forensic Sci.* 55 (1): 215–220.
245. Gao D, Li F, Song J et al. (2009) One step to detect the latent fingermarks with gold nanoparticles. *Talanta* 80: 479–483.
246. Hussain I, Hussain SZ, Habib-ur-Rehman et al. (2010) *In situ* growth of gold nanoparticles on latent fingerprints—From forensic applications to inkjet printed nanoparticle patterns. *Nanoscale* 2: 2575–2578.
247. James JD, Pounds CA, Wilshire B. (1991) Magnetic flake fingerprint technology. *J. Forensic Ident.* 41 (4): 237–247.
248. James JD, Pounds CA, Wilshire B. (1991) Flake metal powder for revealing latent fingerprints. *J. Forensic Sci.* 36: 1368–1375.
249. Haque F, Westland AD, Milligan J, Kerr FM. (1989) A small particle (iron oxide) suspension for detection of latent fingerprints on smooth surfaces. *Forensic Sci. Int.* 41 (1–2): 73–82.
250. Home Office Scientific Development Branch. (2006) Additional fingerprint development techniques for adhesive tapes. *Fingerprint Dev. Imaging Newsletter*, Vol. 23, pp. 1–12.
251. Hlady V, Buijs J. (1996) Protein adsorption on solid surfaces. *Curr. Opin. Biotechnol.* 7: 72–77.
252. Chen Q, Kerk WT, Soutar AM, Zeng XT. (2009) Application of dye intercalated bentonite for developing latent fingerprints. *Appl. Clay Sci.* 44: 156–160.
253. Lim AY, Ma Z, Ma J, Rowell F. (2011) Separation of fingerprint constituents using magnetic silica nanoparticles and direct on-particle SALDI-TOF-mass spectrometry. *J. Chromatogr. B* 879: 2244–2250.
254. Feigl F, Anger V. (1978) *Spot Tests in Inorganic Analysis*, 6th edn. Amsterdam, the Netherlands: Elsevier, p. 424 (physical developer).
255. Morris JR. 1975. The detection of latent fingerprints on wet paper samples. Atomic Weapons Research Establishment—Chemistry Division, Memo No. 36. Aldermaston, U.K.
256. Burow D, Seifert D, Cantú AA. (2003) Modifications to the silver physical developer. *J. Forensic Sci.* 48: 1094–1100.
257. Burow D, Seifert D, Cantú AA, Ramotowski RS. (2001) Unpublished work done at the U.S. Secret Service. Paper read at *International Fingerprint Research Group Meeting—Third Biennial Meeting*, Wiesbaden, Germany.
258. Ramotowski RS, Holgrave S, Andress M. (2009) A Comparison of Aged Physical Developer Working Solutions. Presentation given at the 2009 meeting of the International Fingerprint Research Group in Lausanne, Switzerland.
259. Cantú AA, Leben DA, Wilson K. (2003) Some advances in the silver physical development of latent prints on paper. Paper read at *Proceeding of SPIE—Sensors, and Command, Control, Communications, and Intelligence (C3I) Technologies for Homeland Defense and Law Enforcement II*, Orlando, FL, pp. 164–167.
260. Land EH. (1947) A new one-step photographic process. *J. Opt. Soc. Am.* 37 (2): 61–77.
261. Levenson GIP. (1977) Diffusion transfer and monobaths. In: *The Theory of the Photographic Process*, 4th edn, ed. TH James. New York: McMillan Publishing Co., Chapter 16.
262. Wade DC. (2002) Development of latent prints with titanium dioxide (TiO_2). *J. Forensic Ident.* 52: 551–559.
263. Williams NH, Elliot KT. (2005) Development of latent prints using titanium dioxide (TiO_2) in small particle reagent, white (SPR-W) on adhesives. *J. Forensic Ident.* 55: 292–301.
264. Schiemer C, Lennard C, Maynard P, Roux C. (2005) Evaluation of techniques for the detection and enhancement of latent fingermarks on black electrical tape. *J. Forensic Ident.* 55: 214–238.
265. Cucè P, Polimeni G, Lazzaro AP, De Fulvio G. (2004) Small particle reagents technique can help to point out wet latent fingerprints. *Forensic Sci. Int.* 146S: S7–S8.
266. Polimeni G, Feudale Foti B, Saravo L, De Fulvio G. (2004) A novel approach to identify the presence of fingerprints on wet surfaces. *Forensic Sci. Int.* 146S: S45–S46.

267. Sahai N. (2002) Biomembrane phospholipid–oxide surface interactions: Crystal chemical and thermodynamic basis. *J. Colloid Interface Sci.* 252 (2): 309–319.
268. Nygren H, Tengvall P, Lundström I. (1997) The initial reactions of TiO_2 with blood. *J. Biomed. Mater. Res. A* 34 (4): 487–492.
269. Topoglidis E, Campbell CJ, Cass AEG, Durrant JR. (2001) Factors that affect protein adsorption on nanostructured titania films. A novel spectroelectrochemical application to sensing. *Langmuir* 17 (25): 7899–7906.
270. Choi MJ, Smoother T, Martin AA et al. (2007) Fluorescent TiO_2 powders prepared using a new perylene diimide dye: Applications in latent fingermark detection. *Forensic Sci. Int.* 173: 154–160.
271. Walls HJ, Attridge GG. (1977) Basic photo science: How photography works. In: *The Manual of Photo-Technique*, 2nd edn. London, U.K.: Focal Press, pp. 304–305 (titanium dioxide).

14

Friction Ridge Detection from Challenging Crime Scenes

Della Wilkinson

CONTENTS

14.1 Introduction

Latent friction ridges are typically comprised of chemicals secreted by the eccrine and sebaceous glands plus miscellaneous contaminants [1]. The pores of the eccrine glands are located directly on the friction ridges, whereas the sebaceous materials are transferred to the fingers by frequent contact with the face, neck, and scalp where the sebaceous glands occur in high density. Subsequently, friction ridge residues are comprised of the chemicals contained in the sweat and sebum. The composition of eccrine sweat is in excess of 98% water but it also contains a wide variety of inorganic (e.g., salts and trace elements such as magnesium and zinc) and organic (e.g., amino acids, proteins, and lipids) material. For friction ridge detection, the compounds of primary interest within sweat are amino acids such as serine, glycine, ornithine, and alanine, which react with ninhydrin [2], 1,8-diazafluoren-9-one (DFO) [3], and 1,2-indanedione [4] to produce colored and/or fluorescent reaction products that can be visualized and recorded. Sebum composition shows much variation between individuals but the major lipid components have been identified as fatty acids

(37.6%), wax esters with diglycerides (25%), triglycerides with monoglycerides and cholesterol esters (21%), squalene (14.6%), and cholesterol (3.8%). These sebaceous components are valuable for latent friction ridge detection because they persist, even in the presence of water, and can be detected by a wide variety of physical and chemical techniques such as powders [5], physical developer [6], iodine [7], small particle reagent (SPR) [8], and cyanoacrylate (CA) [9].

The chemical reactivity of these friction ridge components has been exploited by crime scene examiners who utilize optical, physical, and/or chemical means to develop visible images of latent friction ridge impressions. Table 14.1 shows a summary of friction ridge reactivity and common development techniques.

In most crime scenes, this friction ridge reactivity is used to detect latent impressions. In a challenging crime scene where the environment might be contaminated with other materials such as chemical, explosive, or drug residues, these functional groups may also react with the contaminant. Latent friction ridges that have been exposed to such environments may suffer from reduced reactivity to detection chemicals. For the purpose of this review, challenging crime scenes have been restricted to crime scenes or exhibits exposed to arson, explosive residues, radioisotopes, chemical and biological warfare agents, and the decontamination agents used to neutralize them.

14.2 Arson

14.2.1 Introduction

Law enforcement agencies have much to gain by partnering with the first responders who can be trained to recognize items with evidentiary value and take steps to protect them from damage due to fire or fire suppression. The initial observations of first responders can also provide investigators with a starting point for evidence collection and preservation efforts [22]. Actions taken at the outset of a fire investigation can play a pivotal role in the successful resolution of the case and thorough intelligence-led investigation is the key to ensuring that potential physical evidence is not overlooked, tainted, or destroyed.

It is often misstated that physical evidence will be completely consumed during the progress of the fire [23] and subject matter experts often assume that charred or soot-covered fire debris offers no hope for the detection of friction ridge impressions or DNA evidence [24]. While there is no doubt that the physical and chemical properties of friction ridge impressions will be affected by the extreme environment created by fire, such as elevated temperatures, water exposure, and high levels of gases (e.g., carbon monoxide and carbon dioxide), both casework and research indicated that friction ridge impressions [25] and more recently DNA [26] can survive such exposure. Recent work has demonstrated that objects close to the seat of the fire may yield friction ridge impressions if the surface has been covered by soot or debris to protect it from the flame [24]. Even badly damaged objects should be considered, as the underside may be relatively undamaged and yield friction ridge impressions. For many fire investigations, proving that arson was committed is relatively easy compared to proving that a particular person was involved in the case [27]. Forensic examination of arson scenes should be pursued so that valuable physical evidence, such as friction ridge impression and DNA evidence that could be used to identify the suspect, is not overlooked.

TABLE 14.1
Reactivity of Common Friction Ridge Development Techniques

Component	Reagent	Detection Method	Detection Conditions	Reference
Sebum	Powders	Physical	White light	[5]
	Fluorescent powders	Physical	FLS	[10]
	Molybdenum disulfide (SPR)	Physical	Black deposit, white light	[8]
	Vacuum metal deposition (VMD)	Physical	White light, back lighting	[11]
	Multimetal deposition (MMD)	Physical	Gray deposit, white light	[12]
	Iodine	Physical	Brown stain, white light	[7]
	Gentian violet	Physical	Purple stain, white light	[13]
	Oil Red O	Physical	Red stain, white light	[14]
	Physical developer (PD)	Physical/chemical	Gray deposit, white light	[6]
Sebum (unsaturated organic components)	Ruthenium tetraoxide (RTX)	Chemical 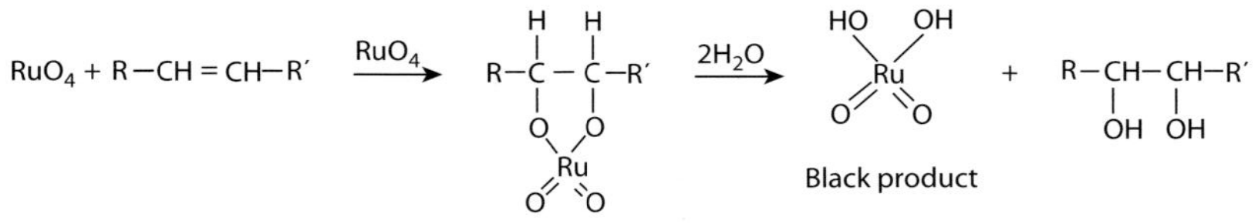	Black product, white light	[15]

(*continued*)

TABLE 14.1 (continued)
Reactivity of Common Friction Ridge Development Techniques

Component	Reagent	Detection Method	Detection Conditions	Reference
Sebum/sweat	Cyanoacrylate/ dye stains	Chemical 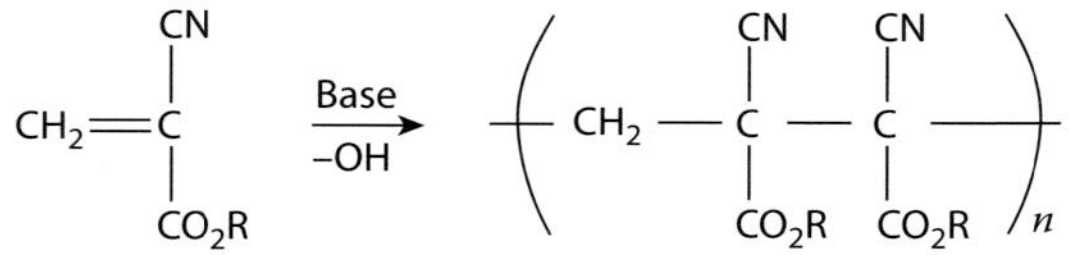	White polymer, white light/ colored fluorescence, FLS	[9]
Sweat (chloride ion)	Silver nitrate	Chemical $AgNO_3 + NaCl \longrightarrow AgCl + NaNO_3$; $AgCl \xrightarrow{\text{Light}} Ag$	Gray deposit, white light	[16]
Sweat (amino acids)	Ninhydrin	Chemical 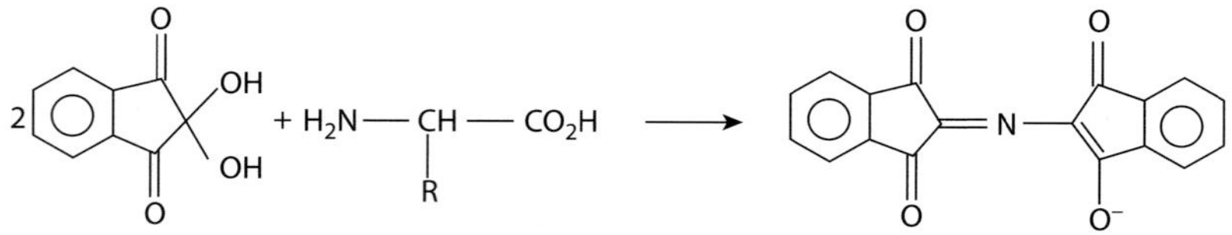	Purple product, white light	[2]
	Ninhydrin/zinc chloride	Chemical 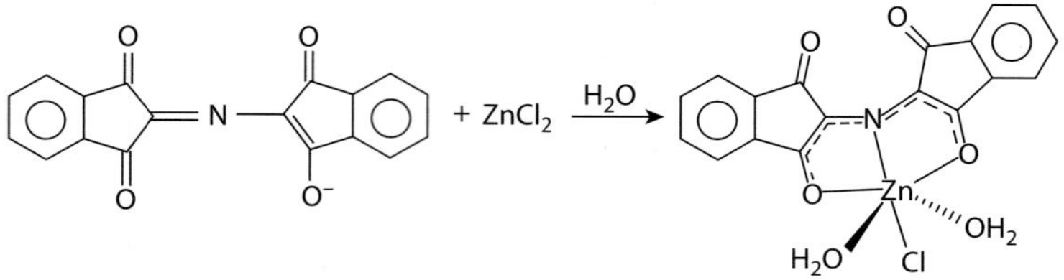	Pink product, yellow fluorescence, FLS	[17]

	1,8-Diazafluoren-9-one (DFO)	Chemical	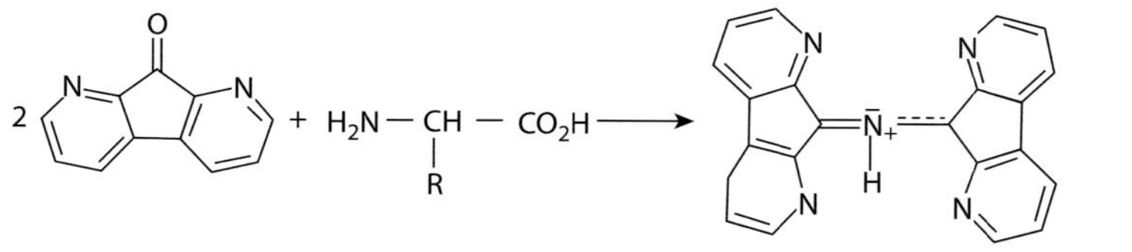	Pink product, yellow fluorescence, FLS	[3]
	1,2-Indanedione	Chemical	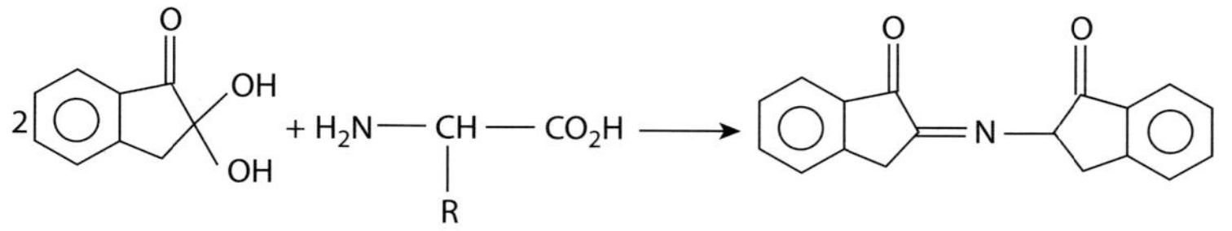	Pink product, yellow fluorescence, FLS	[4]
Blood (heme protein)	Acid black 1 (amido black)	Physical		Blue–black stain, white light	[18]
Blood (heme protein)	Hungarian red	Physical		Red stain, white light	[19]
Blood (peroxidase)	Leucomalachite green (LMG)	Chemical	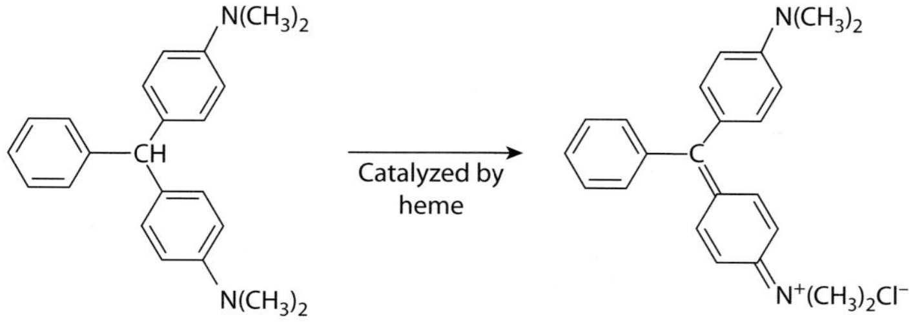	Green product, white light	[20]

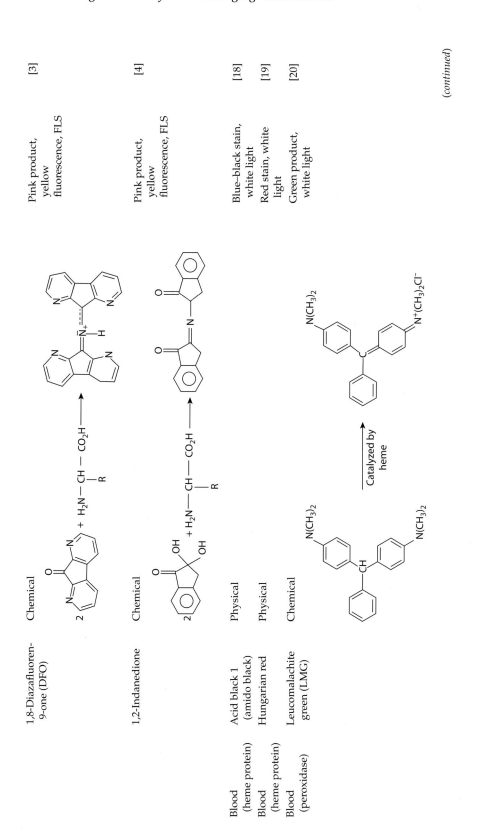

(continued)

TABLE 14.1 (continued)

Reactivity of Common Friction Ridge Development Techniques

Component	Reagent	Detection Method	Detection Conditions	Reference
Blood (hematin)	Luminol	Chemical 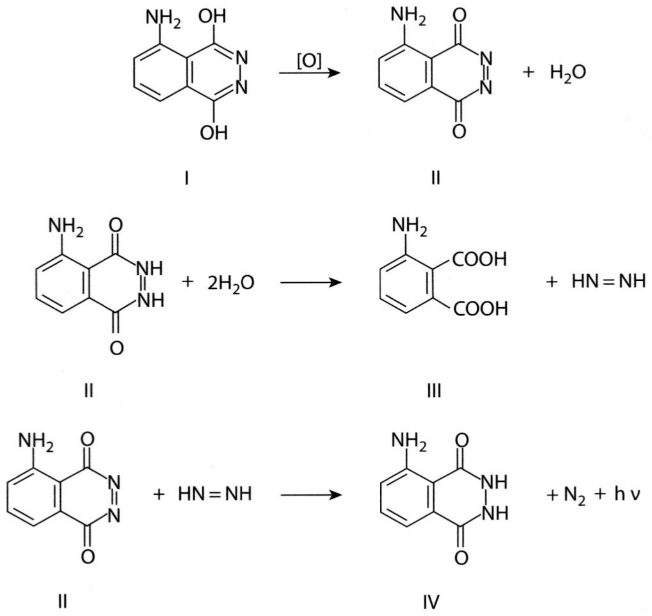	Blue chemiluminescent product, dark conditions	[21]

14.2.2 Soot Removal Techniques

Often the first step in examining arson exhibits for friction ridge impressions involves soot removal. In 1938, Harper developed friction ridge impressions by simply brushing the soot off the surface allowing the carbon particles to adhere to the oily residues in the ridges [28]. He further explored the effect of elevated temperatures on friction ridge impressions placed on a variety of different substrates including glass, porcelain, metal plates, enameled metal, and painted and unpainted wood. He observed that friction ridges quickly covered with a layer of soot were more likely to survive than exposed impressions, as the soot appeared to prevent evaporation of the friction ridge matrix. In addition, Harper exposed soot-covered friction ridges on metal surfaces, to temperatures reaching approximately 500°C and discovered that on washing with water, the ridges appeared to be "burned into the surface" and could not be removed even by rubbing. After the surfaces dried, soot removal was completed by gentle brushing. Although this study did not accurately record experimental conditions or thoroughly examine the effects of elevated temperatures on the recovery of aged friction ridges, the paper does refer to 3 month old friction ridge samples that were exposed to fire. After being covered in soot, they were developed by washing, drying, and brushing clean. If the print was allowed to evaporate to dryness, as a result of the fire, prior to soot deposition, then the friction ridges could not be recovered.

The first report describing retrieval of latent friction ridge impressions from an arson case did not appear in the literature for several decades [29]. In 1978, McCloud described the processing of a soot-covered, unbroken soda bottle that was purported to be a Molotov cocktail, recovered from a partially burned apartment building. The debris and soot were removed by brushing the surface with a fiberglass fingerprint brush using soft, gentle strokes, which revealed soot-developed friction ridge impressions on the rippled glass bottleneck. Remaining soot was removed by washing with soap and water. The texture and color of the surface created difficulties for photography, and sufficient contrast for successful recording of the friction ridge impression was only achieved by inserting a rolled sheet of white glossy paper into the bottle. The identifiable friction ridge impression, recovered from the soot-covered Molotov cocktail, is illustrated in Figure 14.1.

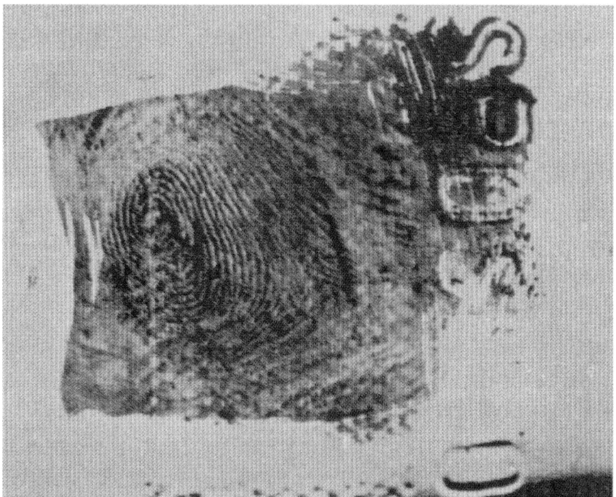

FIGURE 14.1
Latent friction ridge impression on glass from a Molotov cocktail developed by removing soot using a soft brush. (Reprinted With permission. from McCloud, V.D., *Ident. News*, 28, 3, 1978.)

Attempts to lift the impression from the surface resulted in unidentifiable images due to the rippled texture of the substrate.

One year later, Vaughan promoted rinsing soot-covered exhibits such as glass, doorknobs, flammable liquid containers, and car door handles under running water, claiming that fingerprints appeared "etched" into the glass [30]. The presence of gasoline and/or kerosene on the surface of the substrate was reported to decrease the effectiveness of this recovery method, most likely due to the hydrophobic nature of these fuels that would have repelled the water from the surface.

Soot removal techniques were further developed by Thornton and Emmons who suggested the use of lifting tape to remove soot remaining on friction ridge impressions that were only partially revealed by water rinsing [31]. The method was reported to work well for soot-covered latents on metal and glass surfaces. For instances where friction ridge impressions were faintly visible and not soot-covered, the authors recommended a guttural breath technique to re-humidify the dried-out ridges prior to the application of fingerprint powders.

In 1994, Spawn field tested the water rinsing technique using deliberately set incendiary fires involving everyday household items with latent fingerprints deposited on to the surfaces [27]. A kerosene–gasoline mix was used to start the fires and typical fire suppression techniques were employed after intense heat and thick black soot was allowed to develop. No accurate data were published relating to the temperatures experienced by the substrates or the duration of the fire burn prior to being extinguished. Items closest to the fire revealed no ridge impressions on visual examination, whereas surfaces exposed to only heat and soot but no flame revealed many friction ridge impressions following water rinsing. One notable exhibit was a metal light fixture directly above the seat of the fire. Water rinsing revealed several fingerprint impressions which were further enhanced by the application of lifting tape. These impressions were "burned onto" the surface and could not be removed by aggressive rubbing. Again it was observed that soot acted as a protective layer, providing it formed on the latent friction impression before the surface experienced flames. In some circumstances, the formation of the soot layer helped to bake the friction ridge impression onto the metal surface.

The use of a high-frequency sonic bath with a variety of solvents (water, gasoline, toluene, xylene, chloroform, ethanol, acetone, hexane, dilute sulfuric acid at pH 4, and two brands of detergent) was investigated for soot removal by the Israeli National Police [32]. For both friction ridge impressions previously immersed in gasoline and those left untreated, the use of a toluene-filled ultrasonic bath was observed to reveal more latent friction ridge impressions compared to the other solvents.

Wyllie reported immersing soot-covered latent friction ridge impressions on glass into a 2% sulfosalicylic acid solution to "fix" the latent ridges [33]. The glass was then immersed into a sonic bath containing 0.1 M sodium hydroxide solution to remove the soot layer from the "baked-on" fingerprints. The technique was tested using a mock living-room fire scene in which the neutral plane of the fire was allowed to reach floor level before the fire was extinguished. This allowed significant smoke to develop. A total of 18 sets of fingerprints were recovered from the glass bottles using this soot removal method, which were processed with either powder or with CA and Brilliant Yellow 40 (BY40).

Based on successful field experiences using sodium hydroxide wash solutions to remove soot layers without significantly damaging friction ridge impressions, Stow and McGurry published an extensive study of soot removal techniques, including sodium hydroxide wash solutions (1% and 2%), ultrasonic water bath, and vacuum suction [34]. Pure gasoline and a 1:1 mixture of gasoline and motor oil were used to contaminate fingermarks as well as being the flammable component within the glass incendiary devices. In the initial laboratory tests,

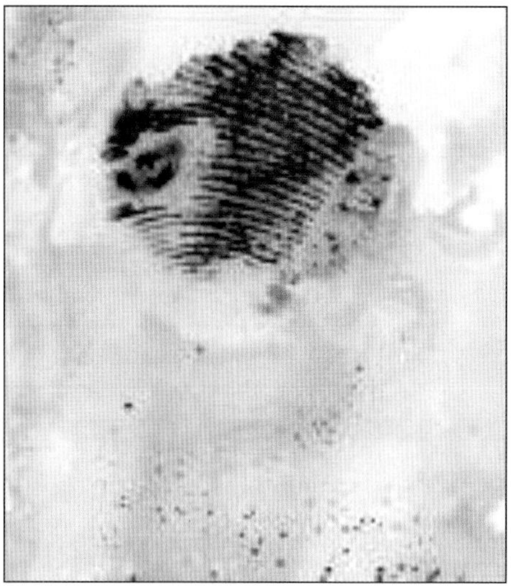

FIGURE 14.2
Soot removal using 2% NaOH solution from glass surfaces exposed to a petrol-fueled Molotov cocktail. Friction ridges were developed using CA/BY40. (Reprinted with permission from Stow, K.M. and McGurry, J., *Sci. Justice*, 46, 3, 2006. With permission from Elsevier.)

contaminated and natural fingermarks on glass substrates that had been subjected to controlled burns were examined using aluminum powder, SPR, and Sudan black. Similar tests involving burning of a cotton/polyester sheet to produce soot were performed to compare the soot removal methods. Washing the soot with 1% or 2% sodium hydroxide solutions allowed recovery of both contaminated and natural fingermarks. The 30 min water ultrasound bath failed to produce fingermarks with the gasoline/motor mix (1:1), but was successful for all other tests. In field tests, friction ridge recovery was attempted after the glass incendiary devices were detonated which resulted in much heavier contamination due to the accelerant. Under these conditions, the ultrasonic water bath, the vacuum, and soft brush soot removal techniques did not perform as well as the 1% and 2% sodium hydroxide wash solutions. The researchers observed that when applying the sodium hydroxide solutions care must be taken to avoid washing away ridge detail. Figure 14.2 shows a photograph of a partial friction ridge impression developed using CA/BY40 from glass, recovered from an ignited petrol-fueled Molotov cocktail, that had been cleaned using 2% NaOH.

Bleay and coworkers compared numerous soot removal processes including many that have already been described: washing under running water; ultrasonic water bath; washing with sodium hydroxide followed by lifting tape; light brushing; lifting tape; and pencil eraser [25,35]. They also tested commercial soot removal methods: Clean-Film™ (a natural latex stabilized with ammonia for cleaning masonry); cleaning sponge; Absorene® (a doughlike material consisting of flour, salt, water, and mineral salts and used for cleaning paper); and Mikrosil™ (a silicone rubber casting compound). A sequential soot removal process was recommended in which the least destructive methods must be tried initially, followed by those considered most likely to destroy both fingerprints and DNA. Recommended soot removal techniques for nonporous and porous surfaces are shown in Figures 14.3 and 14.4, respectively.

For all substrates, light brushing with a soft fingerprint brush to remove loose debris was recommended so that subsequent soot removal techniques would be more effective. If the nonporous surface is flat and the exhibit has a simple shape, then application of flexible lifting tape using a roller is found to work best (see Figure 14.3). If the nonporous

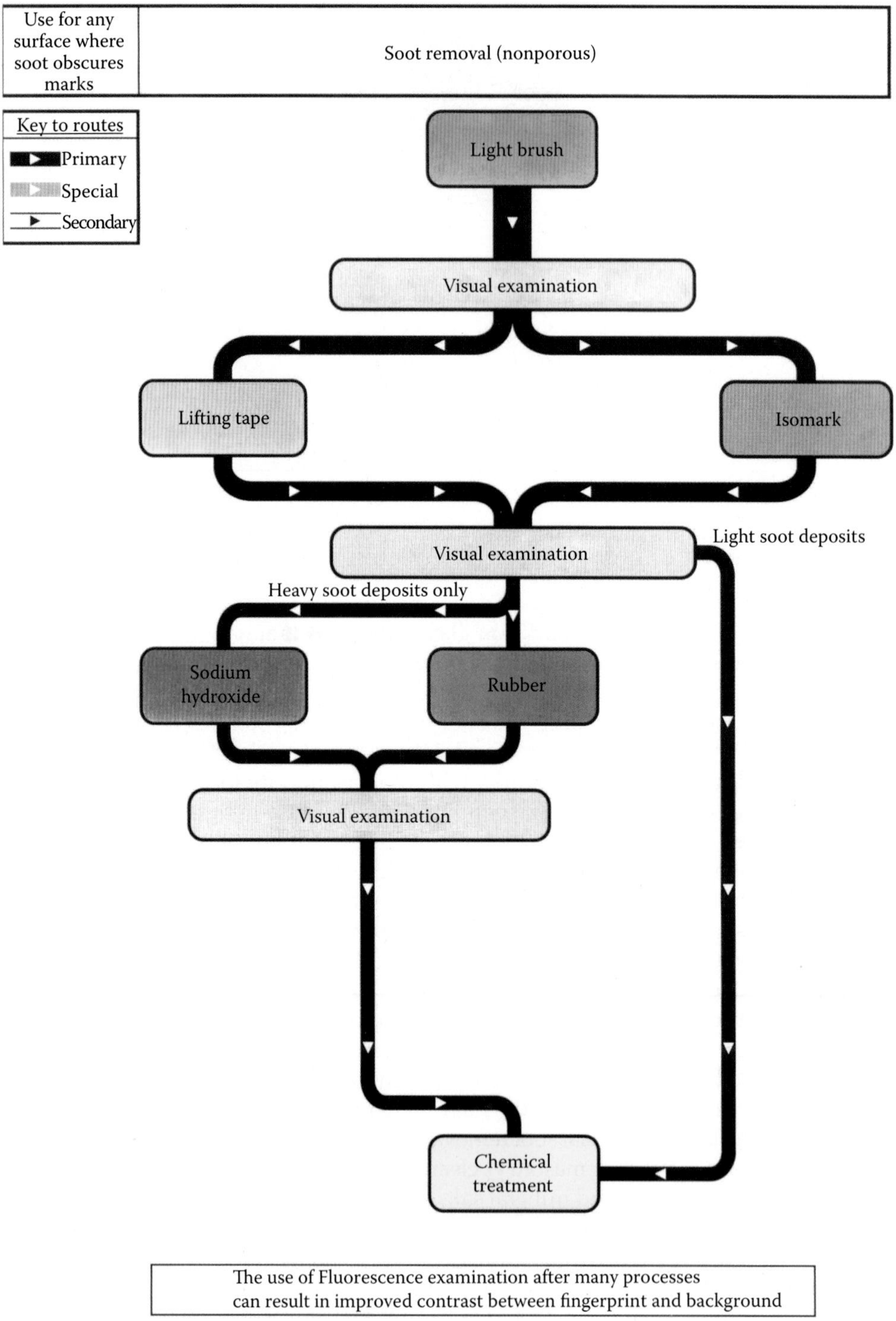

FIGURE 14.3
Flowchart for soot removal from nonporous surfaces. (Reproduced from Bleay, S.M. et al., *Fingerprint Development and Imaging Newsletter: Special Edition Arson*, Home Office, St. Albans, U.K., 2006. Crown Copyright. With permission of HOSDB.)

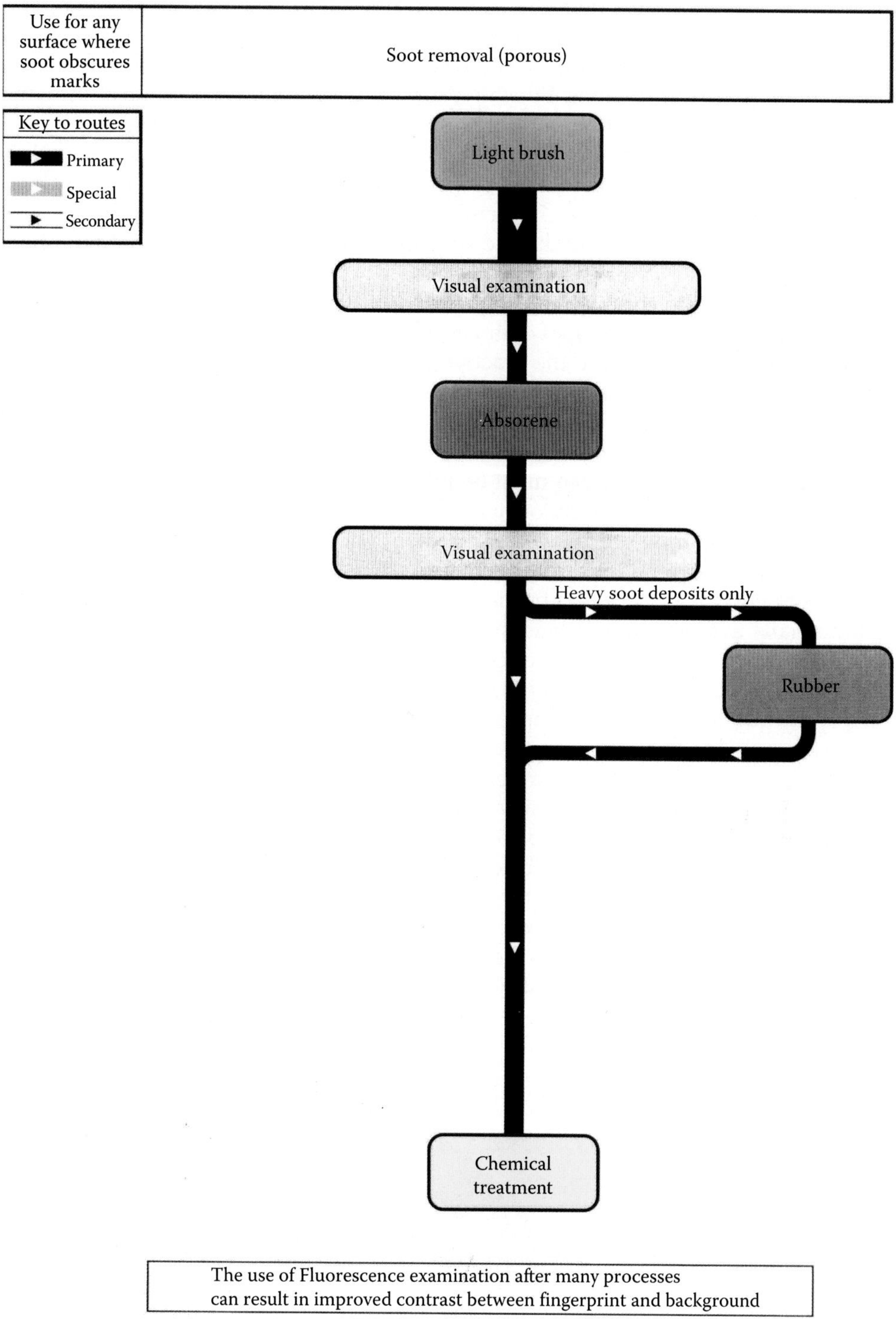

FIGURE 14.4
Flowchart for soot removal from porous surfaces. (Reproduced from Bleay, S.M. et al., *Fingerprint Development and Imaging Newsletter: Special Edition Arson*, Home Office, St. Albans, U.K., 2006. Crown Copyright. With permission of HOSDB.)

surface has a complex shape, then the use of casting materials, such as Mikrosil, is preferred. The soot is removed when the tape or the dried silicone casting material is peeled from the substrate. It is important to examine both the cleaned surface and the silicone cast for friction ridge impressions. Repeated applications of tape or silicone casting material were possible. After each attempt at soot removal, the exhibit should be examined for fingerprints and photographs should be taken. For some surfaces that have heavy deposits, a more aggressive process should be considered. Although sodium hydroxide is detrimental to DNA evidence, immersing or washing exhibits in sodium hydroxide was observed to loosen or make the soot more "transparent" for photography. An alternative method was to use a soft pencil rubber to rub away the heavy soot layer, but this technique is only recommended for "baked-on" marks. For porous surfaces, there were not as many options for soot removal since water-based methods are known to dissolve amino acids, which are the reactive components detected by the friction ridge detection techniques DFO, ninhydrin, and 1,2-indanedione (see Figure 14.4). Bleay et al. recommended Absorene, a commercial product for removing soot and dust from paper products. Figure 14.5 illustrates soot removal from a paper label on a glass bottle using Absorene. The doughlike material must be manipulated until it is soft and pliable, then it is wiped repeatedly in one direction across the soot-covered surface. Figure 14.6 shows soot-covered wallpaper before and after treatment with Absorene. In extreme situations, a soft pencil rubber can be used after Absorene, but care must be taken as this will be more damaging to the surface and friction ridges.

Commercially available liquid latex was successfully used by Larkin et al. to remove soot from large surfaces of a homicide scene to allow for fingerprint and bloodstain examination [36]. The liquid latex was applied without the addition of thickener or colorant using a spray gun attached to a compressor with an air regulator at 30 psi. Repeat applications were possible but care was taken to avoid "skinning over" which could result in latex being removed before the undercoat has dried. When the latex appears clear or slightly opaque, typically after 5–10 min, it can be peeled away from the surface without leaving a residue. Numerous fingerprints were developed by the action of the soot from the fire and were recovered from a variety of surfaces under forensic light source examination. This technique has been further tested by U.S. fire investigators and shown to be a very effective soot removal method for large surfaces such as drywall and glass [37]. Fingerprints developed as a result of the soot deposition but no further fingerprints were observed after soot removal and treatment with ninhydrin (drywall) or black fingerprint powder (glass).

(a) (b) (c)

FIGURE 14.5
Soot removal from a porous substrate using Absorene®: (a) before cleaning, (b) single pass with Absorene, and (c) after full cleaning. (Reproduced from Bleay, S.M. et al., *Fingerprint Development and Imaging Newsletter: Special Edition Arson*, Home Office, St. Albans, U.K., 2006. Crown Copyright. With permission of HOSDB.)

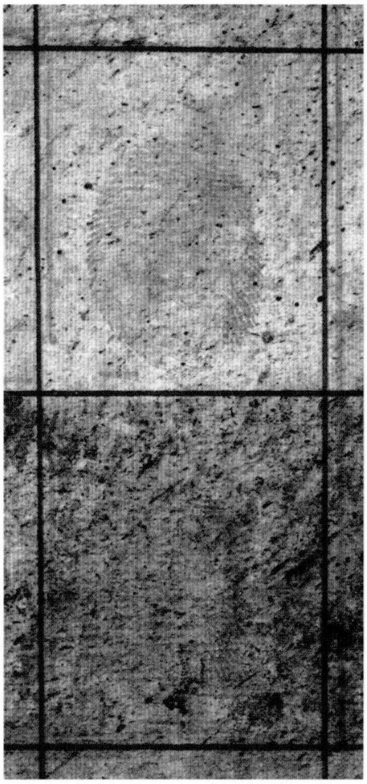

FIGURE 14.6
Soot removal from wallpaper: (a) friction ridge impression after cleaning with Absorene® and (b) as retrieved from the fire scene. (Reprinted from Bradshaw, G. et al., *J. Forensic Ident.*, 58, 54, 2008. With permission.)

A summary of the soot removal techniques tested on friction ridge impressions is shown in Table 14.2.

14.2.3 Effects of Flammable Liquids on Latent Friction Ridge Impressions

The presence of flammable liquids on the surface of the substrate has been reported to decrease the effectiveness of soot removal techniques. The recovery of soot-developed friction ridges by water rinsing described by Vaughan was compromised by liquids such as gasoline and kerosene [30]. As mentioned earlier, the hydrophobic nature of these flammable liquids repels water from the surface impeding soot removal.

In contrast, Tyranski and Petraco believed that the presence of gasoline in a plastic bowl, used to transport and distribute gasoline throughout an apartment that was subsequently set on fire, had created a plastic friction ridge impression in the rim of the plastic bowl [38]. The plastic bowl was slightly soluble in the gasoline and the action of carrying the gasoline-filled vessel had resulted in a molded impression being left in the plastic. The impression was retrieved using silicone casting materials to create a three-dimensional impression, which was transferred to white paper by covering the surface with black ink. The friction ridge impression was identified to a suspect in the arson case.

The belief that inflammable liquids such as gasoline, kerosene, diesel oil, and turpentine destroy latent friction ridge impressions by dissolving the fatty constituents was challenged in the mid-1990s by an Israeli National Police research team [39]. They briefly

TABLE 14.2
Methods of Soot Removal

Reference	Brushing	Water Wash	Lifting Tape	Sonification: Solvents	Sonification: Water	Sodium Hydroxide Wash	Others
Harper [28]	■	■					
McCloud [29]	■	■					
Vaughan [30]		■					
Thornton et al. [31]		■	■				
Spawn [27]		■					
Shelef et al. [32]				Toluene, xylene, chloroform, ethanol, acetone, hexane, dilute sulfuric acid (pH 4), detergents	■		
Wyllie [33]				Sodium hydroxide 0.1 M			
Stow [34]					■	Sodium hydroxide (1% and 2%) Sodium hydroxide (2%) soak	Vacuum suction
Bleay et al. [25]	■	■	■		■	Sodium hydroxide (0.5%)	Pencil eraser, clean film, cleaning sponge, Absorene, Mikrosil
Larkin et al. [36]							Liquid latex
Wright Clutter et al. [37]							Liquid latex

Note: The shaded regions indicate that this method was included in the study referenced.

immersed freshly deposited impressions into several fire accelerants and using SPR and CA, they detected the friction ridge impressions several days after being immersed. Although the team established that immersing friction ridge impressions in gasoline significantly impaired soot removal, they were still able to recover identifiable friction ridge impressions on 34% of the glass slides previously immersed in gasoline [32].

Research conducted by the Bundeskriminalamt (BKA) in Germany into soot removal techniques also considered the effects of three fuel mixes on friction ridge detection [40]. A male donor deposited latent friction ridge impressions on the glass neck and body (glass and paper label) of glass bottles that were subsequently filled with one of the following three accelerants: super unleaded gasoline, a gasoline/diesel (6:4) mix, or gasoline/engine oil (7:3) mix. The samples were un-ignited or ignited and thrown against a test wall. The ignited bottles were either allowed to burn out or extinguished. The soot removal methods involved the use of compressed air, brushing, and adhesive foil tape lifts. They observed that the fuel mixes left greasy residues on the glass which could be removed by the adhesive tape but that long-term immersion in fuel tended to destroy the friction ridge

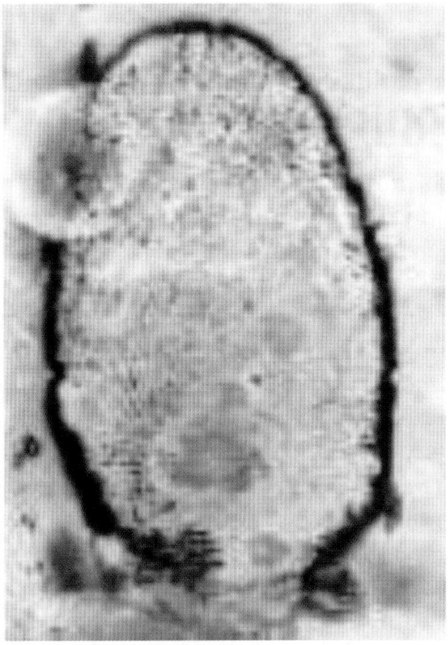

FIGURE 14.7
Effect of petrol/motor oil (1:1) fuel mix on friction ridges developed with CA/BY40 after soot removal using 2% NaOH. (Reprinted from Stow, K.M. and McGurry, J., *Sci. Justice*, 46, 3, 2006. With permission from Elsevier.)

impressions on glass. This is in contrast to the Israeli results, but may depend on the length of time the latent friction ridge is immersed in the accelerant.

Stow and McGurry prepared Molotov cocktails using clean glass bottles that had both good and poor quality friction ridge impressions placed on the glass and plastic label surfaces [34]. The bottles were carefully filled with gasoline or a gasoline/motor oil (1:1) mix and a cotton/polyester wick was inserted into the neck. Each Molotov cocktail was ignited, thrown against a pre-cleaned detonation area, and allowed to burn out naturally. Over 90% of the contaminated glass fragments from each bottle were recovered and subjected to different soot removal techniques before friction ridge recovery with CA/BY40. The researchers observed that it was particularly difficult to develop marks which had been exposed to the gasoline and motor oil mix due to the persistence of the oil on the surface. They observed the greatest success at recovery from these heavily contaminated friction ridge impressions when the glass fragments were soaked in 2% sodium hydroxide, sometimes for up to 30 min. Figure 14.7 shows a photograph of a friction ridge impression developed using CA/BY40 from glass, recovered from an ignited petrol/motor oil–fueled Molotov cocktail, that had been cleaned using 2% NaOH. The researchers were able to recover friction ridge impressions from all but one of the detonated bottles, including both the glass and plastic substrates.

14.2.4 Recovery of Latent Friction Ridge Impressions

Olsen noted the accidental development of latent fingerprints on magazine paper resulting from the heat of a fire and illustrated fingerprint impressions that were identified to the arsonist [7]. References to this method, dating back to the 1940s, were also discussed but the technique as an intentional fingerprint development method was dismissed despite the case work success. Some recent articles have revisited the application of heat as a latent fingerprint development technique for porous surfaces [41–43]. Brown et al. observed that rapid heating of latent fingerprint impressions on a variety of porous surfaces in air, over a temperature range of 220°C–300°C, resulted in fingerprints that initially could be seen to fluoresce under green illumination (505 nm) but with continual heating would eventually appear dark brown under white illumination until they lost contrast due to background charring [41]. The researchers noted that these observations held for both eccrine- and sebaceous-rich impressions. In contrast a study involving a variety of aged latent fingerprint impressions deposited onto white recycled paper, exposed to longer heating regimes at lower temperatures (160°C–180°C) compared to Brown et al., showed that only the eccrine component fluoresced [42]. In a further article, these researchers suggested sequential development protocols for exhibits recovered from arson crime scenes that involved visual examination under forensic light sources to detect the fluorescent product resulting from the heat of the fire [43]. The temperature range for this study was 50°C–200°C with exposure times ranging from 10 to 320 min and was restricted to white recycled paper. The results demonstrated that when no charring or color change was observed on the paper surface and if the substrate remained dry throughout, sequential treatment starting with fluorescent examination using green irradiation (473–548 nm) with a viewing filter of 549 nm should be followed by DFO, then ninhydrin, and finally physical developer. If charring were observed and if the substrate remained dry, then ninhydrin should be removed from the sequence as insufficient contrast would be obtained from the Ruhemann's purple product and the charred background surface. If the exhibit had been wet as a result of fire suppression, regardless of the presence or absence of charring, the fluorescent examination should be followed only by physical developer.

Many of the articles already discussed in this review included some comparison of the performance of friction ridge detection chemicals for substrates exposed to heat and soot [31–34,40].

In the early 1980s, it was suggested that simply breathing onto the arson exhibit could rehydrolyze dried friction ridges and improve the adhesion of fingerprint powders [31].

Shelef et al. examined the ability of several friction ridge detection techniques, including SPR, CA/BY40, silver-black powder, crystal violet, and forensic light source examination (λ_{Ex} = 450 nm, λ_{Em} = 550 nm), to detect freshly deposited impressions that had been briefly immersed in a variety of fire accelerants [39]. Some of the friction ridges following exposure to the accelerant were left for several days before being processed. The researchers were able to recover 80%–90% of the 5 day old impressions and 50%–60% of the 13 day old impressions using either SPR or CA. Although the CA process showed a slightly improved performance compared to SPR, the CA technique was abandoned as it was difficult to implement at the scene. Further work by the group resulted in an optimized SPR formulation for latent friction ridge impressions on glass surfaces that have been washed with accelerant fluids [44]. The new formulation (shown in Table 14.3 alongside the standard formula [13]) has been used effectively by the Israeli National Police since 1996.

TABLE 14.3

Differences in the Formulation for SPR Optimized for Friction Ridge Recovery from Arson Scenes

Chemical Component	Standard SPR Formula [13]	Optimized SPR Formula [39]
Molybdenum disulfide	50 g	200 g
Detergent	7.5 mL Aerosol OT	8–12 mL Tergitol
Water	3 L	1 L

Simulated Molotov cocktail exhibits prepared by filling glass bottles with different fuel mixes were thrown against a test wall and either were allowed to burn out, were extinguished, or were not ignited [40]. The glass surface was examined using the following sequence of techniques: visual examination under white light, forensic light source, and CA followed by vacuum metal deposition (VMD). It was reported that removal of the soot layer without impairing the friction ridge impressions was difficult. No data on the performance of specific detection techniques were provided, except that ninhydrin proved to be very effective at recovering latent friction ridge impressions on the paper labels.

Glass bottles, on which latent friction ridge impressions had been placed, were also tested by Wyllie using a mock living-room fire scene in which significant smoke was allowed to develop before the fire was extinguished [33]. The areas known to have friction ridge impressions were examined using white and ultraviolet (UV) radiation prior to soot removal with 2% sulfosalicylic acid and 0.1 M sodium hydroxide rinsing solutions. The glass was reexamined with white and UV radiation before half of the bottles were treated with aluminum powder and the remaining bottles were treated with CA/BY40. A total of 18 sets of fingerprints were recovered from the glass bottles using this soot removal method and either powder or CA/BY40. The author did not indicate how many latent sets were deposited, which makes interpretation of this work more difficult. There appeared to be no difference in performance between the powder and the CA method of fingerprint detection in these experiments.

In another experiment, aluminum powder, SPR, and Sudan black were used to detect both natural friction ridge impressions and those contaminated with gasoline and a gasoline/motor oil mix (1:1) that had been subjected to controlled burns and sodium hydroxide wash solutions for soot removal [34]. Both aluminum powder and SPR performed well, although adding motor oil to the incendiary mixture resulted in residue on the glass surface that prevented either development technique from being effective. In field tests, friction ridge recovery was attempted using CA/BY40 after the glass incendiary devices were detonated, which resulted in much heavier contamination of accelerant. Under these conditions, friction ridge recovery was compromised but still possible.

A recently published comprehensive study regarding the recovery of friction ridge impressions from arson was reported by Bleay and coworkers [25]. Rather than comparing existing methods of friction ridge recovery, the researchers first tried to establish the range of temperatures and exposure times for which latent friction ridges can survive. They developed a best practice for soot removal and subsequent friction ridge recovery on a variety of nonporous and porous substrates likely to be encountered at typical arson scenes. Extensive laboratory trials established that a wide variety of methods included in the HOSDB Manual of Fingerprint Development Techniques [13] will develop friction ridges that have been exposed to temperatures up to 200°C, although their effectiveness may be reduced especially with increased exposure time. All arson examinations should begin with a thorough visual inspection since the action of heat and soot can develop friction ridge impressions on exhibits. The development may be due to preferential soot deposition onto ridges, heat development of friction ridges on paper, and impressions being "baked" onto metal surfaces. Black or white powder suspensions proved to be the best treatment for nonporous surfaces exposed to temperatures up to 200°C. These methods were also effective for adhesive substrates. For nonporous substrates above 200°C, superglue fuming was most effective, providing the surface was dry and VMD was the technique of choice if the surface had been wet. For porous substrates, DFO was the best performing method, providing the surface had not been exposed to water. Physical developer was the reagent recommended for porous substrates that had been wet. Figure 14.8 illustrates friction ridge

(a) (b) (c)

FIGURE 14.8
Friction ridges developed on the inner tray of a match box using physical developer: (a) before the fire, (b) after the fire, and (c) physical developer friction ridges. (Reprinted from Deans, J., *Sci. Justice*, 46(3), 153, 2006. With permission from Elsevier.)

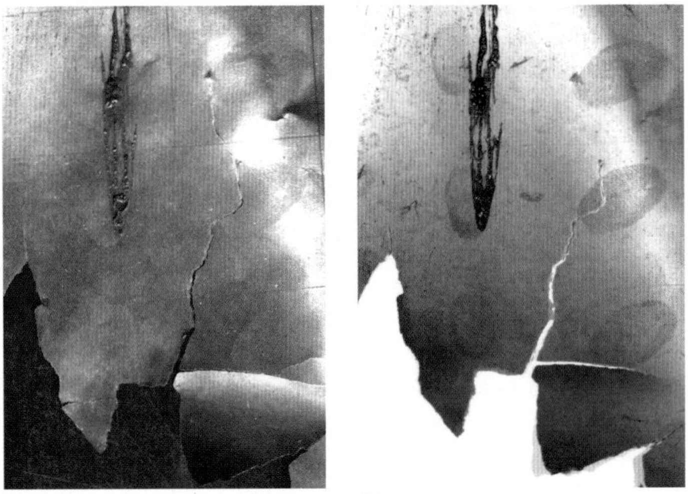

(a) (b)

FIGURE 14.9
Charred paper exhibit treated with physical developer and illuminated with Tungsten light: (a) imaged without IR filter and (b) imaged with RG850 filter. (Reproduced from Bleay, S.M. et al., *Fingerprint Development and Imaging Newsletter: Special Edition Arson*, Home Office, St. Albans, U.K., 2006. Crown Copyright. With permission of HOSDB.)

impressions developed by physical developer on the inner cardboard tray of a matchbox recovered from a controlled fire that had been suppressed using water. Near-infrared imaging using a near-infrared-sensitive camera and filter (cut-on wavelengths of 715nm or above) proved useful for charred paper. Figure 14.9 shows friction ridge impressions developed by physical developer on charred paper using near-infrared imaging.

The friction ridge detection techniques that have been tested on arson exhibits are summarized in Table 14.4.

14.2.5 Recovery of Friction Ridge Impressions in Blood

Blood can either be detected by a chemical reaction with the heme constituent in the hemoglobin protein or by the use of a protein stain. Examples of heme-specific reagents include

TABLE 14.4
Friction Ridge Detection Techniques Tested on Arson Exhibits[a]

	Nonporous Substrates						Porous Substrates			Blood				
Reference	**λ**	**SPR**	**CA**	**Powders**	**VMD**	**Others**	**DFO**	**Ninhydrin**	**PD**	**Acid Black 1**	**Acid Violet 17**	**Acid Yellow 7**	**SPR[b]**	**VMD[b]**
Shelef et al. [32,39,44]	450 nm	Optimized		Silver black		Crystal violet								
Limmer [40]	White, 450 nm					Compressed air								
Wyllie [33]	UV, white		BY40											
Stow et al. [34]			BY40	Aluminum		Sudan black				CA first				
Bleay et al. [25]	White, 450 nm, IR (λ_{Em} = 715 nm)		BY40			Black and white powder suspensions				Up to 200°C	Up to 200°C	Up to 200°C	Up to 900°C	Up to 900°C

[a] Dark gray shading indicates that friction ridges contaminated with fuels were included in the study.
[b] At these temperatures, it is no longer possible to state that the friction ridge impression was made in blood.

leucomalachite green [20] and luminol [45]. The catalytic action of the heme cleaves hydrogen peroxide into two hydroxyl ions that oxidize the blood reagents into their colored form. Examples of protein dyes include acid black 1 (also known as amido black) [18], acid violet 17 [46], and a dye that produces a fluorescent yellow product, acid yellow 7 [47].

The effect of heat and soot on the recovery of blood from arson scenes has not received much attention in the literature. Amido black was used successfully to recover friction ridges in blood following detonation and soot removal with 2% sodium hydroxide [34]. Two glass bottles with four blood depletion impressions were detonated with gasoline or gasoline/motor oil mix (1:1) and allowed to burn. The glass debris was treated with sodium hydroxide, followed by amido black. The gasoline/motor oil mix bottle was also subjected to a 2% 5-sulfosalicylic acid solution prior to soot removal. Good quality impressions were recovered in both instances.

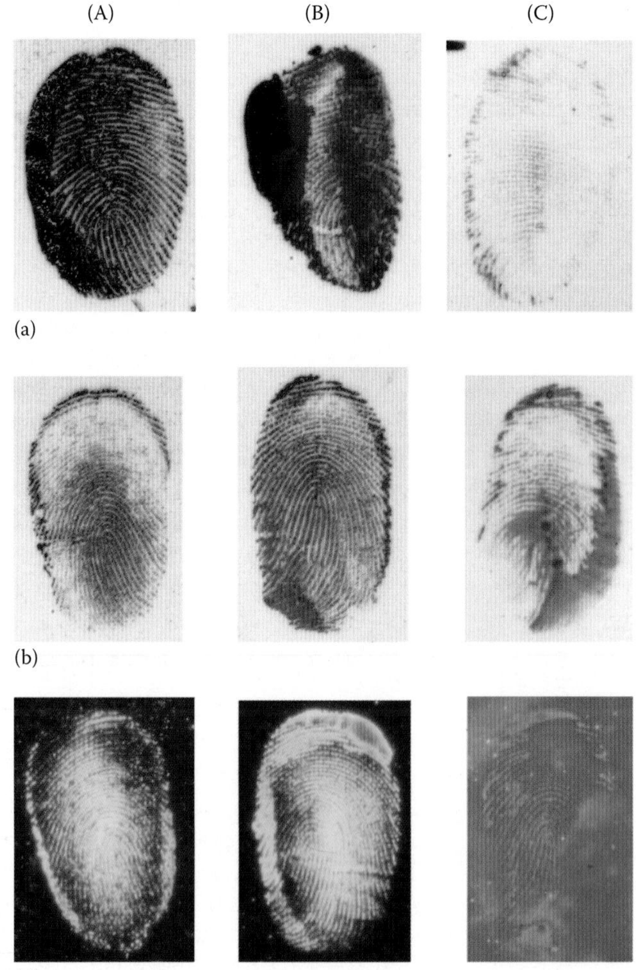

FIGURE 14.10
Effect of heat on blood friction ridge impressions; (a) acid black 1, (b) acid violet 17, and (c) acid yellow 7. Column A—control sample, column B—8 h at 100°C, and column C—8 h at 200°C. (Reproduced from Bleay, S.M. et al., *Fingerprint Development and Imaging Newsletter: Special Edition Arson*, Home Office, St. Albans, U.K., 2006. Crown Copyright. With permission of HOSDB.)

The characteristic chemiluminescent reaction between BlueStar®, a commercial formulation of luminol (5-amino-2,3-dihydro-1,4-phthalazinedione), and blood is frequently used to observe transfer patterns within a crime scene and, although the use of such chemicals for friction ridge recovery is unlikely, it is possible that palm prints or sole impressions may be observed. Collins described the use of BlueStar to detect footwear impressions from a homicide scene that had been burnt to conceal the crime [48]. The blue chemiluminescence that results when BlueStar reacts with blood was observed despite all surfaces being covered in a creosote-type soot produced by a mattress that had been burnt within the scene.

Bleay and coworkers described the range of temperatures and exposure times for which blood detection was possible and published best practices for recovery of friction ridge impressions in blood from arson environments [49]. The researchers observed that when blood was exposed to temperatures above 200°C, none of the known development processes for recovering fingerprints in blood remain effective. Figure 14.10 shows photographs of friction ridge impressions in blood that have been treated with either acid black 1, acid violet 17, or acid yellow 7, after being subjected to 100°C or 200°C for 8 h compared to a control set that were not subjected to heat. Heme-specific leucocrystal violet (LCV) failed at temperatures between 100°C and 150°C. The maximum temperature at which blood was still observed to react with protein dyes was shown to be surface-dependent and may be related to the reactive materials in the surface (e.g., copper and zinc in brass) catalyzing the breakdown of the blood proteins relative to inert surfaces (e.g., ceramic). Before burning off, blood deposits formed a protective layer on the surface creating a difference in the surface oxidation where ridge detail existed and the unprotected area. Processes sensitive to surface differences such as VMD were able to detect fingerprints in blood heated to 900°C, although it is no longer possible to state that the marks were originally blood. Black powder suspension was also observed to enhance contrast.

14.3 CBRNE

14.3.1 Introduction

The release into a crowded Tokyo subway car of a highly toxic nerve agent by the Japanese religious doomsday sect, The Aum Shinrikyo, in 1995 resulted in 12 deaths and about 5500 persons seeking medical treatment [50]. This attack illustrated the type of modern day terrorist threat that no government could ignore. Many government agencies created chemical, biological, radiological, nuclear, and explosive (CBRNE) response teams as part of a CBRNE event management strategy. These response teams are multidisciplinary, comprised of numerous individuals with varied and specialized knowledge who are responsible for mitigating and investigating such an event. Peace Officers such as explosive disposal specialists and forensic identification specialists would typically be members in a CBRNE response team, tasked with explosive mitigation and crime scene examination, respectively. Scientists and public health officials are also part of the CBRNE response team to provide the expertise and equipment required to identify chemical, biological, or radiological agents and to manage safely the ensuing public health crisis.

The distribution of letters containing viable *Bacillis anthracis* spores throughout the United States Postal Service in October 2001 demonstrated a lack of interoperability between the public health and the law enforcement sectors [51] and further heightened public concern toward chemical and biological terrorism. Consequently, CBRNE response teams are now better trained, frequently participating in multiagency exercises designed to practice the protocols for sampling and analysis of both the agent and the physical evidence that may help to identify the perpetrators.

Scientific staff within law enforcement agencies have worked hard to understand how the presence of chemical and biological warfare agents, as well as the decontamination agents used to neutralize them, will affect the performance of chemicals used to enhance friction ridge and footwear impression evidence; however, the topic is highly specialized and there are few published articles.

14.3.2 Chemical Contamination

Chemical warfare (CW) agents can be utilized by small groups of disaffected citizens who have no significant funding or expert knowledge. In today's Internet world, numerous websites provide detailed descriptions on how to manufacture CW agents. Several precursors have common industrial applications and could easily be obtained by determined groups. The utility of chemicals for terrorist activity by independent groups includes consideration of several criteria such as toxicity, quantities required, ease of acquisition, ease of transportation, and ease of dissemination. The chemical structures of selected CW agents are shown in Table 14.5 and include examples of the different categories of CW agents (i.e., irritants, blister, blood, choking, and nerve agents). This categorization of CW agents is based on the effect of the chemical on the human body. Nerve agents are particularly toxic and are further subdivided; the G-series was developed in the 1930s and because absorption occurs through the skin and respiratory tract (e.g., sarin) they are more lethal and faster acting than mustard gas; the V-series, developed in the 1950s, are even more toxic and persistent than the G-series (e.g., VX); and binary agents.

The reactive components within friction ridge residues commonly used to detect friction ridge impressions are amino acids, lipids, and in the case of blood-contaminated latent impressions, heme proteins. Table 14.5 shows the chemical structures of several CW agents. Their structures suggest that some CW agents would react with the functional groups in friction ridge residues, and latent friction ridges that have been exposed to such agents might show reduced detection rates. It is also possible that the CW agents might display reactivity toward the chemicals used for friction ridge detection. Several recent papers have described the effects of CW agents on friction ridge development [52,53], DNA recovery [54,55], and footwear impression enhancement [56].

In 2005, a study was published that described the effects of nine CW agents, including at least one example of each type of agent (e.g., blister, blood, choking, irritant, and nerve), on the detection of friction ridge impressions using common development methods. Due to the difficulty of removing contaminated evidence from CBRNE-contaminated crime scenes, the researchers considered only portable techniques that offered good performance on a wide variety of substrates [52]. The following friction ridge reagents were studied: DFO, ninhydrin, CA/BY40, chemist gray powder, magna black powder, gentian violet, chemist gray/Photo-Flo, amido black, Hungarian Red, and leucomalachite green. Friction ridge impressions on paper, plastic, glass, metal, wax cartons, electrical tape, masking tape, and blood impressions on linoleum were aged for 1, 7, and 14 days prior to exposure to CW

TABLE 14.5

Chemical Structures for Selected Chemical Warfare Agents

Chemical Warfare Agent	Chemical Structure	Agent Type
Hydrogen cyanide	$H - C \equiv N$	Blood
Phosgene	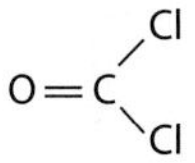	Choking
Chlorine	$Cl - Cl$	Choking
Dimethyl sulfate	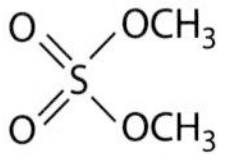	Blister
Sulfur mustard	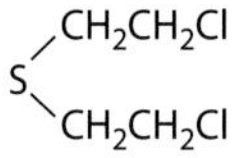	Blister
Lewisite I	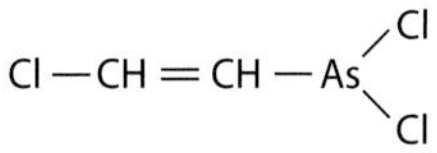	Blister
Sodium fluoroacetate	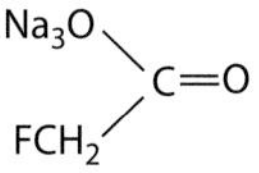	Irritant
Sarin	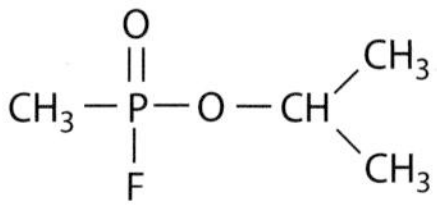	Nerve
Diazinon®	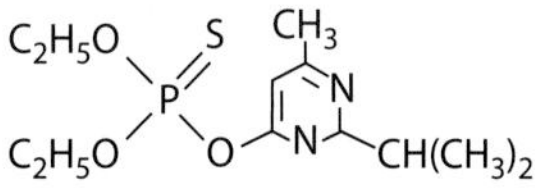	Irritant

Source: Wilkinson, D. et al., *J. Forensic Ident.*, 55(3), 326, 2005.

agents. Once exposed, the friction ridge impressions were detected immediately or after periods of 24 and 48h. Performance was compared to a control set of aged friction ridge impressions created under identical circumstances, but not exposed to CW agents. The control set was developed 24h after the experiment had begun. For CW agents that could be dispersed as either a liquid or vapor, both exposure methods were tested. As the time between exposure to CW agents and friction ridge development increased, fewer identifiable latent friction ridge impressions were recovered relative to the control set. When used for hydrogen cyanide–contaminated nonporous evidence, the fluorescent technique CA/BY40 developed more identifiable latent friction ridge impressions compared to powder. DFO also developed more friction ridge impressions when used for hydrogen cyanide–, sarin–, or sodium fluoroacetate–contaminated porous evidence compared to ninhydrin. Whether these results offer a significant advantage to warrant the use of fluorescent techniques for the examination of a chemically hazardous crime scene, given the fatigue factor of performing this type of examination as well as the logistics of using forensic light sources in a contaminated scene, must be decided by CBRNE-trained crime scene examiners. In general, all common friction ridge development techniques could be utilized with the exception of blood peroxidase techniques such as leucomalachite green.

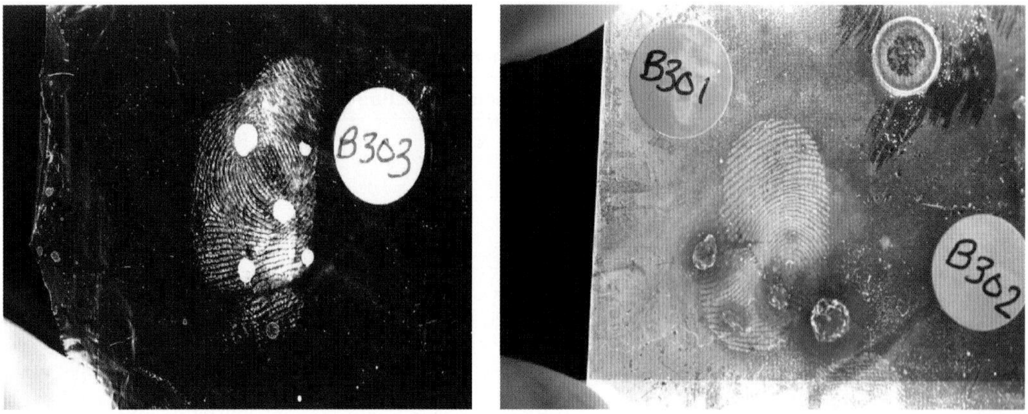

(a) (b)

FIGURE 14.11
Effects of liquid CW agents on friction ridge impressions: (a) masking of ridges on a metal substrate and (b) destruction of ridges on a glass substrate. (Reprinted from Wilkinson, D. et al., *J. Forensic Ident.*, 55(3), 326, 2005. With permission.)

Contamination of friction ridge impressions with liquid microdroplets was found to be highly destructive compared to vapor exposure. Figure 14.11 shows photographs of friction ridge impressions that have been exposed to sodium fluoroacetate. In Figure 14.11a, the sodium fluoroacetate reacts with the CA/BY40 development technique and obscures the friction ridges in the area where the CW residue is located. In another example, shown in Figure 14.11b, the friction ridge detail has been destroyed by contact with the sodium fluoroacetate. From the observed effects of liquid contamination, the recovery of friction ridge impressions from areas within the scene that indicate previous splashing or spilling of a liquid agent was determined to be unlikely.

Miskelly and coworkers further investigated the influence of chlorine and hydrogen chloride (HCl) gas on latent friction ridge impressions after their interest was piqued by the surprising ability of ninhydrin and DFO to detect amino acids following chlorine exposure [53]. HCl would most likely be encountered at clandestine methamphetamine laboratories, when it is generated during the salting out of the hydrochloride form of methamphetamine in the final stage of the drug synthesis. The researchers used single donors to place predominantly eccrine-rich or sebaceous/eccrine friction ridges onto glass and photocopy paper substrates for chlorine exposure and glass slides for HCl studies. The friction ridge impressions were exposed to HCl at varying concentrations (8%–19%) for 5 h and left overnight before being treated with magnetic bichromatic powder or CA/BY40. Powder dusting of sebum-rich friction ridge impressions was successful under all conditions, although increased background was observed as the HCl concentration rose above 12% due to condensation forming on the glass surface. CA fuming was not possible at HCl concentrations above 8%, which was confirmed by the lack of bands attributed to the ester group (1746, 1150, and 1110 cm^{-1}) and the nitrile group (2248 cm^{-1}) in the FTIR spectrum. The inhibition of CA by acidic conditions is well-established and the researchers were able to observe CA development by pretreatment of the friction ridges with alkaline vapors, most notably ethanolamine and triethylamine prior to CA fuming. Figure 14.12 shows photographs that illustrate the effect of extensive chlorine exposure on friction ridge impressions on glass substrates, including the redemptive effect of triethylamine vapors for successful friction ridge recovery. Soaking samples in 2% sodium hydroxide for 20 min

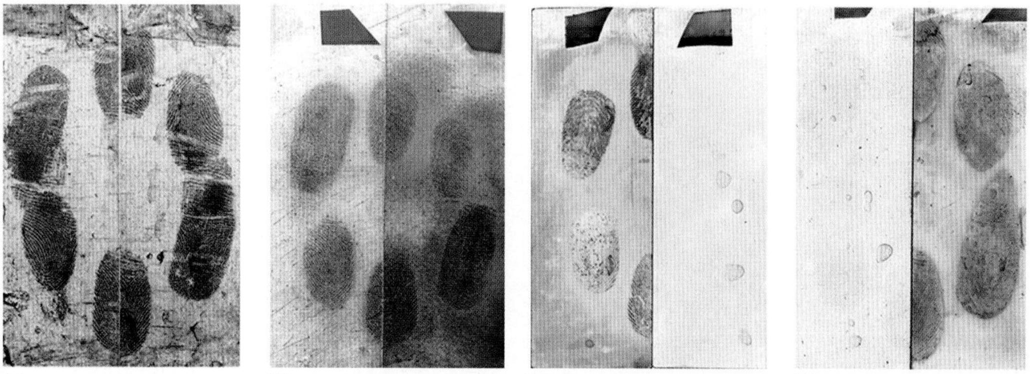

(a) (b) (c) (d)

FIGURE 14.12
Effect of chlorine on enhancement of fingerprints on glass. For images (a–c), the left-hand side is a control which has not been exposed to chlorine, while the right-hand side was in an atmosphere containing 4×10^{-4} mol/L chlorine for 20 min prior to enhancement: (a) SPR, (b) magnetic powder, (c) CA, and (d) both sides were exposed to 4×10^{-4} mol/L chlorine with the right-hand side being exposed to triethylamine vapors for 3 h before both sides were fumed with CA/BY40. (Reprinted from McDonald, D. et al., *Forensic Sci. Int.*, 179, 70, 2008. With permission from Elsevier.)

as recommended for soot removal from arson exhibits led to friction ridge enhancement using CA, but with significant background development.

Friction ridge impressions were exposed to extremely high levels of chlorine for 20 min (10,000 ppm v/v, well above the immediately dangerous to life or health (IDLH) level of 10 ppm). Latent prints on the nonporous substrates were developed using powder, SPR, or CA fuming. The SPR performed well under all conditions (ambient humidity, 60% and 100%); the powder showed increased background with increased humidity levels; and CA fuming failed to develop friction ridges after chlorine exposure. Ninhydrin developed friction ridges on paper under all conditions, although the reaction product appeared pink-red rather than dark purple as is usual for the reaction product Ruhemann's purple [2]. Figure 14.13 shows photographs of friction ridge impressions that illustrate the effect of extensive chlorine exposure compared to unexposed control impressions. Exposure to chlorine and HCl resulted in acidification of samples to such an extent, especially under conditions of high humidity, that enhancement of friction ridge impressions with CA was inhibited. Under these circumstances, pretreatment with a base prior to using these enhancement techniques or use of alternatives such as SPR was recommended.

The contrast in CA performance following chlorine exposure is likely attributable to the experimental conditions. In the Wilkinson et al. study, the exhibits were actively exposed to chlorine gas for 10 min in a low humidity environment, which was intended to mimic friction ridge impressions exposed on a device during release of chlorine gas. The Miskelly and coworkers' experiments involved exposure to chlorine at very high concentrations (10,000 ppm) for 20 min with the humidity level increasing from ambient to 100%.

14.3.3 Biological Contamination

Bioterrorism is the intentional use or threatened use of viruses, bacteria, fungi, or toxins from living organisms to produce death or disease in humans, animals, or plants, and fear within society [57]. Biological agents can be grouped into three risk categories, based on their potential for adverse public health impact. Category A or risk group 3 organisms can

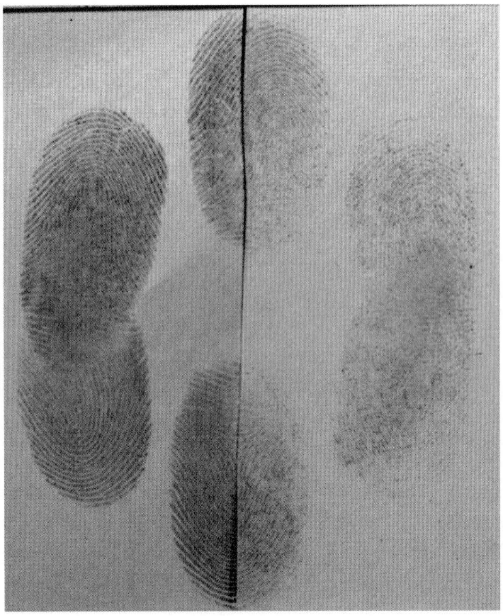

FIGURE 14.13
Effect of chlorine on enhancement of fingerprints on paper with ninhydrin. The right-hand sample was in an atmosphere containing 4×10^{-4} mol/L chlorine for 20 min prior to enhancement. The left-hand sample is the control. Both were dipped in ninhydrin and developed overnight at room temperature. (Reprinted from McDonald, D. et al., *Forensic Sci. Int.*, 179, 70, 2008. With permission from Elsevier.)

easily be disseminated or transmitted from person-to-person and require special action for public health preparedness. Category B or risk group 2 organisms are moderately easy to disseminate and require specific enhancements of diagnostic capacity and enhanced disease surveillance. Category C or risk group 1 organisms are not readily transmitted from person-to-person and pose the least impact on public health. Unlike chemical agents such as sarin, the nerve agent used to attack public spaces in Japan, biological agents show no immediate effect and in the case of *B. anthracis* (anthrax) will persist as an endospore resisting UV light, disinfectants, and desiccation, to cause disease upon eventual exposure.

Hoile et al. contaminated latent friction ridge impressions on porous and nonporous items with viable anthrax spores and then subjected these contaminated exhibits to formaldehyde gas, a common and effective decontamination procedure for biological safety cabinets [51]. The experimental design was intended to observe the effects of the decontamination process on the friction ridge development and the biological agent was only present to determine if the fumigation had successfully destroyed the spores. The friction ridges were deposited daily over a 7 day period prior to exposure, using three volunteers to create triplicates for each time period. Researchers inoculated the samples with a 10 μL aliquot of *Bacillus thuringiensis* var. *kurstaki* (BT) spores (140 cfu/μL) and allowed them to air-dry. The inoculated friction ridge samples were exposed to the standard formaldehyde formulation (30 mL 37% w/v formalin, 10 g $KMNO_4$) or to a revised formulation (15 mL 37% w/v formalin, 7.5 g $KMNO_4$) both at 65% relative humidity for 40 min. Both methods of decontamination were shown to be effective at destroying the spores in reasonable time frames. Latent friction ridge recovery involved DFO, ninhydrin, 1,2-indanedione and physical developer for paper surfaces, and CA/BY40, gray powder, and magna black powder for glass surfaces. The nonporous development techniques, fingerprint powders and CA/BY40, were largely successful (75% and 87.5%, respectively) and showed no differences in performance between the standard and revised formaldehyde methods. In contrast, all three amino acid reagents, DFO, ninhydrin, and 1,2-indanedione, failed to recover any friction ridge impressions with the standard method and showed compromised detection rates relative to the controls for the revised formaldehyde method (33%, 66%, and 8%, respectively). Physical developer showed either minimal or no effect to the decontamination methods. The researchers observed the effects of formaldehyde gas on serial dilutions of four amino acids. They concluded that this biocidal agent, known to inactivate microorganisms by reacting with carboxyl, amino, hydroxyl, and sulfhydryl groups of proteins as well as amino groups of nucleic bases, likely acts as an alkylating agent on the amino group of the amino acids within fingerprint residues. Once this happens, the amino group is effectively blocked from reacting with DFO, ninhydrin, and 1,2-indanedione.

Given the challenges of working with risk group 3 agents, microbiologists often use low-risk organisms as simulants for more pathogenic risk group 3 organisms [58] in order to gain familiarity with a technique and to resolve potential problems. This approach was used by Wilkinson et al. in a 2009 publication that describes the effects of aerosolized bacteria on the recovery of friction ridge evidence [59]. Latent and blood-contaminated friction ridge impressions on a variety of surfaces were exposed to aerosolized *Bacillus globigii* (spore), *Bacillus atrophaeus* (veg), and *Pantoea agglomerans* (veg) using an aerosol test chamber. Sampling methods established that the bacterial agents were in the agent-containing particles per liter of air (ACPLA) range of 10^3, which is the predicted concentration required to kill 50% of exposed people (LD_{50}) and is representative of levels anticipated in a biological attack. A selection of standard chemical techniques was used to detect the contaminated latent and blood friction ridge impressions: paper (DFO and ninhydrin); linoleum (amido black, Hungarian Red, and leucomalachite green); electrical and duct tape (powder suspension); plastic and wax cardboard (CA/BY40); glass and metal (powder). One and seven day old friction ridge impressions were exposed to the bacteria for 24 and 48 h periods. The researchers observed no effect of bacterial exposure to the amino acids within a fingerprint residue on porous exhibits (100% recovery for both DFO and ninhydrin compared to the control set). The nonporous enhancement techniques (powders and CA) were mainly unaffected by exposure to bacterial agents (100% and 97%, respectively). Adhesive substrates, as is typical due to their more challenging surface, showed varied results. However, for the six tests involving adhesive substrates, the only below average result was recorded for duct tape exposed to *P. agglomerans* (veg). The blood detection chemicals also performed well with Hungarian Red showing the highest recovery rate (97%) and leucomalachite green the lowest (86%), relative to the control samples. There appeared to be no effect as a result of increased exposure time to bacteria on performance of friction ridge detection techniques.

14.3.4 Radiological

Colella et al. studied the impact of ionizing radiation on the detection of latent fingerprints on a range of substrates including glass, hard and soft plastic, aluminum, and paper under conditions designed to mimic the illegal possession and trafficking of radioactive materials [60]. Fingerprint samples were exposed to high doses of gamma irradiation ranging from 1 to 1000 kGy before and after treatment with a variety of substrate-specific development techniques. Nonporous samples were processed with one of the following methods: CA/rhodamine 6G, CA/BY40, and black fingerprint powder. The paper substrates were processed with one of the following methods: ninhydrin, DFO, 1,2-indanedione, and PD. The impact of ionizing radiation appears to be substrate-specific with little to no effect on fingerprint detection being observed for glass or aluminum for any of the methods utilized.

A significant color change was noted for glass. In contrast, polyethylene, polystyrene, and paper showed considerable effects of ionizing radiation at high doses (>100 kGy) which was mainly attributed to radiolytic-induced changes within the fingermark as well as degradation of the substrate. Several previous studies into the effects of ionizing radiation on physical evidence focused on the use of electron beam irradiation as a decontamination technique for biological materials [61–63]. Consequently, the doses of ionizing radiation were similar to those used to sanitize mail and these works are discussed further in Section 14.3.5.

14.3.5 Decontamination

Decontamination is the destruction and removal of chemical and/or biological agents. For chemical agents, decontamination may be accomplished by physical removal and/or chemical neutralization (conversion of the toxic chemical into a harmless product through chemical reaction). Physical removal can be achieved by flushing the surface with water or aqueous solutions, scrubbing, or scraping bulk agent from the surface. In addition to mechanically removing the CW agent, application of large quantities of water or aqueous solutions may slowly hydrolyze the agent. However, the limited solubility of CW agents in water will limit the hydrolysis reaction in the absence of hypochlorite solutions. The most important category of chemical decontamination is oxidative chlorination (i.e., hypochlorite solutions, which act universally against organophosphorus and mustard agents). Chemical hydrolysis is most effectively achieved under alkaline conditions when the hydroxide ion initiates nucleophilic attack of the phosphorus atoms in VX and G-agents. The reaction rate is dependent on the chemical structure and environmental conditions such as pH, temperature, presence of catalytic agents and solvents.

For biological agents, decontamination includes both sterilization (the complete destruction of all microorganisms, including bacterial spores) and disinfection (the destruction and removal of specific types of microorganisms). Methods of sterilization include application of heat, chemicals, irradiation, high pressure, or filtration. Disinfection can be defined as cleaning an object of some or all of the pathogenic organisms which may cause infection. Ideally, CBRNE-trained crime scene examiners would be able to examine exhibits after decontamination, so it is important for them to understand how the presence of decontamination agents used to neutralize biological and chemical agents affects the performance of friction ridge reagents. In an ideal world, CBRNE-trained crime scene examiners would be able to remove exhibits from the scene after decontamination and safely examine them back at the forensic identification laboratory using the full complement of detection techniques available.

Electron beam irradiation was selected by the U.S. Postal Service to sanitize mail in response to the anthrax letters in part because of its well-studied use within the food decontamination industry. Several papers have therefore investigated the effect of electron beam irradiation on physical evidence such as fingerprints [61], DNA [62], and writing inks [63].

In a comprehensive study, Ramotowski and Regen examined 320 latent friction ridge impressions deposited by five donors onto two types of porous substrate (Xerox and white, blue lined paper) and three types of nonporous substrates (PVC, Ziploc bags, and black polyethylene garbage bag material) [61]. The deposited friction ridge impressions were aged for at least 7 days before being cut in two; one half was used as a control and the other was irradiated. Porous exhibits were treated with ninhydrin, DFO, physical developer, iodine, black powder, magnetic black powder, and silver nitrate. Nonporous samples were treated with CA, CA/RAM, CA/BY40, MMD, VMD, gentian violet, Sudan black, nonmagnetic and magnetic black powder. Although the exact conditions and irradiation doses were not specified due to operational security, the doses were sufficient to produce a range

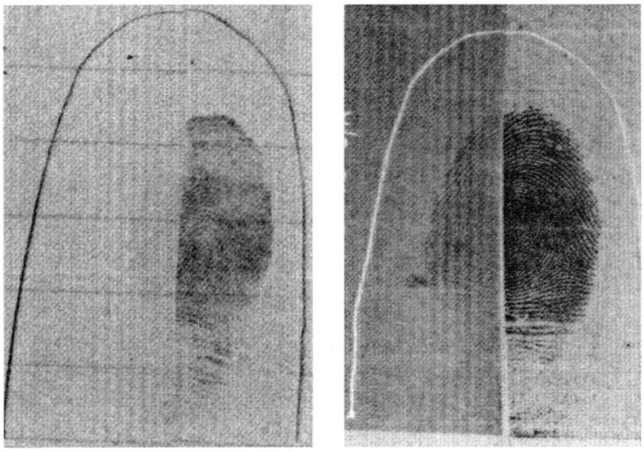
(a) (b)

FIGURE 14.14
(a) The difference in initial DFO color development between the irradiated samples (left) and the control sample (right) and (b) an example of the difference in DFO fluorescence intensity between the irradiated (left) and control (right) samples. (Reprinted from Regen, E.M. and Ramotowski, R., *J. Forensic Sci.*, 50(2), 298, 2005. With permission.)

of effects on the substrates, including discoloration of porous substrates to a faint yellow compared to the controls and wrinkling of the polyethylene garbage bags. For porous substrates, these changes were accompanied by noticeable decreases in the intensity of both the colored Ruhemann's purple product observed with ninhydrin and the fluorescent product for DFO. Figure 14.14 shows photographs that illustrate the effect of irradiation on DFO-developed friction ridge impressions. Iodine and both nonmagnetic and magnetic black powder did not produce good results and silver nitrate failed to produce any friction ridge detail on the irradiated samples. In contrast, physical developer showed improved development for the irradiated samples. The friction ridge impressions shown in Figure 14.15 have been developed with physical developer and illustrate improved development following irradiation. Nonporous samples exhibited significant physical changes as a result of irradiation; PVC was severely discolored and PE became physically wrinkled. For the CA- and dye-stained samples, the intensity and quality of ridge detail was compromised by irradiation. Gentian violet-treated irradiated samples did not develop ridge detail. Sudan black failed to develop on both the irradiated and control samples and neither powder showed good results. In contrast, MMD developed slightly better friction ridges on the irradiated samples compared to the controls. Figure 14.16 shows two friction ridge impressions processed with multimetal deposition. It has been suggested that the effects of electron beam irradiation to both the substrate and the performance of latent friction ridge detection techniques occur due to the complex chemical reactions resulting from the large amount of energy generated by electron beam irradiation. These reactions may produce ions, activated atoms, and molecules that promote processes such as depolymerization, chain scission, deamination, and decarboxylation. Such reactions could explain the reduced performance of latent friction ridge techniques such as ninhydrin, DFO, and CA. The good performance of the two colloidal techniques, PD and MMD, may result from the stability of the ionic salts within the latent print residue.

A further study on ionizing radiation as a biological decontaminant (doses in the 200–40,000 Gy range) demonstrated that latent fingerprints on both nonporous (glass and

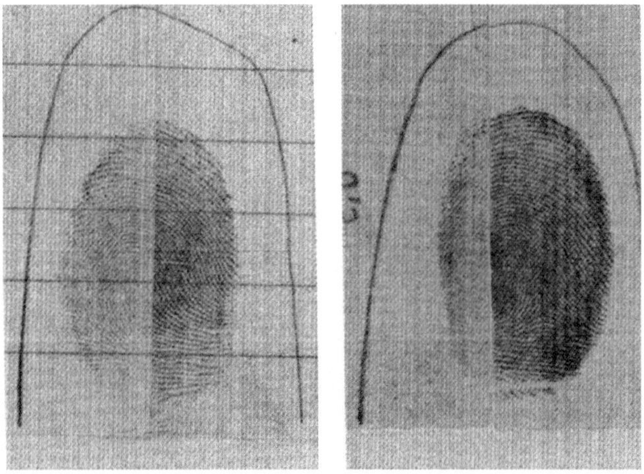

(a) (b)

FIGURE 14.15
(a) The difference between the intensity of PD development between the irradiated (right) and control (left) samples and (b) a similar example in which there is also a noticeable difference between the irradiated (right) and control (left) samples. (Reprinted from Regen, E.M. and Ramotowski, R., *J. Forensic Sci.*, 50(2), 298, 2005. With permission.)

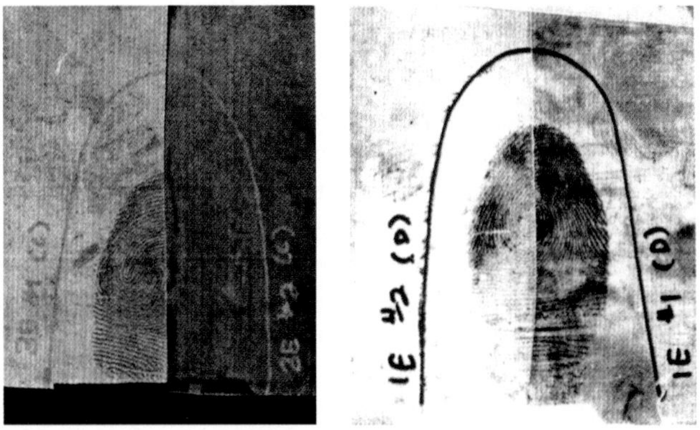

(a) (b)

FIGURE 14.16
(a) The difference between irradiated (right) and control (left) samples on polyethylene that have been processed with the VMD technique and (b) the difference in intensity between the irradiated (left) and control (right) samples on PVC. (Reprinted from Regen, E.M. and Ramotowski, R., *J. Forensic Sci.*, 50(2), 298, 2005. With permission.)

polycarbonate samples treated with either CA or black fingerprint powder) and porous (paper and cardboard samples treated with either ninhydrin, DFO, 1,2-indanedione, or physical developer) samples showed no detrimental effects [64]. This research established that biological decontamination of viable *Bacillus* spores at a gamma dose of >3000 Gy was effective on the chosen substrates with limited adverse affects on the recovery and attribution of human DNA.

Formaldehyde gas is an effective biocidal agent that is commonly used to decontaminate biological safety cabinets, but it proved to be extremely destructive to friction ridge impressions on porous substrates [51]. Both the standard method (30 mL 37% w/v formalin, 10 g $KMNO_4$) as well as a less destructive modified method (15 mL 37% w/v formalin, 7.5 g $KMNO_4$) had a significant negative impact on the recovery of the amino acid residues

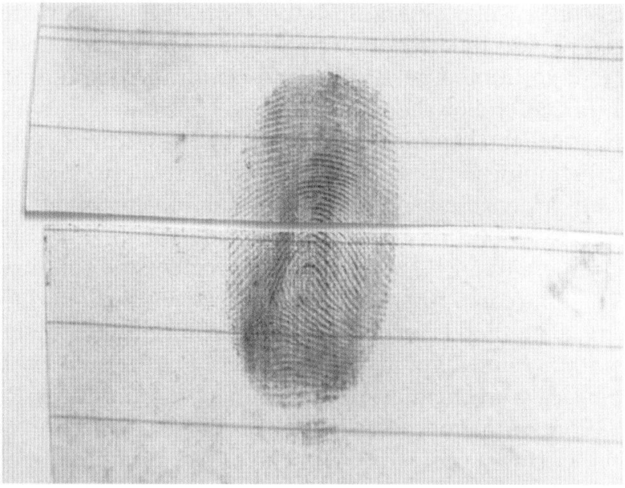

FIGURE 14.17
Development of a friction ridge impression using physical developer after decontamination with standard formaldehyde formulation (top half only). (Reprinted from Hoile, R. et al., *J. Forensic Sci.*, 52(5), 1097, 2007. With permission.)

in latent fingerprints. Figure 14.17 shows the effect of standard formaldehyde treatment on a friction ridge impression developed by physical developer. Physical developer was unaffected by pretreatment with formaldehyde.

Mixed-threat decontamination procedures have also proven to be destructive to fingerprint [52] and footwear [56] impression evidence. Canadian Aqueous System Chemical/Biological Agent Decontamination (CASCAD™) is a bleach-based decontamination agent containing buffers and surfactants. MDF LSA-100 is a similar product manufactured in the United States. The purpose of such decontamination agents is to inactivate the CW and/or BW agent. A consideration when decontaminating following fingerprint development is the possibility that the CW agent may become trapped within the matrix of the fingerprint development medium and could off-gas at a later time.

Wilkinson et al. applied CASCAD to friction ridge impressions on a variety of substrates contaminated with different CW agents both before and after development with appropriate detection techniques [52]. Of the 31 fingerprints passively decontaminated with CASCAD (i.e., no scrubbing) following treatment with a variety of development techniques, 25 survived. The majority of the destroyed fingerprints had been treated with powder before decontamination. Decontamination of exhibits prior to fingerprint development significantly reduced the number of identifiable fingerprints recovered. Tests using control samples that were not exposed to any CW agents before decontamination with CASCAD showed that the number of friction ridge impressions recovered was significantly reduced. The same observation is true when considering the sample set exposed to sarin before decontamination and subsequent fingerprint development. Although not tested on friction ridge impression evidence, MDF LSA-100 was tested along with CASCAD on oil- and salt-contaminated footwear impression evidence. When applied prior to footwear development, both decontamination agents destroyed the latent impressions. When applied after treatment with the appropriate development method (iodine and silver nitrate, respectively), both decontamination methods destroyed the oil impressions, but the salt impressions survived the MDF LSA-100 exposure. This suggests that the MDF LSA-100 might be less aggressive to latent friction ridge impressions compared to CASCAD, and at least the salts within the residue may survive passive exposure.

For radiological agents, such as cesium 137, strontium 90, and americium 241, Colella and coworkers optimized two decontamination procedures for use on paper; one physical and one chemical [65]. Due to limited availability of strontium 90 and americium 241, strontium 85 and uranium 238 (yellowcake [U_3O_8]) were considered as suitable surrogates as they have similar physical and chemical properties. The physical decontamination method involved the physical scraping of the surface with a hard, straight edge (e.g., scalpel or knife) followed by the use of a pencil eraser. This process is recommended when the contaminating radioisotope is in a solid form (i.e., yellowcake). The chemical technique involved 5 min of sonification in either a 2% aqueous or 2% cyclohexane solution of decontaminating agent DEZ-1. When the contaminating radioisotope is in the liquid form (i.e., cesium or strontium), the chemical method is recommended. It is important to note that the researchers did not observe 100% removal of any contaminating radioisotope from the paper surface for either the physical and chemical decontamination procedures. Rather they suggest that both of these decontamination procedures be consider primarily as reducing the levels of contamination. Further consideration of the radiological clearance standards of the appropriate authorities was recommended to determine whether the post-decontamination evidence could be classified as "safe." For the Australian Nuclear Science and Technology Organisation's (ANSTO) radiological clearance standards, the decontaminated samples were classified as having safe levels of radiation. With respect to the affect of these two decontamination procedures on the detection of latent fingerprints, no technique was successful following decontamination. The fingerprint detection methods studied included DFO, ninhydrin, 1,2-indanedione/zinc chloride, and physical developer. DFO and physical developer were able to detect fingerprints when the chemical decontamination procedure followed the fingermark development. The physical decontamination procedure had no impact when applied after any fingerprint development techniques tested in the study.

14.3.6 Explosives

Despite the high number of terrorist events involving explosive materials, few articles have been published that examine the effects of explosion and explosive residues on the recovery of latent friction ridge impressions.

In 2006, Lanagan deposited sebaceous-rich friction ridge impressions on metal and plastic surfaces within a vehicle as well as on metal exhibits placed on the front and rear seats [66]. All latent friction ridge impressions were clearly visible using oblique lighting. A galvanized pipe bomb containing 0.25 lb of Semtex (an ammonium nitrate–based dynamite) was positioned under the dashboard in the area of the foot pedals. A second device containing 2.5 lb of composition B (mixture of cyclotrimethylenetrinitramine [RDX] and trinitrotoluene [TNT]) was positioned between the front seats. The vehicle was subjected to both detonations prior to evidence recovery. All recovered items were examined for friction ridges using a Reflected UltraViolet Imaging System (RUVIS), followed by CA fuming and powders. The momentary exposure of the latent impressions to the heat and flames of the explosions was sufficient to destroy most of the friction ridge detail and the remaining fragments were unsuitable for comparison. More recently, Gardner described the detection of a latent fingerprint from a detonated improvised explosive device (IED) using RUVIS [67]. The fingerprint, located on a plastic bottle used to hold a mixture of nitromethane and gasoline, was identified to the individual who had constructed the IED. The individual had not been instructed to deposit fingerprints onto the device during construction, so the detection implied that under these conditions latent fingerprints could survive the explosion.

A controlled experiment examined how the distance of the latent impressions from the blast affected friction ridge recovery using CA [68]. Aluminum and steel plates containing latent friction ridge impressions were located 0.25–1 m from a 0.7 kg charge of composition B and between 0.125 and 0.5 m from a 0.09 kg explosive charge of composition B. Four friction ridge impressions were deposited on each side of the polished metal plates which were positioned so that one side was oriented away from the explosive charge. Following each detonation, the plates were recovered and processed with CA and Ardrox 970 P25 before being examined using UV radiation. The researchers observed that damage was greater on the aluminum plates compared to the steel plates, even though they were the same distance from the blast. They postulated that the lighter-weight Al plates were carried by the blast, resulting in an increased exposure to the shockwave that caused greater damage from the excessive blast pressure and heat. Post-blast, the steel plates were observed in their original location. Aluminum is less stiff than steel and will more easily deform under such loading. The researchers determined that there was an approximate correlation between the survivability of latent fingerprints and the distance that the friction ridge impression was located from the blast. They were able to recover latent friction ridge impressions using CA and Ardrox on both sides of the plates when they were located 0.75 m from the 0.7 kg charge and 0.5 m from the 0.09 kg charge. Friction ridge impressions were recovered from all plates, even those severely deformed by the blast. Figure 14.18 shows an aluminum plate after exposure to a 0.7 kg explosive charge located 0.25 m away and the friction ridge impression that was developed on the surface by CA/Ardrox.

The effect of different types of explosive materials on the recovery of fingerprint evidence from post-blast debris is described by Sanders [69]. Blood-contaminated, plastic, and latent fingerprints, comprised of a loaded mixture of eccrine and sebaceous residues, were purposefully placed onto the IED during construction. After detonation and evidence collection, the debris was processed with CA and one of the following methods: magna powder, black fingerprint powder, Wetwop™, LCV, or amido black. Five identifiable fingerprints were developed out of the 42 fingerprint controls that had not been subjected to detonation. From the IED debris, five fingerprints were recovered using CA followed by black fingerprint powder (two latent impressions), magna powder (one latent impression), Wetwop (one latent impression), and LCV (one latent impression). No fingerprints

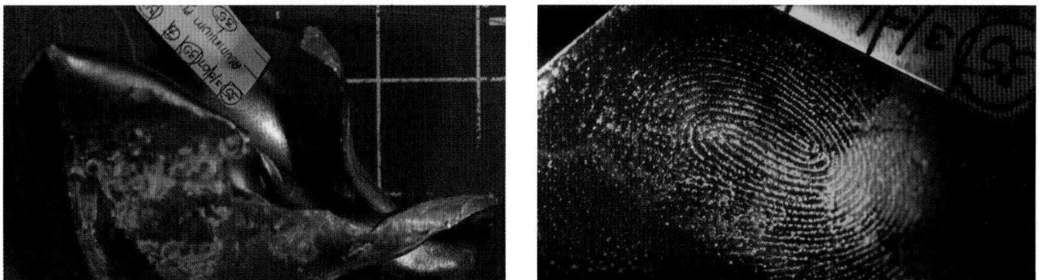

(a) (b)

FIGURE 14.18
An aluminum plate after exposure to blast located 0.25 m away from 0.7 kg explosive charge (a) and friction ridge impression developed on the plate using CA/Ardrox photographed under UV light (b). (Reprinted from Kuznetsov, V.A. et al., *Proceedings 1st International Conference on Forensic Applications and Techniques in Telecommunications, Information and Multimedia*, January 21–23, Adelaide, Australia, Vol. 25, p. 4, 2008. With permission.)

were recovered from devices built with smokeless powder which was attributed to the increased thermal effect of this material compared to the commercial explosives (C-4 plastic explosive, Kinepak, and TNT boosters) utilized in the IEDs where latent fingerprints were detected.

14.4 Conclusions

Based on a review of the combined published work for friction ridge impression recovery from crime scenes compromised by arson, explosives, radioisotopes, chemicals, biologically hazardous materials, and decontamination agents, a few general trends can be observed.

First, CA fuming is the only friction ridge detection method that has been tested in some manner on nonporous exhibits exposed to all of the above hazardous environments. More importantly, researchers were able to successfully recover latent friction ridge impressions for these challenging environments under certain conditions using CA fuming and dye staining. Successful detection of latent fingerprints by CA following exposure to ionizing radiation (cobalt 60 gamma irradiator) was shown to be substrate-dependent. Glass and metal could be effectively treated with CA even after exposure to high dose rates of above 1000 kGy whereas plastics such as polyethylene and polystyrene showed reduced recovery rates above 500 kGy. For environments known to inhibit CA polymerization, such as the formation of acidic conditions from Cl and HCl exposure, CA was still successfully used following ethanolamine pretreatment. Fingerprint powders and powder suspensions were less widely studied but proved to be effective techniques.

For porous substrates, traditional methods such as DFO and ninhydrin produced excellent results, but it was the performance of PD that was consistently noted to recover latent friction ridge impressions under a wide range of extreme conditions, including improved performance following electron beam irradiation. Attempts to develop latent fingermarks on paper exposed to ionizing radiation at doses above 500 kGy failed for all fingerprint detection methods due to the significant degradation in the mechanical properties of the substrate.

Although limited, the research to date supports the inclusion of CBRNE-trained crime scene examiners as members of CBRNE response teams since several studies established that treatment of exhibits for friction ridge impressions was more successful before decontamination of the substrate is attempted.

Author

Della Wilkinson received a PhD in chemistry from Cambridge University and has been providing scientific and technical support to the forensic identification community since the early 1990s. She has been the recipient of several research grants, and her diverse interests have ranged from recovering fingerprints from human skin to finding physical evidence in the aftermath of a chemical or biological attack. She has published many scientific papers in national and international peer-reviewed journals, has delivered numerous conference papers, and has had two patents. She is an adjunct professor with the University of Toronto's Forensic Science Program, a member of SWGFAST, and serves as the current editor of *Identification Canada*.

References

1. Ramotowski RS. (2001) Composition of latent print residue. In: Lee, HC, Gaensslen, RE, Eds. *Advances in Fingerprint Technology*, 2nd edn. CRC Press, Boca Raton, FL.
2. Hewlett DF, Sears VG, Suzuki S. (1997) Replacements for CFC113 in the ninhydrin process: Part 2. *J Forensic Ident* 47(3):300–306.
3. Hardwick S, Kent T, Sears V, Winfield P. (1993) Improvements to the formulation of DFO and the effects of heat on the reaction with latent fingerprints. *Fingerprint Whorld* 19(73):3–10.
4. Hauze DB, Petrovskaia OG, Taylor B, Joullié MM, Ramotowski RS, Cantu AA. (1998) 1,2-Indanediones: New reagents for visualizing the amino acid components of latent prints. *J Forensic Sci* 43(4):744–748.
5. Cassidy M. (1979) Technique for brushing up latents. *RCMP Gazette* 41(4):20–21.
6. Lee HC, Gaensslen RE. (2001) Methods of latent print development. In: Lee, HC, Gaensslen, RE, Eds. *Advances in Fingerprint Technology*, 2nd edn. CRC Press, Boca Raton, FL.
7. Olsen RD. (1978) *Scott's Fingerprint Mechanics*. Charles C Thomas, Springfield, IL.
8. Frank A, Almog J. (1993) Modified SPR for latent fingerprint development in wet, dark objects. *J Forensic Ident* 43(3):240–245.
9. Olenik JH. (1983) Super Glue®: A rapid method. *Ident News* 33(1):9–10.
10. Kerr FM, Barron IW, Haque F, Westland AD. (1983) Organic based fluorescent powders for latent fingerprint detection on smooth surfaces, part II. *Can Soc Forensic Sci J* 16(1):39–44.
11. Batey GW, Copeland J, Donnelly DL, Hill CL, Laturnus PL, McDiarmid CH, Miller KJ, Misner AH, Tario A, Yamashita AB. (1998) Metal deposition for latent print development. *J Forensic Ident* 48(2):165–176.
12. Schnetz B, Margot P. (2001) Technical note: Latent fingermarks, colloidal gold and multimetal deposition (MMD). Optimization of the method. *Forensic Sci Int* 118(1):21–28.
13. Kent T. (2001) *Manual of Fingerprint Development Techniques*, 2nd edn. Home Office, Sandridge, U.K.
14. Beaudoin A. (2004) New technique for revealing latent fingerprints on wet, porous surfaces: Oil Red O. *J Forensic Ident* 54(4):413–427.
15. Mashiko K, Miyamoto T. (1998) Latent fingerprint processing by the ruthenium tetraoxide method. *J Forensic Ident* 48(3):279–290.
16. Margot P, Lennard C. (1994) *Fingerprint Detection Techniques*, 6th revised edn. Université de Lausanne, Lausanne, Switzerland.
17. Kobus HJ, Stoilovic M, Warrener RN. (1983) A simple luminescent post-ninhydrin treatment for the improved visualization of fingerprints on documents in cases where ninhydrin alone gives poor results. *Forensic Sci Int* 22:161–171.
18. Sears VG, Prizeman TM. (2000) Enhancement of fingerprints in blood—Part 1: Optimization of amido black. *J Forensic Ident* 50(5):470–484.
19. Theeuwen ABE, van Barneveld S, Drok JW, Keereweer I, Limborgh JCM, Naber WM, Velders T. (1998) Enhancement of footwear impressions in blood. *Forensic Sci Int* 95(2):133–151.
20. Spalding RP. (2005) Presumptive testing and species determination of blood and bloodstains. In: James, SH, Kish, PE, Sutton, TP, Eds. *Principles of Bloodstain Pattern Analysis Theory and Practice*. Taylor & Francis, Boca Raton, FL.
21. Lytle LT, Hedgecock DG. (1978) Chemiluminescence in the visualization of forensic bloodstains. *J Forensic Sci* 23:550–555.

22. Rau RM, Boyd DG, Samuels JE. (2000) Fire and arson scene evidence: A guide for public safety personnel. National Institute of Justice report. https://www.ncjrc.gov/pdffiles1/nij/181584.pdf (accessed on April 24, 2012).
23. Sandercock PML. (2008) Fire investigation and ignitable liquid residue analysis—A review: 2001–2007. *Forensic Sci Int* 176(2–3):93–110.
24. Deans J. (2006) Recovery of fingerprints from fire scenes and associated evidence. *Sci Justice* 46(3):153–168.
25. Bradshaw G, Bleay S, Deans J, NicDaeid N. (2008) Recovery of fingerprints from arson scenes: Part 1—Latent fingerprints. *J Forensic Ident* 58(1):54–82.
26. Tontarski KL, Hoskins KA, Watkins TG, Brun-Conti L, Michaud AL. (2009) Chemical enhancement techniques of bloodstain patterns and DNA recovery after fire exposure. *J Forensic Sci* 54(1):37–48.
27. Spawn MA. (1994) Effects of fire in fingerprint evidence. *Fingerprint Whorld* 20(76):45–46.
28. Harper WW. (1938) Latent fingerprints at high temperatures. *J Crim Law Criminol* 29(4):580–583.
29. McCloud VD. (1978) Processing glass bottles for latent prints in arson cases (Molotov cocktails). *Ident News* 28(11):3–4.
30. Vaughan MA. (1979) How to lift fingerprints from soot covered articles. *J Fire Eng* 3:14.
31. Thornton JE, Emmons BW. (1982) Development of latent prints in arson cases. *Ident News* 32(3):5–6.
32. Shelef R, Levy A, Rhima I, Tsaroom S, Elkayam R. (1996) Recovery of latent fingerprints from soot-covered incendiarized glass surfaces. *J Forensic Ident* 46(5):565–569.
33. Wyllie J. (2006) The recovery of fingerprints from arson scenes. *Fingerprint Whorld* 32(124):86–92.
34. Stow KM, McGurry J. (2006) The recovery of finger marks from soot-covered glass fire debris. *Sci Justice* 46(1):3–14.
35. Bleay SM, Bradshaw G, Moore JE. (2006) *Fingerprint Development and Imaging Newsletter: Special Edition Arson*. Home Office, St. Albans, U.K.
36. Larkin TPB, Marsh NP, Larrigan PM. (2008) Using liquid latex to remove soot to facilitate fingerprint and bloodstain examinations: A case study. *J Forensic Ident* 58(5):540–550.
37. Wright Clutter S, Bailey R, Everly JC, Mercer K. (2009) The use of liquid latex for soot removal from fire scenes and attempted fingerprint development with ninhydrin. *J Forensic Sci* 54(6):1332–1335.
38. Tyranski W, Petraco N. (1981) An interesting arson case involving a plastic fingerprint. *Ident News* 31(6):9.
39. Shelef R, Levy A, Rhima I, Tsaroom S, Elkayam R. (1996) Development of latent fingerprints from unignited incendiary bottles. *J Forensic Ident* 46(5):556–560.
40. Limmer S. (2001) Personal Communication, Wiesbaden, Germany.
41. Brown AG, Sommerville D, Reedy BJ, Shinnon RG, Tahtouh M. (2008) Revisiting the thermal development of latent fingerprints on porous surfaces: New aspects and refinements. *J Forensic Sci* 54(1):114–121.
42. Dominick AJ, Nic Daéid N, Bleay SM, Sears V. (2009) The recoverability of fingerprints on paper exposed to elevated temperatures—Part 2: Natural fluorescence. *J Forensic Ident* 59(3):340–355.
43. Dominick AJ, Nic Daéid N, Bleay SM, Sears V. (2009) The recoverability of fingerprints on paper exposed to elevated temperatures—Part 1: Comparison of enhancement techniques. *J Forensic Ident* 59(3):325–339.
44. Shelef R, Rhima I, Elkayam R. (1996) Optimization of small particle reagent for the development of latent fingerprints from glass surfaces washed in accelerant fluid. *J Forensic Ident* 46(5):561–564.
45. Laux DL. (2005) The detection of blood using luminol. In: James, SH, Kish, PE, Sutton, TP, Eds. *Principles of Bloodstain Pattern Analysis Theory and Practice*. Taylor & Francis, Boca Raton, FL.
46. Sears VG, Butcher CPG, Prizeman TM. (2001) Enhancement of fingerprints in blood—Part 2: Protein dyes. *J Forensic Ident* 51(1):28–38.
47. Sears VG, Butcher CPG, Fitzgerald LA. (2005) Enhancement of fingerprints in blood part 3: Reactive techniques, acid yellow 7, and process techniques. *J Forensic Ident* 55(6):741–763.

48. Collins S. (2007) BlueStar© application at a homicide scene following arson. *Ident Canada* 29(4):137–141.
49. Moore J, Bleay S, Deans J, NicDaeid N. (2008) Recovery of fingerprints from arson scenes: Part 2—Fingerprints in blood. *J Forensic Ident* 58(1):83–108.
50. Ohbu S, Yamashina A. (1997) Sarin poisoning on Tokyo subway. *South Med J* 90:587–593.
51. Hoile R, Walsh SJ, Roux C. (2007) Bioterrorism: Processing contaminated evidence, the effects of formaldehyde gas on the recovery of latent fingermarks. *J Forensic Sci* 52(5):1097–1102.
52. Wilkinson D, Hancock J, Lecavalier P, McDiarmid C. (2005) The recovery of fingerprint evidence from crime scenes contaminated with chemical warfare agents. *J Forensic Ident* 55(3):326–361.
53. McDonald D, Pope H, Miskelly GM. (2008) The effect of chlorine and hydrogen chloride on latent fingermark evidence. *Forensic Sci Int* 179:70–77.
54. Wilkinson DA, McDiarmid C, Larocque S, Lecavalier P, Handcock J, Cairns S, Sweet D et al. (2006) Recovery of physical evidence from crime scenes contaminated with chemical and biological warfare agents. *Proceedings of American Academy of Forensic Sciences 58th Annual Meeting*, February 20–25, Seattle, WA, pp. 122–123.
55. Wilkinson DA, Sweet D, Fairley D. (2007) Recovery of DNA from exhibits contaminated with chemical warfare agents: A preliminary study of the effect of decontamination agents and chemical warfare agents on DNA. *Can Soc Forensic Sci J* 40(1):15–22.
56. Wilkinson D, Larocque S, Lecavalier P, Cairns S. (2005) The recovery of footwear evidence from crime scenes contaminated with chemical warfare agents. *Ident* Canada 28(4):4–19.
57. What is Bioterrorism? www.bt.cdc.gov/bioterrorism/overview.asp (Centers for Disease Control and Prevention, accessed February 12, 2007).
58. Hilsen RE, Kournikakis B, Ford B. (2005) Inactivation of microorganisms by gamma irradiation. Technical Memorandum DRDC Suffield TM 2005-236.
59. Wilkinson D, Larocque S, Astle C, Vogrinetz J. (2009) The effects of aerosolized bacteria on fingerprint impression evidence. *J Forensic Ident* 59(1):65–79.
60. Colella M, Parkinson A, Evans T, Lennard C, Roux C. (2009) The recovery of latent fingermarks from evidence exposed to ionizing radiation. *J Forensic Sci* 54(3):583–590.
61. Ramotowski R, Regen EM. (2005) The effect of electron beam irradiation on forensic evidence. 1. Latent print recovery on porous and non-porous surfaces. *J Forensic Sci* 50(2):298–306.
62. Withrow AG, Sikorsky J, Downs U, Fenger T. (2003) Extraction and analysis of human nuclear and mitochondrial DNA from electron beam irradiated envelopes. *J Forensic Sci* 48(60):1302–1308.
63. Ramotowski R, Regen EM. (2007) The effect of electron beam irradiation on forensic evidence. 2. Analysis of writing inks on porous surfaces. *J Forensic Sci* 52(3):604–609.
64. Hoile R, Banos C, Colella M, Walsh SJ, Roux C. (2010) Gamma irradiation as a biological decontaminant and its effect on common fingermark detection techniques and DNA profiling. *J Forensic Sci* 55(1):171–177.
65. Parkinson A, Colella M, Evans T. (2010) The development and evaluation of radiological decontamination procedures for documents, document inks, and latent fingermarks on porous surfaces. *J Forensic Sci* 55(3):728–734.
66. Lanagan SR. (2006) Explosive effects on latent fingerprint evidence. *J Forensic Ident* 56(1):18–23.
67. Gardner E. (2010) Using a reflected ultraviolet imaging system to recover friction ridge impressions on post-blast material. *J Forensic Ident* 60(1):104–118.
68. Kuznetsov VA, Sunde J, Thomas M. (2008) Explosive blast effects on latent fingerprints. *Proceedings of the 1st International Conference on Forensic Applications and Techniques in Telecommunications, Information and Multimedia*, January 21–23, Adelaide, South Australia, Australia, Vol. 25, p. 4.
69. Sanders N. (2011) Recovery of fingerprint evidence from post-blast device materials. *J Forensic Ident* 61(3):281–295.

15

Statistics and Probabilities as a Means to Support Fingerprint Examination

Cedric Neumann

CONTENTS

15.1 Introduction

Finger impressions dating from the Neolithic period have been observed at various archaeological sites. While these impressions may have been left by accident, intentionally deposited ones have been observed on artifacts from ancient Babylon, China, and India. More specifically, the presence of fingerprints on clay seals dating from this period seems to indicate that they were already used as a sign of personal identity. In more recent history, several European scientists noted the presence of friction ridges on fingers, but did not investigate further their practical use (other than their primary utility of grasping and handling objects) [1–3].

In 1858, Sir William Herschel, a British administrator for the East India Company, started to use hand impressions as a fraud deterrent: natives were asked to stamp their hands on contracts. At first, Herschel's sole intention was to inspire enough apprehension among his contractors to ensure that they would honor their commitments; Herschel then realized the potential of finger impressions for the verification of the identity of known individuals and proposed a classification system. During his subsequent appointment as a magistrate and collector in Calcutta, Herschel implemented the systematic recording and use of finger impressions for all administrative tasks in his district [1,2,4].

Finger impressions appear to have been more specifically used in connection with the detection and identification of criminals since the nineteenth century and the original work of Paul-Jean Coulier [5], Dr. Henry Faulds [6], and Sir Francis Galton [7]. Their pioneering work led to the replacement of anthropometry (or *bertillonage*) as a means of personal identification of repeat offenders. Several systems for the classification of all 10-finger impressions from individuals were proposed to this extent. Among those, the systems proposed by Vucetich and Sir Edward Henry were widely implemented around the world. The *Henry classification system* was implemented in England in 1901 and was eventually adopted in Europe and most Anglo-Saxon countries, while the system proposed by Vucetich became prevalent in Spanish-speaking countries [8,9].

In parallel to the development of systems for the verification of individuals' identity, law enforcement agencies began to recover and use finger impressions inadvertently left at crime scenes in order to confront suspects and detect offenders. The first identification of an offender in a criminal case has been credited to Juan Vucetich and Eduardo Alvarez in 1892 in Argentina in what is known as the *Rojas murder case* [1,2]. The first convictions of offenders based on the comparison of finger impressions recovered from crime scenes with control impressions taken from known individuals were for murder in India in 1898, burglary in England in 1902, and murder in France during the same year. One of the first records of the use of fingerprints in the United States relates to a case in New Jersey in 1905 [1,2].

The original intent behind the use of finger impressions in modern history was the verification of the identity of individuals for administrative or legal purposes. This verification process still represents the vast majority of the fingerprint work performed today.* In this process, rolled impressions from all 10 fingers of an individual of interest (also known as a *10 print card*) are recorded in controlled conditions and compared to 10 print cards

* The U.S. Federal Bureau of Investigation (FBI) is responsible for the maintenance and handling of one of the largest fingerprints collection in the world. This collection includes the records of approximately 70 million individuals, or 700,000,000 fingers. In 2010, the Criminal Justice Information Services (CJIS) division of the FBI received a daily average of 168,000 requests for the verification of individuals' alleged identities through the comparison of the individuals' 10-finger impressions against their 10-finger reference collection. In contrast, approximately 430 friction ridge impressions recovered on crime scenes were processed by the CJIS division during the same period [10].

previously collected under controlled conditions from individuals associated with known identity. Examiners verifying the identity of individuals, based on impressions from their 10 fingers, take advantage of the presence of a significant quantity of good quality information. The quality and quantity of information that can be observed on these 10 print cards proves to be highly discriminating and allows for reaching undisputed conclusions of identity [11].

By contrast, examiners attempting to identify offenders from impressions inadvertently left at crime scenes are usually provided with partial, potentially distorted and degraded impressions, which must then be compared to 10 print cards from known individuals. These examiners have presumably much less information available to perform their task and to infer the identity of offenders from crime scene impressions. In addition, this information is most often of poor quality (see Figure 15.1) [12,13].

The question of the inference of the identity of the source of friction ridge impressions recovered from crime scenes is the main topic of this chapter. More specifically, this chapter does not expand on the practical aspects of the examination process that can be found elsewhere [14] but rather focuses on the various decisions taken during the examination process by examiners once all the relevant friction ridge information

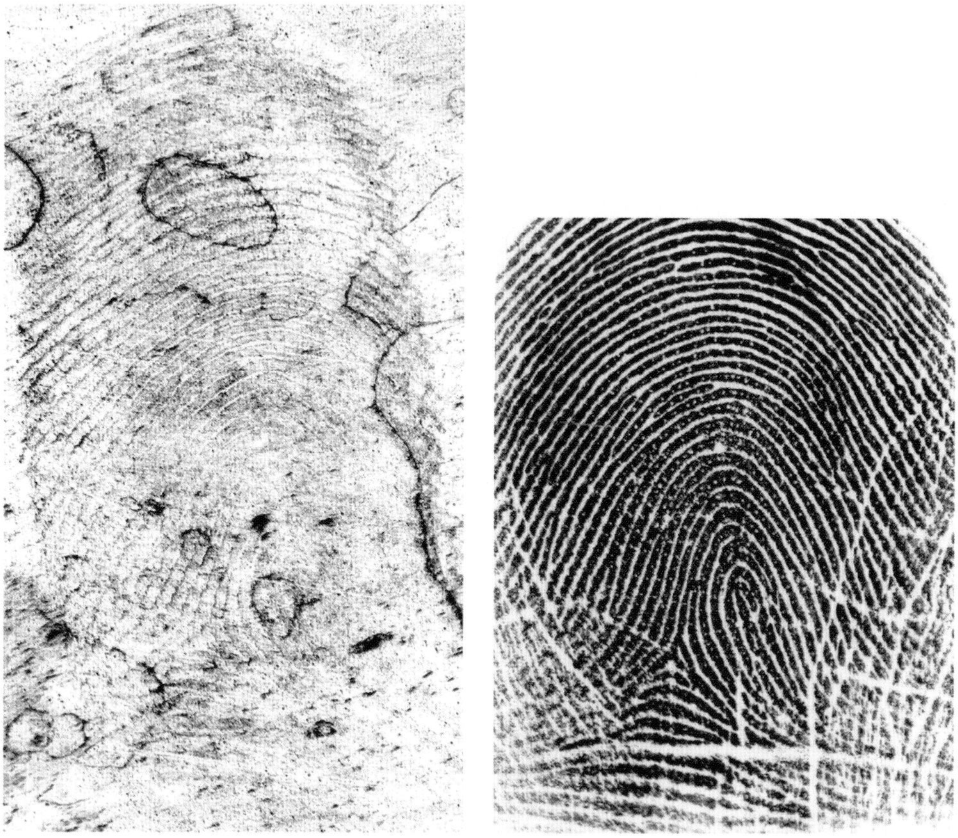

(a) (b)

FIGURE 15.1
Comparison between an example of a friction ridge impression of crime scene quality (a) and a friction ridge impression taken under controlled conditions from the same individual (b). The crime scene quality impression has only part of the information present on the control impression and may display distortion or various effects from the technique used to develop it, the surface on which it was deposited, etc.

has been gathered or compared. All forensic examinations are by nature aimed at investigating and minimizing the uncertainty linked to traces resulting from wrongdoings. Conclusions resulting from forensic examinations are therefore probabilistic in nature and are supported by a logical inference process [15,16], which should be relying on statistical data. Several authors [17–22] and a recent report published by the U.S. National Academy of Science [12] have argued that the scientific foundations of the examination of fingerprints need strengthening by the collection and use of statistical data within a probabilistic framework.

This chapter explores (a) the logical process behind the decisions of identity of source currently made by examiners based on the comparison of crime scene and control impressions, (b) the challenges raised against this decision-making process by legal and scientific scholars, and (c) some future perspectives involving the use of statistics to support the inference process and address some of the criticisms.

15.2 Current Inference Process

This chapter is concerned with the inference of the identity of the source of impressions left by the distal segment of the finger at crime scenes.* This inference results from the careful comparison of features observed on the friction ridge impressions recovered from crime scenes (known as *latent print* in the United States, and *fingermark* or *mark* in the United Kingdom and Europe) with features observed on control impressions from fingers of individuals with a known identity (known as *exemplar prints* in the United States, and *fingerprints* or *prints* in the United Kingdom and Europe).† Figure 15.1 illustrates the differences between marks and prints. The following sections briefly reviews the main aspects of the fingerprint examination process and some key elements that are currently used by examiners to form their conclusions.

15.2.1 Fingerprint Examination Process

When performing their tasks, examiners observe and compare various types of features. These features are commonly classified in three categories [2]. The Scientific Working Group for Friction Ridge Analysis, Standards and Technology (SWGFAST) describes these categories as follows [21]:

1. *First level of detail*: General pattern of the ridge flow and other general morphological information
2. *Second level of detail*: Individual ridge paths and associated events, such as the starting, bifurcation, and ending positions of the ridges. These events are frequently referred to as *Galton points* or *minutiae*. The second level of detail includes the consideration of the morphological relationships between series of minutiae
3. *Third level of detail*: Dimensional attributes and shape of the ridge structure, such as ridge width, edge shapes, and positions and shapes of sweat pores

* Various regions of the body are covered with friction ridges: fingers, palms, toes, and the soles of the feet. However, most impressions recovered on crime scenes are made with the first joint of the finger and it is such impressions that are mainly considered in this chapter. The extension of the theory to other areas of friction ridges can be done by analogy.

† The European nomenclature of *fingermark/mark* and *fingerprint/print* is used in this chapter.

The examination of marks and prints follows a structured process generally known under the acronym ACE-V (for *A*nalysis, *C*omparison, *E*valuation and *V*erification) [2,14,23,24].*

This acronym relates to the different phases followed by fingerprint examiners when gathering and comparing information on marks and prints, and when making decisions related to their identity of source. ACE-V is not always a linear process; however, to ease the comprehension of this process, each phase can be independently and succinctly summarized as follows:

1. *Analysis*: During the analysis phase, examiners assess marks to determine their usefulness based on the *quality* (clarity of features) and *quantity* (amount, specificity and spatial arrangement) of first, second, and third level of details present in the marks. The result of this assessment is affected by elements such as the substrate on which the impressions have been observed, the detection techniques used, the environmental conditions, or the transfer conditions during their depositions (e.g., pressure applied by the finger pad). The analysis phase leads to the determination by examiners of the *suitability* of these marks for further examination.
2. *Comparison*: During the comparison phase, examiners will observe marks and prints side by side and compare them at all levels of details to determine their level of resemblance (or dissimilarity), within some tolerances based on the respective clarity and distortion of the impressions.
3. *Evaluation*: During the evaluation phase, examiners will weigh the *quality* and *quantity* of features in agreement (or disagreement) between pairs of impressions, and based on the specificity of the observed features, will reach conclusions on the identity of their source.
4. *Verification*: In the verification phase, subsequent examiners perform the ACE process on the latent and known prints to either support or refute the conclusions of the original examiner(s).

15.2.2 Conclusions to Fingerprint Examinations

The current culture within fingerprint communities worldwide claims that examiners infer the source of marks by deduction [15] and demands that they report the results of fingerprint comparison as categorical opinions. Resolutions 1979-VII and 1980-V from the International Association for Identification (IAI), while only applying to the members of the association, are representative of this tradition. Before being rescinded in 2010 [25], resolutions taken by the IAI membership in 1979 and 1980 have unambiguously prevented IAI members from reporting less than certain opinions:

> Now therefore be it resolved that any member, officer or certified latent print examiner who initiates or volunteers oral or written reports or testimony of possible, probable or likely friction ridge identification, or who, when required in a judicial proceeding to provide such reports or testimony, does not qualify it with a statement that the print in question could be that of someone else, shall be deemed to be engaged in conduct unbecoming such member …

* The practical implementation of this protocol may vary between agencies. However, fingerprint professionals, and scientific and legal scholars, generally accept that it aims at minimizing the risk of errors and provides a measure of quality assurance. The differences between the different implementations are minimal and have no bearing on the concepts presented in this chapter. The arguments presented in this chapter are valid for all current implementations of this protocol.

Members of the IAI not conforming to this resolution would be exposed to lose their certification, or even their membership to the organization.

Currently, most fingerprint examiners will testify that, following the careful analysis, comparison, and evaluation of two impressions, they can exclude all but one individual, and therefore, that they are absolutely certain that the scene impression was made by the same individual who also provided the control print: the donor of the control print has been *identified* or *individualized* as the donor of the mark [23].

Positive opinions aside, examinations can also lead to negative opinions, whereby examiners will *exclude* the donor of the control print as the source of the mark. These conclusions tend to be noncontroversial, since, following Bertillon [26], one unexplained difference is logically sufficient to declare a lack of identity [23].

A third category of conclusions can be reached for those comparison where examiners consider for various reasons that the evidence is of insufficient quality, or comprises too little detail for an opinion of identification or exclusion to be formed. Those comparisons are qualified as *inconclusive* [23]. When considering current practices, it is important to realize that any comparison for which a state of certainty cannot be reached will be reported as inconclusive, irrespective of the potential corroborative or exculpatory value of the evidence.

15.2.3 Notion of *Sufficiency*

The brief overview of the ACE-V process in Section 15.2.1 shows that a series of determinations and decisions are made at each stage of the process in order to infer the identity of the source of marks recovered from crime scenes. There is no doubt that the sequential assessment of the quantity and quality of information present on finger impressions, the level of similarity between pairs of marks and prints, and the ability to use the observed features to discriminate between impressions of different sources are critical to support fingerprint examiners in their decision-making process. The key issue is related to how these elements are taken into account to make decisions or reach conclusions. At present, the decisions made at each stage of the process are based on the notion of *sufficiency* [23]. This notion essentially consists of using a threshold that must be met in order to move on to the next stage of the process or form a conclusion at the end of the examination. In current practice, we have the following:

1. Assessment of the suitability of a mark during the *analysis phase* aims at determining whether it bears *sufficient* reliable information to proceed with its comparison with control prints, in order to reach a conclusion on its source at the end of the evaluation phase.
2. Assessment of the quality and quantity of features in agreement between a mark and a print during the *comparison phase* aims at judging whether they are *sufficiently* similar to prevent the exclusion of the donor of the print as a potential source for the mark.
3. Assessment of the specificity of the information in agreement between a mark and a print during the *evaluation phase* aims at determining whether the level of agreement between the mark and the print is *sufficiently* high that it cannot be observed between marks and prints originating from different donors.*

* We will see in Section 15.3 that this question is not entirely consistent with the previous two and renders the logical decision-making process inconsistent. Since Section 15.2 is focusing on the current inference process, we consider the decisions currently made by fingerprint examiners.

These three decisions have different purposes. The decision made at the end of the analysis stage mostly affects the operational efficiency of fingerprint units. The definition of suitability is more driven by quality assurance/policy considerations rather than by scientific ones. Some units are required, at the analysis stage, only to consider further and compare fingermarks that are deemed of sufficient quality to reach an individualization conclusion [23]. In those units, the examination of a fingermark cannot result in an inconclusive conclusion unless the control print itself is not considered suitable for comparison. By definition, those units are only meant to consider marks, which bear enough reliable features to discriminate all individuals. At the other end of the spectrum, some units acknowledge that marks can be used for exclusion purposes [23]. In other words, the latter units will consider marks that may not display enough information to discriminate all individuals, but that may be able to exclude particular individuals as their source. For example, a mark only displaying the general pattern of the ridge flow and no other details will not bear enough information to discriminate all individuals, but may be useful to exclude a given individual if that individual has no fingerprint with that general pattern. Overall, examiners will consider crime scene impressions of different levels of quality depending on the operating procedures of their units. Impressions at the higher end of the quality spectrum are less prevalent at crime scenes, are easier to examine, and are more likely to help detect offenders. These units will appear to have better cost/benefit performances, but may be missing valuable evidence. On the contrary, impressions with lower number and poorer quality of friction ridge details are more frequent at crime scenes, require more time and effort to examine, and are less likely to help detect offenders (but may be useful to exclude named individuals). The units considering these latter impressions may be more informative and helpful to resolve legal matters, but will have lower perceived performances and longer turnaround times. The impact of the assessment of suitability during the analysis stage of the examination process has been measured, and a summary of the results is presented in Section 15.4.2.5. The determination of whether marks are suitable or not during the analysis stage is an important question. While this is not necessarily considered in current practice, we will demonstrate that, formally, the determination of suitability during the analysis stage is essentially the same as the determination of sufficiency during the evaluation stage. Indeed, both decisions are (or should be) based on the specificity of the information present on the mark alone.

The second decision (made at the end of the comparison stage) and third decision (made at the end of the evaluation stage) are both more directly related to the logical thought process underlying the inference of the source of crime scene impressions, but have drastically different purposes. Currently, examiners tend to combine these two decisions and determine whether *there is sufficient information in agreement between a mark and a print* to reach a conclusion of identity of source. This statement implies that (a) the features observed on the mark and print need to be sufficiently similar to decide that there is agreement between them and (b), at the same time, this level of agreement should not be possible between marks and prints from different sources.

Thus, the aim of the decision made at the end of the comparison stage is to assess whether or not the features observed on the crime scene impression are compatible with the features observed in the control print. Section 15.2.4 will expand on how the level of similarity is determined. In current practice, the goal of the decision made at the end of the evaluation stage is to determine whether or not the level of agreement observed between the mark and the print at the comparison stage can also be observed between impressions originating from different donors. This is the topic of Section 15.2.5.

15.2.4 Determination of *Sufficiency* at the Comparison Stage

When comparing a mark and a print, an examiner will look for correspondences and differences between the features observed on each of them. Finger impressions are by definition imperfect representations of the friction ridge skin located on fingers. Finger pads are flexible, within limits, and many of the features that can be observed on the skin of finger pads may not be transferred to their impression; alternatively, those features may be transferred but in slightly different ways for every single impression of the pads depending on the pressure and sliding of these pads on the surface. Other elements, such as the nature of the surface, or the method used to visualize the impressions will also affect the presence or appearance of features on finger impressions. As a result, multiple impressions of a given finger, even deposited under controlled conditions, may not be identical but will show variations (see Figure 15.2). The task of fingerprint examiners during the comparison stage of the examination process consists of assessing whether the features observed on a mark fit within the range of variations of the features that can be theoretically observed on multiple impressions of a given finger, when considering elements such as distortion or quality [12,13,27].

Following Bertillon [26], examiners consider that the observation of one difference between the mark and the print excludes *de facto* the donor of the print as being the source of the mark; nevertheless, in practice, the notion of *explainable differences* describes the assessment of whether dissimilarities observed between pairs of marks and prints are part of the natural variation between multiple impressions of the same finger, or whether they indicate that the marks and prints are from different sources. This notion allows for examiners to decide whether characteristics in pairs of impressions correspond or not based on their assessment of the clarity and level of distortion of the mark during the analysis stage.

(a) (b)

FIGURE 15.2
Two different impressions made by the same individual under different pressure conditions. The two impressions are not *identical*; however, they share common features that enable fingerprint examiners to associate them.

This assessment leads to the definition of tolerance levels for deciding that features are (not) corresponding during the comparison stage. In other words, the assessment of the clarity and distortion level of the impressions made during the analysis state enables examiners to *explain away* differences observed between pairs of impressions. Currently, there is no standard for the definition of these tolerance levels. The decision that a particular difference is explainable, or not, and by extension that impressions are *sufficiently* similar, is the prerogative of the examiner based on training and experience.

15.2.5 Determination of *Sufficiency* at the Evaluation Stage

If marks and prints are deemed to be sufficiently similar at the comparison stage, examiners will then move on to the evaluation stage and form their conclusions based on the quantity and quality of information observed during their examination. When there is *sufficient* information in agreement, or to discriminate all individuals, the donors of the prints are identified as the donors of the marks. When there is *insufficient* information, the examination results in an inconclusive conclusion [23].

From the very early days of the discipline, scientists have attempted to define the notion of sufficiency and provide support for the conclusions reached following the comparison of marks and prints. While pioneers considered that the quantification of the weight of friction ridge features during the inference process was continuous, operational requirements quickly reduced this continuum to a threshold-based determination of identity of source. Today, the definition, quantification, and overall use of the notion of *sufficiency* when forming conclusions are at the core of some of the raging criticisms of the fingerprint examination process.

15.2.5.1 Early Days

Sir Francis Galton is credited with the first extensive research published in fingerprints [7]. He collected more than 8000 sets of 10 fingers impressions and showed that pattern and friction ridges are persistent over time. Galton also attempted to demonstrate the specificity of friction ridge details and attempted from the beginning to assign numerical values to the weight of fingerprint evidence. Galton considered already that the inference of the source of marks is a probabilistic process:

> Our problem is this: given two finger prints, which are alike in their minutiae, what is the chance that they were made by different persons?

To answer this question, Galton developed and proposed the first fingerprint statistical model. According to Galton's model, the probability of duplication of the sequence of all minutiae observed on a finger pad would be as low as 1 in 2^{36}, or 1 in approximately 68,000 million.* Galton did not provide much guidance as to how to determine that two finger impressions are "alike" and his model did not directly answer the question of *sufficiency*. Galton's model theoretically allows quantifying the probability of observing fingerprint features on random individuals in a continuous manner; Galton was not concerned with setting up a *sufficiency* threshold, instead he attempted to demonstrate that fingerprints are extremely discriminating in general.†

* Galton reports the figure of 1 in 64,000 million. The actual figure corresponding to 1 in 2^{36} is 1 in 68,719,476,736.

† And not *unique*, as it is often wrongfully claimed.

In 1911, Dr. Victor Balthazard [28], a French professor of forensic medicine, proposed a slightly different model and reached the conclusion that, assuming a world population of 1.5 billion (at the time), a minimum of 17 corresponding minutiae would be needed to conclusively exclude all but one person as the source of a crime scene mark. Similarly to Galton, Balthazard pointed out that the inference of the source of a mark is probabilistic in essence and that the notion of *sufficiency* is continuous (i.e., it depends on the intrinsic characteristics of the mark and may be different for different marks). Importantly, Balthazard's view was that conclusions based on the examination of fingerprints should not only rely on the quantity and quality of information observed on marks, and on the level of agreement between marks and prints, but also on the size of the population of potential suspects.

> In medico-legal duties, the number of corresponding minutiae can be lowered to 11 or 12, if one can be certain that the population of potential criminals is not the entire world population but is restricted to an inhabitant of Europe, a French citizen, or an inhabitant of a city, or of a village, etc.

Since Galton and Balthazard, several authors have attempted to address and quantify the notion of *sufficiency* using statistical models. Their work was critically reviewed in 2001 by Stoney [29], who describes their strengths and weaknesses. For a variety of reasons described by Stoney, these models proved to be unable to provide a satisfactory basis for the definition of the concept of *sufficiency*, or for the quantification of the weight of fingerprint evidence, and none ended up implemented in practice.

15.2.5.2 Numerical Standard

While Balthazard's model was not deployed operationally, Balthazard's work became the basis of the *Tripartite Rule* enunciated by Dr. Edmond Locard [30]. Locard simplified Batlhazard's results and was the first to suggest the use of a predetermined number of corresponding minutiae to declare that two impressions are of common origin. Locard stated that

> If more than 12 concurring minutiae are present and the fingerprint is very clear, then the certainty of identity is beyond debate.
> If 8 to 12 concurring minutiae are found, then identification is marginal and certainty of identity is dependent on: (a) the quality of the fingerprint, (b) the rarity of the minutiae type, (c) the presence of a core and delta in a clear area of the print, (d) the presence of pores, and (e) the perfect agreement of the width of the ridges and furrows, the direction of the ridge flow, and the angular value of the bifurcation.
> If a limited number of characteristics are present, the fingerprint cannot provide certainty for an identification, but only a presumption proportional to the number of points available and their clarity.

Locard was not only the first one to use the notion of *sufficiency*, but he was also the first one to quantify it. And while Galton, Balthazard, and others considered that the determination that two impressions were alike is a different question than the question of the assignment of the probability of duplication of the information observed on any given mark, Locard also appears to be the first one to combine these questions by suggesting the use of the level of similarity between two impressions as a means for the exclusion that a mark could originate from another individual than the donor of a print. With his rules, Locard provided a pragmatic, yet still probabilistic, scheme for inferring the source of a mark.*

In 1912, Alphonse Bertillon published a paper in which he presented several examples of impressions from different individuals displaying multiple similarities [26]. In particular, one example presented the comparison between the ring and middle fingers from two different individuals and displayed 16 points of similarities. In this figure, certain areas of the impressions were edited in order to mask dissimilarities; Bertillon acknowledged the masking in the paper and stated in relation to this particular figure that

> If a larger area [of the prints] were considered, significant differences would appear, which would prevent reaching a conclusion of identity

In his paper, Bertillon made the argument that the absence of dissimilarities is more important than the number of similarities when inferring the identity of individuals based on the examination of fingerprints. This finding later became known as the *one dissimilarity rule* [31], which states that one dissimilarity between two impressions is sufficient to exclude a common origin.

Bertillon's argument was misunderstood, first by the New Zealand Police, and subsequently by New Scotland Yard in England [32]. This misunderstanding led to the establishment of a 16-point numerical standard in 1924 in England and Wales, although this standard was not always followed depending on the circumstances of the case and the level of experience of the examiner [32].

As the acceptance of fingerprints as a means of personal identification spread around the world at the beginning of the twentieth century, specifically trained technicians began to replace scientists for the examination of fingerprints. The use of analysts, who were not trained, or encouraged, to think as scientists, coupled with the need of newly created fingerprint bureaus to maximize the quality of their output within operational constraints (caseload, turnaround time, finances), led many countries to simplify the identification process. These countries adopted some form of numerical point standard as a threshold for the determination that there is sufficient quality and quantity of corresponding features between a mark and a print to declare that they originate from a common source.† In those countries, this adoption was accompanied by the loss of the original probabilistic perspective evoked by Galton [7], Balthazard [28], Locard [30], and others, and by the combination of the determination of the level of similarity between impressions with the assessment of the rarity of such level of similarity. In most cases, only standards similar to Locard's first rule were retained as a proxy for the definition of the notion of sufficiency.

Today, inference processes relying on numerical standards remain practically unchallenged in the many countries where they were adopted. The United Kingdom represents a notable exception. In 1988, the British Home Office commissioned a review of the requirement for the 16-point standard used by fingerprint examiners in England and Wales [32]. The study, conducted by Evett and Williams, provided several recommendations for training, certification, and overall standardized practices [32]. However, the authors found no statistical or logical justification for a point standard of any number. While Evett and Williams did not recommend a change to the 16-point standard,

* While Locard's rules focus on the number of corresponding minutiae, it is assumed that the first level detail (general pattern and overall flow of the ridges) of the impressions corresponds.

† Depending on various factors, some countries adopted different standards and did not strictly follow either Locard or New Scotland Yard. See Champod [14] for a complete list of numerical standards around the world.

this study eventually led England and Wales to abandon the standard in 2001 and to replace it with a more *holistic approach* [14].

15.2.5.3 Holistic Approach

The situation in the United States developed rather differently. Although Locard's rules influenced examiners, they gradually moved away from the notion of a numerical standard and adopted a more holistic approach for the determination of sufficiency. In this approach, examiners compare a more comprehensive range of friction ridge features in addition to general pattern and minutiae, and assess their weight in a more continuous manner [2]. The holistic approach is closer to the original philosophy enunciated by Galton, and is rooted in the lack of scientific justification for a numerical standard, which is seen as a mere "point counting" exercise. The holistic approach considers that depending on the quality and type of features present, and of the specificity of their arrangement in the ridge flow, some impressions will bear more evidentiary value than others.

The holistic approach was used by fingerprint examiners in a fairly informal manner, until 1973, when a review of the concept of numerical standard commissioned by the IAI officially concluded that

> No valid basis exists for requiring that a predetermined minimum number of friction ridge characteristics must be present in two impressions in order to establish identity

The 1973 IAI resolution was further discussed by an international group of scientists participating in a fingerprint symposium in June 1995 in Ne'urim, Israel [33]. The participants essentially agreed with the position from the IAI and made the following statement:

> No scientific basis exists for requiring that a pre-determined minimum number of friction ridge features be present in two impressions in order to establish a positive identification

In 2006, the IAI appointed a committee to investigate whether the 1973 IAI Resolution was still valid in light of the developments of the field over the previous 30 years. The IAI Standardisation 2 Committee concluded its task in 2010 and published its report in 2011 [34]. The committee reviewed a substantial amount of scientific and legal literature and reached globally the same conclusion as the original committee in 1973:

> There currently exists no scientific basis for requiring a minimum amount of corresponding friction ridge detail information between two impressions to arrive at an opinion of single source attribution.

The comparison of the numerical and holistic approaches shows that (a) both combine the determination that two impressions are sufficiently similar with the determination that the level of similarity excludes that the impressions were made by different individuals and (b) both infer the identity of the source of the mark by deduction: since a given level of similarity cannot be observed between impressions from two individuals, it naturally flows that the donor of the print is also the source of the mark.

The main difference between the two approaches is that one quantifies the notion of sufficiency, while the other one does not. Proponents of the holistic approach claim that examiners following that approach take into account and compare more types of friction ridge features than proponents of the numerical standard and that they have more flexibility to use the intrinsic specificity of these features (e.g., spatial relationships between minutiae). While there is some truth in this argument, it appears that, contrary to the approach using a numerical standard, the holistic approach has no explicitly defined quality standard for deciding whether or not pairs of marks and prints have sufficient information in agreement to conclude that the same areas of friction ridges made them. In his book, which is still used as a textbook by many fingerprint trainees, Ashbaugh describes, explains, structures, and clarifies many issues related to fingerprint examination [2]. However, Ashbaugh fails to properly tackle the concept of *sufficiency* in the holistic approach. Ashbaugh addresses the notion of sufficiency with the following circular argument:

> How much is enough: Finding adequate friction ridge formations in sequence that one knows are specific details of the friction ridge skin, and in the opinion of the friction ridge identification specialist that there is sufficient uniqueness within those details to eliminate all other possible donors in the world, is considered enough. [...]. The identification was established by the agreement of friction ridge formation in sequence having sufficient uniqueness to individualise [2].

Neither the 1973 IAI committee nor the scientists cosigning the Ne'urim declaration supplemented their statements with any indication on how "single source attribution" or "positive identification" should be established. The 2006 IAI committee provided several recommendations, including the need for a "single internationally accepted examination methodology and standard methodology," and for establishing "a measurable threshold requirement for identification of latent prints, with the intent of achieving a standard." However, it similarly failed to provide any guideline, or indication on how to achieve those goals. The notion of *sufficiency* in the holistic approach has no defined scientific support and does not relate to any objectively measurable quantity. It remains a very personal and subjective decision and is subject to differences between examiners.

15.2.6 Summary

Section 15.2 briefly described that the comparison of pairs of marks and prints relies on different types of friction ridge features, commonly classified in three categories, and that the technical process used for this purpose had four stages: analysis, comparison, evaluation, and verification. The section expanded on the decisions and conclusions reached by examiners during the first three stages of the examination process. All these decisions rely on the same notion of *sufficiency*. We saw that the definition of what constitutes sufficiency can vary depending on

1. Which stage of the examination process is considered
2. Operational considerations
3. The use of a numerical or holistic approach

Overall, the inference of source of marks is currently considered as being a deduction and conclusions are reported with certainty: an examiner will consider whether the level of similarity between a mark and a print is such that it is possible to exclude the possibility that the mark could have come from anybody else than the donor of the print; therefore, the examiner can be absolutely certain that the donor of the print is also the source of the mark.

From the review of the historical perspective, it appears that the fingerprint examination community does not have the necessary foundation to justify, quantify, or appropriately use a sufficiency threshold in fingerprint examination. The following section describes some of the challenges, criticisms, and concerns regarding the current deductive inference process, the notion of sufficiency, and the categorical conclusion scheme.

15.3 Limitations of the Current Fingerprint Examination Process

15.3.1 Introduction

In 1993, the Supreme Court of the United States issued a watershed decision on the admission of scientific evidence and testimony. *Daubert v. Merrell Dow Pharmaceuticals, Inc.* [35] became renowned for laying down a series of criteria for evaluating the admissibility of such evidence.

The reliability and scientific foundations of some forensic disciplines had already been challenged prior to this decision; however, the dicta in the Daubert case triggered a renewed interest in the reliability and admissibility of various types of forensic evidence and, more specifically, of fingerprint evidence [18–22,27,36–38]. A recent Congressionally commissioned report from the National Academies of Science (NAS) on the state of forensic science in the United States [12] has also brought attention to these matters (e.g., [39,40]). Several criticisms have been made regarding various aspects of the examination process and resulting conclusions. These criticisms generally follow three broad lines of argument:

1. The selection and use of fingerprint features to support the decisions made during the examination process are usually poorly documented and lack transparency. In addition, the background, training, and experience of examiners can affect the reproducibility of the examination process. These elements render the process sensitive to a variety of biases that can limit its objectivity.
2. The deductive logic behind the examination process and the conclusion scheme invokes the necessity to be absolutely certain of the source of the mark. Such logic cannot be rationalized and leads examiners to overstate the weight of fingerprint evidence when reporting their findings.
3. The accuracy and precision of fingerprint examination are not fully understood and have not been extensively measured.

The first line of arguments requests establishing well-defined, transparent, scientifically sound, and community-wide standards for the selection, documentation, and evaluation of fingerprint features during the examination of fingerprint evidence. Since the early challenges in the late 1990s and 2000s [18,41–45], researchers and the fingerprint community have made significant progress in addressing concerns raised by scientific and legal scholars: study of the origin of friction ridge on fingers [46–48], study of elements potentially affecting the reliability of fingerprint examination [49–51], development of standard procedures [23,52–55] and accreditation processes, and the provision of training and continuing education. The use of statistical data to support fingerprint examination will require to record fingerprint features in a standardized way: it will therefore impact the training and documentation required from fingerprint examiners. However, statistics and probability are not directly involved in answering criticisms related to these topics.

On the contrary, statistics and probability can provide helpful tools and data to support fingerprint examiners when addressing arguments from the second and third categories. More specifically, statistics and probability are critical to address the central issue of the evaluation of the weight of fingerprint evidence. One can only agree with the recommendation of the IAI Standardisation 2 Committee that a uniform standard must be established and accepted across the fingerprint examiner community [34]. Statistics and probability can help explain the logical framework for the inference of the source of crime scene marks and propose a new uniform and consistent framework. The following sections present some of the limitations of the current inference process and introduce how statistics and probability may be used to overcome them.

15.3.2 Shortcoming in the Current Logical Framework Supporting Fingerprint Examinations

In Section 15.2, we explored the claims made with respect to the decision-making process used in current practice:

1. This process is deductive.
2. The process relies on the notion of sufficiency.
3. The results of fingerprint examinations need to be reported using one of three possible conclusions: identification, exclusion, or inconclusive. The first two conclusions are only reported when examiners are certain of the identity of the source of the mark; any examination with less than certain results is reported as inconclusive.

15.3.2.1 Fingerprint Examination as a Deductive Process

Examiners commonly claim that the decision-making process supporting the examination of fingerprints is a deduction, which relies on the two notions of *uniqueness* and *individualization*. The concept of uniqueness is based on the premise that nature does not duplicate itself and, therefore, that no two individuals share identical fingerprints. The concept of individualization combines the idea that the possible source of a mark can only be one individual with the absolute certainty associated with this determination.* In this section, we discuss that the arguments supporting the claim of a deductive reasoning are flawed and that the process is, in fact, inductive.

In practice, examiners draw on the notion of uniqueness to support the claim of individualization: given two friction ridge impressions that are *sufficiently* similar, the idea that they must come from the same donor is directly deducted from the belief that no two individuals share the same fingerprints. Cole has called this argument the "fingerprint examiner's fallacy." Following Saks and Koehler [38], Cole [27] demonstrates that the notion of uniqueness is largely irrelevant and unproven.

* While some forensic scientists define *identification* as the association of a particular trace with a given class of sources, it is often used interchangeably with *individualization* when it comes to fingerprint evidence. Within the fingerprint community, some examiners consider that the notion of *identification* represents a more modest claim than the notion of *individualization*. For these examiners, an *identification* allows for the theoretical and remote possibility that, in the absence of any other evidence in the case, the mark may not have actually originated from the donor who has been identified as the source of the mark.

The observation of the mark and print in Figure 15.1 shows that the notion of uniqueness is irrelevant: fingerprint examiners are rarely concerned with comparing pairs of impressions collected under controlled conditions, but rather by the examination of partial, distorted, and degraded impressions recovered from crime scenes. It may well be true that no two individuals share similar friction ridge skin on their finger pads and that friction ridge skin is genuinely unique because of the biological process involved in its creation; furthermore, it may equally be true that finger pad impressions taken under controlled conditions display enough of the features present on the pads that they can be uniquely attributed to their donors; however, the relevant question facing examiners is whether any particular potentially degraded and distorted mark bears enough features to discriminate all individuals. In other words, examiners are concerned with the number of individuals, who could have left the mark, taking into account elements, such as distortion, the surface from which the mark was recovered, or the development technique used.

Even if uniqueness was relevant, it remains to be proven. Fingerprints are thought to be unique in part because of the biological origin of friction ridge skin, and in part because of the claim that out of the millions of comparisons performed every year, no two impressions have ever found to be alike [27]. This statement is interesting and provides valuable statistical data supporting the reliability of forensic fingerprint examination. This statement relies on the fundamental assumptions that examiners understand the notion of sufficiency well enough to define what *similar* means, and that they have never made errors. These assumptions cannot resist scrutiny: current practice shows that erroneous identifications or exclusions have been made, that clerical errors are reported, and that the notion of similarity between impressions is far from being transparently defined (see Section 15.2.4). But even if these assumptions do not hold, the statement still implies that it is very unlikely to find pairs of friction ridge impressions in casework that did not originate from the same source, but are similar enough to fool examiners. This is very powerful data, but it is not sufficient to demonstrate the uniqueness of fingerprints because of the overwhelmingly large number of comparisons that such a demonstration would require.

The statement that "out of the millions of comparisons performed until now, no two fingerprints have been found to be alike" can be compared to the well-known "Birthday problem." The Birthday problem focuses on the probability that two individuals share the same birthday. The underlying argument is that this probability will vary depending on the phrasing of the question (see Table 15.1):

TABLE 15.1

Probability Assigned to the Different Questions Asked in the Birthday Problem and Number of Comparisons Performed

Number of Individuals in the Considered Population	10	20	23	57	100
Probability that a randomly selected individual shares the same birthday as Mr. X	0.27%	0.27%	0.27%	0.27%	0.27%
Number of comparisons performed	1	1	1	1	1
Probability that at least one individual shares Mr. X's birthday	2.7%	5.3%	6.1%	14.4%	23.9%
Number of comparisons performed	10	20	23	57	100
Probability of observing a pair of individuals with the same birthday	11.7%	41.1%	50.7%	99%	99.99%
Number of comparisons performed	45	190	253	1596	4950

1. What is the probability that an individual selected at random in a population shares the same birthday as Mr. X? The answer to this question corresponds to the probability of being born any particular day of the year (1 chance in 365).
2. What is the probability that the population includes one person, who has the same birthday as Mr. X? The answer to this question is related to the number of individuals in the considered population and to the probability of being born any particular day of the year.
3. What is the probability of finding a pair of individuals sharing their birthday in this population (irrespective of the actual birthday)? The answer to this question is slightly more complex: it depends on the total number of pairs of individuals that can be formed in the considered population and on the probability of being born on any particular day of the year.

The important element in the Birthday problem is that the number of comparisons performed between the considered individuals varies significantly between the different questions. In the first question, only one pair of individuals is considered: Mr. X and a randomly selected individual. This number remains the same regardless of the size N of the considered population. In the second question, Mr. X's birthday is compared to the birthday of every one of the N individuals in the population, and the number of comparisons is equal to N. In the third question, the number of comparisons considers the total number of pairs that can be made between the individuals in the population. This number can be computed using the well-known formula

$$\binom{N}{2} = \frac{N(N-1)}{2} \tag{15.1}$$

Table 15.1 shows that the probabilities assigned to each question vary vastly depending on the question and on the size of the population. In particular, we can see that it is extremely likely to observe two individuals sharing the same birthday, even when considering that the probability of being born any particular day of the year is small.

The Birthday problem relates by analogy to the examination of fingerprints in the following ways:

1. First question corresponds to the *one to one* comparison performed between a mark recovered from a crime scene and a print from a given individual.
2. Second question corresponds to the *one to many* comparisons performed when searching a given mark in a fingerprint reference database.
3. Third question would correspond to the systematic comparison of the fingerprints of all individuals on planet Earth.

The statement that "no two impressions have ever been found to be alike out of the millions of comparisons performed every year" corresponds to the tasks performed in the first two situations. However, inferring that "fingerprints are unique" from this statement would require performing an experiment designed to answer the third question. Not only is such an experiment not practical, but, as we have seen for the Birthday problem, the probability of observing two similar fingerprints is much higher in the third case than in the first two ones. Table 15.2 assumes a remote probability of duplication of fingerprint

TABLE 15.2

Probability Assigned to Different Fingerprint Questions When Considering the U.S. National Fingerprint Database and the Earth's Population, and the Number of Comparisons Performed

Number of Individuals in the Considered Population	U.S. National Fingerprint Database: 70 Million Individuals	Population of the Earth: 7 Billion Individuals
Probability that a randomly selected individual has a similar fingerprint to Mr. X	1 in 70 billion chances	1 in 70 billion chances
Number of comparisons performed	1	1
Probability that an individual in the population has a similar fingerprint to Mr. X	0.09%	9.5%
Number of comparisons performed	70,000,000	7,000,000,000
Probability of observing a pair of individuals with similar fingerprints	~100%	~100%
Number of comparisons performed	2.45 quadrillion	24,500 quadrillion

features of one in the number of fingers in the human population (~70 billion fingers) and compare the probability of observing two individuals with the same fingerprint (a) in the U.S. national fingerprint database and (b) on Earth. The probability assigned to the first question is quasi-null in both cases. The probability assigned to the first question can be considered remote when considering the U.S. national fingerprint database, but is almost 10% when considering the entire human population. When considering the third question, we observe that we are theoretically almost certain to find two individuals having the same fingerprint in a database as large as the U.S. national one. This result is due to the overwhelming number of comparisons that are taken into account. This number of comparisons is so large that it would take a system as efficient as the one supporting the U.S. national fingerprint database (61 million searches annually/4.3 quadrillion fingerprint comparisons annually*) approximately 6 months to compare each individual in the database against all others, and approximately 6000 years to compare each individual on Earth against everybody else.†

Since the notion of uniqueness cannot support the state of certainty required by the individualization process, it needs to be supplemented by another argument. Several authors following Stoney [56] describe the existence of a "leap-of-faith" that examiners need to

* One search consists of the search of the 10 fingerprints of an individual against the 70 million 10 print records in the database; in other words, one search is equivalent to 70 million comparisons (see Note 12). Therefore, 61 million searches correspond to 4.3×10^{15} comparisons.

† The numbers reported here and in Table 15.2 are obviously based on a number of assumptions. For example, it is assumed that the 61 million yearly searches performed by the FBI are from 61 million different individuals; it is assumed that individuals are compared against individuals: the aforementioned numbers do not account for the possibility that the fingerprints of two different fingers of the same individual are similar; it is also assumed that *similar fingerprint* means that the impression of one given person's finger is similar to the impression of the corresponding finger of another person (e.g., right thumb vs. right thumb); finally, it is likely that the random match probability of 1 in 70 billion is underestimating the actual specificity of fingerprint patterns. Nevertheless, these assumptions are reasonable to illustrate the point made in this example.

take when making conclusions regarding the source of marks. This leap-of-faith is by definition incompatible with certainty and with a deduction process. The achievement of that state of certainty, as described by Saks and Koehler [38], and Cole [27], is a question of epistemology: it cannot be rationalized scientifically, except in trivial situations, and leads to an overstatement of the evidence when presented in court. As Kwan [57], followed by Champod and Evett [15] and Champod [16], demonstrated, apart from these trivial situations, the determination of the source of marks from their comparisons with control prints is an inductive process that needs to be supplemented by statistical data on the variability of fingerprint features. When considering a given pair of mark and print, the inductive inference process, as described by Champod and Evett, considers (a) whether the mark and the print are indistinguishable (considering knowledge and data that can explain differences) and (b) how likely it is that another person would have friction ridge patterns indistinguishable from the mark. More particularly, the following two questions need to be considered:

1. How similar can different impressions from the same finger appear, and can the differences be explained by data gathered on the influence of distortion, surface, or development technique?
2. How many individuals could produce impressions displaying similar features when taking into account elements such as distortion, surface, or development technique?

These questions are very similar to the question already formulated by Galton in 1892 and reported in Section 15.2.5.1. In fact, fingerprint examiners are also currently considering these questions during the comparison and evaluation stages. The leap-of-faith, which is in essence the decision that the answer to the second question is only one individual, only intervenes in the very last moments of the current inference process. The inductive process described by Champod and Evett is very close to the current process and mainly requires a change in the way examiners conceptualize their inference process, as opposed to significant technical changes in the examination process.

15.3.2.2 Quantification of the Notion of Sufficiency

In current practice, examiners rely on the notion of sufficiency to answer both questions laid down at the end of the previous section. We saw in Sections 15.2.3 through to 15.2.5 that examiners define tolerance levels based on their training and experience to answer the first question, and that they use either a numerical standard or a holistic approach to answer the second one. This section revisits the notion of sufficiency and shows that, aside from not being supported by data, it has also not been properly defined. Ultimately, we advocate that the notion of sufficiency cannot be used to support fingerprint examination, and that it should be replaced by the continuous quantification of the specificity of configurations of friction ridge features.

Proponents of the numerical standard benefit from an explicit quantification of the number of corresponding features between marks and prints, which are needed to declare that only one individual can be considered as the source of both impressions. The numerical standard is a policy decision that can vary between different jurisdictions. Furthermore, the numerical approach lacks a clear and community-wide definition of which features can and should be taken into account. In the numerical standard approach, the question of the quantification of the notion of sufficiency is related to the scientific determination of what the standard should be, in order to minimize the chance of observing two random individuals sharing the same fingerprint features. Properly quantifying the notion of sufficiency in the numerical standard approach would require designing an experiment that would systematically compare all fingerprints in the world as explained in the previous section. The value of the numerical standard would then be one more feature than the maximum number of features found in agreement between two different impressions from two random individuals. Such an experiment, which could scientifically define the numerical standard, is not feasible. Alternatively, the numerical standard should be quantified by measuring the average specificity of fingerprint features and by deciding that, collectively, a certain number of features are specific enough that the probability of observing these features in the fingerprints of two different individuals is vanishingly small. A numerical standard defined according to such an experiment would certainly be supported by data; however, it would remain the result of a policy decision.

The holistic approach is presented as being more exhaustive in the quality and type of information taken into account during the examination process, but it relies entirely on decisions that cannot be properly defined, explained, or communicated. Proponents of the holistic approach have not quantified the notion of *sufficiency*, and this notion is likely to vary significantly depending on case, examiner, or various other circumstances. In practice, the notion of sufficiency in the holistic approach is driven neither by policy nor by data but by a cognitive process relying on training and experience. Ideally, the quantification of the notion of sufficiency should be related to the transparent estimation of the specificity of fingerprint features observed on marks and prints in each case. This would require the development of some model to measure this specificity on a case-by-case basis.

Regardless of the approach, the concept of sufficiency needs to be supported by measuring the specificity of configurations of friction ridge features that can be observed on marks and prints. This quantification could then be the basis for policy decisions or to support a cognitive process. There are three issues with the quantification of the specificity of fingerprint features: the definition of what needs to be measured, its subsequent measurement, and how it should be used to define the notion of sufficiency.

Currently, *sufficiency* is defined as the level of agreement between a mark and a print. The argument goes as follows:

1. There is agreement between the mark and the print.
2. This level of agreement is such that it cannot be observed between two impressions originating from different donors.
3. The source of the print is also the source of the mark.

This is a different argument:

1. There is agreement between the mark and the print.
2. The features observed on the mark are so specific that they can only be observed in one individual.
3. The source of the print is also the source of the mark.

This may seem to be a question of semantics; however, the focus of the decision is different between these two arguments. In the first case, the focus is set on the level of agreement between the mark and the print, while in the second case, the focus is set directly and solely on the information observed on the mark. It is important to realize that the change of focus, which exists in current practice between the comparison and evaluation stages, renders the overall decision-making framework inconsistent. From a statistical point of view, the difference between the two following statements is critical:

1. Mark and the print have sufficient information in agreement to conclude that the donor of the print is also the donor of the print.
2. Information observed on the mark is sufficient to discriminate between all individuals.

The first statement considers a random variable that describes the level of agreement between marks and prints. The second statement considers a random variable that measures directly the information present on marks. Current practice considers the second variable during the analysis stage and the first variable during the evaluation stage. A consistent framework should consider the same variable during the entire process. Hence, such a framework should consider the following decision at the evaluation stage:

> The assessment of the specificity of the information in agreement between a mark and a print during the *evaluation phase* aims at weighing whether the information observed on the mark is sufficiently discriminative to exclude any other individual (than the donor of the print) as the source of the mark.

This decision is consistent with the one made during the analysis stage, since it avoids shifting the definition of the notion of sufficiency in-between different stages of the examination process. This decision is also consistent with the questions raised by early fingerprint scientists, such as Galton and Balthazard (Section 15.2.5), and it seems that focusing on the level of agreement occurred solely as a result of a misinterpretation of Locard's tripartite rule. Table 15.3 summarizes the types of decisions expected at the different stages of the examination process in current practice and in a fully consistent logical framework. Naturally, the definition of a consistent framework in either approach needs to separate explicitly the determination of similarity made during the comparison and evaluation stages, as opposed to combining them (see Section 15.2.3). In both approaches, the question of the similarity between marks and prints during the comparison stages needs to be asked separately than the question of the specificity of the features observed on the marks.

Assuming that sufficiency has been properly defined and quantified, it can be then used by the numerical standard and holistic approaches, in different manners, but toward the same goal: to decide whether a mark is sufficiently discriminative to exclude all individuals but one.

Since, in most cases, this decision is impossible to make based on scientific data alone, and is the result of some policy decision or cognitive process, we advocate that the inductive inference process described in Section 15.3.2.1 should not rely on the notion of sufficiency (which is ultimately unsustainable), but on a continuous approach

TABLE 15.3

Comparison between the Types of Decisions Made at Each Stage of the Fingerprint Examination Process

	Current Practice	Consistent Logical Framework
Analysis stage	Determination whether there is sufficient information in the mark to pursue the examination	Determination of the discrimination potential of the mark's features, and determination whether it is worth pursuing the examination
	Both types of decisions are equivalent, albeit stated in slightly different ways	
Comparison stage	Estimation of the level of agreement between the mark and the print	Estimation of whether the mark's features fit within the range of variations that could be observed between multiple impressions of the donor of the print
	Both types of decisions can be considered equivalent, despite the numerous inexplicit assumptions made in current practice[a]	
Evaluation stage	Assessment of the probability of observing such level of agreement between marks and prints from different donors	Assessment of the probability of observing the features present on the mark in anyone else than the donor of the print
	These decisions cannot be considered equivalent. Decisions made in current practice focus on the level of agreement, while decisions made in a consistent framework remain focused on the information directly observed on the mark	
	The decisions made in the consistent framework at the analysis and evaluation stages are essentially equivalent: highly specific features will by definition not be observed on many individuals	

Note: The decisions made in current practice are summarized in the left-hand side column and the decisions that would be made in a consistent logical framework are summarized in the right-hand side column.

[a] Several assumptions are made when comparing marks and prints. The two most important assumptions are (1) the print is representative of the friction ridge skin on the finger pad and (2) based on training and experience, examiners are able to infer, from the observation of the print, the range of variations that would exist between multiple trace impressions made by the donor of the print.

directly based on the quantification of the specificity of fingerprint features. In this new approach, the decision made at the evaluation stage should be restated as follows:

> The assessment of the specificity of the information in agreement between a mark and a print during the *evaluation phase* aims at weighing the specificity of the information observed on the mark and determining how many individuals (other than the donor of the print) could be considered as the source of the mark.

This decision symbolizes the paradigm shift from a process based on policy decisions and opaque cognitive processes toward a more transparent, data-driven, and logically defendable inference process. This continuous approach enables moving away from the traditional conclusion scheme, which is needed for the reasons presented in the next section.

15.3.2.3 Conclusion Scheme

Section 15.2.2 introduces the three types of conclusions that are traditionally reported following the examination of fingerprints: identification, inconclusive examination, and exclusion. Whenever the mark and the print are not *sufficiently* similar (or *sufficiently* dissimilar) to conclude with certainty that the donor of the print is (not) the source of the mark, examiners will report that the examination is inconclusive. This conclusion scheme suffers from two main limitations:

1. The thresholds separating the different categories require a leap-of-faith that cannot be supported by scientific data alone.
2. While the identification and exclusion categories exaggerate the weight of fingerprint evidence, the inconclusive category prevents reporting valuable evidence.

We discussed in Section 15.3.2.1 that the achievement of the state of certainty cannot be rationalized, that fingerprint examination is an inductive probabilistic process, and that reaching conclusions of identifications or exclusions required some leap-of-faith to supplement the use of the notion of sufficiency. It is clear that reaching the state of certainty when excluding individuals as the source of marks requires a much smaller leap-of-faith than when identifying individuals. Indeed, the accumulation of manifestly different observations between pairs of marks and prints permits to exclude that they originate from the same source, even when taking into account elements such as distortion or development technique. As discussed in the previous section, this leap-of-faith is addressed differently between the proponents of the holistic and numerical standard approaches. In the first approach, the leap-of-faith is an entirely cognitive process that cannot be quantified in a transparent and reproducible way. It depends on the training, experience, and other personal circumstances of the examiners and on the intrinsic elements of the case at hand. In the second approach, the leap-of-faith is policy driven. It depends on operating procedures set by some governing body. In both situations, the data alone cannot justify the existence of the exclusion and identification categories.

Whenever examiners cannot reach either identification or exclusion conclusions, they revert to the last category: inconclusive results. In these situations, examiners implicitly acknowledge that the marks could have originated from more than one individual, but generally cannot provide any information on the number of individuals that could be considered. It seems intuitively logical that whenever a mark is associated to an individual and that very few other individuals could also be considered as the source of the mark, the fingerprint evidence is much more probative than when many other individuals could also be associated with the mark. Nevertheless, when reporting inconclusive results, examiners are not providing any information on the probative or exculpatory value of the examinations that were performed. Inconclusive results are neither transparent nor helpful, but the rationale behind them can be understood when considering an ethical perspective or from an operational point of view:

1. The prejudice to a suspect/defendant resulting from the reporting of *less than certain* evidence may outweigh the value of the reported evidence, and therefore it may not be ethical to report such evidence.
2. If fingerprint units were to examine all marks that are currently deemed of insufficient quality, they may end up having to handle an exponential increase in the number of marks. Units simply do not have the necessary resources to process all these additional marks (see Section 15.4.2.5).
3. By definition, inconclusive results include all results that are less than certain. It can be argued that from a quality assurance point of view, the current conclusion scheme is helping to reduce the rates of erroneous identifications and exclusions of fingerprint examination.

Overall, the current conclusion scheme cannot be justified by data alone and is the result of the complex combination of ethical, policy, and quality assurance considerations, with the level of confidence that examiners associate with their results. This makes the conclusion scheme very difficult to describe and defend. Furthermore, this categorical conclusion scheme prevents the reporting of potentially valuable information to customers of fingerprint examiners.

As discussed earlier for the notion of sufficiency, it would be possible to use data relative to the quantification of the specificity of fingerprint features to create well-defined categories. These categories would remain driven by policy decisions, but would be transparent and easier to describe and justify. Alternatively, it is possible to consider using a continuous reporting scheme in conjunction with the continuous quantification of the specificity of fingerprint features discussed earlier.

The continuous reporting scheme would be consistent with Galton's, Locard's, and others' view on the topic. Indeed, Galton was suggesting that the weight of fingerprint evidence should be reported using a continuous variable; even Locard, who first suggested using a sufficiency threshold, allowed for a continuous reporting scheme with his third rule:

> If a limited number of characteristics are present, the fingerprint cannot provide certainty for an identification, but only a presumption proportional to the number of points available and their clarity.

Such a scheme would have numerous advantages; among these, it would not require a leap-of-faith and would enable the reporting of all useful information to the legal system. Some statistical models, such as the ones presented in Section 15.4.2.2, enable such a continuous scheme.

15.3.3 Error Rates for the Examination of Fingerprints

The (lack of) measurement of the rates of error in fingerprint examination represents a major challenge for the fingerprint community. Data on the accuracy and precision of the fingerprint examination process has been requested by courts, and by legal and scientific scholars. For a long time, fingerprint examiners have claimed that the "rate of error was 0" [37]. The fingerprint community used to claim that the error rate of the process was different than the error rate of the examiners performing the process. Examiners claimed that the process was infallible. Erroneous conclusions on the source of marks could only be observed as a result of a human error, and that human error could only be caused by lack of relevant training, or by some sort of bias. Since the process was error free and that it was not possible to predict when examiners would encounter a case beyond their abilities, or when they could be biased, it was irrelevant to even attempt to measure error rates.

As discussed by Cole, this reasoning is illogical: fingerprint examiners are the process. The ACE-V process in itself is not detailed enough to provide guidance to examiners as to what decision to make based on their observations. They are the ones who decide which features to use and which decisions to make at each stage of the examination process based on the observation of these features.

However, examiners have a point when they challenge the relevance of error rates and their ability to measure them. SWGFAST defines four categories of error rates [52]:

1. Error rates* of each single individual
2. Error rates of a fingerprint unit
3. Error rates of categories of examiners, such as examiners having gone through the same training
4. Error rates of the community

While the first error rates are the most relevant in a single case, they are also the most variable. Error rates for a given individual may vary depending on training, background, and experience but also depending on personal circumstances (e.g., stress, fatigue, personal situation). To be entirely relevant, the error rates for that individual should be measured continuously, which is obviously not realistic. On the other end of the spectrum, the error rates of the community may be practically measurable but will only represent some average measure, which will not account for specific type of training, length of experience, or type of cases performed.

In addition, error rates are commonly measured according to statistical hypothesis testing theory, and result in the measurement of false positive and false negative error rates. Unfortunately, this theory cannot be directly applied to the examination of fingerprint evidence. Indeed, hypothesis testing usually considers the hypothesis to be tested, called the *null hypothesis*, and a mutually exclusive alternative hypothesis. Based on a statistic, the test assesses whether the data fails to reject the null hypothesis, or whether it accepts the alternative hypothesis. Such a test is not directly applicable to fingerprint examination due to the categorical reporting scheme, which includes three categories.

Finally, there is a controversy as to what constitutes an error. Erroneous identifications and exclusions are obvious errors. However, other types of decisions may be inappropriate. For example, the classification of the results of an examination as inconclusive may be inappropriate if other examiners consider that the examination should have resulted in an identification. The question is whether missed identifications, missed exclusions, or other types of inappropriate decisions should be considered as error or not. SWGFAST defines these decisions as "nonconsensus decisions" and proposes example calculations for rates of errors and nonconsensus decisions for the four categories of error rates listed earlier [52]. In parallel, a few research studies have been conducted; their results are presented in Section 15.4.3.

Error rates only exist within a categorical conclusion scheme. When considering a continuous reporting scheme, error rates cannot exist since conclusions cannot be on the wrong side of thresholds. However, this does not mean that the conclusions are always right. Neumann et al. [58] have defined the situations when a conclusion supports the wrong hypothesis (e.g., hypothesis of different sources when the impressions are truly from the same finger) as being misleading evidence in favor of the prosecution or the defense.

* As discussed in the SWGFAST standard [52], there are several possible types of error. With respect to the examination of fingerprint, the most fundamental ones are erroneous identifications and erroneous exclusions.

15.3.4 Summary

The examination of fingerprints for forensic purposes has been heavily challenged over the past decade. This section shows that some of the claims made by the fingerprint community do not resist careful scrutiny. The use of statistics and probability theory needs to fit into a bigger picture, which should include training, certification, and the development of community-wide standards. Nevertheless, statistics and probabilities can help redefine and support the fingerprint examination process by

1. Providing a logical reasoning framework for the inductive inference of the source of marks recovered from crime scenes
2. Providing data to measure the variability and the specificity of fingerprint features
3. Providing data for rendering the current reporting scheme more robust, reproducible, and transparent or for proposing a new continuous reporting scheme
4. Measuring and reporting error rates

15.4 Use of Statistics and Probabilities to Support Fingerprint Examination

15.4.1 Introduction

Statistics and probability theory can be used in many different areas to support and demonstrate the reliability of the fingerprint examination process. Some arguments made by challengers of the fingerprint community have been presented in the previous section. In this section, we will focus on two main areas, which have been requested by critics, where statistical data have already been presented in court:

1. The quantification of the weight of evidence of fingerprint comparisons and the use of statistical data as a support for the inference process
2. The measurement of error rates

15.4.2 Statistical Data for the Support of the Decision-Making Process

Statistics and probabilities have been used in many ways in several attempts to support the inference of the source of marks recovered from crime scenes. In a previous edition of this book [29], Stoney summarized several research projects or studies aimed at developing statistical models acquiring data on the frequency of fingerprint features. Stoney's conclusions were that none of the proposed models have been subjected to extended empirical validation studies and that

1. The models did not capture the spatial relationships between fingerprint features
2. Most models relied on the untested assumption of independence between features
3. The models focused on the estimation of the specificity of fingerprint features but did not account for tolerances due to distortion or clarity of the marks
4. The effect of the representativeness and the composition of the databases for these models (e.g., general pattern, fingerprint number, ethnic origin, sex) has not been addressed

Since Stoney's review, many research projects have been conducted and are summarized in the following paragraphs.

15.4.2.1 Descriptive Statistical Data on Fingerprint Features

Since 2001, a series of papers have been published on research projects investigating the influence of genetic factors on fingerprint features. A study conducted by Reed et al. [59] focused on the heritability of arch patterns by studying monozygotic and dizygotic twins. Results suggest a very high heritability of 91%. Another research project conducted by Steinman [60] focused on the role of genetic and environmental factors influencing the general pattern of friction ridge skin in twins, triplets, quadruplets, and quintuplets. The results show that the similarity of the general pattern is higher between twins (88%) than triplets (84%), quadruplets (74%), and quintuplets (71%). Steinman suggests that the potential for mutation is higher between larger sets of fetuses. These two studies confirm the results observed by previous authors on the heritability of general patterns of friction ridge skin. Jain et al. [61] studied the discriminative power of fingerprint features to measure the limits of biometric-based verification systems. The research proposed to measure the level of similarity between the general pattern and minutiae configurations observed on fingerprints obtained from 94 pairs of twins, and on unrelated individuals. Jain found that while the fingerprints of pairs of twins are more similar to each other than those of unrelated individuals, he also made the point that the same level of similarity can be observed between pairs of fingerprints from unrelated individuals when they have the same general pattern. This study also supports the hypothesis that genetic and other local factors influence the general pattern of fingerprints, but indicates that similarities between other levels of details are more driven by the general pattern than by genetic relationships. Similar research has been conducted by Srihari et al. [62] and by Liu and Srihari [63] with similar results.

Other studies have focused on the underlying distributions of fingerprint features in various populations and provide descriptive statistical data of these features. Notably, Gutièrrez et al. [64] analyzed the general pattern and the number and type of minutiae in fingerprints from 200 index fingers (100 from males and 100 from females) obtained from the Spanish population. The results show that ridge endings are the most common type of minutiae followed by bifurcations. Minutiae were not homogeneously distributed: their density was greater around the cores and deltas than in the periphery of the various patterns. Furthermore, there is a correlation between general pattern and number of minutiae: whorls displayed the highest number of minutiae, followed by loops and arches. This study was expanded in 2011 [65] by using fingerprints from 200 individuals from the Spanish population (100 males and 100 females, 2000 fingerprints total). Among other findings, this study shows that general pattern and fingerprint number are highly correlated, that minutiae frequency was different between the sexes and between finger numbers, and that minutiae are not homogeneously located on the patterns. These results rejoin the observations made by Champod [66], Chen and Jain [67], Ross et al. [68], and Srihari [69].

Overall, these studies provide interesting descriptive data on fingerprint features; however, it is not clear how they can help and support the inference process. The results obtained during these research projects show that fingerprint features are highly variable, and indicate some of the parameters (e.g., sex, finger number, general pattern) that need to be taken into account when quantifying the weight of fingerprint evidence in individual cases, but do not provide a means to perform that quantification. This can only be achieved through the modeling of the joint distributions of these features on marks.

15.4.2.2 Fingerprint Statistical Models

On the one hand, and contrary to forensic DNA profiling, there is no easily definable and quantifiable set of features that can be used to characterize friction ridge skin. In Section 15.2.1, we introduced the three levels of details commonly used to describe fingerprint features. For each of these levels of details, a multitude of variables can be selected. For example, minutiae cannot only be described by their locations on the ridge flows, but also by their types, their directions, the shapes of their edges, and their spatial relationships with other features. In agreement with Champod [66] and Stoney [29], the independence between minutiae cannot be assumed since the relationships between those variables are not known. Developing statistical models for the quantification of the weight of fingerprint evidence appears to be a challenging task.

On the other hand, developers of Automatic Fingerprint Identification Systems (AFIS) have been very successful at designing and implementing algorithms measuring the level of similarity between impressions, at associating impressions from the same source, and at discriminating impressions from different sources [70]. This measure of similarity, which corresponds to the level of similarity expressed by fingerprint examiners and discussed in Section 15.3.2.2, is expressed as a univariate score. In other words, this score captures enough of the variability between several different types of fingerprint features to successfully associate or discriminate impressions. Following projects presented in other areas of forensic science, some authors have proposed to use similarity scores as a basis for the development of fingerprint statistical models. Neumann et al. [58,71] presented a model, which enabled them to assign weight to any mark configurations with 3–12 minutiae.

Following Champod [66], the model relies on the likelihood ratio approach advocated for other types of forensic evidence such as trace and DNA. It is designed to provide an answer to the two main questions that need to be considered when examining fingerprints that were introduced in Section 15.3.2.1:

1. How similar can different impressions from the same finger appear, and can the differences be explained by data gathered on the influence of distortion, surface, or development technique?
2. How many individuals could produce impressions displaying similar features when taking into account elements such as distortion, surface, or development technique?

In essence, the model attempts to answer the first question by assigning a probability to the likelihood of observing a mark feature in multiple impressions of a considered individual's finger; and the second question by assigning the probability of observing the same mark feature on randomly selected individuals.

Neumann et al.'s model accounted for spatial relationships between minutiae and finger pads' distortions, but did not capture other sources of variability, such as the quality of the marks or the variability between users. The results of the project indicated that, even when considering a reduced number of types of features (minutiae types, locations, and directions), configurations observed on marks with a low number of features can be highly specific and carry significant evidential value. The results also showed that the specificity of marks increased with the number of features observed on those marks. Nevertheless, large variations were observed between the weight of configurations with the same number of features, indicating that the number of features itself is not a sufficient indicator of the specificity of the marks.

Importantly, the model proposed by Neumann et al. suffers from the same inconsistency as the one described in Section 15.3.2.2 for the current fingerprint examination process. Indeed, the model considers the level of similarity between pairs of marks and prints as a random variable, but assigns probabilities to this variable using probability density functions based on a different random variable (the specificity of the mark features among impressions from the donor of the prints, and among impressions from randomly selected individuals).

Egli [72] further pursued the concept of using scores to assign weight to fingerprint evidence and designed a model directly based on an AFIS algorithm. Egli attempted to address the inconsistency of Neumann et al.'s model and assigned the probability associated with the aforementioned first question by generating probability density functions of scores computed between multiple pairs of pseudo-marks and prints deposited by the same finger. In order to reduce the amount of impressions required from individuals suspected of being the source of crime scene marks, Egli studied the parameters of these density functions and showed that they were correlated with the number of features. Unfortunately, Egli did not achieve the transition from Neumann et al.'s model toward a completely consistent model: while Egli considers the level of similarity between marks and prints as the random variable, and while the probability density functions addressing the first question are based on the same random variable, the probability density functions addressing the second question are still directly based on the specificity of the mark features. Indeed, a completely consistent model would have generated probability density functions for the second question based on the similarity scores computed between pairs of pseudo-marks and prints deposited by different individuals, as opposed to generating them from the scores computed between the considered crime scene mark and prints from randomly selected individuals. Nevertheless, Egli's results, based on a very large database of fingerprints (over 600,000 fingerprints), confirmed that fingerprint evidence is very powerful, even when considering marks with a low number of features.

As mentioned in Section 15.3.2.2, the difference between Neumann et al.'s and Egli's models is subtle but nevertheless critical. Neumann et al. attempted to address the following two questions:

1. What is the probability of observing a mark (with all its features) if it was deposited by a given individual?
2. What is the probability of observing the same mark if somebody else deposited it?

While Egli has addressed the following two questions:

1. What is the probability of observing this level of similarity between the mark and print if the mark has been deposited by the same individual who deposited the print?
2. What is the probability of observing this level of similarity between the mark and the print if different individuals deposited them?

The focus of these two pairs of questions, and therefore the choice of the random variable and probability density functions, is different.

It is interesting to note that the National Institute of Standards and Technology (NIST) has generated data enabling the construction of a statistical model assigning probabilities to the level of similarity between marks and prints as proposed by Egli. In 2011, NIST released a report [70] on the evaluation of the current generation of matching algorithms for marks. The aim of the research project conducted by NIST was not to design a statistical model for fingerprints; however, in order to compare the accuracy of the most recent search and matching algorithms from the main AFIS providers, the similarity scores between marks and prints originating from the same fingers, and from different fingers, were generated. These two sets of scores are the ones enabling the generation of the probability density functions for the model proposed by Egli. By extension, it also means that all agencies using AFIS to search latent prints against databases of suspects already have a tool, which could enable them to assign probabilities to comparisons between marks and prints. As part of their daily work, examiners matching prints in these agencies generate scores between matched marks and prints, and between marks and non-corresponding prints. As for the NIST research, these scores would allow them to build a statistical model for assigning weight to fingerprint comparisons.

Statistical models considering the level of similarity between pairs of marks and prints as the random variable are easy to design and readily available. That said, they have two significant shortcomings:

1. Weight of the evidence will vary significantly depending on the control print used for the comparison: different control prints from the considered individual will produce different similarity scores, which in turn will produce different weights of evidence for a given mark.
2. Weight of the evidence for a given mark represents some average weight of evidence that is valid for all pairs of marks and prints with the same level of similarity. The weight of evidence is in fact not directly dependent on the specificity of the considered mark.

In 2012, Neumann et al. [73] proposed an updated version of Neumann et al.'s 2007 model. The new model focuses on the specificity of the mark features as the random variable and assigns the two required probabilities using consistent probability density functions. The model relies on probability density functions generated by comparing, on the one hand, the crime scene mark to pseudo-marks deposited by the considered individual, and on the other hand, the crime scene mark to pseudo-marks deposited by other individuals. Neumann et al.'s 2012 model accounts for finger pad distortion and user variability; in addition, it considers spatial relationships between minutiae. The model does use similarity scores to compare the crime scene marks to the pseudo-marks, but does not use the similarity between the mark and the print as a random variable to assign the weight of the evidence. Instead, Neumann et al.'s 2012 model relies on a complex weighting function to perform a Monte Carlo integration to assign the probability of observing a mark feature in both probability density functions. The weighting function was optimized to minimize the rates of misleading evidence of the model, but is considered as a weakness of the model. Neumann et al. validated their model using 364 sets of data, each of which consisted of a mark recovered from a U.K. crime scene, a control print identified by a U.K. examiner as originating from the finger that made the mark, and a close nonmatching print obtained by searching the mark in the U.S. national fingerprint database and retrieving the most similar non-corresponding control print. Figure 15.3 presents some of the results obtained by Neumann et al. These results were obtained by re-sampling configurations of 3–12 minutiae from minutiae detected on the 364 marks and their corresponding prints.

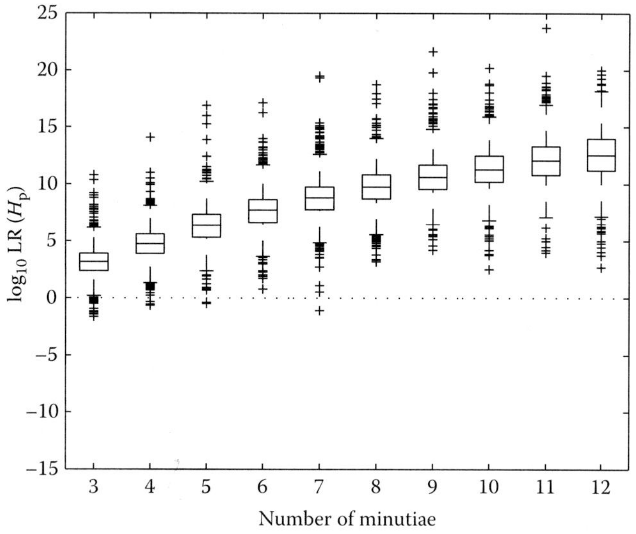

FIGURE 15.3
Results obtained by Neumann et al. in 2012 [73]. The figure presents the weight of evidence (log 10 of the likelihood ratios calculated by their model) obtained for configurations of 3–12 minutiae sampled in pairs of corresponding marks and prints.

The main findings of this study can be drawn from Figure 15.3:

1. First and foremost, the results show that the expected weight of evidence of marks increases with the number of features that can be observed in these marks. In addition, the expected weight of evidence for the largest configurations is extremely strong.
2. Nevertheless, the range of evidential values obtained for the various number of minutiae considered overlap significantly.
3. In fact, some minutiae configurations with a low number of features can be very specific and carry significant evidentiary value; sometimes, they can be considered more powerful evidence than configurations with a higher number of minutiae.

These findings certainly do not unveil groundbreaking revelations on the foundations of the examination of fingerprint evidence; however, for the first time, some claims made by fingerprint examiners are justified by this data. The results obtained by Neumann et al. [73] support the claims that

1. Fingerprint evidence is extremely powerful, and that, if examined correctly, will provide valuable evidence.
2. There is no scientific basis to justify the existence of a numerical standard.
3. The weight of evidence of each mark needs to be assigned based on its own merits.

In addition, Neumann et al.'s model shows that it is possible to quantify the specificity of features observed on marks in individual cases, and that this quantification produces continuous results, supporting that the notion of sufficiency cannot be justified by data alone as advocated previously.

The current state of the art of fingerprint statistical models relying on similarity scores shows that those models suffer from technical limitations (the weighting function used by Neumann et al. [73]) or from practical limitations (average weight of evidence and variability for the level of similarity model). Overcoming these limitations seems to be feasible only by using an analytical model, which would directly model the joint distribution of friction ridge skin features.

Several authors have attempted to develop such models. The models proposed by Pankanti et al. [74], Zhu et al. [75], and Dass et al. [76] propose an analytical solution to the distribution of friction ridge features on fingerprint patterns by modeling the joint distributions of minutiae locations and directions, and the way minutiae cluster depending on the general pattern. Since these models were designed to study the problem of fingerprint uniqueness, the authors of these research projects only focused on the probability of random correspondence between pairs of pseudo-marks generated by these models. They did not seem to have applied their models to the measurement of the specificity of features observed on real marks to assign the probability of observing them by random chance. In addition, these models only studied the question of correspondence between impressions from different fingers. The question of the association between multiple impressions from a given finger was handled by the definition of tolerance levels, which only weakly accounts for finger distortion, clarity, and user variability. Finally, these models assumed independence between minutiae.

In a series of papers summarized in Refs [69,77], a research project lead by Srihari took inspiration from the research by Pankanti et al. [74], Zhu et al. [75], and Dass et al. [76] and attempted to address some of the issues of the previous models. Most notably, Srihari's model does not assume independence between minutiae. Instead, the model considers configurations of minutiae organized around a centroid as in Neumann et al. [71,73]. Srihari's model still relies on tolerance levels for the associations of impressions deemed to be from the same source, but was used to predict the chance of random correspondence of real latent prints. Albeit tested on a very small database, Srihari's model shows that the modeled probabilities of random correspondence follow the ones obtained empirically and that these probabilities are reduced when the number of features is increased.

15.4.2.3 Fingerprint Quality Model

The models presented in the previous section focused on the quantification of fingerprint features and on the estimation of the specificity of marks. Several authors have discussed the impact of the quality of the marks on the ability of fingerprint examiners to reliably draw conclusions from the examination of fingerprints, and on the ability of fingerprint matching algorithms to accurately compare finger impressions. Promising research projects have been conducted with the aim of automatically assessing the quality of marks. In particular, Hicklin et al. [78] presented the results of a survey on the process used by fingerprint examiners to evaluate the quality of marks and prints. Based on their results, Hicklin et al. proposed useful guidelines, metrics, and software tools for assessing fingerprint quality. Other authors are concerned with the assessment of the quality of finger impressions for biometric purposes and have presented effective algorithms for this intent.

So far, these quality metrics are developed separately from the quantitative metrics presented in the previous section. We anticipate that qualitative and quantitative algorithms will be combined in the near future.

15.4.2.4 Validation/Calibration

Validating fingerprint statistical models is a critical step prior to their acceptance by the fingerprint, scientific, and legal communities. The validation of fingerprint statistical models must consider the following three elements:

1. Robustness of the underlying assumptions
2. Precision of the outputs
3. Accuracy of the outputs

The validation of statistical models, or any new theory or technology, can belong to either of the following two categories:

1. A technology should be validated by verifying its underlying assumptions against well understood and verified theories, and by measuring the precision and accuracy of its outputs against expected outputs, which are either theoretically predicted, or have been empirically measured.
2. Pragmatically, a technology can be validated by comparing its performances against those of the previously validated technique(s) it intends to replace.

The validation of forensic DNA profiling belongs to the first category. DNA statistical models for the quantification of DNA evidence benefit from robust assumptions, which are supported by population genetics, and their output can be predicted theoretically. Additionally, DNA statistical models consider variables that can be easily quantified: allele designations. This critical element enables DNA statisticians to perform population studies and practically estimate a gold standard of the expected output of their models. This gold standard can then be used to measure the precision and accuracy of the outputs of the model.

Unfortunately, this is not possible for fingerprint statistical models. The formation of friction ridge skin does not appear to be highly correlated to genetic factors; on the contrary, it is mostly a process influenced by local circumstances affecting the fetus between the very first weeks of its development. The number of parameters influencing the development of friction ridge skin on the fetus is such that it may never be understood well enough to be able to theoretically predict friction ridge features. Furthermore, there is no simply identifiable and measurable set of variables to describe fingerprint patterns; hence, it is practically impossible to create a gold standard estimation of the frequency of particular fingerprint features.

The validation of analytical techniques typically belongs to the second category. Assuming that the assumptions underling the new technique have been previously validated (e.g., they are the same as the previous technique), its performances, in terms of accuracy, precision, and limit of detection, but also costs, user-friendliness, and health and safety, are compared to the performances of the previous technique(s). This strategy is also not applicable to the validation of fingerprint statistical models due to the lack of a previously validated model.

Since it is not be possible to validate fingerprint statistical models by comparing their outputs to predicted outputs, or outputs from previously validated models, their validation appears to be a significant empirical endeavor. Importantly, we also need to recognize at this point that, in the absence of a theoretical foundation such as the one supporting DNA models, every fingerprint model is based on a series of assumptions and incorporates subjective elements related to the background and knowledge of its designers: different models may have different outputs that may all be valid.

We have presented earlier that fingerprint statistical models need to assign two kinds of probabilities:

1. Probability of observing the features on the mark if it was left by the same finger as the print
2. Probability of observing the features on the mark if a different individual, other than the one who left the print, deposited it

It is important to appreciate that both aspects need to be tested for every model. Too often, a lack of understanding of the forensic problem leads scientists to consider only the second probability. In other words, the ability of models, or techniques, to discriminate between objects originating from different sources is the only focus of validation studies. However, it is equally crucial to validate the ability of models, or techniques, to associate objects originating from the same source.

Twins studies have been proposed to validate fingerprint examination (e.g., [62,63,69]). These studies are typical examples of this lack of understanding of the forensic problem. The basic premise behind these studies is that if fingerprint examination or fingerprint statistical models are able to discriminate between finger impressions from twins, then the hypothesis that fingerprints are unique is supported. Apart from the fact that uniqueness is irrelevant, as discussed in Section 15.3.2.1, the only finding from these studies is that finger impressions are not highly genetically dependent (except for general pattern type [59,60]). This is by no means an indication that fingerprints are unique, nor an indication that fingerprint examiners (or models) are capable of associating marks and prints when they have been deposited by the same fingers, or even discriminate between marks and prints when they have been left by different fingers.

As discussed earlier, the validation of models needs to consider three elements: the robustness of their underlying assumptions and the precision and accuracy of their outputs. Considering each assumption separately may enable the design of experiments that allow for comparing predicted and calculated values. Once comfortable with the robustness of a model, it is possible to test its precision by repeatedly quantifying the weight of a given set of fingerprint features under different conditions. For example, it seems imperative to study the precision of the model under the following conditions:

1. Influence of multiple users selecting the same set of fingerprint features
2. Reproducibility of the weights of a set of given fingerprint features observed on multiple replicate impressions from the same finger when those impressions have been deposited under different pressure and distortion conditions, on different surfaces, and revealed by different development techniques
3. Influence of the size of the reference database used to estimate the frequencies of the features, and representativeness of that database

In the absence of a fundamental theory allowing the prediction of friction ridge skin features, and in the absence of a gold standard, the accuracy of fingerprint models can be assessed against *desired* outputs.

Neumann et al. [73] have proposed a stress test for their model: they have designed an experiment that compares the outputs of the model (a) when comparing impressions from

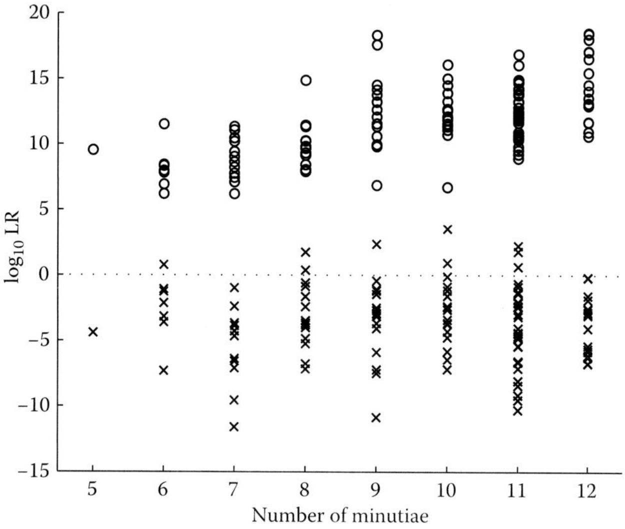

FIGURE 15.4
Results obtained by Neumann et al. [73]. The O's represent the outputs of the model when comparing impressions from the same finger; the X's represent the outputs of the model when comparing impressions from different fingers.

the same finger and (b) when comparing highly similar impressions from different fingers. Note that this design allows the measurement of the ability of the model to associate, as well as to discriminate. The idea behind the test was to put the model in the worst possible situation by taking highly similar impressions from different origins with a desire to observe a clear separation between the two categories of outputs. Figure 15.4 shows the results obtained by Neumann et al. The separation between the two categories of outputs is well defined and the desired result has been achieved.

Other authors have proposed to calibrate the outputs of statistical models [79–81]. These authors suggest running experiments to record the outputs of models when comparing impressions (a) from the same finger and (b) from different randomly selected fingers and then to apply a function to these outputs in order to satisfy some criteria, such as minimizing the rates of misleading evidence produced by the model, or rendering it more favorable to defendants. Overall, these criteria need to have some *utility*. The notion of *utility* discussed by Biedermann et al. [82] is interesting from several perspectives. In particular, it explicitly states that statistical models (or any other process) cannot be used in isolation but need to be seen as part of a bigger picture. The calibration of statistical models to produce desired outputs is a potentially dangerous practice. Calibrating models could be seen as "tweaking" them, and could undermine the confidence from the fingerprint and legal communities in the models: it could be seen as replacing one subjective and opaque practice with another one. The greatest transparency and rigor are needed when performing these calibration exercises, and care should be taken to discuss their needs with respect to the notion of utility described by Biedermann et al.

Overall, the creation of a gold standard is something that needs to be further investigated. While conceptually and technically challenging, this seems to be the safest, most robust, and scientific way of assessing the accuracy of statistical models. We are not blind to the fact that this gold standard will itself rely on several assumptions; however, it should be possible to use current AFIS technology, and large fingerprint databases, to estimate empirically the frequency of various fingerprint features.

15.4.2.5 Operational Impact of the Use of Statistical Models to Quantify the Weight of Fingerprint Evidence

The use of statistical models for quantifying the weight of fingerprint evidence allows for moving away from the traditional categorical conclusion scheme, and for reporting fingerprint evidence using a continuous scale. In Section 15.3.2.3, we alluded to the operational implications of the current reporting scheme. More specifically

1. It provides control over the amount of marks considered by fingerprint units by allowing them to dismiss marks of poor quality or those that are heavily distorted.
2. It allows for only reporting results that are deemed certain.

The results obtained by Neumann et al. [73], presented in Figure 15.3, indeed show that

1. It is possible to observe marks with a low number of features and strong evidentiary value; hence, marks of poor quality should theoretically be considered and processed.
2. It is possible to observe marks with a higher number of features but weaker evidentiary value. If reported as identified, these marks would have their weight of evidence clearly exaggerated.

Neumann et al. [83] conducted a large-scale research project, in partnership with the Bureau of Criminal Apprehension (BCA) of the State of Minnesota, in order to study the operational implications of the use of fingerprint statistical models. Among other elements, Neumann et al. investigated

1. The amount of potentially useful evidence that is dismissed by examiners when following current operating procedures
2. The strength of evidence of the marks that are currently reported as being identified

In their study, Neumann et al. recovered more than 3600 friction ridge impressions that had been rejected by BCA laboratory technicians at the recovery stage, or by BCA examiners at the analysis stage (unsuitable marks) or at the evaluation stage (inconclusive evidence). The study design and a summary of the results are presented in Figure 15.5.

Neumann et al. reprocessed 1689 marks and found that approximately 3% (58 marks) could potentially be associated with an individual relevant to the case. Out of these 58 marks, only five were truly new detections (i.e., an individual who has not been previously associated with another mark in the same case). And out of these five marks, only one was associated with a suspect; the other four were associated with victims or elimination prints from individuals with legitimate access to the crime scene.

The findings of the study are that the proportion of poor quality impressions that could be practically associated with individuals in operational settings is very low. It is certain that some of the 58 marks, by their relevance to the case, may have been important and can be considered *missed evidence*; nevertheless, it is difficult to argue that all of the 3600 poor quality marks that were recovered in this study could be useful. Selecting the marks that are relevant to the case from the mass of friction ridge impressions that can potentially be recovered from crime scenes is therefore of upmost importance. Implementing a Case pre-Assessment and Interpretation (CAI) framework can achieve this [84]. Such a framework would allow for selecting and examining the mark with the most relevance and potential,

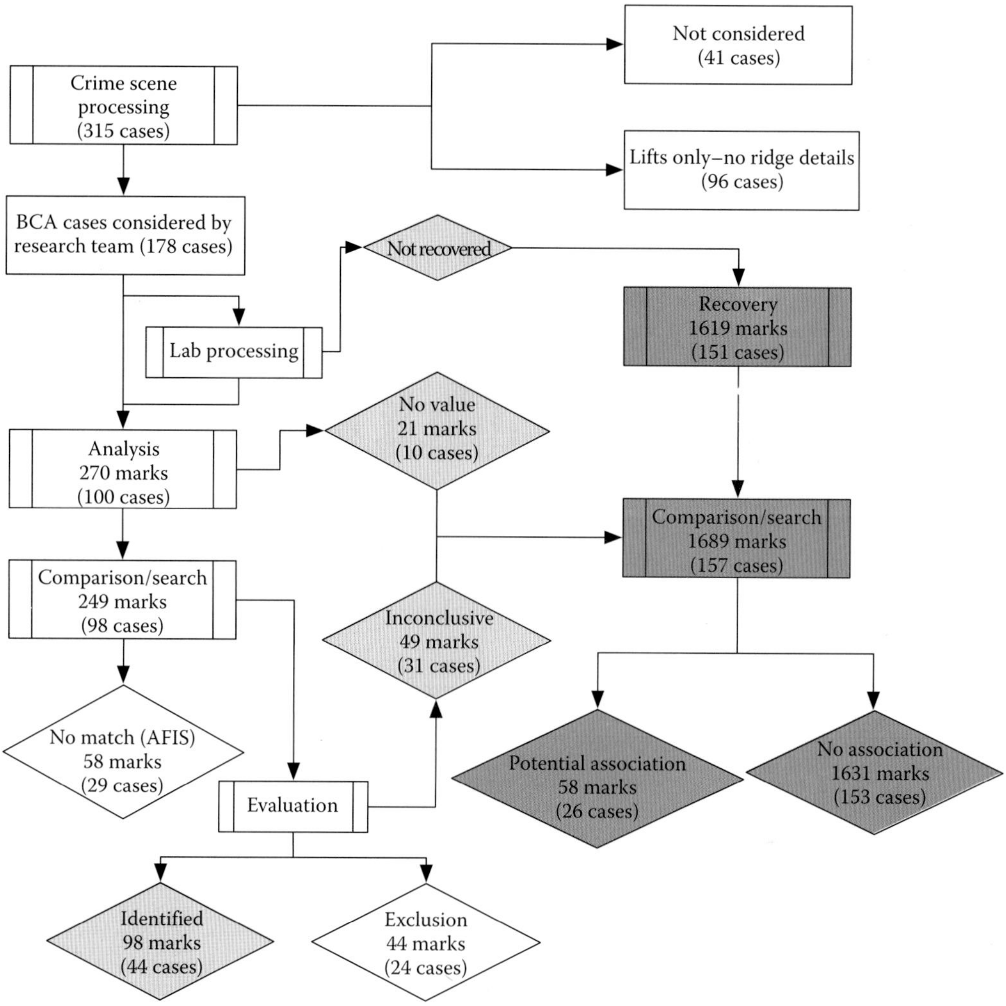

FIGURE 15.5
Study design and summary of the number of marks/cases considered in Neumann et al. [83]. The BCA process is shown in white; the research process is shown in blue. The yellow boxes show the interfaces between both processes. (From Neumann C, Mateos-Garcia I, Langenburg G, Kostroski J, Skerrett JE, Koolen M. (2011) Operational benefits and challenges of the use of fingerprint statistical models: a field study. *Forensic Science International* 212: 32–46. With permission from Elsevier.)

and would permit fingerprint units to balance their workloads, while maximizing the evidence that they would provide to their customers.

Additionally, and supporting the use of a continuous reporting framework, Neumann et al. found that 20 out of the 58 potential new evidence were the marks that had been considered by BCA examiners, but deemed inconclusive. These 20 marks include the one mark that was associated to a new suspect. Had a continuous scheme been in place at the BCA, these 20 marks would have been reported with no additional burden to the workload, since these 20 marks had already been examined.

With respect to the strength of the evidence of marks currently reported as identified, Neumann et al. found that the vast majority of identifications reported by examiners had more than 12 minutiae in agreement between marks and prints (Figure 15.6a). In other words,

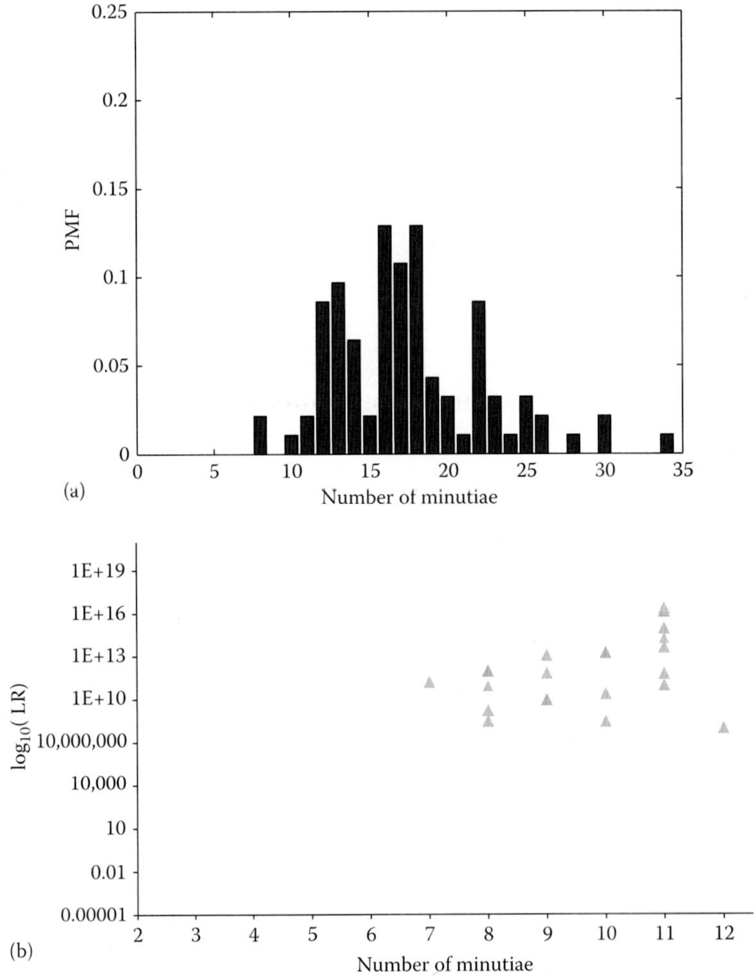

FIGURE 15.6
(a) Histogram of the number of minutiae in agreement for the marks reported as identified by BCA examiners in Neumann et al. [83]. (b) LRs calculated for the marks reported as identified by BCA examiners in Neumann et al. [83], and which had few features in agreement. (From Neumann C, Mateos-Garcia I, Langenburg G, Kostroski J, Skerrett JE, Koolen M. (2011) Operational benefits and challenges of the use of fingerprint statistical models: a field study. *Forensic Science International* 212: 32–46. With permission from Elsevier.)

most of these identifications have a weight of evidence way beyond the ones reported in Figure 15.3 and in Section 15.4.2.2. BCA examiners currently assume a deductive inference process. However, even within a proper logical framework as discussed in Section 15.3.2.2, this finding implies that the amount of features used to support the vast majority of identifications reported in current practice by BCA has a vanishingly small probability of being observed on impressions from different individuals than the true donors of the marks.

With respect to the small proportion of identifications made by BCA based on 12 features or less, Figure 15.6b shows that these identifications also carry strong weight and are not part of the comparisons displaying larger numbers of features in agreement but lower evidentiary value in Figure 15.3.

The results obtained during the research project reported by Neumann et al. [83] address some of the main concerns of the fingerprint community. These results show that the current process is efficient in filtering out the friction ridge details that would not result in useful information to the case, and is successful in selecting the ones that would. The results also support the hypothesis that most identification conclusions currently reported, while theoretically exaggerating the weight of the evidence carried by the comparisons, are extremely strong evidence from a pragmatic point of view. Critically, the data obtained during this study shows that the use of fingerprint statistical models to support the inductive inference process would result neither in an unmanageable amount of additional fingerprint evidence to process nor in a reduction of the power of fingerprint evidence. On the contrary, the use of such models, together with a continuous reporting scheme, would allow the reporting of more evidence for the same amount of effort.

15.4.3 Error Rates

In the previous sections, the possibility to replace the current tradition categorical reporting scheme was considered and data on the operational benefits of such a change was presented. Nevertheless, in the current context, the critical question of error rates in latent print examination remains to be successfully resolved. This particular issue continues to be raised by legal and scientific scholars (e.g., [38,39,85,86]).

We mentioned in Section 15.3.3 that the tripartite categorical conclusion scheme prevents a straightforward application of traditional decision theory to the measurement of error rates. In addition, the theory does not account for prints that are recovered but not deemed suitable for comparison, and for which no conclusions are reported. To take an extreme example, an examiner, who systematically deems that 100% of the prints are either of no value or inconclusive, would be guaranteed to never report false-positive or false-negative conclusions. In this case, it is evident that an "error-free" claim misrepresents the performance of the examiner, since this person never contributes to the resolution of criminal investigations. It would be equally as misleading to claim that this examiner has a 100% error rate, since some of the prints may genuinely be of no value or inconclusive (or the examiner may lack the training needed to reach conclusions in certain circumstances, for example, for highly distorted prints). The decisions made by the examiner may be inappropriate and unhelpful; however, they can hardly be considered as erroneous.

The traditional binary decision-making table cannot account for the overall lack of contribution of examiners not making decisions. Furthermore, it cannot weigh this lack of results against the presence of genuine no value and inconclusive prints in the considered set of prints. This need for tailored definitions of rates of errors and inappropriate decisions as they relate to the practice of the fingerprint discipline has been addressed in a recent (draft) SWGFAST standard [52]. This standard classically defines erroneous exclusions or identifications as false negatives and false positives, respectively. In addition, it defines *rates of nonconsensus decisions* for those cases where (a) examiners deem prints to be of value or of no value when they should not have done so; (b) they deem prints to be inconclusive when they should have reached one of the other two conclusions; or (c) they reach identification/exclusion conclusions when there are, in fact, not enough features in the prints to support those conclusions.

Another important challenge faced when attempting to measure error rates for the examination of latent prints is tied to the testing conditions. Three different generic approaches have been reported. These approaches are summarized later.

The first approach was reported by Cole [37] and focused on inventorying known and publicized misidentified fingerprints. This approach has some merit since it is based on real casework data and conditions. Cole accounted for 22 cases of misidentifications and suggested that this represented only "the tip of the iceberg." This claim is probably justified; however, while Cole's data provides us with a minimum false positive rate of 22 in several million comparisons performed over the past century, this figure is not accurate enough to be informative in court. In addition, Cole's data does not provide any information on the rate of erroneous exclusions or inappropriate decisions. Overall, this data simply highlights that erroneous identifications are made.

Several authors [37,49,50,86–89] have attempted and discussed the second approach. It consists of reviewing the performance of latent print examiners when performing routine proficiency tests. This approach benefits from the fact that the ground truth results are known for each comparison submitted to the examiners (as opposed to casework conditions). It also benefits from the wide distribution of the tests and the centralization of the answers. Error rates measured using data from proficiency tests vary: 0.2%–2.5% for Cole [37], 1.5% false positives for Wertheim et al. [49], 0.25% false positives for Gutowski [88], 2% for Peterson and Markham [89], and 0.5% for Langenburg et al. [50]. Both critics and supporters of the fingerprint community have heavily criticized this approach. The main arguments are centered around (a) the test conditions: the examiners know that they are being tested and it is not possible to control who takes the test (e.g., trainee) and how (e.g., by consensus vs. individually); (b) the test material is not representative of casework material and varies from year to year; (c) the lack of differentiation between genuine erroneous identifications and other errors (e.g., clerical errors); and (d) the absence of data on false negatives and inappropriate decisions.

The third approach is similar to the second one. However, instead of reviewing past results of proficiency tests, a test is specifically designed to measure error rates. This approach benefits from the fact that the ground truth is known for each comparison. It allows for controlling many variables such as (a) the training, experience, and certification of each examiner invited to take the test; (b) the time spent on each exercise; or (c) the level of difficulty of the comparisons. On the negative side, examiners know that they are being tested, and that they are tested for errors. This may create some bias and push examiners to err on the side of caution. In addition, the recurrent issues of the quality of the test material and of the test conditions can be raised. Hicklin and coworkers [90] conducted a large-scale research project based on this approach. The study involved 169 examiners, each of whom performed 100 comparisons. Overall, six erroneous identifications were made (0.1% false positive). The false negative rate was reported to be 7.5%.

The SWGFAST standard mentioned earlier [52] considers a different approach for the systematic measurement of all rates of errors and inappropriate decisions. This approach consists of auditing fingerprint cases from the archives of law enforcement agencies. It is not novel in itself since it is commonly used in the forensic (and fingerprint) communities to review past performances of agencies/individuals when needed (see Ref. [91] for an example). The novelty lies in the systematic auditing of case files to measure, for the wider community, all rates of errors and inappropriate decisions at various stages of the fingerprint examination process.

The SWGFAST standard does propose definitions and processes; however, it does not report error rates. It is now up to the community, and to legal and scientific scholars to join forces, measure them, and demonstrate that this novel method procures reliable and valid results. Overall, we believe that both approaches are somewhat complementary and that putting the two lines of research together should result in a more solid and convincing body of research than either could provide alone.

The last major challenge faced when attempting to measure error rates of latent print examination is linked to access to data (or test subjects) [85]. The impact of this element is especially important when attempting to measure error rates in casework conditions.

As mentioned in the previous paragraphs, all reported studies on error rates generally point toward relatively low error rates. Nevertheless, the community is showing some natural reticence to openly participate in these studies and to contribute data. Most studies reported earlier were performed on a limited sample, on laboratory data, and under potentially biasing test conditions. Furthermore, most studies were performed by either challengers or supporters of the community. This has led to endless arguments on the representativeness, implications, and reliability of their results. This demonstrates that a representative participation of the community, access to real casework data, and a robust experimental design can only be obtained by earning the trust of the community, and by ensuring that examiners openly collaborate with scientific and legal scholars. In addition, the anonymity of the origin of the data should be maintained as much as possible.

This review of the research problem shows that there is a need to conduct a large-scale research project aimed at properly defining and measuring community-wide rates of errors and inappropriate decisions under casework conditions. This project would need to systematically study the elements influencing these rates, such as the sufficiency of features in the prints and the presence of clerical errors. In addition, this project would need to gather data measuring the effectiveness and reliability of new processes designed to reduce the occurrence of errors (e.g., blind verification [54], more rigorous examination procedures [23]). Finally, such a project would need to have the support of the community and would require the open collaboration between latent print examiners, scientists, and legal scholars.

15.5 Conclusions: Changes in Current Practice

This chapter introduced the reader to the examination of fingerprint evidence. The fingerprint community currently claims that the inference of the source of a mark following its comparison with a print is a deductive process, which relies on the notion of sufficiency. We have seen that this claim does not resist careful scrutiny and that in fact, the inference process is an inductive one. In addition, we also demonstrated that the notion of sufficiency cannot be justified by logic alone, but is the result of policy decisions or cognitive processes that cannot be described.

Following several authors, such as Champod and Evett [15,16], we advocate that this inductive inference process should be supported by statistical data. In this chapter, we presented research projects aimed at designing statistical models that enable the gathering of the necessary data. We also discussed studies designed to measure the error rates of fingerprint examiners when comparing fingerprints, which show that, when using appropriate procedures, fingerprint examinations are reliable.

More importantly, we recommend that the fingerprint examination process should move away from the notion of sufficiency and use the results obtained from fingerprint statistical models to propose a continuous quantification of the specificity of fingerprint features. This continuous quantification would enable examiners to report the results of fingerprint examinations using a continuous reporting scheme. The potential benefits and limitations of such a scheme have been presented and show that the benefits for the justice system outweigh the potential limitations due to the number of additional marks that would need to be considered by fingerprint units.

It is interesting to observe that, while the results from the various research projects conducted since Galton have not had a significant impact on the current fingerprint

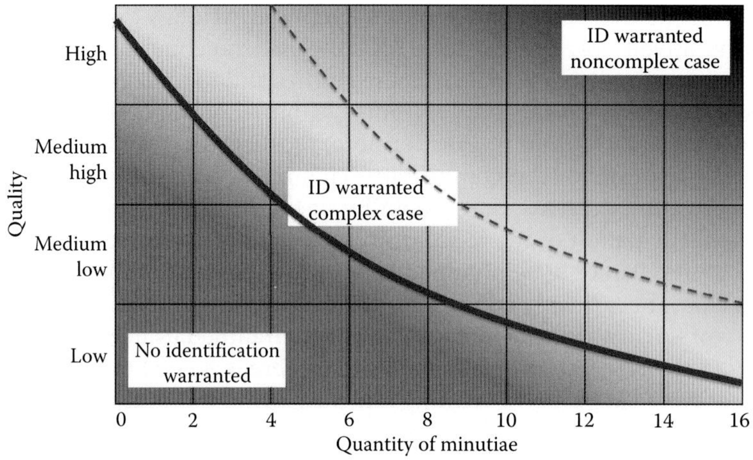

FIGURE 15.7
SWGFAST sufficiency graph [23]. This graph proposes guidelines for the determination of the suitability of marks during the analysis stage and for the forming of conclusions at the end of the evaluation stage.

examination process, the results of the research projects conducted over the past 15 years have been taken into account in the design of the newest operating procedures. Indeed, the newest SWGFAST standard for the examination of friction ridge impressions considers that the inference process is inductive and probabilistic in essence [23]. The standard includes a *sufficiency graph* for the assessment of the suitability of marks during the analysis stage, and for the forming of conclusions at the end of the evaluation stage (Figure 15.7). This sufficiency graph is based on the most recent statistical findings on the specificity of fingerprint features. The standard and its sufficiency graph are a significant step toward the recommended continuous inference scheme.

Similarly, the 2004 report from the Interpol European Expert Group on Fingerprint Identification recognizes the basic principles of fingerprint examination and incorporates detailed guidelines for the application of general scientific principles to fingerprint examination [24]. The Expert Group ultimately proposed a transparent and reproducible process, which includes criteria for the assessment of the value of fingerprint features.

It is clear that significant cultural changes and discussions need to happen within the fingerprint community in order to best implement the proposed paradigm shift. Professional organizations such as the IAI, the Scientific Working Group on Friction Ridge Analysis, Study and Technology (SWGFAST), and the fingerprint Working Group of the European Network of Forensic Science Institutes (ENFSI-FPWG) have a significant role to play in designing the new operating procedures and leading their implementations. Significant research efforts are still needed to further develop fingerprint statistical models to combine the qualitative and quantitative assessments of marks, and to add additional features such as general pattern [92], finger number [93], and other levels of details [94]. Naturally, research is needed to validate these models. Additional research needs to be performed to gather statistical data on the distributions of the various levels of fingerprint features in different populations, and to deepen the understanding of the cognitive process, which remains an important part of the inference process. Finally, research is needed in order to identify the best and fairest way of reporting fingerprint evidence in the proposed scheme.

Author

Cedric Neumann received his PhD in forensic science from the University of Lausanne (Lausanne, Switzerland) for his research on the interpretation of ink evidence. In 2009, the results of this thesis provided the foundations of the Digital Ink Library of the United States Secret Service. For this work, Cedric was awarded the 2009 Emerging European Forensic Scientist Award and a Certificate of Appreciation from the U.S. Department of Homeland Security.

As head of the R&D Statistics and Interpretation Research Group of the Forensic Science Service in the United Kingdom, Cedric was involved in the development and validation of a statistical model for the quantification of fingerprint evidence. The model and its results have already been used in U.S. courts to support the admissibility of fingerprint evidence.

In 2010, Cedric accepted a position as a professor of statistics in the Forensic Science Program at The Pennsylvania State University (University Park, Pennsylvania), where he pursues his research in the area of the statistical interpretation of forensic evidence, more specifically fingerprint, shoeprint, and traces. Cedric is a member of the International Association for Identification (IAI) and of the Scientific Working Group on Friction Ridge Analysis, Study and Technology (SWGFAST).

References

1. Barnes JG. (2011) History. In *The Fingerprint Sourcebook*, A McRoberts (Ed.). National Institute of Justice, Washington, DC, pp. 7–22.
2. Ashbaugh DR. (1999) *Quantitative–Qualitative Friction Ridge Analysis: An Introduction to Basic and Advanced Ridgeology*. CRC Press, Boca Raton, FL.
3. Berry J, Stoney DA. (2001) History and development of fingerprinting. In *Advances in Fingerprint Technology* (2nd edn.), HC Lee, RE Gaensslen (Eds.). CRC Press, Boca Raton, FL, pp. 1–40.
4. Herschel WJ. (1916) *The Origin of Finger-Printing*. Oxford University Press, London, U.K.
5. Margot P, Quinche N. (2010) Coulier, Paul-Jean (1824–1890): A precursor in the history of fingermark detection and their potential use for identifying their source (1863). *Journal of Forensic Identification* 60: 129–134.
6. Faulds H. (1880) On the skin-furrows of the hand. *Nature* 22: 605.
7. Galton F. (1892) *Finger Prints*. Macmillan & Co., London, U.K.
8. Henry E. (1900) *Classification and Uses of Finger Prints*. George Routledge & Sons Ltd., London, U.K.
9. Hutchins LA. (2011) Systems of friction ridge classification. In *The Fingerprint Sourcebook*, A McRoberts (Ed.). National Institute of Justice, Washington, DC, pp. 97–199.
10. U.S. Federal Bureau of Investigation. (2011) Integrated automated fingerprint identification system—Fact Sheet. http://www.fbi.gov/about-us/cjis/fingerprints_biometrics/iafis/iafis_facts (accessed on December 23, 2011).
11. Hicklin AR, Korves H, Ulery B, Zoepfl M, Bone M, Grother P, Micheals R, Otto S, Watson C. (2004) Fingerprint Vendor Technology Evaluation 2003: Summary of Results and Analysis Report, NISTIR7123. National Institute of Standards and Technology, Gaithersburg, MD.
12. National Research Council of the National Academies. (2009) *Strengthening Forensic Science in the United States: A Path Forward*. The National Academies Press, Washington, DC.
13. Campbell A. (2011) *The Fingerprint Inquiry*. APS Group, Scotland, U.K.

14. Champod C, Lennard C, Margot P, Stoilovic M. (2004) *Fingerprints and Other Ridge Skin Impressions*. CRC Press, Boca Raton, FL.
15. Champod C, Evett IW. (2001) A probabilistic approach to fingerprint evidence. *Journal of Forensic Identification* 51: 101–122.
16. Champod C. (2000) Identification/individualization: Overview and meaning. In *Encyclopedia of Forensic Sciences*, JA Siegel, PJ Saukko, GC Knupfer (Eds.). Academic Press, London, U.K., pp. 1077–1083.
17. Champod C. (2008) Fingerprint examination: Towards more transparency. *Law Probability and Risk* 7: 111–118.
18. Cole S. (2004) Grandfathering evidence: Fingerprint admissibility rulings from Jennings to Llera Plaza and back again. *American Criminal Law Review* 41: 1189–1276.
19. Saks M, Koehler JJ. (2005) The coming paradigm shift in forensic identification science. *Science* 309: 893–894.
20. Zabell S. (2005) Fingerprint evidence. *Journal of Law and Policy* 13: 143–170.
21. Haber L, Haber RN. (2008) Scientific validation of fingerprint evidence under Daubert. *Law Probability and Risk* 7: 87–109.
22. Kaye DH. (2010) The good, the bad, and the ugly: The NRC report on strengthening forensic science in America. *Science & Justice* 50: 8–11.
23. Scientific Working Group on Friction Ridge Analysis Study and Technology (SWGFAST). (2011) Standards for examining friction ridge impressions and resulting conclusions, version 1.0. http://swgfast.org/Documents.html (accessed on December 23, 2011).
24. Interpol European Expert Group on Fingerprint Identification II (IEEGFI II). (2004) *Part 2: Detailing the Method Using Common Terminology and Through the Definition and Application of Shared Principles*. Lyon, France.
25. International Association for Identification. (2010) Resolution 2010–18. *Identification News* 40.
26. Bertillon MA. (1912) Les empreintes digitales, notes et observations medico-légales. *Archives d'Anthropologie Criminelle, de Médecine Légale et de Psychologie Normale et Pathologique* 27: 36–52.
27. Cole S. (2009) Forensics without uniqueness, conclusions without individualization: The new epistemology of forensic identification. *Law, Probability and Risk* 8: 233–255.
28. Balthazard V. (1911) De l'identification par les empreintes digitales. *Comptes Rendus des Academies des Sciences* 152: 1862–1864.
29. Stoney DA. (2001) Measurement of fingerprint individuality. In *Advances in Fingerprint Technology*, HC Lee, RE Gaensslen (Eds.). CRC Press, New York.
30. Locard E. (1914) La preuve judiciaire par les empreintes digitales. *Archives d'Anthropologie Criminelle, de Médecine Légale et de Psychologie Normale et Pathologique* 29: 321–348.
31. Thornton JI. (1977) The one-dissimilarity doctrine in fingerprint identification. *International Criminal Police Review* 306: 89–95.
32. Evett IW, Williams RL. (1996) A review of the sixteen point fingerprint standard in England and Wales. *Journal of Forensic Identification* 46: 49–73.
33. Margot P, German E. (1995) *Ne'urim Declaration, Internation Symposium on Fingerprint Detection and Identification*. Ne'urim, Israel.
34. Polski J, Smith R, Garrett R. (2011) The Report of the International Association for Identification. Standardisation II Committee, National Institute of Justice, Washington, DC.
35. Daubert v. Merrell Dow Pharmaceuticals, Inc. (1993) 509 US 579, 589.
36. Cole S. (2008) Out of the Daubert fire and into the Fryeing pan? Self-validation, meta-expertise and the admissibility of latent print evidence in Frye jurisdiction. *Minnesota Journal of Law Science & Technology* 9: 453–542.
37. Cole S. (2005) More than zero, accounting for error in latent fingerprint identification. *Journal of Criminal Law and Criminology* 95: 985–1078.
38. Saks M, Koehler JJ. (2008) The individualization fallacy in forensic science evidence. *Vanderbilt Law Review* 61: 199–219.
39. Kaye DH, Bernstein DA, Mnookin JL. (2011) *The New Wigmore on Evidence: Expert Evidence* (2nd edn.). Wolter Kluwers, New York.

40. Risinger M. (2010) Whose fault? Daubert, the NAS report, and the notion of error in forensic science. *Fordham Urban Law Journal* 38: 519.
41. United States v. Mitchell, 365 F.3d 215 (3d Cir. 2004).
42. United States v. Havvard, 260 F.3d 597 (7th Cir. 2001).
43. United States v. Llera Plaza, 188 F.Supp.2d 549 (E.D. Pa. 2002), vacating Cr. No. 98-362-10, 11, 12, 2002 U.S. Dist. LEXIS 344 (E.D. Pa. January 7, 2002).
44. State of Maryland v. Bryan Rose, The Circuit Court for the Baltimore County, K06-0545, 2008.
45. State of Minnesota v. Jeremy Jason Hull, District Court—Seventh Judicial District, No. 48-CR-07-2336, 2010.
46. Wertheim K, Maceo A. (2002) Friction ridge and pattern formation during the critical stage. *Journal of Forensic Identification* 52: 35–85.
47. Maceo AV. (2011) Anatomy and physiology of adult friction ridge skin. In *The Fingerprint Sourcebook*, A McRoberts (Ed.). National Institute of Justice, Washington, DC, pp. 25–50.
48. Wertheim K. (2011) Embryology and morphology of friction ridge skin, anatomy and physiology of adult friction ridge skin. In *The Fingerprint Sourcebook*, A McRoberts (Ed.). National Institute of Justice, Washington, DC, pp. 51–76.
49. Wertheim K, Langenburg G, Moenssens A. (2006) A report of latent print examiner accuracy during comparison training exercises. *Journal of Forensic Identification* 56: 55–93.
50. Langenburg G, Champod C, Wertheim P. (2009) Testing for potential contextual bias effects during the verification stage of the ACE-V methodology when conducting fingerprint comparisons. *Journal of Forensic Science* 54: 583–590.
51. Dror IE, Charlton D, Peron A. (2006) Contextual information renders experts vulnerable to making erroneous identifications. *Forensic Science International* 156: 74–78.
52. Scientific Working Group on Friction Ridge Analysis Study and Technology (SWGFAST). (2011) Standard for the definition and measurement of rates of errors and inappropriate decisions in friction ridge examination, version 1.1. http://swgfast.org/Documents.html (accessed on December 23, 2011).
53. Scientific Working Group on Friction Ridge Analysis Study and Technology (SWGFAST). (2011) Standard for the technical review of friction ridge examinations, version 1.0. http://swgfast.org/Documents.html (accessed on December 23, 2011).
54. Scientific Working Group on Friction Ridge Analysis Study and Technology (SWGFAST). (2011) Standard for the application of blind verification, version 1.0. http://swgfast.org/Documents.html (accessed on December 23, 2011).
55. Scientific Working Group on Friction Ridge Analysis Study and Technology (SWGFAST). (2011) Standard for the validation and performance review of friction ridge impression development and examination techniques (Validation of Research and Technology), version 1.0. http://swgfast.org/Documents.html (accessed on December 23, 2011).
56. Stoney DA. (1991) What made us ever think we could individualize using statistics? *Journal of the Forensic Science Society* 31: 197–199.
57. Kwan QY. (1977) Inference of identity of source, PhD thesis. University of California, Berkeley, CA.
58. Neumann C, Champod C, Puch-Solis R, Egli N, Anthonioz A, Meuwly D, Bromage-Griffiths A. (2006) Computation of likelihood ratios in fingerprint identification for configurations of three minutiae. *Journal of Forensic Sciences* 51: 1255–1266.
59. Reed T, Viken RJ, Rinehart SA. (2006) High heritability of fingertip arch patterns in twin-pairs. *American Journal of Medical Genetics Part A* 140A: 263–271.
60. Steinman G. (2001) Mechanisms of twinning: I. Effect of environmental diversity on genetic expression on monozygotic multifetal pregnancies. *The Journal of Reproductive Medicine* 46: 467–472.
61. Jain AK, Prabhakar S, Pankanti S. (2002) On the similarity of identical twin fingerprints. *Pattern Recognition* 35: 2653–2663.
62. Srihari SN, Srinivasan H, Fang G. (2008) Discriminability of fingerprints of twins. *Journal of Forensic Identification* 58: 109–127.

63. Liu Y, Srihari SA. (2009) Computational discriminability analysis on twin fingerprints. *Lecture Notes in Computer Science* 5718: 43–54.
64. Gutièrrez E, Galera V, Martínez JM, Alonso C. (2007) Biological variability of the minutiae in the fingerprints of a sample of the Spanish population. *Forensic Science International* 172: 98–105.
65. Gutièrrez-Redomero E, Alonso-Rodriguez C, Hernandez-Hurtado LE, Rodriguez-Villalba JL. (2011) Distribution of the minutiae in the fingerprints of a sample of the Spanish population. *Forensic Science International* 208: 79–90.
66. Champod C. (1996) Reconnaissance automatique et analyse statistique des minuties sur les empreintes digitales, PhD in forensic science. Institut de Police Scientifique et de Criminologie, Université de Lausanne, Suisse, Switzerland.
67. Chen Y, Jain A. (2009) Beyond minutiae: A fingerprint individuality model with pattern, ridge and pore features. *Lecture Notes in Computer Science* 5558: 523–533.
68. Ross A, Shah J, Jain AK. (2007) From template to image: Reconstructing fingerprints from minutiae points. *IEEE Transactions on Pattern Analysis and Machine Intelligence* 29: 544–560.
69. Srihari SN. (2010) *Quantitative Assessment of the Individuality of Friction Ridge Patterns*. National Institute of Justice, Washington, DC.
70. Indovina M, Hicklin RA, Kiebuzinski GI. (2011) *ELFT-EFS Evaluation of Latent Fingerprint Technologies: Extended Feature Sets [Evaluation #1]*. National Institute of Standards and Technology, Gaithersburg, MD.
71. Neumann C, Champod C, Puch-Solis R, Egli N, Anthonioz A, Bromage-Griffiths A. (2007) Computation of likelihood ratios in fingerprint identification for configurations of any number of minutiae. *Journal of Forensic Sciences* 52: 54–64.
72. Egli NM. (2009) Interpretation of partial fingermarks using an automated fingerprint identification system, PhD thesis. Faculty of Law and Criminal Sciences, University of Lausanne, Lausanne, Switzerland.
73. Neumann C, Evett IW, Skerrett J. (2012) Quantifying the weight of evidence from a forensic fingerprint comparison: A new paradigm. *Journal of the Royal Statistical Society (Series A)* 175: 1–26.
74. Pankanti S, Prabhakar S, Jain AK. (2002) On the individuality of fingerprints. *IEEE Transactions on Pattern Analysis and Machine Intelligence* 24: 1010–1025.
75. Zhu Y, Dass SC, Jain AK. (2007) Models for assessing the individuality of fingerprints. *IEEE Transaction on Information Forensics and Security* 2: 391–401.
76. Dass SC, Pankanti S, Prabhakar S, Zhu Y. (2009) Individuality of fingerprints. In *Encyclopedia of Biometrics*, SZ Li, A Jain (Eds.). Springer Verlag, New York, pp. 741–751.
77. Su C, Srihari SN. (2011) Generative models and probability evaluation for forensic evidence, pattern recognition. In *Machine Intelligence and Biometrics*, P Wang (Ed.). Springer, New York.
78. Hicklin RA, Buscaglia J, Roberts MA, Fellner W, Burge MJ, Monaco M, Vera D, Pantzer LR, Unnikumaran TN. (2011) Latent fingerprint quality: A survey of examiners. *Journal of Forensic Identification* 61: 385–418.
79. Brummer N, du Preez J. (2006) Application independent evaluation of speaker detection. *Computer Speech and Language* 20: 230–275.
80. Gonzalez-Rodriguez J, Rose P, Ramos D, Toledano TD, Ortega-Garcia J. (2007) Emulating DNA: Rigorous quantification of evidential weight in transparent and testable forensic speaker recognition. *IEEE Transactions on Audio Speech and Language Processing* 15: 2072–2084.
81. Ramos-Castro D. (2007) Forensic evaluation of the evidence using automatic speaker recognition systems, PhD thesis. Universidad Autonoma de Madrid, Madrid, Spain.
82. Biedermann A, Bozza S, Taroni F. (2008) Decision theoretic properties of forensic identification: Underlying logic and argumentative implications. *Forensic Science International* 177: 120–132.
83. Neumann C, Mateos-Garcia I, Langenburg G, Kostroski J, Skerrett JE, Koolen M. (2011) Operational benefits and challenges of the use of fingerprint statistical models: A field study. *Forensic Science International* 212: 32–46.
84. Cook R, Evett IW, Jackson G, Jones P, Lambert JA. (1998) A model for Case Assessment and Interpretation. *Science & Justice* 38: 151–156.

85. Mnookin J, Cole S, Dror IE, Fisher B, Houck M, Inman K, Kaye D et al. (2008) The need for a research culture in the forensic sciences. *UCLA Law Review* 58: 725–779.
86. Koehler JJ. (2008) Fingerprint error rates and proficiency tests: What they are and why they matter. *Hastings Law Journal* 59: 1077–1098.
87. Haber L, Haber R. (2004) Error rates for human latent fingerprint examiners. In *Advances in Automatic Fingerprint Recognition*, N Ratha, R Bolle (Eds.). Springer-Verlag, New York, pp. 337–358.
88. Gutowski S. (2006) Error rates in fingerprint examination: The view in 2006. *Forensic Bulletin* (Autumn 2006): 18–19.
89. Peterson J, Markham P. (1995) Crime laboratory proficiency testing results: 1978–1991 II. *Journal of Forensic Sciences* 40: 1009–1029.
90. Ulery BT, Hicklin RA, Buscaglia J, Roberts MA. (2010) Accuracy and reliability of forensic latent fingerprint decisions. *Proceedings of the National Academy of Sciences of the United States of America*. 108: 7733–7738.
91. Pinkerton J. (2009) HPD: Lots of fingerprint errors, but no misidentifications. chron.com http://www.chron.com/disp/story.mpl/metropolitan/7022293.html (accessed on December 23, 2011).
92. Neumann C, Evett IW, Skerrett JE, Mateos-Garcia I. (2012) Quantitative assessment of evidential weight for a fingerprint comparison II: Generalisation to take into account the general pattern. *Forensic Science International* 214: 195–199.
93. Neumann C, Evett IW, Skerrett JE, Mateos-Garcia I. (2011) Quantitative assessment of evidential weight for a fingerprint comparison I: Generalisation to the comparison of a mark with set of ten prints from a suspect. *Forensic Science International* 207: 101–105.
94. Anthonioz A, Egli N, Champod C, Neumann C, Puch-Solis R, Bromage-Griffiths A. (2008) Level 3 details and their role in fingerprint identification: A survey among practitioners. *Journal of Forensic Identification* 58: 562–589.

16

Digital Imaging

Bruce Comber, Gemma Payne, and Chris Lennard

CONTENTS

16.1 Introduction

Images have always been a requirement with the application of forensic science for the recording of scenes, evidential items, and associated observations. Images recorded for this purpose may be in the form of drawings, photographs produced from strips of negatives, and, more recently, digital data. Recording with photographic film and the subsequent processing of the images required knowledge of silver-based film, photographic paper, light, and various associated methods for printing and developing that would optimize the results obtained. However, there has been a significant shift in technological capabilities and knowledge toward imaging in the digital domain.

With conventional photography, the film that is in the camera is sensitive to light over its entire surface. In the case of digital imaging, instead of film there is an integrated circuit sensor chip, such as the "charge-coupled device" (CCD) invented in 1969. Sensor chips used in digital cameras consist of a large number of very small light-sensitive picture elements (referred to as *pixels*) arranged in a two-dimensional array. The electronic responses from each sensor pixel are converted into numbers that represent the amount of light detected at each pixel location. The result is a digital representation of the image that was projected on the sensor by the camera's optics. One of the biggest advantages afforded by digital imaging technologies is the ability to quickly and easily apply a range of image processing tools.

Digital cameras were initially low-resolution, bulky devices that offered a relatively fast method of image acquisition. For example, early versions of the Sony Mavica® recorded an image, with a limited color range, directly onto a floppy disk. At that time, due to significant limitations, digital imaging did not pose a significant threat to film photography. Sensor and associated camera technologies developed rapidly to provide a range of low-resolution cameras for the nonprofessional market. At the same time, scientific cameras progressed from vidicon tubes to cooled, CCD-based devices of varying configurations. Higher-resolution digital cameras became available but their expense placed them out of reach of most individuals. Today, high-end single-lens reflex (SLR) cameras and scientific-grade, laboratory-based cameras have significantly improved performance at a reduced cost, making them accessible to forensic laboratories as a realistic alternative to conventional photography.

Digital image capture and image processing evolved concurrently with the development of faster computers and more sophisticated data analysis techniques [1]. The development of computers progressed rapidly within a short period of time, making greater processing power available to more people at reduced costs. This led to an explosion of computer usage and awareness and a conscious move toward digital methods. The significance for forensic work is that capabilities that were previously available only to computer engineers (e.g., for applications such as astronomy) were now available to practitioners at the click of a mouse button.

However, with this relative freedom of access to digital methods, there needs to be an understanding of valid digital recording and processing methods that are adapted for work with established fingermark development and visualization methods. Digital images are easily manipulated, and, since the mid-1990s, the issue of acceptance of digital images for forensic use has grown in importance. The application of digital imaging and image processing to forensic science in the context of this chapter is with reference to the recovery of fingermark evidence through a number of digital methods. It is not the purpose of this chapter to provide an exhaustive coverage of digital imaging techniques.

16.2 Digital Imaging Principles

16.2.1 Digital Images

Items in the real world are able to be seen by the human eye due to their interaction with electromagnetic radiation in the visible range (visible light). The light that we see or subsequently record is dependent on the color and intensity of the incident light, and the subject's color and reflectance properties. Variations in incident light and surface characteristics are boundless, and, therefore, the reflected light we see is also limitless in terms of

FIGURE 16.1
X- and *Y*-axes that reference the pixels in a digital image.

the variations possible. The visual features (color and intensity) are said to be "continuous" or "analogue" in nature; that is, they are infinite in their variability.

> Regardless of whether light focused on a specimen ultimately impacts on the human retina, a film emulsion, a phosphorescent screen or the photodiode array of a CCD, an analog image is produced. These images can contain a wide spectrum of intensities and colors. Images of this type are referred to as continuous tone because the various tonal shades and hues blend together without disruption, to generate a diffraction limited reproduction of the original specimen [2].

By comparison, digital images are constrained in terms of the variability that can be recorded. Digital images are images that have been converted into a computer-readable binary form consisting of logical 0s and 1s. They are obtained by converting continuous signals into a discrete digital format [3]. The term "image" refers to a two-dimensional light-intensity function, denoted by $f(x,y)$, where the value or amplitude of "f" at spatial coordinates (x,y) gives the intensity (brightness) at that point [4] (Figure 16.1). Each of these discrete points is referred to as a pixel (picture element). The result—a two-dimensional array of pixels (with each pixel value representing light intensity at that point)—will appear as a photographic representation of the subject.

Images can be described in terms of the light that emanates from the subject [3]. *Reflection* images sense radiation that has been reflected from the surfaces of objects. The information that is gathered from these images is in relation to the surface shape, texture, color, reflectance, etc., of the subject. *Emission* images are derived from subjects that are inherently luminous. *Absorption* images are obtained as a result of the radiation being partly absorbed by the subject. The emission and absorption images are indicative of the nature of the subject. Latent fingermark visualization takes advantage of each of these types of images through the combined use of optical, chemical, and physical development techniques and the appropriate use of light and optical filters.

16.2.2 Resolution and Quantization

The term *resolution* is defined in a number of contexts, two being:

> the act or process of resolving or separating into constituent or elementary parts

and

> the degree of sharpness of a computer-generated image as measured by the number of dots per linear inch in a hard-copy printout or the number of pixels across and down on a display screen [10].

With reference to digital imaging, resolution refers to how faithfully an image can represent the subject photographed. This will be with respect to representation of the light intensity and the reproduction of shapes and fine detail. Resolution, therefore, is further divided into two categories: *spatial resolution* and *intensity resolution*.

Spatial resolution is determined by the *sampling* process. Sampling is the process of converting a continuous-space signal into a discrete-space signal [3]. In terms of spatial resolution, the field of view is represented by a finite set of pixels arranged in a rectangular array, as per the previous definition of an image. The number of pixels will limit the degree of detail that can be recorded and recognized. In simple terms, the more pixels you have after sampling, the finer the detail that can be recorded. The *Nyquist sampling theorem* dictates that, if a signal is to be reconstructed perfectly, it must be sampled at least twice its upper frequency, otherwise "aliasing" artifacts can be generated [3]. The implication for digital imaging is that, for an image with a finite number of pixels, there will be a lower limit to the amount of detail that the level of spatial resolution can reproduce. This limit must be considered when deciding on a camera, lens, and distance from the subject when a photograph is taken. Spatial resolution also needs to be considered where images may be used for the generation of geometric data (e.g., measurements of distances and areas) and the associated precision that is required.

Intensity resolution is determined by the *quantization* process. For any given digital camera, there is a process by which light intensities as measured by the sensor (e.g., CCD) are converted to a numerical value. The light measured is a continuous quantity represented by the number of photons detected by the sensor for each pixel. The presence of photons (considered as continuous) generates an electrical charge that is sampled by an *analogue-to-digital* converter (ADC) within the camera. The output will be a value within a specified range, which is generally from zero to a maximum value that is determined by the resolving ability of the ADC. Typically, this results in 256 levels of intensity (8 bits per pixel). This action of converting a light intensity to a number is the quantization process. The consideration for recording an image is whether or not the subject's light levels can be adequately represented by the chosen camera. For most applications, commercially available cameras may be adequate. For specialized functions, such as low-light subject recording or chemical imaging (reviewed later in this chapter), scientific cameras with greater bit depth (e.g., 16 bits per pixel, or more) may be required.

The quantization process in the camera can produce noise that is inherent to the camera. Most commercially available cameras are designed for use in ambient light or with the assistance of a camera flash. The recording of fingermark images involves subjects with small surface areas, a low depth of field, and often low or very low levels of light. "Dark current"—the background signal that exists in the absence of light—causes electronic noise that is generated by the CCD operation, even in total darkness [5]. This generally appears as graininess in the image. Long exposures for low-light subjects increase the dark noise, thereby reducing the signal-to-noise ratio. Scientific cameras that cool the CCD have a significantly reduced dark current. Amplification of the signal by increasing the ISO rating does not overcome CCD insensitivity as this action also amplifies the dark noise produced.

16.2.3 Data Compression and File Formats

Digital images are saved as digital files that may be in a variety of formats, depending on the purpose of the file and the type of data being stored. The compression of image data, designed to reduce the amount of space needed to store, process, or transmit image information, can be achieved in a variety of ways. Compression schemes may be either "lossless" or "lossy," depending on whether or not data is irreparably altered. Lossless compression means that no data is lost in the process of shrinking or expanding an image file. On the other hand, lossy compression changes the original data in a destructive manner, resulting in data loss. In most cases, the data loss is not significant and the difference may be difficult to discern with the naked eye. However, lossy compression can result in image degradation and the production of compression artifacts. The benefit of lossy compression algorithms is that they provide much better compression ratios compared to lossless processes.

Some of the more common image data file formats are as follows:

- *Tagged image file format (TIF)*—A very common image format, supported by all computer platforms and many digital cameras that can employ the Lempel–Ziv–Welch (LZW) lossless compression method. TIF can also store "proprietary tags" that allow for the retention of data specific to applications, such as marked regions of interest.
- *Bitmap (BMP)*—A widely recognized format made popular by the Microsoft Windows® operating system. Although this format supports compression, most programs do not take advantage of it.
- *Graphics Interchange Format (GIF)*—A format commonly used to display graphics and images on the Internet (World Wide Web). It is a compressed format that is only capable of reproducing 256 colors.
- *JPEG (JPG)*—Developed by the Joint Photographic Experts Group (JPEG), this is the most popular lossy compression format that is supported by most digital cameras and software packages. With this format, the degree of compression can be varied. Moderate compression levels result in little to no obvious degradation. However, high compression levels can lead to reduced image quality and noticeable compression artifacts.

Most digital cameras provide the option of recording images in one of at least two cross-platform file formats (e.g., TIF and JPG). In addition, there may be the option of saving the data in a proprietary camera format (RAW), which records a raw image to the camera's media card. Software capable of reading this format is required, although popular image processing packages such as Photoshop® can read most RAW formats.

The most important implication of compression is the possibility of data loss and compression artifacts. For this reason, compressed data, the compression of data using lossy processes, is generally not encouraged for evidentiary images. However, with improvements in compression methods and the increasing sizes of images (i.e., number of pixels), detrimental compression effects are becoming less significant.

The need to store data within imaging systems requires, in some instances, the compression of data for those systems to be a viable proposition. For example, such requirements lead to the development of a high-performance compression algorithm for the preservation of fingerprint data: wavelet-scalar quantization (WSQ). Implementation of the WSQ has the potential to vary the appearance of very fine details in a fingerprint image, but no more than could be expected from the variation in application of a fingermark development technique (e.g., application of a fingerprint powder, cyanoacrylate fuming). The consideration, in the context of the evidence being presented, is whether or not the possible variation in the image is significant.

The National Institute of Standards and Technology (NIST) (www.nist.gov) provides a standard image format for the transmission of images and image data, including data related to fingermarks and 10-print fingerprint images. This format is predominantly used in Automated Fingerprint Identification Systems (AFIS) and allows for the exchange of data between organizations.

16.3 Capture Devices and Software

16.3.1 Digital Cameras

The choice of camera needs to be based on the intended application. Field-based image recording requires portability and flexibility, which leads inevitably to the use of handheld SLR cameras. These cameras may also be used in the laboratory; however, other cameras may be better suited depending on the application. With specialized photographic requirements (e.g., low-light levels, small field of view), considerations should include cameras other than SLRs. Microscopy and high-speed imaging cameras offer extra capabilities beyond SLRs in terms of cooled CCDs, extended exposures, or multiple-averaged images (to reduce image noise and therefore improve the overall signal-to-noise ratio).

Computer-controlled cameras provide a live preview of the image on the computer screen prior to image capture. Tools in the camera software allow for indications of correct focus and exposure before the image is acquired. These systems do not generally meet the spatial resolution capabilities of SLR cameras; however, an image that is focused and well exposed can be acquired in a single capture. There is therefore a trade-off between control of the image acquisition, image size, and the convenience of having only one type of camera. For convenience in terms of training and system implementation, the use of an SLR camera for all purposes offers a relatively simple solution that will accommodate most requirements.

CCD-based cameras are typically monochrome (black and white) or color. Color is achieved by the acquisition of data in the three color channels: red, green, and blue (RGB). This is done by either using three CCD sensor arrays (one for each channel) and splitting the incident light with a prism or—more commonly—by placing a Bayer filter on a single CCD chip. The Bayer filter contains RGB elements that coincide with the individual photosites of the CCD chip, thereby permitting the recording of discrete RGB responses across the field of view. Raw data from the acquired image is then interpolated to produce the "true color" image. The recording of fingermarks often uses filters in front of the camera to facilitate recording using selective absorption or photoluminescence. If a color camera is used that employs a Bayer-filtered CCD, there will be a limited response depending on the filter used. For example, if a 530 nm band-pass filter is placed on the camera, there will be little, if any, response from the red- and blue-filtered photosites, representing half of the image data collected. For this reason, a monochrome camera is generally better suited for fingermark applications, particularly where photoluminescence methods are employed. However, given the high resolution of modern CCD sensors in SLR cameras, color images can be successfully employed for most applications.

16.3.2 Image Processing Software

There is a large range of software that can be used to process images. The choice of software should be governed by the intended application and the level of expertise of the person using it. Software can be divided into a number of categories according to the primary purpose, including graphic design and image analysis. Generally, graphic design software allows the user to construct images using other images or data from multiple sources and to directly edit images. Image analysis software allows the user to extract, highlight, or suppress data within the one image. Image processing for forensic purposes is generally contained within the image analysis category.

It is beyond the scope of this chapter to provide a comprehensive list of available software packages. Some representative examples are provided as follows:

- *Adobe Photoshop* (http://www.adobe.com)—This is one of the most widely accepted and employed programs in the imaging industry. Whilst Photoshop is a graphics design program, it is relatively simple to use and has an ability to document processing steps through "Actions" and maintain the integrity of the original image through "Adjustment Layers." Photoshop has a wide selection of imaging functions and has a facility for "plug-ins" from third parties. Batch processing of images can also be performed.
- *V++* (http://www.digitaloptics.co.nz)—This is an image analysis program that has a wide range of menu-selectable functions. It also has a scripting facility based on Pascal that is simple to use and allows high flexibility. Through the scripts, the user can access Windows functions and user-defined DLLs (dynamic link libraries) and operate devices such as filter wheels, cameras, and other peripheral devices. This is an excellent program where flexibility of process and design for research purposes are requirements. Forensic documentation requirements are easily met with the use of scripts, with an ability for these to be recorded and used at a later time to demonstrate process repeatability.
- *ImageJ* (http://rsbweb.nih.gov)—This is similar to V++ in function, but is written and scripted in Java. The program and plug-ins are available at no cost from the National Institutes of Health (NIH) website. There are many plug-ins available from an active online community.
- *Thumbs Plus* (http://www.cerious.com)—This provides an image handling facility in a Windows Explorer–type environment. The program has a range of simple image enhancement and editing functions and is a good addition in a digital image handling environment where the power of Photoshop is not required.

16.4 Image Processing and Enhancement

16.4.1 Image Enhancement Principles

The conditions set before the taking of a photograph and any "enhancement" subsequently carried out on a recorded image should be appropriate to the purpose for which the photograph is taken and must suit the purpose of any subsequent examination that may be required. Careless photographing and the reliance on automatic image processing will often result in the loss of valuable detail and the introduction of unwanted "noise."

Enhancement methods prior to image capture include the optimization and control of lighting when the photograph is taken, and the use of appropriate optical filters (colored, polarizing, UV, etc.). The digital file that results from the capture of an image using a digital camera can then undergo any number of treatments given the vast array of digital processing software available on the market and the sophistication of some of these packages. The printing of hard-copy photographs then allows for further post-capture enhancement with the use of various grades of paper, burning and dodging, contrast and brightness alteration, and color balance. Digital minilabs allow for many of these processes to be readily performed through a user interface and some degree of automation. Modern computer printers (e.g., based on inkjet technologies) are also capable of producing high-quality photographic prints.

Professional digital image processing has become highly specialized and a logical step in the work performed by criminalistics laboratories [1]. Whilst image processing methods were developed and established in various other fields, their application to the forensic sciences was seen as inevitable from an early time.

Moler et al. described image enhancement as follows [6]:

> The principle idea behind image enhancement techniques is to process an image so that the result is more suitable than the original for a specific application. The enhancement process does not increase the inherent information in the data. However, it does increase the dynamic range of the chosen features so that they can be readily detected.

In a recorded image, there are two main components: (1) the "signal," which constitutes the elements of the image that are of interest and are to be examined, and (2) the "noise," which is any other part of the image that makes the signal difficult to see. In any given image, there is a "signal-to-noise" ratio that generally needs to be increased. As Blackwell and Crisci [1] have stated, noise limits the potential in an image:

> The practical limit to all quantitative or photointerpretative measurements on a properly encoded image is the presence of noise. The essence of noise removal in an image is to isolate and remove the various identifiable and characterisable noise components as rigorously as possible so as to do a minimum amount of damage to the actual image data.

Enhancements need to be carried out in a considered manner to ensure that noise is not enhanced along with the signal. If, for example, one was to apply a sharpening filter to an image containing noise, such as JPG artifacts, the effect would be not only to sharpen features of the signal but also to enhance the blocky artifacts caused by the compression (Figure 16.2). Enhancements that seek to improve the image may, if applied inappropriately, reduce the signal-to-noise ratio. Simply put, the aim is to suppress noise and enhance the signal of interest so as to maximize the recovery of useful information from the image.

Image enhancement techniques generally operate either in the "spatial domain" or in the "frequency domain." The spatial domain operates on the pixels in the image as we see it. The enhancement functions may operate on individual pixels (point processing) or on groups of pixels under a "mask" (neighborhood processing) positioned over a central pixel. The output of these functions is a change to the pixel values that will depend on the initial pixel values and the particular mathematical function applied. Examples of such processes are brightness, contrast, gamma, color balance, smoothing, and sharpening.

The frequency domain displays the image as a sum of its spatial-frequency components. Typically, rapid changes in spatial intensity (i.e., sharp contrast) imply the presence of high frequencies in the data, whereas gradual changes in contrast require only low frequencies to be well represented [7]. The frequency domain image (power spectrum) displays the spatial domain image data in an alternative but mathematically equivalent format,

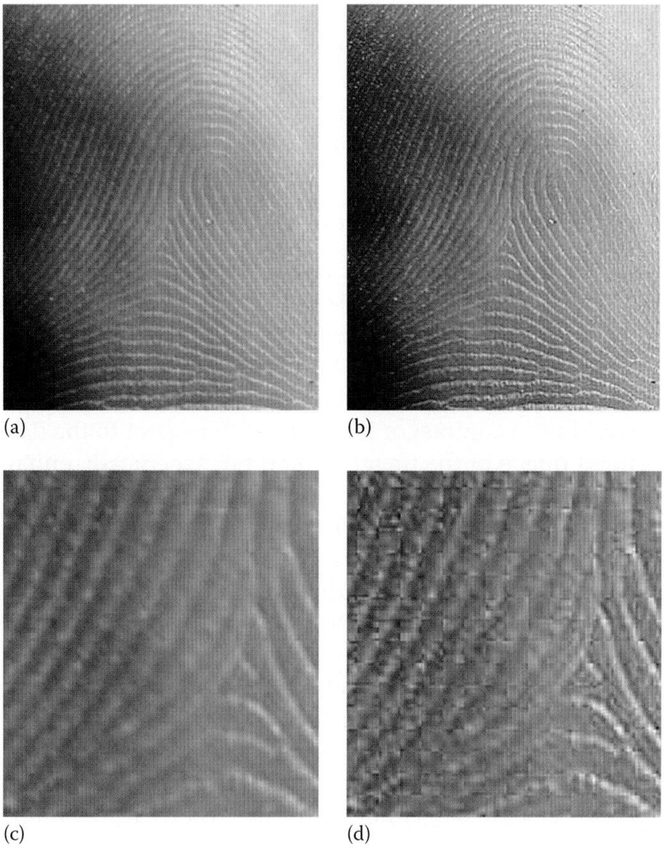

FIGURE 16.2
Processing of an image to enhance detail can also enhance noise: (a) shows the original image and (c) detail from that image, (b) shows the original image after a sharpening filter has been applied, and (d) shows how the JPEG artifacts have been enhanced due to the sharpening.

in which frequency, regularity, and direction of features in the image detail can be interpreted. An image can be transformed from the spatial domain to the frequency domain by the fast Fourier transform (FFT) function. Once in this domain, relevant frequency elements can be amplified, isolated, suppressed, or otherwise filtered with an intention to enhance, isolate, or remove specific detail in the corresponding spatial image. After editing the image in the frequency domain, the inverse transform (inverse FFT) is performed to return the image to the spatial domain with the changes incorporated.

16.4.2 Methods for Fingermark Enhancement

16.4.2.1 General Approach

There are many approaches that can be taken to solve any given enhancement problem. For fingermark imaging, the chosen approach should encapsulate the nature of the fingermark itself (e.g., color and/or luminescence), the image capture process, and the processing of that data. Whilst instances of images requiring enhancement generally fall into similar categories (low contrast, uneven illumination, color balance, repetitive interfering noise, etc.), the enhancement solution for any individual case image will be specific to that image. There needs to be an assessment of that image with knowledge of the various capture and enhancement techniques available, and the most appropriate methods applied. The enhancement methods described later are not to be seen as being comprehensive, but simply examples of how a practitioner may choose to enhance a fingermark.

16.4.2.2 Point Processing: Contrast, Brightness, Gamma, and Histograms

The characteristics of an image, in terms of its brightness or contrast, can be seen in the image's histogram. This shows the distribution of the pixel values as a graph that plots the intensity values (grayscale levels) on the *X*-axis and the number of pixels at each intensity level on the *Y*-axis. On inspection of a histogram, the degree of brightness and contrast that exists in an image can be assessed (Figure 16.3). Often the unprocessed image of a fingermark will be lacking in contrast or intensity with respect to the data of interest. The production of a printed image of the fingermark, if not specifically enhanced for the purpose of a fingerprint examination, may not optimize the available evidential information. It is possible that an image may lose detail in certain areas in order to best enhance and represent the fingermark itself.

Contrast variations cause a change in the distribution of pixel intensities in the original image. An increase in contrast causes the distribution of pixel values to be broader than that of the original image. A contrast reduction results in a narrower distribution. Brightness adjustments cause all pixel values in the image to be adjusted by a particular value. If the value is positive, the image becomes brighter and the histogram is seen to shift to the right. If the value is negative, the image becomes darker and the histogram shifted to the left. With contrast and brightness adjustments, there is a risk that the degree of enhancement will cause the response values to be greater than or less than the maximum dynamic range

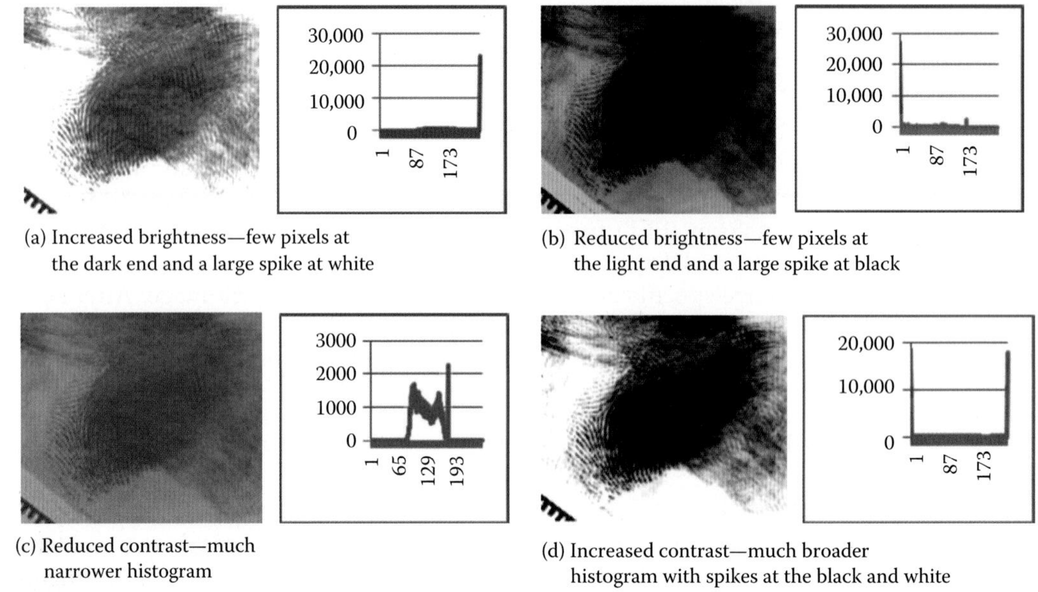

(a) Increased brightness—few pixels at the dark end and a large spike at white

(b) Reduced brightness—few pixels at the light end and a large spike at black

(c) Reduced contrast—much narrower histogram

(d) Increased contrast—much broader histogram with spikes at the black and white

FIGURE 16.3
Histograms of pixel intensity distribution for bright images (a), dark images (b), and low and high contrast images (c and d).

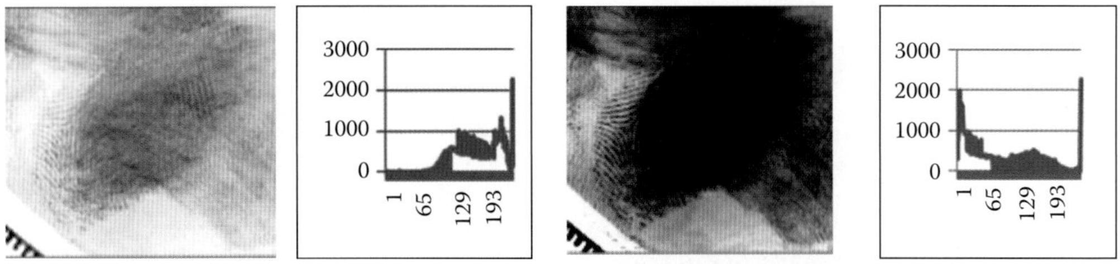

(a) Increased gamma—histogram is moved to the lighter values

(b) Reduced gamma–histogram is moved to the darker values

FIGURE 16.4
Histograms of pixel intensity distribution for gamma adjusted images, showing gamma increased (a) and reduced (b).

for that image type. This will cause all pixels of potentially greater or lesser values than the dynamic range to be rendered as white and black, respectively. The use of gamma enhancement causes an increase in contrast at one end of the histogram and a decrease in contrast at the other (Figure 16.4).

Contrast adjustments can also be applied through histogram equalization. This function aims to transform an image such that it has a histogram with a pixel value distribution as close to uniform as is possible across the intensity range. The result is an image with better improved contrast than a simple contrast stretch; however, if the range intensities are not distributed evenly across the area of the image, optimal contrast enhancement may not be achieved. This means that all discernable detail in the image may not be effectively enhanced. An extension of this is a local histogram equalization (Figure 16.5). This performs the same function, but via a moving window across the original image. Sub-images are taken in sequence across the entire image, with each of these having the histogram equalization function applied. The effect is that greater detail in large areas of single pixel value will be visible; however, the variance of pixel values across the image will diminish.

16.4.2.3 Neighborhood Processing: Digital Filtering

The main difference between digital filters and point operations is that filters generally use more than one pixel from the source image for computing each new pixel [8]. Filtering requires an input image and a filter mask. The mask is an array of values with x- and y-dimensions. The mask is moved over the image sequentially so that the center of the mask is coincident with each pixel in the input image, and a calculation for the output image performed at each pixel location. The values of each of the pixels under the mask are multiplied by the corresponding mask value, and then these values are summed to give the final output pixel value. There may also be a scaling factor applied to the sum to keep the output pixel value within the image's intensity range.

Digital filters perform a number of functions including smoothing, sharpening, and noise removal. Smoothing and sharpening are *linear filters* that use a mask with predetermined values. Fine noise removal uses a *median* filter, which is a *nonlinear filter.* This filter takes all of the values of the input image under the mask and returns the middle value (when all of the values are placed in ascending order).

Fingermark images may contain noise that can be removed by way of filtering (Figure 16.6). This can be, for example, from weave patterns, wood grain, flare from surface particles, paper fibers, etc. Smoothing and median filters can remove such noise,

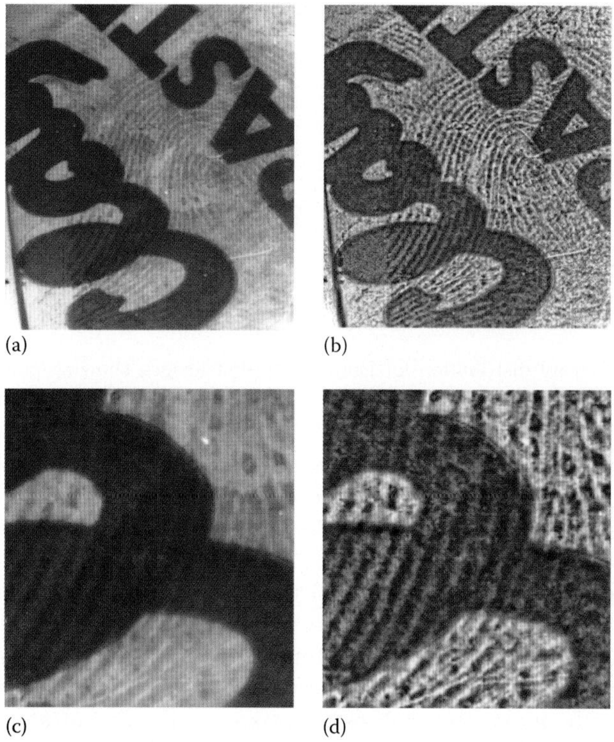

FIGURE 16.5
Result of local histogram equalization can provide greater contrast enhancement across the entire image when there already exists large variations in pixel intensities in the image. (a) Original image, (b) original image after local histogram equalization, (c) detail of original image, and (d) detail of enhanced image. (Images courtesy of the Western Australia Police, Perth, Western Australia, Australia.)

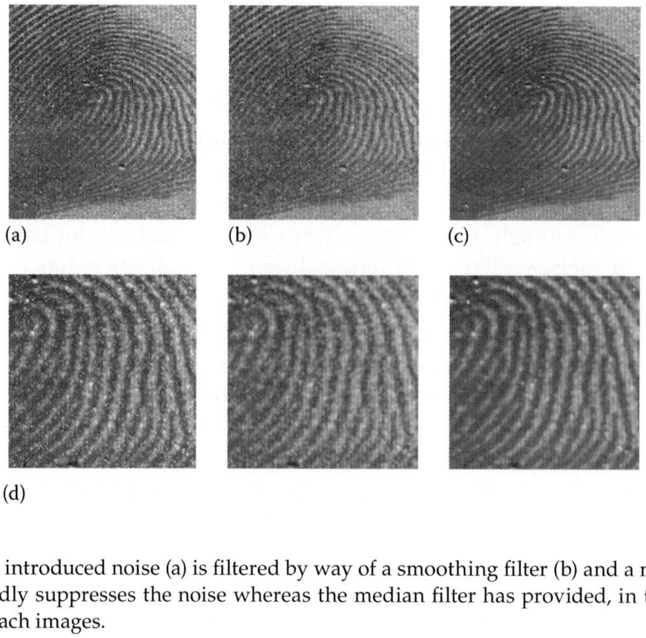

FIGURE 16.6
Original image with introduced noise (a) is filtered by way of a smoothing filter (b) and a median filter (c). The smoothing filter mildly suppresses the noise whereas the median filter has provided, in this case, a superior result. (d) Detail of each images.

depending on how these filters are implemented. Recognition needs to be given not only to what a particular filter can do to remove noise but also to what the filter may do in terms of signal suppression.

16.4.2.4 Use of Multiple Images

To capture only a single image of a subject is to record only one approximation of it. An image is representative of the subject but it is affected by the quantization and sampling processes. A second capture of the same field of view with the same lighting, lens, camera, and subject will produce a similar but nonidentical image. There will always be a degree of variation in the image produced. If a number of images of a subject are captured, with an identical configuration of the camera, optics, subject, and field of view, the images can be combined to generate an image that is a better representation of the subject. The capturing of a series of images and taking the average can produce a better representation of the subject while reducing the effect of noise [3].

Since digital images are essentially arrays of numbers, they can be processed mathematically to achieve a desired result [9]. Noise may be in the form of reflections (flares) or shadows within the image that interfere with the visualization of a fingermark. A series of images is captured and summed to produce a new image of the same dimensions, but of a type that can accommodate large numerical pixel values. To be visible via most computer programs, the summed image needs to be converted to a byte type (gray scale or RGB). To do this, the summed image is divided by the number of captured images, with the decimal places rounded off and the image converted to a byte format.

Two or more images can be combined, and each image may include changes of lighting. When the direction of the incident light is changed, the shadows cast by the subject and the reflection of that light from the subject also changes. By keeping the subject and the camera still, and keeping the same lens and filters, multiple images of the subject will be in perfect registration (i.e., they will line up with each other). If multiple images (e.g., more than 10) are averaged whilst the incident light is moved, the shadows and flares will tend to be eliminated. Experimentation with the lighting angle before the capture of images can optimize the results. The images acquired are then averaged to produce the final result. An example is provided in Figure 16.7. The subject in this example is a hammer treated with cyanoacrylate fumes. The narrow handle is an uneven wooden surface that has been finished with a high gloss varnish. Under white light, the handle showed excessive reflection; shadows and flares were impossible to avoid due to the handle's small radius. In this example, the light was moved in a path around the hammer with the light directed at the handle, with the image data accumulated to produce a single final image.

Images can be added or subtracted from each other. With this possibility in mind, images can be captured that contain detail for a specific function. Such images can be combined mathematically to suppress noise or boost detail. The principle of this, with respect to fingermark enhancement, can be demonstrated by way of the following simple equation:

$$\mathrm{FMN} - \mathrm{N} = \mathrm{FM} \tag{16.1}$$

where

FMN is the image containing the fingermark and the background noise

N is the image containing only the noise

FM is the desired image containing only the fingermark (with the background noise suppressed)

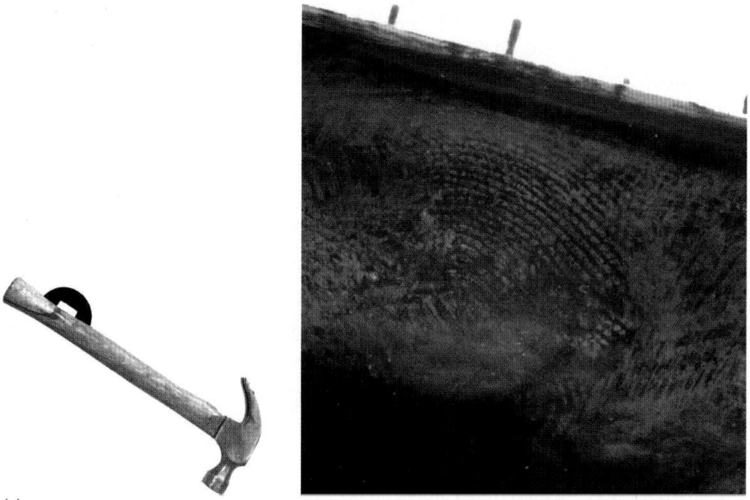

(a) (b)

FIGURE 16.7
Subject bearing the fingermark in this instance is very difficult to illuminate without flare and shadow, and the mark is weak and difficult to visualize. In this instance, accumulating multiple images of the subject whilst changing the angle of illumination causes the shadow and flare to be minimized and the mark enhanced. (a) Location image of the hammer—the fingermark is adjacent to the white label (b) detail of the averaged image.

The subtraction can be achieved by the subtraction function or by inverting one image before adding it to the other.

Equation 16.1 can be extended to involve variable proportions of each image:

$$i \times \mathrm{FMN} - j \times \mathrm{N} = \mathrm{FM} \tag{16.2}$$

where

i is the multiplication factor for the image FMN
j is the multiplication factor for the image N

Where the application of light can cause fingermark detail to become more or less visible against a noisy background, two images can be captured: (1) one image where the detail visibility is maximized and (2) a second image where the detail is minimized (i.e., the visibility of the background is maximized). Depending on the relative tonal values of the image detail, the images can be added or subtracted to suppress the noise. In the example depicted in Figure 16.8, the subject is a multicolored tin lid with a semigloss surface that has been treated by cyanoacrylate fuming. The fingermark in question was most visible using oblique lighting and an image was captured using this illumination. By directing the light away from the subject and bouncing it off a nearby white surface, the subject was illuminated in a manner that minimized the fingermark's visibility. A second image was captured under these conditions. The images were then subtracted in proportions that significantly suppressed contributions from the background (to maximize the visibility of the fingermark).

High-density resolution (HDR) images use multiple images combined to give improved image quality in the low and high ranges of the image intensity. This is achieved by combining a number of images that have exposures above, at, and below the ideal exposure

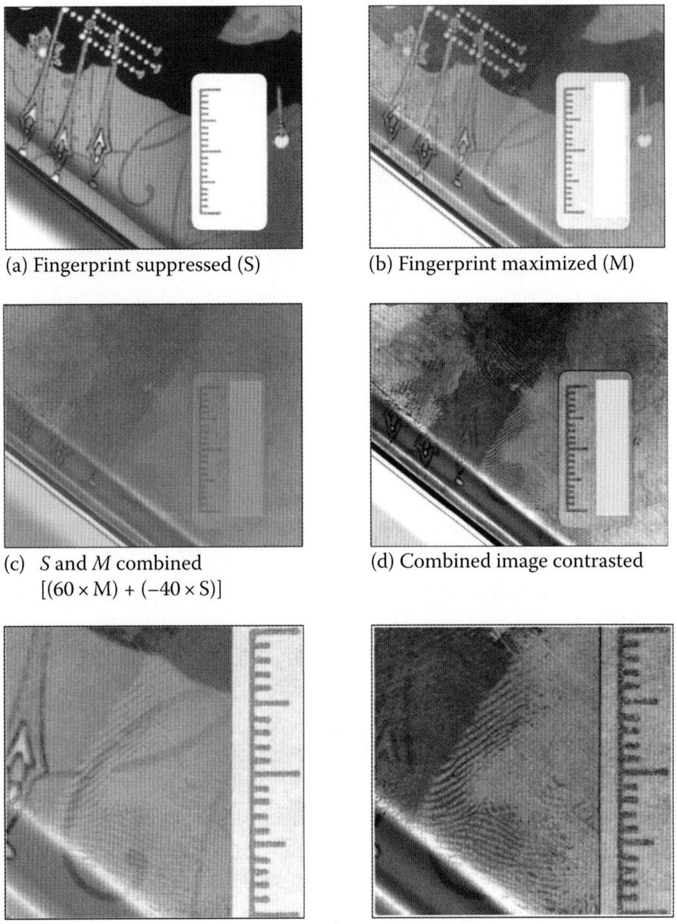

(a) Fingerprint suppressed (S)

(b) Fingerprint maximized (M)

(c) S and M combined [(60 × M) + (−40 × S)]

(d) Combined image contrasted

(e) Detail of M

(f) Detail of final result

FIGURE 16.8
Varying illumination (by color or angle of incidence) produces variations in the image recorded. Controlling the illumination to obtain specific results and combining those resultant images can suppress noise in the image. In this example, (a) and (b) show fingermark detail minimized and maximized. (c) and (d) show the images combined and contrasted. (e) and (f) show the detail in the original and enhanced images.

level. By combining these images, image data is acquired in the dark areas that would normally be underexposed and in the bright areas that would normally be overexposed. When the images are combined, the poorly exposed areas are compensated for by the multiple exposures and the improved densities achieved. HDR images can be generated in Photoshop through the use of images with varied exposures that are imported into layers. A combined average results from varying the exposure on the stream of images. Specialized software for this task is also available.

16.4.2.5 Fourier Transform

The Fourier transform is a complex algorithm that involves the spectral analysis of data. It is applied to images as well as other digital signals such as sound. In its original form, it was computationally intensive; however, with a modification of the transform, the FFT,

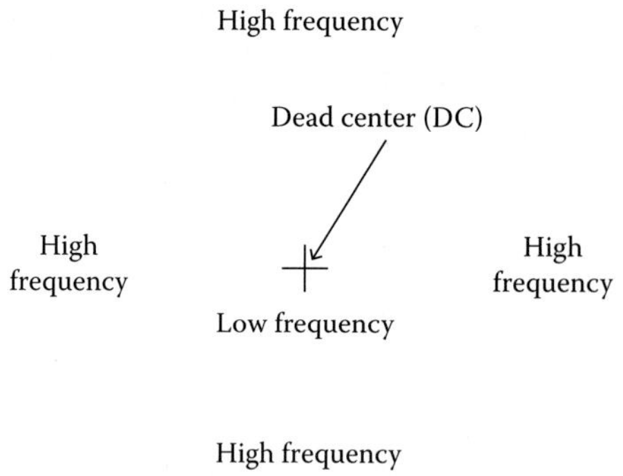

FIGURE 16.9
Power spectrum is interpreted in terms of the location of the spectral data (spikes) in the image. Spikes near the center of the power spectrum represent low-frequency data whereas spikes further out represent higher frequencies.

and the further development of computer technology, there is increased application of Fourier transforms and it is relatively simple to apply.

In the previous sections of this chapter, the processing of images was undertaken in the spatial domain, where the images appear as they would if viewed normally. In the spatial domain, objects within the image are discernable through variations in intensity and the rates of change of intensity, which produce gradients or edges. In turn, these spatial elements give rise to shapes. The combination of shapes constitutes what we see as the image. Fourier transform mathematically transforms the image data to appear in what is known as the frequency domain. The transformed image is known as the "power spectrum."

An image in the frequency domain appears vastly different to the corresponding spatial domain image. The frequency domain displays the image's content in terms of how often it appears (or could appear) in the image; that is, how repetitive it is, the direction in the image that the repetition takes (e.g., the direction of pattern flow), and how regular the repetition is. Objects that are large in an image, such as a face in a portrait, cannot be repetitive as they may not fit in the image more than once, whereas the weave pattern on fabric is fine and has a definable texture to it that is consistent and clearly visible. The detail that is large or non-repetitive will be located toward the center of the power spectrum. As the repetitive aspect (frequency) increases, the corresponding detail in the power spectrum will be further away from the center. Figure 16.9 illustrates the variation in the position of the "spikes" (bright data points) in relation to the frequency of the corresponding image detail.

Figure 16.10 illustrates the relationship between the direction of ridge flow in a fingermark and the orientation of the spikes in the power spectrum. The spikes occur on an axis that is at right angles to the ridge flow. The example in Figure 16.11 shows the relationship between frequency of image detail and the distance that the spikes occur from the center. In this example, the friction ridge frequency is less than that of the printed dots that make up the background image. As a result, the spikes for the printed dots are further from the center than the spikes for the fingermark ridges. The circle superimposed on the power spectrum largely divides the spikes for the dots (printed background) and the spikes for the ridges (fingermark of interest), with the lower frequency ridge spikes being inside the circle, close to the center.

Figure 16.12 contains three fingermark images and their respective power spectra. Figure 16.12a and c contains friction ridge detail from palm impressions. In each image, the ridges are mostly parallel, with ridge flow in one general direction and with a very similar distance between the ridges. Therefore, the frequency and period of the ridges is fairly constant in each image. Because the occurrence of the ridges is regular, they appear distinct in the

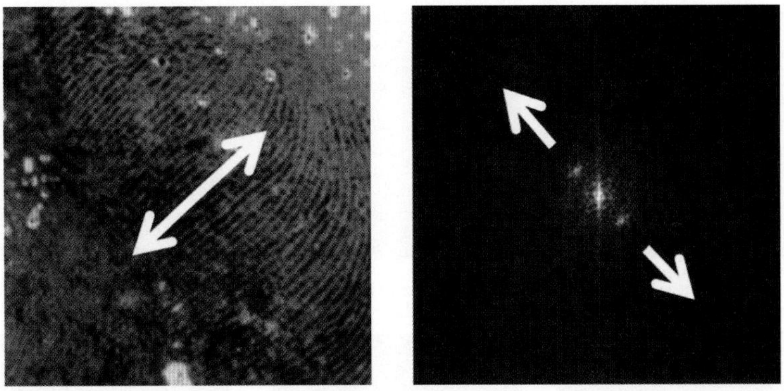

(a) (b)

FIGURE 16.10
Direction of the repetitive information in an image will determine the orientation of the corresponding spikes: (a) shows the direction of the flow of the friction ridges, whereas (b) shows the spikes in an orientation at 90° to the ridge flow.

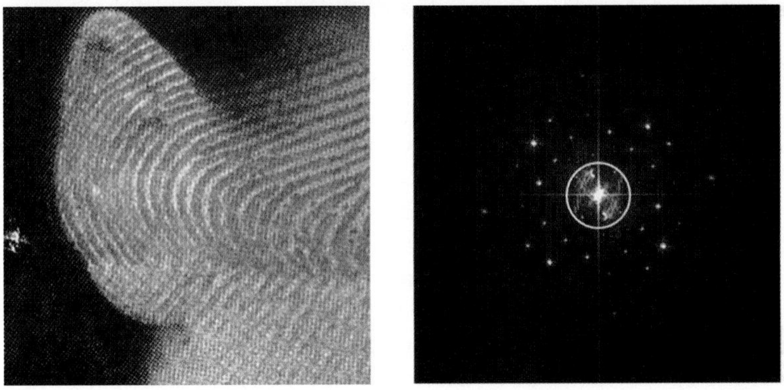

(a) High-frequency detail in the printed background and low-frequency detail in the fingermark

(b) Spikes corresponding to the fingermark are inside the circle and spikes for the printed background are outside the circle, further from the center

FIGURE 16.11
Frequency of occurrence of the information in an image determines how far from the center of the power spectrum the spikes will occur: (a) shows repetitive detail in the form of printed dots and a fingermark and (b) shows where their respective spikes occur in the corresponding power spectrum. (Images courtesy of the Western Australia Police, Perth, Western Australia, Australia.)

corresponding power spectrum as strong spikes. The location of the spikes is determined by the direction of the ridge flow and the frequency of the ridge pattern. Figure 16.12a has the ridges running from bottom left to top right. The spikes appear in a line at right angles to this ridge flow, as can be seen in Figure 16.12b. The ridges in Figure 16.12c are aligned in a different direction to Figure 16.12a, and the resultant power spectrum is seen in Figure 16.12d. Again, the location of the spikes in Figure 16.12d reflects the direction of the ridge flow in Figure 16.12c and the frequency of the ridge pattern. The fingermark in Figure 16.12e has a whorl classification, which has ridges that flow in a radial manner (i.e., all directions). The corresponding power spectrum in Figure 16.12f reflects this ridge flow with what appears to be a circular continuous spike around the center. Note that the spacing of the ridges horizontally is less than the spacing vertically (so the horizontal ridge frequency is higher than

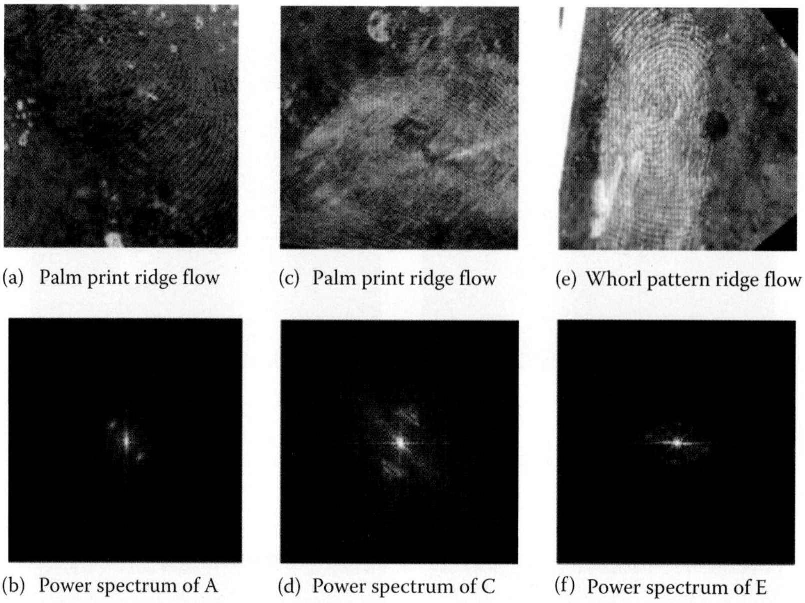
(a) Palm print ridge flow
(c) Palm print ridge flow
(e) Whorl pattern ridge flow
(b) Power spectrum of A
(d) Power spectrum of C
(f) Power spectrum of E

FIGURE 16.12
Examples of the power spectra for different ridge flow: (a) and (c) show palm prints in different orientations and their corresponding power spectra in (b) and (d), and (e) shows a whorl pattern and its corresponding elliptical power spectrum in (f).

the horizontal frequency), which has resulted in the frequency representation being oval shaped, with the height of the oval shape being less than its width.

Information in the frequency domain can be edited to suppress, isolate, or amplify elements of an image. To achieve this, an image must first undergo a Fourier transform to convert it from the spatial domain to the frequency domain. The resulting power spectrum is edited and then an inverse Fourier transform applied to return the image to the spatial domain where the affect of the editing can be seen. If spikes are cut from the power spectrum, the corresponding detail will be suppressed in the spatial domain image. Figure 16.13a provides an example of a fingermark on the frame of a fly screen. Due to grooves in the surface, lines are visible that run diagonally across the image. These are represented in the power spectrum as a fine line running from the bottom left to the top right, crossing through the center. If this spike is removed, the inverse transformed image appears as in Figure 16.13c. If the spike is isolated, with everything else removed leaving only that spike, the inverse transformed image appears as in Figure 16.13d. Given this ability to apply Fourier transform, interpret and edit the power spectrum, and apply an inverse FFT, images can be significantly enhanced to improve the signal-to-noise ratio. However, operators must exercise caution when using such processes as inappropriate use can introduce artifacts that can interfere with the detail being enhanced.

Spikes can be cut from a power spectrum by defining individual regions using a mouse or it can be done by multiplying the power spectrum by a filter or a mask image. The filter causes low or high frequency to be retained or for a band between two frequencies to be retained. The filter image will have values between and including 0 and 1. Where the power spectrum is multiplied by 0, the corresponding part of the power spectrum becomes zero. When multiplied by 1, that area remains at its original value. Where the values vary between 0 and 1, the result is that fraction multiplied by the filter value.

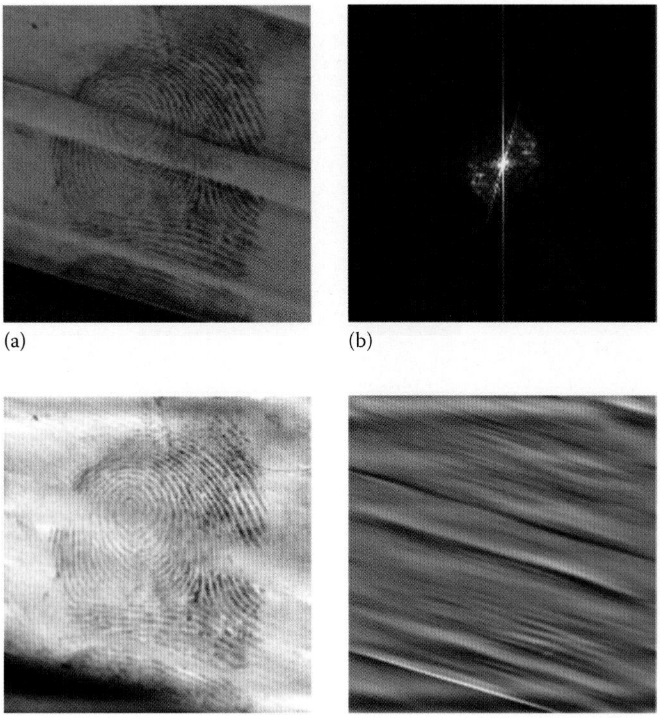

(a) (b) (c) (d)

FIGURE 16.13
Power spectrum is edited to suppress, isolate, or enhance specific detail. (a) shows an original image and (b) its power spectrum. The diagonal line of spikes from the top right to the bottom left corresponds to the grooves in the surface supporting the fingermark. The spikes have been edited to remove the grooves, resulting in (c), and to isolate the grooves, resulting in (d).

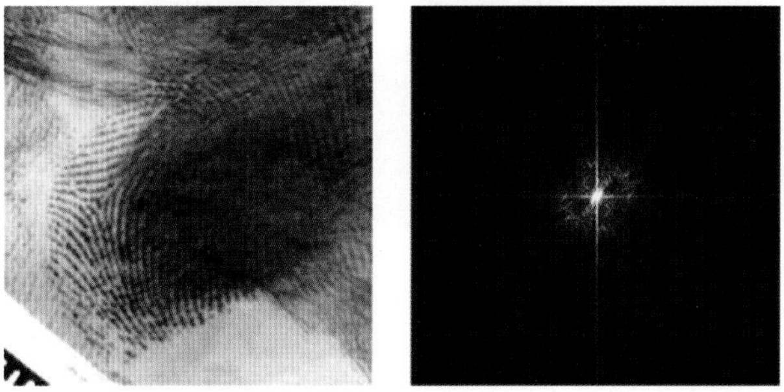

(a) (b)

FIGURE 16.14
Original fingermark image (a) and its power spectrum (b).

Figure 16.14 shows an example of a fingermark and its corresponding power spectrum. Figure 16.15 shows a series of filters (low, high, and band pass) that are multiplied by the power spectrum image in Figure 16.14. The images on the left are the products of that process. The low-pass filter retains the dark and light components of the image (low frequencies), whereas the high pass retains the fine sharp detail (high frequencies). The band pass, given the correct radii, has the ability to highlight the data frequencies that contain the friction ridges.

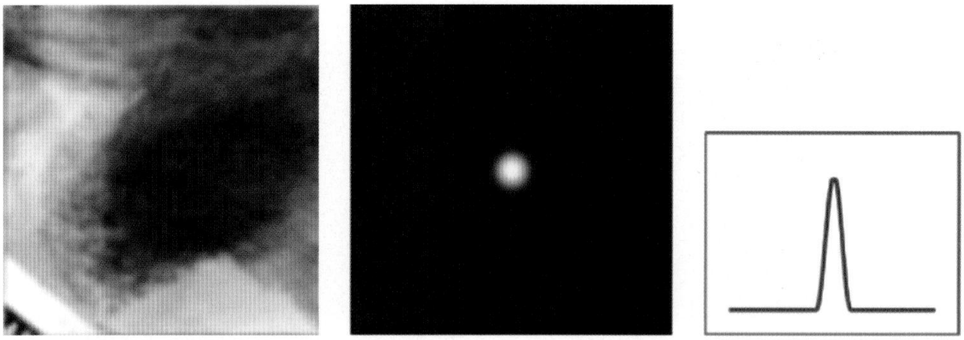

(a)

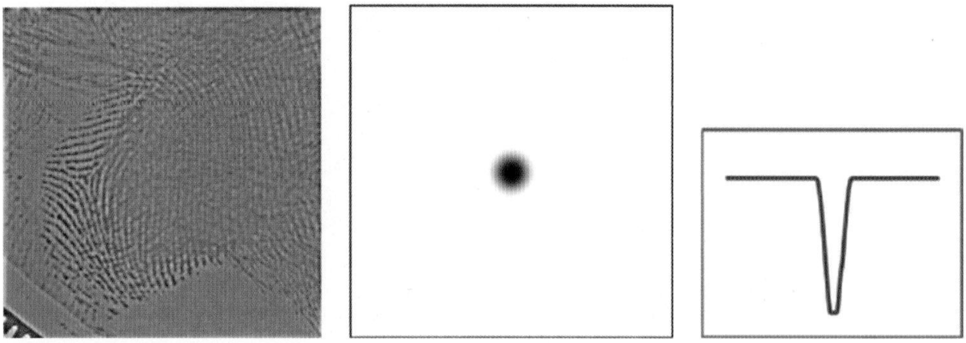

(b)

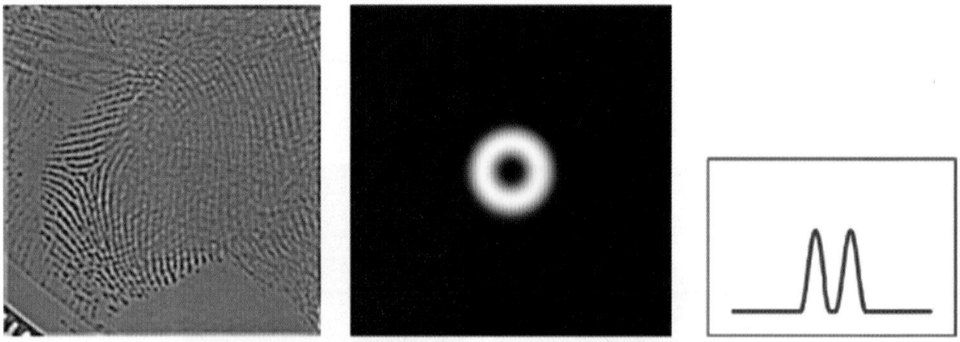

(c)

FIGURE 16.15
Power spectrum can be edited by way of multiplying it by a mask image whose value varies between 0 and 1. Using the fingermark image in Figure 16.14 as the original image, (a) shows the result of a low-pass filtered image, its corresponding filter image, and the profile across the middle of the filter image; (b) shows a high-pass filtered image, its corresponding filter image, and its profile; and (c) shows a band-pass filtered image, the filter image, and its profile.

Figure 16.16 is a worked example. The subject is a latent fingermark in blood on a shirt with a fine weave (Figure 16.16a). Whilst the mark and the ridge flow are visible, that visibility is inhibited by the weave pattern. Initially, the image was divided into two overlapping parts, top and bottom, to allow FFT processing on the requisite square images. The images underwent forward FFT and the power spectra obtained. Spikes representing the weave pattern were identified as high frequency components and were removed. The inverse FFT

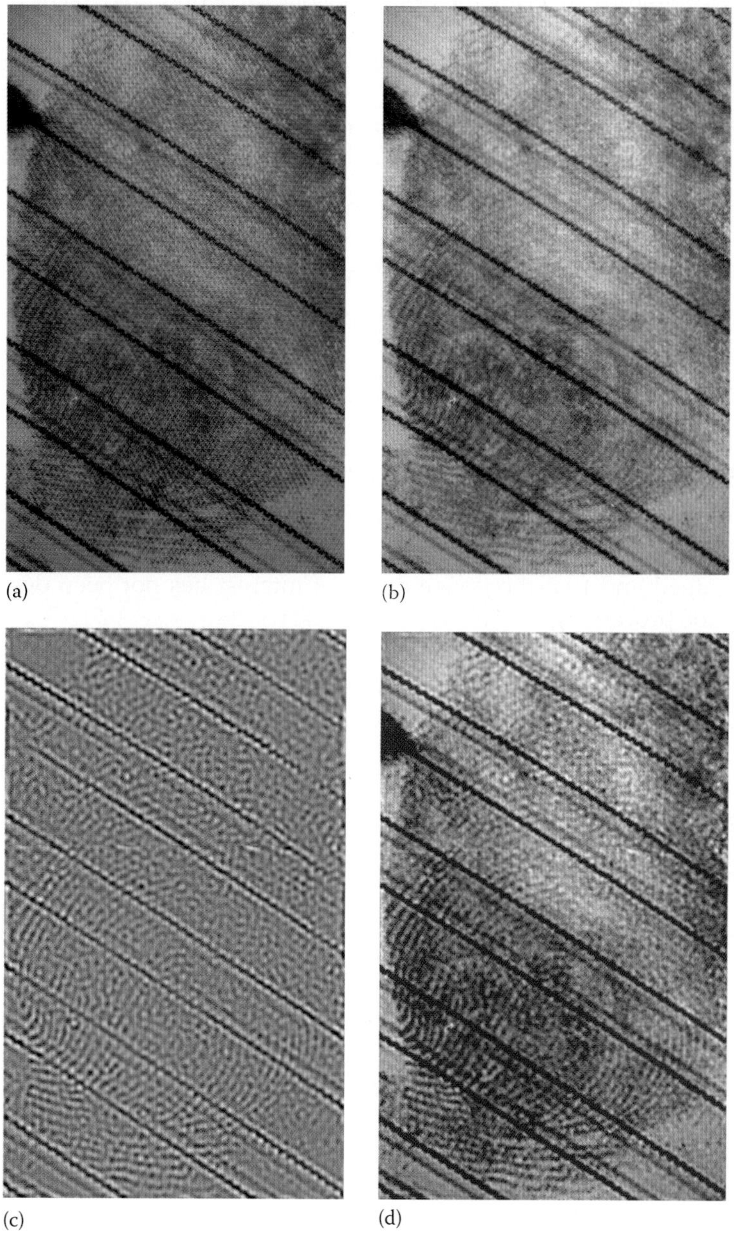

FIGURE 16.16
Worked example where the weave pattern of a fabric substrate is suppressed and the periodic aspect of the fingermark is enhanced. A fingermark in blood was visible before digital enhancement took place but the weave pattern of the support significantly affected examination of the friction ridge detail. Suppression of the weave pattern and combination with a band-pass-filtered image lead to a significant improvement. (a) Original image. (b) Weave pattern suppressed. (c) Band-pass filtered image. (d) Final image combining the suppressed weave and band-pass filtered images. (Images courtesy of the New South Wales Police, Parramatta, New South Wales, Australia.)

produced images with suppressed weave as shown in Figure 16.16b. A band-pass filter was constructed with a radius covering the frequency of the friction ridges. The original power spectra were multiplied by the band-pass filter, producing an image as shown by Figure 16.16c. The images in Figure 16.16b and c were combined in proportions of 65% and 35% to produce the image in Figure 16.16d. The process carried out was established through experimentation and then recorded as an image processing macro that could be reviewed, audited, and run automatically.

When applying such processes, it is recommended that operators

- Carefully examine the spatial domain image
- Identify the noise required to be suppressed
- Identify the signal to be amplified
- Anticipate where the corresponding detail will appear in the power spectrum
- Apply a forward FFT on the image
- Locate the spikes needing editing and edit them
- Apply an inverse FFT on the power spectrum
- Examine the resulting spatial domain image to verify that expected results have been obtained and that the image detail of interest has not been degraded as a result of the processing

It is generally expected that a number of attempts will be required to optimize the enhancement, with each iteration of the earlier process being an improvement on the last. Final processing should be carefully documented to ensure its repeatability.

16.5 Chemical Imaging

16.5.1 Introduction to Chemical Imaging

One application of digital imaging is the combination of this technology with molecular spectroscopy to result in a technique known as chemical imaging (otherwise known as spectral imaging, imaging spectroscopy, multispectral imaging, and hyperspectral imaging). Chemical imaging utilizes both molecular spectroscopy and digital imaging for the analysis of materials. The combination of these analytical tools into a single instrument allows for spatial (imaging) and spectral (chemical) information to be collected simultaneously. The results are represented in the form of a dataset or data cube. These three-dimensional datasets contain a full image at each individual wavelength and a full spectrum at each individual pixel. This concept is demonstrated in Figure 16.17. The spectra of individual pixels can be examined, or multiple pixels selected to produce an average spectrum for a particular region of interest (ROI; Figure 16.18).

Chemical imaging is a fairly broad term that is applied to a wide variety of instrumentation. These instruments vary in terms of the area of the electromagnetic spectrum that is examined, the scanning method, and componentry (such as the spectrometer and detector). Chemical imaging can encompass a wide variety of spectroscopic techniques. These include visible spectroscopy (absorption and luminescence), infrared spectroscopy, and

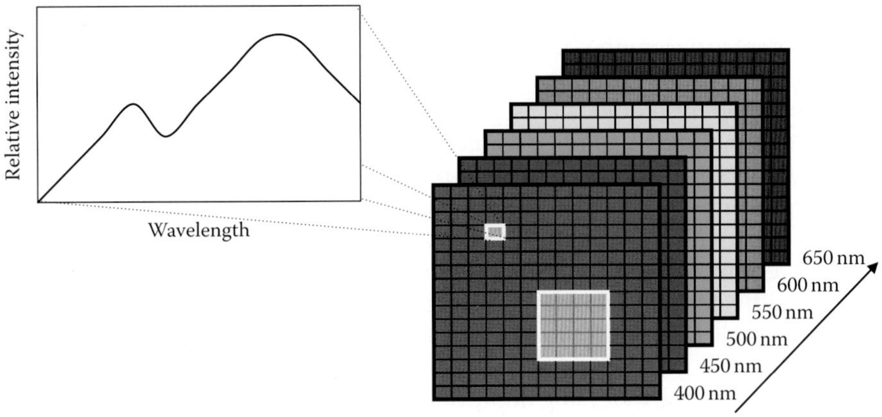

FIGURE 16.17
Representation of a chemical imaging dataset.

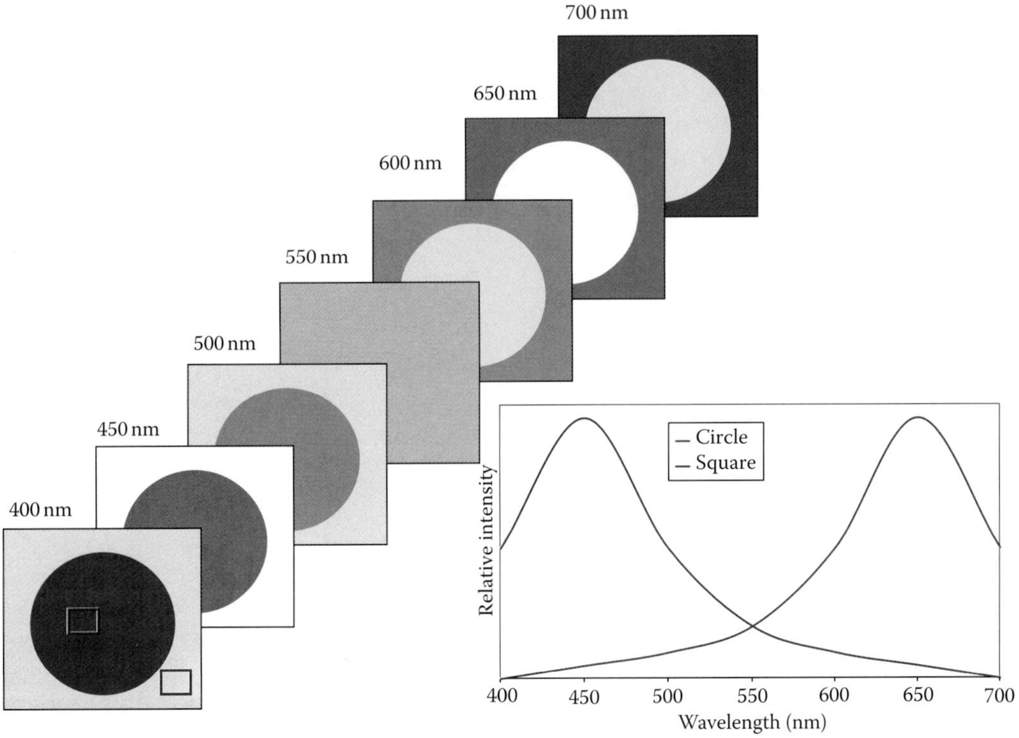

FIGURE 16.18
Chemical imaging data can be viewed as images or spectra.

Raman spectroscopy. The one aspect that remains the same for chemical imaging instruments is that both spatial and spectral information is collected.

A chemical imaging dataset can be built using a number of different methods, including point-by-point, line scanning, and wide-field spectral imaging. In point and line scanning, the three-dimensional dataset is built by the sequential collection of data at single points or lines across the sample. These methods tend to require extended experimental times. In wide-field imaging, an entire image is captured at a time. The dataset is built by collecting an image at a number of different wavelengths. Wide-field imaging is more rapid than point and line scanning methods, making this technique more applicable for forensic applications [11].

A number of different methods exist for spectral selection in chemical imaging instrumentation. These methods include prisms, gratings, interferometers, sets of interference filters, circular variable filters, and tunable filters [12]. The development of tunable filters has had a significant effect in the field of chemical imaging [13]. Tunable filters can be defined as devices that have a range of spectral transmissions that can be controlled electronically [14]. The most significant advantage of these types of filters is that wavelengths are selected rapidly and with no moving parts [15]. Examples of tunable filters include the liquid crystal tunable filter (LCTF) and the acousto-optic tunable filter (AOTF) [12].

Detectors enable the conversion of optical information into digital information, allowing for the computer-based viewing and processing of generated data. The type of detector required is dependent on the region of the electromagnetic spectrum being examined [16]. Some common detectors include silicon CCD and mercury cadmium telluride (MCT) focal-plane arrays (FPA) [17].

16.5.2 Forensic Applications of Chemical Imaging

Chemical imaging has been widely applied to medical, pharmaceutical, agriculture, and military applications. However, the application of all forms of chemical imaging in forensic science has been somewhat limited to-date, despite the potential benefits. Chemical imaging has been applied to the analysis of

- Paint [18]
- Tapes and adhesives [18]
- Fibers [18]
- Questioned documents [19]
- Firearm propellants [18]
- Drugs [20]
- Lubricants [21]
- Bruises [22]
- Fingermarks [23–25]

The most prevalent forms of chemical imaging that have been used for forensic applications have operated in the visible, near-infrared (NIR), and mid-infrared (MIR) regions of the electromagnetic spectrum. The application of chemical imaging in forensic science offers many advantages that have been previously documented [21,23]. One advantage is the capacity to capture both spatial and spectral information on a single instrument. Using a single instrument minimizes the chance of sample loss and contamination. Another benefit is the ability to scan a wide spectral range, which is particularly useful if the spectral characteristics of the sample are unknown. Spectral and spatial information obtained from forensic samples is easily displayed side by side, which can be helpful when presenting evidence in court, especially to lay persons such as jury members. Most chemical imaging techniques are relatively rapid, which is of particular interest to operational forensic laboratories. Chemical imaging techniques are nondestructive, which is beneficial when dealing with trace amounts of evidence. The ability to apply chemometric processes, such as principal components analysis (PCA), has been shown to be especially useful for the exploitation of small variations in the data. Finally, chemical imaging is applicable to a wide range of forensic evidence types, making the technique a potentially universal tool in a forensic laboratory.

16.5.3 Capture and Enhancement of Fingermark Images

Chemical imaging has been shown to be an effective method for the visualization of fingermarks on a variety of different surface types. The technology has been applied over a number of wavelength ranges, including the visible, the NIR, and the MIR (Table 16.1). The benefits that chemical imaging provides to fingermark detection are significant. The ability to capture data at multiple wavelengths allows for chemometric processes to be applied, which can extract otherwise subtle information from the data. Another benefit is the ability to target particular wavelengths depending on surface properties and the nature of any fingermark treatment. This is particularly useful when the spectral properties of the treated fingermarks are known.

16.5.3.1 Visible Region

Chemical imaging in the visible region (approximately 400 to 700 nm) has been successfully applied for the detection and visualization of fingermarks. Exline et al. [23]

TABLE 16.1

Summary of Surface Types and Chemical Treatments for Which Improved Fingermark Detection was Demonstrated Using Chemical Imaging

Surface Type	Treatment	Chemical Imaging Type
Newspaper	DFO	Visible
	Ninhydrin	Near-infrared
	Ninhydrin plus zinc post treatment	
White paper	Untreated	Visible
	DFO	Near-infrared
	Ninhydrin	
	Ninhydrin plus zinc post treatment	
	Indanedione	
Yellow paper	Untreated	Visible
	Ninhydrin	Near-infrared
	Indanedione	
Glossy paper	Powder	Near-infrared
Plastic	Powder	Visible
	Cyanoacrylate plus stain	Near-infrared
Glass	Untreated	Visible
	Powder	Near-infrared
	Cyanoacrylate	Mid-infrared
	Cyanoacrylate plus stain	
Polymer banknotes	Cyanoacrylate	Mid-infrared
Aluminum drink can	Cyanoacrylate	Mid-infrared

Sources: Exline, D.L. et al., *J. Forensic Sci.*, 48(5), 1047, 2003; Payne, G. et al., *Forensic Sci. Int.*, 150(1), 33, 2005; Maynard, P. et al., *Aust. J. Forensic Sci.*, 41(1), 43, 2009; Tahtouh, M. et al., *J. Forensic Sci.*, 50(1), 64, 2005; Tahtouh, M. et al., *J. Forensic Sci.*, 52(5), 1089, 2007.

conducted research using a Condor™ chemical imaging macroscope (ChemImage; http://www.chemimage.com). In this work, three surface types (paper, plastic, and glass) were investigated. Latent fingermarks and fingermarks subjected to a variety of chemical treatments were examined using the Condor and a conventional imaging system (Poliview; Rofin Australia; http://www.rofin.com.au). Several data processing techniques were investigated, including the chemometric method of PCA. Compared to conventional imaging, the chemical imaging system was shown to improve the visualization of fingermarks on paper (untreated and treated with DFO), plastic (treated with cyanoacrylate and a luminescent stain), and glass (treated with cyanoacrylate and a luminescent stain). The authors concluded that the chemical imaging system was a potentially valuable tool for the analysis of untreated fingermarks or weak fingermarks that have undergone chemical treatment.

Payne et al. [24] built on the work by Exline and further examined the applications of visible chemical imaging for fingermark visualization. In this research, a wide range of surface types, chemical treatments, and fingermark conditions were examined. Each fingermark was examined using the Condor (ChemImage) and a conventional imaging system (AxioCam HRM digital camera; Zeiss; http://www.zeiss.com). Different chemometric processes were evaluated on the chemical imaging data in an attempt to reveal ridge detail that was unable to be detected by the conventional imaging method. The authors concluded that chemical imaging was a superior technique for examining weak fingermarks on difficult surfaces, such as surfaces that produce highly luminescent backgrounds. Untreated fingermarks on yellow paper, fingermarks on white and yellow paper treated with ninhydrin, and fingermarks on newspaper treated with ninhydrin and DFO were found to benefit the most from chemical imaging visualization. Figures 16.19 through 16.23 demonstrate some of the results obtained from this study.

These examples demonstrate how chemical imaging, combined with chemometric data processing techniques, can extract subtle information from otherwise poor data. With traditional fingermark visualization methods, only a single image is collected at a

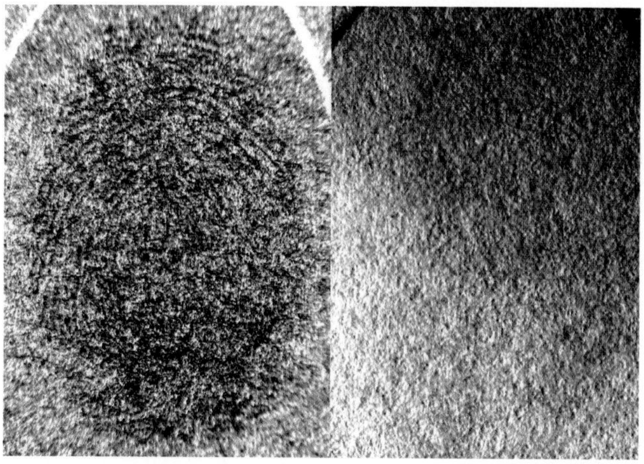

(a) (b)

FIGURE 16.19
An untreated, fresh fingermark on yellow paper. Chemical imaging result (a) compared with conventional imaging (b). The chemical imaging data was collected from 400 to 720 nm in 10 nm steps using white light illumination. The image was processed using zero offset and normalization; data was then extracted from 460 to 480 nm and averaged before mapping (adjustment of brightness and contrast for display).

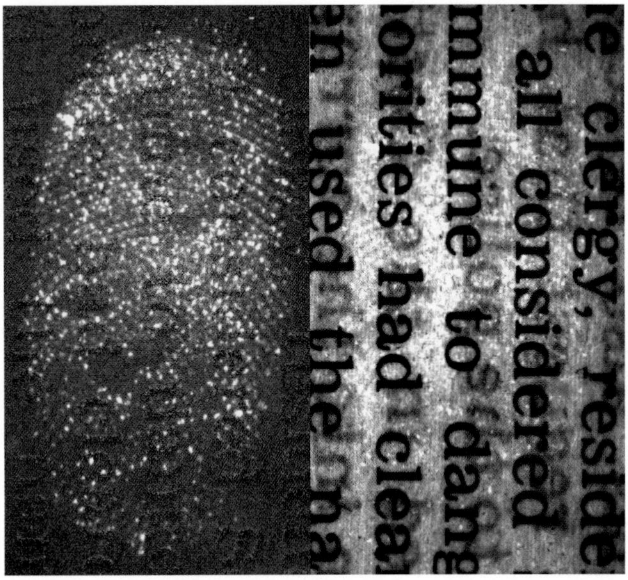

(a) (b)

FIGURE 16.20
One week old fingermark on newspaper with a text background, treated with DFO and visualized in the luminescence mode. Chemical imaging result (a) compared with conventional imaging (b). The chemical imaging data was collected from 570 to 660nm in 5nm steps using 530nm excitation. The image was processed using zero offset and normalization before using PCA. The third PC was extracted and mapped.

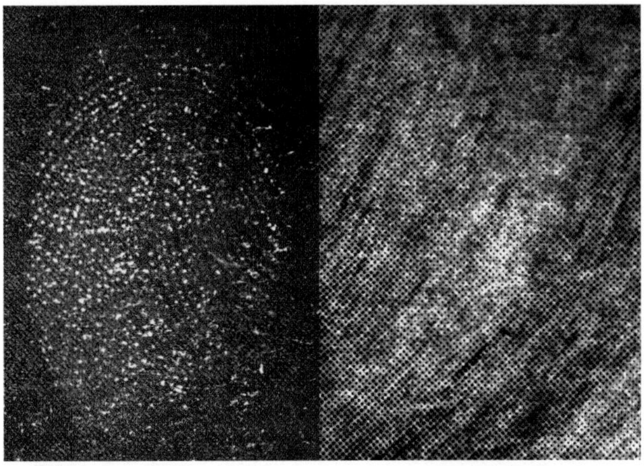

(a) (b)

FIGURE 16.21
Two month old fingermark on newspaper with a picture background, treated with DFO and visualized in the luminescence mode. Chemical imaging result (a) compared with conventional imaging (b). The chemical imaging data was collected and treated in the same manner as for the left image in Figure 16.20.

time and generally only under one set of conditions (e.g., at a specific observation wavelength). The ability to generate a data cube and conduct chemometric processes, such as PCA, enables more information to be extracted from the images. Whilst this ability has no advantage for the imaging of good quality fingermarks, this method has been proven to be beneficial for fingermarks that are weak (e.g., Figure 16.19) or on difficult surfaces

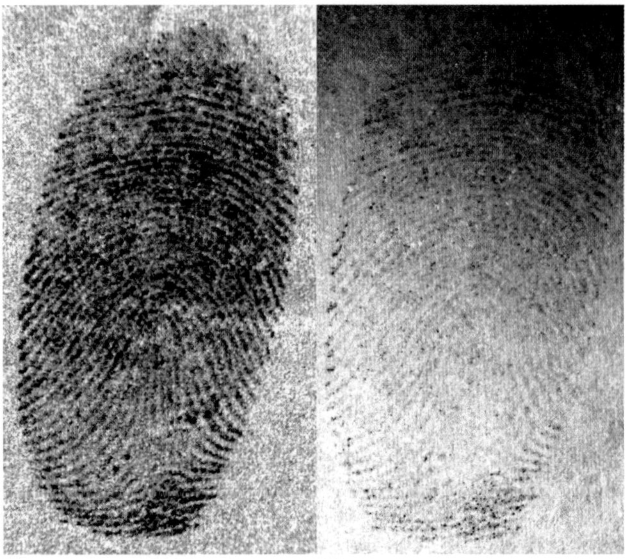

(a) (b)

FIGURE 16.22
Two month old fingermark on white paper, treated with ninhydrin. Chemical imaging result (a) compared with conventional imaging (b). The chemical imaging data was collected from 490 to 620 nm in 5 nm steps using white light illumination. A new image was created using the spectrum of the background. This background image was blurred and the original image was then divided by it. The resulting image was then treated with zero offset, normalization, and PCA. The second PC was extracted and mapped.

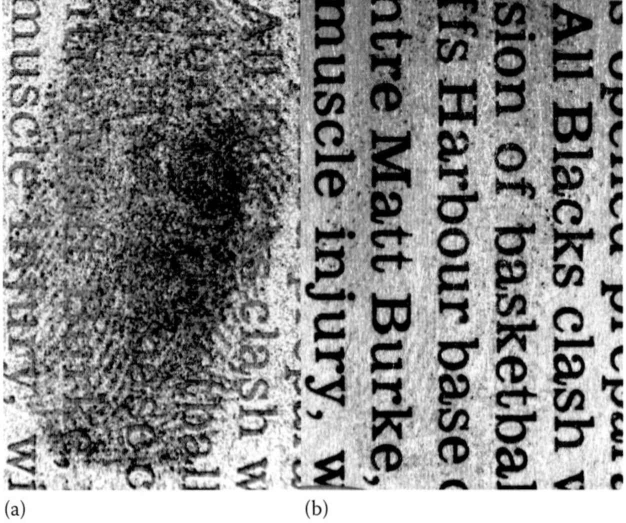

(a) (b)

FIGURE 16.23
Two month old fingermark on newspaper with a text background, treated with ninhydrin. Chemical imaging result (a) compared with conventional imaging (b). The chemical imaging data was collected from 490 to 620 nm in 5 nm steps using white light illumination. The image was first treated with PCA and the second PC extracted. This was then reversed and mapped for display.

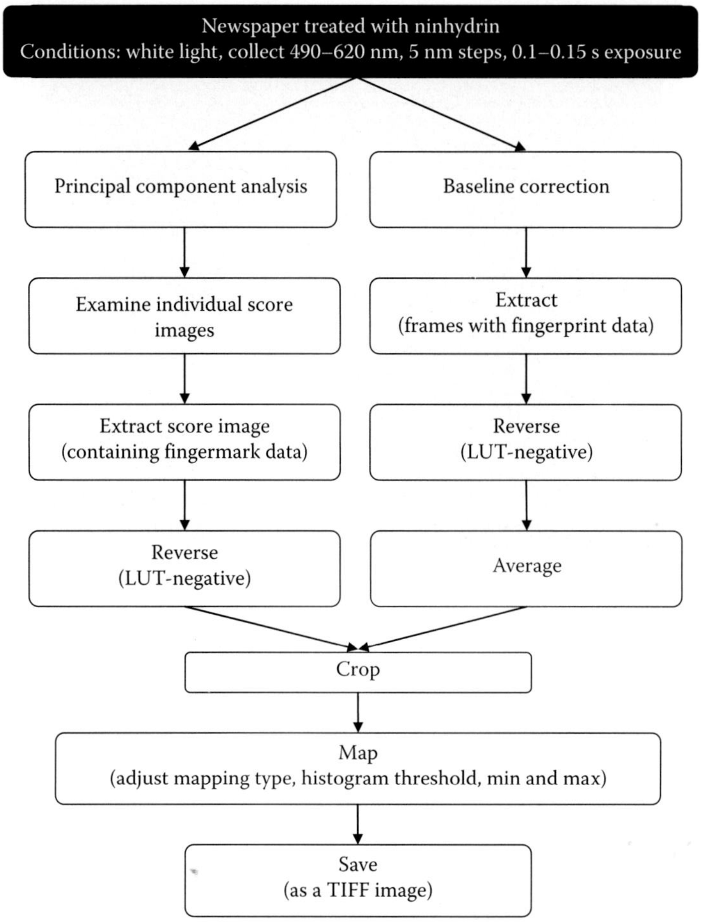

FIGURE 16.24
Recommended procedure for the processing of chemical imaging data collected from ninhydrin-treated fingermarks on newspaper.

(for example, Figure 16.20). This research work has led to the development of a number of recommended chemical imaging procedures, an example of which is given in Figure 16.24.

16.5.3.2 Near-Infrared Region

Recent research has been undertaken to establish the usefulness of NIR chemical imaging in the detection of latent fingermarks [25]. A variety of traditional chemical treatments were used to develop fingermarks on a selection of nonporous, semi-porous, and porous substrates in an effort to determine if chemical imaging could enhance fingermarks in the NIR region. The authors of this study concluded that the chemical imaging system evaluated (Condor; ChemImage) was able to acquire data rapidly in the NIR region. The ability to process chemical imaging data with chemometric methods, such as PCA, also enabled the visualization of ridge detail on surfaces that are traditionally problematic when conventional imaging is employed. Figure 16.25 demonstrates some of the results obtained from this study.

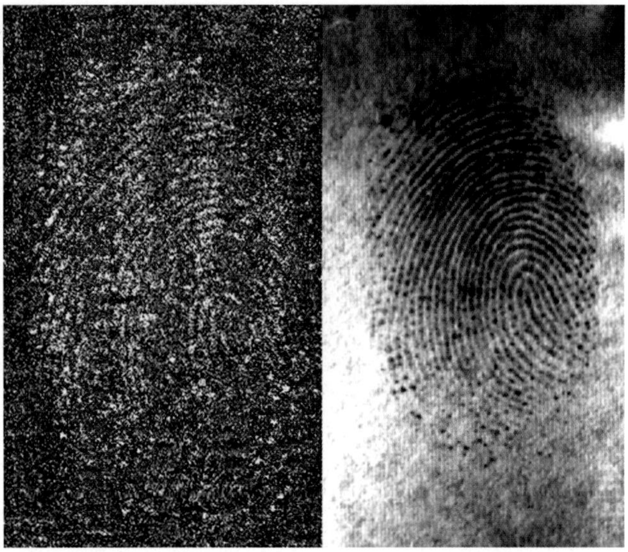

(a) (b)

FIGURE 16.25
Chemical imaging results in the near-infrared for a fresh fingermark on newspaper treated with DFO (a) and a fresh fingermark on white paper treated with ninhydrin (b). The DFO chemical imaging data has been collected from 650 to 1100nm in 10nm steps using 555nm excitation. The data was then treated with PCA and the sixth PC extracted and mapped for display. The ninhydrin chemical imaging data was collected from 650 to 1100nm in 10nm steps using white light illumination. The data was also treated with PCA and the first PC extracted and mapped.

16.5.3.3 Mid-Infrared Region

Chemical imaging in the visible and NIR is an effective tool for the visualization of fingermarks on a number of surfaces. However, this region of the electromagnetic spectrum is somewhat broad and unspecific. When chemical imaging is employed in a region such as the MIR, specific chemical groups can be targeted.

Tahtouh et al. [26,27] have made significant progress with respect to the utilization of MIR chemical imaging for fingermark visualization. This work investigated the use of a Fourier transform infrared (FTIR) imaging spectrometer (Digilab Stingray) fitted with a 64 × 64 pixel FPA detector. Various surfaces and fingermark treatments were examined. Untreated fingermarks on infrared reflective glass slides were found to be effectively imaged at approximately 3000 cm^{-1}, due to C—H stretching in the fatty acid residues located in the untreated fingermarks. It was acknowledged by the authors that imaging untreated prints using the C—H stretching frequency is limited to surfaces such as metals and ceramics that do not absorb in this region.

The authors subsequently identified the use of the C≡N functional group (at approximately 2200 cm^{-1}) to potentially image cyanoacrylate-treated fingermarks. However, it was revealed that, on polymerization, this MIR absorption band for this functional group disappeared. Another area of interest was identified at approximately 1750 to 1800 cm^{-1} (extracted from the second or fourth derivative of the data). This frequency is attributed to C=O stretching in the polymerized cyanoacrylate ester. It was this frequency "slice" that was subsequently used for the successful imaging of cyanoacrylate fingermarks on Australian polymer banknotes and aluminum beverage cans. Using this region, most background interferences (such as printing) were effectively removed.

Whilst the use of MIR chemical imaging is more specific than visible or NIR chemical imaging, there remain several limitations such as instrument cost and data collection times. MIR chemical imaging requires much longer collection time (hours) compared to imaging in the visible or NIR (minutes).

16.6 Standards and Evidentiary Requirements

Acquired images that contribute to a forensic investigation must adhere to the same evidential requirements as for other items of evidence. This has implications for training, equipment selection and maintenance, standard operating procedures, evidence handling, and continuity. The development of digital technology has advanced to a point where it is in the reach of many forensic practitioners in terms of equipment availability, cost, and familiarity. This advancement needs to be paralleled by an advanced awareness of digital applications as a part of the latent fingermark development process and the pitfalls of digital misuse through either impropriety or ignorance. There is a wide range of cameras and software that is readily available on the market. Digital images and processing results of variable quality may therefore find their way into forensic work and the courts. Users need to be aware of technological capabilities, limitations, and relevant evidential requirements with respect to the application of digital imaging in the forensic environment.

It is (also) essential that the methods employed are constantly reviewed and improved to keep pace with the ongoing advances in technology. This is particularly so with respect to digital imaging given that its associated technologies permit digital images to be easily duplicated, manipulated, contaminated, or altered. It is self-evident that digital imaging is assuming an ever increasing importance within the judicial process today and this situation will no doubt continue well into the future. In light of this, it is imperative for forensic science practitioners and agencies to be able to validate the origin and integrity of not only the digital images themselves but also the image capture and handling procedures employed in gathering, processing, and analyzing this type of evidence, especially when digital images are to be used for evidentiary purposes [28].

Policies and procedures must be in place for the digital capture, storage, retrieval, display, and transmission of friction ridge images retained as evidence. This standard establishes requirements for the preservation of identity, authenticity, integrity, and security of friction ridge digital images. Prior to conducting digital imaging tasks in friction ridge examination cases, examiners shall have completed training appropriate to each task before them [29].

Digital imaging procedures must be in place to be able to satisfy a court such that

- The practitioner capturing the image is sufficiently trained and competent to carry out the task
- The equipment used throughout the process is appropriate and fit-for-purpose
- The image is properly captured, preserved, and presented
- There are established procedures for the handling of digital evidence images
- The processes employed have been validated for the purposes required

Important elements of the digital imaging process include the following:

- A requirement to adhere to a standardized process for producing evidential images.
- Preparation of the subject and capture of the image. Choice and control of lighting and the appropriate selection of a camera contribute greatly to the quality of the information of interest in the image recorded. "The image capture devices should be capable of rendering an accurate representation of the item or items of interest" [30].
- Saving, archiving, and exhibiting of original images must be done to ensure the secure maintenance of that digital data in its original state over an extended time. Working copies of the images should be made to make the content available for enhancement or analysis whilst preserving the original data. Note that original images are considered to be exact copies of the first image data recorded in memory [31].
- Post-capture processing of images must be done on a copy or working image and should be repeatable. Categories of processing can be considered to be basic (contrast, brightness) or advanced (FFT, image averaging) [32], with each requiring different degrees of documentation. Advanced processing techniques should be sufficiently documented such that an appropriately qualified and independent person can repeat the enhancement process. Enhancement processes should be validated before use. There should be no limitations on the methods of image processing applied as long as novel processes can be justified and validated.
- Output of the image data needs to be done in a manner that allows for the details of interest to be faithfully reproduced as captured. Displaying of images on screens or in hard-copy form does not guarantee that such detail will be adequately reproduced. This is as vital a component of the digital process as capture (or any other part). If an image is to be properly analyzed, it must be able to be displayed in a form that contains sufficient reproduced detail.

16.7 Conclusions

Modern digital cameras, computer equipment, and image processing software can be combined to provide significant operational advantages for the capture and enhancement of fingermark evidence. Optimized image capture and the correct application of image processing techniques can result in the recovery of fingermark evidence that may go undetected by other means. The result is that digital imaging has become a viable alternative to conventional photography and a valuable tool for this important forensic application.

Chemical imaging further extends the advantages that can be gained through digital capture. Image collection over a wavelength range (hyperspectral imaging), together with the chemometric processing of this data, can result in the significant enhancement of fingermark detail. This is an emerging area that is likely to impact on a number of forensic science disciplines as the technology improves and as the associated equipment costs are reduced.

Digital image capture and image processing techniques have, however, resulted in questions being raised as to the validity and acceptability of "photographic" evidence presented in criminal proceedings. Practitioners need to follow standard operating procedures to ensure that acquired images adhere to the same evidential requirements as for other items of evidence. Original digital images must be safeguarded, with any post-capture processing of images only conducted on working copies. In addition, each step in an image processing sequence must be recorded and must be capable of being reproduced (e.g., in court) if questions arise as to the integrity of any image submitted as evidence. What is required is an unbroken "digital image chain of custody" that demonstrates the production of an enhanced image from the original digital recording.

Authors

Bruce Comber, a senior scientific officer, received his master of information sciences from the University of Canberra in 2012. He commenced his career in 1990 with the Western Australia Police Fingerprint Bureau. In 1995, he was awarded the status of fingerprint expert by the Australian Board of Fingerprint Examiners. Bruce joined the Australian Federal Police (AFP) Fingerprint Team, Canberra, Australia, in 2000. He has played an active role in AFP fingerprint activities since this time, with involvement in notable investigations, including incidents where disaster victim identification (DVI) was required. Bruce conducts and supervises fingerprint research, is an assessor for the Australasian Forensic Field Sciences Accreditation Board, and is a member of the Scientific Working Group (Fingerprints) under the National Institute of Forensic Science. He has been involved in digital imaging and image enhancement of fingerprint evidence for more than 15 years.

Gemma Payne graduated with a bachelor of applied chemistry (honors, forensic science) in 2003 from the University of Technology Sydney, Ultimo, New South Wales, Australia. Gemma continued her studies, completing her PhD on the forensic applications of chemical (hyperspectral) imaging in 2009, which extended the scope of her honors research in this area. This research assessed the suitability of the technique for the forensic examination of fingermarks, writing inks, firearm propellants, bruises, and textile fibers. In 2005, Gemma joined the Australian Federal Police Forensic and Data Centres as a forensic chemist. In this role, Gemma now specializes in the analysis and interpretation of various types of trace evidence.

Chris Lennard has a PhD in chemistry from the Australian National University (1986) for research on the chemical detection of fingermarks. After completing his PhD, he undertook postdoctoral work at the School of Forensic Science, University of Lausanne, Lausanne, Switzerland, where he gained the position of associate professor in criminalistics in 1989. He returned to Australia in 1994 to take up a position with Forensic Services, AFP. Chris left the AFP in October 2006 to take up his current position as professor of forensic studies at the University of Canberra, where he is head of the forensic studies discipline.

References

1. Blackwell RJ, Crisci JD. (1975) Digital image processing and its application in forensic sciences. *J Forensic Sci* 20(2):288–304.
2. Hazelwood KL, Olenych SG, Griffin JD, Murphy CS, Cathcart JA, Davidson MW. (2011). Introduction to Digital Imaging in Microscopy. Part I: Basic Imaging Concepts. Retrieved from Hamamatsu Learning Centre. Concepts in Digital Imaging Technology. http://learn.hamamatsu.com/articles/microscopyimaging.html (accessed on October 5, 2011).
3. Bovik A. (2005) *Handbook of Image and Video Processing* (2nd edn.). Academic Press, New York.
4. Gonzalez RC, Woods RE. (1992) *Digital Image Processing*. Addison-Wesley, Reading, MA.
5. Spring KR, Fellers TJ, Davidson M (2011). *Introduction to Charge-Coupled Devices*. Nikon MicrtopscopyU Fundamentals of Digital Imaging. http://www.microscopyu.com/articles/digitalimaging/ccdintro.html (accessed on October 5, 2011).
6. Moler E, Ballarin V, Pessana F, Torres S, Olmo D. (1998) Fingerprint identification using image enhancement techniques. *J Forensic Sci* 43(3):689–692.
7. Bramble SK, Jackson GR. (1994) Operational experience of fingermark enhancement by frequency domain filtering. *J Forensic Sci* 39(4):920–932.
8. Burger W, Burge MJ. (2008) *Digital Image Processing—An Algorithmic Introduction Using Java*. Springer-Verlag, New York.
9. Comber BA. (2003) Reduction of background features in images of fingerprints using combinations of images acquired under different lighting conditions. *J Forensic Ident* 53(2):198–208.
10. Dictionary.com. http://dictionary.reference.com
11. Garcia D, Nelson MP, Treado PJ. (2002) Applications of Raman chemical imaging to polymeric systems. *Polym Prepr* 43(2):1271–1272.
12. Garini Y, Young IT, McNamara G. (2006) Spectral imaging: Principles and applications. *Cytometry A* 69(8):735–747.
13. Morris HR, Hoyt CC, Miller P, Treado PJ. (1996) Liquid crystal tunable filter Raman chemical imaging. *Appl Spectrosc* 50(6):805–811.
14. Gat, N. (2000) Imaging spectroscopy using tunable filters: a review. In: H.H. Szu, M. Vetterli, W.J. Campbell, J.R. Buss, Eds. *Wavelet Applications VII, Proceedings of SPIE*, Vol. 4056. SPIE, Bellingham, WA, pp. 50–64.
15. Morris HR, Hoyt CC, Treado PJ. (1994) Imaging spectrometers for fluorescence and Raman microscopy: Acousto-optic and liquid crystal tunable filters. *Appl Spectrosc* 48(7):857–866.
16. Kerekes JP, Schott JR. (2007) Hyperspectral imaging systems. In: Chang C-I, Ed. *Hyperspectral Data Exploitation: Theory and Applications*. Wiley, Hoboken, NJ.
17. Treado PJ, Levin IW, Lewis EN. (1994) Indium antimonide (InSb) focal plane array (FPA) detection for near-infrared imaging microscopy. *Appl Spectrosc* 48(5):607–615.
18. Payne G, Wallace C, Reedy B, Lennard C, Schuler R, Exline D, Roux C. (2005) Visible and near-infrared chemical imaging methods for the analysis of selected forensic samples. *Talanta* 67(2):334–344.
19. Ostrum RB. (2006) Application of hyperspectral imaging to forensic document examination problems. *J Am Soc Quest Doc Exam* 9(2):85–93.
20. Exline DL, Treado PJ. (2002) Forensic examination to trace evidence using Raman, UV–vis, and fluorescence chemical imaging. *Proceedings of the American Academy of Forensic Sciences Annual Meeting*, Vol. 8. American Academy of Forensic Sciences, Atlanta, GA.
21. Wolfe J, Exline DL. (2003) Characterization of condom lubricant components using Raman spectroscopy and Raman chemical imaging. *J Forensic Sci* 48(5):1065–1074.
22. Payne G, Langlois N, Lennard C, Roux C. (2007) Applying visible hyperspectral (chemical) imaging to estimate the age of bruises. *Med Sci Law* 47(3):225–232.

23. Exline DL, Wallace C, Roux C, Lennard C, Nelson MP, Treado PJ. (2003) Forensic applications of chemical imaging: Latent fingerprint detection using visible absorption and luminescence. *J Forensic Sci* 48(5):1047–1053.
24. Payne G, Reedy B, Lennard C, Comber B, Exline D, Roux C. (2005) A further study to investigate the detection and enhancement of latent fingerprints using visible absorption and luminescence chemical imaging. *Forensic Sci Int* 150(1):33–51.
25. Maynard P, Jenkins J, Edey C, Payne G, Lennard C, McDonagh A, Roux C. (2009) Near infrared imaging for the improved detection of fingermarks on different surfaces. *Aust J Forensic Sci* 41(1):43–62.
26. Tahtouh M, Kalman JR, Roux C, Lennard C, Reedy BJ. (2005) The detection and enhancement of latent fingermarks using infrared chemical imaging. *J Forensic Sci* 50(1):64–72.
27. Tahtouh M, Despland P, Shimmon R, Kalman JR, Reedy BJ. (2007) The application of infrared chemical imaging to the detection and enhancement of latent fingerprints: Method optimization and further findings. *J Forensic Sci* 52(5):1089–1096.
28. http://www.nifs.com.au/2004%20Digital%20Imaging%20Guidelines.pdf (accessed on October 5, 2011).
29. http://www.swgfast.org/documents/imaging/090914_Standard_Imaging_1.1.pdf (accessed on October 5, 2011).
30. http://www.theiai.org/guidelines/swgit/guidelines/section_1_v3-3_20100611.pdf (accessed on October 5, 2011).
31. http://www.parliament.the-stationery-office.co.uk/pa/ld199798/ldselect/ldsctech/064v/st0503.htm (accessed on October 5, 2011).
32. http://www.theiai.org/guidelines/swgit/guidelines/section_11_v1-3_20100115.pdf (accessed on October 5, 2011).

Index

D

G

T

V

W

X

Z